.ıs book is to be returned on or before
the last date stamped below.

KT-195-271

Schlichter and Horan (1981) described how the behaviour of some institutional staff undermined the goals of a self-control programme for young offenders. The programme aimed to teach young offenders how to control their aggression. Unfortunately, this programme was undermined not only by staff who modelled aggression when they were exposed to provocation, but also by other staff— operating from a different theoretical perspective—who actively encouraged the expression of anger. Hollin (1995) noted that this situation must have been "entirely confusing and counterproductive" (p. 197). The third process described by Hollin was "programme non-compliance". This process occurs either when changes are made to the content of the programme or when targets of a session are altered or discarded without reference to the theoretical principles that underpin the programme. The final result is far removed from the original aims. Hollin eloquently summarized this process:

> The final product of all this is rather like the last murmur in a game of Chinese Whispers. There may be some vestige of the original message, but the original meaning is lost forever (Hollin, 1995, p. 197).

Factors that Enhance Treatment Integrity

Having established some of the processes by which treatment integrity is threatened, we will now consider those approaches that should—when applied to treatment programmes—ensure high levels of programme integrity and thereby maximize the outcome of offender treatment programmes. Although understanding of these issues is not complete, there is sufficient knowledge available to provide guidance: as Harris and Rice (1997) noted, "Many of the puzzle's pieces have been found" (p. 386). In the remainder of this chapter we will consider the key issues that have been identified in the literature; we will consider the requirement of a coherent theoretical framework, the importance of a programme manual, the need for institutional commitment, the necessity of proper facilities for delivery, the importance of staff characteristics—with an emphasis on the selection and training, support and supervision of staff—the necessity of multi-disciplinary treatment of programme staff, the importance of support and supervision, the role of non-programme staff, the requirement of contingency plans and, finally, the need for ongoing monitoring and evaluation.

The Theoretical Framework

The meta-analytic studies have indicated that the success of a programme is dependent on its theoretical basis. Treatment programmes should be designed according to an empirically validated theoretical framework. Harris and Rice (1997), in their very helpful review of treatment programmes for mentally disordered offenders, indicated that the ideal programme would ensure that:

Identified criminogenic needs would become treatment targets, and for each, an explicit plan would specify how change is to be accomplished and measured. The framework should serve as a guide for both programme developers and practitioners about what to target and how (p. 383).

The Programme Manual

One mechanism through which treatment integrity can be maintained is the development of a comprehensive treatment manual: this manual is then the gold standard against which practice must be compared to determine whether treatment integrity is being maintained. Hollin (1995) indicated that a programme manual should explicitly define the treatment goals and provide a description of the programme curriculum, i.e. how the goals are to be achieved.

> A good manual is one that is firmly based on a respectable theory and is itself meticulously researched and evaluated by proficient researchers and practitioners. A sound manual will contain detailed guidelines for the design, setting up, running and evaluation of a given treatment programme (Hollin, 1995, p. 199).

A coherent and effective manual should specify, in detail, the number of sessions to be delivered and provide specific lesson plans for each session. The manual should define not only the learning objectives but also the techniques that should be used to achieve specific learning outcomes. The means by which change can be evaluated; for example, through systematic pre–post evaluations of key variables, should be stated.

Institutional Commitment

It has long been recognized that organizational barriers may exert a negative impact on treatment programmes (e.g. Laws, 1974). Gendreau (1996) argued that the implementation of treatment programmes can be threatened by the "MBA management syndrome". This occurs where institutional administrators and managers are "generalists" who may be capable of effective management but who have little or no knowledge about the prediction or treatment of offending (Gendreau, 1995; Hamm & Schrink, 1989). Given these lacunae, the managers and administrators are unable to determine whether their staff are doing their jobs properly, whether treatment programmes are well designed or whether the programmes are being implemented in a manner that ensures integrity. Furthermore, attempts to evaluate the service will be ill-informed and may target inappropriate factors (Harris & Rice, 1997).

There is a tension, however, if programmes are not linked to the central management structures of the institution or organization. In the past, treatment programmes have not been considered integral to prison and their exclusion from the mainstream management structure has, directly or indirectly, militated against treatment integrity.

Too many rehabilitative or offence-related programmes are dealt with as bolt-on activities that exist at the periphery of mainstream activity. This marginalisation tends to make programmes vulnerable to the vagaries of resourcing and competing demands, suspicion and antagonism from staff and inmates not involved, and a cultural bias against success (Hollin, 1992a, cited in McDougall, 1996, p. 95).

It is important to gain the commitment of the host institution so that the programme is considered part of the institution; this commitment should reduce the deleterious impact of institutional factors. One mechanism by which the institution can enhance its commitment to the treatment programme is by providing the funding for the programme (Gendreau & Goggin, 1996). By providing funding the host organization and its managers are accountable for the outcome of the treatment programme (Harris & Rice, 1997). The possibility of financial loss due to programme failure may motivate managers to support treatment programmes more rigorously.

It is essential that the institution gives priority to treatment programmes. Understandably, operational and security concerns are uppermost within prison and other secure settings; nonetheless, it is important that these concerns do not diminish rehabilitative efforts. McDougall (1996) illustrated this point: she argued that in prisons, problems such as overcrowding can make security and control the main priority. In these circumstances, staff may be required for non-programme duties to ensure that the security, and other institutional concerns, are dealt with—the consequence is that programmes can be disrupted and integrity thereby threatened.

Facilities for Delivery

The programme should be well resourced. This may appear to be self-evident. However, experience suggests that this requirement is more honoured in the breach than in the observance. The treatment environment must be conducive to the delivery of the treatment programme, e.g. an adequately sized room which has the correct seating capacity, which permits the discussion of sensitive issues, and where there is privacy and confidentiality. Aids such as audio visual equipment should be available when needed.

Programme Staff

There is consensus in the treatment literature that staff have a critical role in influencing the outcome of programmes and, in particular, they have a crucial role in maintaining the integrity of treatment programmes (Cooke, 1989, 1997; Hollin, 1992b; Woodward, 1997; Harris & Rice, 1997).

Staff Selection

The success of treatment programmes is fundamentally linked to staff characteristics—it is essential that programme staff are equipped to deliver treatment programmes—requiring both skill and knowledge (with obvious implications for staff training). The attitudes of staff towards treatment and their ability to deliver treatment is also of critical importance. Lösel (1996) argued that when there is a mismatch between the attitudes and competence of staff, and the goals and content of the programme, the treatment integrity and effectiveness of the programme is lowered.

Staff selection procedures should attend to the attitudes, knowledge, motivation, and experience of staff to ensure that they are compatible with the demands of the programme. Rehabilitation staff should possess warmth, empathy, and tolerance. The should employ a "firm but fair" approach to their interactions with clients (Andrews & Kiessling, 1980; Harris & Rice, 1997). Programme staff should also be flexible and sensitive to institutional rules.

Staff morale and staff relationships with prisoners have been identified as influential factors in rehabilitative efforts (Andrews & Kiessling, 1980; Andrews et al., 1990; Averbeck & Lösel, 1994; Cooke, 1989, 1997; McDougall, 1996). These can be improved by both training and by the supportive management of programme staff.

The Programme Leader

The programme director or leader can have a disproportionate impact on treatment integrity. The treatment programme should be led by an individual with a high level of expertise. The leader should possess the appropriate skills and qualities of an effective manager and have the ability to function within the demands and constraints of the organizational environment. What is the leader's role? Harris and Rice (1997) suggested the following:

> A committed leader inside the organization who will fight to maintain interest, motivation, enthusiasm and accountability is important as well. Experience from several impressive psychosocial programs indicates that programmes often die when their innovators move on (p. 383).

Ideally, the programme leader should be internal to the institution or organization. An internal leader will be informed about, and familiar with, institutional routines and institutional priorities, including work commitments, meal times, counts, and other institutional practices. This knowledge will facilitate the design of treatment programmes, and thereby minimize conflict between institutional and treatment priorities; it may enhance co-operation from non-treatment staff.

The programme leader must participate in all stages of programme delivery to oversee the implementation of the programme and to ensure programme integrity. Meta-analyses have shown that treatment efficacy is associated with the level of involvement of the investigator. For example, Gensheimer Mayer, Gottschalk, and Davidson (1986) calculated an ES of $r = 0.37$ for programmes characterized by high levels of involvement of the investigator. Highly involved investigators, who oversee the implementation of the treatment programme, can help ensure that the programme is being delivered properly, thereby ensuring treatment integrity (Lipsey, 1995).

Multi-Disciplinary Training

Treatment programmes for offenders can involve professionals from a diverse range of backgrounds. In order to avoid difficulties, programme staff should receive joint training; this not only builds the cohesion of the team but also ensures that individual members are knowledgeable about the goals and methods of the treatment programme. McDougall (1996) argued that the integrity of a treatment programme is strengthened by ensuring that all staff undergo joint training and adopt a team approach.

Support and Supervision

Treatment integrity is likely to be enhanced by the provision of support and supervision for programme staff. Programme staff should be supervised to ensure that they are implementing the programme correctly. Good supervision has been identified as a "vital ingredient" to ensuring the integrity of a treatment programme (Hollin, 1995; Lösel, 1996). It is important that staff have adequate support because long periods of delivering treatment may result in "burn-out" or, indeed, "rust-out" if boredom is allowed to set in. It is important, from both an ethical and a treatment integrity perspective, that staff who are no longer functioning adequately are supported if they wish to resign from their duties in the treatment programme.

Non-Programme Staff

Non-programme staff have a key role in rehabilitation efforts; this may be particularly true in prison settings. The primary role of the prison officer is as custodian—issues of security and control are paramount—nonetheless, it is important for treatment intergrity that those staff not directly involved in treatment are committed to rehabilitation attempts. Mathias, Mathews, and Sindberg (1989) referred to the "turf wars" that result when treatment staff and security staff are divided. There are many examples of this in the literature. Some time ago, Corsini and Miller (1954) noted that prison staff often failed to ensure that prisoners were available for treatment programmes. More recently, McDougall, Boddis, Dawson, and Hayes (1990) found that officers responsible for organizing an anger-management programme in a young offenders' institution frequently found themselves having to negotiate for rooms and resources. Those treating offenders in secure settings other than prisons may also be subject to such difficulties.

The problem of sabotage of treatment needs to be tackled proactively. It is crucial that non-programme staff are familiar with the programme and its aims. The execution of "staff awareness" campaigns can engage the institutional staff in the promotion of the programme. Non-programme staff should be knowledgeable about the purposes and mechanisms of a treatment programme.

Contingency Plans

Prisons and other secure settings are volatile environments. Security concerns can result in full "lock-ups" of the institution which may result in the cancellation of a programme session. If the treatment integrity of a programme is to remain intact it is essential that the planned programme takes account of these possibilities and that there are plans in place to ensure that unforeseen events do not significantly disrupt the programme. Contingency plans should be in place for the equally important—though less dramatic—disruptions to programme delivery. There should be an appropriate staffing level to ensure that the treatment programme is unaffected by either staff leave or absence through sickness. Continued absences of programme staff can be disruptive and is, therefore, likely to impede the integrity of the programme.

Monitoring and Evaluation

To determine whether programme leaders and staff are maintaining fidelity to the programme, explicit procedures for monitoring and evaluation should be built in. Monitoring of programmes is not the "icing on the cake"—an optional extra—it is a fundamental process by which treatment integrity is maintained. The continuous monitoring of programmes facilitates the implementation of strategies to counter any attacks on the integrity of the programme. Furthermore, as information emerges, adjustments to the programme can be implemented without delay. Negative outcomes are thereby minimized.

Monitoring and evaluation should be done by considering multiple data sources. Programme staff, clients, and independent experts should evaluate the implementation of the treatment programme (Hollin, 1995). Harris and Rice (1997) suggest that the ideal programme:

> Would have a system to ensure its own integrity; this would entail measurement of outcomes, objective measurement of clinical gain for each therapeutic activity... and measurement and explicit feedback on the quantity of the staff members' performance of their clinical duties. There would also be contingent application of rewards to staffers and managers for appropriate performance on all three areas (p. 384).

A valuable tool for this purpose is the Correctional Program Evaluation Inventory (CPEI) (Gendreau & Andrews, 1991). The CPEI is a brief instrument used to improve documentation and process evaluation.

Conclusions

The above provides a summary of the current understanding of the development and maintenance of treatment integrity. This is an issue that requires to be pursued if significant improvement in offender programmes is to be achieved. There is no doubt that therapeutic nihilism is misplaced. Treatment can work with offenders. It can have a significant impact not only on recidivism rates, but also on the life of offenders and their potential victims.

REFERENCES

Andrews, D. (1989). Recidivism is predictable and can be influenced: Using risk assessments to reduce recidivism. *Forum on Corrections Research*, *1*, 11–18.

Andrews, D. (1995). The psychology of criminal conduct and effective treatment. In J. McGuire (Ed.), *What works: Reducing reoffending—guidelines from research and practice* (pp. 35–62). Chichester, UK Wiley.

Andrews, D. A., Bonta, J., & Hoge, R. D. (1990). Classification for effective rehabilitation. *Criminal Justice and Behaviour*, *17*(1), 19–52.

Andrews, D. A., & Kiessling, J. J. (1980). Programme structure and effective correctional practices: A summary of the CaVIC research. In R. R. Ross & P. Gendreau (Eds), *Effective correctional treatment* (pp. 35–53) Toronto, Canada: Butterworths.

Andrews, D. A., Zinger, I., Hoge, R. D., Bonta, J., Gendreau, P., & Cullen, F. T. (1990). Does correctional treatment work? A clinically relevant and psychologically informed meta-analysis. *Criminology*, *28*, 369–404.

Antonowicz, D. H., & Ross, R. R. (1994). Essential components of successful rehabilitation programs for offenders. *International Journal of Offender Therapy and Comparative Criminology*, *38*, 97–104.

Averbeck, M., & Lösel, F. (1994). Subjective theories on juvenile delinquency. In M. Steller, K. P. Dahle, & M. Basque (Eds.), *Straftaterbehandlung Argumente für Eine Revitalisierung in Forschung and Praxis* (pp. 213–226). Pfaffenweiler: Centaurus.

Bailey, W. C. (1966). Correctional outcome: An evaluation of 100 reports. *Journal of Criminal Law, Criminology and Police Science*, *57*, 153–160.

Basta, J. M., & Davidson II, W. S. (1988). Treatment of juvenile offenders: Study outcomes since 1980. [Special issue: Juvenile delinquency]. *Behavioral Sciences and the Law*, *6*, 355–384.

Blackburn, R. (1980). Still not working? A look at recent outcomes in offender rehabilitation. Paper presented at the Scottish Branch of the British Psychological Society's Conference on "Deviance", University of Stirling, UK.

Blackburn, R. (1993). *The psychology of criminal conduct*. Chichester, UK: Wiley.

Cohen, J. (1988). *Statistical power analysis for the behavioural sciences* (2nd ed.). New York: Academic Press.

Cooke, D. J. (1989). Containing violent prisoners. *British Journal of Criminology*, *29*, 129–143.

Cooke, D. J. (1995). Diversion from prosecution: A Scottish experience. In J. McGuire (Ed.), *What works: Reducing reoffending—guidelines from research and practice* (pp. 173–192). Chichester, UK: Wiley.

Cooke, D. J. (1997). The Barlinnie Special Unit: the rise and fall of a therapeutic experiment. In E. Cullen, L. Jones, & R. Woodward (Eds.), *Therapeutic communities in prison* (pp. 101–120). Chichester, UK: Wiley.

Cooke, D. J., & Michie, C. (1998). Predicting recidivism in a Scottish prison sample. *Psychology, Crime & Law*, *4*, 169–211.

Corsini, R. J., & Miller, G. A. (1954). Psychology in prisons, 1952. *American Psychologist*, *9*, 184–185.

Garrett, J. C. (1985). Effects of residential treatment on adjudicated delinquents. A meta-analysis. *Journal of Research in Crime and Delinquency*, *22*, 287–308.

Gendreau, P. (1995). Technology transfer in the criminal justice field: Implications for substance abuse. In T. E. Baker, S. L. David, & G. Soucy (Eds.), *Reviewing the behavioural science knowledge base on technology transfer* (NIDA Research Monograph No. 155). Rockville, MD: National Institute on Drug Abuse.

Gendreau, P. (1996). Offender rehabilitation: What we know and what needs to be done. *Criminal Justice and Behavior, 23*(1), 144–161.

Gendreau, P., & Andrews, D. A. (1990). Tertiary prevention: What the meta-analyses of the offender treatment literature tell us about "what works". *Canadian Journal of Criminology, 32*(1), 173–184.

Gendreau, P., & Andrews, D. A. (1991). *Correctional Program Evaluation Inventory* (2nd ed). New Brunswick, Canada: University of New Brunswick.

Gendreau, P., & Goggin, C. (1996). Principles of effective correctional programming. In L. Motuik & T. Murphy (Eds.), *Forum on corrections research* (pp. 38–41). Ontario, Canada: Research Division of Correctional Research and Development, Correctional Service of Canada.

Gendreau, P., Little, T., & Goggin, C. (1995). *A meta-analyses of the predictors of adult offender recidivism: Assessment guidelines for classification and treatment*. Ottawa, Canada: Ministry Secretariat, Solicitor General of Canada.

Gensheimer, L. K., Mayer, J. P., Gottschalk, R., & Davidson II, W. S. (1986). Diverting youths from the juvenile justice system: A meta-analysis of intervention efficacy. In S. J. Apter & A. Goldstein (Eds.), *Youth violence: Programs and prospects* (pp. 39–57). Elmsford, NY: Pergamon Press.

Glass, G. V., McGraw, B., & Smith, M. L. (1981). *Meta-analysis in social research*. Beverly Hills, CA: Sage.

Gottschalk, R., Davidson, W. S., Mayer, J. P., & Gensheimer, L. K. (1987). Behavioural approaches with juvenile offenders: A meta-analysis of long-term treatment efficacy. In E. K. Morris & C. J. Braukmann (Eds.), *Behavioural approaches to crime and delinquency: A handbook of application, research and concepts* (pp. 399–422). New York: Plenum.

Hamm, M. S., & Schrink, J. L. (1989). The conditions of effective implementation: A guide to accomplishing rehabilitative objectives in corrections. *Criminal Justice and Behaviour, 16*, 166–182.

Harris, G. T., & Rice, M. E. (1997). Mentally disordered offenders: What research says about effective service. In C. D. Webster & M. A. Jackson (Eds.), *Impulsivity, theory, assessment and treatment* (pp. 361–393). New York: Guilford.

Hollin, C. R. (1992a, September). *Treatment integrity: What is it and how do we achieve it?* Paper presented at the Conference "What Works 1992": Next Steps…Progress in Effective Work With Offenders, University of Salford, Manchester, UK.

Hollin, C. R. (1992b, July). *Training for behavioural work with young offenders in a residential setting*. Paper presented at The IVth World Congress on Behaviour Therapy, Queensland, Australia.

Hollin, C. R. (1995). The meaning and implications of "programme integrity". In J. McGuire (Ed.), *What works: Reducing reoffending—guidelines from research and practice* (pp. 195–208). Chichester, UK: Wiley.

Izzo, R. L., & Ross, R. R. (1990). Meta-analysis of rehabilitation programs for juvenile delinquents: A brief report. *Criminal Justice and Behavior, 17*, 134–142.

Johnson, V. S. (1981). Staff drift: A problem in treatment integrity. *Criminal Justice and Behavior, 8*, 223–232.

Kassenbaum, G., Ward, D., & Wilner, D. (1971). *Prison treatment and parole survival: An empirical assessment*. New York: Wiley.

Laws, D. R. (1974). The failure of a token economy. *Federal Probation, 38*, 33–38.

Lipsey, M. W. (1992a). Juvenile delinquency treatment: A meta-analytic inquiry into variability of effects. In T. D. Cooke, H. Cooper, D. S. Cordary, H. Hartmann, L. V. Hedges, R. L. Light, T. A. Louis, & F. Mosteller (Eds.), *Meta-analysis for explanation: A casebook.* (pp. 83–127) New York: Russel Sage Foundation.

Lipsey, M. W. (1992b). The effect of treatment on juvenile delinquents: Results from meta-analysis. In F. Lösel, D. Bender, & T. Bliesener (Eds.), *Psychology and law: International perspectives* (pp. 131–143). Berlin, Germany: New York: de Gruyter.

Lipsey, M. (1995). What do we learn from 400 research studies on the effectiveness of treatment with juvenile delinquents? In J. McGuire (Ed.), *What works: Reducing reoffending—guidelines from research and practice* (pp. 63–78). Chichester, UK: Wiley.

Lipton, D., Martinson, R., & Wilks, J. (1975). *The effectiveness of correctional treatment: A survey of treatment evaluation studies.* New York: Praeger.

Lloyd, C., Mair, G., & Hough, M. (1994). *Explaining reconviction rates: A critical analysis.* London: HMSO.

Lösel, F. (1993). The effectiveness of treatment in institutional and community settings. *Criminal Behaviour and Mental Health, 3*(4), 416–437.

Lösel, F. (1995a). Increasing consensus in the evaluation of offender rehabilitation? Lessons from syntheses. *Psychology, Crime, & Law, 2*, 19–39.

Lösel, F. (1995b). The efficacy of correctional treatment: A review and synthesis of meta-evaluations. In J. McGuire (Ed.), *What works: Reducing Reoffending—guidelines from research and practice* (pp. 79–111). Chichester, UK: Wiley.

Lösel, F. (1996, September). Effective correctional programming: What empirical research tells us and what it doesn't. *Forum on Corrections Research, 6*, 33–37.

Lösel, F. (1998). Treatment and management of psychopaths. In D. J. Cooke, A. E. Forth, & R. D. Hare (Eds.), *Psychopathy: Theory, research and implications for society* (pp. 303–354). Dordrecht, Netherlands: Kluwer Academic.

Lösel, F., & Köferl, P. (1989). Evaluation research on correctional treatment in West Germany: A meta-analysis. In H. Wegener, F. Lösel, & J. Haisch (Eds.), *Criminal behaviour and the justice system, Psychological perspectives* (pp. 334–355). New York Springer-Verlag.

Martinson, R. (1974). What works?—Questions and answers about prison reform. *The Public Interest, 10*, 22–54.

Mathias, R. E., Mathews, J. W., & Sindberg, R. M. (1989). Programs for prisons: Nihilism or pragmatic planning. *International Journal of Offender Therapy and Comparative Criminology, 33*, 141–149.

McDougall, C. (1996). Working in secure institutions. In C. R. Hollin (Ed.), *Working with offenders. Psychological practice in offender rehabilitation* (pp. 94–115). Chichester, UK: Wiley.

McDougall, C., Boddis, S., Dawson, K., & Hayes, R (1990). Developments in anger control training. In M. McMurran (Ed.), *Applying psychology to imprisonment: Young offenders.* (Issues in Criminological and legal psychology No. 15). Leicester, UK: The British Psychological Society.

Murphy, B. C. (1972). *A test of the effectiveness of an experimental treatment program for delinquent opiate addicts.* Ottawa, Canada: Information Canada.

Ogloff, J. R. P., Wong, S., & Greenwood, A. (1990). Treating criminal psychopaths in a therapeutic community. *Behavioural Sciences and the Law, 8*, 181–190.

Redondo, S. (1994). *El tratamiento de la delinqencia en Europa: Un estudio meta-analatico [Delinquency treatment in Europe: A meta-analysis]* (Tesus Doctoral) Spain: Universidad de Barcelona.

Rice, M. E., Harris, G. T., & Cormier, C. A. (1992). An evaluation of a maximum security therapeutic community for psychopaths and other mentally disordered offenders. *Law and Human Behavior, 16*, 399–412.

Robinson, J., & Smith, G. (1971). The effectiveness of correctional programs. *Crime and Delinquency, 17*, 67–80.

Rosenthal, R., & Rubin, D. B. (1982). A simple general purpose display of magnitude of experimental effect. *Journal of Educational Psychology, 74*, 166–169.

Ross, R. R., & Fabiano, E. A. (1985). *Time to think: A cognitive model of delinquency pre-*

vention and offender rehabilitation. Johnson City, TN: Institute of Social Sciences and Arts.

Schlichter, K. J., & Horan, J. J. (1981). Effects of stress inoculation on the anger and aggression management skills of institutionalised juvenile delinquents. *Cognitive Therapy and Research, 5*, 359–365.

Waldo, G., & Griswold, D. (1979). Issues in the measurement of recidivism. In L. B. Sechrest, S. O. White, & E. D. Brown (Eds.), *The rehabilitation of criminal offenders: Problems and prospects* (pp. 225–250). Washington, DC: National Academy of Sciences.

Whitehead, J. T., & Lab, S. P. (1989). A meta-analysis of juvenile correctional treatment. *Journal of Research in Crime and Delinquency, 26*, 276–295.

Woodward, R. (1997). Selection and training of staff for the therapeutic role in the prison setting. In E. Cullen, L. Jones, & R. Woodward, *Therapeutic communities for offenders* (pp. 223–252). Chichester, UK: Wiley.

Chapter 3

To Treat or Not to Treat? A Financial Perspective

Mark A. Cohen
Vanderbilt University, Nashville, USA

INTRODUCTION

Throughout this text, the position is advanced that some interventions can be successful in reducing rates of recidivism in offender populations. However, even if we accept that a treatment program is successful in reducing the incidence of recidivism, a key policy question is whether or not the costs of the program can be justified relative to its benefits. That is the subject of this chapter. First, we review the existing literature on the costs and benefits of offender treatment programs. Next, we provide the researcher and/or practitioner with the basic tools to analyze the costs and benefits of alternative treatment programs. The chapter concludes with a brief discussion of the limitations of this approach.

Conducting a cost–benefit analysis can be intimidating for even the trained economist or policy analyst—not to mention a practitioner who occasionally dabbles in this highly subjective art form which is sometimes labeled as science! Nonetheless, I argue in this chapter that any amount of quantification and evaluation is better than none. You do not have to be trained in the dismal science to do a credible first-cut analysis of the benefits and costs of program alternatives. Thus, the fact that you will not have all the information in the form that would be best for policy analysis should not deter you from doing the analysis. As I will discuss later in the chapter, there are methods explicitly to recognize and deal with these uncertainties and unknowns.

Handbook of Offender Assessment and Treatment. Edited by C. R. Hollin.
© 2000 John Wiley & Sons Ltd.

REVIEW OF THE LITERATURE ON COSTS AND BENEFITS OF TREATMENT

The existing literature on the benefits and costs of treatment alternatives generally takes either one of two forms: "cost-effectiveness" or "cost–benefit" studies. A cost-effectiveness study seeks to answer questions such as, "What is the cost per successfully treated offender who does not recidivate?" or "What is the cost per crime averted?" These questions require a thorough understanding of costs and the probability of a successful outcome. They do not, however, require the analyst to monetize the successful outcome. To do so would be to conduct a "cost–benefit" analysis.

It is worth noting that some analysts ask questions such as "What is the cost per offender?" Although important, this is purely a "cost" analysis and should not be construed as a "cost-effectiveness" study. In order to be a cost-effectiveness study, one must measure outcomes (e.g. crimes averted, recidivism rate), not just inputs (e.g. number of offenders admitted to the program). More importantly, to focus solely on costs can easily result in a conclusion to fund a program even if it has few benefits.

To date, there have been few published studies that attempt to either conduct cost-effectiveness or cost–benefit studies of offender treatment programs. Instead, most researchers stop at the question of whether or not a treatment program reduces recidivism at all. If so, it "works". The fact that there have been few such studies to date is not surprising, given the fact that researchers involved in program evaluation are seldom economists, and are not necessarily trained to analyze costs and benefits. A few studies do exist, however, and a brief sampling is shown below.

Cost-Effectiveness Studies

Although not technically examining a "treatment" program, Greenwood et al. (1994) compared various incarceration alternatives under consideration during the "three strikes" debate in California. In comparing five different alternatives, they found the "cost per serious crime prevented" to range from $11 800 (life in prison for the third violent offense) to $16 300 (life in prison for the third serious felony). Thus, if one were interested in the most "bang for the buck", focusing only on violent offenders would appear to be an appropriate policy decision. However, such a study does not tell us if it is worth $16 300 or more to avert one more serious crime. In fact, one might be able to avert more crimes with the more expensive program. In that case, if the "benefit" from averting one more serious crime exceeds $16 300, then it might be worth it to institute the more expensive alternative. Similarly, Greenwood Model, Rydell, and Chiesa (1996) compared four different child and youth intervention programs: home visits to new mothers and day care for their young children; parent training; high school graduation incentives; and delinquent supervision. In comparing these four alternatives, they found that per million dollars spent, graduation incentives prevented the largest number of serious crimes (258 crimes per million dollars), followed by parent training (157 crimes), delinquent supervision (72 crimes) and home visit/day care (11 crimes). Once again, although one might begin to prioritize spending on the basis of such a study, it does not tell us if *all* or only some of these programs should be adopted.

Thus, while the Greenwood et al. (1994) and Greenwood et al. (1996) studies can help us determine which approach is most cost effective, they are not equipped to answer the more basic question of whether any one approach is socially desirable. The policy analyst must make a subjective determination that the option being considered is worthwhile. That does not mean, however, that cost-effectiveness studies such as this one are without merit. They may also provide important information about the relative benefits of two or more programs being compared. For example, consider the study by Rydell and Everingham (1994), comparing supply-control drug strategies (e.g. drug seizures) to demand-control strategies (e.g. drug treatment). Although they were comparing apples to oranges in terms of programs, Rydell and Everingham were able to place these two approaches on equal footing by estimating the reduced cocaine consumption from each alternative. They found that a 1% reduction in cocaine consumption could be obtained by either spending $34 million on treatment or $246 million on domestic drug enforcement (Rydell & Everingham, 1994, p. 24, Table 3.2). Even higher costs were associated with drug interdiction or source-country control. This study is often cited as providing evidence that treatment is seven times more cost effective than drug control programs.

Cost–Benefit Studies

To date, few researchers have gone beyond cost-effectiveness analysis to compare explicitly the monetary costs to the monetary value of benefits. Perhaps the main reason for this scarcity of cost–benefit studies has been the reluctance of many analysts to place monetary values on the benefits of treatment programs. What is the value of reducing recidivism? What is the value of reducing drug dependence? Although these are difficult questions to answer, economists have developed methods for estimating the monetary value of goods or services that are not traded in the marketplace. For example, there are now estimates available of the monetary value of the costs and consequences of being a victim of crime (see Cohen, 1988; Cohen, Miller, & Rossman, 1994; and Miller, Cohen, & Wiersema, 1996). Table 3.1 reproduces the "cost-of-crime" estimates based on a study of injuries and losses suffered by victims of crime in the United States.

One of the more difficult issues when conducting a cost–benefit analysis is how to analyze fully the "non-monetary" costs and benefits—those that are not normally bought and sold in a marketplace. As shown in Table 3.1, the cost-of-crime estimates include both "tangible" costs such as medical costs, lost wages, and

Table 3.1 The cost of crime to victims

Crime	Tangible ($)	Intangible ($)	Total per crime ($)
Rape	5900	94 400	100 000
Robbery	2700	6 600	9 300
Aggrevated assault	1800	9 000	10 800
Burglary	1300	300	1 600
Larceny	430	0	430
Motor vehicle theft	4100	300	4 400

Note: Numbers may not add due to rounding.
Source: Dollar estimates taken from Miller, Cohen, and Wiersema (1996, Table 2), updated to 1997 dollars.

other out-of-pocket losses, as well as "intangible" costs such as pain, suffering, and reduced quality of life.

Some cost–benefit studies stop at tangible benefits. However, this can easily lead to unrealistic results. For example, Austin (1986) studied an early prison release program and concluded that the savings from building fewer prisons were greater than the costs of repeat victimization by those early releasees who recidivated when they would otherwise have been in prison. However, the only costs included in Austin's study were the costs of processing the recidivist offender through the criminal justice system, and the tangible (out-of-pocket) costs to victims. In the case of rape victims, the "tangible" cost was thus only about $350. To conclude that this early release program was worthwhile is tantamount to balancing the state budget on the backs of crime victims.

Rajkumar and French (1997) compare the costs and benefits of drug treatment programs, where the benefits are estimated to be the monetary value of reduced crime committed by rehabilitated drug abusers. Based on the Treatment Outcome Prospective Study (TOPS) of 11 750 drug abusers, they estimated the monetary value of reduced crime one year following treatment to the cost of the program. They concluded that the cost of treatment for one drug abuser was far outweighed by the benefit of reduced crime. A study of more recent drug treatment programs (Center for Substance Abuse Treatment, 1997) suggests that there are other substantial benefits from treatment, including reduced medical costs, increased employment, and reduced welfare benefits.

O'Farrell et al. (1996) compared the costs and benefits of three different approaches to outpatient alcoholism treatment. Benefits were measured as the reduced health expenses associated with inpatient hospitalization and reduced legal costs associated with days in jail for alcohol-related reasons. Thus, these are primarily out-of-pocket benefits. They found that two alternatives had positive benefit–cost ratios, while a third actually had smaller benefits than costs. They also conducted a cost-effectiveness study, estimating various outcomes per $100 investment. For example, individual counseling was found to be significantly more cost effective than a program that combines individual counseling with behavioral modification treatment.

A somewhat different approach was taken by Cohen (1998), in which the generic question was asked, "What is the monetary value of saving a high risk youth" from a life of crime, drug abuse, or dropping out of high school. In other words, if a treatment program targeting high-risk youth were to "save" one from going down the wrong path, then what were the monetary benefits of such a success? Cohen estimated the value of saving one high-risk youth from a life of crime to be $1.3 to $1.5 million in 1997 dollars (discounted to present value). Comparable estimates are $370 000 to $970 000 for a heavy drug abuser and $243 000 to $388 000 for a high school drop-out. These estimates provide a basis for others who would like to conduct a benefit–cost analysis of their own program.

COST–BENEFIT ANALYSIS MADE SIMPLE (?)

Although the last two examples suggest that a cost–benefit analysis of a treatment program is as simple as estimating the number of crimes averted and tallying up their monetary values, it is more complex than that. Cost–benefit analysis is an art that is built on many important underlying assumptions. It is important to understand some of these assumptions before attempting to conduct such a study. In particular, in order to address the costs and benefits of alternative treatments, the following questions need to be answered:

1. *From whose perspective* are these costs and benefits to be measured?
2. *Costs of treatment program:* What are the fixed costs and incremental costs per participant?
3. *Benefits of treatment program:* What short-term and long-term benefits are expected from this program? How can these benefits be expressed in monetary terms?
4. *Replication and comparability issues:* Is there a difference between the targeted group for this proposed treatment and the group exposed to treatment in earlier studies? Is there evidence that the treatment alternative being considered has been or can be replicated?

Each of these issues will be considered in turn. Before doing so, however, it is useful to set forth a simple hypothetical program evaluation that can be referred to throughout the remainder of this chapter. We will follow the annual budget deliberations of the hypothetical city of New Hope, and their decision about whether or not to fund the "New Hope Drug Treatment Program". This will enable us to move from abstract concepts to implementation in a real-world setting.

The New Hope Drug Treatment Program

The city of New Hope is located in the county of Wellchester. It is the largest city in Wellchester, and home to the county prison and county government agencies.

Table 3.2 Budgetary implications of the New Hope Drug Treatment Program

New Hope Drug Treatment Program costs	($)
Fixed costs (annual)	
Annual lease on facility	60 000
Full-time administrator and secretary	120 000
Incremental costs (per patient)	
Counseling (average 50 visits × $120)	6 000
Drug testing (average 50 weeks × $20)	1 000
Probation costs (average 50 weeks × $25	1 250

New Hope Drug Treatment Program—costs savings	
Fixed costs (annual)	
Prison expansion averted	$20 000 annualized cost of construction per prison bed
Incremental costs (per participant)	
Incarceration savings (average 5 months at $1200/month)	$6 000

Wellchester is otherwise a relatively poor rural county with the highest unemployment rate in the country and few social services for its residents other than those paid for by the federal government. New Hope's mayor, Joan Caring, is concerned about a recent increase in property crime and violent crime that appears to be related to an increase in the use of crack cocaine. Mayor Caring asked John Pennypincher, her chief financial officer, to investigate whether or not the city should offer a drug treatment program as an alternative to incarceration. The program would only be offered to first-time offenders of non-violent crimes who tested positive for illegal drugs.

Table 3.2 lists the program costs of the New Hope Drug Treatment Program. The program requires office space at an annual lease cost of $60 000 and a full-time administrator and secretary at an annual cost of $120 000. Treatment consists of an average of 50 intensive counseling sessions per offender, ongoing drug testing, and periodic reports to a probation officer. All of these costs are incurred on a per offender basis, since all labor and services are contracted for directly with service providers. As shown in Table 3.2, the average cost of counseling is expected to be $6000 per offender, drug testing $1000, and probation supervision $1250. The average offender who is diverted to drug treatment would have been incarcerated for about five months, at a cost of $40 per day or $1200 per month.

From Whose Perspective?

Before estimating costs and benefits, it is important to identify the party to whom the costs and benefits matter. At one extreme, for example, the policymaker might care about all social costs and benefits. In this case, we might care about costs and benefits to both the taxpayers and to victims of future crimes that might be averted. On the other hand, the proposed treatment program might be evaluated solely on the basis of the costs to the funding agency. In that case, one might only care about the cost of the treatment and the reduced expenditures from the future need to treat a recidivist offender.

The treatment outcome adopted might differ considerably depending on which scenario is adopted. For example, as shown in Table 3.2, the chief financial officer of New Hope is not considering the reduced crime committed by successful drug treatment participants, nor the increased crime resulting from the reduced incarceration. However, it is well known that drug addicts have a high propensity to commit property crimes—often to support their habits. Although crime reduction benefits are important social benefits, they might not enter into the decision calculus of the chief financial officer of New Hope. These are social costs—but they are not directly borne by the city through its budgetary process.

The issue of which perspective to consider when calculating costs and benefits is far more complex than suggested by this example. For example, some of the funds for this program might come from a federal government grant that would not otherwise be given to New Hope if they continued incarcerating such offenders. This might sway the balance in favor of drug treatment even if it is not socially beneficial.

If the interests of the decision maker are narrow enough, there may be no need to consider the monetary benefits of alternative programs. For example, consider the problem confronting the chief administrative officer of a social service agency charged with reducing the incidence of drug addiction. Given a fixed budget of $100 million per year, the administrator might consider which combination of treatment programs adds up to $100 million per year and also is the most effective at reducing drug addiction. Unless there is some important heterogeneity of addictions that call for different weights for different addictions, from the perspective of this agency, there is no need to consider the benefits of reduced drug addiction. Instead, they can simply look for the combination of the most effective drug addiction reduction programs. Of course, this does not guarantee a socially optimal solution. First, we do not know if the budget is too big or too small (and hence we are devoting too few or too many resources to fighting this social ill). Secondly, if the social service agency also allocates part of its scarce resources towards fighting other social ills, it might be useful to identify and to quantify the full costs and benefits of drug treatment programs (as well as the other programs administered by the agency). This will assist the administrator in allocating her agency's scarce resources in a socially optimal manner.

For the remainder of this chapter we abstract away from the above issue by considering the full social costs and benefits of treatment. We do not consider the more "narrow" focus of the administrator who cares solely about her budget and reducing her targeted social ill.

The Costs of Treatment Programs

This section considers the costs of treatment programs in more detail. It does not include the benefits of reduced recidivism or other anti-social behavior. Conceptually, all costs of a treatment program should be included in the cost analysis *if* those costs would not be incurred in the absence of the program. In practice, this is often a subtle task of delineating costs that are not often thought about in that manner. It requires an understanding of *incremental* (or *marginal*) costs versus *fixed* costs. It also requires an understanding of opportunity costs.

In Table 3.2, we identified certain expenditures as being fixed, i.e. they do not vary with the number of participants in the program. In this case, an annual lease and one-year contract with employees are considered to be fixed. Other costs— such as the cost of drug testing or counseling—do vary with the number of participants. These are considered incremental (or marginal) costs.

It is important to identify these different types of costs and to understand which are fixed and which are incremental. Different questions require different uses and combinations of these costs. For example, if we are interested in the *average* cost per participant, we first need to know how many particpants we expect. As shown in Table 3.3, the average cost will generally decline with the number of program participants. Thus, if New Hope expects to service 50 offenders per year, the average cost is $11 850 per offender. However, if they expect to service 200 offenders per year, that cost is reduced to $9150. The reason, of course, is that the fixed costs of $180 000 are allocated over a larger number of participants.

When are we interested in average costs? Average costs are relevant whenever we are comparing one option with another, *and* when all of the fixed and incremental costs may vary with our decision. However, there is a more important—and more fundamental—principle at work here that needs to be elaborated on at this point:

> When comparing two options, consider only the costs (and benefits) that will vary with the decision you are about to make.

This is a very general rule that can be applied throughout this chapter. As we will see, implementing this rule is often less than straightforward, and requires a careful analysis of which costs and benefits vary with the decisions. For example, if we are considering whether or not to start up or to renew the New Hope Drug Treatment Program, we want to compare the *average* cost of treatment to the alternatives we are considering. We consider average costs, since both the fixed and incremental costs will vary with the decision about whether or not to start up (or renew) this program. Suppose the alternative is incarceration for those offenders, and there is adequate prison space available. In that case, we would compare the *average* cost of the drug treatment program to the *incremental* cost of incarceration. Since there are plenty of prison beds available, the fixed costs associated with prison construction do not vary with our decision about whether

Table 3.3 Average cost of the New Hope Drug Treatment Program

Expected number of participants	Total cost ($)	Average cost ($)
50	180 000	
	412 000	
	592 500 / 50 =	11 850
100	180 000	
	825 000	
	1 005 000 / 100 =	10 050
200	180 000	
	1 650 000	
	1 830 000 / 200 =	9 150

Note: Fixed costs = $180 000; Incremental costs = $8250/participant.

or not to institute this drug treatment program. Hence, the fixed costs of incarceration are irrelevant in this case. Of course, this may not be true if the alternative to a drug treatment program is to build new prisons.

In some instances, average costs are irrelevant. For example, suppose the New Hope Drug Treatment Program is already operational, and there is adequate physical capacity to expand. The administrator is considering whether to expand the program to a broader population of offenders. In this case, the only relevant costs to this decision are the *incremental* costs of adding program participants—$8250 per participant.

Note also that when estimating the cost of incarceration (or savings due to less incarceration) we have only included the $1200 required monthly to maintain a prisoner—not the annualized cost of a prison cell. By doing so, we have assumed that the "opportunity cost" of the prison cell is zero. In other words, we assume that the prison is already operating and is not at full capacity. In that case, the cost of the prison space itself is a "sunk" cost that is not relevant to the costs and benefits of the proposed treatment program. We will incur the financing cost of the prison regardless of whether or not we incarcerate another drug abuser; thus, we will not "save" that amount if we divert the drug abuser to a non-incarcerative treatment program. On the other hand, if we were operating at full capacity and lack of prison space were forcing us to incarcerate fewer individuals than would otherwise be the case, then we might consider the $20 000 annualized cost of the prison cell to be an "opportunity cost" that is saved by diverting the offender. In that case, we are indeed saving $20 000 by not having to build another cell and/or by not enduring a higher crime rate due to our inability to incarcerate other offenders.

The Benefits of Treatment Programs

In many cases, the main benefits associated with treatment programs will be the cost savings from not putting the offender into an alternative program or facility. For example, in the previous section we considered some of the cost savings associated with the New Hope Drug Treatment Program, such as reduced prison expenditures. These cost savings could also be labeled as "benefits". Since we will subtract cost savings from new costs and compare benefits to costs, it does not matter whether they are labeled cost savings or benefits—the result is the same.

However, if New Hope decides to start a drug treatment program, city officials are presumably expecting to see benefits beyond simply the cost savings due to reduced incarceration. In particular, New Hope officials would expect to see some long-term benefits from offenders who successfully complete the drug treatment program. For example, a recent study of drug treatment programs listed benefits such as: reductions in crime; improvements in employment; decreases in homelessness; improvements in physical and mental health; reductions in medical costs; and reductions in risky sexual behavior (Center for Substance Abuse Treatment, 1997). Table 3.4 lists some of the potential benefits from the New Hope Drug Treatment Program. The largest tangible benefit is likely to be the savings from reduced incarceration—estimated to be $6000 per participant. However, one must also consider the possibility that some participants will recidivate and require other expenditures such as arrest, processing, jail, and re-incarceration.

In some offender populations, the benefit from reduced criminal activity (other than illegal drug sales themselves) will be the largest benefit. For example, Rajkumar and French (1997) estimate the tangible benefits from crime control to be at least $5128 per treated offender in 1992 dollars (or about $6000 in 1997 dollars). Tangible benefits include the medical costs and lost wages that victims would otherwise endure. They are actual out-of-pocket costs to somebody— either the victim, an insurance company, or government program. If intangible benefits are included (pain, suffering, and reduced quality of life), this figure increases to $14 273 (or $16 500 in 1997 dollars).

It is tempting to address some of the larger potential benefits of treatment

Table 3.4 Potential benefits of the New Hope Drug Treatment Program

Benefits to community
• Reduced incarceration costs
• Reduced crime
• Reduced welfare payments
• Reduced government-subsidized medical costs
• Income tax revenue

Additional benefits to participants
• Physical and mental health benefits to participants
• Reduced medical costs
• Increased employment

programs such as reducing the public's fear of crime or the return of residents to inner cities. However, in reality, most individual programs are too small to affect a large enough percentage of the population of offenders and ultimately to affect some of these larger social problems. Thus, a more appropriate analysis is to consider only the costs and benefits that accrue based on each individual program participant.

Replication and Comparability Issues

In most situations, the program being evaluated for potential implementation will be based on another effectively proven model program. Using information obtained from another program to estimate the benefits of a newly proposed program adds a new complexity to the equation, since the two programs will rarely be identical to each other. The treatment populations might differ (e.g. demographics or frequency of offending), the treatment protocols might differ (e.g. number of sessions, length of session, type of counseling), the program personnel might differ (e.g. educational background, experience, commitment), and the time periods might differ. Any one of these factors might alter the effectiveness of the proposed program. Given differences in these programs, success rates are likely to vary, as are the benefits conditional on success.

One method for dealing with this replication problem is to conduct a sensitivity analysis of the results. For example, suppose previous studies have found a treatment program to be 20% effective at reducing crime committed by those who complete the program, and that the benefits of the program exceed its costs. Instead of assuming a 20% effectiveness rate, one might vary this assumption to see how sensitive the cost–benefit analysis is to that rate. We would be much more confident in the program if it also passes a cost–benefit test with only a 10% success rate. However, we would be much less sanguine if only a slight reduction in effectiveness reversed the cost–benefit equation.

Another problem of comparability often arises when the benefits of a program will not be realized for many years into the future. For example, investing in a program that treats young offenders involves expenditures today, but might yield benefits over a 10-, 15-, 20-year time span or more. Since a dollar spent today is not the same as a dollar received 15 years from now, future benefits must be discounted to present value when compared with the costs borne today. Programs that require a multi-year funding commitment might also be evaluated by discounting future costs to present value. Although there is no general consensus of the appropriate discount rate for purposes of policy analysis, a commonly used rate is 2% per year, which is consistent with the "real" (i.e. net of inflation) discount rate for worker wages over time, and the real consumer interest rate over time.[1] Some government agencies, however, have routinely used net discount

---

[1] Note that these are "net" discount rates, since they already account for inflation. Thus, for example, a 2% discount rate would be consistent with long-term cost of living increases of 4% and long-term interest rates of 6%.

Table 3.5 Discount rate "factors"

Year	2% rate	10% rate
1	1	1
2	0.98	0.91
3	0.96	0.83
4	0.94	0.75
5	0.92	0.68
6	0.91	0.62
7	0.89	0.56
8	0.87	0.51
9	0.85	0.47
10	0.84	0.42
11	0.82	0.39
12	0.80	0.35
13	0.79	0.32
14	0.77	0.29
15	0.76	0.26
16	0.74	0.24
17	0.73	0.22
18	0.71	0.20
19	0.70	0.18
20	0.69	0.16
21	0.67	0.15
22	0.66	0.14
23	0.65	0.12
24	0.63	0.11
25	0.62	0.10

Note: The formula for discounting to present value is $1/[(1 + r)^{n-1}]$ where r is the discount rate and n is the number of years. For example, the present value of $1 in year four discounted at a 2% rate is $1/[1 + 0.02)^3] = 1/(1.02 \times 1.02 \times 1.02) = 1/1.06 = 0.94$; If a program is expected to have a \$100 000 benefit in year 4, the present value of that benefit is thus \$94 000.

rates of around 10%. The higher the discount rate, the lower the present value of future benefits. Table 3.5 provides discount rate factors for both a 2% and 10% rate. For example, if a program is expected to have a benefit of \$100 000 in years one through four, the present value of that \$400 000 benefit stream (at a 2% discount rate) is \$388 400.

NEW HOPE DRUG TREATMENT PROGRAM (HYPOTHETICAL EXAMPLE, CONTINUED)

Returning to the New Hope Drug Treatment Program, we can now analyze both the costs and benefits of this proposed change in government policy. Table 3.6 illustrates three scenarios. The first scenario assumes there will be 100 program

Table 3.6 Hypothetical costs and benefits of the New Hope Drug Treatment Program

	Scenario 1 ($)	Scenario 2 ($)	Scenario 3 ($)
A. Costs	1 005 000	1 005 000	592 500
Benefits (tangible only)			
• Incarceration savings	600 000	600 000	300 000
• Crime reduction benefit	600 000	300 000	150 000
B. Total Benefits	1 200 000	900 000	450 000
Net Benefits (B − A)	195 000	(105 000)	(142 500)
Benefit/Cost Ratio (B/A)	1.2	0.9	0.76
Benefits (including intangibles)			
• Incarceration savings	600 000	600 000	300 000
• Crime reduction benefit	1 650 000	825 000	412 500
D. Total Benefits	2 250 000	1 425 000	712 500
Net Benefits (D − A)	1 245 000	420 000	120 000
Benefit/Cost Ratio (D/A)	2.2	1.4	1.2

participants per year and that these participants would otherwise spend an average of five months in jail. Thus, the total cost of the program is $1 005 000 (from Table 3.3), compared with a cost savings from reduced jail expenses of $600 000 (from Table 3.2). Without any other benefits, the program costs exceed its benefits by $400 000. However, it is also estimated that the drug treatment program will reduce crime. Based on the estimate in Rajkumar and French (1997), the tangible benefits alone are estimated to be about $600 000, while total benefits (including intangibles) are $1.65 million. Either way, accounting for the crime control reductions brought about by the drug treatment program now yields projected benefits that exceed the cost of the program. The "net benefits" (benefits minus costs) are positive in either case, and the "benefit–cost ratio" (benefits divided by costs) exceeds 1.0.

The second scenario assumes only half the crime reduction benefit that Rajkumar and French estimate. This is an example of sensitivity analysis. We now find that costs exceed tangible benefits, for a benefit–cost ratio less than one. However, if intangible costs are included, the benefit–cost ratio now increases to 1.4.

The final scenario also assumes only half the crime reduction benefits as in scenario two. Now, however, a smaller program is envisioned, whereby there are only 50 participants per year instead of 100. Once again, the benefit–cost ratio is less than one (0.76) for tangible benefits, and slightly more than one (1.2) when including intangible benefits. Note that this example—when compared with scenario two—also illustrates the fact that smaller scale programs are less likely to pass a benefit–cost test because they have to allocate fixed costs over a smaller number of participants. Recall that the New Hope Drug Treatment Program had fixed costs of $120 000—regardless of the number of participants.

Finally, it is important to note that Table 3.6 ignores the question of "who pays" for the costs of the program. Despite the fact that several of these scenarios have benefit–cost ratios greater than one, less than half of the benefits of the program are received directly by the City of New Hope through cost savings or increased tax revenue. Instead, the main beneficiaries of the program (aside from the offenders themselves) are the potential victims of crime. Although these potential victims might be taxpayers and/or voters, they are not immediately identifiable, and thus are not organized. Thus, if the only costs and benefits considered are those that are directly paid by taxpayers, none of these drug treatment programs will pass the benefit–cost test.

CONCLUDING REMARKS

This chapter has demonstrated the importance of considering both the costs and the benefits of treatment programs. Although the practitioner might think in terms of "cost per treated offender", the more relevant cost is "cost per unit of benefit" where the benefit might include reduced crimes, successful drug treatment, high school completion, etc. Even if a treatment program has been shown to reduce recidivism, it is important to know at what cost and at what benefit. It does little good to know that a program costs $10 000 per offender treated without knowing the corresponding benefit received for that $10 000.

Unfortunately, few program analysts and even fewer practitioners will have adequate information at their disposal to conduct a rigorous cost–benefit analysis. Nevertheless, some items can be quantified more readily than others. I have argued in this chapter that it is important to identify these costs and benefits conceptually even if you cannot quantify all of them. Once the likely cost and benefit categories have been identified, you can begin to compare the known quantifiable costs with your best estimate of the magnitude of the costs or benefits that are subject to more uncertainty. I have also provided a cookbook approach to dealing with issues such as uncertainty and the fact that benefits may accrue over long periods of time.

The techniques used in this chapter have been used for many years in other areas of public policy—including environmental, health, and safety regulation. They are just beginning to penetrate the criminal justice policy arena. The technique is not "ideological", but instead can be an important tool in the public policy debate. Both the hard-line view of "three strikes and you're out" and the more compassionate view of focusing on prevention instead of punishment can be subjected to rigorous cost–benefit analyses in addition to political rhetoric.

REFERENCES

Austin, J. (1986). Using early release to relieve prison crowding: A dilemma in public policy. *Crime and Delinquency, 32*, 404–502.

Center for Substance Abuse Treatment (1997). *National treatment improvement evaluation study (NTIES)* [On-line]. Substance Abuse and Mental Health Services Administration. Available: URL http://www.health.org/nties97/index.htm.

Cohen, M. A. (1988). Pain suffering and jury awards: A study of the cost of crime to victims. *Law and Society Review, 22*(3), 538–555.

Cohen, M. A. (1998). The monetary value of saving a high risk youth. *Journal of Quantitative Criminology, 14*(1), 5–33.

Cohen, M. A., Miller, T. R., & Rossman, S. B. (1994). The costs and consequences of violent behavior in the United States. In A. J. Reiss, Jr & J. A. Roth (Eds.), *Volume 4: Consequences and control of understanding and preventing violence* (pp. 67–166) National Research Council. Washington, DC: National Academy Press.

Greenwood, P. W., Model, K. E., Rydell, C. P., & Chiesa, J. (1996). *Diverting children from a life of crime: Measuring costs and benefits.* Santa Monica, CA: Rand Corp.

Greenwood, P. W., Rydell, C. P., Abrahamse, A. F., Caulkins, J. P., Chiesa, J., Model, K. E., & Klein, S. P. (1994). *Three strikes and you're out: Estimated benefits and costs of California's new mandatory-sentencing law.* Santa Monica, CA: Rand Corp.

Miller, T. R., Cohen, M. A., & Wiersema, B. (1996, February). *Victim costs and consequences: A new look* (National Institute of Justice Research Reports, NCJ-155282).

O'Farrell, T. J., Choquette, K. A., Cutter, H. S. G., Floyd, F. J., Bayog, R., Brown, E. D., Lowe, J., Chan, A., & Deneault, P. (1996). Cost–benefit and cost-effectiveness analyses of behavioral marital therapy as an addition to outpatient alcoholism treatment, *Journal of Substance Abuse, 8*(2), 145–166.

Rajkumar, A. S., & French, M. T. (1997). Drug abuse, crime costs, and the economic benefits of treatment. *Journal of Quantitative Criminology, 13*(3), 291–324.

Rydell, C. P., & Everingham, S. S. (1994). *Controlling cocaine: Supply versus demand programs.* Santa Monica, CA: Rand Corp.

Part II

Risk Assessment

Chapter 4

Risk Assessment of Child Abuse

Martin Herbert
University of Exeter, Exeter, UK

INTRODUCTION

"Is it possible to identify, with a reasonable degree of certainty, children who are at risk of being abused, thus making it possible to intervene at an early stage with their families, with effective preventive, or remedial programmes?" This question, or variations on the theme, has challenged child care professionals and researchers for several decades. Sadly, it has to be admitted at the very outset of this review, that the search for a relatively straightforward, economical, and reliable set of predictive procedures or instruments has proved to be a chimera. Not only has such a narrowly focused search proved to be futile, it is always likely to be thus. Given the over-inclusive nature of the term "child abuse", the absence of a consensus on definitions, and the multidimensional precursors, maintenance influences, and outcomes of acts of maltreatment towards children, the desire for "short cuts" was bound to remain frustrated. This is not, however, a counsel of despair! A good case can be made out for the systematic application of our not inconsiderable knowledge of predisposing and precipitating factors in child abuse, in order to initiate broadly based assessments and interventions pre-emptively (or early) with potentially "risky" families. Inevitably, in a chapter of this brevity, a review of the evidence is bound to be circumscribed in scope.

Handbook of Offender Assessment and Treatment. Edited by C. R. Hollin.
© 2000 John Wiley & Sons Ltd.

DEFINITIONS

For the purposes of the review, child abuse is defined in terms of three of the four categories for placing children on the protection register as defined by the Department of Health and Social Security (1986). They are:

- *Physical abuse:* physical injury to a child. This might be due to excessive corporal punishment. It also includes deliberate poisoning, where there is definite knowledge, or a reasonable suspicion, that the injury was inflicted, or knowingly not prevented.
- *Sexual abuse:* the involvement of dependent, developmentally immature children and adolescents in sexual activities they do not truly comprehend, to which they are unable to give informed consent, or which violates social taboos concerning family roles.
- *Emotional abuse/neglect (combined by the author):* the severe adverse effect on the behaviour and emotional development of a child caused by persistent or severe emotional ill-treatment or rejection. As all abuse involves some emotional ill-treatment, this category is used where it is the main or sole form of abuse. Neglect involves the persistent or severe neglect of a child (for example, exposure to dangers such as cold and starvation, which results in serious impairment of the child's health or development, including non-organic failure to thrive).

FAMILY VIOLENCE AND THE PHYSICAL ABUSE OF CHILDREN

It is particularly difficult to predict precisely the likelihood of family violence (which may involve the child as victim) as some members resort to violence inconsistently, while others do so consistently, especially at times of extreme stress. Nevertheless, we can draw on research which has identified factors that are usually present when aggressive incidents and violent interactions occur (e.g. Patterson, 1982; Webster-Stratton & Herbert, 1994). An understanding of the major causes of family violence might (as secondary prevention) lead to a risk strategy of routinely screening all families who come into contact with social and health services with the purpose of targeting special help on "high-risk" families. The expectation is that specialist services (e.g. parenting skill groups) will reduce coercive interactions and aversive communications, and thus bring about a decrease in the physical maltreatment of children, notably temperamentally difficult youngsters. Research (see Moffitt & Caspi, 1998) indicates that maltreatment and witnessing parental aggression during early childhood predict that children are likely to develop conduct problems. Conduct problems, in turn, predict later partner violence, which first emerges in adolescent dating experiences. Rates of partner violence double among young couples who move from dating into cohabiting, and who bear children at a young age so that aggressive behaviour becomes highly stable across the life course of individuals, and is transmitted from generation to generation within families.

Methods for Detecting Risk Factors

In earlier times it was claimed that an "early warning system" could begin in the labour room, and that potentially abusive parents could be predicted with 76% accuracy from attributes detected during the first 24 hours after birth (Gray, Cutler, Dean, & Kempe, 1977). Checklists of early warning signs proliferated, notably in the 1970s (e.g. Daniel, Newberger, Reed, & Kotelchuck, 1978; Lynch, Roberts, & Gordon, 1976; Lynch & Roberts, 1977). The early enthusiasm for such lists and the uncritical trust in their reliability and validity for routine monitoring of potential child-abusing parents, have diminished in the face of critical reviews (Barker, 1990; Howitt, 1992) and prospective studies (e.g. Browne & Saqi, 1988).

The picture which emerges from a plethora of studies of the different forms of aggression expressed between family members is that family violence is a many-sided phenomenon, caused and maintained by a wide range of mechanisms. There are no *simple* solutions! Certainly, the research literature reveals that certain characteristics are common to those who abuse. They tend to have low self-esteem; a sense of personal incompetence (low self-efficacy); and a sense of being unsupported and helpless. Other features include (*inter alia*) depression; social isolation; a tendency to be aggressive; and little demonstration of warmth or empathy. Their predisposition to violence is exacerbated by their impulsivity and poor self-control. Many experience difficulties in their marriages or cohabitations. Such perpetrators have themselves, as children, frequently been victims of abuse. These are but a few of the characteristics which emerge from research into family violence (see Azar, Ferraro, & Breton, 1998; Skuse & Bentovim, 1994). Browne (see Browne & Herbert, 1997) has identified a list of screening characteristics for child abuse (Table 4.1). Small wonder, when one looks at the defining characteristics for child abuse which are present in non-abusing families, that the risk assessor is faced with a major problem of false positives and false negatives in his/her predictions.

It is important to bear in mind that a correlation does not necessarily imply causation. Correlations are sometimes found between criminality, alcoholism, drug abuse, low intelligence, and various forms of family violence. Obviously, there are many people who drink heavily, or have criminal records, but never abuse children, wives, or grandparents. Causation is a difficult concept: some factors may set the stage (predispose) a person towards abusive behaviour (for example, a childhood experience of being maltreated oneself), while others trigger or precipitate particular incidents of assault. Many causal agents ("multifactorial causation") operate in cases of family violence, as in so many other areas of family dysfunction.

These factors illustrate why no one theory provides a complete rationale (and

Table 4.1 Relative predictive value of screening characteristics for child abuse as determined by discriminant function analysis. (Ranked in order of importance with percentage prevalence)

Checklist characteristics n = Parents with a child under 5 (baseline)	Abusing families (%) (n = 106)	Non-abusing families (%) (n = 14.146)	Conditional probability[a] (%) 0.7
1. History of family violence	30.2	1.6	12.4
2. Parent indifferent, intolerant or over-anxious towards child	31.1	3.1	7.0
3. Single or separated parent	48.1	6.9	5.0
4. Socio-economic problems such as unemployment	70.8	12.9	3.9
5. History of mental illness, drug or alcohol addiction	34.9	4.8	5.2
6. Parent abused or neglected as child	19.8	1.8	7.6
7. Infant premature, low birth weight	21.7	6.9	2.3
8. Infant separated from mother for more than 24 hours post-delivery	12.3	3.2	2.8
9. Mother less than 21 years old at time of birth	29.2	7.7	2.8
10. Step-parent or cohabitee present	27.4	6.2	3.2
11. Less than 18 months between birth of children	16.0	7.5	1.6
12. Infant mentally or physically handicapped	2.8	1.1	1.9

[a] "Conditional probability" refers to the percentage of families with a particular characteristic that later abuse and/or neglect their newborn in the first five years of life.
Source: Browne and Herbert, 1997.

certainly not an all-embracing, integrated explanation, or set of highly discriminative risk criteria) for the diverse and individual abusive acts. A particular goal of risk assessment is to assess parenting responses to child rearing needs (Azar & Wolfe, 1989). With physical abuse, in addition to the influence of parental psychological functioning and situational stressors, there is a strong link between the abuse and events that, in some manner, involve the child (e.g. disciplinary situations, Wolfe, 1985). The majority of cases of physical abuse involve relatively minor physical injuries, and most of these take place in what parents perceive to be disciplinary encounters. This allows us to set a realistic, but optimistic, agenda for child abuse interventions (Frude, 1991; Herbert & Wookey, 1998; Webster-Stratton & Herbert, 1993, 1994; Wolfe, 1987). Relevant to the risk assessment issue is Frude's opinion that a high level of concern, both by the public and by professionals, with regard to the serious and dramatic injuries sustained by *relatively* few children, may prove to have the most welcome effect of increasing the general community support available for the very large number of troubled parents and their children. However, this is unlikely to happen if undue attention is drawn to those parents who systematically and sadistically torture their children. Frude is concerned that this distorted image of the abusing parent may lead to the withdrawal of any sympathy towards *all* parents involved in non-accidental injury and their stigmatization as "monsters", "inhumane", and "a race apart".

An understandable public concern, and a professional preoccupation with narrow-focused risk indicators, should not *blind* us to the individuality of parents who abuse, and the normality of some of their predicaments. This is *not* to condone maltreatment, but to argue for keeping a sense of proportion. Wolfe (1987) states that the conceptualization of physical abuse as impulsive, yet not necessarily malicious, forms a major basis for contending that abusive parents are not marked by major forms of psychopathology, but rather demonstrate critical defects within the boundless possibilities of what can go wrong for any parents in the course of rearing children. In some homes, violence is accepted as the "norm". One needs to consider potentially explosive situations such as a socially isolated, inexperienced, single parent, often living in poor accommodation and trying to manage a persistently difficult, crying baby. Fortunately, there is a great deal that can be done to help parents with these so-called disciplinary problems (Herbert, 1993, 1998; Patterson, 1982; Webster-Stratton & Herbert, 1993, 1994).

Psychometric Instruments

Some instruments exist for examining physical abuse potential (e.g. the Child Abuse Potential Inventory, Milner, 1986, 1989). The validity of these instruments is limited and therefore it is advisable to use them with caution and simply as adjuncts to more comprehensive assessment procedures, a matter we return to.

In the study in Browne and Herbert (1997) referred to earlier (see also Browne, 1988; Browne & Saqi, 1988), with its accompanying statistical table (Table 4.1), the checklist detection rate meant that for every 14252 births screened in the study, it would be necessary to distinguish between 72 true risk cases and 892 false positives in the 1964 cases identified as high risk. This follows from the finding that fully completed checklists, with the relative weighting for each factor taken into account, could correctly classify 86% of cases. The screening procedure was sensitive to 68% of abusing families, and correctly specified 94% of the non-abusing families. Surprisingly, nearly one-third of the abusing families had few risk-factor characteristics of any weight, and were incorrectly identified as "low risk" around the time of birth. The most worrying aspect of the checklist is that 6% of the non-abusing families were incorrectly identified as high risk for potential child abuse, since they were found to have a number of heavily weighted risk factors.

The relatively low prevalence of child abuse (seven children in every 1000 in

Browne's five-year follow-up study) combined with even the most optimistic estimates of screening effectiveness, implies that a screening programme would yield
large numbers of false positives. As outlined by Browne and Herbert (1997) the
chances of situational stressors (risk factors) resulting in child abuse and other
forms of family violence are mediated by, and depend on, the interactive relationships within the family. A secure relationship between the parent and child
may well "buffer" any effects of stress and facilitate coping strategies by the
parents. In contrast, an insecure or anxious relationship is less likely to "buffer"
the parent under stress, and any overload, such as an argument or a child being
particularly defiant or demanding, may result in a physical attack. Overall, this
will have a negative effect on the existing parent–child relationship—a downward spiralling sequence that reduces any protective effects still further. Thus, it
is more likely that stress will overcome the parent yet again. This may lead to a
situation where stress results in repeated physical assaults on the child. Indeed,
stress in family functioning (notably the so-called "coercive spiral") has been
shown to be an important predictor of child abuse potential (Abidin, 1990;
Patterson, 1982).

SEXUAL ABUSE

"Sexual abuse" is not a diagnosis. It is an *event*, or a series of events, which occurs
in a relationship in which the child is involved. However, the physical or psychological consequences may be "diagnosed" and may be deemed to be consistent with sexual abuse. Among the different aims involved in the evaluation of
sexual abuse, investigations may be carried out in order to determine whether or
not an individual has been abused, or information sought in order to provide
proof, or evidence, of abuse for legal purposes. Investigating an allegation of
sexual abuse would lead to the gathering of evidence; investigating a suspicion
of sexual abuse would rely on a clinical diagnosis or an examination of the effects
of sexual abuse. Conducting evaluations useful to legal proceedings requires
special skills (see Azar, 1992; Azar & Bengit, 1994). Expert testimony is often
solicited in such cases and requires a knowledge of both legal criteria and measurement. Special techniques and knowledge may be needed (e.g. use of anatomi-
cally correct dolls—a matter discussed below). The literature is just beginning to
develop in this area.

Definitions of sexual abuse (e.g. Finkelhor & Korbin, 1988) have excluded
abuse by adolescents or peers, but there has been a shift towards definitions that
include this as a form of sexual abuse. Most abuse is committed by men; some
5–15% of abuse is perpetrated by women. Recognition of sexual abuse depends
upon a child's account of her or his experiences, and less frequently on physical
findings. Thus, the child's account is of prime importance. To achieve an adequate
assessment, it is essential that high-quality multidisciplinary working practices are
developed, in which interviews with children mesh with other parts of the multidisciplinary process of assessment. Interviews with children are supplemented

by enquiries in other areas of the child's life, including family life. There is a growing literature on the child as witness. (For a discussion of these issues, see Smith & Bentovim, 1994; Vizard, 1991).

Vizard (1991) provides guidelines for the conduct of interviews with potential child witnesses. The search for "core symptoms" as indicators has not been notably successful. Among these have been behavioural regression, somatic complaints, fearfulness, bedwetting, and others (Conte, 1991). However, these problems are indicators of stress in childhood which parallel those of children experiencing other life-event traumas. Stressors might be any of a number of events, including, but not exclusively, victimization by sexual abuse. One of the effects of sexual abuse can be some form of inappropriate sexual behaviour on the part of the child. Yet again, as with other behavioural disturbance, not all abused children exhibit sexualized behaviour, while some non-abused children do.

One line of research might be the development of a standardized measure, based on developmental psychological theory of children's knowledge about sex, to assess the appropriateness of their knowledge. Another avenue of investigation is the negative effect of sexual abuse on self-esteem. There has been little in the way of measurement of the cognitive effects of sexual abuse in children, although there is some work on its effect on scholastic achievement (Tong, Oates, & McDowell, 1987). Most popular among the assessment procedures are rating scales (e.g. the Louisville Behavior Checklist (LBC), Miller, 1981), child behaviour profiles and symptom checklists, or questionnaire assessments. The use of projective techniques as an adjunct to psychological investigation of sexual abuse merits special attention.

Babiker (1982) used a battery of indirect psychological measures to test whether they would differentiate accurately between children who had been sexually abused and children who had not. The study aimed to answer the following questions:

1. What psychological measures might be of use in the detection of sexual abuse in children and adolescents?
2. Which combination of psychological measures had the best predictive value in identifying sexual abuse?

Three groups of children (sexually abused, physically abused, and non-abused) were compared using blind interviewing for their responding on measures of human figure drawing (HFD) and an exploratory, sexual-abuse-orientated modification of the word association test (WAT). The younger children were also compared on anatomical doll play (ADP). This study attempted to address the issue of adequately matching sexually abused children with comparison groups on important covariants of abuse. Towards this end, all the children ($n = 49$) were the subject of care orders by Social Services and living away from home. The three groups were matched as closely as possible with respect to age and sex. The three study measures were investigated by means of univariate and multivariate analyses. The findings of the univariate analyses were that while the utility of WA as a measure received minimal support, none of the three tests discriminated adequately between sexually abused children and other groups. However, multivariate analysis indicated that combinations of all three variables were significant predictors in the study sample of correct classification by abuse groups. Physically abused subjects were in some ways more reserved than the other groups: they demonstrated no sexual activity with dolls, and significantly longer search times with words. Non-abused subjects did not emerge as significantly less disturbed than the two abused groups. It is possible that whatever reasons led to their being taken into care, while not constituting abuse, were nevertheless traumatic. But whether trauma, which may be common to all three groups, comprises specific effects in each group, remains to be determined. Therefore, although there were some interesting differences observed in the results of the analyses, none of these appeared sufficiently powerful to suggest that any single measure could be used in isolation to detect sexual abuse. Although the retrospective discriminant function analyses appear fairly promising, before any conclusions can be reached as to the meaningfulness of the combinations of variables they contain, the models generated must be replicated (i.e. cross-validated) on an independent sample.

It is important to remember that sexual abuse takes place within a socio-cultural context, and assessment decisions are greatly influenced by the estimated costs of a false "diagnosis". The cost is determined to a large extent by decisions about the trade-off between the two types of error: the risk of misclassifying children who are being abused, and possibly subjecting them to further trauma of repeated interviews, versus the risk of misclassifying children who are not being abused and possibly subjecting them and their families unncessarily to the stress of intervention. Professionals are encouraged to combine the use of standardized measures with the traditional interview in their work with sexually abused children for the general purposes of research and the clinical identification of those in need of help in these areas. It is advisable to refrain from using, in isolation, the kinds of measures for which so little empirical evidence has been unearthed (see Aber, Allen, Carlson & Cicchetti, 1989; Babiker, 1983, and Babiker & Herbert, 1998, for a review of instruments).

EMOTIONAL ABUSE AND NEGLECT

The concept of emotional abuse is in danger of being over-inclusive and far too vague. It is therefore an advantage to have tangible indicators to pinpoint its presence (see Garbarino, Goffman, & Seeley, 1986). Emotional abuse:

- entails punishment of positive operant behaviour such as smiling, mobility, manipulation
- is behaviour which results in discouragement of parent–infant bonding (for example, pushing children away every time they seek proximity, comfort, and affection)

- involves the punishment of self-esteem as when parents endlessly criticize their child
- is parental behaviour leading to the punishing of those interpersonal skills (for example, friendliness) which are vital for acceptance in environments outside the home; for example, school, peer groups.

In assessing risk it has to be recognized that the different types of child abuse, as described earlier, and that are under present discussion, often co-occur, and their interactive effect is not well understood. There is a growing consensus among professionals that emotional abuse (perhaps better-named, maltreatment) is at the core of all major forms of abuse. It requires particular attention to disentangle emotional from physical acts of maltreatment (Garbarino et al., 1986). The association between types of abuse is illustrated in Farmer and Owens' (1995) study. They found that the existence of secondary concerns was a factor significantly related to the placement of a child's name on the protection register. For example, in a third of cases where the main concern was neglect, there were also concerns about physical abuse; in a fifth of cases where the main concern was physical abuse, there were also concerns about neglect; in a quarter of cases where the main concern was sexual abuse, there were also concerns about neglect; in a sixth of cases where the main concern was sexual abuse, there were also concerns about physical abuse; and in a quarter of cases where the main concern was physical abuse, there were also concerns about emotional abuse.

Risk assessment in the area of emotional abuse is complicated by the vague criteria which resist rigorous operational definition. It can include both acts of omission and commission. Some professionals have concentrated on parental behaviour that is considered deleterious (e.g. McGee & Wolfe, 1991); others have proposed that parental behaviour is an inadequate predictor of emotional damage and have attended rather to outcomes in the child (e.g. Kavanagh, 1982). Kavanagh is of the opinion that emotional deprivation to be abusive has to cause obvious physical syndromes such as failure to thrive (see also Iwaniec, 1995).

With regard to outcomes, a child is thought to be "in need" if (in today's legislation)

1. he/she is unlikely to achieve or maintain, or to have the opportunity of achieving, or maintaining, a reasonable standard of health or development, without the provision for him/her of specified services by a local authority (see Part III of the Children Act); or
2. he/she is likely to be significantly impaired, or further impaired, without provision of such services; or
3. he/she is disabled.

"Development" means physical, intellectual, emotional, social, or behavioural development; and "health" means physical or mental health. Concepts of maltreatment are linked to knowledge of a child's developmental needs and attain-

ments. There is a wealth of evidence from various studies that psychological maltreatment affects children's development or leads to psychological disturbance
(e.g. Cicchetti, 1990; Clausen & Crittenden, 1991; Egeland & Erikson, 1987; Hart
& Brassard, 1991).

Professionals carrying out a risk assessment need a sound empirical knowledge base for their recommendations and decisions (see Schaffer, 1990). It is vital
to be clear about what questions are being posed in the assessment, its purpose
and, therefore, objectives. For example, the needs of children who needs involve
two kinds of functions are potentially at risk (if not responded to consistently)
are of two kinds, those involving:

1. survival functions such as the need for food, shelter and physical care, and
2. psychosocial functions, including the child's requirements of love, security,
    attention, new experiences, acceptance, education, praise, recognition, and
    belongingness.

The Children Act uses the concept of "reasonable parents". In referring to care
orders, Section 31 specifies that the care must be "what it would be reasonable
to expect a parent to give".

If an assessment of these matters is to be trusted, the methods or risk-
indicators used, and their application, should meet certain criteria:

*   They should have the appropriate coverage—breadth and specificity—and
    should, for example, be of a representative sample of the client's behaviour
    occurring in specific situations.
*   They should provide indicators or measures that are fair. The assessment
    should not apply to a biased or narrow aspect of the client's activities or
    attitudes, nor should one use tests or questions that are culture-bound
    (ethnocentric) and which therefore discriminate unfairly against particular
    individuals.
*   They should provide accurate indicators or measures, which means that they
    should be reliable (and, if circumstances allow, repeatable). They should also
    be translated into precise statements and descriptions as opposed to vague,
    global terminology.
*   They should provide indicators or measures that are relevant. Relevance is
    critical if assessments are to be valid. This means that assessments should
    measure or indicate what they purport to measure/indicate.
*   They should be practicable in the sense of not being unwieldy, excessively
    time-consuming, or esoteric.
*   They should be ethical—a *sine qua non* of all practice.

When it comes to emotional abuse, the professional may have a nagging
concern about a child who is failing to thrive or cope, and/or parents who appear
ignorant or unwilling to face up to the possible harm to their child because of
the state of his or her health or development. At *least* the professional must have
reasonable cause to suspect that the child is suffering, or is likely to suffer,
significant harm (see Herbert, 1993).

Table 4.2 The quality of parental care

Emotional needs	Some defining criteria
1. Affection	Affection includes physical contact, admiration, touching, holding, comforting, making allowances, being tender, showing concern, communicating.
2. Security	Security means continuity of care, a predictable environment, consistent controls, settled patterns of care and daily routines, fair and understandable rules, harmonious family relationships, the feeling that one's home and family are always there.
3. Responsibility	Responsibility involves discipline appropriate to the child's stage of development, providing a model to emulate/imitate, indicating limits, insisting on concern for others.
4. Independence	Independence implies making opportunities for the child to do more unaided and make decisions, first about small things but gradually about larger matters.
5. Responsiveness	Responsiveness means prompt, consistent, appropriate actions to meet the child's needs.
6. Stimulation	Stimulation means encouraging curiosity and exploratory behaviour by praising, by responding to questions and play, by promoting training/educational opportunities and new experiences.

An important aspect of risk assessment is an exploration of the social and emotional context in which the child is cared for, and brought up. Parental responsiveness is a key concept here, and is a complex and many-sided phenomenon. There are at least three different elements which make for what one might assess to be *sensitive responsiveness: a tendency to react promptly*, *consistently*, and *appropriately*, to their offspring. A professional would be concerned if parents continually failed to show these reactions in response to their child's hunger, pain, crying, or other communications and actions. Of particular concern in assessing emotional abuse is the quality of parental care for the child's emotional needs (see Table 4.2).

Parent–Child Attachment

A question of sensitive or insensitive responsiveness has been linked, in part, with the quality of the emotional "bond" or "attachment" that develops between the parent and baby. Obviously, the infant's survival depends upon a loving and long-term commitment by adult care-givers. Professionals are on the look-out, at this stage in the child's early life, for signs of rejection, neglect, and abuse. This is not the place to review the complex and detailed studies of bonding (see Sluckin, Herbert, & Sluckin, 1983; Sluckin & Herbert, 1986). However, there seems to be no reliable evidence that the once-fashionable risk-indicator involving skin-to-skin contact between mother and child during a critical period after birth, is necessary for the development of mother love, or for the prevention of later emotional abuse. It was suggested (but is less so these days) that separation of the mother and infant for several weeks immediately after birth may not only irreversibly damage the subsequent mother–child relationship, but also predisposes such mothers to child abuse. In fact, the evidence for such far-reaching claims is simply not available; these notions do not stand up to painstaking enquiry and investigation (Sluckin et al., 1983).

Emotional abuse is "signposted" by parental indifference; the outward and visible sign, all too often, is the deep-seated emotional rejection of the child, not infrequently involving hostility. However, as Garbarino, Goffman and Seeley (1986) point out, the same parental act of rejecting, terrorizing, ignoring, isolating, and corrupting will have different effects on children depending on their developmental stage: infancy, early childhood, school age and adolescence. Older children might find help emotionally (or escape) by having access to supportive school teachers, the peer group, or sport and youth leaders. Younger children, however, have limited opportunities to receive emotional nurturing outside the home unless there is extended family support from grandparents or uncles and aunts, and they are therefore particularly vulnerable to rejection and neglect.

It has been hypothesized that maltreatment during infancy produces an insecure attachment over a period of time that adversely affects a child's later intellectual and socio-emotional development (Belsky, 1980). Two patterns of insecure attachment have been identified: anxious-avoidant infants and anxious-resistant infants. Anxious-avoidant infants treat the mother and stranger alike and avoid the mother upon reunion in the Ainsworth Stranger Separation Test. Anxious-resistant infants show little curiosity about their surroundings, and they often struggle and become rigid when being comforted. It is suggested that anxiously attached infants are more difficult to care for, and in turn their mothers are found to be less sensitive and less responsive to their babies. While this is a factor to investigate in a risk assessment, the cautions described above with regard to the heterogeneity of parental deficits and child outcomes apply here; a single, over-confident assessment strategy is likely to be risky.

Psychometric Instruments

Few scales are available for assessing neglect issues. There are family resource scales as well as rating scales of home, cleanliness, safety, and health (see Azar, Ferraro, & Breton, 1998). Herbert (1997) has developed a child resource pack dealing with children's needs and parental responses to these needs. Assessment of parent–child interactions should be systemic and include both self-report and structured observations (see Herbert, 1993, 1998). Children's developmental histories may disclose antecedents to maltreatment. For example, precipitants of abuse may occur in developmental periods of children's increasing autonomy (e.g. the notorious "terrible two's" phase of toddlerhood) or during periods of illness or parental life events which debilitate and traumatize the care-givers. Various measures exist for selected parental skill assessments (e.g. parent problem-solving, anger management, behaviour management, and attitudes). The Parent Opinion Questionnaire has been found to distinguish abusive and neglectful mothers from controls (Azar & Rohrbeck, 1986). Among the functions of risk assessment and formulations about psychological maltreatment within families is the desire to target a variety of preventive and remedial skills:

- Improving parenting skills, increasing responsiveness and positive child-management strategies (e.g. Herbert & Wookey, 1998)
- Increasing self-control (relaxation training and anger management)
- Improving communications within families.

CONCLUSIONS

It is clear that there is no simple or single method for predicting children at risk of abuse. As we have seen, the definitions of abuse vary; furthermore, we are not dealing with a homogeneous concept. To make predictions of risk even more perilous, the following dimensions may complicate the predictive "equation":

- The meaning (e.g. schema) the child puts upon his or her experience (see McGee, Wolfe, Yuen, & Wilson, 1995; O'Connell Higgins, 1994)
- The severity of maltreatment
- Its frequency
- Its chronicity
- The developmental period of a child's life when the abuse occurs
- The number of perpetrators
- Their relationship to the child
- Society's response to disclosure (substitute care arrangements, having to give testimony in court against a parent, etc.)
- The presence or absence of protective factors (intrinsic and extrinsic).

It is apparent that the concept of significant harm being done to a child is a difficult one to be precise about. There is little empirical guidance for deciding on the weightings for assessment strategies. Some degree of safety lies in carrying out a comprehensive, multilevel and multidisciplinary approach using, wherever possible, the evidence about the precursors and consequences of different forms of child abuse that are scattered about in the literature. Efforts to integrate this evidence have been made in several reviews (e.g. Azar, Ferraro & Breton, 1998; Browne & Herbert, 1997; Skuse & Bentovim, 1994; Smith & Bentovim, 1994). It is advisable to examine both the functioning of individual family members and the family as a system in the larger community. It would be advisable to rule out psychiatric disturbance and substance abuse in calculating risk. Physical and neurological examinations might have their place since head injuries and neurological disturbances have been linked with impulsivity and aggression.

The McMaster model of family functioning may serve as a useful framework for organizing the systems assessment (Epstein, Bishop, & Baldwin, 1982). This model suggests that there are three levels of tasks that families must accomplish:

1. Basic tasks which involve the fundamental needs of survival.
2. Developmental tasks which involve adjusting to the shifting developmental needs of the family members.
3. Emergency tasks which involve the family's capacity to deal with crises.

Six domains of family functioning are required to master these tasks: problem-solving, behavioural control, affective responsiveness, affective involvement, communication, and an adequate distribution of family roles. Abusive families may have disturbances in all these areas. Assessments of environmental stress and social support would be included in this approach.

Another model is that of Belsky (1980) which is an ecological approach to the study of child development. This hypothesizes an integrated series of interactions between influences measured at various levels:

1. *The micro-system*: this comprises the child's own characteristics and immediate environment.
2. *The exo-system*: this includes social factors that impinge on the family at risk of abuse.
3. *The macro-system*: this is the larger cultural fabric which comprises broad societal attitudes to violence and related matters.

At each level of this complex interacting system, influences known to be associated with increased risk are examined. The assumption underlying this model is that certain attributes of the abuser may predispose him or her to indulge in abusive behaviour. That person's style of parenting will, in turn, reflect his or her own developmental history, knowledge of child-rearing, mental state, and social milieu (Skuse & Bentovim, 1994).

Skuse and Bentovim (1994) have this to say:

> One way of approaching the question of which are the important antecedents of child abuse is to examine factors that are associated with a broader range of parenting difficulties. Evidence suggests that there is little specificity about the antecedents of abusive behaviour as such; it may more accurately be considered an aspect of parenting failure in the broader sense. Accordingly, when considering relevant risk factors, and how they operate, it may be useful to outline those aspects of parenting that make for satisfactory non-abusive relationships (p. 216).

This chapter began with a question: "Is it possible to identify, with a reasonable degree of certainty, children who are at risk of being abused, thus making it possible to intervene at an early stage with their families, with effective preventive or remedial programmes?" There is no easy answer to that question, but it is clear that no single, facile approach with a narrow focus will work. Fortunately, there is sufficient evidence of a wide range of systemic and individual influences which act as precursors to, and maintenance factors in, different aspects of child abuse. While there is no integrated theory or model of practice in relation to child abuse, it is still possible to conduct a comprehensive, multilevel assessment (perhaps along the McMaster or Belsky lines) which will give child-care personnel a sense of reasonable confidence (if not certainty) in their risk assessments.

REFERENCES

Aber, J. L., Allen, J. P., Carlson, V., & Cicchetti, D. (1989). The effects of maltreatment on development during early childhood: Recent studies and their theoretical, clinical, and policy implications. In D. Ciccetti & V. Carlson (Eds.), *Child maltreatment: Theory and research on the causes and consequences of child abuse and neglect.* Cambridge, UK: Cambridge University Press.

Abidin, R. (1990). Manual for the parenting stress index (PSI) (3rd ed.). Charlottsville, VA: University of Virginia, Pediatric Psychology Press.

Azar, S. T. (1992). Legal issues in the assessment of family violence involving children. In R. T. Ammerman & M. Hersen (Eds.), *Assessment of family violence* (pp. 47–70). New York: Wiley.

Azar, S. T., & Bengit, C. L. (1994). A cognitive perspective on ethnicity, race and termination of parental rights. *Law and Human Behavior, 18,* 249–268.

Azar, S. T., Ferraro, M. H., & Breton, S. J. (1998). Intrafamilial child treatment. In T. H. Ollendick & M. Hersen (Eds.), *Handbook of child psychopathology* (pp. 483–504). New York: Plenum.

Azar, S. T., & Rohrbeck, C. A. (1986). Child abuse and unrealistic expectations: Further validation of the Parent Opinion Questionnaire. *Journal of Consulting and Clinical Psychology, 54,* 867–868.

Azar, S. T., & Wolfe, D. (1989). Child abuse and neglect. In F. J. Mash & R. A. Barkley (Eds.), *Treatment of childhood disorders* (pp. 431–489). New York: Guilford.

Babiker, G. (1982). *Psychological measurement and the identification of sexual abuse in children and adolescents.* Unpublished Ph. D. Thesis, University of Bristol, UK.

Babiker, G. (1983). Projective testing in the evaluation of the effects of sexual abuse in childhood: A review. *British Journal of Projective Psychology, 38,* 45–53.

Babiker, G., & Herbert, M. (1998). Critical issues in the assessment of Child Sexual Abuse. *Clinical Child and Family Psychology Review, 1,* 231–252.

Barker, W. (1990). Practical and ethical doubts about screening for child abuse. *Health Visitor, 63,* 14–17.

Belsky, J. (1980). Child maltreatment: An ecological integration. *American Psychologist, 35,* 320–335.

Browne, K. D. (1988). The nature of child abuse and neglect: An overview. In K. Browne, C. Davies, & P. Stratton (Eds.), *Early prediction and prevention of child abuse* (pp. 15–30). Chichester, UK: Wiley.

Browne, K. D., & Herbert, M. (1997). *Preventing family violence.* Chichester, UK: Wiley.

Browne, K. D., & Saqi, S. (1988). Approaches to screening families at high risk for child abuse. In K. Browne, C. Davies, & P. Stratton (Eds.), *Early prediction and prevention of child abuse* (pp. 57–85). Chichester, UK: Wiley.

Cicchetti, D. (1990). The organisation and coherence of socio-emotional, cognitive, and representational development. In R. Thompson (Ed.), *Nebraska Symposium on Motivation: Vol. 36* (pp. 259–366). Lincoln, NE: University of Nebraska Press.

Clausen, A. E. I., & Crittenden, P. M. (1991). Physical and psychological maltreatment: Relations among types of maltreatment. *Child Abuse and Neglect, 15*, 5–18.

Conte, J. R. (1991). Child sexual abuse: Looking backward and forward. In M. Q. Patton (Ed.), *Family sexual abuse: Frontline research and evaluation.* London: Sage.

Daniel, J. H., Newberger, E. H., Reed, R. B., & Kotelchuck, M. (1978). Child abuse screening. *Child Abuse and Neglect, 2*, 247–259.

Department of Health and Social Security (1986). *Working together.* London: HMSO.

Egeland, B., & Erikson, E. (1987). Rising above the past: Strategies for helping new mothers break the cycle of abuse and neglect. *American Journal of Orthopsychiatry, 56*, 29–35.

Epstein, N. B., Bishop, D. S., & Baldwin, I. M. (1982). McMaster model of family functioning. In F. Walsh (Ed.), *Normal family process* (pp. 115–141). New York: Guilford.

Farmer, E., & Owen, M. (1995). Child protection practice: Private risk and public remedies—decision making, intervention and outcomes. *Protection work.* London: HMSO.

Finkelhor, D., & Korbin, J. (1988). Child abuse as an international issue. *Child Abuse and Neglect, 12*, 2–24.

Frude, N. (1991). *Understanding family problems: A psychological approach.* Chichester, UK: Wiley.

Garbarino, J., Goffman, E., & Seeley, J. A. (1986). *The psychologically battered child.* San Francisco: Jossey-Bass.

Gray, J. O., Cutler, C. A., Dean, J., & Kempe, C. H. (1977). Prediction and prevention of child abuse. *Child Abuse and Neglect, 1*, 45–58.

Hart, S. N., & Brassard, M. R. (1991). Progress achieved. *Development and psychopathology, 3*, 62–69.

Herbert, M. (1993). *Working with children and the Children Act.* Leicester, UK: BPS Books (British Psychological Society).

Herbert, M. (1997). *Childcare and family resource pack.* Exeter, UK: Impact Publications. P.O. Box No. 342, Exeter, EX67ZD.

Herbert, M. (1998). Family treatment. In T. H. Ollendick & M. Hersen (Eds.), *Handbook of child psychopathology* (pp. 557–580). New York: Plenum.

Herbert, M., & Wookey, J. (1998). *Child-wise parenting skills manual.* (revised edn.) Exeter, UK: Impact Publications, P.O. Box No. 342, Exeter EX67ZD.

Howitt, D. (1992). *Child abuse errors: When good intentions go wrong.* Hemel Hempstead, UK: Harvester Wheatsheaf.

Iwaniec, D. (1995). *The emotionally abused and neglected child.* Chichester, UK: Wiley.

Kavanagh, C. (1982). Emotional abuse and mental injury: A critique of the concepts and a recommendation for practice. *Journal of the American Academy of Child Psychiatry, 21*, 171–177.

Lynch, M., & Roberts, J. (1977). Predicting child abuse. *Child Abuse and Neglect, 1*, 491–492.

Lynch M., Roberts, J., & Gordon J. (1976). Early warning of child abuse. *Developmental Medicine and Child Neurology, 19*, 373–387.

McGee, R. A., & Wolfe, D. A. (1991). Between a rock and a hard place: Where do we go from here in defining psychological maltreatment. In D. Ciccetti (Ed.), *Development and psychopathology: Vol. 3* (pp. 119–124). Cambridge, UK: Cambridge University Press.

McGee, R. A., Wolfe, D. A., Yuen, S. A., & Wilson, S. K. (1995). The measurement of maltreatment: A comparison of approaches: *Child Abuse and Neglect, 19*, 233–249.

Miller, L. C. (1981). *Louisville behavior checklist.* Los Angeles: Western Psychological Services.

Milner, J. S. (1986). *The child abuse potential inventory manual* (2nd ed.). DeKalb, IL: Psytec.

Milner, J. S. (1989). Additional cross-validation of the child abuse potential inventory. *Psychological Assessment, 1*, 219–223.

Moffitt, T. E., & Caspi, A. (1998). Implications of violence between intimate partners for child psychologists and psychiatrists. *Journal of Child Psychology and Psychiatry, 39*, 137–144.

O'Connell Higgins, O. (1994). *Resilient adults: Overcoming a cruel past.* New York: Jossey-Bass.

Patterson, G. (1982). *Coercive family process.* Eugene, OR: Castalia.

Schaffer, H. R. (1990). *Making decisions about children: Psychological questions and answers.* Oxford, UK: Basil Blackwell.

Skuse, D., & Bentovim, A. (1994). Physical and emotional maltreatment. In M. Rutter, E. Taylor, & L. Hersov (Eds.), *Child and adolescent psychiatry: Modern approaches* (pp. 209–229). Oxford, UK: Blackwell Scientific Publication.

Sluckin, W., & Herbert, M. (Eds.) (1986). *Parental behaviour.* Chichester, UK: Wiley.

Sluckin, W., Herbert, M., & Sluckin, A. (1983). *Maternal bonding.* Oxford, UK: Basil Blackwell.

Smith, M., & Bentovim, A. (1994). Sexual abuse. In M. Rutter, E. Taylor, & L. Hersov (Eds.), *Child and adolescent psychiatry: Modern approaches* (pp. 230–251). Oxford, UK: Blackwell Scientific Publications.

Tong, L., Oates, K., & McDowell, H. (1987). Personality development following sexual abuse. *Child Abuse and Neglect, 11*, 371–383.

Vizard, E. (1991). Interviewing children suspected of being sexually abused: A review of theory and practice. In C. R. Hollin & K. Howells (Eds.), *Clinical approaches to sex offenders and their victims* (pp. 117–148). Chichester, UK: Wiley.

Webster-Stratton, C., & Herbert, M. (1993). What really happens in parent training? *Behavior Modification, 17*, 407–456.

Webster-Stratton, C., & Herbert, M. (1994). *Troubled families: Problem children. Working with families: A collaborative process.* Chichester, UK: Wiley.

Wolfe, D. A. (1985). Child-abuse parents. An empirical review and analysis. *Psychological Bulletin, 97*, 461–482.

Wolfe, D. A. (1987). *Child abuse: Implications for child development and psychopathology.* Beverley Hills, CA: Sage.

Chapter 5

Assessing Violence Risk in Mentally and Personality Disordered Individuals

Christopher D. Webster
*University of Toronto, Toronto, Simon Fraser University,
Vancouver, and Earlscourt Child and Family Centre,
Toronto, Canada*
and
Gerard Bailes
Norvic Clinic, Norwich, UK

INTRODUCTION

Questions surrounding the prediction of dangerousness seem to change each decade or so. Also, the language in which those questions are framed alters subtly with the accumulation of scientific knowledge, altered professional practice, and changing political and legal realities.

THE 1950s, 1960s, 1970s

In the 1950s, dangerousness had not surfaced as a topic of much interest in forensic psychology and psychiatry. It was generally assumed by judges and administrators that mental health and correctional professionals knew which individuals were apt to be dangerous and which ones were not. The 1960s brought about a sudden change in outlook. This was largely due to the inspired study of Steadman and Cocozza (1974). As many readers will know, these investigators had the wit to take advantage of a "naturally occurring experiment". This exper-

Handbook of Offender Assessment and Treatment. Edited by C. R. Hollin.
© 2000 John Wiley & Sons Ltd.

iment centred on the case of Johnny Baxstrom. Baxstrom had been confined in New York's Dannemora State Hospital for the criminally insane. Toward the end of his detainment he was civilly committed because authorities were unwilling to release him. Baxstrom contested this added confinement, eventually to the United States Supreme Court. There it was decided that, indeed, Baxstrom had been improperly held. The court ordered his release and took the extraordinary step of requiring a further 966 persons released outright or removed to conditions of lowered security. In this way, the better part of 1000 persons, most or all of whom had been detained on the grounds that they represented a danger to the public, were abruptly reclassified with many eventually reaching the community.

Ninety-eight patients were followed in the community for two to three years. Few of these individuals had further contact with the law (about 20% were arrested) and even fewer were involved in violent acts (2%). This finding suggested very strongly that violence had been over-predicted, at least in that particular institution. Attention became focused on the "false positive problem", the idea that clinicians had too often perceived "dangerousness" where it did not exist. That such over-prediction of dangerousness occurred in the Baxstrom patients was recognized by Steadman and Cocozza as being at least partly due to low overall rates of violence during the follow-up period. It was generally thought at the time that predicting future violence was an almost impossible task because of the difficulty of forecasting events with a low frequency of occurrence.

The Steadman and Cocozza (1974) book, called, aptly enough, *Careers of the Criminally Insane*, excited considerable interest upon its publication. It was also received with scepticism in some quarters. Yet its main conclusion was amply reinforced just five years later in a 1979 parallel case in Pennsylvania (Dixon v. Attorney General of the Commonwealth of Pennsylvania). Again, there was a court-ordered release of a large cohort of persons earlier deemed to have committed violent acts due to mental illness. The patients were followed by another pair of investigators, Thornberry and Jacoby (1979). Exactly the same major finding emerged from the study; very few former patients acted violently during the four-year follow-up. There was again, then, the general conclusion that violence had been over-predicted. Some influential authorities began publishing articles during the period with titles like "flipping coins in the courtroom" (Ennis & Litwack, 1974). There were suggestions that forensic psychiatrists and psychologists would be best advised to get out of the business of predicting violence (e.g. as described by Stone, 1985).

THE 1980s

The late 1970s and early 1980s initiated a different line of thought. The distinguished American psychologist, the late Saleem Shah, began to note in places as prominent as the *American Psychologist* (1978) that mental health professionals were more or less obliged to render opinions about dangerousness at many junctures in general psychiatric, forensic psychiatric, and correctional systems. He also expressed the view that it was unlikely that clinicians are uniformly poor at predicting future violence. In his own words: "To say something is difficult to do (namely, to achieve high levels of accuracy in predicting events with very low base rates) is *not* the same as asserting that the task is impossible and simply cannot be done" (1981, p. 161, parentheses and emphasis in original). Shah also made the vital point that individual assessors tend to have little or no idea as to the relative accuracy of their predictions.

Doubtless influenced to some extent by Shah, Monahan published in 1981 his book called *Predicting Violent Behavior: An Assessment of Clinical Techniques.* This text was influential at the time and has remained so. Aside from a compelling summary of the literature then extant, Monahan organized his text largely around the distinction between actuarial and clinical prediction. This distinction, explored early by Meehl (1954), enabled Monahan to stress the importance of both kinds of variables. His point was that it makes sense to ground predictions of violence in easy-to-establish background "static", demographic-type factors. It was, even at that time, apparent that certain actuarial variables like past crime—particularly violent crime—age, sex, socioeconomic status, and alcohol or drug abuse have at least some demonstrable link to subsequent dangerous acts. Moreover, certain variables like family, employment, peer relations, availability of victims, and availability of weapons, could be presumed to have associations with future violence risk. In his book Monahan viewed mental illness as a *non-correlate* of violence. As noted later in this chapter, this particular observation later required another look. What is perhaps most surprising is that the text as a whole has worn so well over the years. It has provided a blueprint for much of the research conducted over the better part of the last two decades.

In this text, and in subsequent articles (1984, 1988), Monahan called for prediction-outcome studies conducted over relatively short periods. This so-called "second generation" research placed insistence on clearly defined predictor and outcome measures. Studies began to appear suggesting that, high though the false positive problem might remain, there was at least some possibility of showing sustainable correspondences between prediction and outcome (e.g. Convit, Jaeger, Lin, Meisner, & Volavka, 1998; Sepejak, Menzies, Webster, & Jensen, 1983).

How is predictive power shown when it comes to gauging the accuracy of violence forecasts? As explained by Monahan in 1981, the most usual way of going about the task is to place individuals following evaluation in one of two categories; dangerous or not dangerous. Similarly, at eventual outcome days, weeks, months, or even years later, persons are again grouped into two categories; those known not to have behaved violently and those known to have committed harm. This gives rise to a 2×2 contingency table under which there are two ways of being correct and two ways of being wrong. It is possible to predict that the person will be danger-free over the study period and be correct in that assertion (true negative); it is possible to predict a non-violent outcome and be wrong in that forecast (false negative); it is possible, as was found in the aftermaths of Baxstrom and Dixon, to predict violence but not find it at follow-up (false positive); and, finally, it is possible to predict violence and have that prediction confirmed (true positive). This scheme for organizing data, though not without its limitations (Hart, Webster, & Menzies, 1993), can be quite useful. Through the use of the basic chi-square statistic, it is easy to determine whether the scores distributed across the four cells depart from chance. This way it can be shown, for example, whether or not particular variables like previous violence, age at time of offence, and global clinical opinion about dangerousness yield "statistically significant" effects (e.g. Sepejak et al., 1983).

Helpful though chi-square and related statistics may be to those with a statistical bent, it soon becomes apparent that the effects of a false negative error are markedly different from those of a false positive error (Walker, 1991). In the former case, some bureaucrat, some judge, or some mental health professional stands a chance of being held accountable for an "error". As a result of miscategorization, there is now a victim. In the latter case, improper classification results in the undue detention of the individual. Small wonder then that there is a tendency for clinicians and administrators, in their understandable reluctance to be stuck with false negative errors, to drive up the level of false positives in a corresponding way. There is one other point about the 2×2 table which merits note. It is that in the usual course of events, persons viewed during assessment as dangerous tend to be confined—that is, the prediction is not tested. A related matter is that even if the individual is free to act violently during the follow-up period, and does in fact do so, there is a good chance that such violence, unless extremely serious, may remain unreported. So what would actually be a true positive if the full facts were known can enter the data analysis as a false positive.

The yes/no characteristic of the chi-square table can be overcome with use of correlation coefficients according to which a *range* of predictor scores can be associated with a *range* of outcome scores. A correlation coefficient yields a maximum correspondence of +1.0 (or −1.0). A correlation of zero implies no correspondence whatever between prediction and outcome. At least in theory it ought to be possible to build a prediction instrument which would show a close to +1.0 correlation between prediction and outcome. In the late 1970s, early 1980s, one of us (CDW), with others, attempted to elucidate a couple of dozen factors which might conceivably link prediction to outcome (Menzies, Webster, & Sepejak, 1985a). Such factors were organized into a scheme called the Dangerous Behaviour Rating Scheme (DBRS). Typical items in this device were called "anger", "rage", "hostility", "manipulative", and "violence increased under alcohol". When forensic psychiatric patients were followed first after two years and later after six (Menzies, Webster, McMain, Staley, & Scaglione, 1994), correlations between DBRS scores at assessment and follow-up tended to be of the order of +0.24. This led us to conclude that it was more or less impossible to break a "sound barrier" of around 0.40 (Menzies, Webster, & Sepejak, 1985b). The DBRS itself, though yielding statistically significant chi-squares and correlations, did not, as we had hoped, yield strength much, if any, more impressive than a handful of easy-to-obtain and score demographic variables (see Menzies & Webster, 1995).

These findings of our own in the mid 1980s seemed fairly consistent with those of other investigators active at the time. Generally, overall prediction-outcome correlations were unimpressive, with a preponderance of false positives. One result of the DBRS venture did, though, catch our attention. This was that, as Shah (1981) had previously suggested, individual clinicians varied markedly in their ability to forecast violence. Some performed at chance levels, others were able to yield positive correlations of around +0.25 or even +0.35, and a few even yielded negative correlations. When we published our results in 1985 we stressed the limited validity of the DBRS. To our surprise, we were deluged with requests for the manual on which the scale was based. Practising clinicians seemed undaunted by its lack of demonstrated reliability and validity. This taught us that, although the DBRS was not "it", there would potentially be acceptance of an instrument that was reasonably succinct and acceptably grounded in clinical and research practice.

THE 1990s

It was the realization that there is a demand for practical down-to-earth instruments that began to lead us and others in a new direction starting in the early 1990s. In 1994 we published *The Violence Prediction Scheme* (Webster, Harris, Rice, Cormier, & Quinsey). This short book was written explicitly for use by mental health and correctional professionals. It was based on an earlier work by Harris, Rice and Quinsey (1993). These authors, based at the maximum-secure "Oak Ridge" Division of the Penetanguishene Mental Centre in Ontario, Canada, published data on some 600 men, all of whom had previously committed at least one serious violent offence. Using statistical techniques more sophisticated than those mentioned above in this chapter, they were able to pool the effects of several actuarial variables (i.e. through discriminant function analysis). The men in this study had been released for seven years and the investigators had been able to determine which men had failed violently during follow-up and which ones had not. Harris et al. had no difficulty in this important study in showing that it was possible to break the +0.40 "sound barrier" referred to earlier.

The overall prediction scores in the "Oak Ridge" population were derived retrospectively from files kept at the hospital. These scores were organized by the researchers, on the basis of comprehensive statistical analysis, into a device named the Violence Risk Appraised Guide (VRAG). All 12 items individually correlated with the outcome measure ("failed violently" over seven and later 10 years vs. "did not fail violently"). The 12 items in the VRAG listed here in terms of strength of correlations against outcome were as follows:

1. Psychopathy Checklist Score
2. Elementary School Maladjustment
3. DSM-III Diagnosis of Personality Disorder
4. Age at Index Offence

5. Separated from Parents under Age 16
6. Failure on Prior Conditional Release
7. Non-violent Offence History
8. Never Married
9. DSM-III Diagnosis of Schizophrenia
10. Victim Injury
11. Alcohol Abuse
12. Female Victim in Index Offence.

The correlations between combined predictor variables and outcome scores across the whole population were +0.45 (ranging up to +0.53 in one subsample).

An impressive part of the write-up of the Harris et al. (1993) study was the use of a histogram depicting the main results. Supported by the main statistical analyses, the authors chose to plot on the ordinate the probability of violent failure. On the abscissa they showed VRAG scores divided into nine equal-sized bins. The result is a visually pleasing correspondence with the bars running from low left to high right. Though not quite as "tight", a second plot based on only seven variables yielded the same basic pattern. These seven variables were included based merely on their ease of scoring (e.g. age at index offence, never married). This observation is reminiscent of that by Menzies et al. (1994) mentioned earlier (i.e. that a few actuarial variables do possess surprising predictive power).

A little attention needs now to be focused on the single most powerful predictor isolated by Harris et al. (1993), psychopathy. Psychopathy as indexed by Hare's Psychopathy Checklist—Revised—PCL—R (1991) can be measured according to 20 items, each scored on a 0 (absent), 1 (possibly present), or 2 (definitely present) scale. The items, as many readers will know, are:

1. Glibness/superficial charm
2. Grandiose sense of self-worth
3. Need for stimulation/proneness to boredom
4. Pathological lying
5. Conning/manipulative
6. Lack of remorse or guilt
7. Shallow affect
8. Callous/lack of empathy
9. Parasitic lifestyle
10. Poor behavioural controls
11. Promiscuous sexual behaviour
12. Early behaviour problems
13. Lack of realistic long-term goals
14. Impulsivity
15. Irresponsibility
16. Failure to accept responsibility for actions
17. Many short-term marital relationships

18. Juvenile delinquency
19. Revocation of conditional release and
20. Criminal versatility.

Statistical analyses based on the PCL—R data show consistently that psychopathy is actually a composite of two factors: one centring on affective/interpersonal considerations and the other dealing with impulsivity, irresponsibility, unstable lifestyle, and persistent violation of social norms. Other studies have shown that the PCL—R, or its more recent short adaptation (Hart, Hare, & Forth, 1994; Hart, Cox, & Hare, 1995), links as well, or better than, any other single predictor of violence yet isolated (e.g. Hill, Rogers, & Bickford, 1996). With its careful description, its "manualization' (Kazdin, 1997), and a body of knowledge to support it, psychopathy at least for the moment would seem to be the 'flagship' variable in the area of violence risk prediction. It is worth noting that the construct was not originally intended by Hare to become a prediction device. It is also worth noting that, interesting and helpful though the device may have become in the area of risk prediction, it is easily subject to misuses of various kinds (Hare, 1998). For example, although the device likely taps the kinds of variables of interest to decision-makers faced with making parole release recommendations, there can be a regrettable tendency to consider an exceptionally low or exceptionally high psychopathy score to be *all* that is needed. As well, it may even be that the use of the term "checklist" leads administrators and even professionals to think that the scale can be used rapidly and without the required extensive training. Hare has himself recently remarked that the notion of psychopathy is more complex than it looks and that, originally based in clinical observation (Cleckley, 1941), its assessment requires a substantial degree of clinical sophistication and training (Hare, 1998).

There are other points to be noted about the critically important work of Harris et al. (see Quinsey, Harris, Rice, & Cormier, 1998; Rice, 1997). One is that childhood variables turn out to be quite powerful. Early childhood maladjustment is a key factor (see Hodgins, 1994), as is separation from parents before the age of 16 years. Another point is that schizophrenia shows a *negative* correlation with violent failure during follow-up. It is worth stressing that the Harris et al. findings likely have applicability to *men* destined for corrections as well as mental hospitalization. This is because their population included not just men sent to Oak Ridge for treatment but also men who were sent there for evaluation before being routed to correctional interventions. It may well be found, as was the case with the PCL—R, that the VRAG has applicability well beyond men found not guilty by reason of insanity. It is the kind of device, given its already strong support, that will merit close study with other groups into the future. The question of "How well can dangerousness be predicted?" dissolves into another question, "How well able is the VRAG able to predict violence in this or that context?" Such questions can be answered with relative ease given the existence of the requisite detailed coding manual (Cormier, 1994).

Another study of the same vintage as that by Harris et al. is that by Lidz, Mulvey, and Gardner (1993). This was based on a general psychiatric population. It is a thorough and important study. The outcome measures were particularly strong, based as they were in part on information about violence provided by friends and relatives ("collaterals"). The study is among a few to show that global clinical opinion about the likelihood of future violence can be valid. Yet, what was surprising about the outcome of this study was that predictions made on behalf of women were on the whole largely inaccurate. Since in this conventional psychiatric sample women made up about half the population, the effectiveness of successful predictions made about men was greatly attenuated by the unsuccessful ones about women. The difficulty was that the assessors markedly underestimated the base rate of violence in these woman (i.e. they made far too many false negative errors).

The year 1994 not only saw the publication of the *Violence Prediction Scheme* but, importantly, it was also marked by the publication of *Violence and Mental Disorder: Developments in Risk Assessment* by Monahan and Steadman. This is an edited volume containing much hitherto unpublished data and commentary. Of special importance perhaps is preliminary material from the MacArthur risk assessment project. This is a multi-site study using prediction and outcome data (see Steadman et al., 1994). As well, there is in the book ample evidence to suggest that Monahan's (1981) earlier assertion about mental disorder being a *non*-correlate of violence is incorrect (see also Monahan, 1992). It is now more accurate to say that mental disorder has a low to moderate association with violence; one, though, which is substantially less than that between alcohol and drug abuse and violence.

In early 1995, one of us (CDW) joined with others to produce a broad-spectrum, workable manual for the assessment of risk of violence (Webster, Eaves, Douglas, & Wintrup, 1995). In so doing, we took a leaf from Robert Hare's book by opting for 20 items scored simply as 0, 1 or 2. The rationale was straight-forward: 20 is a seemingly reasonable number of items for clinicians completing busy assessment schedules. And a three-point scoring system does not oblige colleagues to make distinctions which might be altogether too fine (e.g. our experience with the DBRS, based on a 5-point system, was not entirely satisfactory). The scheme has become known as the "HCR-20". There are 10 "historical" (H) items (influenced to some extent by the VRAG), five current clinical items and five future-oriented risk items. A modified version of the scheme was published two years later (Webster, Douglas, Eaves, & Hart, 1997a, 1997b). Items in the scheme are currently labelled as follows: H1, Previous violence; H2, Young age at first violent incident; H3, Relationship instability; H4, Employment problems; H5, Substance use problems; H6, Major mental illness; H7, Psychopathy; H8, Early maladjustment; H9, Personality disorder; H10, Prior supervision failure; C1, Lack of insight; C2, Negative attitudes; C3, Active symptoms of mental illness; C4, Impulsivity; C5, Unresponsive to treatment; R1, Plans lack feasibility; R2, Exposure to destabilizers; R3, Lack of personal support; R4, Non-compliance with remediation attempts; and R5, Stress. Such limited data supporting the validity of the HCR-20 as are available are listed in the manual. Much of what has so far been reported is of a retrospective nature (e.g. Douglas & Webster, 1999; Belfrage, 1998).

Although as yet in its infancy, the HCR-20 has attracted notice (e.g. Borum, 1996). It may well turn out that, aside from the value of the scheme itself, the HCR-20's main benefit derives from the effort to draw together the results of scientific investigations, on the one hand, with the actualities of clinical practice, on the other. As was said in the manual, "The challenge in what remains of the 1990s is to integrate the almost separate worlds of research on the prediction of violence and the clinical practice of assessment. At present the two worlds scarcely intersect" (Webster et al., 1997b, p. 1). Certainly, it is anticipated that the scheme will require revision from time to time. It has to be seen as a starting place for research, not an end in itself (though see Douglas, 1998). As was true of the DBRS a decade or more earlier, there has been a considerable demand for the manual. It has also been observed that some colleagues have found the device useful not so much as an assessment scheme in itself, but as a means of measuring the effects of interventions and treatments over weeks and months.

Emboldened to some extent by the "success" of the HCR-20, we have developed other similar scales to examine specific topics like spousal assault (Kropp, Hart, Webster, & Eaves, 1995; Kropp & Hart, 1997), sex offending (Boer, Wilson, Gauthier, & Hart, 1997; Boer, Hart, Kropp & Webster, 1998) and the potential of correctional inmates to attempt suicide (Polvi, 1997). Impulsivity seems a central feature of many persons with mental or personality disorder. That, at any rate, is an impression gleaned from the content of the American Psychiatric Associations's *Diagnostic and Statistical Manual* (APA, 1994). For that reason, we have also proposed a 20-item scheme for measuring clinical impulsivity (Webster & Jackson, 1997). Indeed, with reference to the so-called Impulsivity Checklist (ICL), we opted quite deliberately to define the construct based largely on *clinical* experience. Just as Hare relied on Cleckley's *Mask of Sanity* (1941) as a starting point, we chose to depend upon Harold Wishnie's 1977 book *The Impulsive Personality: Understanding People with Destructive Character Disorders*. In the most general way, we have found it instructive to rely upon well-expressed clinical opinion as we have tried to place metrics on the variables of seeming greatest interest. To us it seems vital that, as the next important step, there be a renewal of emphasis on establishing scientist–practitioner models (Webster & Cox, 1997). At present there seems a regrettable tendency for researchers to talk one language and clinicians another. Researchers are often insensitive or unknowledgeable about clinical realities and clinicians too often are ill-informed about the results of dependable, informative, research studies.

The rise in importance of psychopathy as a construct over the past 10 or 15 years is a good case in point. Psychopathy is a clinical notion, or actually a pair of notions. Hare has found a convenient, scientifically sound, way of making these notions intelligible and useful to clinicians. Recently, as noted above, we have made a similar attempt with psychopathy's sister concept, impulsivity (Webster & Jackson, 1997). But there must be many other constructs, all used daily (but mostly in different ways) by clinicians. It seems to us self-evident that the accuracy of risk evaluations will not improve very greatly until more attention is paid to the definition of terms. Just as had been mistakenly assumed that there was a low "sound barrier" for prediction–outcome correlations in this type of work, it may well be that with continued emphasis on the definition of terms and the logic of prediction (Jackson, 1997) much greater accuracy can be obtained than now seems possible. In saying this, we recognize that in the future it may prove expedient to find altogether new types of prediction model (e.g. Marks-Tarlow, 1993).

Quite aside from the importance of being able to demonstrate greater prediction accuracy than is currently possible, increased attention must surely now be focused on how best to encourage true collaboration between clinicians and researchers (Polvi & Webster, 1997). Perfect prediction schemes are not going to fly from the brows of researchers or from clinicians. In this respect, the gradual evolution of devices designed to predict critically important human behaviours may follow exactly the same pattern as is found in applied engineering tasks. The process ought to be the same. Consider, for example, the task of creating a device to clean institutional walls and floors. First, the task must be defined. Then an idea, likely involving chemicals, pumps, nozzles, and sprays must be sketched on a drawing board (the initial design phase). Then, with plans in hand, the task is moved to the machine shop where a prototype is fabricated (the working model phase). The model must then be applied to the task proper (the trial phase). Since it is unlikely that the new device will perform in a completely satisfactory way during initial testing, it is almost certain that there will have to be a return to the design and prototype phases. Actual full-scale production of the cleaning device will be at some considerable remove from the initial concept. Only rarely are short-cuts available. As we have evolved Version 2 of the HCR-20 from Version 1, we have been surprised at the effort required to revisit the design, model, and trial phases.

Recently, we set ourselves the challenge of creating a 20-item scheme for assessing violence potential in children under 12. The need for such a device seemed self-evident. And it was not as if prominent researchers had done no work in the area (e.g. Eron, 1997; Farrington, 1997). At a routine clinical level we were already using at the Earlscourt Child and Family Centre in Toronto, a 50-item yes/no checklist (yet with no attempt at reliability or validity checking). It took some time to isolate 20 factors on the basis of the published literature, the underdeveloped prototype checklist, and the opinions of colleagues who work daily with under-12 children and their families. Our eventual list of six Family (F) items, 12 Child (C) items and two Amenability (A) items is as follows: F1, Household circumstances; F2, Caregiver continuity; F3, Supports; F4, Stressors; F5, Parenting style; F6, Antisocial values and conduct; C1, Developmental problems; C2, Onset of behavioural difficulties; C3, Trauma; C4, Impulsivity; C5, Likeability; C6, Peer socialization; C7, School functioning; C8, Structured community activities; C9, Police contact; C10, Antisocial attitudes; C11, Antisocial behaviour; C12, Coping ability; A1, Family responsivity; and A2, Child treatability.

As we developed the items and corresponding descriptions, we came to the realization that different versions would have to be created for boys and girls. After identifying and defining in a draft manual the seemingly most essential 20 items, we tried them out on 21 consecutive cases (prototype test). Round-table discussion among all participants resulted in the dropping of some items, the addition of others, and the reworking of many others (back to the drawing board). Further testing followed in the clinic and production of the so-called Early Assessment of Risk List—Boys' Version (EARL-20B) has now taken place (Augimeri, Webster, Koegl, & Levene, 1998). No one claims for this more than a starting point for much needed research. Yet, in our view, the "two worlds phenomenon" means that, regrettably, the task often does not get started, let alone finished.

Our general point, then, is that there has been a marked shift in outlook with respect to risk prediction over the past two decades. Although some still argue strenuously that mental health and correctional researchers do more harm than good with their attempts to improve precision in decision making (e.g. Mathiesen, 1998), the general current view from experienced and thoughtful psychiatrists and psychologists is that it is well within our grasp to assess and manage violence risk at standards appreciably higher than those presently in routine use (see Monahan, 1996; Snowden, 1997).

REFERENCES

American Psychiatric Association (1994). *Diagnostic and statistical manual of mental disorders* (4th ed.). Washington, DC: Author.

Augimeri, L., Webster, C. D., Koegl, C., & Levene, K. (1998). The early assessment of risk list for boys' (EARL-20B) (Version 1, Consultation edition). Toronto, Canada: Earlscourt Child and Family Centre.

Belfrage, H. (1998). Implementing the HCR-20 scheme for risk assessment in a forensic psychiatric hospital: Integrating research and clinical practice. *Journal of Forensic Psychiatry*, 9, 328–338.

Boer, D. P., Hart, S. D., Kropp, P. R., & Webster, C. D. (1998). *The SVR-20 manual*. Vancouver, Canada: Family Violence Institute.

Boer, D. P., Wilson, R. J., Gauthier, C. M., & Hart, S. D. (1997). Assessing risk for sexual violence: Guidelines for clinical practice. In C. D. Webster & M. A. Jackson (Eds.), *Impulsivity: Theory, assessment, and treatment* (pp. 326–342). New York: Guilford.

Borum, R. (1996). Improving the clinical practice of violence risk assessment: Technology, guidelines, and training. *American Psychologist*, 51, 945–956.

Cleckley, H. (1941). *The mask of sanity*. St. Louis, MO: Mosby.

Convit, A., Jaeger, J., Lin, S. P., Meisner, M., & Volavka, J. (1988). Predicting assaultiveness in psychiatric inpatients: A pilot study. *Hospital and Community Psychiatry*, 39, 429–434.

Cormier, C. (1994). *Offender psycho-social assessment manual correctional model*. Penetanguishene, Ontario, Canada: Ontario Mental Health Centre.

Douglas, K. (1998, March). The HCR-20 violence risk assessment scheme: A summary of research findings. Paper presented at the biennial meeting of the American Psychology-Law Society, Redondo Beach, CA.

Douglas, K. S., & Webster, C. D. (1999). The HCR-20 violence risk assessment scheme:

Concurrent validity in a sample of incarcerated offenders. *Criminal Justice and Behavior, 26*, 3–19.

Ennis, B. J., & Litwack, T. R. (1974). Psychiatry and the presumption of expertise: Flipping coins in the courtroom. *California Law Review, 62*, 693–752.

Eron, L. D. (1997). The development of antisocial behavior from a learning perspective. In D. M. Stoff, J. Breiling, & J. D. Maser, *Handbook of antisocial behavior* (pp. 140–147). New York: Wiley.

Farrington, D. P. (1997). A critical analysis of research on the development of antisocial behavior from birth to adulthood. In D. M. Stoff, J. Breiling, & J. D. Maser (Eds.), *Handbook of antisocial behavior* (pp. 234–240) New York: Wiley.

Hare, R. D. (1991). *Manual for the Hare Psychopathy Checklist—Revised*. Toronto, Canada: Multi-Health Systems.

Hare, R. D. (1998). The Hare PCL—R: Some issues concerning its use and misuse. *Legal and Criminological Psychology, 3*, 99–119.

Harris, G. T., Rice, M. E., & Quinsey, V. L. (1993). Violent recidivism of mentally disordered offenders: The development of a statistical prediction instrument. *Criminal Justice and Behavior, 20*, 315–355.

Hart, S. D., Cox, D., & Hare, R. D. (1995). *Manual for the screening version of the Hare Psychopathy Checklist—Revised (PCL: SV)*. Toronto, Canada: Multi-Health Systems.

Hart, S. D., Hare, R. D., & Forth, A. E. (1994). Psychopathy as a risk marker for violence: Development and validation of a screening version of the Revised Psychopathy Checklist. In J. Monahan & H. J. Steadman (Eds.), *Violence and mental disorder: Developments in risk assessment* (pp. 81–97). Chicago, IL: University of Chicago Press.

Hart, S. D., Webster, C. D., & Menzies, R. J. (1993). A note on portraying the accuracy of violence predictions. *Law and Human Behavior, 17*, 695–700.

Hill, C. D., Rogers, R., & Bickford, M. E. (1996). Predicting aggressive and socially disruptive behavior in a maximum security forensic hospital. *Journal of Forensic Sciences, 41*, 56–69.

Hodgins, S. (1994). Status at age 30 of children with conduct problems. *Studies on Crime and Crime Prevention, 4*, 41–61.

Jackson, J. (1997). A conceptual model for the study of violence and aggression. In C. C. Webster & M. A. Jackson, *Impulsivity: Theory, assessment and treatment* (pp. 233–247). New York: Guilford.

Kazdin, A. E. (1997). A model for developing effective treatments: Progression and interplay of theory, research, and practice. *Journal of Clinical Child Psychology, 26*, 114–129.

Kropp, P. R., & Hart, S. D. (1997). Assessing risk for violence in wife assaulters: The Spousal Assault Risk Assessment Guide. In C. D. Webster & M. A. Jackson (Eds.), *Impulsivity: Theory, assessment, and treatment* (pp. 302–325). New York: Guilford.

Kropp, P. R., Hart, S. D., Webster, C. D., & Eaves, D. (1995). *Manual for Spousal Assault Risk Assessment Guide* (2nd ed.). Vancouver, Canada: British Columbia Institute on Family Violence.

Lidz, C. W., Mulvey, E. P., & Gardner, W. (1993). The accuracy of predictions of violence to others. *Journal of the American Medical Association, 269*, 1007–1111.

Marks-Tarlow, T. (1993). A new look at impulsivity: Hidden order beneath apparent chaos? In W. G. McCown, J. L. Johnson, & M. B. Shure (Eds.), *The impulsive client: Theory, research and treatment* (pp. 119–138). Washington, DC: American Psychological Association.

Mathiesen, T. (1998). Selective incapacitation revisited. *Law and Human Behavior, 22*, 453–467.

Meehl, P. E. (1954). *Clinical versus statistical prediction*. Minneapolis, MN: University of Minnesota Press.

Menzies, R., & Webster, C. D. (1995). Construction and validation of risk assessments in a six-year follow-up of forensic patients: A tridimensional analysis. *Journal of Consulting and Clinical Psychology, 63*, 766–778.

Menzies, R. J., Webster, C. D., McMain, S., Saley, S., & Scaglione, R. (1994). The dimensions of dangerousness revisited: Assessing forensic predictions about violence. *Law and Human Behavior, 18*, 1–28.

Menzies, R. J., Webster, C. D., & Sepejak, D. S. (1985a). The dimensions of dangerousness: Evaluating the accuracy of psychometric predictions of violence among forensic patients. *Law and Human Behavior, 9*, 35–56.

Menzies, R. J., Webster, C. D., & Sepejak, D. S. (1985b). Hitting the forensic sound barrier: Predictions of dangerousness in a pre-trial psychiatric clinic. In C. D. Webster, M. H. Ben-Aron, & S. J. Hucker (Eds.), *Dangerousness: Probability and prediction, psychiatry and public policy* (pp. 115–143). New York: Cambridge University Press.

Monahan, J. (1981). *Predicting violent behavior: An assessment of clinical techniques.* Beverly Hills, CA: Sage.

Monahan, J. (1984). The prediction of violent behavior: Toward a second generation of theory and policy. *American Journal of Psychiatry, 141*, 10–15.

Monahan, J. (1988). Risk assessment of violence among the mentally disordered: Generating useful knowledge. *International Journal of Law and Psychiatry, 11*, 249–257.

Monahan, J. (1992). Mental disorder and violent behavior. *American Psychologist, 47*, 511–521.

Monahan, J. (1996). Violence prediction: The last 20 and the next 20 years. *Criminal Justice and Behavior, 23*, 107–120.

Monahan, J., & Steadman, H. J. (Eds.) (1994). *Violence and mental disorder: Developments in risk assessment.* Chicago, IL: University of Chicago Press.

Polvi, N. (1997). Assessing risk of suicide in correctional settings. In C. D. Webster & M. A. Jackson (Eds.), *Impulsivity: Theory, assessment and treatment* (pp. 278–301). New York: Guilford.

Polvi, N., & Webster, C. D. (1997). Challenging assessments of dangerousness and risk: The recent research. In J. Ziskin (Ed.), *Coping with psychiatric and psychological testimony* (Supplement to 5th ed., pp. 148–164). Los Angeles, CA: Law and Psychology Press.

Quinsey, V. L., Harris, G. T., Rice, M. E., & Cormier, C. A. (1998). *Violent offenders: Appraising and managing risk.* Washington, DC: American Psychological Association.

Rice, M. E. (1997). Violent offender research and implications for the criminal justice system. *American Psychologist, 52*, 414–423.

Sepejak, D. S., Menzies, R. J., Webster, C. D., & Jensen, F. A. S. (1983). Clinical predictions of dangerousness: Two-year follow-up of 408 pre-trial forensic cases. *Bulletin of the American Academy of Psychiatry and the Law, 11*, 171–181.

Shah, S. A. (1978). Dangerousness: A paradigm for exploring some issues in law and psychology. *American Psychologist, 33*, 224–238.

Shah, S. A. (1981). Dangerousness: Conceptual, prediction, and public policy issues. In J. R. Hays, T. K. Roberts, & K. S. Solway (Eds.), *Violence and the violent individual* (pp. 151–178). New York: SP Medical and Scientific Books.

Snowden, P. (1997). Practical aspects of clinical risk assessment and management. *British Journal of Psychiatry, 170*, 32–34.

Steadman, H. J., & Cocozza, J. J. (1974). *Careers of the criminally insane: Excessive social control of deviance.* Lexington, MA: Lexington Books.

Steadman, H. J., Monahan, J., Appelbaum, P. S., Grisso, T., Mulvey, E. P., Roth, J. H., Robbins, P. C., & Klassen, D. (1994). Designing a new generation of risk assessment research. In J. Monahan & H. J. Steadman (Eds.), *Violence and mental disorder: Developments in risk assessment* (pp. 297–318). Chicago, IL: University of Chicago Press.

Stone, A. A. (1985). The new legal standard of dangerousness: Fair in theory, unfair in practice. In C. D. Webster, M. H. Ben-Aron, & S. J. Hucker (Eds.), *Dangerousness: Probability and prediction, psychiatry and public policy* (pp. 13–24). New York: Cambridge University Press.

Thornberry, T. P., & Jacoby, J. E. (1979). *The criminally insane: A community follow-up of mentally ill offenders.* Chicago, IL: University of Chicago Press.

Walker, N. (1991). Dangerous mistakes. *British Journal of Psychiatry, 138,* 752–757.

Webster, C. D., & Cox, D. N. (1997). Integration of nomothetic and ideographic positions in risk assessment: Implications for practice and the education of psychologists and other mental health professionals. *American Psychologist, 52,* 1245–1246.

Webster, C. D., Douglas, K. S., Eaves, D., & Hart, S. D. (1997a). Predicting violence in mentally and personality disordered individuals. In C. D. Webster & M. A. Jackson (Eds.), *Impulsivity: Theory, assessment, and treatment* (pp. 251–277). New York: Guilford.

Webster, C. D., Douglas, K. S., Eaves, D., & Hart, S. D. (1997b). *HCR-20: Assessing risk for violence, Version 2.* Vancouver, Canada: Mental Health, Law, and Policy Institute, Simon Fraser University.

Webster, C. D., Eaves, D., Douglas, K. S., & Wintrup, A. (1995). *The HCR-20 scheme: The assessment of dangerousness and risk.* Vancouver, Canada: Simon Fraser University and British Columbia Forensic Psychiatric Services Commission.

Webster, C. D., Harris, G. T., Rice, M. E., Cormier, C., & Quinsey, V. L. (1994). *The violence prediction scheme: Assessing dangerousness in high risk men.* Toronto, Canada: University of Toronto, Centre of Criminology.

Webster, C. D., & Jackson, M. (1997). A clinical perspective on impulsivity. In C. D. Webster & M. A. Jackson (Eds.), *Impulsivity: Theory, assessment, and treatment* (pp. 13–31). New York: Guilford.

Wishnie, H. (1977). *The impulsive personality: Understanding people with destructive character disorders.* New York: Plenum.

Chapter 6

Sex Offender Risk Assessment

R. Karl Hanson
Department of the Solicitor General of Canada, Ottawa, Canada

INTRODUCTION

Last year, you saw Mr Smith for three sessions of couples counselling. Mr Smith has just pleaded guilty to his second attempted rape, for which he could face life imprisonment. His lawyer now wants you to testify at his sentencing hearing.

You are working with a mother and her two daughters as part of child protection services. The eldest daughter has recently disclosed being sexually abused by a neighbour. You learn that the mother's new boyfriend was convicted 15 years ago for molesting his step-daughter. You have no power to prevent him from moving in. Should you remove the children from the home?

You are a probation officer with a specialized caseload of 60 sexual offenders. Two of your cases worry you. Yesterday, a 50-year-old repeat child molester began talking openly about his sexual attraction to a particular boy. Today, you learn that a 22-year-old date rapist was evicted from treatment for denying he had done anything wrong. You have the opportunity to make one more home visit this week. Which one would you choose?

The need for accurate risk assessment permeates clinical practice. Given the serious consequences of sexual victimization (Hanson, 1990; Koss, 1993), special care is justified in the evaluation of sexual offenders. Evaluators are most often concerned about new sexual offences, but sexual offenders also have considerable potential for inflicting other forms of damage. Sexual offenders, particularly rapists, are as likely to recidivate with a non-sexual violent offence as with a sexual offence (Hanson & Bussière, 1996, 1998). The predictors of sexual offence recidivism, however, appear to be different from the factors that predict non-sexual violent recidivism (Hanson & Bussière, 1998; Hanson, Scott, & Steffy, 1995). Consequently, the careful clinician should evaluate separately the risk for sexual and for non-sexual recidivism. Since the assessment of general, violent

Handbook of Offender Assessment and Treatment. Edited by C. R. Hollin.
© 2000 John Wiley & Sons Ltd.

recidivism is addressed elsewhere (Bonta, Law, & Hanson, 1998; Quinsey, Harris, Rice, & Cormier, 1998), the present chapter will focus only on assessing the risk for sexual recidivism.

PREDICTORS OF SEXUAL RECIDIVISM

Future behaviour can never be predicted with certainty. Nevertheless, a growing body of research indicates that well-informed evaluators can predict sexual offence recidivism with at least moderate accuracy (Hanson, 1998; Quinsey, Lalumière, Rice, & Harris, 1995). Risk assessments consider two distinct concepts:

1. enduring propensities, or potentials, to reoffend
2. factors that indicate the onset of new offences.

These offence triggers are not random, but can be expected to be organized into predictable patterns (offence cycles), some unique to the individual and some common to most sexual offenders (see Laws, 1989).

Different evaluation questions require the consideration of different types of risk factors. Static, historical variables (e.g. prior offences, childhood maladjustment) can indicate deviant developmental trajectories and, as such, enduring propensities to sexually offend. Evaluating changes in risk levels (e.g. treatment outcome), however, requires the consideration of dynamic, changeable risk factors (e.g. cooperation with supervision, deviant sexual preferences) (Bonta, 1996). Although age is sometimes considered a dynamic factor, the most important dynamic factors are those that respond to treatment. Dynamic factors can be further classified as stable or acute. Stable factors have the potential to change, but typically endure for months or years (e.g. personality disorder), and, as such, represent ongoing risk potential. In contrast, acute factors (e.g. negative mood) may be present for short durations (minutes, days) and can signal the timing of offending. Most risk decisions require consideration of both static and dynamic risk factors.

Follow-up Studies of Sexual Offenders

The strongest evidence for identifying risk factors comes from follow-up studies (Furby, Weinrott, & Blackshaw, 1989). Even the best study, however, is insufficient to establish that a characteristic is (or is not) a risk factor. Knowledge advances through orderly replication (Lakatos, 1970; Schmidt, 1996). When the same factor is identified in many independent studies, evaluators can be reasonably confident that the risk factor is reliable. Consequently, rather than discuss individual follow-up studies in detail, this section relies heavily on our recently completed meta-analysis of sexual offender recidivism studies (Hanson & Bussière, 1998; for an earlier version see Hanson & Bussière, 1996).

Our quantitative review examined 61 different follow-up studies including a total of 28 972 sexual offenders. Table 6.1 presents the risk factors that were examined in at least four independent settings and correlated with recidivism at $r = 0.10$ or greater. Overall, the strongest predictors of sexual offence recidivism were factors related to sexual deviance. Sexual offenders were more likely to recidivate if they had deviant sexual interests, had committed a variety of sexual crimes, had begun offending sexually at an early age, or had targeted boys, strangers, or unrelated victims. Sexual interest in children as measured by phallometric testing (Launay, 1994) was the single strongest predictor of sexual offence recidivism.

After sexual deviance, the next most important predictors were general criminological factors, such as any prior offences, age, and antisocial personality disorder. These factors mark a dimension common to many criminal populations that has been variously referred to as "low self-control" (Gottfredson & Hirschi, 1990), psychopathy (Hare et al., 1990), or lifestyle instability (Cadsky, Hanson, Crawford, & Lalonde, 1996). There is extensive research linking general criminological factors to non-sexual recidivism among both sexual and non-sexual offender populations (Bonta et al., 1998; Gendreau, Little, & Goggin, 1996; Hanson & Bussière, 1998). Although criminal lifestyle was, in itself, only moderately related to sexual offence recidivism, there is some evidence that the combination of deviant sexual preferences and psychopathy places offenders at particularly high risk for committing further sexual offence crimes (Rice & Harris, 1997).

One of the more interesting findings was that offenders who failed to complete treatment were at higher risk than those who completed treatment ($r = 0.17$). Offenders' verbal reports of treatment motivation had little or no rela-

Table 6.1 Predictors of sexual offence recidivism from Hanson & Bussière (1998)

Risk factors	Average r	Sample (studies) size
Sexual deviance		
Sexual interest in children as measured by phallometry	0.32	4 853 (7)
Any deviant sexual preference	0.22	570 (5)
Prior sexual offences	0.19	11 294 (29)
Any stranger victims	0.15	465 (4)
Early onset of sex offending	0.12	919 (4)
Any unrelated victims	0.11	6 889 (21)
Any boy victims	0.11	10 294 (19)
Diverse sex crimes	0.10	6 011 (5)
Criminal history/lifestyle		
Antisocial personality disorder/psychopathy	0.14	811 (6)
Any prior offences (non-sexual/any)	0.13	8 683 (20)
Demographic factors		
Age (young)	0.13	6 969 (21)
Single (never married)	0.11	2 850 (8)
Treatment history		
Failure to complete treatment	0.17	806 (6)

tionship to recidivism (average $r = 0.01$ based on three studies), but those offenders who actively engaged in treatment recidivated less often than treatment drop-outs. Such findings have sometimes been attributed to the effectiveness of treatment (e.g. Hall, 1995), but could also indicate that the highest risk offenders fail to complete treatment. In particular, it is well known that antisocial personality, lifestyle instability, and general impulsiveness are reliable predictors of treatment attrition (Cadsky et al., 1996; Wierzbicki & Pekarik, 1993).

Notably absent from the list of risk factors were any measures of subjective distress or general psychological symptoms (e.g. low self-esteem, depression). Overall, the average correlation with recidivism for general psychological variables was virtually zero (average $r = 0.01$, with 95% confidence interval of -0.02 to $+0.04$) (Hanson & Bussière, 1998). As will be discussed later, this does not mean that subjective distress plays no role in the recidivism process. Mood could be an acute, but not a long-term, risk factor. Since sexual offenders recidivated years after the assessments, rapidly changing factors, such as mood, would not be expected to predict long-term recidivism.

In summary, follow-up studies have identified a number of static (e.g. prior offences) or highly stable factors (e.g. deviant sexual preferences) that can usefully identify an enduring propensity for sexual offending. Follow-up studies have not identified any acute risk factors, nor have they identified many variables that would be useful for clinicians looking for treatment targets. Early research suggested that decreasing sexual deviance reduced recidivism (Quinsey, Chaplin, & Carrigan, 1980), but with extended follow-up, recidivism was predicted by pre-treatment, not post-treatment, deviance scores (Rice, Quinsey, & Harris, 1991).[1]

Dynamic Risk Factors

If evaluators wish to maintain high levels of certainty, the discussion of dynamic risk will be extremely short: there are no well-established dynamic risk predictors for sexual offence recidivism. Dynamic factors, however, are too important to ignore. Consequently, this section will provide some discussion of variables that could potentially be useful dynamic risk factors.

My suggestions regarding dynamic risk factors were guided by social cognitive theory (e.g. Bandura, 1977; Fiske & Taylor, 1991) as has been applied to general criminal behaviour (e.g. Andrews & Bonta, 1994) and sexual offending (Johntson & Ward, 1996; Laws, 1989). In this model, recidivistic sexual offenders would be expected to hold deviant schema, or habitual patterns of thought and action, that facilitate their offences. The likelihood that an offender will invoke such schema would increase if the schema were well rehearsed, were triggered by common circumstances, were considered socially acceptable, and were consistent with the offender's personality and values. Each offender's crime cycle

---

[1] In general, the reduced variability in post-treatment scores would be expected to restrict the extent to which they could predict recidivism.

would be unique. Nevertheless, certain characteristics would be expected to provide fertile ground for the development and maintenance of deviant sexual schema. An outline of some of these potential dynamic risk factors is presented in Table 6.2.

Among the more promising dynamic risk factors are problems with intimacy and attachment (Marshall, 1993; Seidman, Marshall, Hudson, & Robertson, 1994;

Table 6.2   Potential dynamic predictors of sexual offence recidivism

Predictor	Level
Intimacy deficits	low: a stable romantic relationship with an appropriate partner, and several constructive long-term friendships moderate: some intimate relationships, but short-term or unsatisfying high: no intimate relationships, or relationships only with wholly inappropriate partners (e.g. children)
Negative peer influences	low: all significant people are positive influences moderate: a mixture of positive and negative influences high: overtly deviant peer groups (e.g. paedophile exchange members, bike gang)
Attitudes tolerant of sexual assault	low: identifies no situations in which sexual assault is justified. Consistently views sexual offending as wrong moderate: generally disapproves of sexual crimes, but occasionally will express excuses/justifications (e.g. mature child, victim asked for it) high: sees little wrong with sexual offending; able to justify in many situations (e.g. age of consent laws are "arbitary")
Emotional/sexual self-regulation	low: has consistently coped with stressful situations without resorting to sexual fantasies or high-risk behaviour moderate: occasionally lapses into sexual fantasies (deviant or otherwise) and/or high-risk behaviour when stressed high: negative mood/stress consistently trigger sexual imagery, and feels urge to act upon them. Frequently feels sexually frustrated and is unable/unwilling to delay gratification
General self-regulation	low: consistently cooperative with supervision and/or treatment. Avoids high-risk situations, even when it involves personal sacrifices moderate: recognizes need to self-regulate, but little commitment or weak implementation. Attends treatment but not highly motivated. Occasional missed appointments/rescheduling high: disengaged, or overtly manipulative in supervision. Feels no need to change/self-monitor or feels "out of control". Frequent non-attendance or treatment drop-out. Commonly exposed to high-risk situations

Ward, Hudson, & McCormack, 1997). Normative sexuality involves mutually consenting behaviour within a relationship of trust. In contrast, the social interactions connected with sexual offending are, by definition, problematic. The victims are either incapable of mutuality (child molesting), or the contact is overtly hostile (rape), or extremely detached (voyeurism, exhibitionism). Such problems with the initiation and development of sexual relationships has been referred to as courtship disorder (Freund, Seto, & Kuban, 1997) or as heterosexual social skills deficits (McFall, 1990).

Recidivism studies provide some evidence that relationship deficits increase recidivism risk. In general, the closer the pre-existing relationship with the victim, the lower the recidivism rate (incest < acquaintances < strangers) (Hanson & Bussière, 1998). As well, offenders who have never been married/common-law are at increased risk for sexual offence recidivism compared with married offenders. Frisbie's (1969) follow-up study similarly found that "grave difficulties in establishing meaningful relationships with adult females" (p. 163) was one of the most important recidivism risk factors.

Group comparisons between sexual offenders and non-sexual offenders also support the importance of intimacy deficits. In comparison with non-sexual offenders, sexual offenders receive little satisfaction from their intimate relationships (Seidman et al., 1994), lack empathy for women (Hanson, 1997b), and prefer sex in uncommitted relationships (Malamuth, 1998).

A careful examination of the full range of sexual offenders' personal relationships is not only useful for identifying intimacy deficits, but may also reveal direct social support for sexual offending (e.g. paedophile rings; peer support for rape). There is extensive research indicating that having criminal companions is a strong predictor of criminal behaviour (Gendreau et al., 1996). Similarly, there is some evidence that sexual offenders are likely to have friends and relatives who are sexual offenders (Hanson & Scott, 1996). In a recent study of sexual offenders on community supervision (total, $n = 408$), we found that the recidivists were more likely than the non-recidivists to have predominantly negative social influences (43% versus 21%, respectively, Hanson & Harris, 1998, in press).

Attitudes or values tolerant of sexual assault should also be considered potential dynamic predictors. Among community samples, there is consistent evidence that men who admit to sex offending also endorse "rape myths" or attitudes that condone such behaviour (Dean & Malamuth, 1997; Malamuth, Sockloskie, Koss, & Tanaka, 1991). The research with convicted sexual offender samples has not always been consistent, but there is some evidence that deviant sexual attitudes are common among both child molesters and rapists (Bumby, 1996; Hanson, Gizzarelli, & Scott, 1994). Typically, sexual offenders state that sexual offending is wrong but provide justifications and excuses that mitigate the seriousness of their own crimes. Those rare offenders who directly challenge the morality of existing sexual laws should be considered particularly high risk (e.g. paedophile club members).

According to relapse prevention theory, a common trigger for sexual offending is negative mood or stress (Pithers, Beal, Armstrong, & Petty, 1989). Offenders are considered to cope with stress through sexual fantasies, which may eventually be acted upon. In support of this position, repeated assessments of inpatient sexual offenders has found that deviant sexual fantasies tended to follow stressful events (McKibben, Proulx, & Lusignan, 1994; Proulx, McKibben, & Lusignan, 1996). Cortoni, Heil, and Marshall (1996) similarly found that sexual offenders reported using sexual fantasies (both deviant and non-deviant) as coping mechanisms much more often than did other types of offenders. Given that sexual offenders may feel justified or entitled to act out their sexual feelings with little "courtship" (Freund et al., 1997; Hanson et al., 1994), it is easy to imagine how sexual responses to stress could be an important risk indicator. The overall level of subjective distress does not appear to be important in predicting recidivism (Hanson & Bussière, 1998). What do seem more important are the mechanisms used by sex offenders for regulating their emotional and sexual feelings. In particular, sexual offenders should be considered at high risk to reoffend if (a) many circumstances, including negative affect, arouse sexual imagery; and (b) offenders feel deprived or frustrated if they are unable quickly to satisfy their urges.

In addition to problems with emotional/sexual self-regulation discussed above, offenders may also have problems with general self-regulation or self-control strategies. Offenders who are motivated to prevent reoffence and can effectively manage their own behaviour should be able to reduce their recidivism risk. This dimension overlaps with the criminal lifestyle variables previously discussed, but includes additional indicators. In our recent study we found that some of the best predictors of recidivism while on community supervision related to poor self-management strategies. In particular, recidivists, in comparison with non-recidivists, were perceived as failing to acknowledge their own potential for reoffence, exposing themselves to high-risk situations, being unmotivated for treatment, and being uncooperative with community supervision (Hanson & Harris, in press).

Combining Risk Factors

Since no single factor is sufficient to determine whether offenders will or will not recidivate, evaluators need to consider a range of relevant risk factors. There are three plausible methods by which risk factors can be combined into overall evaluations of risk:

1. empirically guided clinical evaluations
2. pure actuarial predictions, and
3. clinically adjusted actuarial predictions.

The empirically guided clinical evaluation begins with the overall recidivism base rate, and then adjusts the risk level by considering factors that have been empirically associated with recidivism risk. The risk factors to be considered are explicit, but the method for weighing the importance of the risk factors is left to the judgement of the evaluator (e.g. Boer, Wilson, Gauthier, & Hart, 1997).

Actuarial approaches, in contrast, explicitly state not only the variables to be considered, but also the precise procedure through which ratings of these variables will be translated into a risk level. In the pure actuarial approach, risk levels are estimated through mechanical, arithmetic procedures requiring a minimum of judgement. The "adjusted" actuarial approach begins with a pure actuarial prediction, but then raises or lowers the risk level based on consideration of relevant factors that were not included in the actuarial method. As research develops, actuarial methods can be expected consistently to outperform clinical predictions (Grove & Meehl, 1996). With the current state of knowledge, however, both actuarial and guided clinical assessment approaches can be expected to provide risk assessments with moderate levels of accuracy.

Actuarial Risk Scales for Sexual Offence Recidivism

The starting point for all risk prediction should be the expected recidivism base rate. The rate at which sexual offenders are reconvicted for sexual offences is much lower than is commonly believed. In our meta-analytic review (Hanson & Bussière, 1998) 13.4% of the sexual offenders recidivated with a sexual offence ($n = 23\,393$; 18.9% for 1839 rapists and 12.7% for 9603 child molesters) during the average four-to-five-year follow-up period. These rates should be considered underestimates since many sexual offences, particularly those against children, are never reported (Bonta & Hanson, 1994). With longer follow-up periods, the rate increases to 35%–45% after 15–25 years (Hanson et al., 1995; Prentky, Lee, & Knight, 1997; Rice & Harris, 1997). The long-term rate for child molesters is similar to that of rapists, although there is a tendency for rapists to recidivate somewhat earlier after release.

Actuarial scales further refine base-rate predictions by estimating the recidivism rates for sub-groups of sexual offenders (e.g. incest offenders, boy-object child molesters with prior sexual offence convictions). Efforts to develop actuarial risk scales are just beginning but the initial results are encouraging.

One of the more promising scales is the Minnesota Sexual Offender Screening Tool (SOST; Epperson, Kaul, & Huot, 1995). The original version contained 21 items related to sexual and non-sexual criminal history, substance abuse, marital status, and treatment compliance. In the replication sample, the original scale correlated 0.27 with sexual offence recidivism. A revised 17-item version is reported to be more accurate than the original version (ROC area of 0.77), but it has yet to be validated on a new sample (D. Epperson, personal communication, October 21, 1997). SOST scores are difficult to translate into recidivism rates, however, since the SOST studies over-sampled recidivists to create artificially high base rates (35%–50%).

Her Majesty's Prison Service (UK) has also developed a brief scale for assessing risk for sexual offence recidivism (David Thornton, personal communication, March 11, 1997). The scale categorizes offenders into three risk levels (low, medium, high) based on sexual and non-sexual criminal convictions, and the type of victim in the sexual offences (males, strangers). The scale was developed to predict both sexual and violent recidivism; nevertheless, in a replication sample drawn from the UK prison population, the scale correlated 0.33 with sexual offence recidivism (David Thornton, personal communication, March 11, 1997). This result is encouraging, but further work is required to determined the extent to which the scale generalizes to other settings.

I have also constructed a brief actuarial risk scale for sexual offence recidivism by reanalysing the data from eight different follow-up studies (total sample of 2604) (Hanson, 1997a). The Rapid Risk Assessment for Sexual Offence Recidivism, or RRASOR, contains four items: prior sexual offences; age less than 25; any male victims; and any unrelated victims. Each item is worth one point, except for prior sexual offences, which can be worth up to three points. Overall, the RRASOR showed moderate predictive accuracy (average $r = 0.27$, area under ROC curve = 0.71), with little variability between the development and validation samples. Each increase in RRASOR scores was associated with an increase in recidivism rates. The estimated five-year rate was 4.4% for the lowest risk category, which increased to 49.8% for the highest risk group. The estimated 10-year recidivism rates were correspondingly higher (6.5% and 73.1% for the lowest and highest risk groups, respectively). The vast majority of the offenders fell in the lower risk groups (average five-year recidivism rate of 12.6%).

The available research suggests that it is possible to assess an offender's long-term risk potential using brief actuarial scales. The predictive accuracy of these scales is only moderate, however, and none claim to be comprehensive. Consequently, the prudent evaluator would start with the rates estimated by the actuarial scales, and then consider whether important factors have been omitted. Evaluators should be exceedingly cautious, however, about adjusting actuarial predictions given the poor track record of clinical risk evaluation (Grove & Meehl, 1996).

SUMMARY AND CONCLUSIONS

Different risk assessment contexts call for different combinations of static and dynamic risk predictors. The follow-up research has identified a number of reliable risk factors related to sexual deviance, criminal lifestyle, and treatment compliance. Almost all of the identified risk factors are static or highly stable. Such factors are useful for assessing enduring propensities to reoffend, but they cannot be used to assess treatment outcome or monitor risk on community supervision. Although the research support is tentative, there are several factors that may be useful dynamic risk factors, including intimacy and attachment deficits, deviant peer groups, poor emotional/sexual self-regulation, and general self-regulation problems.

All risk evaluations should be grounded in the expected recidivism base rates. Evaluators can then adjust their predictions based on the presence or absence of relevant risk factors. Several actuarial scales have been developed that may be useful for assessing long-term risk potential. There are no validated scales, however, for assessing changes in the risk for sexual offence recidivism. Consequently, the available information is better at identifying high-risk offenders than it is at determining how to intervene, or whether the interventions have been effective.

ACKNOWLEDGEMENTS

The views expressed are those of the author and do not necessarily represent the views of the Ministry of the Solicitor General of Canada. I would like to thank Andrew Harris for comments on an earlier version of this chapter. Correspondence should be addressed to R. Karl Hanson, Corrections Research, Department of the Solicitor General of Canada, 340 Laurier Avenue, West, Ottawa, Ontario, Canada, K1A 0P8, or by e-mail to hansonk@sgc.gc.ca.

REFERENCES

Andrews, D. A., & Bonta, J. (1994). *The psychology of criminal conduct.* Cincinnati, OH: Anderson.

Bandura, A. (1977). *Social learning theory.* Englewood Cliffs, NJ: Prentice-Hall.

Boer, D. P., Wilson, R. J., Gauthier, C. M., & Hart, S. D. (1997). Assessing risk for sexual violence: Guidelines for clinical practice. In C. D. Webster & M. A. Jackson (Eds.), *Impulsivity: Theory, assessment, and treatment* (pp. 326–342). New York: Guilford.

Bonta, J. (1996). Risk–needs assessment and treatment. In A. T. Harland (Ed.), *Choosing correctional options that work* (pp. 18–32). Thousand Oaks, CA: Sage.

Bonta, J., & Hanson, R. K. (1994). *Gauging the risk for violence: Measurement, impact and strategies for change* (User Report No. 1994-09). Ottawa, Canada: Department of the Solicitor General of Canada.

Bonta, J., Law, M., & Hanson, R. K. (1998). The prediction of criminal and violent recidivism among mentally disordered offenders: A meta-analysis. *Psychological Bulletin, 123,* 123–142.

Bumby, K. M. (1996). Assessing the cognitive distortions of child molesters and rapists: Development and validation of the MOLEST and RAPE scales. *Sexual Abuse: A Journal of Research and Treatment, 8,* 37–54.

Cadsky, O., Hanson, R. K., Crawford, M., & Lalonde, C. (1996). Attrition from a male batterer treatment program: Client-treatment congruence and lifestyle instability. *Violence and Victims, 11,* 51–64.

Cortoni, F., Heil, P., & Marshall, W. L. (1996, November). Sex as a coping mechanism and its relationship to loneliness and intimacy deficits in sexual offending. Presentation at the 15th Annual Conference of the Association for the Treatment of Sexual Abusers, Chicago.

Dean, K., & Malamuth, N. M. (1997). Characteristics of men who aggress sexually and of men who imagine aggressing: Risk and moderating variables. *Journal of Personality and Social Psychology, 72,* 449–455.

Epperson, D. L., Kaul, J. D., & Huot, S. J. (1995, October). *Predicting risk for recidivism for incarcerated sex offenders: Updated development on the Sex Offender Screening Tool (SOST).* Poster session presented at the annual conference of the Association for the Treatment of Sexual Abusers, New Orleans, LA.

Fiske, A., & Taylor, S. (1991). *Social cognition* (2nd ed.). New York: McGraw-Hill.

Freund, K., Seto, M. C., & Kuban, M. (1997). Frottuerism and the theory of courtship disorder. In D. R. Laws & W. O'Donohue (Eds.), *Sexual deviance: Theory, assessment, and treatment* (pp. 111–130). New York: Guilford.

Frisbie, L. V. (1969). *Another look at sex offenders in California.* (California Mental Health Research Monograph No. 12). California: State of California Department of Mental Hygiene.

Furby, L., Weinrott, M. R., & Blackshaw, L. (1989). Sex offender recidivism: A review. *Psychological Bulletin, 105*, 3–30.

Gendreau, P., Little, T., & Goggin, C. (1996). A meta-analysis of the predictors of adult offender recidivism: What works! *Criminology, 34*, 575–607.

Gottfredson, M. R., & Hirschi, T. (1990). *A general theory of crime.* Stanford, CA: Stanford University Press.

Grove, W. M., & Meehl, P. E. (1996). Comparative efficiency of informal (subjective, impressionistic) and formal (mechanical, algorithmic) prediction procedures: The clinical–statistical controversy. *Psychology, Public Policy, and Law, 2*, 293–323.

Hall, G. C. N. (1995). The preliminary development of a theory-based community treatment for sexual offenders. *Professional Psychology: Research and Practice, 26*, 478–483.

Hanson, R. K. (1990). The psychological impact of sexual victimization on women and children. *Annals of Sex Research, 3*, 187–232.

Hanson, R. K. (1997a). *The development of a brief actuarial risk scale for sexual offense recidivism* (User Report No. 1997-04). Ottawa, Canada: Department of the Solicitor General of Canada.

Hanson, R. K. (1997b). Invoking sympathy: Assessment and treatment of empathy deficits among sexual offenders. In B. K. Schwartz & H. R. Cellini (Eds.), *The sex offenders: New insights, treatment innovations and legal developments* (Vol. 2, pp. 1:1–1:12). Kingston, NJ: Civic Research Institute.

Hanson, R. K. (1998). What do we know about sexual offender risk assessment. *Psychology, Public Policy, and Law, 4*, 50–72.

Hanson, R. K., & Bussière, M. T. (1996). *Predictors of sexual offender recidivism: A meta-analysis* (User Report 96-04). Ottawa, Canada: Department of the Solicitor General of Canada.

Hanson, R. K., & Bussière, M. T. (1998). Predicting relapse: A meta-analysis of sexual offender recidivism studies. *Journal of Consulting and Clinical Psychology, 66*, 348–362.

Hanson, R. K., Gizzarelli, R., & Scott, H. (1994). The attitudes of incest offenders: Sexual entitlement and acceptance of sex with children. *Criminal Justice and Behavior, 21*, 187–202.

Hanson, R. K., & Harris, A. J. R. (1998). *Dynamic predictors of sexual recidivism.* (User Report 1998-01). Ottawa, Canada: Department of the Solicitor General of Canada.

Hanson, R. K., & Harris, A. J. R. (in press). Where should we intervene? Dynamic predictors of sex offense recidivism. *Criminal Justice and Behavior.*

Hanson, R. K., & Scott, H. (1996). Social networks of sexual offenders. *Psychology, Crime, & Law, 2*, 249–258.

Hanson, R. K., Scott, H., & Steffy, R. A. (1995). A comparison of child molesters and non-sexual criminals: Risk predictors and long-term recidivism. *Journal of Research in Crime and Delinquency, 32*, 325–337.

Hare, R. D., Harpur, T. J., Hakstian, A. R., Forth, A. E., Hart, S. D., & Newman, J. P. (1990). The Revised Psychopathy Checklist: Reliability and factor structure. *Psychological Assessment, 2*, 338–341.

Johnston, L., & Ward, T. (1996). Social cognition and sexual offending: A theoretical framework. *Sexual Abuse: A Journal of Research and Treatment, 8*, 55–80.

Koss, M. P. (1993). Rape: Scope, impact, interventions, and public policy responses. *American Psychologist, 48*, 1062–1069.

Lakatos, I. (1970). Falsification and the methodology of scientific research programs. In A. Musgrave & I. Lakatos (Eds.), *Criticism and the growth of knowledge* (pp. 91–195). New York: Cambridge University Press.

Launay, G. (1994). The phallometric assessment of sex offenders: Some professional and research issues. *Criminal Behaviour and Mental Health, 4,* 48–70.

Laws, D. R. (Eds.) (1989). *Relapse prevention with sexual offenders.* New York: Guilford.

Malamuth, N. M. (1998). An evolutionary-based model integrating research on the characteristics of sexually coercive men. In J. Adair & D. Belanger (Eds.), *Advances in psychological sciences (Vol. 1): Personal, social and developmental aspects,* 151–184. Hove, UK: Psychology Press.

Malamuth, N. M., Sockloskie, R., Koss, M. P., & Tanaka, J. (1991). The characteristics of aggressors against women: Testing a model using a national sample of college students. *Journal of Consulting and Clinical Psychology, 59,* 670–681.

Marshall, W. L. (1993). The role of attachment, intimacy, and loneliness in the eitology and maintainance of sexual offending. *Sexual and Marital Therapy, 8,* 109–121.

McFall, R. M. (1990). The enhancement of social skills: An information-processing analysis. In W. L. Marshall, D. R. Laws, & H. E. Barbaree (Eds.), *Handbook of sexual assault: Issues, theories, and the treatment of the offender* (pp. 311–330). New York: Plenum.

McKibben, A., Proulx, J., & Lusignan, R. (1994). Relationships between conflict, affect and deviant sexual behaviors in rapists and child molesters. *Behaviour Research and Therapy, 32,* 571–575.

Pithers, W. D., Beal, L. S., Armstrong, J., & Petty, J. (1989). Identification of risk factors through clinical interviews and analysis of records. In D. R. Laws (Ed.), *Relapse prevention with sex offenders* (pp. 77–87). New York: Guilford.

Prentky, R. A., Lee, A. F. S., & Knight, R. A. (1997). Recidivism rates among child molesters and rapists: A methodological analysis. *Law and Human Behavior, 21,* 635–659.

Proulx, J., McKibben, A., & Lusignan, R. (1996). Relationships between affective components and sexual behaviors in sexual aggressors. *Sexual Abuse: A Journal of Research and Treatment, 8,* 279–289.

Quinsey, V. L., Chaplin, F. C., & Carrigan, W. F. (1980). Biofeedback and signaled punishment in the modification of inappropriate sexual age preferences. *Behavior Therapy, 11,* 567–576.

Quinsey, V. L., Harris, G. T., Rice, M. T., & Cormier, C. A. (1998). *Violent offenders: Appraising and managing risk.* Washington, DC: American Psychological Association.

Quinsey, V. L., Lalumière, M. L., Rice, M. E., & Harris, G. T. (1995). Predicting sexual offenses. In J. C. Campbell (Ed.), *Assessing dangerousness: Violence by sexual offenders, batterers, and child abusers* (pp. 114–137). Thousand Oaks, CA: Sage.

Rice, M. E., & Harris, G. T. (1997). Cross-validation and extension of the Violence Risk Appraisal Guide for child molesters and rapists. *Law and Human Behavior, 21,* 231–241.

Rice, M. E., Quinsey, V. L., & Harris, G. T. (1991). Sexual recidivism among child molesters released from a maximum security psychiatric institution. *Journal of Consulting and Clinical Psychology, 59,* 381–386.

Schmidt, F. L. (1996). Statistical significance testing and cumulative knowledge in psychology: Implications for training of researchers. *Psychological Methods, 1,* 115–129.

Seidman, B. T., Marshall, W. L., Hudson, S. M., & Robertson, P. J. (1994). An examination of intimacy and loneliness in sex offenders. *Journal of Interpersonal Violence, 9,* 518–534.

Ward, T., Hudson, S. M., & McCormack, J. (1997). Attachment style, intimacy deficits, and sexual offending. In B. K. Schwartz & H. R. Cellini (Eds.), *The sex offenders: New insights, treatment innovations and legal developments* (Vol. 2, pp. 2:1–2:14). Kingston, NJ: Civic Research Institute.

Wierzbicki, M., & Pekarik, G. (1993). A meta-analysis of psychotherapy dropout. *Professional Psychology: Research and Practice, 24,* 190–195.

Chapter 7

Psychophysiology and Risk Assessment

William D. Murphy
University of Tennessee-Memphis, Memphis, Tennessee, USA

INTRODUCTION

Psychophysiological methods are used to study the relationship between physiological activity and psychological states (Scarpa & Raine, 1997). Within the
general area of criminal and antisocial behavior, the most frequently recorded
response systems are electrodermal activity (primarily skin conductance), heart
rate, and a variety of cortical measures such as EEG and event-related potentials. Autonomic measures are taken in resting stages, during classical conditioning paradigms, and as a measure of the orienting response. Within the sub-area
of sex offenders, the most common paradigm is the measurement of penile
tumescence while subjects are presented specific sexual stimuli.

The purpose of this chapter is to review the literature on the relationship
of psychophysiological measures to risk. There is a very extensive literature on
the use of psychophysiological measures in general antisocial behavior and
specifically with individuals diagnosed as psychopaths (Scarpa & Raine, 1997).
However, little of this literature speaks to issues of prediction of future violence
or criminal behavior. On the other hand, there is very extensive literature on the
relationship of tumescence measures to risk in sexual offenders. Therefore,
although we will briefly touch on the use of psychophysiological measures in non-
sex offender populations, the majority of this chapter will attempt to summarize
the more extensive literature of the relationship of tumescence measures to risk
in the sex offender population.

Handbook of Offender Assessment and Treatment. Edited by C. R. Hollin.
© 2000 John Wiley & Sons Ltd.

CHILD PHYSICAL ABUSE AND DOMESTIC VIOLENCE

Milner, Murphy, Valle, and Tolliver (1998) have recently reviewed several studies related to physiological activity in child physical abusers or individuals at risk for abuse. These studies have generally employed skin conductance or heart rate reactivity to specific child stimuli, such as infant crying or smiling (Frodi & Lamb, 1980) or videotapes involving stressful or non-stressful children's behavior (Wolfe, Fairbank, Kelly, & Bradlyn, 1983). In general, although there are at times inconsistencies across responses systems, these studies have indicated increases in physiological reactivity to various child stimuli in at least some of the physiological systems.

However, Casanova, Domanic, McCanne, and Milner (1994) compared at-risk and low-risk parents on heart rate and skin conductance responsivity with four non-child-related stressors. They found that the at-risk group was more responsive to two of the more stressful stimuli, a cold presser task and a film of an industrial accident. This would suggest a generalized hyperarousal and not just over-responsivity to child stimuli. Data related to physiological measures in child physical abuse are rather limited and the studies were designed to investigate theoretical mechanisms and not designed as classification or prediction studies. As pointed out by Milner et al. (1998), inspection of the data in these studies suggests a good deal of variability and it is unlikely that physiological measures could accurately classify individuals as being at risk for child physical abuse.

Within the area of domestic violence, there is also rather limited data. Jacobson et al. (1994) found no differences between maritally violent and non-violent men on a number of cardiovascular measures during a structured laboratory interaction. In a second study, Gottman, Jacobson, Rushe, and Shortt (1995) used heart rate reactivity to five minutes of a marital conflict interaction in order to type subjects. Subjects who showed a deceleration in heart rate during this five minute interaction were labeled Type 1 batterers, while the other subjects were labeled Type 2 batterers. Heart rate deceleration is generally interpreted to be associated with an increase in attention. Comparison of these two groups on other measures revealed a number of significant differences. The Type 1 batterers were more violent in general, more antisocial, more violent in the relationship, and the violence in their relationships seemed more instrumental than impulsive.

These data are very interesting and if replicated would clearly be related to risk assessment in this population. However, given that this is the only study that could be found related to this concept, it is premature to draw any firm conclusions regarding the use of psychophysiological measures in domestic violence groups.

GENERAL CRIMINAL AND ANTISOCIAL BEHAVIOR

A number of studies (see Scarpa & Raine, 1997 for a review) have found a relationship between a variety of physiological variables collected during childhood or adolescence and later criminal behavior. However, generally these relationships are relatively few and it is likely that any use of these in a clinical situation to screen for prevention would misidentify a large number. For example, Raine, Venables, and Williams (1990) collected a variety of psychophysiological measures on a group of 101 schoolchildren when they were 15 and collected criminal data at age 24. At age 24, approximately 17% of this population had engaged in some criminal behavior. A discriminant function analysis was applied to heart rate level, non-specific skin conductance responses, skin conductance level, amount of slow wave theta activity in the EEG, and correctly classified 74.7% of the subjects. Of the non-criminals 23% were classified as criminals while 35% of the criminal population were classified as non-criminals. Although this function is significant, it is quite clear that as a screening measure this would lead to a large misclassification rate. Two more recent studies (Brennan et al., 1997; Raine, Venables, & Williams, 1996) have investigated psychophysiological reactivity as a protective factor. Raine et al. (1996), again following up the 101 schoolchildren, studied a sub-set of 17 antisocial adolescents who desisted from crime by age 29, 17 who were engaging in criminal activity by 29, and 17 matched non-antisocial controls. The desisters showed better autonomic conditioning and faster electrodermal recovery time than those who continued in a criminal pattern and controls. This pattern of psychophysiological responding would suggest enhanced information processing of emotionally relevant stimuli. Brennan et al. (1997) studied older subjects (59 to 61) who were considered to be at higher risk for criminal behavior based on their fathers' behavior. Skin conductance and heart rate gathered in a learning paradigm indicated that heightened autonomic nervous system responsiveness seemed to be associated with lower likelihood of criminal outcome in high-risk groups.

SEXUAL AROUSAL MEASURES

Psychophysiological assessment of sexual arousal through measurement of penile circumference and volume change has not only been used in the research context, but is frequently used in the clinical context. Psychophysiological assessment of sexual arousal is frequently part of an overall psychological or psychosexual assessment of an offender. Data for such assessments are many times integrated into reports for courts in addition to being used for treatment planning.

Ethical standards for the use of penile tumescence measures have been established (Association for the Treatment of Sexual Abusers [ATSA], 1997) and the technical aspects of the assessment procedure have been described (Farrall, 1992; Laws & Osborn, 1983). There have been a number of detailed reviews and critiques of the literature (Blader & Marshall, 1989; Murphy & Barbaree, 1994; O'Donohue & Letourneau, 1992; Pithers & Laws, 1988; Simon & Schouten, 1992).

General Procedures

Generally, assessments are made with circumferential gauges (either mercury and rubber or metal band strain gauges) or volumetric devices. The circumferential device measures changes in penile circumference and there are few differences in terms of measuring accuracy between the mercury and rubber and the metal band strain gauges (Laws, 1977). The volumetric device measures the total volume of the penis and it is judged to be more sensitive (Freund, Langevin, & Barlow, 1974), although some have questioned this (Wheeler & Rubin, 1987). However, because of cost and ease of use, the majority of clinicians and research laboratories employ the circumferential measure.

Changes in penile tumescence are assessed while subjects are exposed to specific sexual stimuli, generally from 30 seconds to two minutes, and these stimuli vary from study to study on actual sexual content. Stimuli are primarily slides for assessing age preference and audiotapes for assessing preference for types of sexual behaviors and/or degree of violence in the offense. In the United States, there has been significant controversy regarding the use of slides of children because of children's lack of ability to give informed consent (Card & Olsen, 1996; Laws, 1996). This has led many in the United States to cease using visual depictions of children even though this at times makes it difficult accurately to assess age preference. Konopasky (1995; personal communication, February, 1998) has developed computer-generated visual stimuli and a computerized assessment system that will address some of the ethical concerns regarding the use of slides of real people.

There are a number of ways to score erectile data including millimeter circumference change, percentage full erection, ratios of deviant to non-deviant arousal, difference scores between deviant and non-deviant arousal, and ipsative z-scores. It appears that difference scores and z-scores may maximize discrimination between groups (Harris, Rice, Quinsey, Chaplin, & Earls, 1992), although some criticize the z-score method, especially when subjects show little discrimination between any of the stimuli (Barbaree & Mewhort, 1994).

Finally, it should be recognized that there is no one standard measurement procedure. The actual assessment varies on a number of factors including type of stimuli, type of transducer, length of stimulus presentation, scoring method, etc. As pointed out by O'Donohue and Letourneau (1992), the assessment of sexual arousal among offender populations can probably best be viewed as a family of procedures rather than a specific test.

Discrimination of Groups

The ability accurately to classify offenders relates to risk assessment to the extent that various sub-types of offenders have different risk profiles. Previous reviews have clearly indicated that arousal measures separate extrafamilial offenders from normals. Literature since then has continued to support this general position (Card & Dibble, 1995; Chaplin, Rice, & Harris, 1995; Laws, Gulayets, & Frenzel, 1995; Malcolm, Andrews, & Quinsey, 1993), although not all of these studies have used non-offender control groups. Recently, Miner, West, and Day (1995) presented data that suggests that offenders against male children have the most offense-specific pattern as compared with rapists and offenders against female children. It is also those who molest young males who seem to have the highest recidivism. Two studies failed to find any group differences (Hall, Proctor, & Nelson, 1988; Haywood, Grossman, & Cavanaugh, 1990), but the majority of the literature is quite consistent in its findings. The data are also fairly clear that in general incest cases are more similar to normals than they are to extrafamilial child molesters (Barbaree & Marshall, 1989; Lang, Black, Frenzel, & Checkley, 1988; Marshall, Barbaree, & Christophe, 1986; Quinsey, Chaplin, & Carrigan, 1979).

Although it is clear that arousal measures separate offending from non-offending groups, from a clinical standpoint this still does not speak to the sensitivity and specificity of the test for clinical use. Fortunately, most studies find fairly good specificity in the 80%–90% range (Barbaree & Marshall, 1989; Freund & Watson, 1991; Malcolm et al., 1993; Marshall et al., 1986). However, sensitivity tends to be, as might be expected, much less with classification generally in the 45%–60% range (Freund & Blanchard, 1989; Freund & Watson, 1991; Malcolm et al., 1993; Marshall et al., 1986). Chaplin et al. (1995) and Harris et al. (1992) present data that suggest the discrimination can be improved when stimuli that focus on child trauma and also z-score transformations and deviation indices based on difference scores are employed. Using these variations, they report sensitivity close to 90% and specificity close to 100%.

There are also data, however, that would suggest that some of what is considered a lack of sensitivity in measurement is actually a reflection of the heterogeneity in the offender population. Data from other sources (Knight & Prentky, 1990) suggest that there are a variety of typologies of child molesters and that not all may have sexual arousal as a primary motivator. Barbaree and Marshall (1989) provide profile analysis of arousal measures collected in their laboratory and found five profile types with only approximately 35% being what would be considered a typical child molester profile; that is, maximum responding to children with least responding to other stimuli. The rest of the extrafamilial child molesters were fairly evenly divided between normal profile types, non-discriminating profile types, a child–adult type (where arousal is equivalent) and a teen–adult profile (again where arousal is equivalent). Also, it should be noted that Freund and Watson (1991) found better sensitivity among subjects with male victims, and those with more than one victim, and the previously cited study by Miner et al. (1995) suggested that the offenders against males show the most distinctive offense-specific profile. This literature would be consistent with literature related to reoffense in that those with more than one offense and those with male victims tend to have the highest reoffense rates.

The ability to separate rapists from non-offenders has been somewhat more controversial and the data less consistent (Murphy & Barbaree, 1994) leading

Blader and Marshall (1989) seriously to question the value of arousal measures with the rapist population. There have, however, been two meta-analyses completed using slightly different inclusion criteria and both covering a relatively small number of studies. Hall, Shondrick, and Hirschman (1993) found what would be considered a moderate effect size, while Lalumière and Quinsey (1993), in a somewhat more detailed meta-analysis, found a somewhat stronger effect size suggesting a sensitivity greater than 60% when specificity was set at 90%. Again, as with child molesters, Lalumière and Quinsey found that those studies that use the most brutal stimulus sets report the best discrimination (also see Rice, Chaplin, Harris, & Coutts, 1994; Seto & Kuban, 1996). Also, Harris et al. (1992) report that the use of z-scores and deviance indices based on difference scores also led to much better discrimination in the rapist population.

As with the child molester population, there is also a similar argument that the lack of sensitivity in discrimination is due to the natural heterogeneity of the rapist population and that not all offenders have an arousal pattern that suggests a preference for rape (Barbaree & Marshall, 1991). Freund (1990) has argued that there is a sub-set of rapists who are "rape prone", and have a sexual preference for rape, and that this pattern is part of the courtship disorders. Prentky and Knight (1991) also have presented evidence suggesting that only a sub-set of rapists sexually motivated. Barbaree, Seto, Serin, Amos, and Preston (1994), using the Massachusetts Treatment Center typology (Knight & Prentky, 1990), classified a small group of rapists into those thought to have a sexual motivation and those whose motivation was primarily non-sexual. Arousal data suggested that the sexualized group had the more deviant arousal patterns as predicted. In a somewhat different approach, Proulx, Aubut, McKibben, and Côté (1994) investigated a small group of rapists who they classified as "less physically violent" and compared them with normals. It was found in this group that the non-offenders and offenders did not differ on rape depictions involving physical violence, but did differ on those involving humiliation. This suggested that, for the less violent offenders, humiliation and degradation may be a greater motivating factor than physical violence. However, Eccles, Marshall, and Barbaree (1994) did not find a difference between rapists and non-offenders on stimuli depicting degradation, although it is not clear whether they classified their subjects in terms of more or less physically violent.

In reviewing the data related to both rapists and child molesters, we have pointed out that differences in discrimination in groups may be related to procedural variations between studies and/or may be related to heterogeneity within the subject population. The subjects' ability intentionally to suppress their responding also limits the validity of arousal measures. Freund and Watson (1991) found much lower classification rates for non-admitters compared with admitters. Castonguay, Proulx, Aubut, McKibben, and Campbell (1993) found that judicial status (pre-sentence versus post-sentence) had a 0.36 correlation with penile response magnitude.

There have been a number of approaches attempting to control faking including descriptions of characteristics of feigned records (Freund, Watson, & Rienzo,

1988), the use of a signal detection task to distract subjects (McAnulty & Adams, 1991; Proulx, Côté, & Achille, 1993; Quinsey & Chaplin, 1988a), the use of detumescence time as a possible alternative measure that is harder to fake (Malcolm, Davidson, & Marshall, 1985). Regardless of the method employed, none is totally able to control subjects' ability to fake. Therefore, given the various motivations subjects have to appear normal in the laboratory, there will always be some limitations to the validity of this technique. In clinical use, one needs to realize that offenders' lack of responding may convey less information than positive responding.

Relationship to Violence

There have been a small number of studies investigating the relationship between sexual arousal measures and violence or victim damage. Abel, Barlow, Blanchard, and Guild (1977) presented a small study that suggested that sadistic rapists have higher rape indices, i.e. higher ratios of rape arousal to consenting arousal, than non-sadistic rapists. Quinsey and Chaplin (1982) found that although the rape index did not relate to victim damage, a non-sexual violence index (ratio of consensual sex to non-sexual violence) did. Quinsey, Chaplin, and Upfold (1984) provide somewhat mixed support, finding no relationship between erection data and extent of harm to the victim in the most serious offense but finding a small correlation if a dichotomous victim damage variable were used rather than a more continuous variable. Langevin et al. (1985) basically failed to replicate these results.

In terms of child offenders, Abel, Becker, Murphy, and Flanagan (1981) and Avery-Clark and Laws (1984) presented data that were suggestive that a pedophilic aggressive index could separate less aggressive from more aggressive sex offenders. Avery-Clark and Laws (1984) could correctly identify 92% of the more dangerous offenders and 71% of the less dangerous. Marshall et al. (1986) and Barbaree and Marshall (1989) also presented data suggestive of a relationship between arousal measures and force in offense. Marshall et al. (1986) found a 0.32 correlation between force used and pedophile index based on arousal to the adult mutual stimuli and arousal to non-aggressive sexual interactions with children. Lang et al. (1988) failed to replicate this data, although the sample size was rather small and the study may have had insufficient power to detect differences. Quinsey and Chaplin (1988b) provided what appeared to be more mixed support. Although they did find a relationship between victim injury and an index of the difference between adult-consenting and adult-coercive stimuli, they did not replicate the type of index as has been used by Avery-Clark and Laws (1984).

In general, there is some albeit mixed support for the relationship of arousal measures to violence/victim damage. The literature is somewhat problematic in that in different studies different types of indices (e.g. ratio of deviant to non-deviant arousal or differences between these two measures) have been found to be significant while others have not been replicated. In addition, some authors have used a more general definition of force which has been variously defined, others have rated victim damage or victim injury from reading medical reports. These two variables may be linked but are not the same. In addition, because of the many factors besides arousal to aggressive cues that relate to the amount of injury a victim receives or the amount of force used in the offense, there will always be some limitations on the size of relationships between arousal measure and victim damage/force. From a clinical standpoint, one should proceed with caution in making any strong statements regarding the validity of arousal measures to predict the more violent offenders.

The Relationship of Sexual Arousal to Recidivism

To the general public and to probably most individuals in the field, prediction of recidivism is one of the most important factors to consider. Because this variable has been touched on in previous chapters, we will only briefly reiterate the data here for completeness. Since previous reviews (Murphy & Barbaree, 1994; O'Donohue & Letourneau, 1992), there have been a number of studies linked to the relationship of arousal measures to recidivism. These have already been well reviewed by Hanson and Bussière (1996) in a meta-analysis. They were able to identify seven studies that measured sexual preference for child stimuli and in the meta-analysis there was a very strong (0.32) correlation between phallometric derived measures and recidivism. Studies that looked at specific preference to boys have found significant, but much smaller, relationships (0.14) while those that looked at sexual preference to rape alone have not been significant (Hanson & Bussière, 1996). In addition, Quinsey, Rice, and Harris (1995), in a mixed study of child molesters and rapists, found a significant (0.20) correlation between a deviance index defined as the most deviant index whether it was based on child stimuli, non-sexual violent stimuli, or rape stimuli. Recidivism in this case was either sexual reconviction or a violent failure. Similarly, in another presentation of the same data, Quinsey, Lalumière, Rice, and Harris (1995) report a 0.21 correlation between the deviance index defined as the most deviant regardless of stimulus presentation and sexual recidivism.

Therefore, although studies that use a rape index have not found a significant relationship to recidivism, those that use a broader range of deviance indices do seem to find some relationship. This again may suggest a certain amount of heterogeneity in the population of rapists, who at times may be aroused by rape material, where as at other times they are more aroused by violence *per se*. In general, although, as the Hanson and Bussière (1996) study indicates, there is variability across studies, the relationships between arousal measures and recidivism are quite strong within the context of the recidivism prediction. However, it should be made clear that arousal measures in and of themselves should not be used as sole criteria for prediction.

CONCLUSION

This chapter has attempted to review psychophysiological research relating to risk assessment. Outside the sex offender area, this literature has been primarily theoretically driven and its overall use for risk assessment is rather limited. The data in domestic violence using physiological measures to type individuals are interesting but not adequately developed for clinical use. The literature on arousal measures is much more highly developed and clearly can be a valuable tool when appropriately used. Arousal measures do seem clearly to separate extrafamilial offenders from non-offenders, although the data with rapists is more mixed. Better typologies and an increased understanding of the procedural variations that may maximize discrimination are two promising areas where emerging data are helping us to understand inconsistencies in the literature. However, one must be careful that arousal measures are not misused. As pointed out by Murphy and Barbaree (1994), arousal measures are best used as part of an overall assessment process in terms of treatment planning and risk assessment. Arousal measures may at times be useful in assisting subjects to overcome denial, but should not be seen as something that should be used to force subjects to admit to sexual offenses. Also, as has been pointed out frequently (Murphy & Peters, 1992), arousal measures should not be used to determine whether someone has committed or not committed a specific offense, and should not be used to say whether anyone "fits a profile" of an offender. To date, there are no assessment instruments that allow one to make such a stance. Arousal measures need to be used in the context of a general assessment of both criminological and psychological factors.

REFERENCES

Abel, G. G., Barlow, D. H., Blanchard, E. B., & Guild, D. (1977). The components of rapists' sexual arousal. *Archives of General Psychiatry, 34*, 895–903.

Abel, G. G., Becker, J. V., Murphy, W. D., & Flanagan, B. (1981). Identifying dangerous child molesters. In R. B. Stuart (Ed.), *Violent behavior: Special learning approaches to prediction, management, and treatment* (pp. 116–137). New York: Brunner/ Mazel.

Association for the Treatment of Sexual Abusers (1997). *Ethical standards and principles for the management of sexual abusers.* Beaverton, OR: Author.

Avery-Clark, C. A., & Laws, D. R. (1984). Differential erection response patterns of child sexual abusers to stimuli describing activities with children. *Behavior Therapy, 15*, 71–83.

Barbaree, H. E., & Marshall, W. L. (1989). Erectile responses among heterosexual child molesters, father–daughter incest offenders, and matched non-offenders: Five distinct age preference profiles. *Canadian Journal of Behavioral Science, 21*, 70–82.

Barbaree, H. E., & Marshall, W. L. (1991). The role of male sexual arousal in rape: Six models. *Journal of Consulting & Clinical Psychology 59*, 621–630.

Barbaree, H. E., & Mewhort, D. J. K. (1994). The effects of the *z*-score transformation on measures of relative erectile response strength: A re-appraisal. *Behaviour Research and Therapy, 32,* 547–558.

Barbaree, H. E., Seto, M. C., Serin, R. C., Amos, N. L., & Preston, D. L. (1994). Comparisons between sexual and non-sexual rapist subtypes: Sexual arousal to rape, offense precursors and offense characteristics. *Criminal Justice & Behavior, 21,* 95–114.

Blader, J. C., & Marshall, W. L. (1989). Is assessment of sexual arousal in rapists worthwhile? A critique of current methods and the development of a response compatibility approach. *Clinical Psychology Review, 9,* 569–587.

Brennan, P. A., Raine, A., Schulsinger, F., Kirkegaard-Sorensen, L., Knop, J., Hutchings, B., Rosenberg, R., & Mednick, S. A. (1997). Psychophysiological protective factors for male subjects at high risk for criminal behavior. *American Journal of Psychiatry, 154,* 853–855.

Card, R. D., & Dibble, A. (1995). Predictive value of the Card/Farrall stimuli in discriminating between gynephilic and pedophilic sex offenders. *Sexual Abuse: A Journal of Research and Treatment, 7,* 129–141.

Card, R. D., & Olsen, S. E. (1996). Visual plethysmograph stimuli involving children: Rethinking some quasi-logical issues. *Sexual Abuse: A Journal of Research and Treatment, 8,* 267–271.

Casanova, G. M., Domanic, J., McCanne, T. R., & Milner, J. S. (1994). Physiological responses to child stimuli in mothers with and without a childhood history of physical abuse. *Child Abuse & Neglect, 18,* 995–1004.

Castonguay, L. G., Proulx, J., Aubut, J., McKibben, A., & Campbell, H. (1993). Sexual preference assessment of sexual aggressors: Predictors of penile response magnitude. *Archives of Sexual Behavior, 22,* 325–334.

Chaplin, T. C., Rice, M. E., & Harris, G. T. (1995). Salient victim suffering and the sexual responses of child molesters. *Journal of Consulting and Clinical Psychology, 63,* 249–255.

Eccles, A., Marshall, W. L., & Barbaree, H. E. (1994). Differentiating rapists and non-offenders using the rape index. *Behaviour Research & Therapy, 32,* 539–546.

Farrall, W. (1992). Instrumentation and methodological issues in the assessment of sexual arousal. In W. O'Donohue & J. Geer (Eds.), *The sexual abuse of children: Clinical issues* (pp. 188–231). Hillsdale, NJ: Lawrence Erlbaum.

Freund, K. (1990). Courtship disorder. In W. L. Marshall, D. R. Laws, & H. E. Barbaree (Eds.), *Handbook of sexual assault: Issues, theories, and treatment of the offender* (pp. 195–207). New York: Plenum.

Freund, K., & Blanchard, R. (1989). Phallometric diagnosis of pedophilia. *Journal of Consulting and Clinical Psychology, 57,* 100–105.

Freund, K., Langevin, R., & Barlow, D. (1974). Comparison of two penile measures of erotic arousal. *Behaviour Research and Therapy, 12,* 355–359.

Freund, K., & Watson, R. J. (1991). Assessment of the sensitivity and specificity of a phallometric test: An update of phallometric diagnosis of pedophilia. *Psychological Assessment: A Journal of Consulting and Clinical Psychology, 3,* 254–260.

Freund, K., Watson, R., & Rienzo, D. (1988). Signs of feigning in the phallometric test. *Behaviour Research and Therapy, 26,* 105–112.

Frodi, A. M., & Lamb, M. E. (1980). Child abusers' responses to infant smiles and crimes. *Child Development, 51,* 238–241.

Gottman, J. M., Jacobson, N. S., Rushe, R. H., & Shortt, J. W. (1995). The relationship between heart rate reactivity, emotionally aggressive behavior, and general violence in batterers. *Journal of Family Psychology, 9,* 227–248.

Hall, G. C. N., Proctor, W. C., & Nelson, G. M. (1988). Validity of physiological measures of pedophilic sexual arousal in a sexual offender population. *Journal of Consulting and Clinical Psychology, 56,* 118–122.

Hall, G. C. N., Shondrick, D. D., & Hirschman, R. (1993). The role of sexual arousal in sexually aggressive behavior: A meta-analysis. *Journal of Consulting and Clinical Psychology, 61,* 1091–1095.

Hanson, R. K., & Bussière, M. T. (1996). *Predictors of sexual offender recidivism: A meta-analysis* (User Report No. 1996-04). Ottawa, Canada: Department of the Solicitor General of Canada.

Harris, G. T., Rice, M. E., Quinsey, V. L., Chaplin, T. C., & Earls, C. (1992). Maximizing the discriminant validity of phallometric assessment data. *Psychological Assessment, 4,* 502–511.

Haywood, T. W., Grossman, L. S., & Cavanaugh, J. L. (1990). Subjective versus objective measurements of deviant sexual arousal in clinical evaluations of alleged child molesters. *Psychological Assessment, 2,* 269–275.

Jacobson, N. S., Gottman, J. M., Waltz, J., Rushe, R., Babcock, J., & Holtzworth-Munroe, A. (1994). Affect, verbal content, and psychophysiology in the arguments of couples with a violent husband. *Journal of Consulting and Clinical Psychology, 62,* 982–988.

Knight, R. A., & Prentky, R. A. (1990). Classifying sexual offenders: The development and corroboration of taxonomic models. In W. L. Marshall, D. R. Laws, & H. E. Barbaree (Eds.), *Handbook of sexual assault: Issues, theories, and treatment of the offender* (pp. 23–52). New York: Plenum.

Konopasky, R. J. (1995, October). *Is the use of visual stimuli in penile plethysmography ethical and legal? The Canadian solution is "photos" of artificial figures.* Paper presented at the 14th annual meeting of the Association for the Treatment of Sexual Abusers, New Orleans, LA.

Lalumière, M. L., & Quinsey, V. L. (1993). The sensitivity of phallometric measures with rapists. *Annals of Sex Research, 6,* 123–138.

Lang, R. A., Black, E. L., Frenzel, R. R., & Checkley, K. L. (1988). Aggression and erotic attraction toward children in incestuous and pedophilic men. *Annals of Sex Research, 1,* 417–441.

Langevin, R., Bain, J., Ben-Aron, M. H., Coulthard, R., Day, D., Handy, L., Heasman, G., Hucker, S. J., Purins, J. E., Roper, V., Russon, A. E., Webster, C. D., & Wortzman, G. (1985). Sexual aggression: Constructing a predictive equation: A controlled pilot study. In R. Langevin (Ed.), *Erotic preference, gender identify, and aggression in men: New research studies* (pp. 39–62). Hillsdale, NJ: Lawrence Erlbaum.

Laws, D. R. (1977). A comparison of the measurement characteristics of two circumferential penile transducers. *Archives of Sexual Behavior, 6,* 45–51.

Laws, D. R. (1996). Marching into the past: A critique of Card and Olsen. *Sexual Abuse: A Journal of Research and Treatment, 8,* 273–278.

Laws, D. R., Gulayets, M. J., & Frenzel, R. R. (1995). Assessment of sex offenders using standardized slide stimuli and procedures: A multisite study. *Sexual Abuse: A Journal of Research and Treatment, 7,* 45–66.

Laws, D. R., & Osborn, C. A. (1983). How to build and operate a behavioral laboratory to evaluate and treat sexual deviance. In J. G. Greer & I. R. Stuart (Eds.), *The sexual aggressor: Current perspectives on treatment* (pp. 293–335). New York: Van Nostrand Reinhold.

Malcolm, P. B., Andrews, D. A., & Quinsey, V. L. (1993). Discriminant and predictive validity of phallometrically measured sexual age and gender preference. *Journal of Interpersonal Violence, 8,* 486–501.

Malcolm, P. B., Davidson, P. R., & Marshall, W. L. (1985). Control of penile tumescence: The effects of arousal and stimulus content. *Behaviour Research and Therapy, 23,* 273–280.

Marshall, W. L., Barbaree, H. E., & Christophe, D. (1986). Sexual offenders against female children: Sexual preferences for age of victims and type of behaviour. *Canadian Journal of Behavioural Science, 18,* 424–439.

McAnulty, R. D., & Adams, H. E. (1991). Voluntary control of penile tumescence: Effects of an incentive and a signal detection task. *The Journal of Sex Research, 28,* 557–577.

Milner, J. S., Murphy, W. D., Valle, L. A., & Tolliver, R. M. (1998). Assessment issues in child abuse evaluations. In J. R. Lutzker (Ed.), *Handbook of child abuse research and treatment* (pp. 75–115). New York: Plenum.

Miner, M. H., West, M. A., & Day, D. M. (1995). Sexual preference for child and aggressive stimuli: Comparison of rapists and child molesters using auditory and visual stimuli. *Behaviour Research and Therapy, 33*, 545–551.

Murphy, W. D., & Barbaree, H. E. (1994). *Assessments of sex offenders by measures of erectile response: Psychometric properties and decision making.* Brandon, VT: The Safer Society Press.

Murphy, W. D., & Peters, J. M. (1992). Profiling child sexual abusers: Psychological considerations. *Criminal Justice and Behavior, 19*, 24–37.

O'Donohue, W., & Letourneau, E. (1992). The psychometric properties of the penile tumescence assessment of child molesters. *Journal of Psychopathology and Behavioral Assessment, 14*, 123–174.

Pithers, W. E., & Laws, D. R. (1988). The penile plethysmograph: Uses and abuses in assessment and treatment of sexual aggressors. In B. Schwartz (Ed.), *A practitioner's guide to the treatment of the incarcerated male sex offender* (pp. 83–91). Washington, DC: National Institute of Corrections.

Prentky, R. A., & Knight, R. A. (1991). Identifying critical dimensions for discriminating among rapists. *Journal of Consulting and Clinical Psychology, 59*, 643–661.

Proulx, J., Aubut, J., McKibben, A., & Côtè, M. (1994). Penile responses of rapists and non-rapists to rape stimuli involving physical violence or humiliation. *Archives of Sexual Behavior, 23*, 295–310.

Proulx, J., Côtè, M., & Achille, P. A. (1993). Prevention of voluntary control of penile response in homosexual pedophiles during phallometric testing. *The Journal of Sex Research, 30*, 140–147.

Quinsey, V. L., & Chaplin, T. C. (1982). Penile responses to nonsexual violence among rapists. *Criminal Justice and Behavior, 9*, 372–381.

Quinsey, V. L., & Chaplin, T. C. (1988a). Penile responses of child molesters and normals to descriptions of encounters with children involving sex and violence. *Journal of Interpersonal Violence, 3*, 259–274.

Quinsey, V. L., & Chaplin, T. C. (1988b). Preventing faking in phallometric assessments of sexual preference. In R. A. Prentky & V. L. Quinsey (Eds.), *Human sexual aggression: Current perspectives* (Vol. 528, pp. 49–58). New York: Annals of the New York Academy of Sciences.

Quinsey, V. L., Chaplin, T. C., & Carrigan, W. F. (1979). Sexual preferences among incestuous and nonincestuous child molesters. *Behavior Therapy, 10*, 562–565.

Quinsey, V. L., Chaplin, T. C., & Upfold, D. (1984). Sexual arousal to nonsexual violence and sadomasochistic themes among rapists and non-sex offenders. *Journal of Consulting and Clinical Psychology, 52*, 651–657.

Quinsey, V. L., Lalumière, M. L., Rice, M. E., & Harris, G. T. (1995). Predicting sexual offenses. In J. C. Campbell (Ed.), *Assessing dangerousness: Violence by sexual offenders, batterers, and child abusers* (pp. 115–137). Thousand Oaks, CA: Sage.

Quinsey, V. L., Rice, M. E., & Harris, G. T. (1995). Actuarial prediction of sexual recidivism. *Journal of Interpersonal Violence, 10*, 85–105.

Raine, A., Venables, P. H., & Williams, M. (1990). Relationships between central and autonomic measures of arousal at age 15 years and criminality at age 24 years. *Archives of General Psychiatry, 47*, 1003–1007.

Raine, A., Venables, P. H., & Williams, M. (1996). Better autonomic conditioning and faster electrodermal half-recovery time at age 15 years as possible protective factors against crime at age 29 years. *Developmental Psychology, 32*, 624–630.

Rice, M. E., Chaplin, T. C., Harris, G. T., & Coutts, J. (1994). Empathy for the victim and sexual arousal among rapists and nonrapists. *Journal of Interpersonal Violence, 9*, 435–449.

Scarpa, A., & Raine, A. (1997). Psychophysiology of anger and violent behavior. *The Psychiatric Clinics of North America, 20*, 375–394.

Seto, M. C., & Kuban, M. (1996). Criterion-related validity of a phallometric test for paraphilic rape and sadism. *Behaviour Research and Therapy, 34*, 175–183.

Simon, T., & Schouten, P. G. W. (1992). Problems in sexual preference testing in child sexual abuse cases: A legal and community perspective. *Journal of Interpersonal Violence, 7*, 503–516.

Wheeler, D., & Rubin, H. B. (1987). A comparison of volumetric and circumferential measures of penile erection. *Archives of Sexual Behavior, 16*, 289–299.

Wolfe, D. A., Fairbank, J. A., Kelly, J. A., & Bradlyn, A. S. (1983). Child abusive parents' physiological responses to stressful and non-stressful behavior in children. *Behavioral Assessment, 5*, 363–371.

Chapter 8

Psychometric Assessment

Gisli H. Gudjonsson
Institute of Psychiatry, London, UK

INTRODUCTION

In this chapter the author discusses the value of a psychometric assessment in evaluating "risk". In this context the word "risk" refers to two distinct types of evaluation. First, it refers to evaluating the risk of offending or re-offending. This may involve, for example, considering the likelihood that a sex or violent offender will commit further offences after being released from prison. In other words, it is concerned with predicting recidivism by psychometric means. The assessment predicts the likelihood of a particular kind of behaviour occurring in the future. Probably the best illustration of a psychometric measure in this context is the use of the Hare Psychopathy Checklist—Revised (PCL—R) (Hare, 1980, 1991).

Secondly, a psychometric assessment may be used to identify particular strengths or weaknesses which are relevant to evaluating behaviour which occurred in the past in order to prevent the risk of a possible miscarriage of justice. This includes the use of psychometric tests for identifying, and assessing the extent of, psychological vulnerabilities in the context of legal proceedings (Gudjonsson, 1992, 1996a, 1996b). Here, the identification of intellectual deficits, and the personality traits of suggestibility and compliance, may, for example, play an important part in evaluating the credibility of confession statements. This kind of an assessment sometimes involves drawing inferences from test scores about behaviour that happened many years previously (Gudjonsson & MacKeith, 1997).

PSYCHOMETRIC TESTS

A psychological test is best construed as "A standardised or systematic form of examination (e.g. being required to respond to set questions, statements, or other

Handbook of Offender Assessment and Treatment. Edited by C. R. Hollin.

stimuli), in order to determine the presence or absence of a particular skill, knowledge, or characteristic" (Gudjonsson & Haward, 1998, p. 80). Typically, tests are made up of a number of individual items and the examinee's responses are aggregated and presented on a numerical scale. The word "psychometrics" refers to the application of statistical techniques to psychological testing. Thus, psychometric testing includes a structured design, a formal procedure which has to be followed, numerical scoring, standardized norms for different populations, established "error of measurement" and confidence intervals, and validation. One limitation of psychometric tests is that they are restricted in terms of what they measure and they do not allow for idiosyncratic variations in terms of administration and scoring. This lack of flexibility may on occasions reduce the clinical value of psychometric tests.

Allport (1937) argued that personality and abilities can be measured either "ideographically" or "nomothetically". The ideographic approach involves exploring traits within the individual person and how these are integrated. The nomothetic approach, in contrast, involves the development of scales, questionnaires, and inventories, whose purpose is to determine how the scores obtained are distributed in a particular population. Psychometric tests employ the nomothetic approach, whereas projective tests and clinical interviews are ideographic in nature and depend more upon the skills of the examiner than on the standardized format of nomothetic tests.

In contrast to psychometric tests, projective tests traditionally rely on psychodynamic models of understanding and can provide a basis for formulating clinical hypotheses. These clinical hypotheses can subsequently be tested by using psychometric tests or other means of information gathering (e.g. information obtained from informants, behavioural observations). Projective tests are infrequently used in the United Kingdom for forensic assessments, but are still used by psychologists with a psychodynamic orientation, especially in America and Europe (Gudjonsson & Haward, 1998). Heilbrun (1992) makes the point that projective tests have the advantage of overcoming some of the factors which lower the validity of cognitive tests, such as defensiveness, evasiveness, and malingering. The reason for this is that the items which make up psychometric tests are often transparent in terms of what they measure, which makes the test easier to fake if people are motivated to do so, although the subtlety of items does vary considerably across different psychometric tests. In contrast, projective tests are less structured and transparent and are therefore more difficult to fake.

Projective tests tend to suffer from poor inter-scorer reliability, lack validity, and are influenced by a number of contextual factors (Klein, 1992). However, Theilgaard (1996) argues that ideographic methods can provide important clinical insights and a wealth of data on an individual, including motives for crimes, which can be helpful in terms of diagnosis and prognosis in forensic settings.

Theilgaard (1996) makes the valuable point that patients with paranoid tendencies easily feel threatened by psychometric tests and refuse to co-operate, but they will more easily co-operate with projective tests where they feel they have more control.

In order to ensure good co-operation of the patient, it is important to establish good rapport and carefully explain the purpose of the test. Of course, some psychological constructs are subtle and detailed knowledge about the test may invalidate the findings. For example, when measuring how easily people are influenced by suggestions, warning them that their degree of suggestibility is being measured will reduce their susceptibility to suggestions on a test (Gudjonsson, 1992).

THE PURPOSE OF PSYCHOMETRIC TESTS

The main purpose of psychometric testing is to obtain information about an individual in a reliable and valid way. This may need to be achieved for two main reasons. First, psychometric tests discriminate between individuals in relation to particular *abilities* (e.g. intelligence, literacy, memory, neuropsychological functions), *personality traits* (e.g. extraversion, emotional stability, conscientiousness, openness, suggestibility, compliance, attitudes), or *clinical problems* (e.g. anxiety, depression, paranoia, intrusive thought, avoidance behaviours, bizarre or unusual thinking). This is the essence of the measurement of individual differences. The score obtained on a particular test is compared with normative scores for the appropriate population (e.g. the mean scores for persons in the general population) and presented in different ways for interpretation. Typically, the test's raw score is converted to either a *standard score* or a *percentile score*. The standard score for an individual represents the number of standard deviations below or above the mean at which the score falls. The mean (M) is the average score for a normative sample, while the standard deviation (SD) score is a statistical measure of the spread of scores around the mean. The standard score for an individual expresses the number of standard deviations below or above the mean at which the score falls. It is calculated by subtracting the difference between the individual's raw or scaled score (X) from the normative mean (M) and dividing the difference by the normative group's standard deviation (SD).

The following illustration of obtaining the standard score provides an example of the use of a standard score. A client obtained a Full Scale IQ score of 75 on the WAIS–R. The mean and standard deviation scores for the WAIS–R are 100 and 15, respectively. The difference between the individual score (75) and mean score (100) is −25 IQ points, which when divided by the SD of the normative sample (15) gives a standard score of −1.65 (or 1.65 standard deviations below the mean).

A different way of expressing the significance of raw scores (or "scaled scores" on the WAIS–R) is to convert them into percentile ranks. Percentile scores are expressed in terms of the percentage of persons in the standardization groups who fall below or above a given raw or "scaled" score. A percentile score of 50 represents the median (i.e. central tendency). A test score above 50 represents a score above average, whereas a score below 50 falls below average. A score may be said to fall outside the normal range (i.e. it is abnormal) when found in fewer than 5% or more than 95% of the normative population, respectively. This corresponds to the 5th and 95th percentile rank. When placed within the normal distribution it is equivalent to a standard score of 1.65.

A psychometric test can also be used to measure differences in test scores of the same individual on separate occasions. People may need to be tested on more than one occasion. The reasons for this include:

1. monitoring changes in cognitive and personality functioning as a result of treatment intervention (Sigurdsson, Gudjonsson, Kolbeinsson, & Petursson, 1994)
2. situational variations (transitory states) in mood and anxiety which need to be objectively monitored (Spielberger, 1983)
3. investigating the effects of trauma (e.g. head injury or a major psychological trauma) on psychological functioning, and
4. repeated testing in cases of suspected malingering.

There are a large number of psychological tests available for forensic applications. Heilbrun (1992) and Gudjonsson and Haward (1998) provide guidelines for the use of psychological testing in forensic assessments. These guidelines are discussed in what follows.

The Publication of the Test

The test should be published and reviewed in the scientific literature. There should be a manual describing the test's development, standardization, administration, scoring, reliability coefficients, error of measurement, and validity.

The Test's Reliability

The reliability of a test is measured by its consistency. The reliability coefficient obtained for a given test can range from 0 to 1.0. Typically for psychometric tests the coefficients range between 0.80 and 0.90 (Anastasi & Urbina, 1996). Heilbrun (1992) argues that tests whose reliability is less than 0.80 should be used cautiously. The lower the reliability of a test, the poorer the validity due to excessive error variance.

There are three main types of reliability, which are typically referred to as internal consistency, inter-scorer reliability, and test–retest reliabilities, respectively. Internal consistency of the test items refers to the extent to which one part of the test correlates with another part and it is typically measured by Cronbach's alpha.

Some tests, particularly rating scales and behavioural tests, require the scores to be rated by more than one scorer in order to determine the test's inter-scorer reliability. Some behavioural characteristics are easier to score reliably than others. For example, the suggestibility scores on the Gudjonsson Suggestibility

Scales (Gudjonsson, 1997a) have inter-scorer reliability coefficients of about 0.99, whereas confabulatory responses in memory recall are more difficult to score on the same test and the reliability coefficients are between 0.70 and 0.80.

Test–retest reliability refers to consistency of score obtained by the same person when retested with the same test or with an equivalent (alternative) form of the test. The test's test–retest reliability is commonly measured by correlation coefficients. If a test is administered to a person on more than one occasion, the score obtained should be reasonably consistent over time. Typically, the longer the test–retest interval, the lower the reliability scores tend to be. This means that short-term temporal stability is typically greater than long-term stability. The Minnesota Multiphasic Personality Inventory (MMPI or MMPI–2) (Hathaway & McKinley, 1989) serves as a useful example. The MMPI, and recently the revised version, the MMPI–2, is one of the most widely used personality/clinical measures. Its test–retest reliability varies between 0.70 and 0.80 when people are retested within two weeks, but goes down to about 0.35 to 0.45 when the test is readministered after one or more years (Weiner, 1995). Weiner states that low long-term stability of a clinical test, measuring such symptoms as anxiety and depression, does not invalidate the MMPI as a valuable clinical measure, but it poses a problem when a test is aiming to measure presumably stable and endur-ing personality traits, such as extraversion and antisocial attitudes or personality disorder.

The test–retest reliability coefficient makes it possible to compare the relia-bility of different tests and it gives an overall indication of the test's reliability. However, when interpreting individual scores, the most appropriate way of evaluating reliability is by the test's "standard error of measurement". This is comprised of the margin of error that can be expected in an individual score as a result of inherent unreliability of the test (i.e. deviation from the theoretical "true" score). This is computed from the test–retest reliability coefficient of a test and the test's standard deviation score. The standard error of measurement is usually given in the published manual of psychometric tests.

Matarazzo (1990) states that it is very important, when testifying in court, that the psychologist knows the test's standard error of measurement:

> My experience in the courtroom, where more and more psychologists' conclusions are being vigorously challenged by attorneys, has led me to conclude that too many psychologists testifying in the courts today, whether for the plaintiff or defense, are unaware of the standard errors of measurement of the scores (and accompanying confidence intervals) produced by our batteries of tests (p. 1005).

Relevance to the Legal Issues

The test used in a given case must be relevant to the legal issue addressed, or the psychological construct underlying the legal issue. The relevance should be supported by published validation research. However, sometimes, justification for using a particular test may be made on theoretical grounds. As an example of relevance, a psychometric test like the PCL–R is very suitable, on both theoretical and empirical grounds, for measuring the likelihood of future reoffending (also known as "recidivism") (Hemphill, Hare, & Wong, 1998). Similarly, the Gudjonsson Suggestibility and Compliance Scales (Gudjonsson, 1997a) are particularly relevant to measuring psychological vulnerabilities in cases of disputed confessions.

Standard Administration

The standard administration recommended in the test's manual should be used. Typically, this requires a quiet and distraction-free testing environment, which, unfortunately, is not always possible in forensic practice. Indeed, sometimes clients have to be tested in a noisy prison environment. A deviation from the standard and recommended administration of the test will have to be considered when interpreting the findings from the psychometric test.

Specific Purpose

The scores from a given test should not be applied towards a purpose for which the test was not developed (e.g. making inferences about suggestibility from the results of IQ test scores, which does sometimes happen in forensic practice). The interpretation of the test scores should be guided by population and situation specificity. That is, the closer the individual "fits" the population and situation of those described in the validation studies, the greater the confidence one can express in the applicability of the results. Tests used in forensic practice have sometimes only been standardized on non-forensic populations, which limits the generalizability of the results. This is not a problem if one wants to compare the scores of an individual; for example, an offender or a psychiatric patient, with those found for persons in the general population. The findings may, however, tell you very little about how the person's scores compare with those of other offenders.

Using Up-To-Date Norms

The scores on psychometric tests sometimes have to be re-standardized over time, because gradual and subtle changes within the population may change the distribution of scores. For example, it is known that IQ tests have to be re-standardized regularly because of massive gains in performance over generations (Flynn, 1987). This means that norms need to be regularly updated so that the individual's performance can be reliably evaluated with reference to his or her contemporaries' performance. In addition, well-known tests, such as Raven's Standard Progressive Matrices, have unsatisfactory norms which can cause serious problems when interpreting the findings from an individual assessment (Gudjonsson, 1995a, 1995b).

Validity

The validity of a test is decided by the extent to which it measures what it is designed to measure. In order for a test to be valid it must be reliable, but a reliable test need not be valid for the purpose for which it was designed. For example, a test may be internally stable and give consistent scores when people are tested on separate occasions, but it may not be satisfactory in terms of measuring the construct or behaviour for which the test is intended. The three principal types of validity are "content", "criterion-related", and "construct" validity.

"Content validity" refers to the item content of the test and how well it represents the behavioural domain to be measured. This is particularly important with educational tests, but is less relevant for establishing the effectiveness of aptitude and personality tests which more commonly require empirical verification (Anastasi & Urbina, 1996). Grisso (1986) argues that some tests used for clinical and forensic applications have poor content validity. This places a greater burden on their meeting other standards for validity.

"Criterion-related" validity refers to the ability of the test to predict a person's behaviour in specific situations. Test scores are validated against external criteria. These are of two types, known as *concurrent validity* and *predictive validity*. Concurrent validity is measured by the relationship of test scores with another measure of the same type of behaviour given in the same time period. It is more relevant for predicting current status, such as mental state or clinical diagnosis, rather than predicting future behaviour. In contrast, predictive validity is the ability of the test to predict a specified behaviour on an occasion removed from the test situation. For example, in terms of risk assessment it includes the effectiveness of the Hare (1991) Psychopathy Checklist—Revised (PCL–R) to predict the future offending of criminals (i.e. recidivism).

"Construct validity" measures the relationship of the test scores to a relevant theoretical construct or trait. A good example of this is the early work on the Gudjonsson Suggestibility Scale (GSS) (Gudjonsson, 1984), which was concerned with establishing the construct validity of the test as a valid measure of interrogative suggestibility (Gudjonsson, 1992).

Factors Influencing Test Scores

Gudjonsson and Haward (1998) discuss in detail the numerous factors which can influence test scores. These include the client's co-operation, motivation, mental alertness, attention, concentration, depression and anxiety, language and reading problems, cultural factors, malingering, and response bias. Test scores should not be interpreted in isolation to other sources of information. Using a combination of clinical data and actuarial data is preferable in forensic work. It is interesting that clinical judgements of intellectual skills and suggestibility traits are often wrong (Gudjonsson, 1992).

A Test Battery

There are advantages in administering a battery of tests rather than one single test. First, employing tests that measure different aspects of psychological functioning gives a broader base from which inferences can be drawn. For example, administering all 11 subtests from the WAIS–R gives a better measure of the client's intellectual strengths and weaknesses than the individual score from Raven's Standard Progressive Matrices. Secondly, using tests that measure similar aspects of psychological functioning may support the findings from the two tests.

Interpretation of Test Scores

It is unwise to rely on the results from one single test when conducting a forensic evaluation. Test data are generally integrated and interpreted in relation to other sources of data. Grisso (1986) argues that one of the most important precautions in the forensic evaluation is to base interpretations and opinions on more than a single test score or sign. All psychological tests are susceptible to numerous sources of error, including possible malingering, lack of motivation, and socially desirable responding. Therefore, test scores will need to be interpreted with reference to other sources of information in the case. These other sources of data may include educational and family background information on the client, the client's current mental state, his or her demeanour during the assessment, the findings from other similar or parallel tests administered previously or concurrently, information from informants, and documentary evidence such as school reports.

A distinction needs to be made between a statistical abnormality and a diagnosis of mental disorder. A statistical abnormality indicates the frequency with which a specific test score occurs in a given normative population. In contrast, the diagnosis of a psychiatric disorder is based on a clinical opinion of the presence of various signs and symptoms which can be classified as constituting mental disorder.

Forensic psychologists in the United States are increasingly being expected by legal advocates to use the DSM multiaxial classification system (DSM–IV) (American Psychiatric Association [APA], 1994) in their diagnostic evaluation of clients (Valciukas, 1995). The emphasis on mental state evaluation and diagnostic classification makes their psychological evaluation similar to that of psychiatrists. There is no similar development in the United Kingdom. Psychologists in the United Kingdom are not required or expected to place their findings within the DSM–IV or ICD–10 diagnostic classification systems. The exception is in the diagnosis of post-traumatic stress disorder which typically relies upon DSM criteria, as it did in the arbitration cases of the Zeebrugge disaster (Gudjonsson & Haward, 1998).

THE EFFICACY OF PSYCHOMETRIC TESTS IN RISK ASSESSMENT

Blackburn (1993) reminds us that prediction research in criminology has focused on either identifying high-risk groups from early antecedents, or attempting to obtain prediction indices to assist criminal justice decision-making in relation to placement or release decisions. The latter purpose is mainly associated with the prediction of recidivism (i.e. reoffending).

The purpose of identifying risk factors is to maximize the accuracy of prediction and keep both false positive and false negative error rates at a minimum. The efficacy of the predictor is measured by the extent to which it predicts outcome (e.g. offending or reoffending) beyond chance.

The use of psychometric tests allows the use of statistical or actuarial indices for prediction, in contrast to the more subjective evaluation of risk through the use of clinical prediction (Meehl, 1954).

Personality tests, such as the Eysenck Personality Questionnaire (EPQ) (Eysenck & Eysenck, 1975) have been used to discriminate between offenders and non-offenders (Eysenck & Gudjonsson, 1989). This application of personality tests has met with mixed success (Blackburn, 1993; Gudjonsson, 1997b). The EPQ Psychoticism (P) dimension has proved most discriminative, particularly in identifying persistent offenders, but the problem with the Psychoticism dimension is that it suffers from a high false positive error rate (Gudjonsson, 1997b). In other words, it sometimes fails to identify serious and persistent offenders and the correlation between P and Hare's PCL is very low (Hare, 1982).

Other psychometric tests measuring personality variables have also met with limited success, including the Minnesota Multiphasic Personality Inventory (Blackburn, 1993). One of the best psychometric instruments for predicting future offending and recidivism has been the Gough Socialization Scale, which is a measure of antisocial personality characteristics (Schalling, 1978).

The Hare Psychopathy Checklist (PCL–R) (Hare, 1980, 1991), which can be construed as a psychometric instrument, has consistently been found to be a significant predictor of recidivism, although the average correlations between offending and recidivism are very modest. For example, Hemphill et al. (1998) found that the average correlations between PCL–R scores and recidivism were 0.27 for general and violent recidivism, and 0.23 for sexual recidivism.

PSYCHOMETRIC TESTS FOR IDENTIFYING VULNERABILITIES

Psychometric tests are increasingly being used to identify psychological vulnerabilities in cases where a defendant's confession or a witness's version of events is being challenged at trial. The type of vulnerabilities that are often considered important include intellectual abilities, suggestibility, compliance, and acquiescence, all of which can be measured by standardized tests (Clare & Gudjonsson,

1995; Gudjonsson, 1992; Gudjonsson, Clare, Rutter, & Pearse, 1993). The English appellant courts have accepted the psychological tests that measure these concepts (Corre, 1995). Recent appellant judgments in the English and Northern Ireland courts have shown the impact that psychometric test results are having on legal judgments (Gudjonsson, 1999).

Of course, psychometric tests should always be used cautiously and not in isolation from other salient pieces of information. This is particularly important when making inferences about behaviour dating back many years, which is often what happens in cases of a miscarriage of justice. After having been in prison for several years as a result of a wrongful conviction, the appellant's personality and vulnerabilities may have changed markedly and current test scores may give misleading indications when used in isolation (Gudjonsson & MacKeith, 1990). For this reason it is important to obtain as much information as possible about the client's mental state, abilities, and personality at the material time (e.g. when being interviewed by the police and making a confession).

CONCLUSIONS

Psychometric tests sometimes form an important part of the forensic psychologist's evaluation of risk. They can be applied to a range of human behaviour which is relevant to different types of risk. In this chapter the author has focused on the assessment of two broad types of risk. First, the use of psychometric tests for predicting future behaviour, such as reoffending, and secondly to identify psychological vulnerabilities which are relevant to predicting behaviour retrospectively, such as assessing the likelihood that a person made a false confession to the police during interviewing.

Tests such as Hare's Psychopathy Checklist and the Gough Socialization Scale have proved effective in predicting offending and are sometimes used, along with other sources of information, in order to assist criminal justice decision-making in relation to placement or release decisions.

Psychometric tests have been developed specifically to identify psychological vulnerabilities relevant to police interviewing, such as suggestibility and compliance (Gudjonsson, 1997a). These instruments are commonly used to evaluate the credibility of self-incriminating admissions made during police interviewing and are accepted by the appellant and lower criminal courts.

REFERENCES

Allport, G. W. (1937). *Personality: A psychological interpretation*. New York: Holt, Rinehart & Winston.
American Psychiatric Association (1994). *Diagnostic and statistical manual of mental disorders* (4th ed., DSM—IV). Washington, DC: American Psychiatric Association.
Anastasi, A., & Urbina, S. (1996). *Psychological testing* (6th ed.). New Jersey: Prentice-Hall.

Blackburn, R. (1993). *The psychology of criminal conduct. Theory, research and practice.* Chichester, UK: Wiley.

Clare, I. C. H., & Gudjonsson, G. H. (1995). The vulnerability of suspects with intellectual disabilities during police interviews: A review and experimental study of decision-making. *Mental Handicap Research, 8,* 110–128.

Corre, N. (1995). *A guide to the 1995 revisions to the PACE codes of practice.* London: Callow.

Eysenck, H. J., & Eysenck, S. B. G. (1975). *Manual of the Eysenck personality questionnaire (junior and adult).* London: Hodder & Stoughton.

Eysenck, H., & Gudjonsson, G. H. (1989). *The causes and cures of criminality.* New York; London: Plenum.

Flynn, J. R. (1987). Massive IQ gains in 14 nations: What IQ tests really measure. *Psychological Bulletin, 10,* 171–191.

Grisso, T. (1986). Psychological assessment in legal contexts. In W. J. Curran, A. L. McGary, & S. A. Shah (Eds.), *Forensic psychiatry and psychology* (pp. 103–128). New York; F. A. Davis.

Gudjonsson, G. H. (1984). A new scale of interrogative suggestibility. *Personality and Individual Differences, 5,* 303–314.

Gudjonsson, G. H. (1992). *The psychology of interrogation, confessions and testimony.* Chichester, UK: Wiley.

Gudjonsson, G. H. (1995a). The Standard Progressive Matrices: Methodological problems associated with the administration of the 1992 adult standardisation. *Personality and Individual Differences, 18,* 441–442.

Gudjonsson, G. H. (1995b). Raven's norms on the SPM revisited: A reply to Raven. *Personality and Individual Differences, 18,* 447.

Gudjonsson, G. H. (1996a). Psychological evidence in court. Results from the 1995 survey. *The Psychologist, 5,* 213–217.

Gudjonsson, G. H. (1996b). Forensic psychology in England: One practitioner's experience and viewpoint. *Criminological and Legal Psychology, 1,* 131–142.

Gudjonsson, G. H. (1997a). *The Gudjonsson suggestibility scales manual.* Hove, UK: Psychology Press.

Gudjonsson, G. H. (1997b). Crime and personality. In H. Nyborg (Ed.), *The scientific study of human nature. Tribute to Hans J. Eysenck at eighty* (pp. 142–164). Oxford, UK: Elsevier Science.

Gudjonsson, G. H. (1999). The IRA funeral murders: The confession of P. K. and the expert psychological testimony. *Legal and Criminological Psychology, 4,* 45–50.

Gudjonsson, G. H., Clare, I., Rutter, S., & Pearse, J. (1993). *Persons at risk during interviews in police custody: The identification of vulnerabilities* (Royal Commission on Criminal Justice). London: HMSO.

Gudjonsson, G. H., & Haward, L. R. C. (1998). *Forensic psychology: A practitioner's guide.* London: Routledge.

Gudjonsson, G. H., & MacKeith, J. A. C. (1990). A proven case of false confession: Psychological aspects of the coerced-compliant type. *Medicine, Science and the Law, 30,* 329–335.

Gudjonsson, G. H., & MacKeith, J. A. C. (1997). *Disputed confessions and the criminal justice system* (Maudsley Discussion Paper No. 2). London: Institute of Psychiatry.

Hare, R. D. (1980). A research scale for the assessment of psychopathy in criminal populations. *Personality and Individual Differences, 1,* 111–119.

Hare, R. D. (1982). Psychopathy and the personality dimensions of psychoticism, extraversion and neuroticism. *Personality and Individual Differences, 3,* 35–42.

Hare, R. D. (1991). *The Hare Psychopathy Checklist—Revised.* Toronto, Canada: Multi-Health Systems.

Hathaway, S. R., & McKinley, J. C. (1989). *MMPI-2. Manual for administration and scoring.* Minneapolis, MI: University of Minnesota Press.

Heilbrun, K. (1992). The role of psychological testing in forensic assessment. *Law and Human Bahavior, 16*, 257–272.

Hemphill, J. F., Hare, R. D., & Wong, S. (1998). Psychopathy and recidivism: A review. *Legal and Criminological Psychology, 3*, 139–170.

Klein, P. (1992). *Handbook of psychological testing*. London: Routledge.

Matarazzo, J. D. (1990). Psychological assessment versus psychological testing. Validation from Binet to the school, clinic and courtroom. *American Psychologist, 45*, 999–1017.

Meehl, P. E. (1954). *Clinical versus statistical predictions*. Minneapolis, MI: University of Minnesota Press.

Schalling, D. (1978). Psychopathy-related personality variables and the psychophysiology of socialization. In R. D. Hare & D. Schalling (Eds.), *Psychopathic behaviour: Approaches to research* (pp. 85–106). Chichester, UK: Wiley.

Sigurdsson, E., Gudjonsson, G. H., Kolbeinsson, H., & Petursson, H. (1994). The effects of ECT and depression on confabulation, memory processing, and suggestibility. *Nordic Journal of Psychiatry, 48*, 443–451.

Spielberger, C. D. (1983). *Manual for the state-trait anxiety inventory (Form Y)*. Palo Alto, CA: Consulting Psychologists Press.

Theilgaard, A. (1996). A clinical psychological perspective. In C. Cordess & M. Cox (Eds.), *Forensic psychotherapy. Crime, psychodynamics and the offender patient. Volume II: Mainly practice* (pp. 47–62). London: Jessica Kingsley.

Valciukas, J. A. (1995). *Forensic neuropsychology. Conceptual foundations and clinical practice*. London: The Haworth Press.

Weiner, I. B. (1995). Psychometric issues in forensic applications of the MMPI-2. In Y. S. Ben-Porath, J. R. Graham, G. C. N. Hall, R. D. Hirschman, & M. S. Zaragoza (Eds.), *Forensic applications of the MMPI-2* (pp. 48–81). London: Sage.

Chapter 9

Case Material and Interview

Anthony R. Beech
University of Birmingham, Birmingham, UK

INTRODUCTION

Assessment has long been seen as an essential function of those who work with offenders in order to predict the relative likelihood of reoffending/dangerousness of those being assessed. Clinicians are normally reliant upon any information that can be gained from the client at interview and case materials, the latter being any previous information about clients held on file. The information that may be available on file in order to make an assessment includes previous offence history, educational and medical records, depositions from victims, any past parole and probation reports, prison logs, psychological assessments, and any other reports from professionals.

Any serious risk assessment necessitates being comprehensive in order to gather the necessary amount of information. However, it should also be borne in mind that assessment should be a continual process since new material may come to light at a later stage, or an offender may receive treatment for his/her procriminal activities/problems, both of which may have a very real bearing on the level of risk an individual may pose in the future. This chapter will consider both the usefulness and drawbacks of using case material and interview in the process of risk assessment and will hopefully argue the case that any reasonable risk assessment is dependent upon what can be gleaned at interview, information from an offender's history, plus the level of the offender's motivations.

Handbook of Offender Assessment and Treatment. Edited by C. R. Hollin.
© 2000 John Wiley & Sons Ltd.

DEVELOPMENT OF RISK ASSESSMENT

In order to examine the uses and drawbacks of using material derived from interview and case materials, a brief history of how such materials are used in risk assessment is outlined here.

Risk assessment has been seen as a continually evolving process (Bonta, 1996) with perhaps the earliest subjective assessments being gained via intuition or "gut-level" feelings. *A clinical judgement of risk* gained from material gathered at interview with a client can be seen as arising from this type of subjective assessment. A broad criticism of risk assessments using clinical judgement is that the processes involved in coming to a decision are not always necessarily easily observable and may sometimes be difficult to replicate. However, with the development of the clinical judgement models this type of assessment has reached a hitherto unseen level of objectivity. The models that may be used in such an assessment may include:

1. *The linear rationalist model.* Here, clinicians may follow a decision tree or critical pathway to guide them when making decisions concerning future risk of interpersonal violence (e.g. Gross, Southard, Lamb, & Weinberger, 1987). The strength of this type of model is that it provides a clear decision path. The main weakness of such a model is its lack of flexibility, in that other information that may be relevant, such as level of social support and whether the client has successfully completed treatment for offending behaviours, is not necessarily considered.
2. *The hypothetico–deductive model.* (Schon, 1983). Here, the client's problems are assessed more contextually than with the linear model, with the clinician weighing different factors such as past experiences with similar situations and the information available on the current situation. On the basis of this information, hypotheses are constructed and tested regarding current and future risk, which provide a framework in which to assess the likelihood of future offending, and under what circumstances this might occur.

However, the weakness of both of these models is, by their very nature, the over-reliance on the clinician's judgement gained from interview(s). Ideally, any assessment of risk should be undertaken by people trained to be sensitive to factors that might bias their judgement. However, in practice this may not always be the case. For example, Bottomley (1973), in a study of parole decisions, found that an offender's personality and attitudes seen at interview carried more weight in terms of whether an offender would be released than previous offence history, level of family support, and potential employment prospects. In addition, Bonta (1996) argues that over-reliance on clinical judgement, as it is carried out on a case-by-case basis, has an inhibiting effect in terms of furthering knowledge of criminal behaviour and in producing future effective interventions.

With the development of sophisticated statistical analysis, and the ability to analyse large amounts of information through the use of computers, a number of statistical predictions of risk began to be reported in the 1980s, for example, the Salient Factor Score (Hoffman, 1983), and the Statistical Index on Recidivism (Nuffield, 1982). These *actuarial predictions* were set up to be more objective than information solely gleaned from interview and are predicated on the notion that meaningful risk levels can be calculated about the future behaviour of an individual by looking at the rates of offending behaviours of other individuals with a similar historical background to the client being assessed. Here, clinicians/researchers assess the risk factors or risk markers by drawing upon case material about the client.

The general consensus among researchers in the field of risk prediction (Mossman, 1994) is that actuarial prediction is more accurate than clinical judgement. For example, Gottfredson and Gottfredson (1986) note that:

> In virtually every decision making situation for which the issue has been studied, it has been found that statistically developed predictive instruments outperform human judgement (p. 247).

Indeed, there is even evidence to suggest that actuarial risk assessment carried out by trained assistants has stronger predictive validity than therapists' assessment of risk (Menzies, Webster, McMain, Staley, & Scaglione, 1994).

However, it is important to note that such scales only yield a probability, not a certainty, of future offending or non-offending and may suffer from various methodological weaknesses such as inadequate sample sizes, design faults, and measurement errors (Jones, 1996). Because the instruments are not tailored to individual cases they may lead the clinician to ignore relevant information from case files and include irrelevant information. It should also be noted that particular scales are optimized for use on particular populations, i.e. forensic, psychiatric, civil. Prediction may work well with the specific population for which the scale was designed, but cannot be easily applied to other groups. Also, the occurrence of some behaviours in a particular population (i.e. the base rate) is actually very infrequent, and the more infrequent the behaviour the more difficult it is to predict (Lambert, Cartor, & Walker, 1988). As Harris and Rice (1997) point out, the low base rates of violent recidivism in released forensic patients has in the past made it hard to improve upon the prediction that none will commit a further violent offence.

Although, as previously discussed, statistical prediction commonly outperforms intuitive or clinical judgement in criminology, Gottfredson (1987) points out that the seemingly highly random nature of criminal behaviour ensures that prediction scales rarely explain more than 15% to 20% of the recidivism statistics and may never do much better than 30%. Even in more recent studies this has certainly been shown to be the case with violent recidivism—21% (Harris, Rice, & Quinsey, 1993). So the current status of the literature does not suggest that actuarial assessments can precisely define risk, but such instruments wholly based on case material are best used to determine relative risk, i.e. high, medium, low (Richard Laws, personal communication).

A further problem with some actuarial assessment scales is that they are based on historical information, i.e. static variables that cannot be changed. They therefore do not provide any indication of treatment that could be offered to reduce the level of risk of subsequent offending, or allow for the fact that if an offender has had treatment for his/her offending behaviours, this could reduce the level of subsequent risk. In order to address this "history is destiny" problem, the most recent type of risk assessments take into account how an individual's level of risk can be changed. This type of *risk–needs assessment* (Bonta, 1996) goes beyond pure statistical prediction in terms of making a decision about the level of risk and attempts to identify both the level of current risk and what is needed to be done to reduce the level of future offending behaviours. Such risk–needs assessment should identify under what circumstances and in what situations a risk is posed in order that effective plans can be made by the offender so that such circumstances and situations do not arise.

Quinsey, Lalumière, Rice, and Harris (1995) point out that although "static", historical predictors obtained from case material are useful for making an assessment of an offender's overall level of risk, changeable "dynamic" factors such as procriminal attitudes (although the focus of treatment and supervision which may in the end modify the level of risk) have been less well researched. However, it should be noted that Bonta (1996) reports that reductions in dynamic risk factors were associated with reduced recidivism.

This section has tried to give a brief overview of how the notion of risk assessment has developed and how it is necessary for a reasonable risk–needs assessment to use both case materials and interview. Case material provides historical information but also may provide a check as to the veracity of information gathered at interview. Any information gathered at interview (by an experienced clinician) should encompass clinical material, current life situation and circumstances, as well as providing the opportunity to explore in more detail information gathered from case materials. The next two sections of this chapter examine some of the uses and drawbacks of data gathering from such sources.

USES AND LIMITATIONS OF CASE MATERIAL

Case material that may be available on file includes previous offence history, educational and medical records, psychiatric reports, any past parole and probation reports, prison logs, previous criminal convictions, psychological assessments, any other reports from professionals, and (perhaps) depositions from victims. Obviously, the ease of data gathering here is dependent upon the quality of the source material. The strength of such material is usually the relative objectivity of the sources. Case material can also provide important collateral information. In, for example, the Psychopathy Checklist—Revised (PCL–R) (Hare, 1991), case file information helps to evaluate the credibility of the information gathered at interview, determines whether the offender's interpersonal style is representative of his/her usual behaviour, and provides the primary material for scoring some of the behavioural items on the schedule.

Potential weaknesses of such data gathering are the availability, quality, and comprehensiveness of the information available. To use the example of criminal history, this information may not be in the file or the client may have committed previous violent acts for which he/she was not charged, or was just cautioned or not found guilty. And, as Limandri and Sheridan (1995) point out, the accuracy of case material for predicting risk is influenced by a number of factors including:

- the type of violence being predicted (physical assault, sexual assault, intimidation, suicide, property damage)
- the status of the perpetrator to the victim(s) (strangers, intimates, acquaintances)
- the psychological status of the perpetrator (mentally ill, psychopathic, socially deviant, predominantly non-offender) and
- the time period of prediction (immediate or long-term).

Factors commonly considered important for risk prediction that can usually be easily gathered from file information include the following.

A History of Violence

Research into the prediction of interpersonal violence consistently shows that a previous history of violence is one of the best predictors of future violence (Convit, Jaeger, Lin, Meisner, & Volavka, 1988). Similarly, Monahan (1981) identified prior convictions or prior violent incidents as consistent predictors of further violence and murder, noting that: "if there is one finding that overshadows all other areas in the field of prediction it is the probability of future crime increases with each prior criminal act" (p. 104). Thus, clinical predictions of violence will be made more accurately when any past history of violence is taken into consideration.

Psychiatric Illness

Although this has recently been a subject of debate, evidence would seem to suggest that in certain states those suffering from mental disorder are more likely to commit violent acts than those who are not suffering from mental disorder (Swanson, Holzer, Ganju, & Jono, 1990). However, Montandon and Harding (1984) suggest that there is poor inter-rater reliability between psychiatrists in determining the level of risk a mentally disordered patient presents. A reason for this poor level of accuracy may be due to the fact that the presence of previously violent behaviour may have been due to self-injurious behaviours. Therefore, it is important to check out in any case materials or interview (if possible) whether the violence was directed against others or towards themselves.

History of Substance Abuse

A number of studies have documented the link between drug/alcohol and offending behaviours. But most of these, as Limandri and Sheridan (1995) point out, simply describe the co-occurrence of alcohol and other substances with incidents of violence (e.g. Dobash & Dobash, 1979; Norton & Morgan, 1989).

An example of a comprehensive actuarial assessment that incorporates previous violence (in the index offence), psychiatric history, and alcohol use, that is predominantly based on case material[1] is the Violence Risk Appraisal Guide (VRAG) (Webster, Harris, Rice, Cormier, & Quinsey, 1994). This schedule is scored on the basis of the following twelve items:

1. [Not] lived with both biological parents to age 16 (except for death of parent)
2. Elementary school maladjustment
3. History of alcohol problems
4. Never married (or lived in a common-law relationship)
5. Criminal history for non-violent offences
6. Failure on conditional release
7. [Comparatively young age] at index offence
8. Victim injury (for index offence)
9. Any female victim (for index offence)
10. Meets DSM–IV (APA, 1994) criteria for any personality disorder
11. Meets DSM–IV (APA, 1994) criteria for schizophrenia
12. [High] PCL–R score.

The VRAG has a detailed rating system for each item from which a single score is derived. This score can then be compared with normative data so that the individual can be compared in respect of where he falls in terms of the rest of the population. This system illustrates both the strengths and short comings of using case material to derive a level of risk for an individual. In terms of computing risk the procedure is quite straightforward and consists of information that is, for the most part, easily obtainable from case material. In terms of drawbacks, it is very much in the mould of the "history is destiny" school of risk assessments, in that computation of future risk is wholly founded on static variables (life history) and does not take into account that risk levels could change dependent upon current circumstances such as level of social support, therapist interventions, and so forth.

---

[1] In fact, all of these items can be scored from case material if the PCL–R checklist has already been carried out.

USES AND LIMITATIONS OF INTERVIEW IN RISK ASSESSMENT

Interviewers may use many question-and-answer formats which range from the totally structured to the totally unstructured, although most interviews probably use something in between, i.e. a semi-structured format, including prompts for the main subject areas so that all the relevant points are covered. In terms of defining the two ends of interview protocols:

1. *Structured interviews* involve a fixed set of questions which the clinician asks in a previously arranged order. Interviewees are usually asked to choose a response from a fixed set of options (perhaps including rating scales). This type of schedule ensures comparability of questions from interviews with different clients and makes certain that all the necessary topics are covered. However, such a framework leaves little room for exploring issues that may be elicited in the course of the interview.
2. *Unstructured interviews* cover a number of topics but these are not attempted in a fixed order. Instead, they are allowed to develop as a result of exchanges between the clinician and the client. Open-ended questions are used here so that the client can say as little or as much as he likes on a particular topic. However, as Breakwell (1995) notes, it would be a mistake to think that the flexibility of the unstructured interview offers perhaps a deeper analysis than the structured interview, since in both cases the quality of the information is dependent upon the clinician's skills at eliciting information.

In terms of interviewer skills there are a number of fairly straightforward guidelines to follow. The interviewer should make sure that the interview has a natural flow to it which takes the client through a range of questions which are sensibly related. If there is a change of direction between topics it is sensible to link these with reasonable explanations as to why this should happen. However, in some circumstances, such as when an offender is simply giving a highly rehearsed account of their offence, it may be appropriate to "jump about" from topic to topic in order to try to obtain more information. It is also sensible to avoid asking questions that have double negatives, include complex words or jargon, or ask closed questions (i.e. those that can be answered with a simple yes or no).

Interviewing offenders can also have other associated problems. Beckett (1994) points out that such individuals rarely present willingly for assessment and at interview are defensive and possibly minimizing their level of offending behaviours. Therefore, the quality of information obtained is dependent upon the experience and skills of the interviewer in order to encourage disclosure and his/her sensitivity to transference and counter-transference issues that may occur in interview situations. Usually in interviewing situations it is suggested that interviewers avoid asking assumptive questions. However, Beckett suggests that in forensic settings interviewers can effectively use this style of questioning. For example, with those who have committed sexual offences (where the role of fantasy is acknowledged as an important part of a repeated pattern of offending) the interviewer may use such questions as: "It is quite common for those who have committed sexual offences to have fantasized about their victims prior to committing their first offence, we expect this is the case with you. Would you like to tell us about your own fantasies prior to your offences." Such an interviewing style is much more likely to get clients to be honest in their responses. Also implicit in any interview should be an invitation to the client to take responsibility for what he/she has done. If this process is handled correctly, then there should be increased compliance on the part of the client which will greatly improve the quality of information gathered.

The strengths of interviews are that they are a potentially rich source of information, with the client being able to talk about areas of his/her life that may not necessarily be found in official documentation and allowing the client to outline his life history, which enables the clinician/researcher to put historical information drawn from case files into perspective. Information that a client may divulge can include, for example, other crimes that may have come to the attention of the authorities but may not have been proceeded with, a previous history of physical and/or sexual abuse, and so forth. Another strength of interviews is the potential flexibility, which provides different opportunities to explore many aspects of the client's life, and also to focus on the practical issue of preventing violence happening again.

Information gathered here can have an input into a *functional analysis* of the client's offending behaviour. This examines the purpose the behaviour served, why it developed, when it started, what have been the particular offender's learning experiences, what has been the course of the problem behaviour, and what have been the consequences for the client and victims so far. Additionally, in terms of interview it is possible to get the client to fill out standardized psychometric tests. Although beyond the remit of this chapter, from personal experience such initial face-to-face contact with offenders appears to increase the likelihood that a client will complete such an assessment package.

One of the major weaknesses of interviews is that unless there is some collateral information from case files, the clinician/interviewer has to make a judgement about the veracity of the information that the client divulges in interview. For example, the difficulty with interviewing offenders about their offences is that they quite often deny or minimize their culpability for their behaviours in situations where they perceive that this could cause them more problems. Kaplan (1985), for example, found that sex offenders interviewed in a criminal justice setting only admitted 5% of the offences that they subsequently revealed when full confidentiality was offered. Segal and Marshall (1985) also highlighted the discrepancies between self-report and observed behaviour in groups of sex offenders.

ORGANIZATION OF CASE MATERIALS AND INTERVIEW

The final section of this chapter examines how current risk assessment schedules integrate case material and interview in order to assess the level of risk. Probably the most recent risk assessment schedule for doing this is the HCR–20 (Webster, Douglas, Eaves, & Hart, 1997). The authors suggest that the assessment of dangerousness and violence in forensic psychiatric patients is best undertaken by assessing twenty factors. These are grouped under the following headings: Historical (H), Clinical (C) and Risk (R) factors. The factors under each of these three headings are described below:

Historical Variables

These illustrate the type of material that should be obtainable from case material, although it should be noted here that the measurement of psychopathy is not routinely undertaken as readily in the United Kingdom as in the United States and Canada. The authors of the HCR–20 argue that the historical items described below should be allowed strong weight in reaching overall opinions about the risk of future violence, illustrating the strong influence of historical items in determining future behaviour. These items are:

H1. **Previous violence.** As previously discussed this is an important predictor of antisocial behaviour.

H2. **Young age at first violent incident.** This is an important piece of information from case materials since it would appear that the younger the individual starts committing violent offences the more likely the offending will continue (Webster et al., 1994).

H3. **Relationship instability.** This is an important, but perhaps overlooked, historical factor since some form of close relationship appears to act as a protective factor in terms of future violent behaviour (Harris et al., 1993).

H4. **Employment problems.** These have been found by Andrews and Bonta (1995) to be related to general recidivism.

H5. **Substance use problems.** These have been recognized, as previously discussed, as having a connection with violent behaviour.

H6. **Major mental illness.** This has long been recognized as having a connection with violent behaviour as previously discussed.

H7. **Psychopathy.** This is an important historical item. Salekin, Rogers, and Sewell (1996) found that there was a strong relationship between psychopathy and violence in a meta-analysis of 18 studies in this area.

H8. **Early maladjustment (at home and school).** Harris et al. found that poor progress in school was highly correlated with violent recidivism, as did being separated from parents before the age of 16.

H9. **Personality disorder.** Although a diagnosis of personality disorder rests in part on the presence of antisocial behaviour, Harris et al. found a positive correlation between personality disorder and level of violence. Webster et al. (1997) note that various epidemiological studies in the United States and Canada (Bland & Orn, 1986; Robins, Tipp, & Przybeck, 1991) suggest that there is a link between antisocial personality disorder (APD) and violence, important components of APD such as anger, impulsivity, hostility, etc. obviously increasing the likelihood of violence.

H10. **Prior supervision failure.** Committing offences while on conditional release has been found to be associated with future violent behaviour (Harris et al.).

Clinical Variables

Webster et al. (1997) describe their aim as identifying key concepts from the literature, and through conversations with forensic clinicians, concerning what clinical factors might lead to future violent behaviour. However, elicitation of these items may not necessarily be easy and they illustrate the importance of an interview conducted by an experienced clinician. The five areas they see as important to measure in a clinical interview are:

C1. **Lack of insight.** This is the extent to which an individual perceives him/herself to be dangerous, angry, or out-of-control. The amount of insight into his/her behaviour that a client has not only has a bearing on the level of risk an individual poses but may also provide information about the way potential violent behaviour can be controlled.

C2. **Negative attitudes.** Here, Webster et al. suggest that it is important to determine the extent to which a client's attitudes are pro- or antisocial as well as whether the client minimizes or totally denies that his/her offences took place.

C3. **Active symptoms of major metal illness.** The authors also suggest that as an adjunct to the assessment of his/her current psychiatric state, it is important to ascertain the degree to which an individual expresses suicidal thoughts, not only because of its own importance, but also because of its implication in future violent offending.

C4. **Impulsivity.** Here it is important to ascertain the degree of impulsivity of the client, since the actions of a stable person are easier to predict than those of an unstable one. Evidence for this is reported by Barratt (1994) who found a link between impulsivity and violence.

C5. **Unresponsiveness to treatment.** Here, an attempt should be made to find out whether the client has actively sought out help for his/her behaviours; if so, whether treatment has been accepted and, if treatment has been completed, whether it has been successful.

Risk Management Items

The last part of the HCR–20 is focused on risk items. This information can only be gained through careful integration of material gained through interview and suitable file material. The variables of interest here are:

R1. **(Relapse) Plans lack feasibility.** Here it must be ascertained whether the client's relapse prevention strategies are suitable, safe, and realistic.

R2. **Exposure to destabilizers.** Here it is important to gauge whether the client will have easy access to possible victims, weapons, and drugs. Risk obviously increases if an individual gets into a situation that is similar to his/her index offence or associates with antisocial peers (Gendreau, 1995).

R3. **Lack of personal support.** The level of support available in terms of relatives, friends, and professionals is another important area to be gauged at interview and subsequently cross-checked. Of course, if the client is in a new relationship it is important to find out whether the current partner is aware of the extent and degree of the client's previous offence behaviours.

R4. **Non-compliance with remediation attempts.** The potential for violence is reduced if the client can accept and conform to agreed rules. Webster et al. (1997) also suggest that compliance is usually found to be related to the motivation to succeed, willingness to take medication (where necessary), and be involved in treatment.

R5. **Stress.** Here it is important to try and assess possible future stressors which may lead to relapse. Monahan (1981) suggests that attention be given to three major areas from which stress might emanate, i.e. family, peer group, and employment.

It can be seen that these five variables can obviously have a modifying effect on the level of risk a client presents.

Coding of Risk on the HCR–20

In terms of coding, the overall level of risk items are coded on a three-point scale according to the certainty that the risk factors are present, with a "zero" being given when the risk factor is definitely absent, a "1" is given if the risk factor is partially or possibly present, and a "2" is given if the risk factor is definitely or clearly present. As there is a "risk" profile across 20 items (10 historical, five clinical and five risk management items) the clinician can make a judgement as to whether the client is at "low", moderate of "high" risk of future violence. It should be noted that Webster et al. (1997) do not describe a method for reaching an actual decision of the overall level of risk.

In conclusion, Webster et al. describe a system in which there is an interplay between historical items gained from case material, clinical items gained from interview, and risk management items (from both interview and any other sources available). As previously discussed there is a heavy emphasis on the historical items in that the authors see these as carrying the most weight in terms of predicting future behaviour, but both clinical and risk management items may have a moderating effect. To quote the authors,[2] "actuarial risk assessments can anchor clinical judgement, so that clinicians can use dynamic (changeable) information . . . to adjust the risk level computed by the actuarial prediction instrument" (p. 49).

SUMMARY

It has been argued that good risk assessment requires both the use of case material and interview. However, although case materials are fairly objective, it must be borne in mind that the strength of this kind of information is dependent upon the quality and availability of the information. Important historical factors, related to future risk, that should be obtainable from case materials have been outlined. In terms of information gathering at interview, certain basic interviewer skills have been described as well as the potential difficulties of dealing with forensic clients. The interplay between case material and interview has been highlighted in that in an interview situation details available from the case file may be explored in more detail, while case materials can be used to check the veracity of the client's accounts of events. Finally, one of the most recent risk–needs assessment schedules is described—the HCR—20. This instrument illustrates the importance of: using information gathered from *case material* in order to examine the client's history, which may contain important predictors of future risk; using information gathered from *interview* in order to gather material about clinical factors that have been shown to be related to future violent behaviour; integrating both *case material and interview* in order to assess the client's ability to manage his/her level of future risk.

REFERENCES

American Psychiatric Association (1994). Diagnostic and statistical manual of mental disorder (4th ed.). Washington, DC: Author.
Andrews, D. A., & Bonta, J. (1995). *The psychology of criminal conduct*. Cincinnati, OH: Anderson.
Barratt, E. S. (1994). Impulsiveness and aggression. In J. Monahan & H. J. Steadman (Eds.), *Violence and mental disorder: Developments in risk assessment* (pp. 61–79). Chicago, IL: University of Chicago Press.
Beckett, R. C. (1994). Cognitive behavioural treatment for men who sexually assault children. In T. Morrison, M. Erooga, & R. C. Beckett (Eds.), *Sexual offending against children* (pp. 55–80). London: Routledge.
Bland, R., & Orn, H. (1986). Family violence and psychiatric disorder. *Canadian Journal of Psychiatry, 31*, 127–137.

---

[2] quoting Harris et al. (1993, p. 332).

Bonta, J. (1996). Risk–needs assessment and treatment. In A. T. Harland (Ed.), *Choosing correctional options that work* (pp. 18–32). Thousand Oaks, CA: Sage.

Bottomley, A. (1973). Parole decisions in a long-term closed prison. *British Journal of Criminology, 13*, 26–40.

Breakwell, G. M. (1995). Interviewing. In G. M. Breakwell, S. Hammond, & C. Fife-Shaw (Eds.), *Research methods in psychology*. London: Sage.

Convit, A., Jaeger, J., Lin, S. P., Meisner, M., & Volvaka, J. (1988). Predicting assaultativeness in psychiatric inpatients: A pilot study. *Hospital and Community Psychiatry, 40*, 266–271.

Dobash, R. E., & Dobash, R. (1979). *Violence against wives*. New York: Free Press.

Gendreau, P. (1995). Predicting criminal behaviour: What works? Paper presented at the annual meeting of the Canadian Psychological Association, Charlottetown, Prince Edward Island.

Gottfredson, S. D. (1987). Statistical and actuarial considerations. In F. Dutile & C. Foust (Eds.), *The prediction of violence* (pp. 71–81). Springfield, IL: Charles C. Thomas.

Gottfredson, D. M., & Gottfredson, S. D. (1986). The accuracy of prediction models. In A. Blumstein, J. Cohen, A. Roth, & C. A. Visher (Eds.), *Research in criminal careers and "career criminals"* (Vol. 2, pp. 212–290). Washington DC: National Academy Press.

Gross, B. H., Southard, M. J., Lamb, R., & Weinberger, L. E. (1987). Assessing dangerousness and responding appropriately: Hedlund expands the clinician's liability established by Tarasoff. *Journal of Clinical Psychiatry, 48*, 9–12.

Hare, R. D. (1991). *The Hare Psychopathy Checklist—Revised*. Toronto, Canada: Multi-Health Systems.

Harris, G. T., & Rice, M. E. (1997). Risk appraisal and the management of violent behavior. *Psychiatric Services, 48*, 1168–1176.

Harris, G. T., Rice, M. E., & Quinsey, V. L. (1993). Violent recidivism of mentally disordered offenders: The development of a statistical prediction instrument. *Criminal Justice and Behavior, 15*, 625–637.

Hoffman, P. (1983). Screening for risk: A revised salient factor score (SFS81). *Journal of Criminal Justice, 11*, 539–547.

Jones, P. R. (1996). Risk prediction in criminal justice. In A. T. Harland (Ed.), *Choosing correctional options that work* (pp. 33–68). Thousand Oaks, CA: Sage.

Kaplan, M. S. (1985). *The impact of parolees perceptions of confidentiality on the reporting of their urges to interact sexually with children*. Unpublished doctoral dissertation. New York University.

Lambert, E. W., Cartor, R, & Walker, G. L. (1988). Reliability of behavioral versus medical models: Rare events and danger. *Issues in Mental Health Nursing, 9*, 31–44.

Limandri, B. J., & Sheridan, D. J. (1995). Prediction issues for practitioners. In J. C. Campbell (Ed.), *Assessing dangerousness: Violence by sexual offenders, batterers and child abusers* (pp. 1–19). London: Sage.

Menzies, R. J., Webster, C. D., McMain, S., Staley, S., & Scaglione, R. (1994). The dimensions of dangerousness revisited: Assessing forensic predictions about violence. *Law and Human Behavior, 18*, 1–28.

Monahan, J. (1981). *The clinical prediction of violent behavior*. Thousand Oaks, CA: Sage.

Montandon, C., & Harding, T. (1984). The reliability of dangerousness assessments: A decision making exercise. *British Journal of Psychiatry, 144*, 149–155.

Mossman, D. (1994). Assessing predictions of violence: Being accurate about accuracy. *Journal of Consulting and Clinical Psychology, 62*, 783–792.

Norton, R. N., & Morgan, M. Y. (1989). The role of alcohol in mortality and morbidity from interpersonal violence. *Alcohol and Alcoholism, 24*, 565–576.

Nuffield, J. (1982). Parole decision-making in Canada. Ottawa, Canada: Solicitor General of Canada.

Quinsey, V. L., Lalumière, M. L., Rice, M. E., & Harris, G. T. (1995). Predicting sexual offenses. In J. C. Campbell (Ed.), *Assessing dangerousness: Violence by sexual offenders, batterers and child abusers* (pp. 114–137). London: Sage.

Robins, L. N., Tipp, J., & Przybeck, T. (1991). Antisocial personality. In L. N. Robins & D. Reiger (Eds.), *Psychiatric disorders in America* (pp. 258–290). New York: Free Press.

Salekin, R. T., Rogers, R., & Sewell, K. W. (1996). A review and meta-analysis of the Psychopathy Check List and the Psychopathy Check List—Revised: Predictive validity of dangerousness. *Clinical Psychology: Science and Practice*, *3*, 203–215.

Schon, D. (1983). From technical rationality to reflection in action. In J. Dowie & A. Elstein (Eds.), *Professional: A reader in clinical decision making* (pp. 60–77). Cambridge, UK: Cambridge University Press.

Segal, Z. V., & Marshall, W. L. (1985). Self report and behavioural assertion in five groups of sexual offenders. *Behaviour Therapy and Experimental Psychiatry*, *16*, 223–229.

Swanson, J. W, Holzer, C. E., Ganju, V. K., & Jono, R. T. (1990). Violence and psychiatric disorder in the community: Evidence from epidemiologic catchment area surveys. *Hospital and Community Psychiatry*, *41*, 761–770.

Webster, C. D., Douglas, K. S., Eaves, D., & Hart, S. (1997). *HCR—20: Assessing risk for violence, version 2*. Available from the Mental Health, Law, and Policy Institute, Simon Fraser University, Burnaby, British Columbia, Canada, V5 1S6. URL.

Webster C. D., Harris, G. T., Rice, M. E., Cormier, C., & Quinsey, V. L. (1994). *The violence prediction scheme: Assessing dangerousness in high risk men*. Toronto, Canada: University of Toronto, Centre of Criminology.

Part III

Approaches to Treatment

Chapter 10

Behavioral Approaches to Correctional Management and Rehabilitation

Michael A. Milan
Georgia State University, Atlanta, USA

INTRODUCTION

This chapter will examine the contributions of behavioral principles to the management and rehabilitation of youthful and adult criminal offenders in institutional settings. In addition, the chapter will focus on research with offenders who commit the most typical crimes against property (e.g. burglary, theft) and persons (e.g. robbery, assault), rather than with special management offenders, many of whom are addressed elsewhere in this text. Behaviorists devoted considerable attention to the management and rehabilitation of more typical offenders in institutional settings during the 1960s and 1970s. As Haney and Zimbardo (1998) have noted, the United State's concern about the rehabilitation of the typical offender virtually ended in the 1970s:

> The country moved abruptly from a society that justified putting people in prison on the basis of the belief that their incarceration would somehow facilitate their productive reentry into the free world to one that used imprisonment merely to disable criminal offenders ("incapacitation") or to keep them far away from the rest of society ("containment"). . . . In fact, prison punishment soon came to be thought of as its own reward, serving only the goal of inflicting pain (p. 712).

As a result of this pro-punishment, anti-rehabilitation movement in the United States, correctional rehabilitation research programs not only lost their funding but also lost their welcome in correctional institutions. It should therefore not be

Handbook of Offender Assessment and Treatment. Edited by C. R. Hollin.
© 2000 John Wiley & Sons Ltd.

surprising that with the exception of the growing body of social skills research (Hollin, 1989) that has been conducted elsewhere and will not be addressed herein, descriptions of original behavioral research and new behavioral programs with the typical offender have all but disappeared from the literature since the 1970s. This chapter therefore describes much of the early history of behavioral approaches to correctional management and rehabilitation, while other chapters address more recent endeavors with other offenders in other settings. The lack of interest in the typical incarcerated offender is doubly unfortunate, for the incarceration of typical offenders is most certainly on the rise in the United States, if not elsewhere, and the history of behavioral programs for those offenders showed much promise for more effective and more humane management and rehabilitation practices.

Offender management practices and rehabilitation programs are equally important aspects of the justice system (Ayllon, Milan, Roberts, & McKee, 1979). Positive management practices are called for to minimize the often painful (Toch, 1992) and potentially harmful (Paulus, 1988; McCorkle, 1992) effects of imprisonment on offenders, thereby reducing the likelihood that offenders are a greater threat to society when they leave the justice system than they were when they entered it. Effective rehabilitation programs are called for to reduce further the likelihood that released offenders will offend again (Milan & Evans, 1987). Behavioral theories of the origins and continuance of criminal behavior provide direction for both management and rehabilitation efforts. Most behaviorists would undoubtedly agree with the long-standing assumption that the principles of behavior that explain non-criminal behavior also explain criminal behavior (e.g. Milan & McKee, 1974). Two influential theories that elaborate upon that general assumption are those of Hans Eysenck, a psychologist, and Ronald Akers, a sociologist, who have sought to understand better how the principles of conditioning and learning act at the individual and group levels to produce criminal behavior.

BEHAVIORAL THEORIES OF CRIME AND DELINQUENCY

Eysenck's explanation of criminal behavior (Eysenck, 1977; Eysenck & Gudjonsson, 1989) is an outgrowth of his more general theory of personality (Eysenck, 1967, 1981) that emphasizes the interaction of biological and environmental determinants of behavior. The theory postulates one general intelligence factor (g) and three temperamental factors: extraversion, neuroticism, and psychoticism. These dimensions are said to have biological bases that are strongly influenced by genetic factors. The extraversion continuum is considered to be a product of central nervous system functioning, particularly the reticular activating system, and is generally characterized by high to low stimulation-seeking, impulsivity, and irritability. The neuroticism continuum is said to reflect peripheral nervous system functioning, most specifically the limbic system, and is typically manifest in high to low negative affectivity such as heightened reactions to need states or stress, anxiety, depression, and hostility. The psychoticism continuum is postulated to be a product of blood chemistry, and is characterized by high to low social insensitivity, indifferent cruelty to others, and disregard of danger to self. The personality factors are not viewed as the causes of personality and behavior, but instead as predisposing factors. It is the interaction of the unique mix of these factors with unique environmental experiences that determines each individual's adaptation to life and the various forms of psychopathology and criminality they may exhibit.

In general, the principles of conditioning and learning explain the contribution of environmental experiences to adjustment. Eysenck emphasizes the role of respondent (or classical) conditioning during the socialization of children in his understanding of criminal behavior, and seeks to explain why individuals do *not* engage in criminal activities rather than why they do. Eysenck postulates that during the socialization process, children develop a "conscience" as a result of the respondent conditioning components of punishment for misbehavior. Eysenck invokes his personality theory to explain why some children are less affected by the socialization process than others. The lower cortical arousal of individuals high on the extraversion dimension is said to reduce the responsivity to punishment, thereby impeding a punitive socialization process and the development of the conscience. Research on conditionability and crime indicates that criminals do indeed condition more slowly than non-criminals (Raine, 1993). The effects of reduced conditionability are compounded for those high on the neuroticism dimension, where heightened responsivity to need states further increases the likelihood that individuals will engage in prohibited behavior, and/or for those high on the psychoticism dimension, where decreased sensitivity to others and danger to self also decrease the likelihood that individuals will refrain from criminal behavior. Eysenck and Gudjonsson (1989) have reported numerous studies in support of the theory. Its implications are clear: positive reinforcement is to be preferred to punishment and deprivation during both socialization and rehabilitation.

Akers' differential association–reinforcement theory of deviant behavior was initially formulated in conjunction with Robert Burgess (Burgess & Akers, 1966) and has evolved in response to the research it has generated (Akers, 1973, 1977, 1985). It serves as a thoroughgoing example of the manner in which the principles of operant conditioning and learning may be applied to the explanation of criminal behavior. The theory itself is a reformulation of Edwin Sutherland's differential association theory of criminal behavior. The seven original assumptions of the theory are.

1. Criminal behavior is learned according to the principles of operant conditioning.
2. Criminal behavior is learned both in non-social situations that are reinforcing or discriminative and through that social interaction in which the

behavior of other persons is reinforcing or discriminative for criminal behavior.

3. The principal part of the learning of criminal behavior occurs in those groups which comprise the individual's major source of reinforcement.

4. The learning of criminal behavior, including specific techniques, attitudes, and avoidance procedures, is a function of the effective and available reinforcers, and the reinforcement contingencies.

5. The specific classes of behavior which are learned and their frequency of occurrence are a function of the reinforcers which are effective and available, and the rules or norms by which those reinforcers are applied.

6. Criminal behavior is a function of norms which are discriminative for criminal behavior, the learning of which takes place when such behavior is more highly reinforced than non-criminal behavior.

7. The strength of criminal behavior is a direct function of the amount, frequency, and probability of reinforcement.

Akers' (1998) most recent formulation of the theory summarizes its assumptions in the following manner. The probability that persons will engage in criminal and deviant behavior is increased and the probability of their conforming to the norm is decreased when they differentially associate with others who commit criminal behavior and espouse definitions favorable to it, are relatively more exposed in-person or symbolically to salient criminal/deviant models, define it as desirable or justified in a situation discriminative for the behavior, and have received in the past and anticipate in the current or future situation relatively greater reward than punishment for the behavior. The theory therefore explains initial criminal acts as a juvenile or an adult, whether they will continue and, if they do, the modification and elaboration of those activities. It has been employed as the basis for the explanation of a range of criminal activities, including professional crime, drug use, white collar crime, prostitution, and violent assault. The theory emphasizes the importance of the initial socialization process by the family during childhood, and the subsequent competition between continuing socialization by the family and socialization by the peer group during adolescence. Finally, the theory also explains the failure of the socialization process in adulthood. A central component of that explanation is either the lack or loss of non-deviant means of obtaining reinforcement. Akers' review of the research bearing upon the theory provides strong support for its explanatory power.

The following overview of behavioral approaches to correctional management and rehabilitation describes representative examples of its use in institutional settings with those individuals for whom socialization by the family and, subsequently, community agencies in the form of primary and secondary prevention efforts (Milan & Long, 1980) have failed. Experimental single case and group studies will be emphasized. A more detailed review of such programs is also available (see Milan, 1987a, 1987b). The work of Eysenck and Akers indicates that resocialization programs should emphasize positive reinforcement, rather than punishment, to instill pro-social behavior, and that they should focus on building social, academic, and vocational skills that enable those individuals to achievement reinforcement without recourse to antisocial behavior.

PROCEDURES TO DECREASE UNDESIRABLE BEHAVIOR

Time-out and response cost appear to be the most widely examined behavioral management procedures for the reduction of undesirable behavior in correctional settings. In the typical time-out procedure, the individual is either removed briefly from a setting in which social and non-social reinforcers are available freely, or the individual remains in a setting from which those reinforcers are removed briefly. The brief nature of time-out distinguishes it from more punitive administrative procedures, such as detention, segregation, and punitive isolation, that are common in correctional settings. Response cost procedures call for individuals to either relinquish reinforcers, such as money or tokens, as a fine, or increase the amount of effort required to earn reinforcers.

Two early studies of the effectiveness of time-out were conducted by Tyler and his colleagues (Burchard & Tyler, 1965; Tyler & Brown, 1967) in one cottage of a training school. The target behaviors consisted of general rule violations and disruptive misbehavior. In the Burchard and Tyler study, the time-out procedure was explored in a single-inmate case study and consisted of 15 minutes in a small time-out room in the corner of the cottage. The authors reported a 63% drop in offenses. Using a reversal design with 15 inmates, Tyler and Brown replicated the effect in a study in which the procedure was supplemented with reinforcement for appropriate behavior and concluded that the use of swift, brief time-out can be an effective procedure for the control of classroom misbehavior. They hypothesized that the procedure was effective because it was neither so severe that it encouraged peer group support nor so demeaning that it produced resistance from the inmate.

Burchard (1967) provided an example of how response cost may contribute to the control of antisocial behavior, such as stealing, lying, cheating, and fighting, in another study with mentally retarded adolescents and young adults in a residential program. In a reversal design, the loss of tokens in a classroom token economy was first contingent, then non-contingent, and then again contingent upon antisocial behavior. Results indicated lower amounts of antisocial behavior during response cost.

Burchard and Barrera (1972) compared the effectiveness of time-out and response cost with four groups of incarcerated mentally retarded delinquent youths in a token economy classroom. Time-out durations of five and 30 minutes and response cost magnitudes of five and 30 tokens were applied to all groups in counterbalanced sequences. The target behaviors were aggressive acts such as swearing, personal assaults, and destruction of property. The 30-minute time-out and 30-token response cost procedures were most and equally effective in reducing the aggressive acts. Next most effective was a combination of five-minute time-out and five-token response cost, followed by five-minute time-out and finally by five-token response cost. Burchard and Barrera concluded that response cost appears preferable to time-out because it does not terminate participation in the classroom program.

These representative studies make it clear that time-out and response cost are viable alternatives to more severe practices in the management of undesirable behavior in institutional settings. However, when the time-out and response cost procedures are terminated, at least after a short period of use, the suppressed behavior typically reappears. These procedures may therefore be advocated only as ingredients in programs that include procedures for the generalization and maintenance of time-out and response cost effects and, perhaps most importantly, teach skills that are both incompatible with undesirable behaviors and likely to be sustained when the procedures used to instill them are discontinued. Representative procedures used in correctional settings to foster skills and desirable behavior that are incompatible with undesirable behavior are described in the following section.

PROCEDURES TO INCREASE DESIRABLE BEHAVIOR

Helping inmates improve their academic and vocational preparation and, whenever possible, earn a high school degree or its equivalent so that they may qualify for meaningful employment and find a satisfying place in the community upon release is undoubtedly one of the most beneficial uses of a period of incarceration. It should not be surprising that behaviorists have addressed these goals in many of their correctional rehabilitation efforts. In one of the earliest investigations of the applicability of behavioral procedures to an educational classroom in a correctional institution, Burchard (1967) examined the effect of token reinforcement on the appropriate classroom behavior of antisocial retarded students. In a reversal design, tokens were awarded either contingent upon, or independent of, in-seat behavior. As would be expected, the students were in their seats considerably more during the contingent condition.

Subsequent studies have examined the effects of contingency management procedures on the acquisition of academic skills in institutional classroom programs, rather than the maintenance of order and discipline alone. Bednar, Zelhart, Greathouse, and Weinberg (1970) compared traditional and token reinforcement procedures in a between-groups study with incarcerated juvenile delinquents studying programmed educational material. One group worked on the material with no tangible reinforcement. A second group earned tokens for on-task behavior and then for the mastery of the material. In addition, bonus tokens were earned whenever individuals' test scores exceeded the average of their previous week's test score performance. The reinforcement group improved significantly more than the non-reinforcement group in reading and word comprehension on a standardized achievement test.

Graubard (1968) used a reversal design to explore the use of a group contract with emotionally disturbed delinquent youths in a classroom of a residential treatment center. Baseline conditions consisted of traditional teaching strategies involving no tangible reinforcers or group contingencies. During intervention conditions the teacher and students negotiated individual goals, reinforcers, and additional reinforcers that the entire group would earn if everyone met their goals. Substantial decreases in antisocial behavior and substantial increases in academic performance occurred during intervention conditions. Although this study indicates that the use of group contingencies can be an effective strategy for developing positive peer group pressure for appropriate behavior, group contingencies may encourage some group members to apply psychological and physical coercion to individuals who will not or cannot attain the requirements of the group contingency. They should therefore not be utilized unless close and continuing supervision that guarantees the protection of participants is possible and in place.

While each of the previous studies provides an example of the potential of the behavior approach in correctional education, the work of McKee and his colleagues (Clements & McKee, 1968; McKee, 1971; McKee & Clements, 1971; McKee, Jenkins, & Milan, 1977) in a maximum security institution provides a model for the extension of the behavioral approach to academic and vocational instruction. McKee's program begins with a specification of each student's strengths and weaknesses. Training objectives are then specified in behavioral terms; material is presented in a logical sequence of small modules; students respond actively at their own rate to the educational material; and immediate feedback is provided for correct and incorrect answers. McKee (1974) reported that 30% more students completed training with these procedures than was predicted on the basis of previous experience with traditional programs.

McKee (1974) summarized several additional studies going beyond the use of feedback alone and reported that:

1. the performance-contingent opportunity to select items from a "reinforcing event" menu resulted in a doubling of the learning rate with no decline in test scores.
2. the self-recording of performance, supplemented with small monetary awards for sustained outstanding performance, resulted in a marked increase in academic progress and output.
3. a change from contingent to non-contingent monetary consequences resulted in a substantial deterioration in academic test performance, thereby confirming the central role of contingency management procedures in his efforts.

Similarly, McKee et al. (1977) found that students earning monetary reinforcement for academic progress had significantly higher learning rates than a comparable group without contingent reinforcement. Clements and McKee (1968) found that contingency contracts were of approximately equal effectiveness whether prescribed unilaterally by the teachers or negotiated with the students. Finally, accelerated rates of learning have been maintained through reinforcement for protracted periods of time (McKee, 1971), with students averaging gains of 1.4 grade levels on standardized achievement tests for 208 hours of study (McKee & Clements, 1971).

The teaching of academic and vocational skills in the correctional setting appears to be an important ingredient of rehabilitation programs, for it most probably increases the likelihood that inmates will find appropriate employment and earn an adequate wage after release from the institution. In general, research such as has been reported in this and the preceding section indicates that behavioral procedures can be effective in decreasing undesirable behavior and fostering participation in rehabilitation activities in institutional classrooms and shops. As Hollin (1989) has noted, however, there is no evidence that institutional social skills training programs by themselves reduce offending following release from custody, and the same can be said of the efforts described in this and the preceding section. Perhaps what is called for are comprehensive programs that combine all those components, and more. The following section provides examples of more comprehensive programs that incorporate both management and rehabilitation components and operate throughout the inmate's day.

TOWARDS COMPREHENSIVE PROGRAMS FOR MANAGEMENT AND REHABILITATION

Behavioral programs that have combined significant management and rehabilitation components have typically utilized a token economy (Ayllon & Azrin, 1968) to do so. Several large-scale token economies for institutionalized offenders have been described in the literature. Levinson and his colleagues (Ingram, Gerard, Quay, & Levinson, 1970; Karacki & Levinson, 1970) described a program for youthful offenders diagnosed as psychopathic and incarcerated at a federal institution for older, "hard-core" delinquent youths. Inmates earned tokens for appropriate behaviors and for winning in games and contests. A response cost procedure was applied to minor forms of inappropriate behavior, and seclusion was used with more serious and aggressive forms of inappropriate behaviors. Seclusion periods were typically in hours rather than in minutes as is the case with time-out procedures. Outcome measures included the time spent in rehabilitation programs, the occurrence of assaults, and whether an inmate's release from the institution was considered to be "positive" (i.e. paroled or remaining in the institution after completion of the program) or "negative" (i.e. disciplinary transfer or escape). Comparisons between the youths in the program and comparable inmates revealed that all differences favored the youths who were enrolled in the behavioral program, with many of the differences achieving statistical significance.

Hobbs and Holt (1976) evaluated a token economy in the cottages of a residential facility for older delinquent males. Outcome measures included following rules in group games, completing assigned chores, avoiding assaultive behavior, and staying with the group while walking between buildings. A multiple baseline design across cottages indicated that the token economy produced significant improvements in the target behaviors. Hobbs and Holt employed a reversal design to also evaluate the effects of their program on academic performance, including completion of assignments and appropriate social interactions. The token economy was found to produce significant improvements in target behaviors.

Several additional studies examining the effectiveness of token reinforcement procedures were conducted by Ayllon and his colleagues and have been reported by Ayllon, Milan, Roberts, and McKee (1979) in their collaborative description of the Motivating Offender Rehabilitation Environment (MORE) project. MORE extended the scope of the token economy in several studies to include vocational training activities. In one study, MORE explored the effects of incentives on the mastery of instructional material dealing with both the theory underlying auto mechanics and the actual operation of various mechanical parts of the automobile. By alternately reinforcing inmates' mastery of theoretical and applied materials, Ayllon and his colleagues demonstrated that the inmates' efforts could be distributed among these two areas and maintained at high levels of performance. In a second study, MORE examined the effects of a "progressive" differential reinforcement of other behavior (DRO) schedule in a barbering class. In the progressive DRO schedule, progressively more error-free performances earned progressively larger amounts of token reinforcement. The number of errors made in the same amount of time during the progressive DRO reinforcement contingency was less than half the number made during the time that it was not in effect. Unfortunately, no outcome data assessing the effect of the program on post-release adjustment were provided for this and the preceding token economies. Such data were reported for the following four token economy programs.

The Contingencies Applicable to Special Education (CASE) projects and the Karl Holton School for Boys token economy were both large-scale token economies for institutionalized older delinquent youths. Although neither program included systematic investigations of specific program components and motivational strategies, some outcome data were provided. In the CASE projects (Cohen, 1973; Cohen & Filipczak, 1971; Cohen, Filipczak, & Bis, 1970), tokens were earned for academic activities, such as completing assignments and passing examinations, and for engaging in personal hygiene and facility maintenance activities. Perhaps most noteworthy was the effect in the academic program: for every 90 hours of educational work, the inmates increased an average of 1.89 academic months on the Sanford Achievement Test, 2.70 academic months on the Gates Reading Survey, and 12.09 IQ points as assessed by the Revised Beta (Cohen, 1973). Filipczak and Cohen (1972) have asserted that their three-year follow-up indicated that CASE releasees had fewer violator warrants than did similar releasees. Filipczak and Cohen note, however, that trends in the violator warrant data indicate that CASE releasees would eventually recidivate near the national norm.

The Karl Holton token economy (Jesness & DeRisi, 1973) served incarcerated young adults similar to those in the CASE projects. The program used two types of tokens: Karl Holton Dollars that were earned for various academic behaviors and routine hygiene and living hall maintenance activities, and Behavior Change Units that were awarded for progress in the remediation of individual problems. Follow-up involved a comparison of parole violation rates before and after implementation of the program as well as comparisons with a transactional analysis program and two traditional programs, all of which served similar inmates (Jesness, 1979). Jesness found no difference in parole violations between the token economy and transactional analysis programs at the end of the 12-month follow-up period. Parole violation dropped to an average of 33% for the token economy and transactional analysis programs in comparison with 43% for the two traditional programs.

Milan and his colleagues (Milan & McKee, 1976; Milan, Throckmorton, McKee, & Wood, 1979; Milan, Wood, & McKee, 1979) systematically explored the effects of the token economy with an array of management and rehabilitation behaviors in a maximum security correctional institution for adult male felons. Milan and McKee (1976) described the Cellblock Token Economy that served as a basis for their rehabilitation and management efforts. Target behaviors included educational activities during evening and weekend times as well as personal hygiene and cellblock maintenance tasks. All target behaviors were operationally defined, and inmates were provided with instruction in the performance of each. The initial criteria for reinforcement allowed successive approximations of the target behaviors to ensure that inmates earned reinforcement as they mastered the skills required. Backup reinforcers included activities available on the token economy cellblock, such as access to a television room, a pool room and a comfortable lounge, the purchase of coffee, soft drinks, sandwiches, cigarettes and the like in the token economy canteen, and additional activities available off the cellblock, such as movies and recreational athletics. Inmates had access to the backup reinforcers throughout the day. The tokens consisted of tokens credited to inmate checking accounts as they were earned, and the inmates purchased the backup reinforcers by writing and exchanging checks. Accounts were balanced at the end of each day.

The first of the two studies described by Milan and McKee (1976) focused on the management of cellblock maintenance activities normally expected of individuals living in group settings. In an extended withdrawal design consisting of 13 experimental conditions spanning 420 days, the best efforts of a correctional officer to encourage inmates to perform these activities were compared with the effect of the non-contingent award of tokens, the contingent earning of tokens, and an increase in the number of tokens earned. Results indicated that the correctional officer's efforts, which typically consisted of threats and intimidation, and the non-contingent award of tokens were no more effective than the routine conditions of baseline periods. Indeed, the data suggest that performance deteriorated and aggressive behavior increased in response to the correctional officer's intensified efforts. The contingent earning of tokens produced a significant and enduring increase in the performance of the targeted behaviors.

Continued monitoring of performance revealed a gradual and continuing improvement in performance and a reduction in variability over a period of a year.

The second of Milan and McKee's (1976) two studies indicated that reinforcement for participation and performance in the educational program produced an increase in the amount of time spent in the classrooms on the cellblock. In addition, the token economy did not impose a discernible hardship upon the inmates as indexed by their ability to come and go from the token economy cellblock in order to participate in activities elsewhere in the prison. Finally, reinforcement for personal hygiene and cellblock maintenance activities did not produce noticeable increases in the amount of time devoted to these activities, although the quality of each improved. However, a small number of inmates consistently abused the rules governing the operation of the token economy cellblock. Strategies to increase the generality of the token economy so that it encompassed such inmates were examined in subsequent studies.

Milan, Throckmorton et al. (1979) used a reversal design to explore a procedure to encourage adherence to the requirements of the Cellblock Token Economy in the first of their two studies. They chose not to discourage rule violations through punishment but instead to achieve the same result through the reinforcement of its incompatible opposite: adherence to the rules of the token economy. The study focused on the inmates' use of a time clock to record the amount of time they spent away from the token economy cellblock, a backup reinforcer for which they had to pay at the end of the day. During baseline, the amount of time between the time at which inmates were last identified as being on the cellblock during a routine attendance check and the time at which they returned was added to their recorded time off the cellblock. During intervention, inmates earned a half hour of free time off the cellblock each day the routine attendance checks indicated that they were recording all their time away from the cellblock. Results indicated that the reinforcement condition produced a significant increase in adherence to the time clock rule.

Milan, Throckmorton et al. (1979) next explored the relationship between the magnitude of token reinforcement and the performance of target behaviors. The study focused on keeping abreast of current events. During the 11 conditions of their parametric reversal study, the magnitude of token reinforcement for attendance at the evening news program was gradually increased and then decreased. The results showed that the average number of inmates attending the program was functionally related to the magnitude of reinforcement, with progressively more inmates in attendance at the progressively higher magnitudes of reinforcement. Some inmates, however, were unaffected by the magnitude of reinforcement. A strategy to motivate inmates who seemed insensitive to reasonable magnitudes of token reinforcement in token economies was explored in the following study.

The use of response chaining to maximize performance in the cellblock education program when tokens alone produced less than optimal participation and progress was tested by Milan, Wood, and McKee (1979) using an extended reversal design. In the baseline conditions the importance of remedial education activities was emphasized, and inmates were encouraged to participate in the program during their leisure-time hours. Virtually no inmates participated. Next, inmates earned tokens for completing and passing module tests. Participation in the education program increased somewhat, but in general the inmates devoted little time to the educational program and mastered little material. Finally, a chaining procedure was established in which achievement in the education program was a prerequisite for access to selected backup reinforcers. Inmates who mastered material representing 10 hours of study time during a week earned access to the reinforcers for the whole of the following week. Inmates who mastered less material earned access to the reinforcers for proportionately less of the week. The procedure resulted in marked increases in both participation in the educational program and the amount of material mastered. The chaining procedure is an alternative to procedures that use increased magnitudes of token reinforcement in an attempt to increase appropriate behavior when those strategies risk the dilution of the token economy itself by the availability of "cheap money".

Jenkins et al. (1974) reported an 18-month post-release follow-up of Cellblock Token Economy inmates and other inmates who either received vocational training or participated in routine prison activities. During the early months of the follow-up period, the percentage of token economy releasees who were returned to prison for either parole violations or the commission of new crimes was markedly lower than for any of the comparison groups. By the end of the follow-up period, however, the rate of return for the token economy group, although still lowest, approximated those of the comparison groups. None the less, the severity of the offenses for which the Cellblock Token Economy inmates were returned to prison was markedly less than those of the comparison groups, with more of the token economy inmates returned for minor parole violations and fewer returned for serious crimes against persons.

The potential contribution of token economy procedures to the rehabilitation of delinquent soldiers with character and behavior disorders in a closed treatment unit was explored by Colman and his colleagues (Boren & Colman, 1970; Ellsworth & Colman, 1970). The target behaviors consisted of the requirements of military life. Educational offerings involved courses in a variety of practical skills, such as overcoming problems with authority and work projects in which the group worked as a team toward common goals. In his description of the immediate effects of the Walter Reed program, Colman (1970) stated that psychotic episodes and suicidal gestures, previously chronic hazards in the group, stopped completely.

An outcome assessment (Colman & Baker, 1969) compared successful outcomes, defined as either completion of a tour of duty and honorable discharge or continuing satisfactory adjustment in a military unit and unsuccessful outcomes, defined as less than honorable discharge, absence without leave, or presence in a military stockade at the time of follow-up, for 46 soldiers participating in the program and another 48 soldiers who received either general psychiatric treatment or routine disciplinary action. The results indicated that 69.5% of the soldiers who participated in the token economy were successful outcomes, while only 28.3% of the comparison group were successful outcomes.

CONCLUSIONS

The research reported herein indicates that behavioral procedures show much promise in the management of correctional institutions and the operation of rehabilitation programs. When combined in comprehensive token economy programs, these procedures also demonstrate potential to improve adjustment following release from confinement. Taken together, the latter four token economy outcome studies reported continuing, albeit not permanent, effects on offenders' behavior following release from custody. As would be expected, the most promising results were generated by a program in a military setting that returned soldiers to similar military service, supporting the well-established finding (e.g. Miltenberger, 1997) that the more similar the rehabilitation setting is to the setting in which the releasees will find themselves, the more pronounced and enduring will be the effects of intervention.

The lack of more permanent effects of the non-military token economies highlights the need for transition and community programs that maintain and build upon the accomplishments of institutional programs. It is, therefore, discouraging that the social and political climate in the United States has brought correctional rehabilitation efforts to an end and dictates that the criminal justice system will not, for the foreseeable future, build upon the foundation of effective rehabilitation and management practices laid by these early programs so many years ago. For the sake of both incarcerated offenders and their potential victims in the community, one can only hope that era will soon come.

REFERENCES

Akers, R. L. (1973). *Deviant behavior: A social learning approach.* Belmont, CA: Wadsworth.

Akers, R. L. (1977). *Deviant behavior: A social learning approach* (2nd ed.). Belmont, CA: Wadsworth.

Akers, R. L. (1985). *Deviant behavior: A social learning approach* (3rd ed.). Belmont, CA: Wadsworth.

Akers, R. L. (1998). *Social learning and social structure: A general theory of crime and deviance.* Boston, MA: Northeastern University.

Ayllon, T., & Azrin, N. (1968). *The token economy: A motivational system for therapy and rehabilitation.* New York: Appleton–Century–Crofts.

Ayllon, T., & Milan, M. A., with the assistance of Roberts, M. D., & McKee, J. M. (1979). *Correctional rehabilitation and management: A psychological approach.* New York: Wiley.

Bednar, R. L., Zelhart, P. F., Greathouse, L., & Weinberg, S. (1970). Operant conditioning principles in the treatment of learning and behavior problems with delinquent boys. *Journal of Counseling Psychology*, *17*, 402–407.

Boren, J. J., & Colman, A. D. (1970). Some experiments on reinforcement principles within a psychiatric ward for delinquent soldiers. *Journal of Applied Behavior Analysis*, *3*, 29–37.

Burchard, J. D. (1967). Systematic socialization: A programmed environment for the habilitation of antisocial retardates. *Psychological Record*, *17*, 461–476.

Burchard, J. D., & Barrera, F. (1972). An analysis of timeout and response cost in a programmed environment. *Journal of Applied Behavior Analysis*, *5*, 270–282.

Burchard, J. D., & Tyler, V. O. (1965). The modification of delinquent behavior through operant conditioning. *Behaviour Research and Therapy*, *2*, 245–250.

Burgess, R. L., & Akers, R. L. (1966). A differential association-reinforcement theory of criminal behavior. *Social Problems*, *14*, 128–147.

Clements, C. B., & McKee, J. M. (1968). Programmed instruction for institutionalized offenders: Contingency management and performance contracts. *Psychological Reports*, *22*, 957–964.

Cohen, H. L. (1973). Motivationally-oriented designs for an ecology of learning. In A. R. Roberts (Ed.), *Readings in prison education* (pp. 142–154). Springfield, IL: Charles C. Thomas.

Cohen, H. L., & Filipczak, J. A. (1971). *A new learning environment.* San Francisco, CA: Jossey-Bass.

Cohen, H. L., Filipczak, J. A., & Bis, J. S. (1970). A study of contingencies applicable to special education: CASE I. In R. E. Ulrich, T. Stachnik, & J. Mabry (Eds.), *Control of human behavior* (Vol. 2, pp. 51–69). Glenview, IL: Scott, Foresman.

Colman, A. D. (1970). Behavior therapy in a military setting. *Current Psychiatric Therapies*, *10*, 171–178.

Colman, A. D., & Baker, S. L. (1969). Utilization of an operant conditioning model for the treatment of character and behavior disorders in a military setting. *American Journal of Psychiatry*, *125*, 101–109.

Ellsworth, P. D., & Colman, A. D. (1970). The application of operant conditioning principles: Reinforcement systems to support work behavior. *American Journal of Occupational Therapy*, *24*, 562–568.

Eysenck, H. J. (1967). *The biological basis of personality.* Springfield, IL: Charles C. Thomas.

Eysenck, H. J. (1977). *Crime and personality* (3rd ed.). London: Paladin.

Eysenck, H. J. (1981). *A model for personality.* New York: Springer.

Eysenck, H. J., & Gudjonsson, G. H. (1989). *The causes and cures of criminality.* New York: Plenum.

Filipczak, J., & Cohen, H. L. (1972, September). *The CASE II contingency management system and where it is going.* Paper presented at the meeting of the American Psychological Association, Honolulu, HI.

Graubard, P. S. (1968). Use of indigenous groupings as the reinforcing agent in teaching disturbed delinquents to learn. *Proceedings of the 6th Annual Convention of the American Psychological Association* 613–614.

Haney, C., & Zimbardo, P. (1998). The past and future of U.S. prison policy. *American Psychologist*, *7*, 709–727.

Hobbs, T. R., & Holt, M. M. (1976). The effects of token reinforcement on the behavior of delinquents in cottage settings. *Journal of Applied Behavior Analysis*, *9*, 189–198.

Hollin, C. R. (1989). *Psychology and crime: An introduction to criminological psychology.* New York: Routledge.

Ingram, G. L., Gerard, R. E., Quay, H. C., & Levinson, R. B. (1970). An experimental program for the psychopathic delinquent: Looking in the "correctional wastebasket". *Journal of Research in Crime and Delinquency*, *7*, 24–30.

Jenkins, W. O., Witherspoon, A. D., Devine, M. D., deValera, E. K., Muller, J. B., Barton, M. C., & McKee, J. M. (1974). *The post-prison analysis of criminal behavior and longitudinal follow-up evaluation of institutional treatment.* Elmore, AL: Rehabilitation Research Foundation.

Jesness, C. F. (1979). The youth center project: Transactional analysis and behavior modification programs for delinquents. In J. S. Stumphauzer (Ed.), *Progress in behavior therapy with delinquents* (pp. 56–72). Springfield, IL: Charles C. Thomas.

Jesness, C. F., & DeRisi, W. M. (1973). Some variations in techniques of contingency management in a school for delinquents. In J. S. Stumphauzer (Ed.), *Behavior therapy with delinquents* (pp. 196–235). Springfield, IL: Charles C. Thomas.

Karacki, L., & Levinson, R. B. (1970). A token economy in a correctional institution for youthful offenders. *The Howard Journal of Penology and Crime Prevention, 13,* 20–30.

McCorkle, R. C. (1992). Personal precaution to prison violence. *Criminal Justice and Behavior, 19,* 160–173.

McKee, J. M. (1971). Contingency management in a correctional institution. *Educational Technology, 11,* 51–54.

McKee, J. M. (1974). The use of contingency management to affect learning performance in adult institutionalized offenders. In R. Ulrich, T. Stachnik, & J. Mabry (Eds.), *Control of human behavior* (Vol. 3, pp. 177–186). Glenview, IL: Scott, Foresman.

McKee, J. M., & Clements, C. B. (1971). A behavioral approach to learning: The Draper model. In H. C. Rickard (Ed.), *Behavioral interventions in human problems* (pp. 201–222). New York: Pergamon Press.

McKee, J. M., Jenkins, W. O., & Milan, M. A. (1977). The effects of contingency management procedures on the rate of learning. *Quarterly Journal of Corrections, 1,* 42–44.

Milan, M. A. (1987a). Basic behavioral procedures in closed institutions. In E. K. Morris & C. J. Braukmann (Eds.), *Behavioral approaches to crime and delinquency* (pp. 161–193). New York: Plenum.

Milan, M. A. (1987b). Token programs in closed institutions. In E. K. Morris & C. J. Braukmann (Eds.), *Behavioral approaches to crime and delinquency* (pp. 195–222). New York: Plenum.

Milan, M. A., & Evans, J. H. (1987). Intervention with incarcerated offenders: A correctional community psychology perspective. In I. B. Weiner & A. K. Hess (Eds.), *Handbook of forensic psychology* (pp. 557–583). New York: Wiley.

Milan, M. A., & Long, C. K. (1980). Crime and delinquency: The last frontier? In D. Glenwick & L. Jason (Eds.), *Behavioral community psychology: Progress and prospects* (pp. 194–230). New York: Praeger.

Milan, M. A., & McKee, J. M. (1974). Behavior modification: Principles and applications in corrections. In D. Glaser (Ed.), *Handbook of criminology* (pp. 745–775). Chicago, IL: Rand McNally.

Milan, M. A., & McKee, J. M. (1976). The cellblock token economy: Token reinforcement procedures in a maximum security correctional institution for adult male felons. *Journal of Applied Behavior Analysis, 9,* 253–275.

Milan, M. A., Throckmorton, W. R., McKee, J. M., & Wood, L. F. (1979). Contingency management in a cellblock token economy: Reducing rule violations and maximizing the effects of token reinforcement. *Criminal Justice and Behavior, 6,* 307–325.

Milan, M. A., Wood, L. F., & McKee, J. M. (1979). Motivating academic achievement in a cellblock token economy: An elaboration of the Premack principle. *Offender Rehabilitation, 3,* 349–361.

Miltenberger, R. (1997). *Behavior modification: Principles and procedures.* Pacific Grove, CA: Brooks/Cole.

Paulus, P. B. (1988). *Prison crowding: A psychological perspective.* New York: Springer-Verlag.

Raine, A. (1993). *The psychopathology of crime.* San Diego, CA: Academic Press.

Toch, H. (1992). *Mosaic of human despair: Human breakdown in prison.* Washington, DC: American Psychological Association.

Tyler, V. O., & Brown, G. D. (1967). The use of swift, brief isolation as a group control device for institutionalized delinquents. *Behaviour Research and Therapy, 5,* 1–9.

Chapter 11

Therapeutic Community Treatment Programming in Corrections

Douglas S. Lipton
Two World Trade Center, New York, USA

INTRODUCTION

This chapter presents an overview and history of the Therapeutic Community (TC) treatment as applied in the United Kingdom to disturbed offenders and in the United States to incarcerated drug-using offenders. It attempts briefly to describe the principles and program philosophies so as to clarify the differences between them. It focuses on findings from five scientifically sound studies which conclude that TC treatment during custody for serious felons (who are also hard-core drug users) is effective in reducing drug abuse and recidivism.

The utilization of the TC during incarceration is currently viewed by policy makers and correctional administrators in the United States as an important tool capable of yielding substantial reductions in recidivism as well as chronic drug abuse among hard-core addict–offenders. The Federal Congress authorized spending the largest sum ever for correctional rehabilitation, beginning in 1996, (through the Residential Substance Abuse Treatment for State Prisoners Formula Grant Program (RSAT)), namely $270 million over five years to the states for the development of substance abuse treatment programs in state and local correctional facilities. This bipartisan decision was based on accrued research findings (Field, 1984, 1989; Inciardi, Martin, Butzin, Hooper, & Harrison, 1997; Knight, Simpson, Chatham, & Camacho, 1997; Wexler, 1995; Wexler, Falkin, & Lipton, 1988, 1990; Wexler, De Leon, Thomas, Kressel, & Peters, 1998) that prison-based TC programs significantly reduce recidivism and drug relapse and create a

Handbook of Offender Assessment and Treatment. Edited by C. R. Hollin.
© 2000 John Wiley & Sons Ltd.

significant opportunity to alter the drug-using lifestyles of criminal predators with long addiction histories. These offenders are persons who without treatment are highly likely to continue their drug use and criminality after release and who are unlikely to seek treatment for their heroin or cocaine addiction on their own.

AN OVERVIEW OF TC TREATMENT

The history of the TC as it developed in the United Kingdom has been thoughtfully detailed by Roberts (1997). TC treatment mainly emerged as a process for treating military veterans during and just after the Second World War as these patients returned with serious neurotic conditions engendered by their experiences in combat. The term was coined by Tom Main after the war (1946). Employed at The Cassel Hospital, Main pioneered a therapeutic model combining community therapy with ongoing psychoanalytic psychotherapy. This was a modification of therapeutic work developed about the same time by Maxwell Jones (1968) and others (see Roberts, 1997 for the works of Bridger, Anthony, Foulkes, deMare, Casson and Bion) with this difficult population. It is perhaps worthwhile noting that other proto-TCs preceded these efforts. Kennard (1983) reports that The York Retreat had many TC features when it provided treatment to mentally ill patients in *the late eighteenth century*, and Harry Stack Sullivan pioneered the use of community treatment with schizophrenics in the 1930s at Chestnut Lodge in Maryland in the United States. By 1954, TC ideas were influencing wards in UK psychiatric hospitals.

At the same time, however, the use of major tranquilizers began to emerge as the dominant "treatment" for schizophrenia. As patient symptom mitigation became possible through chemistry, drastic reductions in psychiatric beds and other confinement beds occurred as facilities closed down guided by financial and commercial goals, as well as misunderstood research findings about the use of these tranquilizers (Roberts, 1997). With this rapid trend in the 1950s and 1960s, the TC movement shifted toward the other milieus, notably corrections. Jones visited the United States in 1959 where he became involved in the development of TCs with the California Department of Corrections—11 TC projects were established (Jones, 1962, 1979), the most notable of which was at Chino (Briggs, 1972).

Developments in UK Prisons

In the early 1960s the offender programs in the United Kingdom began to be guided by TC principles. This followed legislation, the 1959 Mental Health Act, which granted to psychopathy and personality disorder the status of psychological abnormality, making them "susceptible to treatment", and Grendon Prison was built specifically with a number of wings within which TCs would experimentally operate to provide treatment for psychologically disturbed offenders (see Table 11.1). The TCs in British prisons were also established at Wormwood

Table 11.1   The elements and principles that characterize the classic Maxwell Jones' TC as exemplified at Grendon Prison

Elements	Description
Setting	An assessment unit, five TC wings, and a pre-release unit in a medium security facility in Aylesbury, 55 miles NW of London. (Said to be inadequate space for all activities (Cullen, Jones, & Woodward, 1997).)
Residents	All residents, $N = 245$, serious offenders (38% violent offenders, 27% sex offenders, 28% robbers, 4% theft, 3% arson) with histories of personality disorders (45% said they had been mental hospital in-patients at least once) are volunteers from 50 UK prisons, average sentence seven years, 40% are lifers, most are referred when 2–3 years from parole eligibility. Average age 32, range, 21–60.
Staff	About 220 total, led overall by career prison governor, supported by a director of therapy, a psychiatrist. Each wing team is led by a psychiatrist (or psychotherapist), with a full-time psychologist and a probation officer; majority are 10 basic grade uniformed officers and two senior officers, and one part-time tutor for education per wing.

Principles	Description
• Democratization	The principle of enfranchisement and empowerment ". . . wherein every community member has a direct say in every aspect of how the wing is run" (including the power to vote someone out for a rule breach).
• Permissiveness	A philosophy of tolerance to allow members to make mistakes, and to accept themselves "with all their warts" and support each other "regardless of their warts".
• Communalism	Encouragement of individual and especially collective responsibility and accountability
• Reality confrontation	Continuous, direct, and candid presentation of interpretations of each other's behavior to counteract tendency to distort, deny, or withdraw from interpersonal difficulties or rule breaking
• Peer group influence	Used to control and modify inimical prison cultural values with an important role for "community elders"—members who have successfully completed the transition themselves playing a supportive role
• Focus on	relief of intrapsychic distress developing relationships with women and children developing relationships with figures of authority developing relationships with one another attitudes to offending generally, and specifically to primary offense

continued overleaf

Table 11.1 *(continued)*

Principles	Description
	denial and morality victim awareness, contrition, consequences for victim fantasies and rehearsal in formulating offending cognitions plans and strategies for future offending behavior, i.e. risk and relapse prevention

	Description
Program	The Grendon therapy group, daily small therapy groups of 10 residents (+2 staff), daily community "wing" meetings of 35–42 (as large as 50), "feedbacks" or confrontation sessions; supplemented by conjoint therapies including Psychodrama, Social and Life Skills, Cognitive Skills, Sex Offender Treatment Program, Alternatives to Violence, and education.
Dosage	At Grendon, the treatment program lasts for over two years. Evidence favors longer (12–18 months) rather than shorter periods of therapy.
Outcome	Most of the studies of reconviction (Cullen, 1993; George, 1971; Gunn, Robertson, & Dell, 1978; Marshall, 1997; Newton, 1973; Newton & Thornton, 1994) found that rates of reoffending after two years from release were not significantly lower than before nor significantly different from comparison populations, although a distinct time- in-program function has been consistently seen, i.e. the longer the term in therapy, the lower the rate of reconviction, and greater success occurs more frequently with men over thirty years of age than with younger men.

Scrubs and at a special unit at Barlinnie Prison in Glasgow. It should be noted that while Maxwell Jones' name is strongly credited with these developments, this is perhaps more due to the fact that he published extensively about the TC concept while others worked clinically and published less.

Developments in the United States

Jones' model continues through the 1990s at Grendon Prison in the United Kingdom. This TC model, however, was not the direct origin of the prison-based TC for substance abusers seen chiefly in the United States and increasingly in Europe. The label *TC* has caused some confusion. The term is also used for asylums or sanctuaries, anti-psychiatry communities, residential group homes, and even special schools. Current TCs for addicted persons (both alcoholic and drug addicted) derive from *Synanon* founded in 1958 by Charles Dederich in California. Synanon's immediate roots are in the Oxford movement and Alcoholics Anonymous, with earlier prototypes existing in religious, temperance, and communal healing communities in North America and abroad (Arbiter, 1992). Addiction (also called concept-based) TCs generally subscribe to a self-help, social learning model approach and a holistic human change perspective. In the United States in the mid-1990s, they admit about 80 000 persons annually (TCA, 1994).

It is useful first to discuss what is meant by a community-based, concept-based TC. A typical community-based TC is a residence staffed by a few professionals but primarily by recovered addicts serving as staff. Residents are asked to spend about 9 to 18 months in residence, but the drop-out rate is quite high—usually 60–80% are gone within the first three months. A core characteristic of most community-based TCs is the use of work as an organizing therapeutic activity. This means that residents are involved in all aspects of the community's operations including administration, maintenance, and food preparation. (In the modified TC typically found in US correctional institutions, TC residents cannot be involved in all aspects of the community's operations to the same degree, e.g. maintenance and food preparation are carried out by specialized crews from the general population, although some superficial maintenance of the resident housing area is usually possible—thus, community work as an organizing activity shifts to work on one's own psychological issues.)

Drug abuse is seen as a disorder of the whole person, so the treatment problem to be addressed is the person, not the drug, i.e. drug abuse is seen as a symptom not the essence of the disorder, and the pattern of drug use is less important than the psychological and behavioral disorders. Drug abuse is seen as a symptom of immaturity, thus the abuser is seen as being unable to postpone gratification, unable to tolerate frustration, and has difficulty maintaining stable healthy relationships. Beside immaturity, most abusers have conduct or behavior problems and low self-esteem. These characteristics are targets for the behavior change techniques used by the TC staff and senior residents. Recovery is considered to involve the development of a personal identity and global change in lifestyle, including the conduct, attitudes, and values consonant with "Right Living", and is a lifelong continuing process. Right Living develops from committing oneself to the values of the TC, including both positive *social* values such as the work ethic, social productivity, and communal responsibility, and positive *personal* values such as honesty, self-reliance, and responsibility to oneself and significant others. The goals of treatment are congruent with these values: abstinence from drug use, termination of illicit behaviors, gainful legal employment/or school matriculation, and maintenance of positive stable social relationships (De Leon, 1995).

TCs are hierarchically organized or stratified. Staff and resident roles are aligned in a clear chain of command. New residents are assigned to work teams with the lowest status, but can move up the strata as they demonstrate increased competency and emotional growth. Thus, they have an incentive to earn better work positions, associated privileges, and living accommodations. For success in the TC one must accept the notion of "acting as if", which requires the new residents to suspend judgment and make believe that they accept the basic TC values and rules conduct. The residents then continue to "act as if" until the community values and attitudes become internalized. Maturity develops as roles and responsibilities are taken on and increase. The stratified character of the TC facilitates the working through of authority problems and helps the residents to accept appropriate authority as they move out to assume responsible positions within society. The distinguishing feature of the TC in contrast to other treatment approaches is the "purposive use of the *community* as the primary method for facilitating social and psychological change in individuals" (De Leon, 1995, p. 1611) as it blends confrontation and support to help residents undergo the arduous changes that are necessary. The perception of the *community* is constantly emphasized. The program uses groups and meetings to provide "positive persuasion" to change behavior, and confrontation by peer groups whenever values or rules are breached. On the other hand, peers also provide supportive feedback such as reinforcement, affirmation, instruction, and suggestions for changing behavior and attitudes, and assist the residents during group meetings as they recall painful memories from childhood and adolescence. It should be noted that the TC regimen of today often provides additional services such as family treatment, and educational, vocational, medical, and mental health services, and staffing is augmented by increasing proportions of professionals from the mental health, medical, and education fields (De Leon, 1994).

The chief differences between the Jones' TC model, as used in the United Kingdom and in Canada, and the US TC model are: the US model is less psychoanalytic and psycho-therapeutic; less focused on the criminal offense or on substance abuse *per se*; more holistic, i.e. more concerned with lifestyle changes across more dimensions; uses the community of peers and role models more as the change agents rather than professional clinicians and trained correction officers; is less democratic in operation and more hierarchical in structure. The US model is less psychiatric (and less medical) in origin, emerging from a recovered client self-help background.

A BRIEF HISTORY OF THERAPEUTIC COMMUNITIES IN US CORRECTIONS

Until 1987 and the changes wrought by the US Department of Justice's Bureau of Justice Assistance technical assistance effort, Project REFORM (discussed below), about 25 prison-based TSs had existed in seventeen states and the District of Columbia. Seven TCs had existed in the Federal Bureau of Prisons.

In 1966 the author was involved in establishing the earliest prison-based TC in New York State as a pilot program. It was housed at the then recently closed Dannemora State Hospital for the Criminally Insane (DSHCI) in Dannemora,

NY—which is very close to the Canadian border, where two wards were physically converted to house and treat 100 inmates in a TC. This state hospital was adjacent to Clinton Prison, hence the program's euphemistic name—the Clinton Prison Diagnostic and Treatment Center. Directly administered by the State Department of Correction in cooperation with the State Division of Parole, it was staffed with professionals from Montreal's McGill University forensic psychiatry unit under Bruno Cormier, MD, and by recently laid-off DSHCI correctional officers who had been trained by him for six months, and a few student volunteers from nearby Plattsburgh State College. The model for this program was Dr. Cormier's own variation of the Maxwell Jones-type TC. Its clients were identified prison troublemakers with records of difficult behavior and acting out—said to have serious mental and emotional problems, though not mentally ill—sent eagerly from many of the prisons in New York State. No careful scientific evaluation research study was carried out, but an analysis of arrest records after one year following release from treatment revealed a surprisingly low level of recidivism among these very high-risk offenders (Preiser, Delaney, & Lipton, 1968). Unfortunately, the program received no publicity and thus did not serve as a model for others. Its existence as a TC ended after two years, when the legislature became aware of its high cost and embarrassed that the professional staffing was almost entirely Canadian in "a State with more of our own psychiatrists than any other" at that time.

In 1969 in the federal penitentiary in Marion, Illinois, the first correctional TC began that *served as a model* program. The prison psychiatrist, Dr Martin Groder, designed and developed a TC based on his Transactional Analysis training and his group therapy experience in California. The program combining these two general approaches was named *Aesklepeiain* for the Greek God of healing, Aesculapius. While it did not meet the criteria we now have for this kind of treatment, it still served as a model for the proliferation of correctional-based TCs in federal and several state institutions in the early and mid-1970s.

With the availability of Federal Law Enforcement Assistance Administration funds many new programs began to spring up. Programs began, for example, in four institutions in Arkansas from 1975 through 1977 including one for women offenders, but all were discontinued in 1980. Eight TCs began in Connecticut at about the same time and these were for persons addicted to drugs. Connecticut also established a TC for women at Niantic and one for juveniles at Cheshire, as well as in several community correctional centers. None of these programs followed the Aesklepeiain model, but adapted the Daytop treatment model which was much closer to the current prison-based TC model than Aesklepeiain.

A TC was established in Georgia at the Metropolitan Correctional Institution in Atlanta in 1982. It was closed down in 1985 because of staff burnout and lack of fresh volunteers to staff the program. A TC for women was established in Michigan in 1977 and was moved to a smaller facility in 1982, and closed down in 1984, but reopened in 1988 and continues to today. Missouri launched a "TC" for sex offenders in 1981. Close examination reveals that while separated from other inmates, members never established a community structure and they were dispersed to the general population in 1988. For five years from 1979 to 1984, Nebraska ran a TC at Lincoln Correctional Center. It closed after a variety of problems including friction between the program and the larger institution, an investigative article by a reporter who had received damaging information from a disgruntled discharged resident, overcrowding generally, and declining state revenues. Florida developed the Lantana TC model for youthful offenders which was cited by the federal government as a program exemplar. It lasted about nine years until 1987 by which time it had lost its focus as a TC and its energy as a change agent.

Stay'n Out, using the community-based program Phoenix House as a model, began in 1977 in New York's Arthur Kill Correctional Facility with one unit modified for a prison environment. It now has five units treating 180 males at Arthur Kill and about 40 women at Bayview Correctional Facility. Initial funding was from the state substance abuse agency. After three years and having demonstrated that it was not a threat to safety and some notable success and good press, the state correctional department picked up the cost. The staffing has been from the outset under contract to the Therapeutic Communities of New York, Inc. The cost per year per inmate participant in Stay'n Out is still less than $3000.

Oklahoma began six small TCs in 1973, one of which was for drug offenders. All six were closed when in 1979 the primary exponent retired. The institution in which they were housed was torn down and replaced with a new reception center. Oregon's Cornerstone Program (Field, 1992), located on the grounds of the Oregon State Hospital, is a 32-bed TC for correctional inmates that began in 1975. Somewhat like Stay'n Out, Cornerstone, before it was closed in 1996, had a higher proportion of professional staff and trained correction officers than Stay'n Out, which still has a staff mainly of recovered ex-addict, ex-offenders. The cost of treatment at Cornerstone was greater than in Stay'n Out because of the higher proportion of professional staff. Cornerstone's cost per day per participant at the time of its closing had reached $39, making its cost comparable to that of community-based TCs.

In South Carolina, in 1975, a TC was started which lasted until 1979, by which time it had become overcrowded, corrupted with contraband drugs, and staffed inadequately to supervise and operate the program. In Virginia, a TC, *House of Thought*, was established on the Aesklepeiain model at the James River Correctional Center. After overcoming strong institutional resistance and unfounded rumors of misconduct, the program grew, moved to Powhatan Correctional Center in 1980 and lasted until late 1982 when it was closed after a decline in state revenues forced budget cuts and the supportive director resigned.

Thus, a number of prison-based TCs developed beginning mainly in the 1970s and this process continued through the early 1980s. A variety of models existed: Aesklepeiain, Daytop, Phoenix House. Not all the programs focused on drug abusers, some were used for sex offenders, some for disturbed inmates, some for offenders with no particular disorder other than a history of criminal offending. The life span of the programs averaged around five to seven years. Most closed when executive priorities changed and/or revenue short-falls reduced funding availability. A few became corrupted when supervision weakened and contraband drugs were brought in. Some were never able to develop a true community. Others, like Stay'n Out, which is 20 years old, remain viable today, and some, like Cornerstone, which opened in the 1970s have recently closed their doors. In most cases, however, closed TCs were replaced by a new TC. It is important to note that the theoretical underpinnings of TC practice for most of these early programs, except for the Stay'n Out program and Cornerstone, would have met few of the criteria for TCs in the late 1990s.

Projects REFORM and RECOVERY

The next burst of productive energy that triggered a new wave of expenditure on prison-based drug abuse treatment involving TCs was the launch of two major national technical assistance projects stemming from the Federal Anti-Drug Abuse Act of 1986 i.e. Projects REFORM and RECOVERY. Under the impetus and guidance of Nicholas Demos of the Bureau of Justice Assistance, Project REFORM was launched in 1987 by Lipton and Wexler of the National Development and Research Institutes, Inc. (NDRI) who had recently completed a comprehensive evaluation of the modified prison-based TC, Stay'n Out. Project REFORM was an effort by the federal government to develop comprehensive state-wide correctional drug abuse treatment in selected states. Each state's REFORM involvement was divided into two phases, planning and implementation. During the planning phase, correctional officials developed plans for the initiation or enhancement of substance abuse treatment services system-wide. Upon completion of these plans, each state applied for funds to implement priority interventions listed in their plans, such as model treatment units, treatment infrastructure, staff training, and tracking and evaluation strategies. Assistance was provided to the states of Alabama, Connecticut, Delaware, Florida, Hawaii, New Jersey, Oregon, Washington, California, New York, New Mexico, and Oregon for first setting up, then implementing, the plans. Project REFORM resulted in expanding, improving, and/or implementing 72 assessment and referral programs; 118 drug education programs; 71 drug resource centers; 82 in-prison, 12-step programs; 15 urine monitoring programs; 128 pre-release counseling and referral programs; 49 post-release treatment programs with parole or work release; and 77 modified TC treatment programs (Lipton, 1995, 1996).

It is clear that the comprehensive planning, aided by the technical assistance team (James Inciardi of the University of Delaware, M. Douglas Anglin of the University of California—Los Angeles, George De Leon of NDRI, Richard Dembo of the University of South Florida, Ron Williams of Stay'n Out, Rod Mullen and Naya Arbiter of Amity, George and Camille Camp of the Criminal Justice Institute) helped local state officials assess problems related to the provision of substance abuse services within their correctional systems, and helped them develop appropriate short- and long-range strategies for service enhancement. New service delivery models were created that enhanced the continuity of treatment so that programming begun in the institution could continue after program participants were released to the community. This included developing contracts with community programs to provide counseling and treatment planning assistance to offenders approaching release as well as residential and outpatient treatment after discharge and/or parole to the community.

In 1991, when funding for Project REFORM from the Bureau of Justice Assistance ended after five years, the national effort shifted to the new Office for Treatment Improvement (OTI) of the Alcohol, Drug Abuse and Mental Health Administration of the Department of Health and Human Services. OTI (now the Center for Substance Abuse Treatment (CSAT) of the Substance Abuse and Mental Health Services Administration (SAMHSA)) established Project RECOVERY to provide technical assistance and training services to demonstration prison drug treatment programs and continued the work begun by REFORM. Most of the original REFORM states remained involved in RECOVERY, and an additional seven states participated (Colorado, Georgia, Michigan, North Carolina, North Dakota, Pennsylvania, and Virginia). Texas and Ohio also attended RECOVERY workshops without direct federal funding. RECOVERY continued for 18 months. One net effect of these two projects, insofar as TC development is concerned, is that in 1997 there were 110 TCs operating in state and federal correctional institutions, in addition to a variety of other milieu, cognitive skills training, counseling, relapse prevention, vocational, and educational programs.

In 1994, the single largest initiative to create in-prison treatment for drug abusers began when the United States Congress passed legislation to create the Residential Substance Abuse Treatment for State Prisoners Program (RSATSPP), and $270 million was authorized over a five-year period beginning in 1996. This Act was written in part due to a number of research studies indicating that prison-based TC treatment was yielding consistently positive outcomes with predatory cocaine and heroin users, and also because it received bipartisan support (Lipton, 1995). The Residential Substance Abuse Treatment for State Prisoners Formula Grant Program, part of the Violent Crime Control and Law Enforcement Act of 1994, provides funding for the development of substance abuse treatment programs in state and local correctional facilities. The program encourages states to adopt comprehensive approaches to substance abuse treatment for offenders, including relapse prevention and aftercare services (the latter is, unfortunately, an unfunded mandate).

The fiscal year (FY) 1996 appropriation for this program was $27 million. The authorized amounts through FY 2000 sum to an additional $243 million. Each state may apply for the "block grant" funds and receives a base amount plus an allocation from the remaining funds equal to its proportional share of the total prison population in all participating states. These states, in turn, may make subawards to state agencies and local government units—counties or cities. While not requiring that TCs be established with these funds, the model treatment program criteria that are stipulated—isolated unit, a minimum of six months of treatment, etc.—are based on the findings of the TC evaluation studies produced since the latter half of the 1980s that are noted below.

Findings from Signal Examples of Prison-Based TC Treatment Programming

The Amity at Donovan Program

The Amity Prison TC program which began in 1989 is located at R. J. Donovan Correctional Facility on the Otay Mesa south of San Diego. The evaluation of the program has been under the direction of Harry Wexler and is funded by NIDA as part of NDRI's Center on Therapeutic Community Research, directed by George De Leon.

Approximately 4000 men are housed in five self-contained living areas in the R. J. Donovan medium security facility. All aspects of daily living—housing, sustenance, education, and work—are accommodated within these areas. One 200-man housing unit in one of these areas was set aside for the Amity project. The men who reside in this housing unit participate in daily TC programming mainly conducted by Amity staff in two trailers located near the housing unit. Eligibility criteria include: history of drug abuse; no in-prison assaults or weapon possession within the last five years; no sex-related offenses in prison within the last ten years; no history of child molestation or mental illness; and within 9–15 months of parole.

The program is modeled upon the Stay'n Out program in New York—i.e. a TC modified to fit into a correctional institution (described below). Program residents are housed in a separate residential unit, though they eat in a common dining room and participate in some activities with other inmates who live in the same yard. Participants move through three distinct phases of treatment during the in-prison treatment phase, which lasts about 12 months. The *first phase* of treatment consists of orientation, diagnosis, and an assimilation process. It involves clinical observation, and assessment of resident needs and problem areas, and lasts two to three months. The prison TC procedures are learned and participation occurs in encounter groups, seminars, and similar group activities. Residents are assigned prison industry jobs and are also given limited responsibility in the maintenance of the TC. During the *second phase* of treatment, which lasts about five to six months, residents demonstrating sincere involvement in the program and hard emotional work are given opportunities to earn positions of increased responsibility. More seasoned residents are expected to share their insights by teaching the newer members of the community, and by assisting in the day-to-day operation of the facility. Also, encounter groups and counseling sessions deepen in their content and focus on the areas of self-discipline, self-worth, self-awareness, respect for authority, and acceptance of guidance for problem areas. Seminars take on a more intellectual nature, and debate is encouraged to enhance self-expression and to increase self-confidence. Several components, unique to the Amity TC, then occur: psychodrama groups are used to complement standard TC groups and meetings; video playback is used to raise self-awareness, foster reality of self-perception, and give the residents a chance to see themselves change over time; and, "lifers" are used in counselor roles providing live-in 24-hours-a-day, seven-days-a-week counseling. The lifers are extensively trained, have great commitment, are extremely credible role models, and are treated as regular Amity staff. The *third phase*, community re-entry, lasts about one to three months. During this phase, inmates sharpen their skills in planning and decision making and work with correctional, treatment, and parole staff to design their individual exit plans.

Upon release from prison, graduates of the Amity Prison TC Project are offered the opportunity to continue in residential TC treatment for up to one year in a 40-bed community facility operated by Amity in Vista, California, nearer San Diego. All residents have responsibility for the security, maintenance, and emotional health of the TC. The TC welcomes the families of residents and offers special services to meet their needs as both clients and supporters in the recovery process. The program builds upon that offered in the prison and is individualized for each resident based upon the progress achieved in the prison TC treatment program. Prison TC residents who choose not to continue treatment in the community facility are encouraged to maintain strong ties to the house by joining weekly family groups, attending special functions sponsored by Amity, and by telephoning residents or Amity staff to update the house on their current situation and plans. All graduates of the Amity Prison TC and community TCs are encouraged to participate in treatment activities sponsored by other human service providers in the community (e.g. Alcoholics Anonymous, Narcotics Anonymous). Many program staff are former substance abusers with criminal histories and all are graduates of community TCs.

The prospective outcome study utilizes a quasi-experimental design ($n = 715$ males) in which random selection was closely approximated, and an extensive follow-up. An eligible pool was created by the formation of a waiting list of volunteers who met the admission criteria. Subjects in the voluntary pool were randomly selected and assigned to the treatment condition as bed space became available, and were stratified to create equal ethnic proportions; inmates not selected randomly remained in the pool until they had less than nine months to serve, when they were moved to the no-treatment control group.

A wide variety of background information and psychological data was collected at admission, at six and 12 months while in program, and at 12 and 24 months post-release from prison. These data reported here are based on the 12 and 24 month follow-up using criminal record data obtained from the California Department of Corrections (Wexler et al., 1998).

The no-treatment control group had significantly greater levels of recidivism to prison than the intent-to-treat group (at 12 months, 49.7% vs. 33.9% ($N = 715$), and at 24 months post-release, 67.1% vs. 43.3% ($N = 263$)). Moreover, among the offenders who were returned to prison, the no-treatment controls were reincarcerated in significantly fewer days than the intent-to-treat group (213 mean days vs. 266 mean days).

The residents are hard-core felons with extensive criminal histories. An average of 321 offenses per offender have been committed in their lifetimes. More than 70% have committed a violent crime (assault, kidnapping, manslaughter, rape, or murder)—report they have committed murder and 3% report having committed rape. Many inmates have long criminal histories: half of the study participants were declared delinquent by a juvenile court, and the average inmate has spent more than half of his adult life in prison, in 19 separate incarceration terms.

Recidivism at 12 Months

Treatment subjects and program dropouts were at risk (i.e. had been released from prison) for an average of 16 months. Table 11.2 shows that 8% of the participants who went through both the program and the community-based TC were reincarcerated within one year; 39% of those who completed the prison TC but who dropped out of the aftercare TC were reincarcerated; 40% of the program completers (who did not go to the aftercare TC) were reincarcerated; and 45% of the TC program dropouts were reincarcerated, as were 50% of the control group subjects. The reincarceration results are statistically significant (as are the arrest results, not shown) (Wexler et al., 1998).

Recidivism at 24 Months

Table 11.3 shows that 14% of the participants who went through both the program and the community-based TC were reincarcerated within two years; 60% of those who completed the prison TC but who dropped out of the aftercare TC were reincarcerated; 49% of the program completers (who did not go

Table 11.2 Amity Donovan TC, California: reincarceration one year following parole as of mid-1995

	Untreated control		TC drops		TC completers		TC comp + aftercare drops		TC comp + aftercare comp	
	N	%	N	%	N	%	N	%	N	%
Not reincarcerated	145	**50.3**	54	**55.1**	116	**59.8**	22	**61.1**	89	**91.8**
Reincarcerated	145	**49.7**	44	**44.9**	78	**40.2**	14	**38.9**	8	**8.2**
Total	290	100	98	100	194	100	36	100	97	100

Note: $p < 0.001$. Controlling for gender, race, age, prison history, treatment history, and previous drug use.

Table 11.3 Amity Donovan TC, California: reincarceration two years following parole as of November, 1997

	Untreated control		TC drops		TC completers		TC comp + aftercare drops		TC comp + aftercare comp	
	N	%	N	%	N	%	N	%	N	%
Not reincarcerated	28	**32.9**	17	**42.5**	116	**51.2**	06	**40.0**	37	**86.0**
Reincarcerated	57	**67.1**	23	**57.5**	78	**48.8**	09	**60.0**	06	**14.0**
Total	85	100	40	100	80	100	15	100	43	100

Note: $p < 0.001$. Controlling for gender, race, age, prison history, treatment history, and previous drug use.

to the aftercare TC) were reincarcerated; 58% of the TC program dropouts were reincarcerated, as were two-thirds of the control group subjects. The reincarceration results are statistically significant (as are the arrest results, not shown) (Wexler et al., 1998). At 24 months, then, there is a difference of 23.8% (43.3% vs. 67.1%) in the overall reincarceration rate for the intent-to-treat group over controls.

These Amity recidivism outcomes are similar to the positive results of the New York Stay'n Out prison program, and compare closely with outcome evaluation results of other prison-based TC programs, and compare quite favorably with many community-based TCs. This degree of similarity in outcome is highly unusual in social science research. The level of consistency achieved across programs with different staffs, different mixes of offenders, and in different settings suggests strongly that the overall effects of this form of programming are stable and replicable.

New York's Stay'n Out Program

The results from the New York program, Stay'n Out, have been reported extensively elsewhere, hence it is sufficient to summarize the outcome of this program briefly. In 1984, the National Institute on Drug Abuse provided a grant to NDRI to evaluate the Stay'n Out TC program in New York which had been started in 1977 by recovered addicts who were also ex-offenders (Wexler, Lipton, Falkin, & Rosenblum, 1992). Using a sample of about 2000 subjects from the program, they report that prison-based TC treatment significantly reduced recidivism rates (in terms of rearrest) for both males and females. Stay'n Out was compared with another milieu therapy-based program run by the Department of Correctional Services, a group counseling program, and with no treatment (Wexler, Falkin, & Lipton, 1990).

The evaluation study employed a quasi-experimental design with two types of comparison groups: (1) Inmates who volunteered for the TC program, but never participated, i.e. no-treatment controls (not drop-outs); and, (2) Matched inmates who participated in other types of prison-based drug use treatment programs (counseling and milieu therapy) located elsewhere in the prison system. Parole outcomes were obtained for 1626 male and 398 female inmates in New York State prisons. The male and female no-treatment comparison groups were composed of inmates who had volunteered for the TC program and were placed on waiting lists, but never entered the program.

The samples were quite comparable in terms of background characteristics. As can be seen in Table 11.4, the male TC treatment group had a significantly lower arrest rate (22%) than all the other male groups.

The arrest rate for the male milieu therapy group (35%) was significantly lower than for the male counseling (50%), and male no-treatment groups (51%). The male counseling group's arrest rate did not differ from the male no-treatment group arrest rate. Thus, the male data provided support for the study hypotheses with the TC treatment showing the best results followed by the milieu therapy treatment and then counseling treatment and no-treatment (Wexler, Falkin, & Lipton, 1990). Similar arrest results were found for the female groups, as shown in Table 11.5.

Table 11.4 Stay'n Out males, Arthur Kill Correctional Facility, New York: arrest status at 36-month follow-up by treatment group

	No treatment		Counseling only		Milieu therapy		Stay'n Out	
	N	%	N	%	N	%	N	%
Arrest-free	78	**49**	130	**50**	374	**65**	339	**78**
Arrested	81	**51**	130	**50**	202	**35**	96	**22**
Total	159	100	260	100	576	100	435	100

Note: p < 0.001. Controlling for age, prison history, criminal history, length of treatment, and previous drug use.

Table 11.5 Stay'n Out females, Bayview Correctional Facility, New York: arrest status at 36-month follow-up by treatment group

	No treatment		Counseling only		Stay'n Out	
	N	%	N	%	N	%
Arrest-free	29	**76**	80	**71**	203	**82**
Arrested	09	**24**	33	**29**	44	**18**
Total	38	100	113	100	247	100

Note: p < 0.07. Controlling for age, criminal history, prison history, length of treatment, and previous drug use.

The female TC group had a significantly lower arrest rate than the female counseling and female no-treatment groups combined. Individual comparisons revealed that the female TC's arrest rate (8%) was significantly lower than the female counseling group (33%), but the differences between the notreatment group versus the counseling and TC groups did not reach significance. In fact, the no-treatment group had a lower recidivism rate than the counseling group (Wexler, Falkin, & Lipton, 1990). Thus, the female data indicate that the TC was effective in reducing recidivism rates, but that the counseling treatment showed no such effect. Another significant finding was that the members of the male TC treatment group who subsequently failed *stayed drug and crime free before failing for significantly longer periods than the comparison groups*. Most important, however, is that the females who spent six to nine months in treatment had only an 8% failure rate as compared with the 24% for the controls and 29% for the women who were in the counseling program. The robust central conclusion of the Stay'n Out evaluation is that hard-core drug abusers who remain in the prison-based TC longer are considerably more likely to succeed than those who leave earlier. In addition, nine to 12 months appears to be the optimal duration for the treatment, and that as time in TC treatment increases, recidivism declines significantly.

Oregon's Cornerstone Program

The Cornerstone Program (Field, 1992), located on the grounds of the Oregon State Hospital, is a 32-bed TC for correctional inmates that began in 1975. Somewhat like Stay'n Out, Cornerstone is modeled on the TC concept. However, it has a higher proportion of professional staff and trained correction officers than Stay'n Out, which has a staff mainly of recovered ex-addict, ex-offenders. Two evaluation studies of the Cornerstone program assessed several treatment outcomes, including recidivism (Field, 1984, 1989). In the first study, a three-year, follow-up study, Field compared the groups according to two outcome measures: the percentage not returned to prison and the percentage not convicted of any crime. The program graduates had a significantly higher success rate for both outcome measures than each of the other groups. Of the program graduates, 71% were not reincarcerated three years after release; only 26% of the dropouts avoided reincarceration. The results support the hypothesis that treatment in the Cornerstone program is associated with reduced recidivism (see Table 11.6). Indeed, significance tests of both outcome measures showed that program graduates had significantly better outcomes than the Oregon parole sample (63% of the parolees were not reincarcerated and only 36% were not convicted of any crimes). These differences tend to *understate* the effect of the treatment because the program graduates had significantly more severe criminal histories and substance abuse problems than the Oregon parole sample.

Field's 1989 study produced similar results, using a different research design. The results for the program graduates in this sample were similar to the findings in the earlier evaluation with three-quarters of the graduates not reincarcerated

Table 11.6 Cornerstone Therapeutic Community, Oregon, 1984: reincarceration and conviction three years following parole release

| | Reincarcerated/Convicted for new crime | | |
	Program dropouts %	Parole control %	Cornerstone graduates %
Not reincarcerated	26/14	63/36	71/51
Reincarcerated	74/86	37/64	29/49
Total	100/100	100/100	100/100

Note: G vs. PC Δ = **08**, NS; Δ = 15, *p* < 0.05; G vs. DO Δ = **45**, *p* < 0.01; Δ = 37, *p* < 0.05.

Table 11.7 Cornerstone Therapeutic Community, Oregon, 1989: percentrage reincarcerated three years following parole release

| | Reincarcerated | | |
	Program dropouts %	Program non-grads %	Cornerstone graduates %
Not reincarcerated	15	37	75
Reincarcerated	85	63	25
Total	100	100	100

Note: DO vs. G Δ = 60%, *p* < 0.01; NG vs. G Δ = 38%, *p* < 0.05.

(see Table 11.7). These results compared favorably with the two groups that did not graduate, only 37% of whom were not reincarcerated. The findings for the other dropouts are even more startling. Only 8% of the clients who dropped out in less than two months were not arrested during the three-year follow-up, only 11% were not convicted, and only 15% were not reincarcerated (data not shown). These findings are consistent with the findings on the Stay'n Out program, which showed that increased time in program is associated with more positive treatment outcomes.

The Key–Crest Program in Delaware

The Key–Crest program is a three-stage model program operating within the Delaware correctional system. Only the first two stages have been operationalized. It is built around two TCs, the *Key*, a prison-based TC for men, and *Crest*, a residential *work-release* center for both men and women. The concept of the Key, the primary stage of treatment, is modeled on the Stay'n Out program. This program differs from the others already discussed because of its *secondary* stage of treatment: a "transitional TC"—a TC work-release program. In this stage inmates who are near their release date are allowed to work for pay in the free community while spending their non-working time in the "family setting" similar to a traditional TC. Data from drug-involved offenders receiving the first two stages (prison-based TC followed by work-release TC) are surprisingly good. The research evaluation design contrasts the Key alone, Crest alone, the two combined—Key Crest—against no treatment other than HIV prevention education. The subjects are 81% male, 82% with prior drug treatment, 72% African American, mean age 29.6 years, first arrest at 17 years, and two previous incarcerations. Results after 18 months by treatment groups, controlling for other factors (e.g. days in treatment, follow-up time, previous times incarcerated), show highly positive outcomes in terms of both drug-free and arrest-free status. The percentage *drug-free* (Inciardi et al., 1997) were (see Table 11.8): Comparison, 35%; Key, 53%; Crest, 51%; and Key–Crest, 72%. The percentages *arrest-free* were (see Table 11.9): Comparison, 46%; Key, 43%; Crest, 57%, Key–Crest, 77%.

The results suggest the pattern of improvement with increasing exposure to the TC continuum is maintained after the six-month point, even after controlling for a number of potential covariates. The Crest and Key–Crest groups

Table 11.8 Key–Crest evaluation, Delaware: drug-free at 18-month follow-up by treatment group by 30-day self report and urinalysis

	Comparison		Key		Crest		Key Crest	
	n	%	n	%	n	%	n	%
Drug-free	19	35.0	13	53.0	58	51.0	19	72.0
Not drug-free	91	65.0	24	47.0	67	49.0	6	28.0
Total	124	100	24	100	129	100	38	100

Note: $p < 0.01$. Controlling for gender, race, age, prison history, treatment history, and previous drug use.

Table 11.9 Key Crest evaluation, Delaware: arrest-free since release at 18-month follow-up

	Comparison		Key		Crest		Key Crest	
	n	%	n	%	n	%	n	%
Not rearrested	83	46	16	43	102	57	33	77
Rearrested	97	54	21	57	77	43	10	23
Total	180	100	37	100	179	100	43	100

Note: $p < 0.05$. Controlling for gender, race, age, prison history, treatment history, and previous drug use.

are significantly more likely to be drug-free than the comparison group, but the Key group was not significantly different than the comparison (Inciardi et al., 1997).

The pattern of improvement with increasing exposure may be seen here as well. The outcome data support the relative improvement engendered by the work-release TC, rather than just an in-prison TC, but continue to indicate that the strongest and most consistent pattern of success comes from the group who receive the full continuum of TC treatment as seen in the results from Amity Prison TC Program and Stay'n Out. TC exposure at Key–Crest produced other benefits that can be seen in some additional 18-month outcome data.

These data include significant reductions in the use of injection drugs; in the amount of income from crime in the past year; and fewer returns to prison for new sentences among those who attended Crest compared with those who did not. Inciardi's robust findings, through the two stages of his research, are that length of time in treatment and the degree of involvement in treatment are important for success. Further, that even controlling for these influences, participation in the prison TC/work-release TC treatment continuum significantly improves outcome (Inciardi et al., 1997).

These studies, of the Amity Prison TC program, the Stay'n Out program, the Cornerstone program, and the Key–Crest program are the first large-scale research evaluations to provide solid evidence that prison-based TC treatment can produce significant reductions in recidivism rates among chronic drug abusing felons, *and to show consistency of such results over time.* This is not to say that prison-based TCs have not been successful before, but that formal evaluations meeting tight scientific standards have not been undertaken before publication of these studies.

Recent data from a still unfinished evaluation of the New Vision TC at Kyle Correctional Facility outside of Austin, Texas reveals this trend observed above to be continuing (Knight et al., 1997). This TC is unusual in that it is the first in a privatized facility. The Kyle establishment is run by the Wackenhut Corporation. Stay'n Out, whose leadership provided the training and some of the key staffing during the program design and early implementation phase, is the model for this TC. A matched-groups design was used in which inmates who went to the TC were compared to a group that was similar in demographic composition but did not receive in-prison treatment. Six-month and one-year, post-release, follow-up data were collected from face-to-face interviews, parole officers, biological assays (e.g. urine and hair tests) and official arrest records. Parolees who received in-prison TC treatment showed marked reductions in criminal activity and drug involvement in the following six months after release from prison. Treated inmates were less likely to be rearrested (7%) and more likely to be employed (88%) than parolees in the matched comparison group (arrested 16%, employed 78%) in the six months following release from prison. Of those treated 10% had a cocaine-positive urine screen compared with 22% of the comparison group six months after release. See Table 11.10 below which presents the data at

Table 11.10 New Vision TC in Kyle CF, Texas 1996: percentage reincarcerated at one-year follow-up (preliminary)

| | Reincarcerated | | | | | |
| | No treatment controls | | Program graduates | | Prog + aftercare graduates | |
	N	%	N	%	N	%
Not reincarcerated	50	**67**	158	**71**	119	**82**
Reincarcerated	25	**33**	64	**29**	26	**18**
Total	75	100	222	100	145	100

Note: P + A vs. No treatment Δ = 15% P + A vs. PG Δ = 11%.
Source: Simpson (personal communication, 1997).

one year post-release (Knight et al., 1997). As can be seen, the effect is somewhat attenuated but still significantly different in a favorable direction. Like the findings from the Donovan Amity and the Key–Crest programmes, the TC combined with aftercare produced the most marked success.

CONCLUSION

It is worthwhile noting that the success of this type of holistic treatment is due to dealing with the many factors impeding the return to responsible social functioning, and with the myriad problems associated with the lifestyle of crime and addiction—and is therefore more likely to be successful than treatment programs focusing mainly on one problem, however focal, such as drug abuse, or underlying psychic distress, or anger, or thinking errors. Therefore, it is essential that the treatment staff identify those factors that are likely to impel relapse to harmful conduct after release, what Andrews et al. (1990) call criminogenic factors, and plan how to address all of them.

The cost-effectiveness of the treatment supports its implementation even more. Programs like Stay'n Out cost about $3000 more than the annual correctional cost per inmate. The savings produced in crime-related and drug use-associated costs alone, however, repay the cost of the treatment in about two to three years. Moreover, the higher the investment in rehabilitating the most severe offender–addicts, the greater the probable impact. Substantial reductions in high-volume criminality immediately have an impact on the quality of life. Thus, with appropriate intervention applied for a sufficient duration, more than three out of four offenders will re-enter the community and lead a socially acceptable life. Moreover, the findings are relevant for more than drug offenders since a great many of the successful graduates of these programs in the United States had long histories of serious property crime and violent crime—this has important implications for the use of this modality for other than drug offenders. While it appears that few programs using other methods have been as successful, it is worthwhile noting that our comprehensive examination of the correctional intervention literature clearly shows that methods utilizing variations of the cognitive–behavioral approach produce mostly positive outcomes with offender populations (Lipton, Pearson, Cleland, Charles, & Yee, 1997; Pearson, Lipton, & Cleland, 1997).

REFERENCES

Andrews, D. A., Zinger, I., Hoge, R. D., Bonta, J., Gendreau, P., & Cullen, F. T. (1990). Does correctional treatment work? A clinically relevant and psychologically informed meta-analysis. *Criminology*, *28*, 369–404.

Anglin, M. D., & Maugh, T. H. (1992, February). *Overturning myths about coerced drug treatment*. Report from UCLA Drug Abuse Research Center.

Arbiter, N. (1992, June). *Presentation on the history of the therapeutic community by the clinical director, Naya Arbiter*. Tucson, AZ: Amity Foundation.

Briggs, D. (1972). Chino, California. In S. Whiteley et al. (Eds.), *Dealing with deviants* (pp. 95–171). London: Hogarth Press.

Condelli, W. S., & De Leon, G. (1993). Fixed and dynamic predictors of client retention in therapeutic communities. *Journal of Substance Abuse Treatment*, *10*, 11–16.

Cullen, E. (1993). The Grendon reconviction study, Part 1. *Prison Service Journal*, *90*, 35–37.

Cullen, E., Jones, L., & Woodward, R. (Eds.) (1997). *Therapeutic communities for offenders*. Chichester, UK: Wiley.

De Leon, G. (1994). Therapeutic communities. In M. Galanter & H. Kleber (Eds.), *The American psychiatric press textbook of substance abuse treatment*. Chicago, IL: American Psychiatric Press.

De Leon, G. (1995). Therapeutic communities for addictions: A theoretical framework. *International Journal of the Addictions*, *30*, 1603–1645.

De Leon, G., & Melnick, G. (1992). *Therapeutic community scale of essential elements questionnaire*. (Center for Therapeutic Community Research). NDRI, NY: Community Studies Institute.

Field, G. (1984). The cornerstone program: A client outcome study. *Federal Probation*, *48*, 50–55.

Field, G. (1989). A study of the effects of intensive treatment on reducing the criminal recidivism of addicted offenders. *Federal Probation*, *53*, 51–56.

Field, G. (1992). Oregon prison drug treatment programs. In C. G. Leukefeld & F. Tims (Eds.), *Drug abuse treatment in prisons and jails* (pp. 142–155) (NIDA Monograph No. 118). Washington, DC: USGPO.

George, R. (1971). *Grendon follow-up 1967–68* (Series A Rep. No. 47). Grendon Psychology Unit.

Gerstein, D. R., & Harwood, H. (Eds.) (1992). *Treating drug problems, Volume 2* (National Academy of Sciences, Institute of Medicine). Washington, DC: National Academy Press.

Gostin, L. (1991). Compulsory treatment for drug-dependent persons; Justifications for a public health approach to drug dependency. *The Milbank Quarterly*, *69*, 561–592.

Gunn, J., Robertson, G., & Dell, S. (1978). *Psychiatric aspects of imprisonment*. London: Academic Press.

Hollin, C. R. (1995). The meaning and implications of "programme integrity". In

J. McGuire (Ed.), *What works: Reducing reoffending—guidelines from research and practice*. Chichester, UK: Wiley.

Hubbard, R. L., Marsden, M. E., Rachel, J. V., Cavanaugh, E. R., & Ginzburg, H. M. (1989). *Drug abuse treatment: A national study of effectiveness*. Chapel Hill: University of North Carolina Press.

Inciardi, J. A., Martin, S. S., Butzin, C. F., Hooper, R. M., & Harrison, L. D. (1997). An effective model of prison-based treatment for drug-involved offenders. *Journal of Drug Issues, 27*, 261–278.

Jones, M. (1953). *The therapeutic community: A new treatment method in psychiatry*. New York: Basic Books.

Jones, M. (1962). *Social psychiatry in the community, in hospital and in prisons*. Springfield, IL: Charles C. Thomas.

Jones, M. (1968). *Social psychiatry in practice*. Harmondsworth, UK: Penguin Books.

Jones, M. (1979). The therapeutic community, social learning and social change (pp. 1–9). In R. D. Hinshelwood & N. Manning, *Therapeutic communities, reflections and progress*. London: Routledge & Kegan Paul.

Kennard, D. (1983). *An introduction to therapeutic communities*. London: Routledge & Kegan Paul.

Knight, K., Simpson, D. D., Chatham, L. R., & Camacho, L. M. (1997). An assessment of prison-based drug treatment: Texas" in-prison therapeutic community program. *Journal of Offender Rehabilitation, 24*, 75–100.

Leukefeld, C. G., & Tims, F. M. (Eds.) (1986). *Compulsory treatment for drug abuse: Research and clinical practice* (NIDA Research Monograph No. 86). Washington, DC: USGPO.

Lewis, B. F., & Ross, R. (1994). Retention in therapeutic communities: Challenge for the nineties. In F. M. Tims, G. De Leon, & N. Jainchill (Eds.), *Therapeutic community: Advances in research and application* (pp. 99–116) (NIDA Research Monograph No. 144). Washington, DC: USGPO.

Lipton, D. S. (1995). *The effectiveness of treatment for drug abusers under criminal justice supervision* (NIJ Research Report). Washington, DC: Department of Justice.

Lipton, D. S. (1996, February). Prison-based therapeutic communities: Their success with drug abusing offenders. *National Institute of Justice Journal* (Issue No. 230), 12–20.

Lipton, D. S., Pearson, F. S., Cleland, C., & Yee, D. (1997). *Synthesizing correctional treatment outcomes: Preliminary CDATE findings*. Paper presented at the annual National Institute of Justice Conference on Research and Evaluation in Criminal Justice, Washington, DC.

Main, T. (1946). The hospital as a therapeutic institution. *Bulletin of the Menninger Clinic, 10*, 66–70.

Marlatt, A., & Gordon, J. (1985). *Relapse prevention maintenance strategies in treatment of addictive disorders*. New York: Guilford.

Marshall, P. (1997). A reconviction study of HMP Grendon therapeutic community. *Home Office Research and Statistics Directorate, Research Findings No. 53*. London: Information and Publications Group.

Newton, M. (1973). Reconviction after treatment at Grendon (CP Report Series B, No. 1), London: Home Office, Prison Service.

Newton, M., & Thornton, D. (1994). Grendon re-conviction study, Part 1 update. Unpublished internal correspondence.

Pearson, F. S., Lipton, D. S., & Cleland, C. (1997). *Rehabilitative programs in adult corrections: CDATE meta-analyses*. Paper presented at the annual meeting of the American Society of Criminology, San Diego, CA.

Platt, J. J., Buhringer, G., Kaplan, C. D., Brown, B. S., & Taube, D. O. (1988). The prospects and limitations of compulsory treatment for drug addiction. *Journal of Drug Issues, 18*, 505–526.

Platt, J. J., Perry, G. M., & Metzger, D. S. (1980). The evolution of a heroin addiction treatment program within a correctional environment. In R. R. Ross & P. Gendreau (Eds.), *Effective correctional treatment*. Toronto, Canada: Butterworths.

Porporino, F. J., Fabiano, E. A., & Robinson, D. (1991). *Focusing on successful reintegration: Cognitive skills training for offenders* (Research Rep. No. 19). Ottawa, Canada: Correctional Service of Canada.

Preiser, P., Delaney, J., & Lipton, D. S. (1968). *Preliminary report of the governor's special committee on criminal offenders*. Albany, NY: State of New York.

Rawson, R. R., Obert, J. L., McCann, M. J., Smith, D. P., & Ling, W. (1990). Neurobehavioral treatment for cocaine dependency. *Journal of Psychoactive Drugs, 22*, 159–171.

Roberts, J. (1997). History of the therapeutic community. In E. Cullen, L. Jones, & R. Woodward (Eds.), *Therapeutic communities for offenders* (pp. 3–22). Chichester, UK: Wiley.

Robinson, D., Grossman, M., & Porporino, F. J. (1991). *Effectiveness of the cognitive skills training program: From pilot to national implementation*. Ottawa, Canada: Correctional Service of Canada.

Therapeutic Communities of America (1994). *Paradigms: Past, present and future*. Proceedings of the Therapeutic Communities of America 1992 Planning Conference, Chantilly, VA. Providence, RI: Manisses Communication Group.

Wexler, H. K. (1995). The success of therapeutic communities for substance abusers in American prisons. *Journal of Psychoactive Drugs, 27*(3), 57–66.

Wexler, H. K., De Leon, G., Thomas, G., Kressel, D., & Peters, J. (1999). The Amity prison TC evaluation: Reincarceration outcomes. *Criminal Justice and Behavior 26*, 147–167.

Wexler, H. K., Falkin, G. P., & Lipton, D. S. (1988). *A model prison rehabilitation program: An evaluation of the "Stay'n Out" therapeutic community*. Final Report to the National Institute on Drug Abuse. New York: Narcotic and Drug Research.

Wexler, H. K., Falkin, G. P., & Lipton, D. S. (1990). Outcome evaluation of a prison therapeutic community for substance abuse treatment. *Criminal Justice & Behavior, 17*, 71–92.

Wexler, H. K., Lipton, D. S., Falkin, G. P., & Rosenblum, A. (1992). Outcome evaluation of a prison therapeutic community for substance abuse treatment. In C. Leukefeld & F. Tims (Eds.), *Drug abuse treatment in prisons and jails* (pp. 156–175) (NIDA Monograph No. 118). Rockville, MD: NIDA.

Wish, E. D., & Gropper, B. (1990). Drug testing in the criminal justice system: Methods, research and applications. In M. J. Tonry & J. Q. Wilson (Eds.), *Drugs and Crime* (Crime & Justice Series, Vol. 13). Chicago, IL: University of Chicago Press.

Chapter 12

Programming in Cognitive Skills: The Reasoning and Rehabilitation Programme

David Robinson
and
Frank J. Porporino
T³ Associates, Ottawa, Canada

INTRODUCTION

The Reasoning and Rehabilitation programme, frequently referred to as *R&R* or *Cognitive Skills*, has become a popular correctional treatment intervention offered in a variety of settings in several countries. Since the mid 1980s the programme has been implemented quite broadly throughout Canada and the United States, and as well in England and Scotland, the Scandinavian countries, Spain, the Canary Islands, Germany, Australia, and New Zealand. In this chapter we outline the essential tenets of the R&R programme, including the theoretical and conceptual model on which it is based and the intervention techniques employed in delivering the programme. We then review existing research on the effectiveness of the programme.

First developed and tested with Canadian offender populations (Ross, Fabiano, & Ewles, 1988), R&R is a structured cognitive behavioural approach to facilitating change in offender behaviour. The approach focuses specifically on the thinking skills which guide (or fail to guide) the behaviour of offenders. It attempts to replace maladaptive and well-established thinking patterns with cognitive skills that promote pro-social behavioral choices. There is emphasis on teaching offenders to become more reflective rather than reactive, more anticipatory and planful in their responses to potential problems, and more generally

Handbook of Offender Assessment and Treatment. Edited by C. R. Hollin.

flexible, open-minded, reasoned, and deliberate in their thinking. Using step-by-step instruction and purposeful repetition, skills-building is sequenced and refined as the programme unfolds, and skills-use is integrated and made relevant with concrete examples from offenders' lives. Application of skills is encouraged through constant use of modelling and reinforcement techniques. However, the programme's underlying philosophy is that offenders should be given "choice" to apply the skills they learn. They are told to see one of their pockets as filled with their "old" skills. The programme will attempt to fill their other pocket with "new" skills. They will then have the choice of which pocket they wish to draw from in negotiating problems or conflicts in their lives. In this fashion, the programmme attempts to motivate offenders subtly rather than confrontationally.

The programme focuses on the "how" of thinking. A key concept that has become associated with R&R is that offenders are taught "how" to think, not "what" to think. Another way of saying this is that they are taught the "process" of thinking before attempting to redirect the "content' of their thinking. In this context the term "skill" has been applied to the notion of thinking. The process of learning new methods of thinking, which is most frequently manifested in improved problem-solving skills, allows broad generalization of the skills to a variety of typical living situations involving choices that might lead to pro-social or anti-social outcomes (Fabiano, Porporino, & Robinson, 1990).

The supposition that offenders lack some of the thinking skills necessary for pro-social adaptation is based on a body of empirical evidence drawn from both juvenile and adult offender samples (Ross & Fabiano, 1985; Zamble & Porporino, 1988). For example, in their review of literature, Ross and Fabiano (1985) found a number of studies indicating that thinking processes affect social perceptions and that inter-personal relationships are different across offender and non-offender samples. For example, the evidence presented suggested that many offenders have the propensity to act quickly before thinking, failing to consider the circumstances and emotions of other persons in their choices, and showing cognitive rigidity in their approaches to solving problems. A critical deficit area concerns offender attributions regarding the intentions and actions of other persons. A good example of this phenomenon is illustrated in the work of Dodge and Frame (1982). In contrast to non-aggressive boys, they showed that aggressive boys tend to attribute hostile intent to the ambiguous actions of others. In terms of more general problem-solving deficits that may be linked to thinking skills, Zamble and Porporino (1988) described numerous deficits in the way their sample of incarcerated men solved everyday problems. Their problem-solving was characterized by unsystematic methods that often tended to exacerbate problems, more palliative rather than problem-oriented coping, and a general lack of planful or pro-active behaviour.

According to the theory on which the R&R is based, the skill deficits described above are viewed as playing a role in the onset of criminality and are highly instrumental in the maintenance of offending behaviour. In addition, these skill deficits are viewed as amenable targets of change when addressed using social-learning-based interventions. Again drawing from social learning theory, the model proposes that for many offenders the cognitive skills needed for pro-social adjustment are not acquired as part of the usual socialization process in childhood. Temperamental qualities that can lead to generalized conduct disorder and the early emergence of aggressivity place these individuals particularly at risk. Conceivably, a broad range of skill deficits develops because of the absence of appropriate adult models or the presence of poor parenting practices associated with reinforcement of pro-social skills through childhood and adolescence. Early school failure and delinquent peer-group influence further strengthen an anti-social developmental pattern. At the same time, the R&R approach is based on the assumption that essential skills can be newly acquired or relearned through structured interventions at a later time in adolescence or adulthood. Hence, the programme combines direct training and pro-social modelling techniques to address the skill deficits. The programme also helps offenders to learn to generalize the skills to a variety of situations which have the potential for criminal outcomes when the skills are not applied.

CONTENT OF THE PROGRAMME

The principal targets for the programme include self-control (e.g. thinking before acting), inter-personal problem-solving skills (e.g. early recognition of problems, ability to examine alternatives, assess consequences and interpersonal goals and respond appropriately), social perspective-taking (e.g. acknowledging that the behaviour of others has an impact on ourselves and that there are consequences of one's behavioural choices for other persons), critical reasoning (e.g. evaluating ideas objectively and considering a variety of sources of information in the process of decision-making), cognitive style (e.g. becoming less rigid and narrow in one's thinking and less prone to externalize blame) and values (e.g. acknowledge values that govern one's behaviour and learning to identify inconsistencies between what we believe and how we behave). The R&R programme is delivered in a series of 36 two-hour sessions which are designed to build thinking or "cognitive" skills in a progressive manner but are also designed to move offenders through stages of change—from accepting the existence of problems, decision-making about choices, taking action, maintaining new behaviours, and preventing relapse through learning to monitor and self-correct thinking in new situations. Normally, the programme is delivered to appropriately selected groups of 6–12 participants.

Throughout the 36-session curriculum, there is a consistency in focusing on skills acquisition in all programme content. Programme delivery staff are viewed as "trainers" or "coaches" who teach the requisite skills to the offenders. R&R is multi-modal in that it exposes offenders to a variety of techniques in acquiring the skills. These techniques include role-playing, dilemma games, cognitive exercises (e.g. cognitive puzzles), board games aimed at examining values, and other methods aimed at gaining and maintaining the attention of the participants.

Maximum use is made of the groups setting to break participants into dyads and triads to complete various exercises. Coaches also combine a variety of visual techniques to cover the didactic components of the curriculum, including pictures, posters, overhead transparencies, flip charts, and chalk boards.

Practice and repetition are also important components of the skill acquisition process within the programme. Participants learn many of the social skills which are based on the work of Goldstein (1988) through repeated rehearsal using video-taped feedback to perfect their performance of the skill. Content presented in the programme is frequently repeated and participants are often exposed to rapid reviews of previous material before the introduction of new content. In addition, the importance of memory in learning has been used in the R&R programme through the presentation of skills in a series of steps which participants are encouraged to memorize so that they can easily produce the required behaviours when various situations emerge which call for the performance of the skills. Techniques are used to help students develop memory devices and many of the skills have easily memorized acronyms to assist participant recall. For example, DeBono's (1982) creative thinking skills are employed within the programme to assist offenders in problem-solving. Each skill has a clever acronym (e.g. CAF—Consider All Factors) which participants can easily retrieve when the skill is indicated.

A variety of learning techniques have been purposely integrated within the curriculum of the programme. This approach to the design of the programme was intended to keep skill-learners stimulated, but also to ensure that the diversity of learning styles observed within offender populations is represented. The programme was intended to be delivered at a steady and rather rapid pace. Programme coaches should refrain from lecturing or instructing. Rather, they are trained to teach "Socratically"; not to tell but to elicit answers by asking questions. Ultimate mastery in the delivery of R&R implies that coaches must constantly attend to the diversity of learning styles and ensure that each individual participant is motivated by and able to grasp the material.

The programme is not simply didactic in focus but also incorporates a number of principles of guided discovery whereby participants must pose and answer questions as they master the content. The programme devotes considerable time to problem-solving skills. In learning thinking skills for problem-solving, participants must learn to question in a critical fashion. They must also learn tools of analysis which they can use to make judgements about various pieces of information and choose the best course of action when it is time to make decisions. In teaching problem-solving, R&R coaches provide information on the various steps that must be taken before decision-making is possible. However, they must also use the material generated by the offenders (e.g. problem situations) to guide them through the various steps required to solve a problem. During the training, coaches learn that they must resist the temptation to specify the correct solutions to problems. Rather, they assist the participants in arriving at the best solutions by helping them apply the various cognitive skills covered in the curriculum.

PROGRAMME DELIVERERS

While coaches use their own problem-solving examples and encourage the offender participants to offer scenarios for problem-solving practice, the programme is highly structured. The detailed programme manual guides coaches through the various sessions in a carefully ordered sequence. The programme was not designed to be delivered solely by highly trained professional therapists. In fact, programme coaches are frequently drawn from correctional officer, probation officer, and case management officer ranks within correctional jurisdictions. The possession of the cognitive skills covered in the programme is a key criteria used in selecting coaches. In addition, good rapport with offenders, the ability to manage group situations, and a degree of discipline, flexibility, attentiveness, and exuberance are characteristics of individuals who will become successful coaches. The use of line level correctional staff is a conscious programme implementation principle for many jurisdictions. A benefit of this approach is that support for the objectives of the programme can be more easily obtained when staff from all levels of the correctional setting have ownership and understanding of the programme principles. In this way, line staff can begin to encourage other line staff to support and reinforce the progress of offenders in acquiring the programme skills.

Rather than therapy, R&R is a training programme. While para-professionals are most often used to deliver the curriculum, they must complete an intensive training programme before delivering the programme. Coach preparation consists of at least one week of formal training which includes practicing delivery techniques before trainers and other trainees, and feedback on delivery style and mastery of the programme materials. Following training, new coaches are monitored using video-tapes of their programme sessions and follow-up training assists the coaches to refine their delivery in areas of weakness. A programme of coach certification is regarded as the key to maintaining a high-quality programme delivery system for R&R.

R&R places considerable emphasis on coach training, careful implementation of programme principles, and the ongoing integrity of programme delivery. While the manual is helpful, coaches must prepare each two-hour session in advance so that they are familiar with all the exercises in the session and ready to instil confidence among participants in the content of the programme. The preparation includes set-up of materials and generation of examples or scenarios that are appropriate for the particular group being trained. The programme is not easily "done-on-the-fly", without a full understanding of the sequencing of skills learned and the interdependence between the various programme components. During the training, neophyte coaches receive instruction on each session within the 36-session curriculum. They learn to deal with questions from participants in each of the key areas of the programme. Coaches are also exposed to the group management techniques that are necessary to lead groups of 6–12 participants.

RESEARCH

From its first development, adherents of R&R have emphasized the necessity of research-based knowledge for programme development in corrections. As alluded to above, the selection of the major targets of the programme was based on a review of research on cognitive correlates of criminal behaviour (Ross & Fabiano, 1985). Recently, there have been a number of meta-analyses suggesting that programmes based on cognitive behavioural principles are most promising in treating criminal offenders (Andrews et al., 1990; Izzo & Ross, 1990; Lipsey 1995; Lösel, 1995). The conclusions of these studies have found further empirical support from the preliminary results of the most ambitious meta-analytic review undertaken to date by Lipton and his colleagues (Lipton, Pearson, Cleland & Yee, 1998). Based on more than 900 treatment studies with offender populations, their data suggest that programmes borrowing from cognitive behavioural approaches appear to be more effective than programmes based on alternative models.

Cognitive-based approaches are now quickly becoming the fashion in corrections and criminal justice. However, it is the particular design, and the mode of delivery of a cognitive intervention, that will determine its effectiveness. Regardless of how they are labelled, all programmes should therefore pass the litmus test of controlled research.

There has been considerable commitment by proponents of the R&R to subject the programme to empirical investigations. In particular, there has been an interest in assessing the impact of R&R on participants' post-programme recidivism. In this chapter we concentrate on the research which addresses the impact on recidivism. However, we also draw attention to some studies which have examined more intermediate programme outcomes such as changes in attitudes and indicators of client satisfaction. In our review of the research we examine studies conducted on different offender populations, including adults, juveniles, substance abusers, and mentally disordered offenders.

Adult Offenders

The earliest study conducted on the R&R programme was reported by Ross et al. (1988). At the time of their study they commented that the research represented an "experimental project designed to assess the efficacy of an unorthodox treatment" (p. 29) for high-risk adult probationers. Known as the "Pickering Experiment", the study compared post-programme outcomes of probationers who had been exposed to R&R with the outcomes of a group of offenders who had received "life skills", and a third group of regular probation clients. The offenders ($n = 62$) were all randomly assigned to the three comparison groups. The R&R group showed far superior outcomes than the other two groups in terms of recidivism. For example, only 18.1% of the R&R probationers recidivated compared with 47.5% in the life skills and 69.5% in the regular probation group. In addition, none of the R&R offenders was incarcerated in comparison with 11% of the life skills and 30% of the regular probation groups. Therefore, although the sample size was modest, the first experimental assessment of the effectiveness of the R&R was highly positive.

A series of larger studies on the efficacy of R&R for adult offenders was conducted by researchers at Correctional Service Canada (CSC), where the programme was nationally implemented with Canadian federal offenders. In the Canadian federal system the programme has come to be known as Cognitive Skills Training. For the most part these studies were conducted by the current authors and our colleagues (Fabiano, Robinson & Porporino, 1990; Porporino & Robinson, 1995; Robinson, 1995; Robinson, Grossman & Porporino, 1991) and we relied generally on samples of offenders who had received the programme while they were incarcerated. However, a smaller sub-sample of offenders also had received the programme in community settings.

The introduction of the R&R programme with Canadian federal offenders[1] represented a massive implementation strategy and, in many senses, the strategy has been used as a model by other jurisdictions. The implementation included a commitment to providing resources for delivering the programme across the country in both institutional and community sites. In addition, field staff were given awareness training so that they could support the implementation of the programme. Methods for carefully selecting offenders with the cognitive deficits targeted by the programme were also put in place. Importantly, a large-scale research and evaluation component was included that would provide for an assessment of programme efficacy and ongoing monitoring of programme integrity.

The first research to be reported on CSC's implementation of the programme involved pilot data from initial runs of the programme carried out in 1989 in four sites (Fabiano, Robinson, & Porporino, 1990). Based on a sample of 50 treated offenders and 26 waiting-list comparison offenders, the data provided good evidence that the programme was being targeted to high-risk offenders. Moreover, after 18-month post-release follow-up, there was evidence that the treated group was less likely to be reconvicted (20%) than the comparison group (30.4%). The results remained stable after the initial follow-up was extended for a longer period (mean follow-up = 32.1 months) (Porporino & Robinson, 1995). By this time the overall base rate of recidivism had increased (61%), reflecting the high-risk nature of the treated federal offenders. Of the comparison offenders 70% had been reincarcerated over the follow-up period compared with 57% of the treated group. In addition, the treatment effect appeared to be more marked when official reconvictions were used as the criteria of recidivism, a finding that has been confirmed in several samples with this population of treated offenders. In total, 55% of the comparison group had been reconvicted during follow-up

---

[1] In Canada, offenders who have been sentenced to incarceration for two years or more are under federal jurisdiction. All other offenders are under provincial jurisdictions.

compared with 35% among the offenders who had completed R&R. The difference represented a 36.4% reduction in recidivism for the R&R group. Hence, as the implementation of the programme grew in federal corrections in Canada, the data provided considerable optimism about the efficacy of the programme with high-risk offenders.

In addition to the recidivism data reported for the Canadian pilot study, there was also evidence that the offenders had made positive gains on programme relevant targets as assessed through a number of pre-test/post-test measures (Fabiano, Robinson, & Porporino, 1990). These gains included social perspective-taking, conceptual complexity, generation of solutions to inter-personal conflicts, attitudes toward the law, courts, and police, less tolerance for law violations, and less identification with criminal others. Client satisfaction responses provided by R&R participants also indicated favourable assessment of the programme's ability to assist them with problem-solving, inter-personal relationships, goal setting, controlling anger and other emotions, and handling stress.

The most ambitious effort to assess the effectiveness of the R&R programme was based on a sample of more than 4000 Canadian federal offenders who had completed the programme between 1989 and 1994 (Robinson, 1995). A sub-sample of released offenders ($n = 2125$) had been followed up for a minimum of one year, including 1444 programme completers and 379 offenders who were randomly assigned to a waiting list control group and had never been exposed to the programme. In addition, the follow-up sample included 302 offenders who had terminated their participation in the programme before completion.

As the implementation of the programme proceeded, it became increasingly difficult for the researchers to maintain field commitment to randomly assigning offenders to the waiting list control group. For this reason, the control group failed to grow to a size that was comparable to the treatment group. Nevertheless, the control group size ($n = 379$) remained sufficiently large to allow for a number of tests of moderating variables to identify offender characteristics that were most predictive of positive treatment outcomes. The control group, although differing slightly on some characteristics when compared with treated offenders (e.g. sentence length, frequency of non-violent property offences), was methodologically suitable for conducting controlled comparisons of outcomes. Because of the sample size, minor differences between the two groups could be statistically controlled in most analyses to ensure that treatment effects were not resulting due to the non-equivalence of groups.

The overall base rate of recidivism for the sample remained high as had been observed in the earlier pilot results, a finding that confirmed the high-risk nature of the population under treatment. Among waiting list control group members, 50.1% were readmitted to custody compared with 44.5% among offenders who had completed R&R—a reduction in recidivism of 11.2%. The readmission rate was higher for programme dropouts (58.2%). However, trends showing a positive effect of treatment remained even when the dropouts were included in some of the recidivism analysis. As observed in the pilot study, the impact of the programme appeared to be greatest for official reconvictions (24.8% among controls versus 19.7% among R&R participants). Hence, there was a 20% reduction in new reconvictions associated with programme participation during the first year after release.

As noted above, the CSC sample was sufficiently large to examine a variety of treatment moderator variables. Of particular interest were tests of differential treatment outcome for groups differing on risk for recidivism. The programme implementation model specified that R&R was intended for offenders who possessed the cognitive deficits targeted by the programme and participants should generally be drawn from offenders who were at higher risk for poor outcomes following release. Implementation of the programme by CSC attempted to follow the "risk principle" (see Andrews, Bonta, & Hoge, 1990) for selecting candidates to participate in the programme. This approach recognized that lower risk offenders were less likely to recidivate and would therefore receive no benefits from participating in an intensive intervention such as the R&R programme.

A simple actuarial measure based on criminal history indicators (e.g. previous federal admission, failure while under community supervision, history of property offences, robbery, and young age at admission) was used to divide the R&R sample into "low-" and "high-" risk groups. However, even the low-risk portion of the sample demonstrated relatively high rates of recidivism (36.2% versus 58.2% among high-risk offenders). Somewhat unexpectedly, the programme showed greater efficacy with the lower risk participants. For example, there was a 34.2% reduction in reconvictions associated with participation in R&R among low-risk offenders compared with no reduction in reconvictions among high-risk offenders.

Initially, the findings appeared to contradict the risk principle hypothesis that the R&R programme would be most effective with higher risk cases. However, the results were viewed as more consistent with the risk principle when it was considered that even the so-called "low-" risk cases from this sample returned to prison at relatively high rates. In addition, all of the programme participants had been screened into the programme using selection criteria that ensured that candidates were high need with respect to interventions to develop cognitive skills. In Canada, federal offenders generally present a profile of higher risk and need than offenders under provincial jurisdiction (Robinson, Porporino, Millson, Trevethan, & MacKillop, 1998). Andrews et al. (1990) argued that medium- to high-risk offenders are likely to benefit most from treatment. In examining the full spectrum of risk of Canadian offenders, it was assumed that the so-called "low-" risk cases in the CSC sample actually fall toward the higher end of the risk continuum. Hence, the lower risk CSC cases which responded to the R&R intervention might be described more accurately as medium- to high-risk offenders. The higher risk offenders, for whom no programme effect was produced, are likely to be at the extreme end of the risk continuum representing correctional clientele who are most resistant to treatment.

Another important finding from the 1995 CSC study was that offenders who were exposed to the R&R programme in community settings appeared to benefit more from the intervention than those who had been treated while incarcerated.

A 66.3% reduction in new convictions was observed for offenders treated in the community compared with a 16.2% reduction among those from institutional programmes. While the effect for those treated in institutional programmes could not be dismissed, the data suggested that continued efforts should be made to expand delivery of R&R in community sites. It was also discovered that the higher risk CSC cases, when exposed to the programme in a community, rather than institutional, setting, also benefited from participation. Hence, the data suggested that more resistant clients may benefit when their exposure to the R&R was combined with community supervision.

There were also differential programme effects observed across offence type in the CSC sample. Specifically, in the controlled comparisons offenders with violent, sexual, and drug offences benefited from programme participation to a greater extent than property offenders (e.g. break and enter, and robbery). This effect was partly due to the finding that the highest risk cases were less responsive to the intervention. The property offender group tended to be particularly high in risk for recidivism when compared with offenders with other types of offences. This phenomenon is typical of federally sentenced property offenders in Canada.

Controlled outcome comparisons have also been reported for adult offenders who received the R&R programme while on probation in Britain. The Mid-Glamorgan Experiment, reported by Raynor and Vanstone (1996), compared follow-up results for probationers who had received the R&R programme (referred to as Straight Thinking on Probation, STOP, $n = 107$) with results for offenders who had received a variety of other correctional dispositions, including regular probation and incarceration ($n = 548$). Using an actuarial prediction device to predict reconvictions, Raynor and Vanstone found lower than predicted reconviction rates after 12 months of follow-up (35% versus 42% predicted) for completers of the STOP programme. Offenders with other dispositions (e.g. incarceration, other probation) tended to have similar or higher rates of reconviction when their actual rates were compared with predicted rates. However, the STOP participants failed to show reductions on recidivism when the follow-up period was extended from 12 months to 24 months.

An interesting finding from the Mid-Glamorgan Experiment concerned more pronounced impacts of participating in STOP when offence type and disposition for reconvictions were examined. Compared with the combined sample of offenders who had received custodial sentences, those who had completed the R&R intervention while on probation were much less likely to have a serious offence (8%) than those who had been incarcerated (21%). The more positive effects favouring STOP participation were limited to the 12-month follow-up period and were not observed at the 24-month follow-up point. Another finding concerned an apparent impact of programme participation on judicial dispositions whereby a negligible number of STOP participants (2%) received custodial sentences upon reconviction in comparison with those who had been initially incarcerated (15%).

Juvenile Offenders

The efficacy of the R&R programme has also been tested using juvenile offender populations. One of the first studies to evaluate the programme with juveniles was conducted in Spain (Garrido & Sanchis, 1991). Although the sample size was small (R&R group, $n = 14$; control group, $n = 17$), the study provided preliminary evidence that the programme could produce beneficial results with incarcerated juvenile populations. The authors noted that the control group, which was recruited from alternative custodial centres, presented an overall lower risk profile than the group that had received the programme. However, the R&R subjects improved to a greater extent on a number of measures designed to operationalize the targets used in the programme (e.g. role-taking, problem-solving). The authors also noted that compared with the control group, the experimental group also demonstrated behavioural improvements as measured by staff ratings on a number of dimensions (e.g. social withdrawal, obsessive–compulsive, self-destruction, inattention, aggressive familial relationships).

A second study based on a sample of incarcerated juvenile offenders was reported from the state of Georgia in the United States (Murphy & Bauer, 1996) The recidivism follow-up was based on a sample of 33 offenders who had received the R&R programme and 16 "control" offenders who were "randomly selected" but did not participate in the programme. While the method of random selection was not described, the authors noted that the treatment group tended to have somewhat higher risk characteristics than the controls. After a mean follow-up period of 16 months, 39% of the R&R offenders had been rearrested compared with 75% of the comparison group. Of those who were rearrested, only 67% of the treated juveniles were convicted compared with 83% of the comparison group. The study also included a number of pre-test/post-test measures of programme-relevant targets. Generally, the psychometric data, which included behavioural ratings completed by staff, indicated more positive scores following participation for the R&R group and superior performance relative to the comparison group.

A final study on juvenile offenders was reported by Pullen (1996) and described an intervention used in the context of juvenile intensive probation supervision in the state of Colorado. Unfortunately, the process evaluation of the R&R programme indicated that implementation procedures were lacking in many respects and the author noted that many of the programme delivery staff failed adequately to prepare to deliver the training. The researcher compared pre-test/post-test results for a group of 20 juvenile probationers who were randomly assigned to R&R with 20 probationers who were randomly assigned to a control group. Perhaps as a function of the poor implementation procedures, the data provided only limited evidence of improvement in pre-test/post-test scores on various cognitive measures. In addition, there was little evidence of an impact of programme participation on recidivism. Overall, 50% of the R&R offenders recidivated during supervision compared with 35% among the controls. On the other hand, the rates for post-supervision recidivism were 20% for the R&R group and 25% for the control group.

Substance Abusing Offenders

R&R outcome data from two samples based on substance abusing offenders have been reported. Generally, the data suggests that the R&R programme, when combined with other substance abuse treatment has beneficial recidivism reduction effects. In addition, in one study, the effect of R&R participation was as promising when delivered on its own as was a competing treatment intervention that focused specifically on substance abuse.

The National Council on Crime and Delinquency (NCCD) (Austin, 1997) evaluated the implementation of the R&R programme ($n = 70$) along with a multi-phase drug treatment approach ($n = 65$) by the Northern District of California Probation Service. The latter programme, referred to as the Drug After-care Programme (DAC) included urinalysis, psycho-social assessment, drug counselling, and treatment planning. The efficacy of the two approaches was compared with respect to programme implementation and outcome using a random assignment design. The NCCD was critical of the implementation procedures that were used for the R&R programme, noting that delivery staff did not consistently follow the programme procedures and that there was insufficient implementation support within the programme environment. Despite the lack of integrity in the implementation of R&R in this setting, programme participants were slightly less likely to be arrested (25.3%) during the follow-up than those receiving the DAC (32.3%) intervention. In addition, the report concluded that the R&R programme was most cost-effective in that the per-capita cost of delivering the intervention was less than the cost associated with the alternative drug treatment approach.

A second study focusing on assessing the efficacy of the R&R programme with substance abusing offenders was conducted in Colorado using a randomized experimental method (Johnson & Hunter, 1995). The study compared three groups: regular probation service ($n = 36$); specialized drug offender programme (SDOP) ($n = 51$); and SDOP + R&R ($n = 47$). The SDOP and SDOP + R&R yielded considerable reductions in recidivism when compared against the regular probation condition. In total, 41.7% of regular probationers were revoked compared with 29.4% among SDOP probationers and 25.5% among SDOP + R&R probationers. While the R&R probationers performed only marginally better than the SDOP probationers, offenders who had the most severe drug/alcohol problems appeared to benefit to a much greater extent when exposed to the R&R enhancement of the SDOP. Only 18% of this group were revoked compared with 43% among SDOP probationers and 60% among regular service probationers. There was also evidence that probationers who had received the R&R programme achieved more positive results on a variety of pre-test/post-test measures such as empathy, problem-solving, anti-criminal attitudes, and other targets of cognitive skill training.

Mentally Disordered Offenders

There has been some interest in use of the R&R programme for treating mentally disordered offenders. The programme has been implemented with such populations in the state of New York in the United State and in Germany. A post-programme client satisfaction study was conducted at a forensic psychiatric facility in New York city in order to provide information about how offenders perceived the utility of such programmes (Otis, 1997). Although the sample size was small ($n = 12$), the patients were very positive about their experience in completing the R&R programme. The majority of patients believed that the programme was easy to understand and enjoyable and most indicated that they would recommend the programme to other patients. The efficacy of the programme with this type of offender population awaits empirical investigation.

CONCLUSIONS

The R&R programme is based on a well-defined set of theoretical principles which provide explanations of the link between programme targets and criminal behaviour. The programme is skill-based and stresses the "training" approach that is used to help offenders acquire the thinking skills necessary to obtain pro-social adjustment. The programme is highly structured and programme developers have placed considerable emphasis on effective implementation strategies. Because of the high degree of structure characterizing programme delivery, the programme is highly replicable across sites and para-professional staff can master the techniques for programme delivery given motivation and a base of cognitive skills. The manual and training for the programme provide instructions about the optimal conditions that should be achieved before delivering the programme. This not only includes adequate preparation of materials by programme delivery staff, but also a network of support for the principles of the programme within the correctional setting where R&R is being implemented.

The research reviewed above does not include all of the studies that have been conducted on the programme to date. There are now on-going studies in Sweden, Norway, Finland, and a number of state jurisdictions in the United States. However, the available body of literature on this specific approach to the rehabilitation of criminal offenders suggests that the programme can produce beneficial effects for many groups of offenders. Ideally, the programme is suited to offenders who are at medium to high risk of recidivism and exhibit deficits in the various cognitive skills that are included in the programme. Evidence for effectiveness with high-risk adult offenders, substance abusing offenders, and juveniles is available from the studies conducted to date. As the numbers of offenders who have completed the R&R programme increase, researchers should turn their attention to identifying which offenders appear to benefit most from the programme, and which staff are most effective in delivering this kind of structured cognitive intervention.

The content of the programme covers a broad range of cognitive skills which are not only applicable to offenders, but may be important for a number of categories of individuals who are at high risk for negative social outcomes. In most jurisdictions where R&R has been used, the explicit objective of the intervention is to reduce recidivism among adjudicated offenders. An adaptation of the approach is also now being used as a delinquency prevention programme with adolescent age schoolchildren in Norway. In the most recent adaptation, the R&R principles are being used with an intervention designed to teach chronically "unemployable" individuals the requisite skills for securing and maintaining employment.

REFERENCES

Andrews, D. A., Bonta, J., & Hoge, R. D. (1990). Classification for effective rehabilitation: Rediscovering psychology. *Criminal Justice and Behavior, 17*, 19–52.

Andrews, D. A., Zinger, I., Hoge, R. D., Bonta, J., Gendreau, P., & Cullen, F. T. (1990). Does correctional treatment work? A clinically relevant and psychologically informed meta-analysis. *Criminology, 28*, 369–404.

Austin, J. (1997). *Evaluation of the drug aftercare program and the reasoning and rehabilitation program in California probation.* Unpublished manuscript. Washington DC: National Council on Crime and Delinquency.

DeBono, E. (1982). *DeBono's thinking course.* London: BBC Books.

Dodge, K. A., & Frame, C. L. (1982). Social cognitive biases and deficits in aggressive boys. *Child Development, 53*, 620–635.

Fabiano, E. A., Porporino, F. J., & Robinson, D. (1990). *Rehabilitation through clearer thinking: A cognitive model of correctional intervention, R-04.* Ottawa, Canada: Correctional Service Canada.

Fabiano, E., Robinson, D., & Porporino, F. (1990). *A preliminary assessment of the cognitive skills training programme: A component of living skills programming. Programme description, research findings and implementation strategy.* Ottawa, Canada: Correctional Service Canada.

Garrido, V., & Sanchis, J. R. (1991). The cognitive model in the treatment of Spanish offenders: Theory and practice. *Journal of Correctional Education, 42*, 111–118.

Goldstein, A. (1988). *The prepare curriculum: Teaching prosocial competencies.* Champaign, IL: Research Press.

Izzo, R. L., & Ross, R. R. (1990). Meta-analysis of rehabilitation programmes for juvenile delinquents: A brief report. *Criminal Justice and Behavior, 17*, 134–142.

Johnson, G., & Hunter, R. M. (1995). Evaluation of the specialized drug offender program. In R. R. Ross & R. D. Ross (Eds.), *Thinking straight: The reasoning and rehabilitation programme for delinquency prevention and offender rehabilitation* (pp. 215–234). Ottawa, Canada: AIR.

Lipsey, M. W. (1995). What do we learn from 400 research studies on the effectiveness of treatment with juvenile delinquents? In J. McGuire (Ed.), *What works: Reducing reoffending—Guidelines from research and practice* (pp. 63–78). Chichester, UK: Wiley.

Lipton, D. S., Pearson, F. S., Cleland, C., & Yee, D. (1998). *How do cognitive skills training programmes for offenders compare with other modalities: A meta-Analytic perspective.* Presented at the Stop and Think Conference, Her Majesty's Prison Service, York, UK.

Lösel, F. (1995). The efficacy of correctional treatment: A review and synthesis of meta-evaluations. In J. McGuire (Ed.), *What works: Reducing reoffending—Guidelines from research and practice* (pp. 79–111). Chichester, UK: Wiley.

Murphy, R., & Bauer, R. (1996). *Evaluating the effectiveness of a cognitive skills training programme for juvenile delinquents.* (Unpublished Manuscript) Georgia: Valdosta State University.

Otis, D. (1997). *Kirby Forensic Psychiatric Center Patient Satisfaction of the Cognitive Skills Programme: A Formative Evaluation.* Unpublished Manuscript. New York: Kirby Forensic Psychiatric Center.

Porporino, F. J., & Robinson, D. (1995). An evaluation of the reasoning and rehabilitation programme with Canadian federal offenders. In R. R. Ross & R. D. Ross (Eds.), *Thinking straight: The reasoning and rehabilitation programme for delinquency prevention and offender rehabilitation* (pp. 155–191). Ottawa, Canada: AIR.

Pullen, S. (1996). *Evaluation of the reasoning and rehabilitation cognitive skills development programme as implemented in juvenile ISP in Colorado.* Unpublished Report. Denver, CO: Colorado Division of Criminal Justice.

Raynor, P., & Vanstone, M. (1996). Reasoning and rehabilitation in Britain: The results of the straight thinking on probation (STOP) programme. *International Journal of Offender Therapy and Comparative Criminology, 40,* 272–284.

Robinson, D. (1995). *The impact of cognitive skills training on post-release recidivism among Canadian federal offenders.* No. R-41. Research Branch). Ottawa, Canada: Correctional Service Canada.

Robinson, D., Grossman, M., & Porporino, F. J. (1991). *Effectiveness of the cognitive skills training programme: From pilot to national implementation, B-07.* Ottawa, Canada: Correctional Service Canada.

Robinson, D., Porporino, F. J., Millson, W. A., Trevethan, S., & MacKillop, B. (1998). *A one-day snapshot of inmates in Canada's adult correctional facilities* (Juristat, Vol. 18, no 8). Ottawa, Canada: Canadian Centre for Justice Statistics, Statistics Canada.

Ross, R. R., & Fabiano, E. A. (1985). *Time to think. A cognitive model of delinquency prevention and offender rehabilitation.* Johnson City, TN: Institute of Social Sciences and Arts.

Ross, R. R., Fabiano, E. A., & Ewles, C. D. (1988). Reasoning and Rehabilitation. *International Journal of Offender Therapy and Comparative Criminology, 32,* 29–36.

Zamble, E., & Porporino, F. (1988). *Coping, behaviour, and adaptation in prison inmates.* New York: Springer-Verlag.

Chapter 13

Intensive Supervision in Probation and Parole Settings

Paul Gendreau[1]
Claire Goggin
*University of New Brunswick, Saint John, New Brunswick,
Canada*
and
Betsy Fulton
University of Cincinnati, Ohio, USA

INTRODUCTION

In the authors' view, a potent miasma has infected probation and parole (P/P) services during the last decade, especially in North America. Panaceaphilia (See Gendreau & Ross, 1979), a longstanding problem in corrections, is still alive and well as evidenced by the transient popularity of various quick fix solutions (e.g. scared straight, electric monitoring, etc.) that have recently been proposed to reform offenders. Probation and parole, at times, seem to be operating in an aimless, muddle-headed fashion.

In order to understand why this state of affairs exists we will first engage in a primitive archaeological exercise by examining the traces of an earlier civilization of P/P services and what it had to say about offender reformation. Later, we present some new evidence that unequivocally addresses the issue of whether anything is working in P/P settings in the 1990s.

---

[1] Interested readers can obtain further information on the issues raised in this chapter by contacting the first author at the University of New Brunswick, P.O. Box 5050, Saint John, New Brunswick, Canada, E2L 4L5, fax #: 506-648-5780.

Handbook of Offender Assessment and Treatment. Edited by C. R. Hollin.
© 2000 John Wiley & Sons Ltd.

ANOTHER ERA

At one time, P/P had a strong rehabilitative mandate (Gendreau, Paparozzi, Little, & Goddard, 1993). Let us not, however, be naïve about the "good old days" of the 1950s to 1970s. While the *Zeitgeist* may have been favourable, the quality of the programming in the community was suspect in part due to a sparse knowledge base and the absence of training opportunities for corrections personnel to learn about beneficial interventions (Gendreau, 1996a). Nevertheless, there was good reason for optimism. Some exceptionally well conceptualized programmes of sound therapeutic integrity were implemented in P/P settings: for a detailed compilation and review of these programmes and more recent ones, see Ross and Gendreau (1980) and Gendreau (1996a). The evaluation results were impressive. Reductions in recidivism of 20%–60% were reported. Increases in employment and educational activities doubled or tripled in some instances.

What kinds of programmes were these? First, they had programme designers/supervisors with excellent clinical skills in behavioural assessment and treatment. Secondly, the therapeutic integrity of the programmes was safeguarded (see Gendreau & Ross, 1979, p. 467). In other words, treatment staff appeared to adhere to the principles and techniques of the therapy they were employing. They worked hard; treatment was intense. Not only were staff carefully monitored, but ongoing training was provided. Thirdly, offenders' individual differences in responding to various styles of service delivery were taken into account.

Here are, briefly, three examples of programmes that best illustrate the above. Walter and Mills' (1980) behavioural employment programme for juvenile probationers utilized a token economy, contingency contracting, and life skills interventions. The programme was admirable in that it linked employers and the courts in the treatment design. Employers were trained to be paraprofessional behaviour modifiers. Next, Andrews and Kiessling's (1980) Canadian Volunteers in Corrections Programme used professionals and volunteers in an adult probation supervision programme. The major features of the counselling and supervision practices developed by these authors were the use of authority, anticriminal modelling and reinforcement, and problem-solving techniques. The quality of interpersonal relationships was also a factor in the pairings of offenders and counsellors. The theoretical importance of this study should not be underplayed as their treatment guidelines were instrumental in the continuing development of the principles of effective correctional treatment literature (e.g. Andrews, 1995; Andrews & Bonta, 1994; Gendreau, 1996b; Gendreau & Ross, 1983–1984).

Then, there are the studies by William Davidson, II and colleagues (Blakely, Davidson, II, Saylor, & Robinson, 1980; Davidson, II & Robinson, 1975; Seidman, Rappaport, & Davidson, II, 1980) which featured an amalgam of behavioural techniques, relationships skills training, child advocacy, and matching of offenders and therapists. As pioneering community psychologists, they were among the first researchers to be aware of the need to overcome system-based barriers in delivering effective interventions.

THE PRESENT: GETTING TOUGH

Just as it seemed that progress was being made in propagating effective services for P/P, an insidious counterrevolution was evolving. Its Magna Carta was the declaration that "nothing works" in offender rehabilitation (Martinson, 1974). Rather, the new epoch of punishment-based strategies was upon us (Martinson, 1976). Martinson's (1974) message was propitious[2] because it occurred during a period when, for a variety of reasons, conservative and neo-liberal socio-political forces in the United States were vigorously attacking liberal social policies, including rehabilitative efforts in corrections (Cullen & Gendreau, 1989). Not surprisingly, reports of successful treatment programmes in P/P declined precipitously (e.g. Davidson, II, Redner, Blakely, Mitchell, & Emshoff, 1987; Ross, Fabiano, & Ewles, 1988) as corrections policy-makers embraced "get tough" methods. What began to appear in P/P was a distinct form of "get tough" strategy known as the intermediate sanction. The term "intermediate" was derived from the notion that deterrence strategies based on excessive use of incarceration were too crude and expensive while regular probation was too "soft".[3] The most common form of intermediate sanction was intensive supervision programming (ISP). As Billie J. Erwin so forcefully put it when referring to the Georgia ISP, considered by many to be a model for the United States: "... We are in the business of increasing the heat on probationers ... satisfying the public's demand for just punishment ... Criminals must be punished for their misdeeds" (Erwin, 1986, p. 17).

This new generation of ISPs quickly spread throughout the United States (Gendreau, Cullen, & Bonta, 1994). They turned up the heat by:

1. Greatly increasing contact between supervisors and offenders.
2. Confining offenders to their homes.
3. Enforcing curfews.
4. Submitting offenders to random drug testing.
5. Requiring offenders to pay restitution to victims.
6. Electronically monitoring offenders.
7. Requiring offenders to pay for the privilege of being supervised.

ISPs have employed these sanctions in varying degrees with the major emphasis on increasing contact.

Besides serving a retributive purpose, the expectation was that ISPs would effect prosocial conformity through the threat of punishment (Gendreau et al., 1994). There were also other intuitively appealing facets of ISPs (cf. Cullen,

---

[2] To a lesser degree, and somewhat later than the Americans, the "get tough" agenda was also embraced by other Western countries, although in the case of some (i.e. Australia and Canada) the rhetoric outweighed the reality. Also of note, when Martinson began to recant his views (Martinson, 1979), his revised message was largely ignored.

[3] Some proponents of intermediate sanctions asserted that probation could be even more punishing than prison (Petersilia, 1990).

Wright, & Applegate, 1996). Since corrections were excessively reliant on incarceration, prisons were crowded and operational costs were escalating. ISPs, on the other hand, offered sentencing options to imprisonment. It would be much cheaper to punish offenders in the community.

GETTING TOUGH: IS IT WORKING?

Recent reviews of the cost-effectiveness of ISPs present a rather woeful scenario (Gendreau et al., 1993). They concluded: while more evaluations need to be conducted, there is tentative evidence that some jurisdictions may be widening the net by using ISPs to target seemingly low risk offenders who, routinely, would have received a regular P/P term, less costly than ISPs by a factor of three. In fact, some types of ISPs, like drug testing, have inflated P/P budgets to a marked degree. Furthermore, ISPs have contributed to correctional costs by promoting incarceration. Offenders on ISPs generally receive more technical violations than those on regular probation. ISPs also tend to attract "law and order" types of P/P officers who, in turn, generate higher rates of technical violations (e.g. Paparozzi, 1994). More technical violations lead to more return to prison orders. Please note, however, that so far there is no convincing evidence that technical violations are precursors to more serious offending (Petersilia & Turner, 1993).

When it comes to the matter of reducing offender recidivism, the conclusion is inescapable. ISPs have had little effect on offenders' future criminal activity. The first two authors have been accumulating evidence regarding the effect of ISPs on offender recidivism and assessing the results using meta-analytic techniques. We analysed these data for the purpose of this presentation and Table 13.1 summarizes the results gathered to date. Five different forms of ISPs are listed. Category 1, ISP programmes, were a mixed group of studies. All of them involved increased surveillance/contacts by P/P staff; a few contained one or two of the sanctions in categories 2 to 5. Studies in this latter group relied primarily on the individual sanction noted.

The results in Table 13.1 can be read as follows. In category 1 there were 47

Table 13.1 Intermediate sanctions

Type of sanction (k)	N	Mφ (SD)	CI
1. Intensive supervision programs (47)	19 403	0.00 (0.18)	−0.05 to 0.05
2. Restitution (17)	8 715	−0.02 (0.09)	−0.06 to 0.03
3. Scared straight (12)	1 891	0.07 (0.14)	−0.02 to 0.16
4. Drug testing (3)	419	0.05 (0.12)	−0.24 to 0.34
5. Electronic monitoring (6)	1 414	0.05 (0.07)	−0.02 to 0.12

Note: k = number of effect sizes per type of sanction; N = total sample size per type of sanction; Mφ (SD) = mean phi coefficient and standard deviation per type of sanction; CI = lower and upper limits of the confidence interval about the mean phi coefficient.

comparisons between an ISP programme and a control group of offenders who received a lesser sanction, such as regular probation. There were 19 403 offenders involved in these comparisons. The mean treatment effect size was 0.00 as expressed by the phi correlation coefficient (ϕ). Thus, on average, there was no difference in percentage recidivism rates between the ISP and control groups. The confidence interval (CI) reflects the 95% likelihood that a given range of values, in this case a 5% reduction ($\phi = -0.05$) to a 5% increase ($\phi = 0.05$) in recidivism, contains the population value. If the CI contains 0, one can also conclude that no significant treatment effect exists at the $p < 0.05$ level. As the reader will note, in every instance the CIs of all five types of ISP included 0! Furthermore, the mean effect size across all five categories was 0.01 or a 1% increase in recidivism, with mean ϕ values ranging from -0.02 for restitution to 0.07 for scared straight.

A final comment regarding these results is that they did not vary by type of offender (i.e. risk level, adult or juvenile) or quality of research design. Wherever possible, technical violations were not included among the outcome measures, as they might have biased the results against sanctions.

In summary, the unmistakable conclusion is that the new "get tough" revolution in P/P has been an abject failure when it comes to reducing recidivism. But that is not the end of the story. When we began to review the ISP literature we noticed a few outliers, that is, ISP studies that reported reductions in recidivism (Paparozzi, 1994; Pearson, 1987; Petersilia & Turner, 1993). These were studies that provided a treatment component (e.g. counselling) equal to or greater than that of the ISP employed. So, while coding the ISP literature, we decided to separate those ISPs that included treatment and examine their results. Table 13.2 tells the story. We located 15 ISP–control group comparisons where it was evident that treatment services were a meaningful part of the ISP regimen. In an additional 21 instances there was evidence that some unspecified treatment was provided (it was difficult to determine the nature of the treatment as the reports involved were sketchy on programme detail). There was no indication that treatment was offered in a further 49 comparisons.

The results were remarkably consistent. Under the "no treatment" condition ISPs produced a 7% increase in recidivism. The CI did not include 0; it was 0.03 to 0.11. ISPs that appeared to have had some treatment component tended to

Table 13.2 Intermediate sanctions and treatment services

Treatment condition (k)	N	Mϕ (SD)	CI
1. Counselling: Yes (15)	2 544	−0.10 (0.14)	−0.18 to −0.02
2. Counselling: Possibly (21)	8 574	−0.03 (0.15)	−0.10 to 0.03
3. Counselling: No (49)	20 724	0.07 (0.13)	0.03 to 0.11

Note: k = number of effect sizes per type of sanction; N = total sample size per treatment condition; Mϕ(SD) = mean phi coefficient and standard deviation of the mean phi coefficient per treatment condition; CI = lower and upper limits of the confidence interval about the mean phi coefficient.

produce a slight decline in recidivism of 3%. ISPs that employed more treatment reported a 10% decrease in recidivism. The CI associated with these data was bounded by -0.18 and -0.02; treatment was associated with a significant decline in recidivism.

Unfortunately, we had no way of knowing the quality of the treatment services provided in the above programmes. Our suspicion is that they were treatments with nowhere near the therapeutic integrity of the P/P programmes discussed at the outset. Interestingly, when we examined the non-ISP treatment literature we found reductions in recidivism of similar amounts for programmes that were of unknown suspect quality (Gendreau & Goggin, 1997).

WHERE DO WE GO FROM HERE?

While it is one of the hoariest of clichés, it appears that if we do not learn from the past we will continue to make the same mistakes. The "get tough" revolution in P/P was a fascinating experiment but it is now time to put it to rest if we are interested in providing a cost-effective service delivery system for offenders. How optimistic are we that some of the literature from the "old days" that we referenced will be rediscovered? Please bear in mind that a tremendous amount of political capital has been invested in the "get tough" strategies (Gendreau et al., 1994). Obviously, current practices will not change overnight. Our guess is that it will be at least several years before there will be even a modest resurgence in the availability of treatment services in P/P. Fortunately, there are signs that some constructive knowledge is beginning to be produced. Some cases in point are:

1. Among offenders supervised by P/P officers who were rated higher on (a) the quantity and style of their supervision skills, (b) efficient enforcement of conditions, (c) monitoring of offenders' changes in high risk/need areas, and who (d) delivered the intervention in advance of a crisis situation, recidivism rates were 20%–30% lower (Byrne & Kelly, 1989; Byrne, Lurigio, & Baird, 1995).
2. P/P officers who had a "balanced" supervisory approach produced reductions in recidivism in the range of 10%–40% compared with those who were too punitive or "soft" in this orientation (Paparozzi, 1994).
3. The degree to which the organizational setting supported the planned intervention has been associated with reductions in recidivism of 5%–17% (Paparozzi, 1994).
4. A series of meta-analyses on the prediction of recidivism for large samples of general offenders, as well as special offender populations (e.g. mentally disordered, sex offenders) have produced remarkable consensus as to the most useful factors to be assessed (see Gendreau, Goggin, & Paparozzi, 1996). They report that in addition to criminal history, measures of criminogenic need (those that assess aspects of offenders' attitudes, values, and behaviours supportive of a criminal lifestyle) were the best predictors of

recidivism. Weak predictors included constructs such as anxiety, depression, low self-esteem, and IQ. Amongst risk assessment instruments, the Level of Service Inventory—Revised (LSI-R) (Andrews & Bonta, 1995), a structured interview consisting of 54 items, has generated the strongest correlations with recidivism (Gendreau, Little, & Goggin, 1996). Another promising assessment protocol is the Case Needs Identification and Analysis (CNIA) process developed by the Correctional Service of Canada (Motiuk & Brown, 1994). Measures of criminogenic need are still in their infancy. The most promising of these are reviewed by Gendreau, Goggin et al. (1996).

5. The assessment of responsivity to treatment—the matching of offender and staff characteristics and programme modules—has enormous potential (Kennedy & Serin, 1997; Serin & Kennedy, 1997). The measure they developed consists of 39 constructs that assess treatment readiness and improvements in treatment participation.

6. Measures of programme implementation and organizational supportiveness (Gendreau & Burkhead, 1996) and the quality of treatment practices (the Correctional Program Assessment Inventory (CPAI); Gendreau & Andrews, 1996) are now available. The latter instrument consists of five components: programme implementation, assessment and treatment practices, staff characteristics, and evaluation. Normative data on the CPAI is now available (Gendreau & Goggin, 1997).

7. Andrews and Bonta (1998) have provided a useful guideline that can be adopted to assess how well the P/P officer utilizes effective modelling, reinforcement, and disapproval in supervising offenders. Fulton, Stichman, Travis, and LaTessa (1997) found that, through a comprehensive approach to training, officer attitudes can be modified from a control orientation to one that supports the roles and strategies necessary to effect positive behavioural change. Moreover, there is now a plethora of data supporting the effectiveness of certain styles of service delivery over others (cf. Andrews & Bonta, 1998; Gendreau & Goggin, 1997). Specific guidelines as to what works in this regard have been described (Andrews, 1995; Gendreau, 1996b).

8. Finally, with the support of the American Probation and Parole Association, one of the authors has taken the lead in establishing a prototype for effective service delivery in P/P settings (Fulton, Gendreau, & Paparozzi, 1995; Fulton et al., 1997; Fulton, Stone, & Gendreau, 1994). According to these authors, the characteristics of effective P/P supervision are:

    (a) Higher risk P/P offenders should be targeted for the most intensive supervision. Risk must be identified using a standardized objective measure of proven validity.

    (b) P/P officers should have small caseloads and thorough, systematic case reviews should be routine.

    (c) It is mandatory that P/P officers have substantive contact with their cases. Contact, however, should not be mindless watching of offenders but purposeful surveillance directed at assisting and advocating for problem resolution.

(d)   A wide range of effective interventions should be available. The use of positive reinforcers to motivate behavioural change must predominate.

(e)   Ongoing programme evaluation should be routine, starting with documentation on intermediate changes in offenders' criminogenic needs before the termination of the supervisory period.

In conclusion, we have documented that effective service delivery in P/P settings is possible. The knowledge base, dating back about 30 years, is considerable. The major barriers, as we see them, are political and professional. While we have no special insight into the former, we do know that public support for effective offender treatments still has considerable appeal (Applegate, Cullen, & Fisher, 1997). Hopefully, sooner, rather than later, this evidence will have an impact at the political level. As to professional matters, we see the major issue as one of transferring knowledge to policy-makers and line staff (Gendreau, 1996a). Regrettably, few appropriate training centres on offender assessment and treatment are currently available in North America, even for the profession (i.e. psychology) most involved in designing treatment programmes (Bersoff et al., 1997). At least the resolution to this problem is relatively straightforward.

REFERENCES

Andrews, D. A. (1995). The psychology of criminal conduct and effective treatment. In J. McGuire (Ed.), *What works: Reducing re-offending—Guidelines from research and practice* (pp. 35–62). Chichester, UK: Wiley.

Andrews, D. A., & Bonta, J. (1998). *The psychology of criminal conduct* (2nd ed.). Cincinnati, OH: Anderson.

Andrews, D. A., & Bonta, J. (1995). *LSI-R: The level of service inventory—Revised.* Toronto, Canada: Multi-Health Systems.

Andrews, D. A., & Kiessling, J. J. (1980). Program structure and effective correctional practice: A summary of CaVic research. In R. Ross & P. Gendreau (Eds.), *Effective correctional treatment* (pp. 439–463). Toronto, Canada: Butterworths.

Applegate, B. K., Cullen, F. T., & Fisher, B. S. (1997). Public support for correctional treatment: The continuing appeal of the rehabilitation ideal. *The Prison Journal, 77,* 237–258.

Bersoff, D. N., Goodman-Delahunty, J., Grisso, J. T., Hans, V. P., Poythress, N. G., Jr, & Roesch, R. G. (1997). Training in law and psychology: Lessons from the Villanova conference. *American Psychologist, 52,* 1301–1310.

Blakely, C. H., Davidson, W. S., II, Saylor, C. A., & Robinson, M. J. (1980). Kentfields rehabilitation program: Ten years later. In R. R. Ross & P. Gendreau (Eds.), *Effective correctional treatment* (pp. 319–326). Toronto, Canada: Butterworths.

Byrne, J. M., & Kelly, L. M. (1989). *Restructuring probation as an intermediate sanction: An evaluation of the Massachusetts intensive probation supervision program* (Research program on the punishment and control of offenders). Washington, DC: National Institute of Justice.

Byrne, J. M., Lurigio, A. J., & Baird, C. (1995). The effectiveness of the new intensive supervision programs. *Research in Corrections, 2,* 1–48.

Cullen, F., & Gendreau, P. (1989). The effectiveness of correctional rehabilitation: Reconsidering the "nothing works" debate. In L. Goodstein & D. MacKenzie (Eds.), *American prisons: Issues in research and policy* (pp. 23–44). New York: Plenum.

Cullen, F., Wright, J., & Applegate, B. (1996). Control in the community: The limits of reform? In A. T. Harland (Ed.), *Choosing correctional options that work: Defining the demand and evaluating the supply* (pp. 69–116). Thousand Oaks, CA: Sage.

Davidson, W., Redner, R., Blakely, C., Mitchell, C., & Emshoff, J. (1987). Diversion of juvenile offenders: An experimental comparison. *Journal of Consulting and Clinical Psychology*, *55*, 68–75.

Davidson, W. S., II, & Robinson, M. J. (1975). Community psychology and behavior modification: A community based program for the prevention of delinquency. *Journal of Corrective Psychiatry and Behavior Therapy*, *21*, 1–12.

Erwin, B. (1986). Turning up the heat on probationers in Georgia. *Federal Probation*, *50*, 17–24.

Fulton, B., Gendreau, P., & Paparozzi, M. (1995). APPA's prototypical intensive supervision program: ISP as it was meant to be. *Perspectives*, *19*, 25–41.

Fulton, B., Stichman, A., Travis, L., & LaTessa, E. (1997). Moderating probation and parole officers attitudes to achieve outcomes. *The Prison Journal*, *77*, 295–312.

Fulton, B. A., Stone, S. B., & Gendreau P. (1994). *Restructuring intensive supervision programs—Applying "what works"*. Lexington, KY: American Probation & Parole Association.

Gendreau, P. (1996a). Offender rehabilitation: What we know and what needs to be done. *Criminal Justice and Behavior*, *73*, 144–161.

Gendreau, P. (1996b). The principles of effective intervention with offenders. In A. T. Harland (Ed.), *Choosing correctional options that work: Defining the demand and evaluating the supply* (pp. 117–130). Thousand Oaks, CA: Sage.

Gendreau, P., & Andrews, D. A. (1996). *The correctional program assessment inventory* (6th ed.). Saint John, Canada: University of New Brunswick.

Gendreau, P., & Burkhead, M. (1996). *Correctional program implementation inventory*. Saint John, Canada: University of New Brunswick, Criminal Justice Studies Centre.

Gendreau, P., Cullen, F. T., & Bonta, J. (1994). Intensive rehabilitation supervision: The next generation in community corrections? *Federal Probation*, *58*, 72–78.

Gendreau, P., & Goggin, C. (1997). Correctional treatment: Accomplishments and realities. In P. VanVoorhis, M. Braswell, & D. Lester (Eds.), *Correctional counseling and rehabilitation* (pp. 271–279). Cincinnati, OH: Anderson.

Gendreau, P., Goggin, C., & Paparozzi, M. (1996). Principles of effective assessment for community corrections. *Federal Probation*, *60*, 64–70.

Gendreau, P., Little, T., & Goggin, C. (1996). A meta-analysis of adult offender recidivism: What works! *Criminology*, *34*, 575–607.

Gendreau, P., Paparozzi, M., Little, T., & Goddard, M. (1993). Does "punishing smarter" work? An assessment of the new generation of alternative sanctions in probation. *Forum on Corrections Research*, *5*, 31–34.

Gendreau, P., & Ross, R. R. (1979). Effective correctional treatment. Bibliotherapy for cynics. *Crime and Delinquency*, *25*, 463–489.

Gendreau, P., & Ross, R. R. (1983–84). Correctional treatment: Some recommendations for successful intervention. *Juvenile and Family Court Journal*, *34*, 31–40.

Kennedy S., & Serin, R. (1997). Treatment responsivity: Contributing to effective correctional programming. *ICCA Journal*, *9*, 46–52.

Martinson, R. (1974). What works?—Questions and answers about prison reform. *Public Interest*, *35*, 22–54.

Martinson, R. (1976). California research at the crossroads. *Crime and Delinquency*, *22*, 180–191.

Martinson, R. (1979). New findings, new views: A note of caution regarding sentencing reform. *Hofstra Law Reform*, *7*, 243–258.

Motiuk, L. L., & Brown, S. L. (1994). Offender needs identification and analysis in community corrections. *Forum on Corrections Research*, *6*, 14–16.

Paparozzi, M. A. (1994). *A comparison of the effectiveness of an Intensive Parole Supervision Program with traditional parole supervision.* Unpublished doctoral dissertation, Rutgers University, Brunswick, New Jersey.

Pearson, F. S. (1987). Evaluation of New Jersey's intensive supervision program. *Crime and Delinquency, 34,* 437–448.

Petersilia, J. (1990). When probation becomes more dreaded than prison. *Federal Probation, 54,* 23-27.

Petersilia, J., & Turner, S. (1993). *Evaluating intensive supervision probation/parole: Results of a nationwide experiment* (Research in brief). Washington, DC: National Institute of Justice.

Ross, R. R., Fabiano, E., & Ewles, C. (1988). Reasoning and rehabilitation. *International Journal of Offender Therapy and Comparative Criminology, 32,* 29–35.

Ross, R. R., & Gendreau, P. (1980). *Effective correctional treatment.* Toronto, Canada: Butterworths.

Seidman, E., Rappaport, J., & Davidson, W. S., II. (1980). Adolescents in legal jeopardy: Initial success and replication of an alternative to the criminal justice system. In R. R. Ross & P. Gendreau (Eds.), *Effective correctional treatment* (pp. 101–126). Toronto, Canada: Butterworths.

Serin, R., & Kennedy, S. (1997). *Assessment protocol for treatment readiness, responsivity, and gain.* Ottawa, Canada: Correctional Service of Canada.

Walter, T. L., & Mills, C. M. (1980). A behavioral–employment intervention program for reducing juvenile delinquency. In R. R. Ross & P. Gendreau (Eds.), *Effective correctional treatment* (pp. 185–206). Toronto, Canada: Butterworths.

Chapter 14

Family-Based Treatments

Cynthia Cupit Swenson
Scott W. Henggeler
and
Sonja K. Schoenwald
Medical University of South Carolina, Charleston, USA

INTRODUCTION

Overwhelming evidence supports the view that antisocial behavior in adolescents is multidetermined (i.e. from the interplay of individual, family, peer, school, and community factors) and that family relations play a key role in the development and maintenance of adolescent criminal activity and drug use (Elliott, 1994; Henggeler, 1997; Thornberry, Huizinga, & Loeber, 1995; Tolan & Guerra, 1994). Moreover, in light of the failure of individually-based treatment approaches to realize positive long-term outcomes in treating serious antisocial behavior, reviewers have argued for greater emphasis on addressing difficulties within the key systems in which youths are embedded (Dodge, 1993; Henggeler, 1996; Tate, Reppucci, & Mulvey, 1995). In the vast majority of instances, the family is the key system in which youths are involved—with parents and guardians being the adults primarily responsible for providing their children with the love, structure, and guidance needed for healthy psychosocial adjustment.

Various models of family-based treatment have been applied to the problems presented by antisocial youth. Indeed, meta-analytic reviews have shown that family therapy is effective for resolving a variety of problem behaviors compared with no treatment (Hazelrigg, Cooper, & Borduin, 1987) and alternative treatments (Shadish et al., 1993). Conclusions regarding the efficacy of family therapy, however, are mitigated by the fact that the majority of family-based treatments have received no empirical support. While some family-based treatment approaches have been rigorously evaluated, many others are based primarily on

Handbook of Offender Assessment and Treatment. Edited by C. R. Hollin.
© 2000 John Wiley & Sons Ltd.

unsubstantiated theory and clinical anecdote. In general, family treatment approaches that follow unstructured models, such as client-centered, intergenerational, and psychodynamic, have not evinced the positive outcomes of more structured treatments (Henggeler, Borduin, & Mann, 1993; Kazdin, 1994). A central contention of this chapter is that family work concerned principally with behavioral changes and that has at least some empirical support carries the greatest likelihood of producing positive outcomes for youths and their families.

As such, the purpose of this chapter is to describe family-based approaches that: (a) have been applied to youth who exhibit criminal activity or substance abuse; and (b) have been examined empirically. These approaches include: *family preservation models* (Nelson, 1990); *functional family therapy* (Alexander & Parsons, 1982); *structural family therapy* (Kurtines & Szapocznik, 1996; Minuchin, 1974; Minuchin & Fishman, 1981); *multidimensional family therapy* (Liddle, Dakof, & Diamond, 1991; Liddle, 1995); and *multisystemic therapy* (Henggeler & Borduin, 1990; Henggeler, Schoenwald, Borduin, Rowland, & Cunningham, 1998). For each of these approaches, the theoretical basis, central treatment goals, and an overview of outcome studies is provided.

DEFINING FAMILY-BASED TREATMENT

In general, the underlying assumptions of family-based treatments are that factors within the family maintain problem behavior and, consequently, changes in family interactions can lead to improved youth behavior. In some clinical settings, however, the youth's problem behavior may not be conceptualized as related to family factors, and inclusion of the family may play a different role. Liddle and Dakof (1995), for example, have distinguished between family therapy (family-based treatment) and family-involved interventions. The former addresses the connection between family relationships and the youth's problem of concern, while the latter involves the family in more adjunctive ways, such as providing information. For the purpose of this chapter, the terms family therapy, family-based treatment, and family work are used interchangeably.

Family therapy models that view family relations as an etiological or maintaining factor in youth behavior problems and seek to change interactions within the family as a means for changing youth behavior are presented. A caveat, however, pertains to the first presentation concerning family preservation programs. Like family therapy in the generic, family preservation programs follow a wide variety of treatment models, some of which may or may not address the role of family interactions in youth behavior problems. However, given that services based on this model have expanded at a rapid rate in the United States and many antisocial youth are being served through these programs, the reader should be aware of the effectiveness of family preservation models with antisocial youth.

FAMILY PRESERVATION PROGRAMS

During the past decade, family preservation programs have proliferated in the United States, primarily within child welfare systems. More recently, family preservation models have been applied to youths in the juvenile justice system (Nelson, 1990). Although family preservation may be viewed as an intervention, it is most accurately described as a model of service delivery encompassing a variety of therapeutic interventions and concrete services in the youth's home and community (Schoenwald & Henggeler, 1997). The characteristics of the family preservation model of service delivery differ from traditional office-based counterparts in several important ways: treatment is time limited (1–5 months), sessions are scheduled at times convenient for family members (including weekends and evenings), services are generally provided in the home and other community settings, therapists have low caseloads (2–6 families) and make multiple contacts weekly, and most programs include 24 hour/7 day availability of service providers (Farrow, 1991; Fraser, Nelson, & Rivard, 1997). The intensity of family preservation is designed to help attain the primary goal of preventing an out-of-home placement for the youth. Thus, such an intense (and costly relative to outpatient treatment) treatment can be cost effective if relatively expensive out-of-home placements are avoided.

The nature of the family-based treatment provided in family preservation varies across programs, but three distinct practice models have been identified (Nelson, 1990, 1994):

1. crisis intervention,
2. home-based model, and
3. family treatment model.

Homebuilders is the national prototype of the crisis intervention model. Interventions are very brief (4–6 weeks) and include concrete services (e.g. food, clothing) and counseling that primarily targets family communication, behavior management, and problem-solving skills from a social learning orientation (Kinney, Haapala, Booth, & Leavitt, 1990). Home-based models tend to be more clinically oriented than crisis models, with interventions targeting problematic interactions between family members and between the family and community (Lloyd & Bryce, 1984). Family treatment models share a similar orientation with the home-based models in that interventions are based on family systems theory. The primary difference between the two models is that concrete services are generally provided by case managers rather than therapists and service delivery is in the outpatient office, as well as the home.

Outcome Studies

Family preservation outcome studies consist mainly of program evaluations and studies with quasi-experimental designs. Within these studies, methodological problems (e.g. selection bias, non-equivalent control groups) render the results equivocal. Studies that included appropriate comparison groups (e.g. Mitchell, Tovar, & Knitzer, 1989; Wood, Barton, & Schroeder, 1988) failed to support the effectiveness of family preservation in preventing placement in child welfare, or combinations of child welfare, juvenile justice, and mental health populations. A recent meta-analytic review (Fraser et al., 1997) suggests that family preservation programs may be more successful with older children referred for aggressive or oppositional behavior than with child maltreatment referrals. However, the majority of the family preservation studies conducted with older youths referred for aggressive behavior used multisystemic therapy (MST) as the model of treatment (randomized trials of MST with violent and serious juvenile offenders are presented later in this chapter). Therefore, with the exception of MST, little evidence supports the effectiveness of family preservation programs with youths engaging in antisocial behavior.

Aside from the MST studies, one randomized trial including antisocial youths has been reported in the family preservation literature (Feldman, 1991). In this study, youths and families were referred by multiple agencies (i.e. juvenile justice, child welfare, and community mental health crisis centers) and randomly assigned to the New Jersey Family Preservation Services program, modeled after Homebuilders, or traditional preventive services (e.g. referral to mental health services, agency monitoring of youths). Family preservation services achieved better placement results up to 9 months after service completion, at which time the effects diminished. Families who received the family preservation services also appeared to function at higher levels on measures of family functioning and stress upon case closure, but the improvements were not greater than those of families who received traditional services. Thus, little evidence supports the effectiveness of family preservation, *per se*, in treating youths with serious antisocial behavior.

FUNCTIONAL FAMILY THERAPY

Functional family therapy (FFT; Alexander & Parsons, 1982) was one of the first family-based treatments applied to antisocial youth. Within an FFT framework, the family is viewed as a constellation of interacting groups that behave according to certain principles and these principles can be used to effect change. A central focus of the treatment is on the functions that problem behaviors play and how the family functions interrelate. Treatment targets behaviors that maintain the functions and strives to help families determine how to achieve the same functions through new behavior patterns. For example, if a youth's tantruming behavior serves the function of gaining parental attention, intervention focuses on obtaining attention with more pleasant behaviors. Responsibility for motivation for treatment is with the therapist who must be proficient in three skill categories:

1. conceptual (i.e. understanding the functions of behaviors and the dynamics of interactions);
2. technical (i.e. knowledge of procedures that produce change in perceptions, feelings and behaviors); and
3. interpersonal skills (i.e. how to apply techniques).

FFT combines interventions from behavior therapy, cognitive behavioral therapy, and family systems models to change family interactions, communication, and problem solving in ways that no longer support the maladaptive behavior (Kazdin, 1994).

Outcome Studies

Several outcome studies show that FFT holds promise as a treatment for mild antisocial behavior in adolescents. An initial evaluation of FFT was conducted with first-time male and female status offenders, mainly from middle class Mormon families (Alexander & Parsons, 1973). FFT was effective at reducing further status offenses, but not criminal offenses. Three subsequent quasi-experimental evaluations were conducted with families of status offenders or youths engaged in delinquency (Barton, Alexander, Waldron, Turner, & Warburton, 1985). Interestingly, the treatment was provided by individuals with varied levels of training: (a) undergraduate students (single-group design), (b) probation workers (*post hoc* comparison of FFT and standard probation services), and (c) doctoral students (planned comparison of FFT and behavioral group home treatment). Across these studies, data regarding recidivism favored FFT. Though outcomes appeared positive, the conclusiveness of these studies is limited by the exclusive reliance on archival data and use of non-experimental designs (i.e. absence of random assignment).

The most recent evaluation of FFT with adolescent offenders was conducted using a quasi-experimental design by Gordon and colleagues (Gordon, Arbuthnot, Gustafson, & McGreen, 1988). Fifty-four White juveniles were assigned to either FFT or a no-treatment control condition. Participants had committed status offenses, misdemeanors, or felonies. The FFT group was composed of 15 male and 12 female youths, and the comparison group contained 23 male and 4 female youths. A significant aspect of this study was the delivery of FFT in the families' homes. FFT was provided by graduate students over an average of 5.5 months, and included an average of 16 sessions (ranging from 7 to 38 sessions), each lasting approximately 1.5 hours. Archival data, reviewed after a follow-up period of 27.8 months for the treatment group and 31.5 months for the comparison group, favored FFT for recidivism rates of all types of offenses combined. An examination of adult court records of the original sample was conducted 3 years after the initial follow-up, when most of the youths were in young adulthood. Data favored FFT for misdemeanor but not felony recidivism rates (Gordon, Graves, & Arbuthnot, 1995).

In addressing the problem of youth substance abuse, Friedman (1989) randomly assigned the families of 135 substance-abusing adolescents to either FFT or a parent group. Noteworthy is that in 93% of families in the FFT condition, one or both parents participated, and in 67% of families in the parent group condition, one or both parents participated. Thus, FFT was more effective at engaging parents in treatment. Families received a 6-month course of treatment. Follow-up was conducted at 9 months. Although time effects emerged during the course of the 9-month follow-up (i.e. decreased substance use and psychiatric symptoms, improved family relations), no FFT treatment effects were observed. In a later report, Friedman, Tomko, and Utada (1991) found that positive family relations at the time of intake was a predictor of positive outcomes for families in the FFT condition.

As a whole, the FFT outcome studies suggest promise for this treatment with youths who do not present serious criminal activity and who have relatively positive family relations. The lack of favorable outcomes or rigorous evaluations of FFT with youths presenting serious antisocial behavior, however, limits the external validity of this treatment model.

STRUCTURAL FAMILY THERAPY

Structural family therapy (SFT; Minuchin, 1974; Minuchin & Fishman, 1981) views the family as a system that operates through patterns of interactions. These interactional patterns regulate the behavior of family members and maladaptive patterns prevent achievement of the family's goals. Problem behaviors may result from the family system's way of organizing itself as it attempts to cope with changes and stresses. Thus, problems are viewed as an expression of the family dysfunction (Szapocznik et al., 1988). SFT is an action-oriented, present-focused therapy directed toward changing the organization or structure of the family (e.g. how they interact, alliances, subsystems). Change in the family structure contributes to changes in the behavior of family members.

SFT therapists form a new therapeutic system with the family and use themselves to change the family system in a way that repairs the family's functioning and enables them to better perform the tasks of support, regulation, nurturance, and socialization of members (Minuchin, 1974). Change mechanisms associated with SFT include (a) joining (techniques the therapist uses to enter the family system); (b) diagnosing or identifying maladaptive interactional patterns; and (c) restructuring or changing maladaptive interactions that are related to problem interactions within the family (Kurtines & Szapocznik, 1996).

Outcome Studies

The most conceptually and methodologically rigorous research on SFT has been conducted by Szapocznik and his colleagues, focusing on specialized applications of SFT for Hispanic families (Kurtines & Szapocznik, 1996). Early studies established the efficacy of SFT in reducing drug use among adolescents upon treatment termination (Szapocznik, Santisteban et al., 1986; Szapocznik, Santisteban, Rio, Perez-Vidal, & Kurtines, 1989). Other studies comparing conjoint family therapy and one-person family therapy (both forms of SFT) documented improvements in youth behavior problems and family relations for both groups at termination of treatment and follow-up (Szapocznik, Kurtines, Foote, Perez-Vidal, & Hervis, 1983, 1986).

A subsequent series of studies focused on the engagement of adolescents and their families in treatment. Strategic Structural Systems Engagement (SSSE; Szapocznik & Kurtines, 1989; Szapocznik et al., 1988), designed to begin the work of joining, diagnosing, and restructuring the family on the first contact, was compared with usual engagement techniques (i.e. minimal joining techniques such as expressing polite concern, asking about problems and well-being of the family). SSSE was more effective in engaging and retaining adolescent substance abusers and their families in treatment. Ninety-three percent of the SSSE families engaged in treatment and 75% of those completed treatment, which compares favorably with the engagement (42%) and completion (25%) rates of families in the control condition (Szapocznik et al., 1988). In a later study comparing SSSE with family therapy without SSSE and group therapy without SSSE, Santisteban et al. (1996) replicated the 1988 findings, but also found that SSSE more successfully engaged non-Cuban Hispanic than Cuban Hispanic families. They hypothesized that Cuban Hispanic families were more incorporated into the mainstream US culture, as evidenced by requesting hospitalization and individual therapy for their child.

The work of Szapocznik and colleagues has made a significant contribution to the adolescent substance abuse treatment field, especially with regard to the engagement process and cultural competence. Additional research is needed to assess further the effectiveness and generalizability of the SFT treatment model. That is, scant results have supported the clinical effectiveness of SFT and applicability of extant findings should be extended to other cultural groups.

MULTIDIMENSIONAL FAMILY THERAPY

Multidimensional family therapy (MDFT; Liddle et al., 1991; Liddle, 1995) is an empirically-derived, multicomponent intervention that was developed for treating adolescent substance abuse. The underlying principle of MDFT is that individual behavior change results from change in the family system. Youth behavior problems are defined as developmental detours or behaviors that prevent adolescents from achieving developmentally appropriate milestones. Conceptualization of the problem emphasizes the multiple, interacting social contexts in which the problem forms and solvability of the problem.

MDFT is theme-driven, as it relies on mutually-agreed-upon themes or areas of work that have personal meaning to the youth and parent. Engagement of the youth, parent, and all subsystems is viewed as basic to treatment success and is ongoing and aggressive. The therapeutic alliance and developing mutually-agreed-upon goals are central to engagement. Parental involvement is viewed as critical to change, but MDFT therapists may treat the adolescent alone in an effort to increase engagement. For the youth, drug screens are required and results are revealed to the parent and involved professionals (e.g. probation officer). Service delivery is designed to engage families, and thus treatment is con-ducted in the office, by telephone, or in the home (Liddle, 1995). Interventions target four domains: (a) the youth's intrapersonal and interpersonal functioning (e.g. peers); (b) the parent's intrapersonal and interpersonal functioning (adult peers); (c) parent–youth interactions observed in sessions and reported by the parent and adolescent; and (d) family interactions with extrafamilial sources of influence (e.g. school) (Schmidt, Liddle, & Dakof, 1996).

Outcome Studies

Liddle and colleagues have demonstrated the potential merits of MDFT with substance-abusing adolescents. A controlled clinical trial (Liddle & Dakof, 1995) comparing MDFT with peer group therapy and family education indicated that MDFT was more effective in reducing drug use post treatment and at maintain-ing reductions in use at 1-year follow-up. Youth receiving MDFT also evinced more improvement in school performance relative to youth in the other two treatment conditions. Schmidt et al. (1996) examined the parenting practices of 29 families who completed 16 sessions of MDFT and found significant improve-ment in parenting (i.e. decreased negative practices and affect and increased positive practices and affect) in 69% of parents. Although most parents and ado-lescents improved simultaneously, change patterns varied, with 21% of families experiencing adolescent change without parent change and 10% experiencing parent change without adolescent change. In explaining these patterns, Schmidt and colleagues suggest that if MDFT interventions with the primary target (e.g. the parent) fail, treatment should focus on alternative domains (e.g. the youth). MDFT is noteworthy as it represents a relatively new family-based treatment model that is supported by cogent theory and is being validated by a skilled team of investigators. Thus, the field should be informed by future evaluations of MDFT.

MULTISYSTEMIC THERAPY

Multisystemic therapy (MST; Henggeler & Borduin, 1990; Henggeler et al., 1998) was developed as a treatment for adolescent offenders (Henggeler et al., 1986) and is the only treatment approach to demonstrate long-term reductions in rear-rest and incarceration in randomized clinical trials. The theoretical foundation of MST lies in Bronfenbrenner's (1979) theory of social ecology and pragmatic family systems models of behavior (Haley, 1976; Minuchin, 1974). Individuals are viewed as nested within interconnected systems (i.e. individual, family, extrafamilial, peers) that influence behavior in a reciprocal fashion, and youth behavior problems are viewed as maintained by problematic transactions within and/or between any one or combination of these systems. Thus, interventions target interactions within the family, and between the family and other systems in the youth's and family's natural (e.g. peers, work) and service (e.g. mental health, child welfare) ecologies (Schoenwald, Borduin, & Henggeler, 1998). Nine treatment principles guide the conceptualization of the problem behavior (i.e. how the behavior makes sense in the context of the youth's social ecology) and the development and implementation of interventions individually tailored to meet the specific needs of the youth and family. Specific intervention techniques are integrated from the best of the existing pragmatic and problem-focused child psychotherapy approaches that have at least some empirical support.

In MST clinical trials, considerable attention has been devoted to the applicability of MST to real-world populations seen in community mental health and juvenile justice settings. As such, clinical trials have been conducted in community-based settings, with a home-and-community-based model of service delivery and 3–5 month length of treatment. Providing treatment in places convenient to families (home, school, church, community) has been important in removing barriers to services access and thus, in the low dropout rates in MST studies (see Henggeler, Pickrel, Brondino, & Crouch, 1996). In accordance with a family preservation service delivery model, MST treatment of the youth and family involves frequent, intensive contacts (sometimes daily) and round-the-clock therapist availability. Therapists carry small caseloads of 4–6 families and receive regular (sometimes daily) clinical and supervisory support. Because empirical demonstrations indicate that MST treatment fidelity is essential to obtaining positive outcomes (Henggeler, Melton, Brondino, Scherer, & Hanley, 1997), therapists are provided with extensive training, supervision, and ongoing mechanisms to promote quality assurance.

Outcome Studies

Following several early clinical trials supporting the short-term efficacy of MST with inner-city adolescents (Henggeler et al., 1986), maltreating families (Brunk, Henggeler, & Whelan, 1987), and a small sample of adolescent sex offenders (Borduin, Henggeler, Blaske, & Stein, 1990), several randomized trials have been conducted with youths presenting serious antisocial behavior. In a study conducted through a community mental health center (Henggeler, Melton, & Smith, 1992; Henggeler, Melton, Smith, Schoenwald, & Hanley, 1993), 84 violent and chronic juvenile offenders at imminent risk of out-of-home placement were randomly assigned to MST or usual juvenile justice services. The latter condition included services such as court ordered curfew and referral to community agencies. MST was more effective than usual community services at reducing criminal behavior and out-of-home placement. At a 59-week follow-up, youths who participated in MST had significantly fewer arrests ($M = 0.87$ vs. 1.52) and fewer weeks of incarceration (5.8 vs. 16.2) than youths receiving usual community services. Moreover, in comparison with families receiving usual services, families who received MST reported increased cohesion and decreased peer aggression among their youths. MST treatment effects were maintained at a 2.4-year follow-up, with MST almost doubling the survival rate (percentage of participants not rearrested) of the serious offenders (Henggeler Melton et al., 1993). Finally, a comparison of cost indicated that the cost per client for MST treatment was approximately $3500, which compares favorably with the cost of institutional placement received by over 70% of the youths in the comparison condition.

More recently, Borduin et al. (1995) randomly assigned families of 176 chronic adolescent offenders to MST or individual therapy. Following treatment, adolescents whose families received MST had significantly fewer behavior problems and parents reported greater cohesion and adaptability in family relations— reports that were supported by observational data. Importantly, at a 4-year follow-up evaluating rearrest of participants, MST substantially reduced violent criminal activity, other criminal activity, and drug-related arrests (Borduin et al., 1995).

In a third randomized trial of MST with violent and chronic juvenile offenders (Henggeler, Melton et al., 1997), services were provided across two community-based treatment sites to 155 youths and families. A key aspect of this study was ongoing treatment fidelity checks aimed at promoting adherence to the MST treatment protocol. Although MST improved adolescent symptomology at post-treatment and decreased incarceration by 47% at a 1.7-year follow-up, findings for decreased criminal activity were not as favorable as observed in other recent trials of MST. Analyses of parent, adolescent, and therapist reports of MST treatment adherence, however, indicated that outcomes were substantially better in cases where treatment adherence ratings were high. These results highlight the importance of maintaining treatment fidelity when treating youths with serious antisocial behavior and their families.

In addition to the recent MST trials with violent and chronic juvenile offenders and their families, a randomized trial of MST vs. usual community services has been completed with 118 substance abusing or dependent adolescent offenders. At post-treatment, MST participants showed greater reductions in soft- and hard-drug use; and at 12 months post-referral, youths in the MST condition had fewer days incarcerated and in other out-of-home placements (Henggeler, Pickrel, & Brondino, in press). Moreover, 98% of the families referred to the MST condition completed a full course of treatment—demonstrating the effectiveness of MST engagement and retention strategies (Henggeler et al., 1996). Finally, 1 year following referral, cost analyses indicate that the incremental costs of MST were nearly offset by savings accrued as a result of reductions in days of out-of-home placement (e.g. hospital, residential) in the MST condition relative to usual community services (Schoenwald, Ward, Henggeler, Pickrel, & Patel, 1996).

In summary, several randomized trials with youths presenting serious antisocial behavior have demonstrated the short-term capacity of MST to improve family relations and the long-term ability of MST to reduce rates of rearrest and out-of-home placement. Importantly, some of these studies have been conducted in real-world community contexts. Moreover, findings support the importance of treatment fidelity in dissemination to such contexts as well as the potential cost saving produced by effective family-based treatment models. Current studies are examining the effectiveness of MST with other populations of youths presenting serious problems (e.g. MST as an alternative to the emergency psychiatric hospitalization of youths) and MST provided via other models of service delivery (e.g. outpatient, school-based, within a system of care).

FUTURE DIRECTIONS OF FAMILY-BASED TREATMENT

The family therapy models described in this chapter represent important advances in treating adolescent offenders, substance abusing youths, and their families. The promising short- and long-term outcomes from these studies are especially encouraging after a long history of research demonstrating ineffective results from individually-focused treatment models. Taken together, the family therapy outcome studies provide a number of lessons regarding characteristics of effective interventions for antisocial youth.

1. *Treatment should be provided in the youth's and family's natural environment.* In outpatient settings, services are often underused by child clinical populations, as reflected by retention rates of 50%–70% (Tuma, 1989). In MST studies, where services for antisocial youths and their families were provided in the home and community, treatment completion rates have been as high as 98% (Henggeler et al., 1996). Treatment in the home reduces barriers to service access often faced by multineed families (e.g. lack of transportation or child care) and provides opportunities for the therapist directly to observe family and community interactions. Moreover, families are afforded the chance to practice new behaviors in the settings where they must adapt, which may increase the probability that acquired skills will be maintained.

2. *Treatment should include the primary care giver and principal participants in the various systems in which the youth is embedded.* Interactions within and between systems important to the youth and family may maintain or reduce problem behavior. For example, due to school failure, the youth may leave the school building and once unsupervised, engage in criminal activities. In this case, interventions aimed solely at the family will exclude the very systems that, when targeted, may carry the greatest likelihood of reducing the youth's antisocial opportunities. Traditional family therapy models include the family system but often fail directly to address factors in extrafamilial systems that are crucial to resolving identified problems. Comprehensive interventions that pay careful attention to ecological validity have

empirically demonstrated the importance of addressing needs and building competencies across multiple systems.

3. *Treatment should address the known correlates of antisocial behavior.* Addressing the correlates of a problem behavior requires that services be based on the needs of the youth and family within their ecological context, rather than based on the programmatic or policy needs of the agency or philosophical preference of the provider (Tolan, 1996). As noted earlier, causal models have shown that youth antisocial behavior relates to multiple factors across multiple systems (Henggeler, 1991, 1997). In part, the poor outcomes of individually-focused treatments may be due to their failure to target factors that are maintaining the youth's behavior. For example, if parental substance abuse is a barrier to parental monitoring of youth's behavior, then treatment of the youth alone will have little effect on a major factor that may be maintaining the youth's behavior problems. MST clinical trials have demonstrated that with multineed families presenting complex clinical problems, targeting the multiple correlates of antisocial behavior is possible and essential to obtaining positive outcomes.

4. *Interventions should include techniques whose effectiveness is empirically supported.* According to a national survey, psychological practitioners value research and read research journals (Beutler, Williams, Wakefield, & Entwistle, 1995). However, practicing clinicians report that psychotherapy research holds little value to them (Weisz, Donenberg, Han, & Weiss, 1995) and, as noted by Kazdin, Mazurick, and Bass (1993), few child clinicians rely on research in practice. When therapeutic techniques with no established efficacy are used with families, the probability is increased that services will be of little benefit and may actually exacerbate the problem. To assist practitioners in using empirically validated family-based treatments, researchers may need to collaborate more carefully with service providers to ensure that treatments meet the test of implementation in clinical settings.

5. *Interventions should be sensitive to and informed by an understanding of the youth's and family's cultural beliefs and background* (Tolan, 1996). To facilitate engagement of the family in the treatment process, therapists must develop a critical level of cultural competence (i.e. the ability to share the world view of the family and adapt clinical practice to respect that view) (Abney & Gunn, 1993). By increasing awareness of the family's culturally-influenced beliefs, the therapist may come to understand the important distinction between characteristics of the family that are culturally congruent and those that are dysfunctional (Heras, 1992). The work of Szapocznik and colleagues, demonstrating success in engaging and maintaining adolescents and their families in treatment, is an exemplary model of integrating cultural context into a treatment approach.

In conclusion, future directions for family-based treatment should incorporate lessons learned from current research into clinical practice. Continued progress in research will require procedures to ensure that treatment methods: are transportable to real-world settings; consider the practical needs of families (i.e. service delivery that meets the family's needs); are ecologically valid; and are sensitive to the family's cultural context. Only by integrating the lessons from clinical practice into research and those from research into clinical practice, can effective family therapy models continue to be developed and disseminated.

ACKNOWLEDGMENTS

Preparation of this chapter was supported by the National Institute of Mental Health Grant R01-MH-51852; National Institute on Drug Abuse Grant R01-DA10079; the Center for Mental Health Services, Substance Abuse and Mental Health Services Administration 90FYF0012; and the Annie E. Casey Foundation.

Correspondence concerning this chapter should be addressed to Cynthia Cupit Swenson, Family Services Research Center, Department of Psychiatry and Behavioral Sciences, Medical University of South Carolina, 67 President Street—Suite CPP, P.O. Box 250861, Charleston, SC 29425, USA.

REFERENCES

Abney, V. D., & Gunn, K. (1993). A rationale for cultural competency. *APSAC Advisor*, *6*(3), 19–22.

Alexander, J. F., & Parsons, B. V. (1973). Short-term behavioral intervention with delinquent families: Impact on family process and recidivism. *Journal of Abnormal Psychology*, *81*, 219–225.

Alexander, J. F., & Parsons, B. V. (1982). *Functional family therapy*. Monterey, CA: Brooks/Cole.

Barton, C., Alexander, J. F., Waldron, H., Turner, C. W., & Warburton, J. (1985). Generalizing treatment effects of functional family therapy: Three replications. *American Journal of Family Therapy*, *13*, 16–26.

Beutler, L. E., Williams, R. E., Wakefield, P. J., & Entwistle, S. R. (1995). Bridging scientist and practitioner perspectives in clinical psychology. *American Psychologist*, *50*, 984–994.

Borduin, C. M., Henggeler, S. W., Blaske, D. M., & Stein, R. (1990). Multisystemic treatment of adolescent sexual offenders. *International Journal of Offender Therapy and Comparative Criminology*, *34*, 105–113.

Borduin, C. M., Mann, B. J., Cone, L. T., Henggeler, S. W., Fucci, B. R., Blaske, D. M., & Williams, R. A. (1995). Multisystemic treatment of serious juvenile offenders: Long-term prevention of criminality and violence. *Journal of Consulting & Clinical Psychology*, *63*, 569–578.

Bronfenbrenner, U. (1979). *The ecology of human development: Experiments by nature and design*. Cambridge, MA: Harvard University Press.

Brunk, M., Henggeler, S. W., & Whelan, J. P. (1987). A comparison of multisystemic therapy and parent training in the brief treatment of child abuse and neglect. *Journal of Consulting and Clinical Psychology*, *55*, 311–318.

Dodge, K. A. (1993). The future of research on the treatment of conduct disorder. *Development and Psychopathology*, *5*, 311–319.

Elliott, D. S. (1994). *Youth violence: An overview*. Boulder, CO: University of

Colorado, Institute for Behavioral Sciences, Center for the Study and Prevention of Violence.

Farrow, F. (1991, May). Services to families: The view from the states. *Families in Society: the Journal of Contemporary Human Services, 268*–275.

Feldman, L. H. (1991). Evaluating the impact of intensive family preservation services in New Jersey. In K. Wells & D. E. Biegel (Eds.), *Family preservation services: Research and evaluation* (pp. 33–47). Newbury Park, CA: Sage.

Fraser, M. W., Nelson, K. E., & Rivard, J. C. (1997). The effectiveness of family preservation services. *Social Work Research, 21*, 138–153.

Friedman, A. S. (1989). Family therapy vs. parent groups: Effects on adolescent drug abusers. *American Journal of Family Therapy, 17*, 335–347.

Friedman, A. S., Tomko, L. A., & Utada, A. (1991). Client and family characteristics that predict better family therapy outcome for adolescent drug users. *Family Dynamics Addiction Quarterly, 1*, 77–93.

Gordon, D. A., Arbuthnot, J., Gustafson, K., & McGreen, P. (1988). Home-based behavioral-systems family therapy with disadvantaged juvenile delinquents. *American Journal of Family Therapy, 16*, 243–255.

Gordon, D. A., Graves, K., & Arbuthnot, J. (1995). The effect of functional family therapy for delinquents on adult criminal behavior. *Criminal Justice and Behavior, 22*, 60–73.

Haley, J. (1976). *Problem solving therapy*. San Francisco, CA: Jossey-Bass.

Hazelrigg, M. D., Cooper, H. M., & Borduin, C. M. (1987). Evaluating the effectiveness of family therapies: An integrative review and analysis. *Psychological Bulletin, 101*, 428–442.

Henggeler, S. W. (1991). Multidimensional causal models of delinquent behavior and their implications for treatment. In R. Cohen & A. W. Siegel (Eds.), *Context and development* (pp. 161–181). Hillsdale, NJ: Lawrence Erlbaum.

Henggeler, S. W. (1996). Treatment of violent juvenile offenders—We have the knowledge: Comment on Gorman-Smith et al. (1996). *Journal of Family Psychology, 10*, 137–141.

Henggeler, S. W. (1997). The development of effective drug abuse services for youth. In J. A. Egertson, D. M. Fox, & A. I. Leshner (Eds.), *Treating drug abusers effectively* (pp. 253–279). New York: Blackwell.

Henggeler, S. W., & Borduin, C. M. (1990). *Family therapy and beyond: A multisystemic approach to treating the behavior problems of children and adolescents*. Pacific Grove, CA: Brooks/Cole.

Henggeler, S. W., Borduin, C. M., & Mann, B. J. (1993). Advances in family therapy: Empirical foundations. In T. H. Ollendick & R. J. Prinz (Eds.), *Advances in Clinical Child Psychology*, (Vol. 15, pp. 207–241). New York: Plenum.

Henggeler, S. W., Melton, G. B., Brondino, M. J., Scherer, D. G., & Hanley, J. H. (1997). Multisystemic therapy with violent and chronic juvenile offenders and their families: The role of treatment fidelity in successful dissemination. *Journal of Consulting and Clinical Psychology, 65*, 821–833.

Henggeler, S. W., Melton, G. B., & Smith, L. A. (1992). Family preservation using multisystemic therapy: An effective alternative to incarcerating serious juvenile offenders. *Journal of Consulting and Clinical Psychology, 60*, 953–961.

Henggeler, S. W., Melton, G. B., Smith, L. A., Schoenwald, S. K., & Hanley, J. (1993). Family preservation using multisystemic therapy: Long-term follow-up to a clinical trial with serious juvenile offenders. *Journal of Child and Family Studies, 2*, 283–293.

Henggeler, S. W., Pickrel, S. G., & Brondino, M. J. (1997). *Multisystemic treatment of substance abusing and dependent delinquents: Outcomes, treatment fidelity, and transportability*. Mental Health Services Research.

Henggeler, S. W., Pickrel, S. G., Brondino, M. J., & Crouch, J. L. (1996). Eliminating (almost) treatment dropout of substance abusing or dependent delinquents through home-based multisystemic therapy. *American Journal of Psychiatry, 153*, 427–428.

Henggeler, S. W., Rodick, J. D., Borduin, C. M., Hanson, C. L., Watson, S. M., & Urey, J. R.

(1986). Multisystemic treatment of juvenile offenders: Effects on adolescent behavior and family interaction. *Developmental Psychology, 22*, 132–141.

Henggeler, S. W., Schoenwald, S. K., Borduin, C. M., Rowland, M. D., & Cunningham, P. B. (1998). *Multisystemic treatment for antisocial behavior in youth.* New York: Guilford.

Heras, P. (1992). Cultural considerations in the assessment and treatment of child abuse. *Journal of Child Sexual Abuse, 1*, 119–124.

Kazdin, A. E. (1994). Psychotherapy for children and adolescents. In A. E. Bergin & S. L. Garfield (Eds.), *Handbook of psychotherapy and behavior change* (pp. 543–594). New York: Wiley.

Kazdin, A. E., Mazurick, J. L., & Bass, D. (1993). Risk for attrition in treatment of antisocial children and families. *Journal of Clinical Child Psychology, 22*, 2–16.

Kinney, J., Haapala, D., Booth, C., & Leavitt, S. (1990). The Homebuilders model. In J. K. Whittaker, J. Kinney, E. M. Tracey, & C. Booth (Eds.), *Reaching high risk families: Intensive family preservation in human services* (pp. 31–64). New York: Aldine.

Kurtines, W. M., & Szapocznik, J. (1996). Family interaction patterns: Structural family therapy within contexts of cultural diversity. In E. D. Hibbs & P. S. Jensen (Eds.), *Psychosocial treatments for child and adolescent disorders: Empirically based strategies for clinical practice* (pp. 671–697). Washington, DC: American Psychological Association.

Liddle, H. A. (1995). Conceptual and clinical dimensions of a multidimensional, multisystemic engagement strategy in family-based adolescent treatment. *Psychotherapy, 32*, 39–58.

Liddle, H. A., & Dakof, G. A. (1995). Efficacy of family therapy for drug abuse: Promising but not definitive. *Journal of Marital and Family Therapy, 21*, 511–543.

Liddle, H. A., Dakof, G. A., & Diamond, G. (1991). Adolescent substance abuse: Multi dimensional family therapy in action. In E. Kaufman & P. Kaufman (Eds.), *Family therapy with drug and alcohol abuse* (pp. 120–171). Boston, MA: Allyn & Bacon.

Lloyd, J. C., & Bryce, M. E. (1984). *Placement prevention and family reunification: A handbook for the family-centered service practitioner.* Iowa City, IA: University of Iowa, National Resource Center for Family Based Services.

Minuchin, S. (1974). *Families and family therapy.* Cambridge, MA: Harvard University Press.

Minuchin, S., & Fishman, H. C. (1981). *Family therapy techniques.* Cambridge, MA: Harvard University Press.

Mitchell, C., Tovar, P., & Knitzer, J. (1989). *The Bronx Homebuilders Program: An evaluation of the first 45 families.* New York: Bank Street College of Education.

Nelson, K. E. (1990). Family based services for juvenile offenders. *Children and Youth Services Review, XII*, 193–212.

Nelson, K. E. (1994). Family-based services for families and children at risk of out-of-home placement. In R. Barth, J. D. Berrick, & N. Gilbert (Eds.), *Child welfare research review*, (Vol. 1, pp. 83–108). New York: Columbia University Press.

Santisteban, D. A., Szapocznik, J., Perez-Vidal, A., Kurtines, W. M., Murray, W. J., & LaPerriere, A. (1996). Engaging behavior problem drug abusing youth and their families into treatment: An investigation of the efficacy of specialized engagement interventions and factors that contribute to differential effectiveness. *Journal of Family Psychology, 10*, 35–44.

Schmidt, S. E., Liddle, H. A., & Dakof, G. A. (1996). Changes in parenting practices and adolescent drug abuse during multidimensional family therapy. *Journal of Family Psychology, 10*, 12–27.

Schoenwald, S. K., Borduin, C. M., & Henggeler, S. W. (1998). Multisystemic therapy: Changing the natural and service ecologies of adolescents and their families. In M. H. Epstein, K. Kutash, & A. Duchnowski (Eds.), *Outcomes for children and youth with behavioral and emotional disorders and their families: Programs and evaluation best practices* (pp. 485–511). Austin, TX: PRO-Ed.

Schoenwald, S. K., & Henggeler, S. W. (1997). Combining effective treatment strategies with family preservation models of service delivery: A challenge for mental health. In R. J. Illback, H. Joseph, Jr., & C. Cobb (Eds.), *Integrated services for children and families: Opportunities for psychological practice* (pp. 121–136). Washington, DC: American Psychological Association.

Schoenwald, S. K., Ward, D. M., Henggeler, S. W., Pickrel, S. G., & Patel, H. (1996). MST treatment of substance abusing or dependent adolescent offenders: Costs of reducing incarceration, inpatient, and residential placement. *Journal of Child and Family Studies, 5*, 431–444.

Shadish, W. R., Montgomery, L. M., Wilson, P., Wilson, M. R., Bright, I., & Okwumabua, T. (1993). Effects of family and marital psychotherapies: A meta-analysis. *Journal of Consulting and Clinical Psychology, 61*, 992–1002.

Szapocznik, J., & Kurtines, W. M. (1989). *Breakthroughs in family therapy with drug-abusing and problem youth.* New York: Springer-Verlay.

Szapocznik, J., Kurtines, W. M., Foote, E., Perez-Vidal, A., & Hervis, O. E. (1983). Conjoint versus one-person family therapy: Some evidence for the effectiveness of conducting family therapy through one person. *Journal of Consulting and Clinical Psychology, 51*, 889–899.

Szapocznik, J., Kurtines, W. M., Foote, E., Perez-Vidal, A., & Hervis, O. E. (1986). Conjoint versus one-person family therapy: Further evidence for the effectiveness of conducting family therapy through one person. *Journal of Consulting and Clinical Psychology, 54*, 395–397.

Szapocznik, J., Perez-Vidal, A., Brickman, A. L., Foote, F. H., Santisteban, D., Hervis, O., & Kurtines, W. (1988). Engaging adolescent drug abusers and their families in treatment: A strategic structural systems approach. *Journal of Consulting and Clinical Psychology, 56*, 552–557.

Szapocznik, J., Santisteban, D., Rio, A. T., Perez-Vidal, A., & Kurtines, W. M. (1989). Family effectiveness training: An intervention to prevent problem behaviors in Hispanic adolescents. *Hispanic Journal of Behavioral Sciences, 11*, 4–27.

Szapocznik, J., Santisteban, D., Rio, A. T., Perez-Vidal, A., Kurtines, W. M., & Hervis, O. E. (1986). Bicultural effectiveness training: An experimental test of an intervention modality for families experiencing intergenerational/intercultural conflict. *Hispanic Journal of Behavioral Sciences, 8*, 303–330.

Tate, D. C., Reppucci, N. D., & Mulvey, E. P. (1995). Violent juvenile delinquents: Treatment effectiveness and implications for future action. *American Psychologist, 50*, 777–781.

Thornberry, T. P., Huizinga, D., & Loeber, R. (1995). The prevention of serious delinquency and violence: Implications from the program of research on the causes and correlates of delinquency. In J. C. Howell, B. Krisberg, J. D. Hawkins, & J. J. Wilson (Eds.), *A sourcebook: Serious, violent, and chronic juvenile offenders* (pp. 213–237). Newbury Park, CA: Sage.

Tolan, P. H. (1996). Characteristics shared by exemplary child clinical interventions for indicated populations. In M. C. Roberts (Ed.), *Model programs in child and family mental health* (pp. 91–107). Mahwah, NJ: Lawrence Erlbaum.

Tolan, P. H., & Guerra, N. C. (1994). *What works in reducing adolescent violence: An empirical review of the field.* Boulder, CO: University of Colorado, Institute for Behavioral Sciences, Center for the Study and Prevention of Violence.

Tuma, J. M. (1989). Mental health services for children. *American Psychologist, 46*, 188–189.

Weisz, J. R., Donenberg, G. R., Han, S. S., & Weiss, B. (1995). Bridging the gap between laboratory and clinic in child and adolescent psychotherapy. *Journal of Consulting and Clinical Psychology, 63*, 688–701.

Wood, K. M., Barton, K., & Schroeder, C. (1988). In-home treatment of abusive families: Cost and placement at one year. *Psychotherapy, 25*, 409–414.

Chapter 15

Alternative Interventions for Juvenile Offenders: History of the Adolescent Diversion Project

William S. Davidson II[1]
Stephen D. Jefferson
Aggie Legaspi
Jennifer Lujan
and
Angela M. Wolf
Michigan State University, East Lansing, USA

INTRODUCTION

Although crime and delinquency have always been concerns in American society, the popular responses to this social problem have fluctuated. Since its inception, the juvenile court has struggled with the often mutually exclusive roles of acting in the best interests of youth and protecting the public from juvenile crime (Krisberg & Austin, 1993). The emergence of juvenile diversion from the criminal justice system occurred during the late 1960s. Diversion was born out of the tripartite concerns about ineffective and inefficient correctional practices, violation of the rights of the accused, and concerns for humane treatment. The creation of Youth Service Bureaus (YSBs) through the President's Commission on Law Enforcement Administration of Justice during the late 1960s facilitated the spread of juvenile diversion programs throughout the country (Davidson &

---

[1]Authors are listed in alphabetical order to indicate equal contribution.

Handbook of Offender Assessment and Treatment. Edited by C. R. Hollin.
© 2000 John Wiley & Sons Ltd.

Johnson, 1987; Hudzik, 1984). However, diversion programs were largely unable to fulfill public expectations and their popularity has since waned (Gensheimer, Mayer, Gottschalk, & Davidson, 1985; Palmer & Lewis, 1980). Unlike the 1960s and 1970s, the current trend in juvenile corrections has placed greater emphasis on detainment and punishment, and less emphasis on diversion and rehabilitation (The Economist, 1996; Stansky, 1996; Petersilia, 1995).

Despite the current emphasis on retribution and deterrence in dealing with juvenile crime and the disappearance of most independent juvenile diversion programs, the Michigan State University Adolescent Diversion Project (ADP) has maintained its presence in the community since its inception in 1976. This chapter discusses the factors that have contributed to the ADP's longevity and success. Specifically, this chapter will first examine the historical context of the Project's inception and the rationale for its development. Second, this chapter will describe the Project and the Project values that have contributed to its success. Lastly, this chapter will summarize the results of research concerning the Project's efficacy and contribution to its community.

HISTORICAL PERSPECTIVE

Ironically, the inception of juvenile diversion occurred against the backdrop of dramatic increases in violent crime combined with the fear of social unrest in a very similar Zeitgeist present during the inception of the original juvenile court in the state of Illinois in 1899. Beginning in the early 1960s, reported crime rates increased dramatically. Concerns increased as civil disobedience, urban unrest, and political demonstrations received increasing attention from the public and politicians alike (Hudzik, 1984). Concurrently, the juvenile justice system was criticized for its ineffectiveness in dealing with adjudicated youth and the rising cost of traditional approaches of handling juvenile offenders. Critiques of the juvenile system claimed that contact with the system actually made conditions worse through labeling youth and denial of youth rights (Davidson & Johnson, 1987; Smith, 1990).

In 1967, the President's Commission on Law Enforcement and the Administration of Justice attempted to address these criticisms. The Commission suggested that part of an effective approach would include a focus on the prevention of crime through improved education, the provision of jobs, and increased opportunities for the poor. This led to the development of YSBs, which were to provide an alternative to the formal Juvenile Court. YSBs were to be composed of community representatives and professionals who would design needed services for young people. While widely acclaimed, the empirical evidence for the success of YSBs never emerged. Further more, a few studies suggested that YSBs were not effective *and* served to "widen the net" of the formal juvenile justice system potentially having the exact opposite of their intended effect. There was often conflict between community residents and agency personnel over program goals, and few residents felt that YSBs reflected the needs of the community (Hudzik, 1984; Palmer & Lewis, 1980).

The failure of YSBs to alleviate the problems associated with juvenile crime contributed to the eventual criticisms of youth diversion. In general, diversion fell short of living up to its high expectations and clearly did not eradicate juvenile crime. In response to this perception, public sentiment shifted to the view that violent crimes were due to juvenile offenders who had received too many chances in community-based programs. It was argued that in order to attack effectively the crime problem, youth should be locked up and given fewer chances. In short, the perception was that community-based programs did not offer the protection sought after by the public. This sentiment resonated with the conservative reform agenda which was gaining momentum during the late 1970s and 1980s. These positions dominated debates in the United States over juvenile justice during this period. With an emphasis on deterrence and punishment, vigorous prosecution of youthful offenders was demanded (Palmer & Lewis, 1980).

Despite this hostile environment, ADP continued to survive within this changing political climate. Through rigorous development and evaluation, ADP has continued to demonstrate its effectiveness at reducing youth recidivism, providing a cost-effective alternative to the juvenile justice system. In addition, ADP has provided an ongoing research site for community projects nested within a university setting.

ADOLESCENT DIVERSION PROJECT: PROGRAM DESCRIPTION

This section will describe ADP's current goals, the essential values of ADP, the responsibilities of advocates, training procedures for advocates, and the components of an actual intervention.

Goals of ADP

The primary goal of ADP is to provide intense, effective, and efficient community-based service intervention to youth as an alternative to formal processing in the juvenile justice system. Although the project exists outside the formal structure of the justice system, it is tied to the courts through the referral of youth. The project uses non-professionals as catalysts to institute positive change in the lives of youths and ultimately to decrease recidivism back into the justice system. Currently, ADP uses undergraduate student advocates to provide a one-on-one, individualized, youth-centered intervention in excess of 120 hours to each youth referred. Intervention effort focuses on several environmental and behavioral variables in a youth's life. Specifically, advocates are trained to work with not only the youth, but all the key people in the youth's social environment (i.e. the youth's family, teachers, potential employers, etc.). Advocate training focuses on the use of behavioral contracting and advocacy to create behavior modification and resource attainment within the youths' environments. Careful group supervision of the advocates by staff members not only ensures intervention quality, but also creates a supportive environment for advocates to share their experiences and generate ideas. A more extensive description of the goals and objectives of ADP will be provided in the following sections.

Values of ADP

Several fundamental values are central to the operation of the ADP. These values are derived from the tenets of ecological and community psychology (e.g. Fairweather & Davidson, 1986; Rappaport, 1977). A central notion is the idea that a focus on positive areas of change rather than deficits or pathologies is a more beneficial approach to preventing and decreasing delinquency. The other values of ADP simply elaborate upon this basic premise.

ADP builds upon the strengths of youth by training advocates to focus on solutions rather than problems. Specifically, advocates are instructed to concentrate on utilizing the strengths of each youth to address areas of needed intervention. Reinforcing positive behaviors is thought by ADP to be a far more effective method of behavior modification than punishing negative acts, a strategy over-emphasized by families of delinquent youth and juvenile courts. Emphasizing a youth's strengths helps advocates model a non-blaming approach to behavior change for both parents and youth. This emphasis on strength is likewise more likely to allow the youth and family to experience successful and positive behavior changes.

Second, ADP values suggest that all youths have the right to basic resources in our society. These include resources such as food, shelter, safety, education, free time activities, and due process. Intervention training and implementation specifically focuses on ensuring that advocates are capable of modeling and teaching youths and their families tactics to fulfill these and any other needed resources within their community.

Third, ADP stresses open communication and strict confidentiality between the youth and the advocate. Advocates are not allowed to discuss any details concerning their youths with anyone not affiliated with ADP, a policy that extends even to the court system. Advocates are likewise not allowed to disclose confidential information to parents, teachers, or other significant figures in a youth's environment. This policy is explained to youth during their intake at court, and also during an advocate's first meeting with his/her youth. Open communication and confidentiality foster trust between the advocate and the youth, and protect the youth from social labeling by family and community members. The ADP is very concerned about possible social labeling, for it has been shown to have an adverse effect on this population of youth (Goffman, 1963).

Another key value of ADP is working intensively with youths in their respective communities. Because ADP stresses the importance of environmental influences on the behavior of young people, it is essential that the intervention occurs where these influences are most salient. This means that advocates encourage youths to utilize local resources (e.g. the neighborhood library, neighborhood recreation center, family members, etc.) before more distant or less available ones are considered. Teaching youths to access and control resources in their immediate environments has been found to ensure more longstanding change because such proximal resources are more readily accessible to these youths, and therefore these resources have the potential to exert a stronger and more immediate influence on these youths than more distal resources.

A final value of ADP is that it avoids a victim blaming the approach in dealing with delinquents. Youths are not seen as having innate and intractable personality problems that cause them to become delinquent; rather, these youths are seen as responding to environmental influences. Additionally, these youths are further hampered by unfair formal sanctioning policies and practices. These victim-blaming influences are especially prevalent in many home and school environments. ADP avoids victim blaming by focusing on more empowering approaches such as strengths-based, environmentally appropriate behavior modification, and on resource identification and attainment.

Course Structure and the Advocates

While the ADP model has been tried with paid staff as change agents, community college students as change agents, and community volunteers as change agents, the primary source of advocates has been undergraduate college students (Davidson, Redner, Amdur, & Mitchell, 1990; Smith & Davidson, 1999). This section will focus on the operations and procedures of the ADP when college students have served as advocates. Those interested in operations with alternative change agents are encouraged to contact the authors. To be admitted into the course, students must have attained at least sophomore status. They are required to pass introductory psychology and must attend two orientation sessions before given permission to enroll. Eligible students who enroll in the course commit to participating in a two semester course. The course consists of three major components. First, the students participate in a formal training segment which involves 12 intense weeks of written and oral quizzes, role-playing exercises, and training in direct advocacy and assessment strategies. Second, advocates agree to work with court referred youth for 18 consecutive weeks for 6–8 hours per week. Third, advocates agree to meet once a week throughout the two semesters to discuss their case with a supervisory group of peers and instructors. During this supervisory meeting, an emphasis is placed on peer support and group generation of ideas for each intervention. Finally, in order for students to remain in the course, they must show mastery of all course materials and attend every class meeting.

Using student advocates contributes to the efficiency of the ADP. Furthermore, it insures an energetic pool of fresh change agents each semester. It also avoids the difficulty of breaking traditional role behaviors frequently encountered when asking seasoned professionals to work as change agents in natural community settings.

The Training Component

Advocates are trained to understand human behavior and delinquency through two theoretical models: the behavioral model and the advocacy model. These models were chosen because earlier research has demonstrated each model's efficacy (Davidson, Redner, Blakely, Mitchell, & Emshoff, 1987). Further more, it was determined that student advocates preferred utilizing both models because it allowed for a flexible and comprehensive intervention (Davidson et al., 1990).

The behavioral model emphasizes the importance of a youth's environment in determining his/her actions. It likewise suggests that the focus of change should be the youth's environment and the youth's interaction with their environment, not the individual youth *per se*. The intervention strategy arising from the behavioral model focuses on interpersonal problem solving. Training focuses on gaining the knowledge and skills involved in improving the relationships between the youth and significant others through the use of behavioral contracts and agreements. Additional skills taught to the advocate, the youth, and the family include effective communication and negotiation skills.

The advocacy model emphasizes that delinquency is distributed among all youth and that youth that are unfortunately labeled as delinquent differ from other youth in the material and personal resources available to them. This subset of identified youthful violators often reflects the members of society who are denied social privileges based on race or economic standing. Advocacy training focuses on helping advocates to develop the skills to teach their youths to be proficient in identifying and securing access to various community resources to address unmet needs.

The use of these two models aims to provide the youth and the family with additional skills they may need in responding to the interpersonal and societal challenges of life. These models combined provide the framework for the intervention model of ADP by allowing advocates to work within the youth's natural environment, focus on the youth's strengths, and continuous progress assessment. The reader is referred to Davidson and Rapp (1976), Davidson et al. (1990), and Schillo, Monaghan, and Davidson (1994) for a more detailed description of the intervention models. Further more, the training procedures have been detailed in a 12-unit manual complete with role plays, practice assignments, assigned readings, and text material (available from the authors upon request).

Components of the Intervention

The first 4 weeks of the advocate's involvement with the project are comprised exclusively of training. During week 5 of training, the assignment of youths to advocates begins. Each advocate is assigned one youth from the county serviced by ADP. Once assigned, the first phase of intervention occurs in which the youth, advocate, and significant others within the youth's environment all provide input related to the desired behavioral changes and needed community resources that will be addressed during the course of the intervention. Areas of needed change are usually very specific to each youth; however, some general areas of intervention include improving a youth's academic performance, helping the youth to establish pro-social free time activities, helping the youth secure employment, and helping the youth improve his/her relationship with important adults. The overarching goal of the advocate is to assist the youth and the family in developing the necessary skills to bring about whatever desired changes were identified during the assessment period at the beginning of the intervention.

After identification of intervention areas, the intervention enters phase two in which the advocate assists the youth and family in learning to negotiate and implement behavioral agreements and advocate for resources. Formal behavioral agreements are contracts between the youth and his or her caregiver(s) which allow the youth to earn desired privileges based on his/her performance of some specific responsibility. The implementation of such an agreement occurs during the second phase of the intervention. Also occurring at this time, the youth is taught how to identify and access needed community resources. It is expected that once these two skills are learned, they will remain with both the youth and the family even after completion of the intervention.

The third phase of the intervention consists of a timely review and (if necessary) revision of the intervention efforts up to this point. For example, if a behavioral agreement has been implemented which does not result in the targeted behavioral changes, it would be necessary to revise the contingency between the responsibilities and the privileges until the desired behaviors resulted. A similar process would be used to reassess any advocacy resources that proved to be ineffective in rewarding needed changes in the youth's environment.

The final phase of the intervention consists of preparing the youth for the termination of the intervention. In the last weeks of the intervention, the advocate reviews with the youth and family the work they have done together, and how observed gains may be maintained in the future. Additionally, during the last meeting with their youths, advocates deliver a termination pack or portfolio which is filled with information relevant to the areas of change that were addressed during the previous 18 weeks. Such a pack might include information on study tips, job-hunting skills, reproductive health issues, and so on. Giving youths such a pack contributes to the ultimate goal of teaching the youth and family to be their own advocates of change, even after the 18-week intervention has terminated.

Staff

Project staff consists of a faculty member in community psychology, several graduate students in psychology, and a few seasoned undergraduate students who have previously completed an intervention and received very high evaluations from their supervisors. Staff meet once a week for approximately an hour to discuss training topics and special case issues (e.g. if the two supervisors of an advocate need additional suggestions for how to respond to the unusual circumstances of an intervention). Additional responsibilities for the staff include the assignment of youths to specific advocates, and updating and maintaining course reading material and instructional exercises. Finally, staff are also responsible for establishing and enforcing procedural guidelines for advocates.

Relationship with Other Agencies

Establishing a good working relationship with the probate court is necessary to ensure the continued success of this project. ADP depends on the county's juvenile court officers to refer youth to the program. Because of ADP's relationship with the probate court, open communication is essential to the collaborative enterprise that ADP shares with the court. ADP maintains regular contact with court referees to ensure that important concerns and issues are discussed in a timely manner. In addition to this regular contact, ADP staff and court referees meet once a year for an informal gathering to renew old acquaintances and welcome new staff members.

EVALUATION

One component that is key to the survival of ADP in its community setting is continuous development and evaluation. During its early research and development period, federal funding from the National Institute for Mental Health supported research activities on the ADP model. After over a decade of such funding, ADP had established itself as a successful program for reducing youth delinquency. Its rigorous evaluation was an impetus in obtaining supporting funds from the county which it services. The next section is a summary of the research conducted to evaluate and improve ADP. For a detailed description of the developmental phases of ADP and results refer to Davidson et al. (1987), Davidson and Redner (1988), Davidson et al. (1990), and Smith and Davidson (1999).

Evaluation of the ADP model went through three phases. The first was focused on examining the basic efficacy of the model. The second was determining which components were critical to the efficacy observed. The third was aimed at determining the replicability and durability of the model.

Evidence of Effectiveness: Early Evaluations

Originally developed in Champaign-Urbana, Illinois, the ADP was part of a larger project evaluating the effectiveness of non-professional change agents in servicing a variety of populations including adolescents in legal jeopardy (Seidman & Rappaport, 1974). Only youth considered for petition to the local circuit court were considered for ADP. During a 2-year study, 73 youth met this criteria. These youth were then assigned randomly to undergraduate students who had been trained either in behavioral contracting or child advocacy. Additionally, some of the youth were assigned randomly to an outright release/no treatment control group. Of these 73 youth, 61 were males, 49 were White, and the average age was 14.3. In the year prior to their involvement with ADP, youth were arrested an average of 2.16 times (Davidson et al., 1977).

Undergraduate student advocates received 6 weeks of training which included reading assignments, homework assignments, and practice role plays. The training and supervision of the student advocates was conducted by advanced graduate students who were in turn trained and supervised by two faculty members. Intervention techniques focused on behavioral contracting, child advocacy, and resource mobilization.

There were three important results that emerged from this intervention. First, there was no difference in the efficacy of the behavioral contracting group or the child advocacy group in terms of recidivism or school attendance. Second, both the behavioral contracting and the advocacy groups were superior to the control group in terms of both recidivism and school attendance. Third, these results persisted through a two-year follow-up (Davidson et al., 1977; Davidson & Redner, 1988).

Evidence of Effectiveness: Examining Critical Components of the ADP

An initial replication of the ADP focused on examining the relative efficacy of various elements of the intervention model. In addition, two other comparisons were included. The first study had compared the ADP model with an outright release control group. For this second study, ADP models were compared with usual court processing. Further more, there were concerns for the degree to which the original results were a function of attentional components (i.e. perhaps simply giving delinquent youths positive attention would be enough to effect a reduction in recidivism). As a result, this second study also included an attention placebo condition. In order to accomplish these comparisons, different groups of students received training (10 weeks manual based) and supervision in different intervention models. In the first experimental condition, labeled the *action condition*, the behavioral and advocacy models were combined. Students received 10 weeks of training in the combined model and worked one-on-one with referred youth for 18 weeks. A variation of this model was directed exclusively towards the family and was labeled the *action condition–family focus*. This group utilized advocacy and contracting also, but these principles were applied exclusively with family members. Similar training and intervention intensities applied. A third condition, the *relationship condition*, focused exclusively on the relationship

between the youth and the student advocate and was based on Rogerian principles and emphasized the importance of interpersonal relationships as con-
tributors to youth delinquency. A fourth condition embodied our concern with
examining the transferability of the model to other settings. Labeled the *action
condition–court setting*, students were trained in the action model by project staff
but their work with youth was supervised by staff from the juvenile court. The
action–court setting was administered with the juvenile court setting. The fifth
group was an *attention placebo* group. This group was intended to mirror the
typical model provided by university volunteers and reflect the same intensity of
intervention as was present in the other groups. These students received brief
training covering the history of the juvenile court, theories of delinquency, and
focused on the importance of helping relationships. The intervention was atheo-
retical and mostly recreational, but of similar intensity and duration (Davidson
et al., 1987).

Of the 228 youth that participated in this second study, 83% were males, 26%
were minorities, and the average age was 14.2 years. The youth were arrested an
average of 1.46 times in the year prior to their involvement in the project. Results
indicated that the action group, the action–family focus group, and the relationship groups were all superior in preventing recidivism to the action–court setting,
the attention placebo group, and the control group. The action–court setting was
the least effective in reducing recidivism (Davidson et al., 1987).

These results support the previous conclusion that ADP was effective in reducing delinquency. Moreover, these results indicated that a specified model and
training were critical to providing an effective intervention. Additional findings
of interest indicated that the student advocates strongly preferred the action
intervention resulting in the decision to employ it in future replications.

Another replication of this intervention examined the importance of college
students as the type of advocates employed. In this study, students from a major
university, students from a community college, and volunteers recruited from the
local community all received training in the action model of intervention. They
all received 10 weeks of manual based training and provided 18 weeks of one-
on-one intervention to referred youth and their families. Youth were randomly
assigned to one of the three groups of advocates or a court processed control
group. Using the same criteria for youth participation as in the previous studies,
129 youth were included. Most of the youth were males (83.9%) and 29.8% were
minorities. The average age of the youth was 14.1 years.

The first group of advocates ($n = 47$) consisted of undergraduates recruited
from a large midwestern university had an average age of 21; 51% were female,
the majority were single (91%), and most were White (91%). Most of the participants in this group had some previous human service experience (70%). These
undergraduates received three academic quarters of course credit for their participation. The second group of advocates ($n = 35$) was comprised of students
enrolled in a midwestern community college. Most of these students were White
(91%), female (70%), and single (67%). Sixty-seven percent of this group had
some human service experience. The students in this group received three acad-

emic quarters of course credit for their participation. The last group was comprised of community advocates ($n = 18$). Their training, supervision, and intervention goals were the same as the other two groups but they received no course credits or grades for their participation. Although over 200 potential community advocates approached the project during the recruitment period, the vast majority dropped out before the training started. Of the remaining 18 advocates, most were female (67%), White (100%), and had human service experience (93%). Only 36% of the advocates were single, 43% were married, and 21% were divorced or separated.

A two-year follow-up indicated that all three intervention groups had significantly lower recidivism than the control group. However, there was no significant difference between each of the three intervention groups. These results offer support for the intervention model utilizing populations other than university undergraduates to serve as the service providers. Further more, it was discovered that the students from the major university provided the same level of intervention for significantly lower costs. This was due to the increased recruitment costs required to solicit and retain both community college and community volunteer groups (Davidson et al., 1990).

Evidence of Effectiveness: Replication in a Major Urban Area

Since the first three studies had taken place in medium-sized cities, proponents of the ADP felt it was important to begin exploring replication and dissemination possibilities in a large metropolitan area. As a result, the ADP model was also examined in a fourth study in a large metropolitan area. In addition, two important issues were examined in the fourth study. First, the ADP model was directly (Davidson et al., 1990) compared with an outright release control group and a court processing control group in the same study. This allowed examination of the two control conditions while controlling for the larger environmental influences. Second, the ADP model was implemented by a community agency rather than being based in a university setting. This meant that professional staff served as advocates.

In this fourth study, youth were referred by the police after being charged with an offense that would have normally been referred to the court. After agreeing to participate, 395 youth were assigned to one of three groups: (1) the diversion project, (2) released to parents with no further interventions, and (3) traditional court processing. The mean age of the participants was 14 years. Most of the youth were male (84%) and Black (91%). Professional staff (Bachelors degree level) underwent intensive training similar to the previous stages on assessment, behavioral contracting, and advocacy techniques, and methods to monitor intervention and termination. They each carried a case load of 4–6 cases to allow maintaining the intensity of the intervention for 18 weeks.

Results of this study indicated that the action model was statistically superior in reducing delinquency. In a 1-year follow-up, the ADP group had a significantly lower recidivism rate than either the release to parents or the court processed group. There were no differences in recidivism between the release to parents group and the court processed group (an interesting and controversial finding in its own right).

What Makes ADP Effective?

In addition to the experimental comparisons reported above, there have been several other foci of our program of research aimed at understanding the potent forces operating in the ADP model. A first series of investigations conducted in parallel with the first three studies examined the salient processes operating in both the lives of the adolescent youth and the program. These results emanated from extensive open-ended interviews which were conducted at six-month intervals with the youth involved, their parents, the advocate, and a nominated best friend of the youth. While these results have been reported in great detail elsewhere (e.g. Davidson et al., 1990; Davidson & Redner, 1988) a brief summary is relevant here. Three important findings were identified. First, it appears that the ADP model operates to increase the fit of the youth in pro-social activities. This model has both a social control and social support component. Youth who receive ADP intervention remain relatively more involved in their families, school, and employment settings, and they are relatively less involved in peer activities and legal issues. Second, the ADP model appears to insulate the youth and their families from the negative influences which are exacerbated by court processing. In other words, the ADP model has a direct and positive effect while avoiding a negative effect. Third, it appears that interventions that are characterized as proactive, persistent, and accomplishment oriented are more likely to have positive effects. In other words, when the details of intervention process are examined in relation to outcome, those interventions which proactively addressed issues in the home, school, or employment domain are more likely to see the youth involved and reduce recidivism.

Other attempts to examine factors that contribute to the success of ADP have illuminated the role of labeling in the lives of youth serviced by ADP. As previously mentioned, one of the original goals of diversion programs was to remove the negative stigma applied to youth who came into contact with the criminal justice system. Later, diversion programs were criticized for not fulfilling this promise. Youth who are formally processed by the juvenile court are assumed to be stigmatized by the experience, and this stigma is believed to encourage future acts of delinquency as a function of a self-fulfilling prophecy.

An analysis of interview data from the youth and parent in the fourth study indicated that diversion from the juvenile justice system was successful in reducing the number of people who are aware of a youth's delinquency; however, diversion was positively related to the number of people in the youth's life who suspected further delinquency. Positive family relationships seemed to serve as a buffer against the expectation that families had about further delinquency in that families with better relationships had a lower expectation of future delinquent behavior on the part of the youth. Program participation did not significantly increase pro-social attitudes; however, increased pro-social attitudes were inversely related to the number of people knowing about the delinquency, and the expectation of future delinquency. Others knowing about delinquency was related to expectancies for future delinquency because it was related to attributing a negative reputation to the youth, which was related to the youth then attributing a negative reputation to themselves. Additionally, for two of the three sites in this study, an inverse relationship was found between the number of people aware of delinquent acts and delinquency. Finally, the youth's perception of self as a delinquent was found to generally have a smaller effect on delinquent behavior than negative labeling by others (i.e. parents, neighbors, friends, etc.). This research generally supports the supposition that labeling of delinquent youth can have significant negative consequences for the youth (Smith & Davidson, 1999).

Effects on the Advocates

Juveniles have not been the only focus of ADP research. Additional research has been conducted using the student advocates. In the hope of improving the selection of volunteers to be used as change agents, the first investigation of the advocates examined three key issues. First, the long-term impact on the volunteer of the intervention was examined to assess the possible influence effects the intervention experience may have on the volunteer's future choice of career and education. Second, the volunteer's attitudes toward the client population and related social services were examined over time. Third, the impact of the intervention experience on the volunteer's evaluation of the students' undergraduate education. The only clear finding that emerged was that students who participated in the project, compared with a control group, were significantly more likely to be employed in the human service arena (Davidson et al., 1990).

Later research examined the political empowerment beliefs of ADP advocates before and after completing their work with a court referred youth. The specific beliefs of interest in this study were political awareness, political competence, and political activism. Angelique (1997) expected that participants who actually worked with court referred youth (experimental group) would feel more politically empowered than waiting list participants who were never assigned youths (control group). Again, findings for this study were mixed. Angelique found that participants who were actually allowed to work with youth exhibited an increased level of political commitment compared with advocates in the control group. However, feelings of political efficacy decreased more significantly for the experimental group than for the control group. Despite the latter finding, a general trend was found which suggested that advocates who worked with youth were more likely to aspire to careers in social services.

CONCLUSION

The Adolescent Diversion Project is a community-based service provider which attempts to keep at-risk youth out of the formal juvenile court system by utilizing the efforts of trained undergraduate advocates. Despite significant social and political opposition to diversion programs that can be traced back to the early 1970s, this project has survived and flourished during the past 26 years due to a number of specific factors.

One of the most important contributing factors to ADP's longevity is its strict adherence to the values that guided the original development of the Project. ADP has a set of empirically validated values which permeate all aspects of its implementation. Specifically, ADP endorses the view that delinquency is caused by youths whose needs have been thwarted by an unresponsive environment. This approach avoids victim blaming, and it helps advocates focus on helping youths to capitalize on their strengths. Additionally, ADP endorses the view that the focus of change in a youth's life should be directed at his/her environment rather than the unique personality variables of the youth. Toward this end, advocates center their intervention efforts in the youth's community. Lastly, ADP has a value for self-evaluation and program dissemination. The latter value allows ADP to quantitatively justify its existence, and because it has been able to demonstrate its efficacy, this fact makes it easier to disseminate program information to new communities.

Another important factor that helps to promote ADP's continued existence and dissemination is its low cost and its use of non-federal funding sources. Because ADP is a program with demonstrated efficacy, many county and state agencies are willing to utilize it as an alternative to more expensive, less efficacious options such as building more detention centers or hiring more law enforcement officers. Additionally, ADP is able to keep its costs low because it enlists the aid of para-professionals. These advocates have been found to be effective agents of change, and they are also much less expensive than utilizing more traditional human service professionals. Utilizing non-federal funding sources and enlisting the aid of advocates has helped ADP reduce costs without sacrificing efficacy, and this allows ADP to avoid the criticism leveled at other diversion programs which asserts that such programs are too expensive and ineffective.

Finally, ADP's concerted effort to maintain a very congenial and open relationship with juvenile court officials has also contributed significantly to its survival and ultimate success. By convincing court officials that ADP is a viable sentencing alternative, ADP ensures that these officials will find a place for it in their dispensation decisions.

This chapter has attempted to describe some of the major factors that have contributed to ADP's ability to persevere when so many other diversion programs have been forced to expire. The heart of ADP is that it is a collaborative effort, not only of individuals and institutions, but also of ideas and values. It is a program that is committed to the betterment of youth, and it has had over 20 years to refine this resolve. It is hoped that the information described in this chapter will be useful to other human service workers who may be attempting to start similar projects.

REFERENCES

Angelique, H. L. (1997). *Paths to political empowerment: Evaluation of a comprehensive model and an intervention with university students.* Unpublished doctoral dissertation, Michigan State University.

Davidson, W. S., & Johnson, C. (1987). Diversion in Michigan. Lansing, MI: Department of Social Services, Office of Children and Youth Services.

Davidson, W. S., & Rapp, C. (1976). Child advocacy in the justice system. *Social Work, 21,* 225–232.

Davidson, W. S., & Redner, R. (1988). The prevention of juvenile delinquency: Diversion from the juvenile justice system. *Fourteen Ounces of Prevention* (pp. 123–137). Washington, DC: American Psychological Association.

Davidson, W. S., Redner, R., Amdur, R., & Mitchell, C. (1990). *Alternative treatments for troubled youth.* New York: Plenum.

Davidson, W. S., Redner, R., Blakely, C. H., Mitchell, C. M., & Emshoff, J. G. (1987). Diversion of juvenile offenders: An experimental comparison. *Journal of Consulting and Clinical Psychology, 55,* 68–75.

Davidson, W. S., Seidman, E., Rappaport, J., Berck, P., Rapp, N., Rhodes, W., & Herring, J. (1977). Diversion programs for juvenile offenders. *Social Work Research and Abstracts, 13,* 40–49.

The Economist (1996). Misunderstood youth: Campaign issues: Crime. *The Economist, 340*(7984), 25–26.

Fairweather, G. W., & Davidson, W. S. (1986). *An introduction to community experimentation.* New York: McGraw-Hill.

Gensheimer, L. K., Mayer, J. P., Gottschalk, R., & Davidson, W. S. (1985). Diverting youth from the juvenile justice system: A meta-analysis of intervention efficacy. *Youth Violence.* 39–57.

Goffman, E. (1963). *Stigma: Notes on the management of spoiled identity.* Englewood Cliffs, NJ: Prentice-Hall.

Hudzik, J. K. (1984). *Federal aid to criminal justice: Rhetoric, results, lessons.* Lexington, KY: National Criminal Justice Association.

Krisberg, B., & Austin, J. F. (1993). *Reinventing juvenile justice.* Newbury Park, CA: Sage.

Palmer, T., & Lewis, R. V. (1980). *An evaluation of juvenile diversion.* Cambridge, MA: Oelgeschlager, Gunn, & Hain.

Petersilia, J. (1995). A crime control rationale for reinvesting in community corrections. *Spectrum: The Journal of State Government, 68*(3), 16–28.

Rappaport, J. (1977). *Community psychology: Values, research, and action.* New York: Holt, Rinehart, & Winston.

Schillo, B., Monaghan, T., & Davidson, W. S. (1994). Adolescent diversion project: An alternative to traditional court service for youthful offenders. Unpublished manuscript, Michigan State University.

Seidman, E., & Rappaport, J. (1974). The Educational Pyramid: A paradigm for research, training, and manpower. *American Journal of Community Psychology, 2,* 119–130.

Smith, E. (1990). *Labeling: The process of self-fulfilling prophecy and its effect upon adolescent behavior.* Unpublished doctoral dissertation, Michigan State University.

Smith, E., & Davidson, W. S. (1999). Pygmalion revisited: The role of labeling in juvenile delinquency. Manuscript submitted for publication.

Stansky, L. (1996). Age of innocence: More and more states are telling teens: If you do adult crime, you'll serve adult time. *ABA Journal, 82,* 60–66.

Chapter 16

Delinquency Prevention Programs in Schools

David LeMarquand
and
Richard E. Tremblay
Université de Montréal, Montréal, Canada

INTRODUCTION

Chronic adult offenders commonly begin their criminal careers as chronic juvenile offenders (Lynam, 1996; see also Loeber & Stouthamer-Loeber, 1998). Ideally, intervention strategies for criminal behavior should be initiated early, before violent and criminal behavior becomes a stable part of an individual's repertoire. One method of intervening in treating or preventing chronic juvenile delinquency is through the school (Durlak, 1995; Lane & Murakami, 1987). This strategy may be effective for a number of reasons.

First, longitudinal studies have demonstrated that low intelligence, poor academic achievement, small vocabulary, and poor verbal reasoning are predictors of chronic delinquency (Farrington, 1985, 1987; Hawkins et al., 1998; Loeber & Dishion, 1983). Poor "executive functions", including the ability to plan and sequence behavior, have also been associated with stable aggressive behavior in early-adolescent boys (Séguin, Pihl, Harden, Tremblay, & Boulerice, 1995). Low cognitive ability is commonly thought to precede the development of delinquent behavior; however, it is possible that early aggressive behavior may lead to lower IQ, or that third variables (e.g. parental psychopathology) may account for the cognitive deficit/delinquency association. At present there is not enough evidence to clearly specify a direction of causality (Yoshikawa, 1994). A causal link between low cognitive ability and delinquency might be mediated by academic success and bonding to the school environment. Low bonding to school, truancy

Handbook of Offender Assessment and Treatment. Edited by C. R. Hollin.
© 2000 John Wiley & Sons Ltd.

and school dropout have been related to later delinquency (Hawkins et al., 1998). Low cognitive ability leading to academic failure and reduced bonding to the school may lead to skipping school and dropping out, increasing the time available for becoming involved in delinquent behavior. School interventions designed to improve cognitive functioning could contribute to a reduction in delinquency and provide confirmation of a causal link between reduced cognitive ability and later delinquency.

Second, behavior problems exhibited in school are important targets for intervention in and of themselves. Disruptive behavior in the classroom consumes a teacher's time and energy, and interferes with the learning processes of disruptive and non-disruptive students, which may lead to a classwide reduction in academic achievement. Moreover, classroom behavior problems may represent early expressions of disruptiveness that later develop into delinquent behavior. Childhood aggressive behavior, as well as hyperactivity, attentional difficulties, impulsivity, and oppositional behavior, are related to delinquent behavior in adolescence (Farrington, 1991; Huesmann, Eron, Lefkowitz, & Walder, 1984; White, Moffitt, Earls, Robins, & Silva, 1990). More specifically, teacher-rated aggressive behavior in school is related to later delinquency, particularly in males (Stattin & Magnusson, 1989; Tremblay et al., 1992).

Third, school processes and climate are related to levels of achievement and delinquency (Fiquera-McDonough, 1986; Rutter, 1983). A number of early studies (summarized in Rutter, 1983) have demonstrated a wide variability in delinquency rates across schools, although some of this variability may be a function of school intake characteristics. A school environment characterized by competitive academic achievement, routine handling of discipline and unpredictable supervision (versus a broader definition of success, more specialized discipline, and predictable supervision) is associated with higher rates of minor delinquency (Fiquera-McDonough, 1986).

Another advantage of intervening in schools to impact on delinquency, particularly from a prevention point of view, is that the great majority of children attend school. This facilitates the early identification of children who exhibit aggressive behavior and/or academic difficulties, which are known predictors of later delinquent behavior (Farrington, 1994; Loeber & Dishion, 1983; Stattin & Magnusson, 1989). Following identification, a school intervention can be implemented for indicated individuals with greater ease than if implemented in the home or clinic.

In this chapter, school interventions designed to prevent and treat juvenile delinquency are reviewed. Only those studies implementing a school intervention and assessing juvenile delinquency outcomes using controlled experimental or quasi-experimental designs are included for review. The majority of studies in this review include school interventions implemented before the onset of delinquent behavior, designed to prevent the subsequent development of serious delinquency. Thus, these are prevention studies, as opposed to treatment studies, seeking to reduce criminal behavior in youth already identified as juvenile delinquents. Interest in the prevention of delinquency is growing. Early intervention, before the development of serious delinquent behavior, may avert significantly greater societal and individual suffering than by treating the individual after the development of delinquent behavior.

PRIMARY FINDINGS

Table 16.1 summarizes the studies of school interventions to reduce delinquent behavior. The studies are grouped by type of intervention. Preventive interventions can be classified according to the characteristics of the sample chosen for the intervention (Gordon, 1987). A universal preventive intervention is applied to an entire population, a selective intervention to individuals at above average risk for a disorder, and an indicated intervention to asymptomatic individuals who manifest a risk factor which places them at high risk for the development of a disorder. In the present review, interventions were classified as selective if participants manifested one or more environmental risk factors (i.e. poverty), whereas indicated interventions involved participants manifesting personal risk factors (e.g. disruptive behavior, low IQ) placing them at higher risk for the development of delinquency. Within each intervention type, studies are ordered by decreasing age of the participants.

Also included in Table 16.1 are effect sizes (ESs), calculated for delinquency outcomes. ESs represent the mean of the control group subtracted from the mean of the intervention group, and divided by the pooled within-group standard deviation, and are unweighted (Hedges & Olkin, 1985). They are calculated so that positive scores reflected improvement in the intervention group relative to the controls. ESs of 0.2 are generally considered small, 0.5 medium, and 0.8 large (Cohen, 1977).

Three universal interventions have incorporated school intervention components to prevent juvenile delinquency (among other negative outcomes), including two carried out by Hawkins and his associates involving altering teaching methods to reduce delinquent behavior. A third reported by Farrell and Meyer (1997) involved the implementation of a classroom information curriculum to prevent violent behavior. An additional universal intervention (Kellam, Rebok, Ialongo, & Mayer, 1994) reported on the effects of a classroom-based behavior management strategy on aggressive behavior; however, delinquency outcome data have yet to be reported on this sample. Another large-scale universal intervention designed to prevent bullying in schools found reductions in antisocial behavior after 20 months of intervention; however, this study did not employ a no-treatment control group, using instead a "time-lagged contrasts between age-equivalent cohorts" design (Olweus, 1991).

Hawkins and his associates (Hawkins, Doueck, & Lishner, 1988; Hawkins & Lam, 1987) implemented an intervention experiment in grade seven classrooms of five Seattle middle schools. Three of these schools were randomly assigned to either the intervention or control condition, while the classes of a fourth school were assigned to the intervention and the classes of a fifth school to the control

Table 16.1 School interventions and their effects on delinquent behavior

Author(s)	Number of participants at pretest (I = intervention, C = control)	Age at intervention (years)	Design	Type of intervention	Description of intervention	Context of intervention	Length of intervention	Follow-up: length (years); sample size at follow-up	Results for delinquency for intervention group, compared to controls, at latest assessment (effect size)
Farrell & Meyer (1997)	978	11	random assignment	universal	violence information curriculum	school	18 weeks	0; 698 (385 girls); 348 I, 350 C	• significant decreases in boys' self-reported problem behavior (0.24) and drug use (0.20) • trend for decreased boys' self-reported violent behavior (0.18) • no effect on girls self-reported violent behavior (−0.12), problem behavior (−0.14), and drug use (−0.02)
Hawkins & Lam (1987)	1166 boys and girls; 513 I, 653 C	mean = 13.3	quasi-experimental (partial randomization)	universal	teacher training	school	1 year	0; 766	• negative relationship between teacher practices and school disciplinary reports (0.90), days suspended (0.98), and self-report times suspended or expelled
Hawkins et al. (1999); SSDP	643 (316 girls); 156 full I, 267 late I, 220 C	6	quasi-experimental (partial randomization)	universal	teacher training, child training, parent training	school, family	6 years	6 years; 598 (299 girls); 149 full I, 243 late I, 206 C	• full I significantly reduced self-report violent delinquency (0.23), officially-recorded school misbehavior (0.25) • full I tended to reduce self-report non-violent delinquency (0.11), police arrests (0.14), and official court-recorded delinquency (0.17)

Study	Sample	Age	Design	Type	Intervention	Setting	Duration	Follow-up	Results
Clarke & Campbell (1997); The Abecedarian Project	111 (59 girls); 57 I, 54 C	mean = 4.4 m	random assignment	selective	preschool	daycare	5 years	13 years; 105, 54 I, 51 C	• no differences in officially-recorded adult criminal charges and arrests (including percentage receiving any charge (0.03), mean number of charges, mean number of arrests)
Gottfredson (1987); PCD	360 boys and girls; 184 I, 176 C	14–17; mean = 15.4	random assignment	indicated	group counselling with peers/leaders	school	15 weeks	0	• marginally greater self-report serious delinquency (−0.20) • no difference in police contacts (−0.05) • greater drug use (−0.25)
Gottfredson & Gottfredson (1992); STATUS	247 boys and girls; 120 I, 127 C	12 to 17	quasi-experimental (failed random assignment)	indicated	social studies curriculum	school	1 year	0	• less self-report serious delinquency in junior (0.33) and senior (0.42) schools • marginally lower rates of court contact in junior (0.07) and senior (0.18) schools less drug involvement in junior (0.42) and senior (0.35) schools
Arbuthnot & Gordon (1986)	48 (13 girls); 24 I, 24 C	mean = 14.5	pairing, random assignment	indicated	group discussions around moral reasoning	school	16–20 weeks	1 year; 22, 13 I, 9 C	• no differences in police/court contacts • decreased school absenteeism
Gottfredson (1986); PATHE	869 boys and girls; 468 I, 401 C	11–17	random assignment	indicated	individualized intervention programs, alterations in school management and organization	school	2 years	0	• no change in self-report serious delinquency (0.00), number of court contacts (0.00), school-recorded suspensions (−0.02), expulsions (0.10), disciplinary infractions (0.16) • greater self-report drug involvement (−0.21)

continued overleaf

Table 16.1 *(continued)*

Author(s)	Number of participants at pretest (I = intervention, C = control)	Age at intervention (years)	Design	Type of intervention	Description of intervention	Context of intervention	Length of intervention	Follow-up: length (years); sample size at follow-up	Results for delinquency for intervention group, compared to controls, at latest assessment (effect size)
Ahlstrom & Havighurst (1982)	Group 2: 167 boys; 95 I, 72 C	13–14	random assignment	indicated	individualized classroom education program; work program	school	approx. 5.5 years	0	• higher police-reported arrests in early adolescence (−0.29); slightly lower percentage of arrests in late adolescence (0.04)
Wodarski & Filipczak (1982); PREP	60 (18 girls); 30 (9 girls) I; 30 (9 girls) C	13.2 (grades 7–9)	matching, random assignment	indicated	individualized and small group instruction, social skills training, behavioral contracts with incentives	school	1 year	4 years; 21 I, 19 C	• no differences on 31 I–C comparisons on self- and parent-reported juvenile problem behavior variables • less self-reported participation in gang fights (0.51) greater attempts to avoid trouble (0.52)
Reckless & Dinitz (1972); YDP	1094 boys; 632 I, 462 C	13 (7th grade)	random assignment	indicated	remedial reading, teacher group lesson planning, teacher group discussion, social role-modelling	school	1 year	3 years; 536 I, 379 C	• no differences on police contacts (−0.03) • no differences on self-report delinquency • teacher-rated delinquency lower in one cohort
Stuart et al. (1976)	60; 30 I, 30 C	11–15 (grades 6–10)	random assignment	indicated	behavioral contacts with incentives, costs	school	4 months	0	• no differences in court contacts (0.37)
Bry (1982)	66 (22 girls); 33 I, 33 C	mean = 12.5 (grader 7)	pairing, andom assignment	indicated	behavior contingencies, school monitoring	school	2 years	5 years; 60 (20 girls), 30 I, 30 C	• fewer serious or chronic delinquency probation dept. files (0.51)

Study	Sample	Age	Design	Level	Intervention	Setting	Duration	Follow-up	Results
Lochman (1992)	145 boys; 31 anger-coping (AC), 52 untreated aggressives (UA), 62 nonaggressives (NON)	9–12	random assignment of some cohorts to treatment and control groups	indicated	cognitive–behavioral, anger control	school	4–5 months	2.5–3.5 years	• no differences in self-report general behavioral deviance (0.11, including crimes against persons (−0.12) or general theft (0.19)) between AC and UA boys
Tremblay et al. (1995); MLES	166 boys; 43 1, 82 attention/observation C, 41 C	7	random assignment	indicated	parent training in effective child rearing; social skills training for children	home, school	2 years	6 years	• less self-reported delinquent behaviors 1 to 6 years after end of intervention (0.24) • no difference in court registered delinquent offenses (−0.07)
Schweinhart et al. (1993); Perry Preschool Study	123 (51 girls); 58 (25 girls) 1, 65 (26 girls) C	3–4	random assignment	indicated	preschool; teacher home visits	school, home	1–2 years	22 years	• fewer mean officially-recorded lifetime arrests (0.54) • no differences on self-report misconduct variables (0.29)
Schweinhart & Weikhart (1997); Preschool Curriculum Study	68 (37 girls); 23 Direct Instruction (DI), 22 High/Scope (HS), 23 Nursery School (NS)	3–4	random assignment	indicated	preschool (either DI—teacher-initiated activities, HS—teacher and child planned & initiated activities, or NS—child-initiated activities); teacher home visits	school, home	1–2 years	18 years, 52; 19 DI, 14 HS, 19 NS	• DI had higher self-report mean frequency of work suspensions (0.22 for all self-report delinquency variables, HS vs. other two groups) • DI had higher lifetime arrests, adult arrests, felony arrests (specifically property felonies) and property misdemeanour arrests according to official records (0.21 for lifetime arrests, juvenile and adult, HS vs. other two groups)

condition. The intervention focused on maintaining low achievers in regular class-rooms and modifying teaching practices to provide them with opportunities for active involvement, skills for successful participation, and constant reinforcement for work involvement. Hypothetically, these opportunities would increase school success, increase bonding to school, and decrease disruptive behavior. To this end, teachers were provided with training programs emphasizing proactive classroom management (how to create a learning environment in the classroom), interac-tive teaching (including mastering objectives before moving to higher learning levels), and cooperative learning (grouping students of different abilities to work together). Teachers were also supervised in these instructional methods in the classroom.

Data for the entire sample were analyzed by looking for correlations between the use of the prescribed teacher practices and delinquent behaviors, rather than comparing the intervention and control groups on delinquency outcomes. At the end of the school year, inverse relationships were found between the extent to which teachers employed project teaching practices and the number of school disciplinary reports and days suspended, as well as students' self-report number of times suspended/expelled and high on drugs at school. There were no rela-tionships between use of teacher practices and student self-reports of truancy, school theft, or trouble due to drug/alcohol use (Hawkins & Lam, 1987). In a subset of the entire sample chosen on the basis of low math achievement test scores, the intervention group was suspended or expelled less often than the control group according to school records and self-report (ES = 0.36); however, again there were no group differences in self-report property crimes (ES = 0.06), interpersonal violence (ES = 0.04), serious crime (ES = 0.13), or drug use (ES = 0.11). This despite the fact that intervention students reported more positive atti-tudes toward school and higher expectations for future education (Hawkins et al., 1988). It may be that not enough time had elapsed for the change in atti-tudes and school behaviors to have "trickled down" to impact on delinquency. An additional follow-up might demonstrate the desired effects.

A second, more extensive universal intervention experiment designed to prevent delinquency and other undesirable behavioral outcomes is the Seattle Social Development Project (SSDP) (Hawkins, Catalano, Kosterman, Abbott, & Hill, 1999). First grade classrooms in one Seattle public school were assigned to the intervention condition, classrooms in a second school to the control condi-tion, and classrooms in the remaining six schools were randomly assigned to intervention or control conditions. At the beginning of grade five, the sample was non-randomly expanded with the addition of 18 schools to the late treatment and control conditions, resulting in a quasi-experimental design. The interven-tion was 6 years in length. In this study, the classroom intervention was one component of a multimodal intervention. For this component, teachers re-ceived 5 days of in-service training per year in proactive classroom manage-ment, interactive teaching, and cooperative learning. As a manipulation check, teachers in the intervention and control conditions were observed in the fall and spring of each year to document the use of the targeted teaching strategies.

Greater use of the targeted teaching strategies in the intervention classrooms compared with the control classrooms was confirmed. In addition to the teacher-training component, the intervention included cognitive and social skills training administered to the children by the teachers, as well as parent training in behavior management skills. A recent 6-year follow-up of this study has demonstrated that the full intervention significantly reduced officially-recorded school misbehavior (ES = 0.25) and self-report violent delinquency (ES = 0.23), and tended to reduce self-report non-violent delinquency (ES = 0.11), police arrests (ES = 0.14), and official court records (ES = 0.17) (Hawkins et al., 1999). Since the teacher-training intervention was but one component of a multimodal intervention package, it is not possible to know the proportion of the reduction in disruptive behavior that was due to the school intervention component alone.

Farrell & Meyer (1997) reported on a classroom-based curriculum designed to teach high-school-aged youth about the nature of violence. This program was implemented and evaluated in six of eight middle schools with predominantly low-income African-American students. Classrooms were randomly assigned to the immediate intervention or waiting-list control conditions. The 18-week intervention focused on building trust, teaching respect for individual differences, imparting information on the nature of violence and risk factors, teaching anger management, discussing personal values, discussing the precipitants and consequences of fighting, and generating non-violent alternative responses to fighting. It was implemented in the classroom by four college-educated, African-American male prevention specialists, working in pairs. Post-intervention assessment was completed after those in the immediate intervention condition had finished the intervention, but before the waiting-list control condition received the curriculum. Data were available for 348 students in the intervention condition, and 350 students in the waiting-list control condition.

Three subscales of the Behavioral Frequency Scales were the primary dependent measures: the Violent Behavior Scale, with items such as "been in a fight in which someone was hit", "threatened to hurt a teacher", "threatened someone with a weapon (gun, knife, or club)", "brought a weapon to school", and "been in a fight in which you were injured and had to be treated by a doctor or nurse"; the Problem Behavior Scale, tapping the frequency of vandalism and shoplifting, in addition to violent behaviors; and the Drug Use Scale, assessing the frequency of alcohol, cigarette, and marijuana use. Results showed definite sex effects. Scores on the Problem Behavior and Drug Use scales were significantly decreased for boys (ESs = 0.24 and 0.20, respectively), but not for girls (ESs = −0.14 and −0.02), in the intervention condition compared with the waiting-list control condition. Scores on the Violent Behavior Scale also tended to be lower for boys in the intervention condition relative to controls (ES = 0.18), with no differences for girls (ES = −0.12). The authors speculate that the intervention may have been more effective for boys because they more readily identified with the African-American men who implemented the program.

The only selective intervention located that involved a school component was the Abecedarian project (Clarke & Campbell, 1997). This study is notable, however, in that the intervention was initiated when the participants were born, presumably when the potential for influence on future behavior is greatest. It is distinguishable from other preventive interventions beginning at or near birth (Olds et al., 1997; Seitz, Rosenbaum, & Apfel, 1985) in that it focused specifically on cognitive development through a preschool intervention, whereas the latter interventions were daycare-oriented. One hundred and eleven infants were randomly assigned at birth to receive either 5 years of preschool education in a child-care setting, or no treatment. The infants were considered to be at risk for suboptimal cognitive development due to conditions of poverty, low parental education levels, low parental IQ, and poor maternal social/family support, among others (Campbell & Ramey, 1995). The intervention covered four primary domains: cognitive and fine motor development; social and self-help skills; language; and gross motor skills. Areas within the child care center were set up for art, housekeeping, blocks, fine motor manipulation, language, and literacy. Language instruction was less focused on syntax and more on practical usage. Prephonics training to prepare children for reading was also provided. Follow-up 13 years later (at age 18) failed to reveal significant differences between the intervention and control groups in the (officially-recorded) percentage of participants receiving any criminal charge (ES = 0.03), the percentage receiving violent (ES = 0.08), property (ES = –0.12), drug (ES = 0.01), or other (ES = 0.09) charges, the mean number of total charges, the mean number of specific charges, the mean number of all arrests, or the mean number of specific arrests. This despite the fact that the intervention group had higher IQs, higher reading test scores, fewer students retained in a grade at least once, and fewer students assigned to special education classes relative to the control group at age 15 follow-up (Campbell & Ramey, 1995). These authors have hypothesized that the lack of positive results may have been due to the exclusion of a home visit/parent training component in the intervention.

The remaining 13 studies in this review are indicated or treatment interventions (some study samples contain both individuals at high risk for delinquency, as well as those who have engaged in delinquent behavior already, making classification of the study as an indicated preventive or treatment intervention difficult). Of note, some studies incorporated interventions implemented in schools (e.g. Kolvin et al., 1986) but did not report specifically on delinquent behavior outcomes, and thus were not reviewed below. Studies in the following section are ordered by decreasing age of the sample at the start of intervention.

Gottfredson and Gottfredson (1992) reported on three indicated interventions for adolescents involving school intervention components. The first of these, the Peer Culture Development (PCD) program (Gottfredson, 1987), was a 15-week peer counselling program implemented in three public secondary schools for students ages 14–17 years. The program involved daily group counselling sessions with peers and a leader, and was offered as a social studies course for credit. The principle behind the intervention was that delinquents would learn to conform to societal rules by receiving more social rewards for conformity than non-conformity. The emphasis in the sessions was on problem-solving and conformity to social rules. Equal numbers of students in trouble at school and positive role models were included in the peer groups. Participants (volunteers, or referrals from teachers, peers) were randomly allocated to intervention or control groups separately by gender and within pools of:

1. negative leaders (youths demonstrating leadership and delinquent socialization);
2. positive leaders (youths demonstrating leadership and conventional socialization);
3. students in trouble; and
4. students with no difficulties.

There were 184 intervention and 176 control participants. Post-intervention outcome assessment revealed that the intervention group tended to show higher rates of self-report serious delinquency (ES = −0.20) and significantly greater drug use (ES = −0.25), relative to the control group. There was no effect of the intervention on number of police contacts (ES = −0.05), as derived from archival records.

Another strategy tested to prevent school delinquency involved exposure to an English and law/social studies school curriculum emphasizing instruction in various facets of society, such as the school, human nature and interpersonal relations, the family, social contracts, and the justice system. This intervention was called the Student Training Through Urban Strategies (STATUS) project (Gottfredson & Gottfredson, 1992). Personal responsibility and the importance of order and rules were emphasized. This curriculum involved active participation, including visits to community organizations/agencies, independent and small group research, role-playing and simulation, and guest speakers. Teachers used student teams for tutoring and support, rewarded progress, and created individualized learning plans. The overarching principle behind the intervention was to allow students the opportunity to gain a first-hand appreciation for the functioning of society and their place as citizens within it. This, in turn, would reduce their alienation from learning, increase academic success, and decrease disruptive behavior. This program was implemented in one junior (ages 12–13 years) and one senior (ages 15–17 years) secondary school in California. Participants were recruited through school–staff referrals or self-nominations. Random allocation of students to intervention or control conditions was attempted but not fully achieved due to scheduling difficulties. As such, in the senior cohort, there were more females and African-American students in the intervention group compared with the control group. There were 120 intervention and 127 control students. Results at the end of the school year, controlling for pretreatment differences between the intervention and control groups (where necessary) revealed that, in the junior school, the program reduced self-report serious delinquency (ES = 0.33; non-significant) and drug use (ES = 0.42; significant), and lowered the rate of court contact (ES = 0.07; non-significant). In the senior school, the program significantly reduced self-report serious delinquency (ES = 0.42) and drug use (ES = 0.35), and non-significantly reduced court contacts (ES = 0.18).

A similar intervention by way of its focus on learning personal responsibility was that of Arbuthnot and Gordon (1986). They reported on an indicated preventive intervention to enhance the moral reasoning of adolescents teacher-rated as seriously behavior-disordered. Forty-eight young adolescents were randomly assigned into intervention or no-treatment control groups. The intervention consisted of 16–20 weekly sessions, each one class period (45 minutes) long, in which the intervention participants discussed moral dilemmas in groups of five to eight students. The leader used questioning, role-playing, and perspective-taking techniques to facilitate discussion of moral dilemmas. Active listening, communication, problem-solving, and decision-making skills were taught. At post-intervention, the intervention group demonstrated increases in moral reasoning abilities and grades, as well as decreases in school-recorded disciplinary referrals and tardiness. There was also a significant difference between groups in officially-recorded police/court contacts (ES = 0.66) favoring the intervention group. At one-year follow-up, however, there was no group difference in police/court contacts, as neither group had any recorded contacts (note that the numbers of participants followed-up was low, particularly in the control group). Differences in moral reasoning, academic performance, school behavior referrals, absenteeism, and teacher-ratings of school adjustment were found, again favoring the intervention group.

A third school-based intervention for delinquency presented by Gottfredson and Gottfredson (1992) endeavored to alter school organization and management and intervene directly with high-risk youths (the Positive Action Through Holistic Education, or PATHE, program; Gottfredson, 1986). Youths were identified through teacher referrals and screenings of academic and behavioral records. Once identified, academic and behavioral objectives were defined, and the intervention specialists created individualized treatment programs to work toward the objectives. These treatment plans could include counselling, tutoring services, extracurricular activities (field trips, clubs), peer counselling and rap sessions, and community services for families. Specialists worked with teachers to recommend instructional strategies as well. School organization and management were also altered to increase school bonding and reduce disorder. It was hypothesized that by intervening in such a fashion, commitment to school would increase, and delinquency would decrease.

The program was implemented in seven secondary schools for students from ages 11–17. Four hundred and sixty-eight students were randomized to the treatment group, 401 to the control group. Following two years of intervention (at post-test), there were no changes in self-report serious delinquency (ES = 0.00) or officially-recorded court contacts (ES = 0.00). There were also no changes in school-recorded suspensions (ES = −0.02), expulsions (ES = 0.10), or disciplinary infractions (ES = 0.16). There was, however, greater self-reported drug involvement in the intervention group (ES = −0.21). Thus, the intervention failed to have a positive effect on delinquency, despite improvements in academics (e.g. better grades, better promotion, and graduation rates).

Two interventions implemented in the 1960s to prevent delinquency had school components. Ahlstrom and Havighurst (1982) reported on a combined school/work intervention with 13–14 year-old socially, behaviorally, and educationally maladjusted boys begun in 1962. The intervention began when the boys entered grade eight, and was divided into stages. In stage one, half of each day was spent in the classroom in an educational program geared toward each boy's needs, interests, and personal orientations. The boys had their own teachers. The other half of each day was spent in supervised work programs for token pay (e.g. landscaping, woodworking, and warehouse work). In stage two, at approximately 15 years of age, part-time paid employment in the community was sought for each participant, while the half day of classroom study continued. In stage three, the boys were no longer in the school program, and moved into full-time employment. Control group boys were enrolled in regular classrooms. Post-treatment assessment was done when the boys were 19 years old.

Prior to the eighth grade (i.e. pretreatment), the intervention group had a higher percentage of police reports of arrests relative to the control group (ES = −0.12). From ages 13 to 16, the intervention group continued to show a higher percentage of arrests relative to the control group (ES = −0.29), including a higher percentage of arrests for more than one offense (ES = −0.18) and for serious offenses (ES = −0.24). Between ages 17 and 19, the intervention had a slightly lower percentage of arrests compared with the control group (ES = 0.04), including a lower percentage of arrests for more than one offense (ES = 0.10), and for serious offenses (ES = 0.23). The authors suggest that the absence of an intervention effect on arrest rates in early adolescence may have been due to grouping delinquent boys together in work and classroom settings, an effect that has been found more recently (Dishion & Andrews, 1995; McCord, 1997). They also suggest that the suppressive effect regular school had on arrest rates in the control group in early adolescence was not present in later adolescence.

The Youth Development Project (YDP; Reckless & Dinitz, 1972) investigated whether a one school year intervention with potentially delinquent boys would lower delinquency and dropout rates over a 3-year follow-up period compared with untreated controls. Boys identified by their sixth-grade teachers as likely candidates for future delinquency were randomly assigned to all-boy intervention or control regular classrooms in grade seven. The intervention consisted of remedial reading exercises, teacher group lesson planning in consultation with project staff, teacher group discussion of student behavior problems with a psychiatrist, and role-modelling of social relationships. The intervention failed to have an effect on police contacts in the 3 years following the end of the intervention, relative to controls (ES = −0.03). Project teachers rated the intervention boys as lower in delinquency potential relative to control boys in one cohort of participants 2 years after the seventh grade. Self-report delinquency was not significantly lower in the intervention boys compared with controls at this assessment point either. The authors hypothesized that the intervention may not have been strong enough to effect behavioral change.

At least three school interventions implemented at the middle or early high school level to prevent delinquent behavior have applied behavioral techniques to alter the classroom environment. In one of a number of cohorts of the Preparation through Responsive Educational Program (PREP; Wodarski & Filipczak, 1982; Wodarski, Filipczak, McCombs, Koustenis & Rusilko, 1979), 60 students, mean age 13 years, who exhibited evidence of academic or social problems in the prior year were matched and randomly assigned to either the intervention or a no-treatment control group. The intervention involved individualized and small-group instruction in core courses (reading, English, mathematics), daily social skills training, and family skills training to promote increased parental involvement in school and management programs at home. Behavioral contracts were negotiated for classes taken in the regular school program, with positive reinforcers delivered for academic performance and appropriate social behavior. The intervention lasted for one year. At 4-year follow-up, 40 students were assessed. Of 33 intervention–control comparisons on self- and parent-reported juvenile problem behaviors, only two comparisons were statistically significant. Thus, the intervention was not successful in reducing delinquency in the long term.

A second school intervention based on behavioral principles was the Family and School Consultation Project (Stuart, Jayaratne, & Tripodi, 1976; Stuart & Tripodi, 1973). In this study, 60 students, primarily ages 13–15 years, and referred by assistant principals for prior problem behavior, were randomly assigned to an intervention or placebo control group. The intervention centered around the negotiation of behavioral contracts at school. Special privileges were given for meeting specific responsibilities; sanctions were imposed for lapses in contract compliance. Home-based consequences were made contingent on academic and behavioral outcomes in school and, later, behavioral goals at home. The intervention continued for 4 months. Only one measure of delinquency was reported: court contacts. At baseline, before the intervention, one of 30 participants in the intervention group and none of the 30 control group participants had had contact with the court system. At post-treatment, none of the intervention group and two of the 30 control group participants had court contacts. This difference was not statistically significant (ES = 0.37).

A final intervention using behavioral techniques to alter the classroom environment was reported by Bry and George (1980). They developed an intervention based on the notion that adolescent problem behaviors are preceded by feelings of cynicism concerning the predictability of the world and feelings of decreased coping self-efficacy. They endeavored to create environments in which desired consequences were obtainable through one's actions. Their two-year program was administered to seventh-grade urban adolescents with some combination of: (a) low academic achievement motivation, (b) family problems, or (c) frequent or serious discipline referrals. Participants within the same classroom with similar sixth-grade records were paired and randomly assigned to an intervention or control group. Working closely with teachers, the participants' school behaviors (e.g. attendance, tardiness, disciplinary actions) were closely monitored. Positive reinforcement (e.g. praise, a positive letter sent home, points that allowed the student to participate in a school trip) for decreases in undesirable school behaviors (e.g. tardiness) and increases in desirable behavior (e.g. following rules) was given. Failing these methods, individual schoolwork monitoring sessions were scheduled with a paraprofessional.

At age $15^1/_2$, one year after the end of the intervention, self-reported criminal behavior was significantly lower in the intervention group ($n = 29$) compared with the controls ($n = 29$). At age $19^1/_2$, five years after the intervention, significantly fewer of the intervention participants (three of 30) had county court files, compared with the control group (nine of 30; ES = 0.51) (Bry, 1982).

Two studies have reported on interventions carried out in a school setting, but did not directly involve the alteration of the classroom/school environment or teaching styles of instructors. Lochman (1992) reported on a 3-year follow-up of a cognitive–behavioral anger control intervention in a large number of teacher-nominated aggressive pre-adolescent boys. The intervention involved weekly, hour-long group sessions in school, for four to five months, in which participants learned about using self-statements to inhibit impulsive behavior, identified problems and generated response alternatives to them, watched videotapes of children modelling adaptive problem-solving, planned and made their own videos portraying adaptive problem-solving, and used discussions, role-playing and dialoguing to develop problem-solving skills. Three years post-treatment, relative to untreated aggressive boys, the anger control group did not show differences in their self-reported levels of general behavioral deviance (ES = 0.11), including crimes against persons (ES = –0.12), or general theft (ES = 0.19). There were differences between the anger control and untreated aggressive boys on substance abuse, self-esteem, and problem-solving skills, with the anger control boys fairing better on these dimensions.

An intervention component of the Montréal Longitudinal-Experimental Study (MLES; Tremblay, Kurtz, Mâsse, Vitaro, & Pihl, 1995) was also administered in a school setting. In this indicated intervention to prevent conduct problem behavior, low SES boys who scored high on disruptiveness were randomly assigned to either an intervention, attention/observation control, or no-treatment control groups. The intervention had two components: parent training in effective child-rearing and social skills training in children. The social skills training sessions were administered by professional child-care workers in the schools over lunch period, and involved training in prosocial skills, problem-solving, and self-control in conflict situations. This component was administered in a group format, composed of four to seven school peers, with a ratio of teacher-nominated prosocial to disruptive youth of three to one. The parent training component was administered in the boys' homes. The intervention was 2 years long; after this the groups were assessed yearly for 6 years on self-report delinquency. Court records were also searched for evidence of extreme delinquent behavior. The results indicated a reduction of self-reported delinquency in the intervention group compared with the combined (attention/observation and no-treatment) control group (ES across all six years = 0.24). There were no differences between the intervention and combined control groups on court-registered delinquent offenses, however (ES = –0.07).

The final two indicated school interventions are unique in that they were applied at an early age, similar to the Abecedarian Project (Clarke & Campbell, 1997) reviewed above. These two well-known preschool prevention studies utilized the High/Scope classroom curriculum (Schweinhart, Barnes, & Weikart, 1993; Schweinhart & Weikart, 1997). This curriculum encourages an open-framework approach to education where both the teacher and the child initiate learning activities. Children are encouraged daily to plan, do, and review. One might hypothesize that it may be this continual focus on planning and reviewing that impacts positively on delinquency, particularly given that early-adolescent aggressive boys have been shown to have poorer executive functions, including the ability to plan and sequence behavior (Séguin et al., 1995). Both studies were indicated preventive interventions; the children selected had lower IQs and were from low SES families. In one study, children were paired on IQ and randomly assigned to either the High/Scope curriculum or a no-treatment control group (Schweinhart et al., 1993). In the second study, children were randomly assigned to either the High/Scope curriculum, a Direct Instruction curriculum (characterized as a programmed-learning approach, in which the teacher initiates/instructs and the children respond), or a Nursery School curriculum model (characterized as a child-centered approach, in which the child initiates and the teacher responds) (Schweinhart & Weikart, 1997). Intervention began when the children were 3 to 4 years old, and lasted for one to two years. Children in the first study have been followed for 22 years, to age 27 (Schweinhart et al., 1993), and in the second study for 18 years, to age 22 (Schweinhart & Weikart, 1997). Both studies have demonstrated significant reductions in self-report and officially-recorded delinquency at follow-up (ESs between 0.20 and 0.50; see Table 16).

ON-GOING SCHOOL INTERVENTION TRIALS

Two on-going large-scale preventive interventions for conduct disorder contain prominent school components. The Fast Track Project (Conduct Problems Prevention Research Group, 1992) combines a universal program (a five-year, teacher-led classroom curriculum focusing on the development of emotional concepts, social understanding, and self-control) with an indicated intervention for high-risk children (child social skills training, tutoring in reading, and classroom friendship enhancement, as well as parent-training). This package has been implemented in elementary school children beginning in grade one. Preliminary results indicate that both the universal and indicated components demonstrate positive effects on disruptive behavior after one to two years of intervention (Coie & Conduct Problems Prevention Research Group, 1997; Conduct Problems Prevention Research Group, 1997). It is expected that this sample will be followed into early adulthood, allowing for the assessment of delinquent behavior.

In the Metropolitan Area Child Study (Metropolitan Area Child Study Research Group, 1997), 16 schools have been randomly assigned to one of three increasingly intensive intervention conditions or a no-treatment control condition to test their effects on aggressive behavior in elementary school children.

The first intervention group has received a classroom enhancement program (involving a teacher education program, collaborative support for project staff, and a 40-session social cognitive curriculum for the children); the second has received the classroom enhancement program plus small group social skills training for high-risk children; and the third has received both the classroom enhancement program and small group training plus a family intervention for high-risk children and their families. Preliminary results after two years of intervention reveal reduced aggression in the most extremely aggressive children, with the greatest impact from the full intervention condition. Follow-up into late adolescence will similarly allow for the measurement of delinquent behavior.

WHAT WORKS?

There are a number of advantages to intervening in the schools to prevent delinquency. The majority of children attend school. This facilitates the identification of children exhibiting aggressive behavior at an early age. These children may be targeted for intervention to improve academic achievement and promote prosocial behavior. Children in school are also more accessible for the application of an intervention. Also, variability in delinquency rates across schools (Rutter, 1983) indicates that the potential for effective intervention at the classroom or school level to reduce delinquency exists.

From this review, it is evident that wide variability exists between studies in the types of interventions implemented, the characteristics of the study participants (age, risk factors), the length of the interventions, the length of follow-up periods, and the types of outcome measures. This makes the task of drawing conclusions concerning which school interventions, or components thereof, are effective in reducing delinquency, difficult. A few general conclusions can be advanced, however. The application of behavioral techniques in the classroom may hold promise for the prevention of delinquency. The studies by Hawkins and his associates demonstrate that teacher training in classroom management, interactive teaching, and cooperative learning, particularly in the context of a multimodal intervention package, can lead to reductions in delinquent behavior and other negative outcomes (Hawkins et al., 1988; 1999). Two studies utilizing behavioral contracts for the completion of academic and behavioral goals, with clear rewards for successful completion and costs for breaches, demonstrated both short-term (Stuart et al., 1976) and long-term (Bry, 1982) reductions in delinquency. Notably, and regrettably, one study utilizing behavioral techniques along with other components such as social skills training for a substantial period of time, and with a substantial follow-up, failed to demonstrate effects on delinquency outcomes (Wodarski & Filipczak, 1982). The reasons for this lack of effect are not readily apparent.

School interventions emphasizing moral reasoning or social studies have also demonstrated some efficacy in reducing delinquent behavior. Although Arbuthnot and Gordon (1986) found no effect of their moral reasoning intervention on delinquency after one year, at post-treatment there was a significant reduction in delinquency in the intervention group, similar to that demonstrated in the STATUS project, an intervention emphasizing personal responsibility and the importance of order and rules (Gottfredson & Gottfredson, 1992). It may be that longer, more intensive moral reasoning interventions might reduce delinquency over the long term.

More generally, interventions that incorporate school components along with other components, such as home visits (Schweinhart et al., 1993; Schweinhart & Weikart, 1997), parent training (Hawkins et al., 1999; Tremblay et al., 1995), and child social skills training (Hawkins et al., 1999) appear to be more effective than those with only one component. Intuitively, it makes sense that changing relationships and environments in multiple areas (e.g. school, family, peers) would lead to greater behavioral change than altering one area only. For example, the absence of a home visit component in the Abecedarian Project (Clarke & Campbell, 1997), similar to that implemented in the Perry Preschool and Preschool Curriculum Studies, may have led to the negative findings on crime, despite improvements in IQ, reading ability and grade retention rate. A home visit component may have allowed for the generalization of classroom learning to the home environment, perhaps facilitating continued learning after the completion of the intervention.

Intervening at younger ages, before the development of delinquent behavior, may be the most profitable course of action. Of the studies reviewed, the two multimodal interventions beginning in preschool appear to be among the most effective in preventing delinquency (Schweinhart et al., 1993; Schweinhart & Weikart, 1997). Also, interventions should be relatively lengthy. Studies with larger effects on delinquency in the present review tended to be those with intervention periods greater than one year (e.g. Bry, 1982; Gottfredson & Gottfredson, 1992; Hawkins et al., 1999; Schweinhart et al., 1993; Schweinhart & Weikart, 1997; Tremblay et al., 1995) with some notable exceptions (Ahlstrom & Havighurst, 1982; Clarke & Campbell, 1997; Gottfredson, 1986).

GUIDELINES FOR FUTURE INTERVENTIONS

Ramey and Ramey (1998) recently outlined six principles to inform the design of early interventions to improve cognitive, academic, and social outcomes. From their viewpoint, early interventions should:

1. begin at an early age and continue for a substantial time period;
2. be time intensive (i.e. provide much contact within the intervention period);
3. provide direct intervention (i.e. direct contact with the children, as opposed to, for example, parent training only);
4. be multimodal, providing comprehensive services;
5. be cognizant of individual differences in program benefits (i.e. some children benefit more than others); and

6. provide adequate environmental supports after the end of the intervention to maintain attitude and behavior change.

These principles are directly applicable to the design of preventive interventions for delinquency that incorporate a school component. More research into multi-modal interventions implemented in preschool or the primary grades is warranted. School components within these interventions might incorporate cognitive training (of the type implemented by Schweinhart et al., 1993), social skills training, and teacher training in behavioral principles. Such multi-component interventions implemented early in development appear most likely to have salutary effects on delinquency outcomes later in life.

REFERENCES

Ahlstrom, W., & Havighurst, R. J. (1982). The Kansas City work/study experiment. In D. J. Safer (Ed.), *School programs for disruptive adolescents* (pp. 259–275). Baltimore, MD: University Park Press.

Arbuthnot, J., & Gordon, D. A. (1986). Behavioral and cognitive effects of a moral reasoning development intervention for high-risk behavior-disordered adolescents. *Journal of Consulting and Clinical Psychology, 54,* 208–216.

Bry, B. H. (1982). Reducing the incidence of adolescent problems through preventive intervention: One- and five-year follow-up. *American Journal of Community Psychology, 10,* 265–276.

Bry, B. H., & George, F. E. (1980). The preventive effects of early intervention on the attendance and grades of urban adolescents. *Professional Psychology, 11,* 252–260.

Campbell, F. A., & Ramey, C. T. (1995). Cognitive and school outcomes for high-risk African–American students at middle adolescence: Positive effects of early intervention. *American Educational Research Journal, 32,* 743–772.

Clarke, S. H., & Campbell, F. A. (1997). *The Abecedarian Project and youth crime.* Paper presented at the biennial meeting of the Society for Research in Child Development, Washington, DC.

Cohen, J. (1977). *Statistical power analysis for the behavior sciences* (Rev. ed.). New York: Academic Press.

Coie, J. D., & Conduct Problems Prevention Research Group (1997). *Testing developmental theory of antisocial behavior with outcomes from the Fast Track Prevention Project.* Paper presented at the annual meeting of the American Psychological Association, Chicago.

Conduct Problems Prevention Research Group (1992). A developmental and clinical model for the prevention of conduct disorder: The FAST Track Program. *Development and Psychopathology, 4,* 509–527.

Conduct Problems Prevention Research Group (1997). *Prevention of antisocial behavior: Initial findings from the Fast Track Project.* Symposium (R. J. McMahon, chair) presented at the biennial meeting of the Society for Research in Child Development, Washington, DC.

Dishion, T. J., & Andrews, D. W. (1995). Preventing escalation in problem behaviors with high-risk young adolescents: Immediate and 1-year outcomes. *Journal of Consulting and Clinical Psychology, 63,* 538–548.

Durlak, J. A. (1995). *School-based prevention programs for children and adolescents.* Thousand Oaks, CA: Sage.

Farrell, A. D., & Meyer, A. L. (1997). The effectiveness of a school-based curriculum for reducing violence among urban sixth-grade students. *American Journal of Public Health, 87*, 979–984.

Farrington, D. P. (1985). Predicting self-reported and official delinquency. In D. P. Farrington & R. Tarling (Eds.), *Prediction in criminology* (Vol. 8, pp. 150–173). New York: State University of New York Press.

Farrington, D. P. (1987). Early precursors of frequent offending. In J. Q. Wilson & G. C. Loury (Eds.), *From children to citizens (Vol. III). Families, schools and delinquency prevention* (pp. 27–50). New York: Springer-Verlag.

Farrington, D. P. (1991). Childhood aggression and adult violence: Early precursors and life outcomes. In D. J. Pepler & K. H. Rubin (Eds.), *Development and treatment of childhood aggression* (pp. 5–29). Hillsdale, NJ: Erlbaum.

Farrington, D. P. (1994). Childhood, adolescent, and adult features of violent males. In L. R. Huesmann (Ed.), *Aggressive behavior: Current perspectives* (pp. 215–240). New York: Plenum.

Fiquera-McDonough, J. (1986). School context, gender, and delinquency. *Journal of Youth and Adolescence, 15*, 79–98.

Gordon, R. (1987). An operational classification of disease prevention. In J. A. Steinberg & M. M. Silverman (Eds.), *Preventing mental disorders: A research perspective* (pp. 20–26). Rockville, MD: Department of Health and Human Services.

Gottfredson, D. C. (1986). An empirical test of school-based environmental and individual inter entions to reduce the risk of delinquent behavior. *Criminology, 24*, 705–731.

Gottfredson, D. C., & Gottfredson, G. D. (1992). Theory-guided investigation: Three field experiments. In J. McCord & R. E. Tremblay (Eds.), *Preventing antisocial behavior: Interventions from birth through adolescence* (pp. 311–329). New York: Guilford.

Gottfredson, G. D. (1987). Peer group interventions to reduce the risk of delinquent behavior: A selection review and new evaluation. *Criminology, 25*, 671–714.

Hawkins, J. D., Catalano, R. F., Kosterman, R., Abbott, R., & Hill, K. G. (1999). Preventing adolescent health-risk behaviors by strengthening protection during childhood. *Archives of Pediatrics and Adolescent Medicine, 153*(3), 226–234.

Hawkins, J. D., Doueck, H. J., & Lishner, D. M. (1988). Changing teaching practices in mainstream classrooms to improve bonding and behavior of low achievers. *American Educationnal Research Journal, 25*, 31–50.

Hawkins, J. D., Herrenkohl, T., Farrington, D. P., Brewer, D., Catalano, R. F., & Harachi, T. W. (1998). A review of predictors of youth violence. In R. Loeber & D. P. Farrington (Eds.), *Serious and violent juvenile offenders: Risk factors and successful interventions* (pp. 106–146). Thousand Oaks, CA: Sage.

Hawkins, J. D., & Lam, T. (1987). Teacher practices, social development and delinquency. In J. D. Burchard & S. N. Burchard et al. (Eds.), *Prevention of delinquent behavior: Primary prevention of psychopathologyp* (Vol. X, pp. 241–274). Beverly Hills, CA: Sage.

Hedges, L. V., & Olkin, I. (1985). *Statistical methods for meta-analysis.* New York: Academic Press.

Huesmann, L. R., Eron, L. D., Lefkowitz, M. M., & Walder, L. O. (1984). Stability of aggression over time and generations. *Developmental Psychology, 20*, 1120–1134.

Kellam, S. G., Rebok, G. W., Ialongo, N., & Mayer, L. S. (1994). The course and malleability of aggressive behavior from early first grade into middle school: Results of a developmental epidemiologically-based preventive trial. *Journal of Child Psychology Psychiatry, 35*, 259–281.

Kolvin, I., Garside, R. F., Nicol, A. R., MacMillan, A., Wolstenholme, F., & Leitch, I. M. (1986). *Help starts here.* New York: Tavistock.

Lane, T. W., & Murakami, J. (1987). School programs for delinquency prevention and intervention. In E. K. Morris & C. J. Braukmann (Eds.), *Behavioral approaches to crime and delinquency: A handbook of application, research and concepts* (pp. 305–327). New York: Plenum.

Lochman, J. E. (1992). Cognitive–behavioral intervention with aggressive boys: Three-year follow-up and preventive effects. *Journal of Consulting and Clinical Psychology, 60,* 426–432.

Loeber, R., & Dishion, T. J. (1983). Early predictors of male delinquency: A review. *Psychological Bulletin, 94,* 68–99.

Loeber, R., & Stouthamer-Loeber, M. (1998). Development of juvenile aggression and violence: Some common misconceptions and controversies. *American Psychologist, 53,* 242–259.

Lynam, D. R. (1996). Early identification of chronic offenders: Who is the fledgling psychopath? *Psychological Bulletin, 120,* 209–234.

McCord, J. (1997). *Some unanticipated consequences of summer camps.* Paper presented at the biennial meeting of the Society for Research in Child Development, Washington, DC.

Metropolitan Area Child Study Research Group (1997). *A cognitive–ecological approach to preventing aggression in urban and inner-city settings: Preliminary outcomes.* Manuscript submitted for publication.

Olds, D. L., Eckenrode, J., Henderson, C. R. Jr., Kitzman, H., Powers, J., Cole, R., Sidora, K., Morris, P., Pettitt, L. M., & Luckey, D. (1997). Long-term effects of home visitation on maternal life course and child abuse and neglect: Fifteen-year follow-up of a randomized trial. *Journal of the American Medical Association, 278,* 637–643.

Olweus, D. (1991). Bully/victim problems among schoolchildren: Basic facts and effects of a school based intervention program. In D. J. Pepler & K. H. Rubin (Eds.), *The development and treatment of childhood aggression* (pp. 411–448). Hillsdale, NJ: Lawrence Erlbaum.

Ramey, C. T., & Ramey, S. L. (1998). Early intervention and early experience. *American Psychologist, 53,* 109–120.

Reckless, W. C., & Dinitz, S. (1972). *The prevention of juvenile delinquency: An experiment.* Columbus, OH: Ohio State University Press.

Rutter, M. (1983). School effects on pupil progress: Research findings and policy implications. *Child Development, 54,* 1–19.

Schweinhart, L. L., Barnes, H. V., & Weikart, D. P. (1993). *Significant benefits. The High/Scope Perry School Study through age 27.* Ypsilanti, MI: High/Scope Press.

Schweinhart, L. L., & Weikart, D. P. (1997). *Lasting differences: The High/Scope Preschool Curriculum Comparison Study through age 23.* (Monographs of the High/Scope Educational Research Foundation, 12). Ypsilanti, MI: High/Scope Press.

Séguin, J. R., Pihl, R. O., Harden, P. W., Tremblay, R. E., & Boulerice, B. (1995). Cognitive and neuropsychological characteristics of physically aggressive boys. *Journal of Abnormal Psychology, 104,* 614–624.

Seitz, V., Rosenbaum, L. K., & Apfel, H. (1985). Effects of family support intervention: A ten-year follow-up. *Child Development, 56,* 376–391.

Stattin, H., & Magnusson, D. (1989). The role of early aggressive behavior in the frequency, seriousness and types of later crime. *Journal of Consulting and Clinical Psychology, 57,* 710–718.

Stuart, R. B., Jayaratne, S., & Tripodi, T. (1976). Changing adolescent deviant behavior through reprogramming the behavior of parents and teachers: An experimental evaluation. *Canadian Journal of Behavioral Science, 8,* 132–144.

Stuart, R. B., & Tripodi, T. (1973). Experimental evaluation of three time-constrained behavioral treatments for predelinquents and delinquents. In R. D. Rubin, J. P. Brady, & J. D. Henderson (Eds.), *Advances in behavioral therapy* (Vol. 4, pp. 1–12). New York: Academic Press.

Tremblay, R. E., Kurtz, L., Mâsse, L. C., Vitaro, F., & Pihl, R. O. (1995). A bimodal preventive intervention for disruptive kindergarten boys: Its impact through mid-adolescence. *Journal of Consulting and Clinical Psychology, 63,* 560–568.

Tremblay, R. E., Mâsse, B., Perron, D., LeBlanc, M., Schwartzman, A. E., & Ledingham, J. E. (1992). Early disruptive behavior, poor school achievement, delinquent behavior and delinquent personality: Longitudinal analyses. *Journal of Consulting and Clinical Psychology, 60*, 64–72.

White, J. L., Moffitt, T. E., Earls, F., Robins, L., & Silva, P. A. (1990). How early can we tell? Predictors of childhood conduct disorder and adolescent delinquency. *Criminology, 28*, 507–533.

Wodarski, J. S., & Filipczak, J. (1982). Behavioral intervention in public schools: II. Long-term follow-up. In D. J. Safer (Ed.), *School programs for disruptive adolescents* (pp. 201–214). Baltimore, MD: University Park Press.

Wodarski, J. S., Filipczak, J., McCombs, D., Koustenis, G., & Rusilko, S. (1979). Follow-up on behavioral intervention with troublesome adolescents. *Journal of Behavior Therapy and Experimental Psychiatry, 10*, 181–188.

Yoshikawa, H. (1994). Prevention as cumulative protection: Effects of early family support and education on chronic delinquency and its risks. *Psychological Bulletin, 115*, 28–54.

Chapter 17

Peer Group Therapy

John C. Gibbs
Ohio State University-Columbus, Columbus, OH, USA
Granville Bud Potter
Corrections Consultunt, Columbus, OH, USA
Albert K. Liau
Kent State University, Kent, OH, USA
Angie M. Schock
Ohio State University-Columbus, Columbus, OH, USA
and
Steven P. Wightkin
Ohio State University-Columbus, Columbus, OH, USA

INTRODUCTION

This chapter argues for a multi-component approach in peer group therapy with offenders, with a focus on young offenders. The multi-component approach incorporates cognitive-behavioral skills-training curricula into traditional peer group therapy, such that offenders are not only motivated but also equipped to help one another effectively. Programs (e.g. Positive Peer Culture) exemplifying the traditional peer group therapy approach have sought to motivate antisocial youths to help one another. Generally, the mixed success of the traditional approach may be attributable to its failure to address the challenges represented by the negative youth culture and the helping-skill limitations of antisocial youth. Designed to remedy both the negative culture and skill limitations of such youth is EQUIP (Gibbs, Potter, & Goldstein, 1995), an innovative new group treatment program. The results of a recent outcome study (Leeman, Gibbs, & Fuller, 1993) suggest that traditional peer group therapy should evolve into an integrative or multi-component approach as represented by the EQUIP program, in which youthful offenders help one another to learn to think and act responsibly.

Handbook of Offender Assessment and Treatment. Edited by C. R. Hollin.

THE TRADITIONAL THERAPEUTIC PEER GROUP APPROACH

Although people have been motivated to help one another in groups for thousands of years, the modern format for peer group therapy originated in 1935 with the founding of Alcoholics Anonymous. Mutual-help group formats quickly proliferated. In recent years, approximately 500000 therapeutic peer groups have emerged, involving over 12 million Americans (Hurley, 1988; Wuthnow, 1994). Like Alcoholics Anonymous, many of these group programs address a struggle against an addictive behavior (e.g. Gamblers Anonymous). Other groups are composed of individuals facing stressful or painful situations (e.g. single parenthood, heart disease, widowhood, rape or incest, or murder of a child). Still other groups (e.g. Al-Anon) aim to provide help for friends and relatives of the person with the problem.

Beginning in the 1940s, the therapeutic peer group approach began to be applied to individuals who regularly victimize others and society. At a psychiatric hospital in Great Britain, Jones (1953) innovated techniques for cultivating a "therapeutic community" among sociopathic patients. Independently and concurrently in New Jersey, McCorkle, Elias, and Bixby (1958) applied similar techniques to delinquent boys in an intervention they termed "guided group interaction". These techniques were subsequently refined by Vorrath and Brendtro (1985), who modified the guided group interaction approach and renamed it "Positive Peer Culture", or PPC, to depict its intended goal. Agee (1979) similarly refined guided group interaction for use with severely aggressive adolescents. PPC and other guided group interaction programs represent the traditional way that the therapeutic peer group approach has been applied to antisocial individuals.

The Challenge of a Negative Youth Culture

Offenders represent a formidable challenge to the traditional therapeutic peer group approach. Unlike most mutual-help groups, which are initiated voluntarily by participants, peer groups for young offenders are initiated by adults and typically meet with initial resistance (Ferrara, 1992; Lee, 1995). Researchers and practitioners have noted the negative norms of antisocial youth groups: "Drug use is cool, sexual exploitation proves manliness, and you have to watch out for number one" (Brendtro & Wasmund, 1989, p. 83). In their analysis of a Bronx, New York, high school, Kohlberg and Higgins (1987) termed these negative norms "counter-norms" that attribute blame for antisocial behavior to others: for example, "Look at me the wrong way and you're in for a fight", and "It's your fault if something is stolen—you were careless and tempting me" (p. 110). In correctional settings, the offender culture is "characterized by opposition to institutional rules and goals, norms against informing authorities about rule violations, and the use of physical coercion as a basis of influence among inmates" (Osgood, Gruber, Archer, & Newcomb, 1985, p. 71).

Therapeutic peer group programs must transform this self-centered and harmful culture into one characterized by caring and the provision of constructive help for peers. Peer group therapy assumes that such transformations are possible because many young offenders can become "hooked on helping" as a basis for self-respect. "In reaching out to help another, a person creates his own proof of worthiness" (Vorrath & Brendtro, 1985, p. 6; cf. Reissman, 1990). The thesis is that such helping-induced gains in genuine self-respect should engender gains in responsible conduct.

Evaluations of Traditional Peer Group Therapy

Evaluations of the thesis that peer group programs can promote self-respect or self-esteem and responsible behavior have yielded a mixed picture. Outcome evaluation studies of PPC and related programs have been conducted in schools (public and alternative), juvenile correctional facilities or detention centers, private residential facilities, and community group homes. Many of these programs have found guided peer group programs to be effective in improving self-concept or self-esteem (Atwood & Osgood, 1987; Martin & Osgood, 1987; Vorrath & Brendtro, 1985; Wasmund, 1988). Furthermore, Gottfredson (1987) noted in connection with a controlled study of PPC in Chicago that schools in which guided peer programs operated became "safer over time, school-wide reports of negative peer influence went down, and school-wide beliefs in conventional rules went up" (p. 710). However, the interpetability of other research results was generally undermined by serious methodological flaws, such as the absence of a control group. Significant reduction in recidivism was less likely to be found in the more rigorously controlled studies (Garrett, 1985; Gottfredson, 1987).

This mixed picture is perhaps not surprising in light of other research indicating that such programs often do not operate as intended. To investigate problems and program needs as seen by participants, Brendtro and Ness (1982) surveyed 10 schools and facilities using PPC or related programs. Cited as a problem at 9 out of 10 centers was "abuse of confrontation" (e.g. "harassment, name-calling, screaming in someone's face, hostile profanity, and physical intimidation", p. 322). Yochelson and Samenow (1976, 1977) found that in therapeutic community or milieu therapy groups for offenders at Saint Elizabeth's Hospital in Washington, D.C., "helping" mainly meant keeping quiet about a fellow group member's rule violation or lying on behalf of a group member to help him cover up a crime. The offenders defined their problems not as antisocial behavior but rather as confinement and unsatisfactory institutional conditions; hence, group meetings became gripe sessions or "snow jobs" at best, criminal operations at worst.

It might be argued that evaluations of the traditional peer group approach might be more consistently favorable if institutions more often implemented and operated guided peer group programs as intended. Yet, the widespread abuse of confrontation and helping may signal more basic problems. The formidable challenge represented by the negative culture of offenders has already been noted.

Helping-Skill Limitations of Offenders

An additional basic problem in the application of the therapeutic peer group to the offender population is the helping-skill limitations of such individuals. Can an individual with an anger, stealing, or lying problem be helped by fellow group members who lack the skills for dealing with such problems—and many of whom have such problems themselves? In an important critique of PPC, Carducci (1980) argued that the effectiveness of such programs is undermined from the outset by antisocial youths' limitations. Carducci observed that such youth are generally: first, morally immature, that is, "frequently at a stage of arrested moral/ethical/social/emotional development in which he is fixated at a level of getting his own throbbing needs met, regardless of effects on others" (p. 157); second, cognitively distorted, for example, using "the defense mechanism of [externalization] . . . in which [youths] blame others for their misbehavior" (p. 157); and third, socially unskilled in problem-solving, that is, not knowing "what specific steps, on their part or the part of the owner of the problem, will result in its being solved" (p. 158). The research literature provides striking corroboration for Carducci's observations, documenting among young offenders widespread sociomoral developmental delays (immature moral judgment, age-inappropriate egocentric bias); social-cognitive deficiencies and distortions; and social skill deficiencies (see Gibbs, Potter, Barriga, & Liau, 1996).

THE MULTI-COMPONENT THERAPEUTIC PEER GROUP APPROACH

Negative peer culture and helping-skill limitations, then, can undermine the effectiveness with which offenders help one another. Agee and McWilliams (1984) argued for the feasibility and value of equipping even violent young offenders to help one another:

> The violent juvenile offender, with his long history of sabotaging attempts at intervention and poor interpersonal relationships, would seem to be about as likely to benefit from a therapeutic community as a schizophrenic. The vital difference is that while the interpersonal skills of the violent juvenile offender are characteristically poor, the majority of them can be taught the behaviors necessary to be therapeutic with one another (p. 286).

Kazdin (1995) emphasizes the need for such teaching to be broad-based and multi-component in light of the multifaceted character of the limitations of such youth. The preponderance of helping-skill interventions, however, have been single-component. As Kazdin would predict, single-component interventions have had (like peer group programs) mixed success (see Gibbs et al., 1996).

Exemplifying the multi-component approach in peer group therapy is the EQUIP program (Gibbs, Potter, & Goldstein, 1995). EQUIP is designed both to motivate and to teach young offenders and other antisocial youth how to help one another to think and act responsibly. EQUIP is multi-componential in two senses. First, it combines peer group with skills-training approaches, specifically by helping youth to develop skills in order to facilitate their ability to help group members. Providing a peer-helping rationale for skills training contributes to the motivation to learn those skills: Litwack (1976) found that juveniles were better motivated to acquire skills when they expected to use them later to help other adolescents (of course, development of these skills also promotes self-help, but emphasizing empowerment to help *others* can reduce the offenders' initial defensiveness and resistance to change). Second, the skills taught in EQUIP are themselves multi-componential, addressing the multifaceted limitations noted.

Essentially, then, EQUIP incorporates a skills-training approach or psychoeducational curriculum into a traditional guided peer group format. The EQUIP program encompasses both "mutual help" and "equipment" meetings. In the mutual help meeting, young offenders use two sets of standard terms: first, the Positive Peer Culture list of 12 problem names (authority problem, easily angered, aggravates others, lying problem, etc.); and second, a list of four social–cognitive distortions or "thinking errors" as defined by Gibbs and Potter (1992): these are self-centered, assuming the worst, minimizing/mislabelling, and blaming others (see Table 17.1). For example, group members are required to report not only their "surface" Positive Peer Culture-style behavior problems, but also the underlying thinking errors generative of those problems. Once the group is sufficiently motivated to function as a treatment modality, "equipment" meetings are initiated in order to equip the group with helping skills (moral judgment maturity, accurate social cognition [through avoidance or correction of criminogenic thinking errors], anger management skills, and constructive social skills). Teaching the helping skills not only serves to remediate the limitations of young offenders, but also to transform the group culture toward a positive climate of genuine therapeutic helping.

Case Illustration

An incident from one EQUIP group of incarcerated juvenile offenders (see Gibbs, Potter, & Goldstein, 1995) illustrates the way in which reporting and examining the thinking errors can add depth and power to a mutual-help meeting. One youth, Mac (a chronic juvenile offender incarcerated for murder), reported resisting and yelling profanities at a staff member who, in accordance with institutional policy, had attempted to inspect his carrying bag. Mac was able to report his behavior as an authority problem; identifying the underlying thinking error

Table 17.1 Four categories of cognitive distortion with examples

1. **Self-centered:** According status to one's own views, expectations, needs, rights, immediate feelings, and desires to such an extent that the legitimate views, etc. of others (or even one's own long-term best interest) are scarcely considered or are disregarded altogether.

   Examples:
   If I see something I like, I take it.
   If I lie to people, that's nobody's business but my own.
   Rules are mostly meant for other people.
   When I get mad, I don't care who gets hurt.

2. **Minimizing or mislabelling:** Depicting antisocial behavior as causing no real harm or as being acceptable or even admirable, or referring to others with belittling or dehumanizing labels.

   Examples:
   If you know you can get away with it, only a fool wouldn't steal.
   Everybody lies. It's no big deal.
   Taking a car doesn't really hurt anyone if nothing happens to the car and the owner gets it back.
   People need to be roughed up once in a while.

3. **Assuming the worst:** Gratuitously attributing hostile intentions to others, considering a worst-case scenario for a social situation as if it were inevitable, or assuming that improvement is impossible in one's own or others' behavior.

   Examples:
   You might as well steal. If you don't take it, somebody else will.
   I might as well lie—if I tell the truth, people aren't going to believe me anyway.
   I can't help losing my temper a lot.
   You should hurt people first, before they hurt you.

4. **Blaming others:** Misattributing blame for one's harmful actions to outside sources, especially to another person, a group, or a momentary aberration (one was drunk, high, in a bad mood, etc.), or misattributing blame for one's victimization or other misfortune to innocent others.

   Examples:
   If someone is careless enough to lose a wallet, they deserve to have it stolen.
   People force me to lie when they ask me too many questions.
   I lose my temper because people try to make me mad.
   If people don't cooperate with me, it's not my fault if someone gets hurt.

Note: Adapted from *The EQUIP Program: Teaching youth to think and act responsibly* and from *The How I Think Questionnaire* by J. C. Gibbs, A. Q. Barriga, G. B. Potter and A. K. Liau (in press). Champaign, IL: Research Press. Copyright 1992 Gibbs & Potter. Reprinted by permission.

required some discussion, but provided insight useful to the group in working with Mac on his problems. Mac explained that the bag contained something very special as well as irreplaceable—photos of his grandmother—and that he was not going to let anyone take the photos from him. He thought only of safeguarding his photos; he did not for a moment consider the staff member's perspective, that she was only carrying out institutional policy concerning inspection for contra-band. Nor did he consider that she was not abusive and that he therefore had no reason to assume that the photos would be confiscated. Generating the surface behavior identified as authority problem, then, were Self-Centered and Assum-ing the Worst thinking errors. Mac's anger at staff for his subsequent disciplinary write-up was identified as an Easily Angered problem and attributed to a Blaming Others thinking error (after all, objectively speaking, Mac had only himself to blame for the write-up).

As Mac, with the help of his peers, learned the vocabulary terms for his irresponsible thinking and behavior (along with the application of the social skill Expressing a Complaint Constructively and certain anger manage-ment skills), his anger dissipated considerably. Perhaps most important, he began to regret his verbal assault on the staff member. His remorse emerged as he saw the unfairness of his behavior toward the staff member, empathized with her, and attributed blame to himself. Over the course of subsequent sessions, Mac's authority and easily angered problems manifested themselves less frequently.

Evaluation of the EQUIP Program

Although vivid and encouraging, case illustrations do not provide adequate evaluation of an intervention program's effectiveness. The effectiveness of the EQUIP program was evaluated in a systematic and controlled outcome study (Leeman et al., 1993). The study was conducted at a medium-security cor-rectional facility maintained by the juvenile corrections department of a Midwestern state. Participating as subjects were 57 male juvenile offenders, aged 15–18, who were incarcerated at the facility. The subjects were randomly assigned either to the EQUIP experimental unit or to one of two control groups (a simple passage-of-time control and a control that received a motivational message).

EQUIP was found to stimulate substantial institutional and post-release conduct gains. Institutional conduct gains were highly significant for the EQUIP group, relative to the control groups, in terms of self-reported misconduct, staff-filed incident reports, and unexcused absences from school. These gains corrobo-rated informal observations and comments by institutional staff that the EQUIP unit was dramatically easier to manage than other units. The program's impact was also evident 12 months after subjects' release. The recidivism rate for EQUIP participants remained low and stable, whereas the likelihood of revidivism for the untreated subjects climbed. Specifically, the EQUIP group's recidivism rate was 15.0% at both 6 months and 12 months after release. In contrast, the mean recidivism rate for the control groups was 29.7% at 6 months and increased to 40.5% at 12 months (a significant difference from the experimental group's 15.0% rate).

CONCLUDING COMMENTS

Further research would appear to be warranted on multi-component peer group therapies designed not only to motivate but also to equip offenders to help one another to think and act responsibly. Continued favorable findings would suggest that a certain synergy may result from the integration of skills training into the traditional therapeutic peer group model. In that case, peer group programs in facilities, schools, centers, and group homes would be well advised to add psychoeducational curriculum components. Conversely, psychoeducational programs would be well advised to promote offenders' amenability to treatment through the use of guided peer group processes.

The integration of peer group therapy and skills training can be discerned in various treatment contexts. For example, Recovery Training and Self-Help (National Institute on Drug Abuse, 1993), a program for supporting recovery from alcohol or substance addiction, features "a recovery skills training curriculum in combination with a guided peer support group" (p. 19). A residential group treatment program for juvenile sex offenders (Scavo & Buchanan, 1989) entails not only self-disclosure and supportive confrontation by group members, but enables the group members to help one another more effectively by also including in the group program a psychoeducational component (e.g. interpersonal skills, sex education, and victim awareness). Goldstein, Glick, Irwin, Pask-McCartney, and Rubama's (1989) skills training program for dysfunctional families takes place in a support group context. In "cooperative learning" programs for students with antisocial behavior problems, teaching skills are an implicit consideration insofar as more capable students are included in each cooperative learning group (Carducci & Carducci, 1984). Skills training or preparation is typically provided in youth-to-youth service programs, wherein older youth counsel younger ones.

Any therapeutic program should be monitored and evaluated on a continuing basis. Although the specifics will vary, evaluation procedures should satisfy three basic requirements (Kazdin, 1995). First, program implementers should have available and follow closely a manual that operationally delineates the agreed-upon program. Second, once implemented, the therapeutic program activities should be monitored to ensure that the actual treatment conforms to prescribed procedures. Finally, standard instruments should be used to assess the severity of the client problem (level of offense, etc.) and whether the therapy has been effective in reducing that severity. Applied to the present concerns, then, multi-component peer group therapy programs should be accurately implemented, faithfully maintained, and rigorously evaluated.

REFERENCES

Agee, V. L. (1979). *Treatment of the violent incorrigible adolescent*. Lexington, MA: Lexington Books.

Agee, V. L., & McWilliams, B. (1984). The role of group therapy and the therapeutic community in treating the violent juvenile offender. In R. Mathais (Ed.), *Violent juvenile offenders* (pp. 283–296). San Francisco: National Council on Crime and Delinquency.

Atwood, R. O., & Osgood, D. W. (1987). Cooperation in group treatment programs for incarcerated adolescents. *Journal of Applied Social Psychology, 17,* 969–989.

Brendtro, L. K., & Ness, A. E. (1982). Perspectives on peer group treatment: The use and abuse of guided group interaction/positive peer culture. *Children and Youth Services Review, 4,* 307–324.

Brendtro, L. K., & Wasmund, W. C. (1989). The Positive Peer Culture model. In R. Lyman, S. Prentice-Dunn, & S. Gabel (Eds.), *Residential treatment of emotionally disturbed children* (pp. 81–93). New York: Plenum.

Carducci, D. J. (1980). Positive peer culture and assertiveness training: Complementary modalities for dealing with disturbed and disturbing adolescents in the classroom. *Behavioral Disorders, 5,* 156–162.

Carducci, D. J., & Carducci, J. B. (1984). *The caring classroom: A guide for teachers troubled by the difficult student and classroom disruption.* New York: Bull.

Ferrara, M. L. (1992). *Group counseling with juvenile delinquents: The limit and lead approach.* Newberry Park, CA: Sage.

Garrett, C. (1985). Effects of residential treatment on adjudicated delinquents: A meta-analysis. *Journal of Research in Crime and Delinquency, 22,* 287–308.

Gibbs, J. C., & Potter, G. (1992). *A typology of criminogenic cognitive distortions.* Unpublished manuscript, Ohio State University.

Gibbs, J. C., Potter, G. B., Barriga, A. Q., & Liau, A. K. (1996). Developing the helping skills and prosocial motivation of aggressive adolescents in peer group programs. *Aggression and Violent Behavior, 1,* 285–305.

Gibbs, J. C., Barriga, A. Q., Potter, G. B., & Liau, A. K. (in press). *The How I Think Questionnaire and Profile Form.* Champaign, IL: Research Press.

Gibbs, J. C., Potter, G., & Goldstein, A. P. (1995). *The EQUIP program: Teaching youth to think and act responsibly through a peer-helping approach.* Champaign, IL: Research Press.

Goldstein, A. P., Glick, B., Irwin, M. J., Pask-McCartney, C., & Rubama, I. (1989). *Reducing delinquency: Intervention in the community.* New York: Pergamon.

Gottfredson, G. D. (1987). Peer group interventions to reduce the risk of delinquent behavior: A selective review and a new evaluation. *Criminology, 25,* 671–714.

Hurley, D. (1988, January). Getting help from helping. *Psychology Today,* 63–64, 66–67.

Jones, M. (1953). *The therapeutic community.* New York: Basic Books.

Kazdin, A. E. (1995). *Conduct disorders in childhood and adolescence* (2nd ed.). Newbury Park, CA: Sage.

Kohlberg, L., & Higgins, A. (1987). School democracy and social interaction. In W. M. Kurtines & J. L. Gewirtz (Eds.), *Moral development through social interaction* (pp. 102–128). New York: Wiley Interscience.

Lee, R. E. (1995). Availability to peer group treatment in residential care as a function of relational ethics. *Contemporary Family Therapy: An International Journal, 17,* 343–348.

Leeman, L. W., Gibbs, J. C., & Fuller, D. (1993). Evaluation of a multi-component group treatment program for juvenile delinquents. *Aggressive Behavior, 19,* 281–292.

Litwack, S. E. (1976). *The use of the helper therapy principle to increase therapeutic effectiveness and reduce therapeutic resistance: Structured learning therapy with resistant adolescents.* Unpublished doctoral dissertation, Syracuse University, NY.

Martin, F. P., & Osgood, D. W. (1987). Autonomy as a source of prosocial influence among incarcerated adolescents. *Journal of Applied Social Psychology, 17,* 97–108.

McCorkle, L., Elias, A., & Bixby, F. L. (1958). *The Highfields Story.* New York: Holt.

National Institute on Drug Abuse (1993). *Recovery training and self-help: Relapse prevention and aftercare for drug addicts* (NIDA Publication No. 93-3521). Rockville, MD: National Institute on Drug Abuse.

Osgood, D. W., Gruber, E., Archer, M. A., & Newcomb, T. M. (1985). Autonomy for inmates: Counterculture or cooptation? *Criminal Justice and Behavior*, *12*, 71–89.

Reissman, F. (1990). Restructuring help: A human services paradigm for the 1990s. *American Journal of Community Psychology*. *18*, 221–230.

Scavo, R., & Buchanan, B. D. (1989). Group therapy for male adolescent sex offenders: A model for residential treatment. *Residential Treatment for Children and Youth*, *7*, 59–74.

Vorrath, H. H., & Brendtro, L. K. (1985). *Positive Peer Culture* (2nd ed.). New York: Aldine.

Wasmund, W. C. (1988). The social climates of peer group and other residential programs. *Child and Youth Care Quarterly*, *17*, 146–155.

Wuthnow, R. (1994). *Sharing the journey: Support groups and America's new quest for community*. New York: The Free Press.

Yochelson, S., & Samenow, S. E. (1976). *The criminal personality: A profile for change* (Vol. 1). New York: Jason Aronson.

Yochelson, S., & Samenow, S. E. (1977). *The criminal personality: The change process* (Vol. 2). New York: Jason Aronson.

Chapter 18

Skills Training

Clive R. Hollin
and
Emma J. Palmer
University of Leicester, Leicester, UK

INTRODUCTION

There can be little doubt that social skills training (SST) has proved immensely popular with practitioners working with a vast range of client groups (Hollin & Trower, 1986a, 1986b, 1988). In terms of criminal populations, both young and adult offenders have proved to be popular targets for SST: there are several reviews available (Cunliffe, 1992; Henderson & Hollin, 1983, 1986; Hollin, 1990a; Howells, 1986; Huff, 1987; Spence, 1979; Templeton, 1990), as well as texts to inform the practice of SST with offenders (Priestley et al., 1984; Priestley & McGuire, 1985).

The original social skills model (Argyle & Kendon, 1967) held that socially skilled behaviour, perhaps better termed socially competent behaviour, consists of three related components, namely social perception, social cognition, and social performance (Hollin & Trower, 1986c). Social perception refers to the ability to perceive and understand social cues and signals; social cognition, in this sense, is analogous to social information processing; and social performance is, of course, observable social action. Thus, SST seeks to help the individual develop their social skills in order to function more effectively in their social world.

The application of this way of thinking about social behaviour with respect to offender populations raises two issues. First, is there any evidence to indicate that offenders have particular difficulties in any specific areas of social ability? Second, is an offender's level of social skills related to their offending?

Handbook of Offender Assessment and Treatment. Edited by C. R. Hollin.
© 2000 John Wiley & Sons Ltd.

SOCIAL PERCEPTION

The ability to recognize, understand, and interpret interpersonal cues is central to all social behaviour (Argyle, 1983). In a study of social perception in delinquents, McCown, Johnson, and Austin (1986) investigated the ability of young offenders to recognize emotion from facial expression cues. They found that, compared with non-delinquents, the young offenders could reliably recognize happiness, anger, and fear; but were less able to identify the facial expressions of sadness, surprise, and disgust. In a similar fashion, a body of evidence has accumulated to suggest that children and adolescents who struggle socially, particularly with respect to aggressive behaviour, have difficulties in both the selection and interpretation of social cues (e.g. Akhtar & Bradley, 1991; Dodge, Murphy, & Buchsbaum, 1984; Dodge & Tomlin, 1987). Similarly, a study by Lipton, McDonel, and McFall (1987) suggested that sexually aggressive men may misperceive social cues in male–female social interactions.

The misperception of social cues may in turn lead to misattribution of intent, so that the actions of other people are mistakenly seen as hostile or threatening (Crick & Dodge, 1996; Lochman & Dodge, 1994; Slaby & Guerra, 1988). The way a social encounter is perceived will, in turn, influence the way in which the person deals with a given social encounter.

SOCIAL COGNITION

Following social perception, the individual must decide on a suitable response. This decision-making requires the ability to generate feasible courses of action, consider alternatives, and make plans towards achieving the desired outcome (Spivack, Platt, & Shure, 1976). Several studies have suggested that some offenders, particularly young offenders, may experience difficulties in solving social interaction problems. For example, using the Adolescent Problem Inventory (API; see Palmer & Hollin, 1996), Freedman, Rosenthal, Donahoe, Schlundt and McFall (1978) found that young offenders gave less socially competent responses than non-offenders to a series of social problems. The delinquents used a more limited range of alternatives to solve interpersonal problems, and relied more on verbal and physical aggression. Veneziano and Veneziano (1988) used the API to classify delinquents as "incompetent", "moderately competent", and "competent" in their knowledge of social skills. These three groups differed significantly in the number of behavioural difficulties they experienced, on scores on various measures of personality, and on measures of social values and morality. In general, young people with less knowledge were socially and personally disadvantaged compared with their peers; the delinquents showed a lower knowledge of social skills than a sample of "good citizens". Similarly, Simonian, Tarnowski, and Gibbs (1991), using a revised version of the API, found that API scores were related to delinquent activity (official and self-report). Interestingly, Cole, Chan, and Lytton (1989) found that delinquents accurately perceived themselves as less skilled than their peers.

Gaffney and McFall (1981) developed the Problem Inventory for Adolescent Girls (PIAG), a self-report measure of social competence in dealing with awkward social situations. They reported that delinquent girls gave less socially competent responses with respect to their probable actions in the various social situations. Furthermore, it was found that delinquency was more closely related to skill deficits in interacting with adults in positions of authority rather than in interacting with peers. Ward and McFall (1986), also using the PIAG, found that female young offenders gave less competent responses to the problem situations.

It is clear that, perhaps particularly for children and adolescents, social cognition, including social problem solving, is related to delinquent and antisocial behaviour. There is a weight of research in the tradition illustrated above, that strongly suggests that difficulties in setting social goals, solving social problems, and accurately perceiving social feedback on performance are critical factors in understanding antisocial behaviour (e.g. Akhtar & Bradley, 1991; Crick & Dodge, 1994; Demorest, 1992; Hollin, 1990b; Ross & Fabiano, 1985).

SOCIAL PERFORMANCE

In a typical study, Spence (1981a) compared the social performance skills of young male offenders with non-delinquent controls matched for age, academic performance, and social background. The delinquents showed significantly less eye contact and speech, but more "fiddling" and gross body movements, behaviours shown to relate to poor observer ratings of social skill (Spence, 1981b). On global ratings of social skill, social anxiety, and employability the delinquent group was rated less favourably than the non-delinquents.

In summary, the research suggests that some offenders do experience difficulties with social skills. However, it would be wrong to assume that this is a characteristic of all offenders: clearly offenders are a heterogeneous population with a wide distribution of social ability. Nonetheless, there are offenders with social difficulties and the hypothesis has been formed that there is a link between social ability and offending. If this hypothesis is true, in some cases at least, then remediation of these social difficulties through SST may lead to a reduction in offending. However, as noted in the extant reviews, there is little in the way of convincing evidence that SST has any systematic effect on recidivism. A number of studies have, however, been published since the last reviews and the remainder of this chapter focuses on their contribution to this field.

RECENT EVIDENCE: AN OVERVIEW

The extant reviews give a picture of the field of skills training with offenders up to the 1990s. Since that time it is clear that skills training has increasingly been used as a component of multimodal programmes (e.g. Goldstein, Glick, & Gibbs, 1998) rather than as a "stand alone" intervention. However, several studies with an explicit focus on skills training, published after 1989, were identified and these are discussed below. There are two main groups of studies: the first concerns skills training with general offender groups, the second involves skills training with sex offenders.

Several studies with juvenile offenders have been reported in the post-1989 literature. Lennings (1990) evaluated a social skills programme for three juvenile offenders in a detention centre. The programme focused on enhancing self-esteem, increasing assertion and communication skills, and challenging sex-role behaviours. The evaluation showed that the programme was successful in achieving positive gains in the target areas. Elrod and Minor (1992) also evaluated a programme with juvenile offenders, in which traditional skills training was bundled with outdoor adventure and parent skills training to form "Project Explore". The offending rates of juveniles participating in Project Explore were compared with those of juveniles who received standard probation. At two-year follow-up, both groups showed a reduction in offending, but there was no difference in the offending rates of the two groups. The design of the evaluation makes it impossible to disaggregate the relative effect of the skills training component.

Mathur and Rutherford (1994) took a much narrower focus in an evaluation of a social skills programme designed specifically to improve the conversational skills of female juvenile delinquents. The programme was a clear success in improving a range of conversational skills, such as using names and making positive statements, but did not report offending rates. Leiber and Mawhorr (1995) reported an evaluation of the impact of the "Second Chance" programme with juvenile delinquents. The programme consisted of social skills training, pre-employment training, and exploiting job placement opportunities. The design of the evaluation allowed a comparison of the offending, at one-year follow-up, of juveniles participating in the programme with juveniles who received traditional court juvenile services. The rates of recidivism of the juveniles participating in the Second Chance programme, as measured by official referral to a juvenile or adult court, did not differ significantly from the controls. However, the young people completing the programme, as compared with the controls, were more likely to be charged with *less* severe offences. As Leiber and Mawhorr note, it is not possible to assess the specific effect of the skills training in the general pattern of results. Finally, Wright (1995) reported a study looking at the effectiveness of social skills training (with an explicit cognitive bias) with conduct-disordered boys in residential treatment. The intervention was successful in increasing self-esteem, self-control, and social skills: the lack of a control group makes outcome effectiveness difficult to judge, but there were indications of beneficial effects with respect to later community adjustment and low rates of offending.

Marshall, Turner, and Barbaree (1989) reported an evaluation of a life skills training programme for penitentiary inmates. The focus of the programme was on a range of skills including problem-solving, attitudes towards authority, and

Table 18.1 Summary of recent studies

Study	Offender group	Training methods	Target and generalization measures	Evaluation method and measures	Results
Elrod & Minor (1992)	43 juvenile delinquents: 22 treatment group 21 controls. Males and females. Aged 12–17 years.	Group: instruction, role-play with peers and parents, discussion, homework. 8 weeks plus 3 months a year later. Weekly.	Prevalence of official offending.	Official records. Pre-post training.	Both groups showed a reduction in status and criminal offences over two-year follow-up. No significant differences between the two groups.
Graves, Openshaw & Adams (1992)	18 young sex offenders 12 controls. Aged 12–19 years.	Group: Modelling rehearsal, encouragement, homework. 9 weeks.	Giving and getting feedback, resisting peer pressure, problem-solving, negotiation, following instructions, conversation skills.	Parental self-report scales for parent–child relationship. Adolescent self-concept. Behaviour checklist completed by parents of adolescents. Pre-post training.	Significantly more social skills shown by treatment group than controls after training. Improvement in parent–child communication after training. Some evidence of improvement in social competence by training group, from adolescents' perceptions. Suggestion that self-concept improved for training group.
Hopkins (1993)	8 sex offenders 7 controls.	Group: discussion, observation, role-play, feedback.	Social anxiety, self-esteem, fear of negative evaluation, appropriate social behaviour.	Staff ratings of behaviour. Ratings of videoed interactions with unknown female.	Increased use of appropriate behaviour among treatment group. Increased self-esteem among treatment group.

continued overleaf

Table 18.1 (continued)

Study	Offender group	Training methods	Target and generalization measures	Evaluation method and measures	Results
		6 weeks, 1 hour/week.		Self-report scales. Pre-post training and 6 month follow-up for treatment group only.	Decrease among controls. Decreased social anxiety among treatment group. No change among controls. Decreased fear of negative evaluation among treatment group. Small increase among controls.
Jones & McColl (1991)	12 male offenders. 12 controls taking part in conventional psychotherapy group.	Group: role-play, feedback, self-evaluation. 3 weeks, 2 sessions/week.	Desire for participation in groups. Need for social inclusion, ability to take on group membership roles, ability to take on prosocial group roles, positive feelings about group membership.	Self-report scales. Pre-post training.	Desire to participate in groups increased for both groups. Treatment group took on more roles post-training than controls, especially as pleaser, risk-taker, and director. Roles occupied valued more positively by treatment group.
Leiber & Mawhorr (1995)	Juvenile delinquents: 57 treatment group, 56 matched controls, 85 non-matched controls. Males and	Group: instruction, discussion, homework. 16 weeks.	Official recidivism.	Official referral to court. Pre-post treatment.	No reduction in recidivism at one-year follow-up for any group. However, treatment group referred for less serious offences.

	females. Aged 9–18 years.				
Lennings (1991)	3 male juvenile delinquents. Aged 16–19 years.	Group: role-play. 6 sessions over a 3-month period.	Assertion, self-control, self-esteem, and institutional behaviour.	Self-report scales and staff assessment for behaviour. Pre-post training.	No statistical analysis due to small sample. However, results show change in positive direction on assertion, self-control, and self-esteem. Behaviour showed signs of improvement too.
Marshall, Turner, & Barbaree (1989)	68 male offenders. 22 offender controls.	Group: discussion.	Social interaction, social behaviour, attitudes, and criminal disposition.	Videoed role-play with female confederate. Self-report scales. Pre-post training.	Treatment group showed greater change over time. Controls showed little at all. After training, treatment group was less less tolerant of crime, less under-assertive, more positive towards the police and courts, less concerned about being negatively evaluated, more empathic, less psychopathic, more socially skilled, and less socially anxious.
Mathur & Rutherford (1994)	9 female juvenile delinquents. Aged 13–17 years.	Group: explanation, practise, modelling, role-play, feedback, transfer of skills. 5 phases: baseline, SST & prompting, prompting only,	Using others' names, using manners, making positive statements about self, others, and the present and future.	Direct observation. Throughout all 5 phases.	All targeted behaviours increased during social skills training, although the level decreased after. At follow-up, all target behaviours were at a slightly higher level than the baseline level.

continued overleaf

Table 18.1 (continued)

Study	Offender group	Training methods	Target and generalization measures	Evaluation method and measures	Results
		maintenance, follow-up. SST phase lasted 5 days.			
Valliant & Antonowicz (1991)	19 male sex offenders. 34 male adult non-sex offenders.	Group: instruction, Role-play, discussion. 5 weeks, 2 hours/week.	Anxiety, self-esteem, hostility.	Self-report scales. Pre-post training.	Self-esteem increased, and anxiety and hostility decreased after training. Sex offenders showed higher levels of self-esteem and lower aggression and anxiety than the general offenders.
Valliant & Antonowicz (1992)	45 sex offenders including controls.	Group: instruction, role-play, discussion. 5 weeks, 2 hours/week.	Restructuring of faulty thinking, self-esteem, anxiety, and hostility.	Self-report scales. Pre-post training.	Increased self-esteem among rapists. Decrease in anxiety among rapists and molesters.
Wright (1995)	30 conduct-disordered boys in a residential setting. Aged 8–11years.	Group: modelling, role-play, scripting, coaching, video feedback, homework. One hour/week.	Social skill competency, self-esteem, locus of control.	Self-report scales. Pre-post training.	Social skill competency appeared to increase. There were significant increases in levels of self-esteem, and the boys' locus of control became more internal. Longer-term follow-ups suggest that benefits are maintained.

practical living skills. The skills of inmates participating in the programme improved significantly as compared with controls who did not participate in the programme. Jones and McColl (1991) also evaluated a life skills programme for offenders admitted to a Forensic Inpatient Service. The programme aimed to develop skills in interacting with social groups and adopting prosocial roles, and the evaluation suggested that these aims were, in the main, achieved through the training.

Valliant and Antonowicz (1991) report the findings from an evaluation of an intervention, heavily reliant on SST, with imprisoned offenders, including sex offenders. They found that the treatment programme had positive effects on the offenders' levels of self-esteem and reduced their levels of anxiety. Similarly, Valliant and Antonowicz (1992) reported that cognitive and SST with incarcerated sex offenders increased levels of self-esteem. Graves, Openshaw, and Adams (1992) developed a SST programme for use with adolescent sex offenders. They report that the SST had a number of significant benefits, including improved communication with parents, higher levels of social competence, and positive changes in self-concept. Finally, Hopkins (1993) evaluated the effects of SST with groups of sex offenders in prison, finding a range of positive behavioural and psychological changes following training.

CONCLUDING COMMENTS

Set against the earlier reviews, it appears that SST is still a part of practice in working with offenders, but that its use as the primary means of intervention has decreased markedly. The development of the field over the past decade, and particularly the last five years, has seen the growth of multimodal programmes as the optimum means of working with offenders. While the "single modality" studies of the type discussed here are important, this importance is not based on their effects on recidivism (not measured in most of the studies) but in increasing understanding of the strengths and limitations of SST, thereby moderating unrealistic expectations of what SST can achieve (Hollin & Henderson, 1984). This growth in understanding will, in turn, feed the development of the skills training component of the more complex multimodal programmes.

REFERENCES

Akhtar, N., & Bradley, E. J. (1991). Social information processing deficits of aggressive children: Present findings and implication for social skills training. *Clinical Psychology Review, 11*, 621–644.

Argyle, M. (1983). *The psychology of interpersonal behaviour* (4th ed.). Harmondsworth, UK: Penguin Books.

Argyle, M., & Kendon, A. (1967). The experimental analysis of social performance. In L. Berkowitz (Ed.), *Advances in experimental social psychology* (Vol. 3). New York: Academic Press.

Cole, P. G., Chan, L. K. S., & Lytton, L. (1989). Perceived competence of juvenile delinquents and nondelinquents. *Journal of Special Education*, *23*, 294–302.

Crick, N. R., & Dodge, K. A. (1994). A review and reformulation of social information-processing mechanisms in children's social adjustment. *Psychological Bulletin*, *115*, 74–101.

Crick, N. R., & Dodge, K. A. (1996). Social information-processing mechanisms in reactive and proactive aggression. *Child Development*, *67*, 993–1002.

Cunliffe, T. (1992). Arresting youth crime: A review of social skills training with young offenders. *Adolescence*, *27*, 891–900.

Demorest, A. P. (1992). The role of social cognition in children's social maladjustment. *Social Cognition*, *10*, 211–233.

Dodge, K. A., Murphy, R. R., & Buchsbaum, K. (1984). The assessment of intention-cue detection skills in children: Implications for developmental psychopathology. *Child Development*, *55*, 163–173.

Dodge, K. A., & Tomlin, A. M. (1987). Utilization of self-schemas as a mechanism of interpretational bias in aggressive children. *Social Cognition*, *5*, 280–300.

Elrod, H. P., & Minor, K. I. (1992). Second wave evaluation of a multi-faceted intervention for juvenile court probationers. *International Journal of Offender Therapy and Comparative Criminology*, *36*, 247–262.

Freedman, B. J., Rosenthal, L., Donahoe, C. P., Schlundt, D. G., & McFall, R. M. (1978). A social–behavioral analysis of skills deficits in delinquent and non-delinquent adolescent boys. *Journal of Consulting and Clinical Psychology*, *46*, 1448–1462.

Gaffney, L. R., & McFall, R. M. (1981). A comparison of social skills in delinquent and nondelinquent adolescent girls using a behavioral role-playing inventory. *Journal of Consulting and Clinical Psychology*, *49*, 959–967.

Goldstein, A. P., Glick, B., & Gibbs, J. C. (1998). *Aggression Replacement Training* (Rev. ed.). Champaign, IL: Research Press.

Graves, R., Openshaw, D. K., & Adams, G. R. (1992). Adolescent sex offenders and social skills training. *International Journal of Offender Therapy and Comparative Criminology*, *36*, 139–153.

Henderson, M., & Hollin, C. R. (1983). A critical review of social skills training with young offenders. *Criminal Justice and Behavior*, *10*, 316–341.

Henderson, M., & Hollin, C. R. (1986). Social skills training and delinquency. In C. R. Hollin & P. Trower (Eds.), *Handbook of social skills training, Volume 1: Applications across the life span*. Oxford: Pergamon Press.

Hollin, C. R. (1990a). Social skills training with delinquents: A look at the evidence and some recommendations for practice. *British Journal of Social Work*, *20*, 483–493.

Hollin, C. R. (1990b). *Cognitive–behavioral interventions with young offenders*. Elmsford, NY: Pergamon Press.

Hollin, C. R., & Henderson, M. (1984). Social skills training with young offenders: False expectations and the "failure" of training. *Behavioural Psychotherapy*, *12*, 331–341.

Hollin, C. R., & Trower, P. (Eds.) (1986a). *Handbook of social skills training, Volume 1: Applications across the life span*. Oxford: Pergamon Press.

Hollin, C. R., & Trower, P. (Eds.) (1986b). *Handbook of social skills training, Volume 2: Clinical applications and new directions*. Oxford: Pergamon Press.

Hollin, C. R., & Trower, P. (1986c). Social skills training: Critique and future development. In C. R. Hollin & P. Trower (Eds.), *Handbook of social skills training, Volume 2: Clinical applications and new directions*. Oxford: Pergamon Press.

Hollin, C. R., & Trower, P. (1988). Development and applications of social skills training: A review and critique. In M. Hersen, R. M. Eisler, & P. M. Miller (Eds.), *Progress in behavior modification* (Vol. 22). Beverly Hills, CA: Sage.

Hopkins, R. E. (1993). An evaluation of social skills groups for sex offenders. *Issues in Criminological and Legal Psychology*, *19*, 52–59.

Howells, K. (1986). Social skills training and criminal and antisocial behaviour in adults. In C. R. Hollin & P. Trower (Eds.), *Handbook of social skills training, Volume 1: Applications across the life span*. Oxford: Pergamon Press.

Huff, G. (1987). Social skills training. In B. J. McGurk, D. M. Thornton, & M. Williams (Eds.), *Applying psychology to imprisonment: Theory & practice*. London: HMSO.

Jones, E. J., & McColl, M. A. (1991). Development and evaluation of an interactional life skills group for offenders. *The Occupational Therapy Journal of Research, 11*, 80–92.

Leiber, M. J., & Mawhorr, T. L. (1995). Evaluating the use of social skills training and employment with delinquent youth. *Journal of Criminal Justice, 23*, 127–141.

Lennings, C. J. (1990). Skills training in a juvenile detention centre. *Residential Treatment for Children and Youth, 8*, 39–54.

Lipton, D. N., McDonel, E. C., & McFall, R. M. (1987). Heterosocial perception in rapists. *Journal of Consulting and Clinical Psychology, 55*, 17–21.

Lochman, J. E., & Dodge, K. A. (1994). Social–cognitive processes of severely violent, moderately aggressive and nonaggressive boys. *Journal of Consulting and Clinical Psychology, 62*, 366–374.

Marshall, W. L., Turner, B. A., & Barbaree, H. E. (1989). An evaluation of life skills training for penitentiary inmates. *Journal of Offender Counseling, Services and Rehabilitation, 14*, 41–59.

Mathur, S. R., & Rutherford, R. B. (1994). Teaching conversational social skills to delinquent youth. *Behavioral Disorders, 19*, 294–305.

McCown, W., Johnson, J., & Austin, S. (1986). Inability of delinquents to recognize facial affects. *Journal of Social Behavior and Personality, 1*, 489–496.

Palmer, E. J., & Hollin, C. R. (1996). Assessing adolescent problems: An overview of the adolescent problem inventory. *Journal of Adolescence, 19*, 347–354.

Priestley, P., & McGuire, J. (1985). *Offending behaviour: Skills and stratagems for going straight*. London: Batsford.

Priestley, P., McGuire, J., Flegg, D., Hemsley, V., Welham, D., & Barnitt, R. (1984). *Social skills in prison and the community*. London: Routledge & Kegan Paul.

Ross, R. R., & Fabiano, E. A. (1985). *Time to think: A cognitive model of delinquency prevention and offender rehabilitation*. Johnson City, TN: Institute of Social Sciences and Arts.

Simonian, S., Tarnowski, K. J., & Gibbs, J. C. (1991). Social skills and antisocial conduct of delinquents. *Child Psychiatry and Human Development, 22*, 17–27.

Slaby, R. G., & Guerra, N. G. (1988). Cognitive mediators of aggression in adolescent offenders: I. Assessment. *Developmental Psychology, 24*, 580–588.

Spence, S. H. (1979). Social skills training with adolescent offenders: A review. *Behavioural Psychotherapy, 7*, 49–56.

Spence, S. H. (1981a). Differences in social skills performance between institutionalized juvenile male offenders and a comparable group of boys without offence records. *British Journal of Clinical Psychology, 20*, 163–171.

Spence, S. H. (1981b). Validation of social skills of adolescent males in an interview conversation with a previously unknown adult. *Journal of Applied Behavior Analysis, 14*, 159–168.

Spivack, G., Platt, J. J., & Shure, M. B. (1976). *The problem-solving approach to adjustment: A guide to research and intervention*. San Francisco, CA: Jossey-Bass.

Templeton, J. K. (1990). Social skills training for behavior-problem adolescents: A review. *International Journal of Partial Hospitalization, 6*, 49–60.

Valliant, P. M., & Antonowicz, D. H. (1991). Cognitive behaviour therapy and social skills training improves personality and cognition in incarcerated offenders. *Psychological Reports, 68*, 27–33.

Valliant, P. M., & Antonowicz, D. H. (1992). Rapists, incest offenders, and child molesters in treatment: Cognitive and social skills training. *International Journal of Offender Therapy and Comparative Criminology, 36*, 221–230.

Veneziano, C., & Veneziano, L. (1988). Knowledge of social skills among institutionalized juvenile delinquents: An assessment. *Criminal Justice and Behavior, 15,* 152–171.

Ward, C. I., & McFall, R. M. (1986). Further validation of the problem inventory for adolescent girls: Comparing Caucasian and black delinquents and nondelinquents. *Journal of Consulting and Clinical Psychology, 54,* 732–733.

Wright, N. A. (1995). Social skills training for conduct-disordered boys in residential treatment: A promising approach. *Residential Treatment for Children and Youth, 12,* 15–28.

Chapter 19

Anger Treatment with Offenders

Raymond W. Novaco
University of California, Irvine, USA
Mark Ramm
and
Laura Black
The State Hospital, Carstairs, Scotland, UK

INTRODUCTION

Because anger is an important antecedent of violent behaviour and because it is also a significant aspect of psychological distress associated with many clinical syndromes, advances in anger treatment offer important resources for service providers attending to the needs of various offender groups. Despite the transparent relevance of anger to intervention work with offender populations, clinical research in this field is sparse. In no small measure, this is partly due to the formidable challenges presented by the dispositions of angry and aggressive clients and the contexts in which such clients are typically found.

We present our approach to anger treatment with patients at a maximum security psychiatric hospital, aiming to portray that such work can be done efficaciously, even with severely disturbed clients having long-standing histories of violence and institutionalization for mental disorder. A model differentiating levels of anger treatment is put forth, seeking to clarify how interventions for anger problems are understood and might then be resourced in providing clinical service options.

To frame the presentation, we discuss the prevalence of anger among offender populations, highlighting the role of anger as a violence risk factor. However, in

Handbook of Offender Assessment and Treatment. Edited by C. R. Hollin.
© 2000 John Wiley & Sons Ltd.

addition to clinical interventions for anger being justified by it being a central mediator of aggressive behaviour, it is also the case that anger dyscontrol is a significant component of psychological distress in the clinical profiles of many different types of offenders.

ANGER, AGGRESSION, AND ANGER TREATMENT APPROPRIATENESS

The anger–aggression relationship is a dynamic one. While being neither necessary nor sufficient for aggression, anger is a significant activator of aggression and is reciprocally connected to it. This is generally agreed among a number of theorists (Bandura, 1983; Konecni, 1975; Novaco, 1994; Zillmann, 1983). As a normal emotion, anger does not always result in aggression, because aggressive behaviour is regulated by inhibitory mechanisms engaged by internal and external controls. Regulatory controls on aggression, such as external restraints, expectations of punishment, empathy, or considerations of consequences, can be overridden by disinhibitory influences, such as heightened arousal, aggressive modelling, lowered probability of punishment, biochemical agents, and environmental cues (Bandura, 1983). Aggression can occur independently of anger for instrumental, automatized, or cue-activated reasons.

It is thus readily understood that not all violent offenders are candidates for anger therapy. Howells (1989) cogently discussed the suitability of clients for anger therapy and provided case illustrations of congruities and incongruities. He stated that anger treatment is not indicated for those whose violent behaviour is not emotionally mediated, whose violent behaviour fits their short-term or long-term goals, or whose violence is anger mediated but not acknowledged. We essentially concur with Howells, except to note that persons in the latter category are often found among the type of treatment-resistant clients served by our State Hospital Anger Project.

Across categories of clients, the key issues regarding appropriateness for anger treatment are:

1. the extent to which the person's offending behaviour is an anger regulatory problem, implying that the acquisition or augmentation of anger control capacity would thereby reduce the probability of offending; and

2. whether the person recognizes, or can be induced to see, the costs of his or her anger/aggression routines—i.e. can genuine engagement in treatment be obtained?

Because resolution on the latter issue is so often elusive, an anger treatment "preparatory phase" has been developed and implemented in our work with forensic patients.

ANGER AND INSTITUTIONALIZED OFFENDERS

The presence of anger dyscontrol as a salient characteristic of violent offenders is commonly recognized. Blackburn (1993) gives extensive attention to the involvement of anger in violent crime and as a personal attribute of offenders. Even psychopaths, whose violent offending behaviour might appear to fit with the exclusionary criteria given above, may stand to gain from anger treatment. Blackburn and Lee-Evans (1985) asserted that ". . . psychopaths as a group may be more distinguished by angry reactions to threats or provocation of an inter-personal kind, rather than by reactions to thwarting or frustration" (p. 99). They suggested that anger management interventions might hold promise for their socialization.

Violent criminals are often impulsively aggressive, and anger prompts their harm-doing behaviour by locking-in schemas and scripts associated with threat and retaliation. In Berkowitz's (1986) study of impulsively violent men in Scottish prisons, he found that uncontrolled anger was experienced by 82% of the men before their violent offence. Anger remains salient among prison inmates during long-term incarceration (Zamble, 1992).

The dynamics of anger and violence in prison settings has been aptly charac-terized by Toch (1989), and a number of prison-based studies have assessed anger psychometrically. Selby (1984) examined five measures of anger or hostility for their ability to discriminate violent from non-violent criminals in a study with 204 adult male felons. He found that most of the measures, including the Buss–Durkee Hostility Inventory (Buss & Durkee, 1957), various MMPI hostil-ity scales, and the Novaco Anger Inventory (NAI; Novaco, 1975), discriminated the violent group from the non-violent group and that the NAI did so with 90% accuracy. Kroner and Reddon (1995) assessed anger using the State Trait Anger Expression Inventory (STAXI; Spielberger, 1991) and examined the relationship of that measure's scales to Basic Personality Inventory (BPI; Jackson, 1989) indices. They found that the STAXI Anger-Out scale was significantly correlated with BPI scales of interpersonal difficulties and alienation, while the Anger-In scale was related to nearly all BPI scales, including depression, anxiety, and self-devaluation. These correlations are not surprising. What is noteworthy about the results is that incarcerated felons will self-report anger and these interpersonal and intra-psychic difficulties. Similarly, Welsh and Gordon (1991) found that STAXI Trait Anger was predictive of aggressive behaviour coded from role-plays in a study with a forensic hospital sample (whose psychiatric status was unde-fined). These studies suggest that anger self-report is an avenue of opportunity for treatment engagement.

In addition to these studies with incarcerated offenders, there is anger research on offenders in community settings, such as male batterers court-referred to anger management programmes for domestic violence. For example, Maiuro, Cahn, Vitaliano, Wagner, and Zegree (1988) compared domestically violent males with generally assaultive men and with non-violent controls and found that while the domestically violent men were more likely to be depressed, their anger and hostility scores were very similar to those who were generally assaultive. Indeed, there is a growing body of work pertinent to anger management with male batterers, activated by Gondolf (1985). In contrast, there is very little research on the anger dispositions of young offenders in community custodial settings. Gentry and Ostapiuk (1989) discuss violence in such residential treatment environments and present a case illustration that points to considerable anger involvement, but there is little psychometric research in this area. However, there is noteworthy anger treatment research with adolescents in such settings done by Feindler and her colleagues, discussed later. The broad range of cognitive–behavioural interventions with young offenders can be found in Hollin (1990).

One of the most prolifically studied topics in the psychiatric literature is the violence proneness of in-patients, regarding their functioning in the community and within institutions (cf. Monahan & Steadman, 1994; Mullen, Taylor, & Wessely, 1993). Recent community studies have focused on specific psychotic symptoms, rather than mental disorder in general, as violence risk factors. Swanson, Borum, Swartz, and Monahan (1996), following the work of Link and Stueve (1994), found that the presence of delusions, and, most specifically, threat/control-override symptoms doubled the risk of violence, controlling for other effects. Conceptualization of occurrences of violent behaviour as sequelae of illness pathology gives priority to illness symptomology, such as delusions and hallucinations, as crucial activators of assault. Alternatively, anger may be identified as an important mediator of the psychotic stimulus–violent behaviour relationship.

There is now considerable evidence about the violent conduct of psychiatric in-patients in European and North American institutions (cf. Hersen, Ammerman, & Sisson, 1994; Monahan & Steadman, 1994; Rice, Harris, Varney, & Quinsey, 1989). Haller and Deluty (1988), in a review of assaults on psychiatric staff, asserted that the frequency of such behaviour substantially increased during the course of the previous 10 years. However, such trends may have changed since that review, and there may be substantial variation across institutions. Noble's (1997) data from the records at Maudsley and Bethlem Royal Hospitals for the period of 1970–1995 show that since 1986 the incident rate has levelled after having sharply escalated in the previous years.

Among the variables identified by Haller and Deluty (1988) as potentially predictive of patient assault on staff was "level of anger" (p. 177). In an analysis of physical assault data pertaining to over 4000 civil and forensic psychiatric patients in California State Hospitals, Novaco (1994) found level of anger, indexed by clinician ratings, to be significantly related, concurrently and prospectively, to patient assaultiveness, and the prospective analysis controlled for prior assaultive behaviour. Convergently, Novaco and Renwick (1998) found in a prospective analysis of patient assaultiveness of 125 male forensic patients, studied longitudinally for 30 months, that anger was very significantly predictive of the patient being involved in physical assault incidents and in being the precipitator of physical assault. High anger patients were also less likely to be discharged in that prospective analysis.

EXISTING ANGER TREATMENT STUDIES WITH OFFENDERS

In view of the above research, the provision of anger treatment ought to have a high priority for a clinical service with offenders. Indeed, Rice, Harris, Quinsey, and Cyr (1990) found institutional staff to rate anger as the biggest problem in secure psychiatric facilities. Despite such evidence, the treatment of anger continues to be seriously neglected. Historically-driven conceptualizations of emotional disregulation in the illness process may have obscured seeing the mediating influence of anger on violent behaviour. That is to say, clinical staff in mental health facilities may tend to see assaultive patients as ill rather than lacking the capacity for anger control and thus fail to consider self-control treatments as a means of overcoming such difficulties. In correctional settings, because of the connection between anger and aggression, both prison and mental health staff may be inclined to view anger reactions as associated with bad behaviour and not be oriented psychotherapeutically when presented with anger reactions.

As practitioners working with offenders have been mindful of anger and aggression as significant problems, there has been a modicum of research in the treatment realm, although there has been considerable variability in the content and process of the treatment. Most applications have been based broadly on a cognitive–behavioural approach, initially developed by Novaco (1975, 1977), which utilized the stress inoculation approach (Meichenbaum, 1985). Studies with offender populations that are most closely connected to this approach are those of Stermac (1986), Bornstein, Weisser, and Balleweg (1985), Howells (1989), and Renwick, Black, Ramm, and Novaco (1997), all of which concerned forensic hospital patients, as well as the studies by Schlichter and Horan (1981) with institutionalized juvenile delinquents and by Feindler, Marriott, and Iwata (1984) with non-institutionalized juvenile delinquents.

The study by Stermac (1986) utilized a control group design and involved a group treatment of six sessions for male offenders with personality disorders, remanded to a Canadian psychiatric facility. She found significant changes in anger, impulsivity, and coping strategies in her anger treatment condition, compared with a psycho-educational control group. Bornstein et al. (1985) more fully implemented the stress inoculation approach in a multiple baseline design and obtained significant anger treatment gains with three institutionalized forensic patients, as reflected by ratings of behaviour in videotaped role-play, ward behaviour ratings, and self-reported anger. Howells (1989) reported successful anger treatment using the stress inoculation approach in a case study with a patient who had recurrent admissions to penal and psychiatric facilities due to violent offences and anger.

Most recently, Renwick et al. (1997) extended cognitive–behavioural anger treatment to institutionalized mentally disordered patients at a maximum security forensic hospital. The intervention involved an extension of the Novaco (1993) anger treatment protocol, developed in conjunction with a controlled clinical trial with Vietnam veterans with severe PTSD (Chemtob, Novaco, Hamada, & Gross, 1997). The Renwick et al. project modified and substantially developed the Novaco anger treatment protocol to meet the needs of secure hospital patients and was evaluated with four very angry and assaultive men with long histories of institutionalization, who were then found to make significant treatment gains.

Treatment studies with adolescent offenders have also incorporated the stress inoculation approach to anger problems. Schlichter and Horan (1981) implemented this anger treatment in 10 sessions in an experimental study with institutionalized aggressive delinquents. They obtained significant anger treatment effects, compared with a no-treatment group, on various anger self-report measures and on role-play behaviour ratings. Feindler et al. (1984) conducted a 10-session group anger control intervention with many stress inoculation approach elements with junior high school delinquents, as part of an in-school token economy programme. Feindler, Ecton, Kingsley, and Dubey (1986) further modified the intervention and applied it to aggressive adolescents on a psychiatric ward. Compared with a control group, their anger treatment group was found to have reduced aggressive behaviour on the ward, decreased hostile verbalizations in role-play, improved cognitive performance, and increased staff-rated self-control. The book by Feindler and Ecton (1986) gives a full account of this work, which, while not applied to violent offenders, is oriented behaviourally and offers many useful ideas for clinicians dealing with adolescent anger in outpatient, in-patient, and residential settings. Another valuable approach to cognitive–behavioural treatment of adolescent aggression is that of Goldstein and Keller (1987), who incorporate some stress inoculation anger management procedures in their training of prosocial skills.

At the heart of the stress inoculation approach to anger treatment is a focus on emotional dysregulation and a progressive acquisition of self-control coping skills. Other less complex approaches have been adopted with offenders, notably, a psycho-educational programme for anger management, used by McDougall and her colleagues. McDougall, Boddis, Dawson, and Hayes (1990) obtained improvement in self-report and institutional behaviour in 18 young offenders following the completion of a brief anger control course. Curiously, the authors expressed concern about whether anger, as opposed to aggression, epitomized the nature of participants' difficulties. This may have been due to participant selection being determined by the recommendations of prison officers (i.e. the absence of clinical assessment) or to the intervention failing to address the emotional component of the offenders' violent conduct.

Brief cognitive–behavioural anger management interventions have been implemented with adolescents by Valliant, Jensen, and Raven-Brook (1995) with offenders in open custody and by Dangel, Deschner, and Rasp (1989) in a residential treatment facility. Both of these studies used control group designs. However, highly aggressive persons were dismissed from the latter study (cf. Dangel et al., p. 457), and Valliant et al. did not get treatment effects for their brief anger therapy, which they thought may have been due to lack of participant motivation.

A number of other psycho-educational approaches to anger management for violent offenders have been reported. Serin & Kuriychuk (1994) applied a cognitive–behavioural anger control programme to violent offenders in a Canadian prison. They implemented a 12–16 session programme, but their report of its content, sequence, and results are very cursory. Smith, Smith, and Beckner (1994) conducted a three-session series of 2-hour workshops with women in a medium security prison and found significant reductions in anger inventory scores and mood diary ratings. Their intervention involved education about anger, self-monitoring, relaxation techniques, cognitive review of anger events, and strategies to escape from conflict; however, only one of their participants was in prison for a violent crime. Implementation of these basic elements of the cognitive–behavioural approach was done by Daly (1994) with a patient at a maximum security hospital. That patient had a history of substance abuse, paranoid schizophrenia, and serious violence. His anger and confrontational behaviour diminished with treatment, and he was transferred to a lower security unit.

Other anger management intervention work, linked to the Novaco cognitive–behavioural approach, has been conducted in the British Prison Service. Towl (1995) described the nationally implemented courses designed for groups of six to eight prisoners and run for eight 2-hour sessions. In an evaluative study, Hughes (1995) reported results for a 12-session programme involving 52 offenders in a Canadian federal penitentiary, finding significant pre-post changes in anger, physical symptoms, and irrational beliefs, although there was considerable incompleteness in the psychometric data. However, measures of recidivism were obtained for all those released from prison, and those who completed the anger management programme had a significantly longer latency to rearrest and a lower likelihood for conviction for a violent crime. Fitzharding (1997) reported gains for the participants of a group anger management in work with women prisoners, based on pre-post interviews compared with a group of non-participants.

Clearly, there has been considerable variation in the form of anger therapies; it would seem useful to distinguish various types of intervention, particularly as there is corresponding variation in the requirements and objectives for each type.

THERAPEUTIC INTERVENTIONS FOR ANGER: DIFFERENTIATING LEVELS

Psychotherapeutic interventions for anger occur at several levels, which have different aims and degrees of sophistication. Intervention levels reflect the degree of systematization, complexity, and depth of therapeutic approach. Increased depth is associated with greater individual tailoring to client needs. Correspondingly, greater specialization in techniques and in clinical supervision is required with more complex levels of intervention.

Level 1: General Clinical Care for Anger. A client's problems with anger and aggression may be treated in routine clinical care. Here, the clinician identifies anger as a relevant treatment issue and addresses the anger-related difficulties as part of a wider mental health care programme. This level pertains to general treatment strategies of counselling, psychodynamic therapies, cognitive and behavioural therapies, and/or psychopharmacology applied in an individual, couple, family, or group format. In seeking explicitly to address anger, such intervention work will actively incorporate new knowledge about anger and aggressive behaviour. General clinical care for anger, when its operational characteristics are explicitly designated, may indeed serve as a comparison condition for experimental anger treatment, as was done in the Chemtob et al. (1997) study with Vietnam veterans.

Level 2: Anger Management Provision. It is particularly useful to distinguish this level of intervention from more specialized anger treatment. The term "anger management", which was first used in Novaco (1975) to describe an experimental cognitive–behavioural treatment, can now better be used to designate a *psycho-educational* approach that is less treatment intensive. The content and format of this intervention type may vary considerably, although most existing forms of this approach are guided by cognitive–behavioural principles.

This intervention type is structured by a syllabus of some sort. It imparts information about anger, including its determinants, signs, manifestations, and consequences. It also educates about ways of controlling anger, such as changing perceptions or beliefs, using relaxation, and adopting alternative behaviours for dealing with provocation. It aims to increase the person's self-monitoring capacity by calling attention to "anger triggers" and habitual ways of responding. It seeks to promote new coping skills. This type of intervention is often implemented in a group format, providing a forum for the sharing of anger experiences, peer support, and peer modelling, as well as serving the throughput objectives of a clinical service system.

Compared with "anger treatment", the provision of anger management is more time-limited and is more structured. It is generally homogeneous in procedure, not being individually tailored. While there are occasions for participant discussion, it is less interactive than treatment and more unidirectional in information flow. It involves less client disclosure and is thus less threatening. Correspondingly, and because of its structure, the personal investment for the client is lower. However, it thereby does not address the treatment engagement issues intrinsic to the profiles of treatment-resistant patients. Lastly, while evaluative measures are often employed in conjunction with the intervention, there tends not to be explicit use of individual client assessment data.

Level 3: Anger Treatment Provision. At this level of intervention, anger dyscontrol is approached in terms of the client's core needs. However, anger treatment is not a substitute for psychotherapy and should be understood as an adjunctive treatment. It focuses on psychological deficits in self-regulation and explicitly integrates assessment with treatment. Precisely because it must often overcome client resistance to change and centrally involves clients who are characteristically high in threat-sensing, suspicion, and avoidance, it hinges on the provision of a therapeutic relationship.

Anger treatment targets enduring change in cognitive, arousal, and behavioural systems. It centrally involves substantial cognitive restructuring and the acquisition of arousal reduction and behavioural coping skills. It achieves cognitive and behaviour change in large measure through changing valuations of personal priorities and augmenting self-monitoring capacity. Because it addresses anger as grounded and embedded in aversive and often traumatic life experiences, it entails the evocation of distressed emotions—i.e. fear and sadness, as well as anger. Therapeutic work centrally involves the processes of "transference" (the learning of new modes of responding to cues previously evocative of anger in the context of relating to the therapist) and of "counter-transference" (negative sentiment on the part of the therapist to the frustrating, resistive, and unappreciative behaviour of the client). Regarding the latter, it is characteristic of high anger patients to push people away as part of their external blaming and avoidant styles. Thus, advanced therapeutic skill and supervision is essential in delivering anger intervention at this level.

Level 3R: Anger Treatment Protocol Research. This incorporates all of the attributes of Level 3 intervention, but follows a designated protocol in delivering the treatment. To meet research design requirements, inclusion and exclusion criteria are specified for client participation. This level of intervention is explicitly evaluative and stipulates time points and procedures for assessment. As part of the research design procedure, it incorporates checks on treatment protocol fidelity. In the enterprise of scientific discovery, it seeks knowledge about anger assessment and treatment.

Having made this differentiation in anger interventions, we now turn to the context of our Level 3 and 3R work at a maximum security forensic hospital. Prior to our research there (Renwick et al., 1997), existing anger intervention studies had yet to address the treatment of severely mentally disordered violent offenders. Our project participants have been severely disordered, dangerously violent, and have long histories of institutionalization.

THE STATE HOSPITAL ANGER TREATMENT PROJECT

The State Hospital, Carstairs, is the sole national forensic psychiatric facility serving the populations of Scotland and Northern Ireland. It has up to 240 patients at any one time. In addition to having a determined mental illness, patients must demonstrate dangerous, violent, or criminal propensities to warrant detention there, and most patients usually have an extensive history of criminal activity. Admission to the hospital is from courts, prisons, or other National Health Service facilities and requires legal orders of restriction.

The anger project was established under the direction of Dr Stanley Renwick to develop a protocol to assess and treat anger with this client population. For the target group, emphasis was placed on long-standing aggression associated with an inability to control anger. When referral of such patients was invited, almost one-fifth of the hospital's census was referred.

The State Hospital anger treatment protocol substantially modifies the 12-session anger control, stress inoculation approach progressively developed by Novaco (1975, 1993), which involved the following key components:

1. education regarding anger and aggression;
2. self-monitoring of anger frequency, intensity, and situational triggers;
3. construction of a personal anger provocation hierarchy created from the self-monitoring data;
4. cognitive restructuring by altering attentional focus, modifying appraisals, and using self-instruction;
5. arousal reduction through progressive muscle relaxation, breathing-focused relaxation, and guided imagery;
6. training behavioural coping, communication, and assertiveness through modelling and role-play;
7. practising anger control coping skills through visualizing and role-playing progressively intense anger-arousing scenes from personal provocation hierarchies;
8. practising the new anger coping skills in real everyday situations.

Owing to the severity of the patients' disorders and the institutional context, a number of additions to the basic protocol were required for it to be efficacious. First, a comprehensive assessment was needed of the patient, his anger problems, and treatment goals; second, a treatment "preparatory phase" was developed to engender treatment engagement and basic skill prerequisites, such as emotion awareness, emotion intensity level differentiation, and elementary self-monitoring; and third, the outpatient protocol was extended to a 20-session pro-cedure to address the multi-layered needs of the patients.

COMPREHENSIVE ASSESSMENT

Our assessment involves psychometric scales, such as the STAXI and the NAS, but suitability for treatment and identification of anger regulatory deficits can hardly be ascertained from questionnaire procedures—unlike the all too common anger treatment studies done with college students, who are selected as participants by having upper-quartile scale scores and then volunteer by tele-phone. Assessment with seriously disordered patients must involve: interviews with the patient, doctor, and nursing staff; psychometric testing; observational recordings; examination of case notes; and background reports. Indeed, various members of the clinical team are continually involved in the anger assessment and treatment. A proper assessment of anger problems cannot be gained from psychometric measures alone, particularly when self-reports of anger are given with considerable guardedness.

Assessing therapeutic progress requires evaluation with multiple measures of anger and anger control. This includes self-report psychometric scales, behavioural observation, and scaled ratings by clinical staff. The self-monitoring records of anger experiences maintained by the patients throughout treatment can also provide one form of process measure. Very importantly, we carefully track critical incidents in ward behaviour.

As noted earlier, not all patients are suitable for anger treatment and this treatment approach. Clients who have significant learning difficulties or are acutely psychotic may not benefit. However, they may be suited to adapted protocols or other interventions—for example, Black and Novaco (1993) reported on successful anger treatment of a then hospitalized man with a mild learning disability. Many patients for whom treatment is indicated often refuse to participate in assessment or for various reasons give misleading information. With patience and supportive encouragement this resistance may be overcome. The "preparatory phase" is devised to address engagement issues and to shape the capacity for veridical assessment.

TREATMENT PREPARATORY PHASE

Originally implemented as a five-session procedure (Renwick et al., 1997), this is now a protocol-guided block of seven sessions. The rationale for this "preparatory phase" is to foster therapeutic engagement while conducting further assessment and developing client competencies needed for treatment. Particularly in a forensic setting, patients are likely to be very guarded about self-disclosure and to be motivationally ambivalent. They are not likely to recognize the personal costs that their anger routines incur. Also, they often lack a number of prerequisites for optimal involvement in a self-regulatory, coping skills intervention programme. They may very well have had some training in arousal control, and they may not have much difficulty in identifying emotions or differentiating degrees of intensity. But they are likely to be unaccustomed to making self-observations about their thoughts, feelings, and behaviours, or conduct rudimentary self-monitoring. Many may not recognize the degree to which thoughts, emotions, and behaviours are interconnected. For some patients, the educational aspects of the preparatory phase proceed quite smoothly and are much less crucial than the engagement issues.

The preparatory phase is thus constructed to "prime" the patient motivationally and to establish basic skills of emotion identification, self-monitoring, communication about anger experiences, and arousal reduction. It serves to build trust in the therapist and the treatment programme, providing an atmosphere conducive to personal disclosure and to the collaboration required by this therapeutic approach. While designed to be relatively non-probing and non-challenging, for many patients it elicits considerable distress. Consequently, some follow-up meetings often are needed to support patients in coping with the impact of the sessions. Very importantly, it must be recognized that treatment engagement frequently remains an ongoing issue. The start of the central treatment becomes a second decision to engage, but this issue is likely to be revisited several times throughout the course of therapy.

CENTRAL TREATMENT: MAJOR ISSUES

The completion of the treatment procedure (defined by the completion of the provocation hierarchy) in many cases might be expected to take longer than the 20 meetings specified in the protocol. This can be a function of both institutional circumstances and individual patient conditions that impede scheduled implementation. Clients may override the planned session procedure with their own agenda or resist the therapist's inducements. Importantly, the institutional context must be grasped. In a maximum-security setting, life moves at a slow pace. Forensic hospital patients, in common with prisoners in the penal system, develop strategies to cope with extended periods of incarceration. There is a subtle, but very real, "slowing down". Patients can take a disproportionately long time to complete routine tasks, avoid long-term planning, and live from day to day. Failure to take such needs into account evokes patient resistance. Thus, adjustments have to be made in therapist expectations regarding such things as homework assignments and the number of sessions required to reach therapeutic milestones.

Although essentially cognitive–behavioural, this anger treatment approach views anger dyscontrol as relating to the historically constituted core needs of the person, to ingrained psychological deficits in self-regulation, and to biomedical factors. This Level 3 treatment therefore requires training in a broad-based clinical approach suitable for the evocation of distressed emotions in the therapeutic arena. While this intervention is protocol-driven, we must say, quite emphatically, that its implementation requires clinical sophistication to modulate it.

Being prone to frustration and inclined toward avoidant behaviour, clients may frequently pull back or disengage. It is characteristic of high anger patients that they push people away as part of their avoidant style. As treatment engagement can often be tentative, the therapist must steer a steady course, maintaining focus and patience. As in Motivational Interviewing (Miller & Rollnick, 1993) this is achieved through a gentle therapeutic style and listening to the client's perspective.

For many patients, anger is deeply entrenched in identity, and the costs of chronic anger are discounted. High anger patients are reluctant to surrender this part of their defined sense of self. The anger treatment gives the patients a middle ground. It gives them a way to maintain their self-esteem and also to move on through the system. While fortifying self-worth, it gives the patients a compromise position by allowing them to maintain self-respect and yet enables them to change. The patient thereby finds himself or herself empowered rather than compromised.

Because of the complexity of this work and the potential risk of physical attack when working at an interpersonal level, it is essential that all therapists have adequate clinical supervision and a security plan. Therapists working with such difficult clients need the support and objective eye of another to guard against colluding with the client's view of the world or responding to their hostility with blame or rejection.

FOLLOW-UP

The transition towards coping alone is difficult, particularly as the patient is likely to remain in confinement. As with all established habits, those of angry, aggressive individuals can easily resurface following treatment. Setbacks are to be expected and worked through. Support and refresher sessions in later months are therefore very valuable. This is particularly the case when a person has to deal with a completely new set of circumstances, e.g. when leaving hospital to return to the community or simply being transferred to a less secure facility.

SUMMARY AND FUTURE DIRECTIONS

Given the prevalence of anger and aggression among offender populations, there is a salient need for effective treatment interventions. This is particularly the case for forensic patients who have longstanding difficulties with both mental disorder and violent behaviour. Such severely disordered people do not gravitate to "anger management" interventions and present considerable resistance to engaging and remaining in therapy.

We have here put forward a differentiation of levels of interventions for anger and have described the complexities of providing anger treatment in a high security setting. We also pointed to a newly developed anger treatment protocol, designed for use with Special Hospital patients whose inabilty to control anger presented recurrent, substantial problems for themselves, for care staff, and for society outside the institution. Clinical and empirical data from our preliminary research (Renwick et al., 1997) reflect modest but noteworthy gains in emotional competence, in anger management, and in social–behavioural competencies.

Our most clear indication of treatment success is that our anger project patients are recommended for discharge from the hospital. That this measure of success could be achieved with patients who were so severely disordered is certainly encouraging. These are patients for whom institutions all too easily give up hope, which is quite understandable, given their treatment-resistant characteristics and the institutional incidents that are associated with their behaviour. Having been in and out of many treatment facilities, they are given a poor prognosis by treatment providers, who view them as being "at the end of the line"— so much has been tried, with so little effect. This sense of highly entrenched problems is shared by the patients. We hope that what we have learned in treating such a severely disordered population will be useful for downward extensions anger intervention to less extreme anger clients.

REFERENCES

Bandura, A. (1983). Psychological mechanisms of aggression. In R. G. Geen & E. I. Donnerstein (Eds.), *Aggression: Theoretical and empirical reviews* (Vol. 1, pp. 1–40). New York: Academic Press.

Berkowitz, L. (1986). Some varieties of human aggression: Criminal violence as coercion, rule-following, impression-management, and impulsive behaviour. In A. Campbell & J. J. Gibbs (Eds.), *Violent transactions*. Oxford, UK: Basil Blackwell.

Black, L., & Novaco, R. W. (1993). Treatment of anger with a developmentally handicapped man. In R. A. Wells & V. J. Giannetti (Eds.), *Casebook of the brief psychotherapies*. New York: Plenum.

Blackburn, R. (1993). *The psychology of criminal conduct*. Chichester, UK: Wiley.

Blackburn, R., & Lee-Evans, J. M. (1985). Reactions of primary and secondary psychopaths to anger-evoking situations. *British Journal of Clinical Psychology, 24*, 93–100.

Bornstein, P. H., Weisser, C. E., & Balleweg, B. J. (1985). Anger and violent behavior. In M. Hersen & A. S. Bellack (Eds.), *Handbook of clinical behavior therapy with adults* (pp. 603–629). New York: Plenum.

Buss, A., & Durkee, A. (1957). An inventory for assessing different kinds of hostility. *Journal of Counseling Psychology, 21*, 342–349.

Chemtob, C. M., Novaco, R. W., Hamada, R. S., & Gross, D. M. (1997). Cognitive–behavioral treatment for severe anger in post-traumatic stress disorder. *Journal of Consulting and Clinical Psychology, 65*, 184–189.

Daly, A. (1994). An eclectic approach to nursing an angry young man. *Nursing Times, 90*, 50–51.

Dangel, R. F., Deschner, J. P., & Rasp, R. R. (1989). Anger control training for adolescents in residential treatment. *Behavior Modification, 13*, 447–458.

Feindler, E. L., & Ecton, R. B. (1986). *Adolescent anger control: Cognitive therapy techniques*. New York: Pergamon Press.

Feindler, E. L., Ecton, R. B., Kingsley, R. B., & Dubey, D. R. (1986). Group anger-control training for institutionalized psychiatric male adolescents. *Behavior Therapy, 17*, 109–123.

Feindler, E. L., Marriott, A., & Iwata, M. (1984). Group anger control training for junior high school delinquents. *Cognitive Therapy and Research, 8*, 299–311.

Fitzharding, S. (1997). Anger management groupwork with women prisoners. *Forensic Update, 48*, 3–7.

Gentry, M. R., & Ostapiuk, E. B. (1989). Violence in institutions for young offenders and disturbed adolescents. In K. Howells & C. R. Hollin (Eds.), *Clinical approaches to violence* (pp. 249–266). Chichester, UK: Wiley.

Goldstein, A., & Keller, H. (1987). *Aggressive behavior: Assessment and intervention*. New York: Pergamon Press.

Gondolf, E. W. (1985). *Men who batter*. Holmes Beach, FL: Learning Publications.

Haller, R. M., & Deluty, R. H. (1988). Assaults on staff by psychiatric in-patients: A critical review. *British Journal of Psychiatry, 152*, 174–179

Hersen, M., Ammerman, R. T., & Sisson, L. A. (1994). *Handbook of aggressive and destructive behavior in psychiatric patients*. London: Plenum.

Hollin, C. R. (1990). *Cognitive–behavioral interventions with young offenders*. New York: Pergamon Press.

Howells, K. (1989). Anger-management methods in relation to the prevention of violent behavior. In J. Archer & K. Browne (Eds.), *Human aggression: Naturalistic accounts* (pp. 153–181). London: Routledge.

Hughes, G. V. (1995). Short and long term outcomes for a cognitive–behavioral anger management program. In G. Davies, S. Lloyd-Bostock, M. McMurran, & C. Wilson (Eds.), *Psychology, law, and criminal justice: International developments in research and practice* (pp. 485–494). New York: Walter de Gruyter.

Jackson, D. N. (1989). *The basic personality inventory manual.* Port Huron, MI: Research Psychologist Press.

Konecni, V. J. (1975). The mediation of aggressive behavior: Arousal level versus anger and cognitive labeling. *Journal of Personality and Social Psychology, 32,* 706–712.

Kroner, D. G., & Reddon, J. R. (1995). Anger and psychopathology in prison inmates. *Personality and Individual Differences, 18,* 783–788.

Link, B., & Stueve, C. (1994). Psychotic symptoms and the violent/illegal behavior of mental patients compared to community controls. In J. Monahan & H. Steadman (Eds.), *Violence and mental disorder: Developments in risk assessment* (pp. 21–59). Chicago, IL: University of Chicago Press.

Maiuro, R. D., Cahn, T. S., Vitaliano, P. P., Wagner, B. C., & Zegree, J. B. (1988). Anger, hostility, and depression, in domestically violent versus generally assaultive men and nonviolent control subjects. *Journal of Consulting and Clinical Psychology, 56,* 17–23.

McDougall, C., Boddis, S., Dawson, K., & Hayes, R. (1990). Developments in anger control training. *Issues in Criminological and Legal Psychology, 15,* 39–44.

Meichenbaum, D. (1985). *Stress inoculation training.* Oxford, UK: Pergamon Press.

Miller, W. R., & Rollnick, S. (1993). *Motivational interviewing.* New York: Guilford.

Monahan, J., & Steadman, H. (1994). *Violence and mental disorder.* Chicago, IL: University of Chicago Press.

Mullen, P., Taylor, P. J., & Wessely, S. (1993). Psychosis, violence and crime. In J. Gunn & P. J. Taylor (Eds.), *Forensic psychiatry: Clinical, legal and ethical issues* (pp. 329–372). Oxford, UK: Butterworth–Heinemann.

Noble, P. (1997). Violence in psychiatric in-patients: Review and clinical implications. *International Review of Psychiatry, 9,* 207–216.

Novaco, R. W. (1975). *Anger control: The development and evaluation of an experimental treatment.* Lexington, MA: D. C. Heath.

Novaco, R. W. (1977). Stress inoculation: A cognitive therapy for anger and its application to a case of depression. *Journal of Consulting and Clinical Psychology, 45,* 600–608.

Novaco, R. W. (1993). *Stress inoculation therapy for anger control: A manual for therapists.* Unpublished manuscript, University of California, Irvine.

Novaco, R. W. (1994). Anger as a risk factor for violence among the mentally disordered. In J. Monahan & H. Steadman (Eds.), *Violence and mental disorder: Developments in risk assessment* (pp. 21–59). Chicago, IL: University of Chicago Press.

Novaco, R. W. (1997). Remediating anger and aggression with violent offenders. *Legal and Criminological Psychology, 2,* 77–88.

Novaco, R. W., & Renwick, S. J. (1998). Anger predictors of the assaultiveness of forensic hospital patients. In E. Sanavio (Ed.), *Behavior and cognitive therapy today: Essays in honor of Hans J. Eysenck* (pp. 199–208). Amsterdam: Elsevier Science.

Renwick, S., Black, L., Ramm, M., & Novaco, R. W. (1997). Anger treatment with forensic hospital patients. *Legal and Criminological Psychology, 2,* 103–116.

Rice, M. E., Harris, G. T., Quinsey, V. L., & Cyr, M. (1990). Planning treatment programs in secure psychiatric facilities. In D. N. Weisstub (Ed.), *Law and mental health: International perspective* (Vol. 6, pp. 159–187). Hillsdale, NJ: Erlbaum.

Rice, M. E., Harris, G. T., Varney, G. W., & Quinsey, V. L. (1989). *Violence in institutions: Understanding prevention, and control.* Toronto, Canada: Hogrefe & Huber.

Schlichter, K. J., & Horan, J. J. (1981). Effects of stress inoculation on the anger and aggression management skills of institutionalized juvenile delinquents. *Cognitive Therapy and Research*, *5*, 359–365.

Selby, M. J. (1984). Assessment of violence potential using measures of anger, hostility, and social desirability. *Journal of Personality Assessment*, *48*, 531–544.

Serin, R. C., & Kuriychuk, M. (1994). Social and cognitive processing deficits: Implications for treatment. *International Journal of Law and Psychiatry*, *17*, 431–441.

Smith, L. L., Smith, J. N., & Beckner, B. M. (1994, March). An anger management workshop for women inmates. *Journal of Contemporary Human Services*, 172–175.

Spielberger, C. D. (1991). *State–trait anger expression inventory: Revised research edition.* Odessa, FL: Psychological Assessment Resources.

Stermac, L. E. (1986). Anger control treatment for forensic patients. *Journal of Interpersonal Violence*, *1*, 446–457.

Swanson, J. W., Borum, R., Swartz, M. S., & Monahan, J. (1996). Psychotic symptoms and disorders and the risk of violent behaviour in the community. *Criminal Behaviour and Mental Health*, *6*, 309–329.

Toch, H. (1989). Violence in prisons. In K. Howells & C. R. Hollin (Eds.), *Clinical approaches to violence* (pp. 267–285). Chichester, UK: Wiley.

Towl, G. (1995). Anger management groupwork. *Issues in Criminological Psychology*, *23*, 31–35.

Valliant. P. M., Jensen, B., & Raven-Brook, L. (1995). Brief cognitive behavioural therapy with male adolescent offenders in open custody or on probation: An evaluation of the management of anger. *Psychological Reports*, *76*, 1056–1058.

Welsh, W. N., & Gordon, A. (1991). Cognitive mediators of aggression: Test of a causal model. *Criminal Justice and Behavior*, *18*, 125–145.

Zamble, E. (1992). Behavior and adaptation in long-term prison inmates: Description of longitudinal results. *Criminal Justice and Behavior*, *19*, 409–425.

Zillmann, D. (1983). Arousal and aggression. In R. Geen & E. I. Donnerstein (Eds.), *Aggression: Theoretical and empirical reviews.* New York: Academic Press.

Chapter 20

Relapse Prevention: Reconceptualization and Revision

D. Richard Laws
Adult Forensic Psychiatric Community Services,
Victoria, British Columbia, Canada

INTRODUCTION

The basic model of relapse prevention (RP) (see Daley, 1991; Laws, 1995a; Marlatt & Gordon, 1985; Wanigaratne, Wallace, Pullin, Keaney, & Farmer, 1990) originated in drug and alcohol treatment. While there have been numerous derivatives of this basic model (see, for example, Wilson, 1992) the revised version developed in the sex offender field (Laws, 1989, 1995a, 1995b; Pithers, 1990, 1991; Pithers, Marques, Gibat, & Marlatt, 1983) has probably been the one most widely adopted.

Relapse prevention was a natural outgrowth of the movement in psychology to link traditional behavior therapy with cognitive therapy. One of the basic premises of cognitive–behavior therapy is that behaviors and the thoughts that accompany them are tightly linked. Therefore the main target of relapse prevention has been on the analysis and restructuring of these cognitive–behavioral chains.

BEGINNINGS

The earliest formulation of relapse prevention resulted from the observation by workers in the drug and alcohol field that a variety of treatments could produce

Handbook of Offender Assessment and Treatment. Edited by C. R. Hollin.
© 2000 John Wiley & Sons Ltd.

cessation or at least moderation of behaviors such as heroin, alcohol, or tobacco addiction. The problem was that the probability of continued abstinence was highest when the treatment ended, and this was followed by a process of deterioration. With no further treatment, relapse rates approached 80% over the next 12 months, two-thirds of them occurring with the first three months following the end of treatment (Hunt, Barnett, & Branch, 1971). Marlatt (1980) made a simple conclusion. If a follow-up strategy could be designed to *maintain* the effects of the cessation-oriented treatment, then it was possible that relapses could be prevented. Thus the original formulation of RP was that of a *maintenance strategy*, not a formal treatment (Marlatt & Gordon, 1985). Today RP is more likely to be seen as an umbrella under which a variety of analytical and self-management strategies may be organized, i.e. RP becomes the cessation-oriented treatment *and* the maintenance strategies (George & Marlatt, 1989; Pithers, Martin, & Cumming, 1989; Wanigaratne et al., 1990). The notion that there is little reason to expect treatment effects to persist very much beyond the end of treatment would be particularly true of addictive behaviors (alcoholism, drug addiction, smoking) as well as disorders of impulse control (compulsive sexual behavior, compulsive gambling, sexual deviance, problem drinking, compulsive spending, shoplifting, or interpersonal violence). Following treatment for any of these problems we might expect that the treated person will find him or herself in risky situations and/or in the presence of factors associated with risk. To the extent that the person can deal with these encountered threats, the effects of the cessation-oriented treatment should be able to be maintained.

A COGNITIVE–BEHAVIORAL MODEL OF RELAPSE

The original model of RP advanced by Marlatt (1985a) has been altered very little in the past 20 years. As we shall see, this remains RP's major shortcoming. In its most basic formulation, RP is a step-by-step model of how treated behavior falls apart if there is no further intervention. It starts with the assumption that upon termination of treatment, the client is in a state of *abstinence*. *Self-efficacy* and *expectations for continued success* are high. Sooner or later the client will again come into contact with situations and other conditioned stimuli associated with the terminated behavior. It is here that he or she is likely to make a *seemingly irrelevant decision* (SID). A SID is a minor lapse, a seemingly unintentional slip that brings one into contact with risky situations and stimuli, and takes the person one step closer to a serious lapse or even relapse. If the person stops and reflects at this point and does not make a SID, self-efficacy will be enhanced and the probability of relapse will decrease. If he or she does make the SID, this places the person in a *high-risk situation* that will pose a threat to his or her sense of self-control.

In the original RP model high risk situations (sometimes called high-risk *factors*) are characterized in three ways: as negative emotional states, as interpersonal conflict, and as social pressure to engage in the terminated behavior

(Laws, 1995a; Marlatt, 1985b; Wanigaratne et al., 1990). All of these factors are believed to be precursors of relapse. If the person has put him or herself deliberately in harm's way, then in addition to SIDs the person has also probably been making *maladaptive coping responses* which lead to more lapses. If at this point an *adaptive coping response* can be produced, abstinence can be maintained and further lapses and possible relapse prevented. If the adaptive coping response is not produced, a lapse and backsliding toward the undesired behavior could begin. Since these lapsing behaviors are clearly related to previous patterns of undesirable behavior, the client may experience the *abstinence violation effect* (AVE), sometimes called the *rule violation effect* (RVE) (Wanigaratne et al., 1990). The AVE/RVE is, despite its lofty title, simply a recognition by the client that he or she is failing, that the pledge of abstinence has been broken, that the goal of the cessation-oriented treatment is being defeated. A number of events are hypothesized to occur during the AVE. These are said to take the form of an internal monologue. These include *self-deprecation* ("I'm worthless!"), *failure expectation* ("The treatment didn't work"), the *problem of immediate gratification* aka *The Pig* ("Might as well do it"), or *erroneous attributions* ("It's my fault"). All of these self-statements are believed to contribute to increasing the likelihood of relapse. However, even this far along in the chain toward relapse, if the individual can produce an adaptive coping response, he or she could return to a state of abstinence and possibly ponder the meaning of the AVE. If the coping response cannot be produced, then it is believed that relapse is likely.

THE COGNITIVE–BEHAVIORAL CHAIN

The feature that has emerged as the central element of RP was not part of the original model. The cognitive–behavioral chain (Laws, 1995a; Nelson & Jackson, 1989) developed from clinical practice with sex offenders. Viewed in the context of sexual offending, the chain may be seen as an "offense schematic", a map of how a given individual commits sex offenses. It closely resembles the familiar domestic abuse or sexual abuse cycle (e.g. Freeman-Longo & Pithers, 1992). It may be seen as a sort of pictorial version of the cognitive–behavioral model of relapse. The therapeutic purpose of the chain is to put the client in touch with the complete sequence of behaviors leading from high-risk situations or factors to lapse and ultimately, relapse. The behavioral side of the chain is completed first, usually a sequence of not more than 10 steps. Once this is complete the client is required to add in the cognitions that accompany each behavioral component. Once completed the chain provides graphic evidence that thought and behavior are inextricably linked; that deviant behavior does not "just happen." Figure 20.1 provides an example of a completed cognitive–behavioral chain (Nelson & Jackson, 1989). Marques (personal communication, 7 July 1993) also requires clients to produce credible cognitive and behavioral coping responses to deal with the threats posed by various events in the chain.

EVENT	INTERPRETATION
I get divorced from my fourth wife.	"Women are always messing me over. Yet I've got to be in a relationship with somebody."
I meet a new girlfriend who is already pregnant from another man. She moves in with me because she has nowhere else to stay.	"This isn't exactly what I want, but it's better than nothing. Maybe I can't get anything better than somebody else's throwaways. At least she needs me."
I get laid off my job.	"I keep getting the shaft! I deserve better than this."
My girlfriend's 13-year-old daughter (the victim) moves in with us.	"I really don't like this, but there's nothing I can do about it. I'd rather live alone with my girlfriend."
The victim tells me she was sexually molested. I tell her mother and grandparents, but no one calls the authorities.	"She's sexually experienced. I guess her family doesn't care if she has sex or not."
I see the victim nude when she goes from the bathroom to her bedroom without any clothes on. I tell my girlfriend but she does nothing about it.	"What a ripe and ready body! She sure turns me on! I guess her mom doesn't care what she does."
The victim walks nude into the bathroom while I'm drying off from my shower. I tell her to leave.	"I think she's trying to seduce me. Why else would she come in here like that? God, I can't get much more turned on! I can't stand it . . . got to have her."
I go to the bar and get drunk after having an argument with my girlfriend. I return home late.	"After all I've done for her. She treats me just like all the rest. I can do better than this. I'll just stay out and get drunk. That'll teach her not to make me mad."
When I come home my girlfriend is in bed. The victim is still up watching T.V. I lay down next to her on the floor.	"Whew! She turns me on and I know she wants it. Since her mom doesn't appreciate me, maybe she will after I make her feel good. Screw it! I deserve some pleasure too."

SEXUAL MOLESTATION

Figure 20.1 The cognitive–behavioral chain. Reproduced from Laws (1989) by permission of Guilford Press, New York

RP AND COGNITIVE–BEHAVIOR THERAPY

While I have identified the cognitive–behavioral chain as the element that *I* deem to be central to RP as theory and therapy, there are many additional elements that complement the chain as well as stand apart from it. In reviewing the theoretical structure of RP it becomes apparent that many of its statements are not unique to Marlatt and his colleagues. Concepts such as lapse, relapse, and maladaptive behavior apply to a wide variety of deviant behaviors. Assessment and treatment elements such as autobiographies, self-monitoring, behavioral and cognitive coping strategies, cognitive restructuring, self-efficacy ratings, labeling and detachment, and cognitive reframing are common to many cognitive–behavioral treatments. Other concepts such as relapse fantasies, relapse rehearsal, relapse roadmaps, relapse precursors, seemingly irrelevant decisions, high-risk situations, the cognitive–behavioral chain, urges and craving, decision matrix, urge surfing, reminder cards, and the AVE seem to be unique to RP. It would appear, as Hanson (1996) has argued, that despite a certain specialness of language, RP is right in the mainstream of cognitve–behavior therapy.

Even given the preceding, I think that it is too often ignored that Marlatt and his colleagues have made two major contributions to cognitive–behavior therapy. First, they reconceptualized the relapse process as a learning experience rather than the failure of treatment. As we have seen above, the lapsing client can recover a state of abstinence at any point in the relapse process by emitting adaptive coping responses. This flies in the face of programs insisting upon zero tolerance. Furthermore, Hanson (1996) has noted that RP has presented a model which offender therapists recognize. It clearly says that relapse is an expected and manageable problem. He also stated that RP has inspired an entire generation of offender therapists. I consider that to be a major victory. Second, Marlatt's original model of RP is a clear, concise, and forthright treatment intervention. Laws (1995a) has argued that it ought to be effective, with minor modifications, across a broad range of addictive behaviors and disorders of impulse control.

RECONCEPTUALIZING AND REVISING RP

The very popularity of RP has, I think, been its undoing. In the area with which I am most familiar, sex offender treatment, the popularity of RP has led to its institutionalization. While everyone does local modifications, the basic structure of the model has not changed in 10 years. Its broad acceptance, its ease of implementation, and its striking face validity, have virtually precluded empirical evaluation of the treatment. This sweeping act of faith was further bolstered by Marshall, Jones, Ward, Johnston, and Barbaree's (1991) conclusion that cognitive–behavior therapy was the treatment of choice for sex offenders. This article was widely accepted as the ultimate riposte to the (by then notorious and oft misinterpreted) Furby, Weinrott, and Blackshaw (1989) review of sex offender treatment. I think that few people probably noticed Marshall and Anderson's (1996) evaluation of treatment outcome of RP with sex offenders *specifically*. They concluded that RP did not perform any better than a variety of other treatments and, in some cases, worse. I think that even fewer people noticed that a subversive literature was developing, one that would result in the near total reconceptualization of RP.

Thornton (1997) asked if relapse prevention is really necessary. He acknowledged that RP permits organizing and integrating many treatment approaches, it appears to be applicable to most risks, and it is an excellent framework for community supervision and risk management. Thornton points to three theoretical problems. First, RP makes deviant behavior *too* salient. As indicated above, the RP approach spends a great deal of time focusing upon thoughts, feelings, behaviors, and situations associated with risk. The thought that "I might lapse" is made ever present. Since sex offenders typically offend at a fairly low rate, Thornton believes that RP makes deviance too visible and hence tempting. Second, sex offenders are not highly motivated people. Although RP permits the identification of a huge number of risk factors and development of intricate coping schemes, the question of why the offender should use them remains. Rather, Thornton says, we should help offenders construct non-offending lifestyles sustained by positive reinforcers intrinsic to that lifestyle. As it stands, RP creates a negative picture of things to be avoided and pleasures to be given up. Finally, he says that RP may be a "pseudo-treatment". RP, says Thornton, indicates that risk may be managed by getting the offender to identify it and produce a coping strategy for it. Conceptualizing the coping strategy should be the starting point for developing it as a skill. In fact, skill development is often neglected. Thornton believes that we could do without RP. His approach would be to target criminogenic factors. Specifically, we should

1. use research to identify factors which are liked to offending,
2. determine which of these factors apply to particular offenders, and
3. design interventions to target those factors.

This approach has the advantage that it permits treatment of denying offenders and avoids the salience and motivational problems common to RP.

Without making a great issue of it, Thornton (1997) has identified what has emerged as the basic problem with RP. It was designed for use with people who *want* to change their undesirable behavior. In my judgment the most remarkable work in the area of reconceptualizing and revising RP is being done by Hudson, Ward and their colleagues in New Zealand. This is the first real breakthrough work done, both theoretically and practically, since RP was initially organized for use with sex offenders (Laws, 1989; Pithers et al., 1983). This revision is represented in two major articles. The first (Ward, Louden, Hudson, & Marshall, 1995) was an extensive revision of the cognitive–behavioral chain. The original models of relapse (Pithers, 1990, 1991) and the chain (Nelson & Jackson, 1989) show how a person desiring to be abstinent or dramatically change his or her behavior would progress in identifying risk factors and develop coping responses to manage them. What they did not do was show how unmotivated persons or persons with pro-offending attitudes might progress. In their revision of the offense chain Ward et al. (1995) identified different pathways that would accommodate different types of offenders. Their research into offending patterns identified nine discriminable steps in the offense chain for child molesters. They state that child molesters typically follow one of the three pathways (Ward et al., 1995, pp. 253–254).

> The positive affect pathway has explicit planning, and pro-adult/child sexual contact beliefs. The negative affect pathway has implicit planning, interpersonal neediness, and a sense of entitlement, especially regarding sex, a negative evaluation of offending behavior, and a resolve to avoid such behavior in the future. Finally, some men shift between these two extreme pathways.

The second article is virtually a complete revision of the cognitive–behavioral model of relapse (Ward & Hudson, 1997) and is built directly on the model just described (Ward et al., 1995). The authors refer to this as a *self-regulation model of sexual offending*. They note that self-regulation may be employed to *avoid* certain goals as well as to *achieve* others. In dealing with sexual offending the focus is primarily upon dysfunctional self-regulation (p. 3). There are three types of self-regulation. Individuals may *underregulate* their behavior, becoming disinhibited and losing control. They may *misregulate*, where ineffective strategies are used to achieve goals. Or they may *effectively self-regulate*, where goals are self-serving and not problematic to the offender.

Ward and Hudson (1997, pp. 4–12 *passim*) describe a self-regulation model of the relapse process. Like the earlier model it also consists of nine different phases. They stress that the process is fluid and distinct steps would probably not be detected by the offender. As in the original model of RP for sex offenders (e.g. Pithers, 1990, 1991) the offender can exit the process at any point by using adaptive coping strategies. The relapse process could be relatively brief or could extend over a period of time. Individuals may move back and forth between different points in the offense chain. The phases of the model are:

Phase one: life event. As in the original RP model some kind of life event occurs to an individual who is attempting to remain sex offense-free. This is appraised according to existing beliefs, attitudes, goals, and context. Specific patterns of thoughts, emotions, and intentions are then activated.

Phase two: desire for deviant sex or activity. If a person has a history of sexually abusing women or children such goals might elicit a crude plan for a sexual assault. In this sense deviant fantasizing would constitute what Ward and Hudson call a "mental simulation" of an assault.

Phase three: offense-related goals established. At this stage the offender considers what he should do about his maladaptive desire. Ward and Hudson say that there are two broad classes of goals: avoidance and approach. An *avoidant* goal would be to *not* commit the offense. *Approach* goals, on the other hand, reflect the intention to sexually offend, for whatever reason.

Phase four: strategy selected. The authors specify four offense pathways which are related to the two broad goals of avoidance or approach. These are:

- *Avoidant-passive.* This encompasses both the desire to avoid offending and the failure to prevent it from happening. This is the underregulation or disinhibition pathway, the inability to control deviant sexual behavior. These persons lack coping skills, are more impulsive, and use covert planning.
- *Avoidant-active.* This pathway involves a direct attempt to control deviant thoughts and fantasies that threaten self-control. It is the misregulation pathway in that the strategies selected do not work and increase the likelihood of offending. These persons may be able to plan, monitor, or evaluate their behavior but are unable to evaluate the effectiveness of coping responses.
- *Approach-automatic.* These people have overlearned sexual scripts related to offending. Their behavior seems impulsive and poorly planned. This is an underregulation or disinhibition pathway. This is the type of behavior that Pithers (1990) has referred to as "planned impulsiveness".
- *Approach-explicit.* These are the offenders who carefully plan and execute their sexual offenses. They have good self-regulation skills but use them to abuse others. They maintain or heighten their emotional state through sexual offending. The notion of disinhibition does not apply here.

Phase five: high-risk situation entered. Appraisal processes come into play here as the offender makes contact or finds an opportunity for contact with a victim. This is a critical event. Ward and Hudson (1997, p. 8) state: "For those attempting to control or inhibit their behavior, it signifies failure, and for offenders whose goals are acquisitional ones, it signals the likelihood of success." Avoidant-passive offenders will exhibit automatic, mindless, well rehearsed, and habitual behaviors. Their "self-evaluative processess are effectively disengaged" (p. 8). The avoidant-active offender will perceive control strategies failing leading to a sense of personal inadequacy and negative self-evaluation. The approach-automatic offender will be in the grip of the PIG, focused upon achieving sexual pleasure. Approach-explicit offenders will be focusing on planning strategies to effect the offense.

Phase six: lapse. Here we consider the immediate precursors to the offense. The offender is intending to re-engage in deviant behavior. Although it may be temporary, the avoidant-passive offender may switch to an approach goal, simply giving up their attempt to control themselves. The avoidant-active person will judge his attempts to control deviant sexual desire as a failure, and switch to an approach goal, if only temporarily. Approach-automatic offenders fall victim to situational stimuli and impulsively offend. Approach-explicit offenders will demonstrate careful planning and management of the situation.

Phase seven: sexual offense. Ward and Hudson state that, at the time of the offense, the avoidant-passive and avoidant-active offenders will be self-focused, disinhibited, and focused upon their own goals. Because of the loss of control, they say, the offense may be quite violent. The approach-automatic individual may be impulsive, intimidating, and demeaning. The approach-explicit offender may either construe the sexual offense as mutually consenting or, conversely, humiliate or degrade the victim.

Phase eight: post-offense evaluation. The two avoidant pathways are hypothesized to exhibit the classical AVE response, namely feeling guilt or shame and evaluating themselves negatively. On the other hand, approach offenders will experience positive affect because they have achieved their goals.

Phase nine: attitude towards future offending. Ward and Hudson state that those persons with avoidant goals may do several things. They may once again commit themselves to abstinence, try to regain control, or continue to misregulate their behavior. They may decide that they are unable to stop and simply continue offending. Or, they may choose offending as a lifestyle and switch to an approach goal. The approach-automatic offender will have his sexual offending script reinforced by success. The approach-explicit offender will refine his abusive strategies and adjust his style accordingly. Both approach types will not attempt to restrain their sexual offending in the future.

In addition to this conceptual revision of the relapse process, Hudson and Ward (1997) have developed explicit intervention strategies for each of the four types of self-regulation. Ruth Mann (personal communication, 5 December 1997) has stated that the HM Prison Service Sex Offender Treatment Programme is empirically evaluating the validity of the four pathways model. These and other revisions and expansions of the original RP model greatly enhance our understanding of the relapse process and more precisely identify the points of intervention.

CONCLUSION

The history of RP applied to criminal offenders has much to teach us. The uncritical acceptance of RP served to place it somewhere outside the continuing "what works" argument in criminology. It fit therapists' preconceptions, it seemed to "work", it was accepted, and it was not evaluated. This enthusiasm masked its faults and prevented its evaluation. Now, nearly 20 years on, the basic assumptions of RP are being successfully challenged. What is emerging is a cleaner model, empirically rather than rationally derived, testable rather than merely believable.

REFERENCES

Daley, D. C. (1991). *Kicking addictive habits once and for all*. Lexington, MA: Lexington Books.

Freeman-Longo, R., & Pithers, W. D. (1992). *A structural approach to preventing relapse: A guide for sex offenders.* Brandon, VT: Safer Society Press.

Furby, L., Weinrott, M. R., & Blackshaw, L. (1989). Sex offender recidivism: A review. *Psychological Bulletin, 105,* 2–30.

George, W. H., & Marlatt, G. A. (1989). Introduction. In D. R. Laws (Ed.), *Relapse prevention with sex offenders* (pp. 1–31). New York: Guilford.

Hanson, R. K. (1996). Evaluating the contribution of relapse prevention to the treatment of sexual offenders. *Sexual Abuse, 8,* 209–221.

Hudson, S. M., & Ward, T. (1997, October). *Relapse prevention: Treatment implications.* Paper presented at the 16th annual meeting of the Association for the Treatment of Sexual Abusers, Arlington, VA.

Hunt, W. A., Barnett, L. W., & Branch, L. G. (1971). Relapse rates in addiction programs. *Journal of Clinical Psychology, 27,* 455–456.

Laws, D. R. (Ed.) (1989). *Relapse prevention with sex offenders.* New York: Guilford.

Laws, D. R. (1995a). A theory of relapse prevention. In W. O'Donohue & L. Krasner (Eds.), *Theories of behavior therapy* (pp. 445–473) Washington, DC: American Psychological Association.

Laws, D. R. (1995b). Central elements in relapse prevention procedures with sex offenders. *Psychology, Crime & Law, 2,* 41–53.

Marlatt, G. A. (1980). *Relapse prevention: A self-control program for the treatment of addictive behaviors.* Unpublished manuscript, University of Washington, Department of Psychology, Seattle.

Marlatt, G. A. (1985a). Relapse prevention: Theoretical rationale and overview of the model. In G. A. Marlatt & J. R. Gordon (Eds.), *Relapse prevention* (pp. 3–70). New York: Guilford.

Marlatt, G. A. (1985b). Cognitive factors in the relapse process. In G. A. Marlatt & J. R. Gordon (Eds.), *Relapse prevention* (pp. 128–200). New York: Guilford.

Marlatt, G. A., & Gordon, J. R. (Eds.) (1985). *Relapse prevention.* New York: Guilford.

Marshall, W. L., & Anderson, D. (1996). An evaluation of the benefits of relapse prevention programs with sexual offenders. *Sexual Abuse, 8,* 209–221.

Marshall, W. L., Jones, R. L., Ward, T., Johnston, R., & Barbaree, H. E. (1991). Treatment outcome with sex offenders. *Clinical Psychology Review, 11,* 465–485.

Nelson, C., & Jackson, P. (1989). High-risk recognition: The cognitive–behavioral chain. In D. R. Laws (Ed.), *Relapse prevention with sex offenders* (pp. 167–177). New York: Guilford.

Pithers, W. D. (1990). Relapse prevention with sexual aggressors: A method for maintaining therapeutic gain and enhancing external supervision. In W. L. Marshall, D. R. Laws, & H. E. Barbaree (Eds.), *Handbook of sexual assault* (pp. 343–361). New York: Plenum.

Pithers, W. D. (1991). Relapse prevention with sexual aggressors. *Forum on Corrections Research, 3,* 20–23.

Pithers, W. D., Marques, J. K., Gibat, C. C., & Marlatt, G. A. (1983). Relapse prevention with sexual aggressives: A self-control model of treatment and the maintenance of change. In J. G. Greer & I. R. Stuart (Eds.), *The sexual aggressor* (pp. 214–234). New York: Van Nostrand Reinhold.

Pithers, W. D., Martin, G. R., & Cumming, G. F. (1989). Vermont treatment program for sexual aggressors. In D. R. Laws (Ed.), *Relapse prevention with sex offenders* (pp. 292–310). New York: Guilford.

Thornton, D. (1997, October). *Is relapse prevention really necessary?* Paper presented at the 16th annual meeting of the Association for the Treatment of Sexual Abusers, Arlington, VA.

Wanigaratne, S., Wallace, W., Pullin, J., Keaney, F., & Farmer, R. (1990). *Relapse prevention for addictive behaviours.* Oxford, UK: Blackwell Scientific.

Ward, T., & Hudson, S. M. (1997, October). *Relapse prevention: Conceptual innovations.*

Paper presented at the 16th annual meeting of the Association for the Treatment of Sexual Abusers, Arlington, VA.

Ward, T., Louden, K., Hudson, S. M., & Marshall, W. L. (1995). A descriptive model of the offense chain for child molesters. *Journal of Interpersonal Violence, 10,* 452–472.

Wilson, P. H. (Ed.) (1992). *Principles and practice of relapse prevention.* New York: Guilford.

Chapter 21

Forensic Psychotherapy

Christopher Cordess
University of Sheffield, Sheffield, UK

I knew myself, at the first breath of this new life, to be more wicked, sold a slave to my original evil: and the thought, in that moment, braced and delighted me like wine.
Robert Louis Stevenson (1886, 1979), *The Strange Case of Dr Jekyll and Mr Hyde*

It is neither easy nor agreeable to dredge this abyss of viciousness, and yet I think it must be done, because what could be perpetrated yesterday could be attempted again tomorrow, could overwhelm us and our children. One is tempted to turn away with a grimace and close one's mind: this is a temptation one must resist
Primo Levi, 1988, *The Drowned and the Saved.*

INTRODUCTION

These two quotations raise questions which are central to forensic psychotherapy. How much is known about our "dark" or shadow side and capabilities, in given circumstances, for destructive, antisocial and possibly offending behaviour? To what extent is it a gratification to us (so-called "ego syntonic"), and to what extent conflictual ("ego dystonic")? The answers to these questions will dictate and inform whether, and to what extent, we are motivated to try to change. Finally, are we and our patients (with our help) prepared to "dredge this abyss of viciousness", as described above by Primo Levi?

Although the concept of "evil" is part of another discourse—a moral and theological one—it is at least adjacent to our professional interests. The context of clinical practice with offenders is that of human motivation in its widest aspects. There are major questions to be asked about what motivational drives and what degrees of intentionality lead on to the wide spectrum of offending behaviour. For example, Gilligan (1996) makes a substantial, and intellectually compelling as well as subversive case for the origin of most violent acts in a subjective sense of a desire for "justice"—however misconstrued and mistaken.

Handbook of Offender Assessment and Treatment. Edited by C. R. Hollin.
© 2000 John Wiley & Sons Ltd.

"Forensic psychotherapy" is the not entirely satisfactory term now adopted to describe the psychodynamic treatment of offenders and victims. The coining of this new term implies a new subject, but, in fact, reflects more a new enthusiasm for a subject with a hugely diverse history, which has linked up with, and profited from, the recent growth in interest and resources of forensic psychiatry. Along with the improved conceptual "tools" of contemporary psychoanalysis, it necessarily joins forces with developments in a range of related and cognate disciplines.

At the core of the Forensic Psychotherapy enterprise is the (rather unremarkable) theoretical assumption that behaviour (and, therefore, action) is suffused with personal meaning through the agency of individual thought processes and—intimately entwined—emotional states. Offender patients frequently have only restricted access and ability to reflect upon their subjective mental states: rather they are more prone to "act out" or enact impulsively. Whilst the psychodynamacist acknowledges some (restricted) place for behaviour theory and therapy, and a far greater place for cognitive–behavioural and systemic approaches, he/she places his/her stall in the realm of not only conscious mental events, but also of *pre*conscious and *un*conscious mental activity, including unconscious phantasy. The convention is used here of using the different spellings of *fantasy* and *phantasy* for conscious and unconscious phenomena, respectively. In this context, unconscious phantasy refers to the subliminal mental representation which accompanies all action: using another discourse, it is partly made up of implicit (or procedural) memory, as opposed to autobiographical (event) or explicit memory. Psychodynamic psychotherapeutic practice distinguishes itself by its concerns with these unconscious mental events (as well as conscious events), as they appear within the patient–therapist interaction (the transference–counter-transference relationship): the aim is the gaining of *affective* as well as *cognitive* understanding. The forensic psychotherapist, in addition, pays particular attention to this interaction in the light of possible re-enactment of aspects of the offensive behaviour within the professional relationship. The theoretical stance is taken that by addressing different elements of the way of being, feeling, and thinking within a therapeutic relationship, greater self-understanding and capacity for "reflective self function" (Fonagy et al., 1997), and empathy, will thereby be achieved, and provide alternative coping strategies to those of the offending behaviours. Otherwise "what could be perpetrated yesterday could be attempted again tomorrow, could overwhelm us . . .". Using a different but parallel language, the forensic psychotherapeutic endeavour is largely directed at increasing the capacity to "mentalize" in the so-called "theory of mind" (Frith, 1989; Leslie, 1987).

Confusion arises when there is a failure to distinguish between "causal" and "meaningful" connections in the Jasperian sense (Jaspers, 1963). A significant contemporary clarification is made by Bolton and Hill (1996) who argue that "reasons can be causes". They distinguish between two types of causality: "non-intentional causality", e.g. a genetic defect like Down's Syndrome; and "intentional causality", which they see as unique to biological systems, "whether operating at a physiological or psychological level, and having the properties, among others, of "set goals", purpose, *being driven by information rather than energetics*, and being active rather than passive" (Holmes, 1998).

This rather condensed and—no doubt, to many readers—sweeping claim for the remit of forensic psychotherapy needs justification. This is what I shall attempt in this brief overview chapter—with, however, the expression of certain reservations, especially in regard to outcome research.

Lest our attempts at defining and pathologizing the negative emotions and motivations—which are part of the assumptive terrain of forensic practice—become too focused on the "offender", it is well to be reminded that they are also the stuff of all human kind. The essayist, William Hazlitt, described it well enough in 1828 to be quoted at some length:

> Nature seems (the more we look into it) made up of *antipathies*: without something to *hate*, we should lose the very spring of thought and action. Life would turn to a stagnant pool, were it not ruffled by the jarring interests, the *unruly passions*, of men. The white streak in our own fortunes is brightened (or just rendered visible) by making all around it as dark as possible. . . . Is it *pride*? Is it *envy*? Is it the force of contrast? Is it *weakness* or *malice*? There is a secret affinity, a *hankering* after, evil in the human mind that takes a *perverse* delight in mischief, since it is a never-failing source of satisfaction. Pure good soon grows insipid, wants variety and spirit. Pain is a bitter-sweet, which never surfeits. Love turns, with a little indulgence, to *indifference* or *disgust*: *hatred* alone is immortal. Do we not see this principle at work everywhere? Animals *torment* and worry one another without mercy, children *kill* flies for sport: every one reads the *accidents* and *offences* in a newspaper as the cream of the jest: a whole town runs to be present at a fire, and the spectator by no means exults to see it extinguished . . . and our *feelings take part with our passions rather than with our understandings*. Men assemble in crowds, with eager enthusiasm, to witness a tragedy: but if there were an execution going forward in the next street . . . the theatre would be empty. A *strange cur in a village*, an *idiot, a crazy woman*, are set upon and baited by the *whole community*. Public nuisances are in the nature of public benefits (my italics).

Any clinical response or, indeed, political policy (as in the contemporary mass panic about public protection with proposals for widespread preventative detention), and especially the psychotherapist has to take on board the fact of such human negative attitudes, fantasies, and "failings". Forensic psychotherapy—possibly arrogantly—specializes in them—and most significantly attempts to address the behaviours, and the tragedies of human destructiveness which are their consequences.

One question that arises from this quotation is: "What is the difference between those of us who think and feel these negative emotions, and the offender who acts them out?"—crudely put as "Bad men do what good men dream" (Simon, 1996); another: "Is our fascination with crime and the criminal acts of others a vicarious "substitute" (for the so-called "moral majority") for enacting some of our own criminal fantasies and wishes?" The answer must be almost certainly affirmative.

Contemporary forensic psychotherapy exists predominantly as a discipline working alongside, and within the domain of, forensic psychiatric or related practice, and therefore, too, alongside other psychotherapies. There is little or no place in this massive clinical task for therapists working alone—in theoretical or actual isolation—with the typical offender patient met with in institutional practice, and within the Criminal Justice System. Only the untrained, the inexperienced and unsupervised, the unwary or the foolhardy, would attempt to "go it alone", but sadly such therapeutic risk-taking is not uncommon in private practice, or even in the public services with the "forensic" offender patient (see Travers, 1994, for a, literally, fatal example). Similarly, it is doubtful whether there is a place for "stand alone" clinics that offer only single modalities of treatment, rather than integrated services offering the whole range of therapies, as well as different levels of security from the purely psychotherapeutic out-patient (ambulant), through to low, medium and maximum secure levels. It is necessary to rehearse the obvious: "security" is a complex concept which refers to psychological and emotional containment, as well as physical safety, of both offender–patient and potential victim–society. It essentially depends upon human contact and not locks or bricks and mortar.

Besides the physical dangers of such work, there are those of the potential toll on professionals' own emotional life. Too frequently gainsayed by a system that underestimates or denies these aspects, good work with frequently disruptive, damaged, and dangerous patients should indeed carry the metaphorical equivalent of a "Government Health Warning": safe, as well as creative and integrated work can only happen within the support of the wider system and specifically, clinically, that of the multi-disciplinary team. The alternative is defensive personal detachment, which, however necessary at certain times, impoverishes the very nature of our practice and the therapeutic experience of our patients.

EXAMPLE

To take a simple example. A young female psychologist reported in supervision that she had met with a serial rapist in a secure hospital for an initial assessment for cognitive–behavioural treatment. The patient was reported to be polite, intelligent, and unusually enthusiastic to begin a therapeutic relationship: she too was very keen to try to help him. That night she dreamt of him in the form of a literal, sexual, and violent narrative, which she found surprising and distressing, but clearly also exciting. A preliminary observation by the supervisor was that this man had, by some meeting of unconscious (as well as conscious) minds, effected a powerful intrusion into the psychologist's "private" life—the equivalent of a "mental rape". Clearly the phenomenon is interpersonal and dependent upon therapist as well as patient "variables". This was felt to be neither necessarily good nor necessarily bad, but was important information which at least needed to be acknowledged by the therapist. The more technical question of how this might inform what one may later say to the patient, or what form of management will best take account of this clinical phenomenon, is multidetermined and for discussion.

However, the view of the Forensic Psychotherapist is that a failure to address such exceptional but, none the less in forensic practice, routine meaningful "communication" is potentially perilous: at the very least not to make use of such information within the professional relationship misses out on major therapeutic possibilities, which are central to the forensic psychotherapy task.

The dangers of the therapeutic "system"—whether individual therapist or institution—becoming defensive, rigid, or emotionally "cut off" from the raw contents of the basic subject-matter of forensic clinical practice are evident and ubiquitous. Therapists become blasé and over-confident, or plough a narrow "therapeutic" modality which misses the point but keeps their own anxiety at bay; institutions, likewise, become obsessed with rules of behaviour and administrative matters (necessary as they are) while "Rome burns". A comment made by a visiting psychotherapist to a maximum security hospital makes the point: "The eerie thing about this place", she said, "is that you know that the patients are in some sense raging—unconsciously if not consciously—but the place is so *silent* and suppressed." The defensive rituals and structures of functioning social systems is described in the Health Service, for example, by Menzies Lyth (1988) and in prisons by Hinshelwood (1993). A constructive examination of these institutional dynamics, ritualistic responses, and (partly) necessary defences, as well as dysfunctional practices which are commonly found in the organization of secure hospitals is long overdue: such matters have been touched upon by Cox (1996).

OUTLINE

I will first briefly describe:

1. The origins and historical roots, with reference to the contemporary scene.

Then

2. The general methods and practice, including aspects of practice in out-patient and secure settings; institutional dynamics; therapeutic communities; and family, groups, and individual psychotherapy.

I shall then review some aspects of

3. The vexed area of research, its methodologies, and the place of audit.

Origins and Historical Roots and the Contemporary Scene

Current forensic psychotherapy might best be regarded as largely the product of a body of psychological and psychodynamic ideas, experience, and theory whose roots lie, in outline, within:

1. Theories of the interrelation of criminology with early concepts of the unconscious mind, which preceded Freud's earliest writings. Ellenberger (1970) in
   The Discovery of the Unconscious describes a range of, particularly nineteenth century, psychological/criminological writings, some of which made
   use of concepts like "the self-deception of consciousness by the unconscious".
   The obvious point needs to be emphasized, as illustrated in the quotations
   already cited, that the great writers of world literature have much to say to
   us about the complexities of the human mind and its motivations, and in particular of "the criminal mind".

2. The body of Freudian writing and development. Although Freud wrote
   relatively little specifically on the criminal mind, psychoanalytic theory, with
   its metaphor of mental conflict, lends itself naturally to the investigation of
   the criminal state of mind. The specific papers include: "Criminals from a
   sense of guilt" (1916a) and "The exceptions" (1916b), and especially relevant
   papers include: "Three essays on the theory of sexuality" (1905), the case of
   the judge, Schreber ("Psycho-analytic notes of an autobiographical account
   of a case of paranoia"), (1911). Also, "Group psychology and the analysis of
   the ego" (1921), which reads like a contemporary text even today. Other psychoanalysts in the early days, for example, Theodor Reik—a lawyer and psy-
   choanalyst—wrote directly on the subject; also August Aichhorn, who much
   influenced Edward Glover: Glover, in turn, was effectively the founder of
   what is now the Portman Clinic in London (Cordess, 1992); Glover's most
   relevant papers are collected in a volume entitled *The Roots of Crime* (1960);
   also, Alexander (1935), the Gluecks in the United States, and from a different perspective, Cleckley (1976). These names are purely illustrative.

3. What has been called "the widening scope of psychoanalysis", bringing with
   it a much increased understanding of the interpersonal phenomena of Transference and Counter-transference, especially as a consequence of the psychoanalytic treatment of borderline, psychotic, and also delinquent patients.
   The contributions of Melanie Klein had a particularly powerful influence, in
   the widest sense, via her clinical theories of psychotic functioning of the mind.
   Klein wrote two brief but interesting early papers of specific interest:
   "Criminal tendencies in normal children" (1927), and "On criminality"
   (1934). Some post-Kleinian developments, for example those of Bion, Rosen-
   feld, and Segal, have been specifically applied to offender patients, notably
   by Williams (1982) and Gallwey (1996).

4. The impetus provided by the foundation, in 1931, and the later clinical and
   theoretical work, of the Institute for the Scientific (later, Study) and Treatment of Delinquency (ISTD)—a group of social reformers, psychoanalysts,
   and others of a range of disciplines. With the passing of the National Health
   Act in 1948, the ISTD split into what now continues as the clinical, treatment
   "wing"—the Portman Clinic (previously the Psychopathic Clinic)—and the
   now rather changed social reforming and educational "wing", which retains
   the ISTD name. The *British Journal of Criminology* was founded within this
   organization and continues under its imprimatur (Cordess, 1992).

5. Other less classifiable contributions. For example, those of Donald Winnicott, especially on delinquency, for instance his 1956 paper entitled "The anti-social tendency"; the work of Bowlby (1988) on "attachment", and the consequences of failed attachment (from which, for example, de Zulueta (1993) has coined the phrase "violence as failed attachment"); also, earlier, a classic, empirical study, "Forty-four juvenile thieves" (Bowlby, 1946), is a model for its time.
6. Recent and contemporary contributions. These are comprehensively covered in a recently published compendium of this subject (Cordess & Cox, 1996), in a collection of papers edited by van Marle (1997), and in an edited basic text by Welldon and Van Velsen (1997). These and other recent publications attest to the momentum of this subject, especially in the United Kingdom at the present time. Largely, this is a reflection of need in a growing area of forensic clinical practice across a wide spectrum of organizations and institutions.

The Methods and Practice

General

I increasingly think of the value and significance of psychodynamic ideas within forensic clinical practice in a hierarchy which runs from the most general one of informing, influencing mainstream psychiatric practice and "the system", right down to the relatively rare, and selective, formal psychotherapy of the individual patient.

At the widest level, psychodynamic understanding should inform the way our society and our systems and institutions respond to the challenge of the offender. To what extent, for example, are we in the business of retribution and punishment—societal or personal; to what extent do we invoke the utilitarian arguments of "deterrence"; and how much of our thinking is reparative and aimed at the so-called "rehabilitative ideal"? There is, for example, a conceptual clash between, on the one hand, clinical understanding of individual offence behaviour and a "bespoke" personalized response, and, on the other, the predominantly "just desserts" philosophy of our current judicial system—"to make the punishment fit the crime", rather than the criminal, as it were.

It should be remembered that, beyond the most superficial analysis, offenders are invariably victims of their own anti-social behaviour, as well as frequently victims of others" earlier exploitation. The overlap, therefore, of offending behaviour and victimization is great, and forensic psychotherapy seeks to address both. As Gunn and Taylor (1993) remark,

> Most patients who come to forensic psychiatrists are victims of one sort or another
> ... [they] have often suffered multiple victimisation in the sense that they have suf-
> fered earlier psychological trauma, usually in childhood. [Their] deleterious experi-
> ences include poverty, social deprivation, inconsistent discipline, violence or sexual

abuse, or as adolescents or adults inadequate or harsh treatment for primary problems (such as schizophrenia and behaviour disorders) (p. 2).

Recent surveys of prison and secure hospital populations have confirmed the
very high percentages of offenders who have been brought up in long-term, or
more often, multiple care placements.

Huesmann, Eron, Lekkowitz, and Walder (1984) found that aggression, for
example, was perpetuated in families across three generations, and Mullen
(1990), Mullen, Martin, Anderson, Romans, and Herbison (1993), and Herman,
Perry, and van der Kolk (1989), amongst many others, have recently provided
empirical evidence of some of the long-term sequelae of abuse in childhood. They
include personality disorder, anxiety, depression, and eating disorders, as well as
patterns of abusive behaviour perpetrated against others. Schetsky (1990) has
provided a comprehensive review of the long-term effects specifically of child
sexual abuse.

It should be emphasized that the fact that violent and sexual offenders have
frequently been victims of similar behaviour themselves is not being presented
as necessarily exculpating of responsibility (Cordess, 1993). Indeed, the reasons
and causes for some people appearing to be resilient to what for others are disastrous early experiences of victimization, needs far greater attention than it has
so far received. Clinically, however, histories of multiple, severe emotional impov-
erishment and traumatism are clearly of great significance in the formation of
the culture of "total" institutions specializing in the detention of such offending
people.

Within an NHS forensic psychiatric Secure Unit—where the patients are typically psychotic and have behaved violently, frequently including killing—it is the
nurses and occupational therapists who provide the continuing day-to-day, and
night, patient contact—the so called "other 23 hours" (Stanton & Schwarz, 1954).
They provide the therapeutic front line and are likely to be the first recipients of
a patient's intimate feelings. The staff require supervision by the psychotherapist,
as well as the support of all other staff: a good working relationship between staff
members within such settings is the basis upon which any more specialized family,
group, or individual psychotherapy relies. Interventions may then include
dynamic, systemic cognitive or behaviourally based treatments. Later, after discharge into independent living, a range of these psychotherapeutic interventions
are likely to be necessary at different times.

It is barely necessary to say that the primarily personality disordered patient
requires his or her own specific therapeutic response. This is too large a subject
to review here, but recommended accounts are those of Cleckley (1941), Meloy
(1992) and Dolan and Coid (1993).

The "living learning environment" of the therapeutic community (Jones, 1952)
provides one of the main socio-therapeutic interventions for personality disordered patients. In such settings "the pervasiveness of forensic patients' maladaptive attitudes and behaviour—as it were polluting virtually all areas of their
psychosocial functions—becomes apparent" (Norton, 1996, p. 402), and can be

creatively and positively addressed. Such an institution is the Henderson Hospital, London, which is presently spawning several sister institutions: of rather different conceptual underpinnings are the therapeutic community institutions of the Dutch (combined penal–therapeutic) TBR system. Within the prison system in the United Kingdom, Grendon Underwood Prison provides an adapted version of the therapeutic community ideal, although it has suffered from a relative lack of training of many of its staff. Even so, evaluations of process and outcome speak to an ameliorating effect on patients/inmates (Cullen, 1994; Genders & Player, 1995; Gunn & Robertson, 1982). It is understood that plans are being made for the establishment of a second "Grendon" within the prison system.

More generally, the importance of the multi-disciplinary and team approach to clinical and psychotherapeutic work with offenders in whatever setting—whether penal institution, hospital, or the community—cannot be over-emphasized. Glover (1960), for example, spoke of the benefits of the "distributive transference", when working with frequently difficult, demanding, and sometimes very provocative patients. On the other hand, such team work offers ample opportunity for the "splitting" of staff—particularly, but not by any means exclusively, in residential settings—as the acting out of "part object" relationships (Gabbard, 1989). At its worst this process can result in confusion, demoralization, and consequent withdrawal by staff working within these institutions; in short, "burn out". For this reason, amongst others, our maximum secure hospitals had gained, until the changes in recent years, a reputation for therapeutic bankruptcy. One authority has written—albeit of the American system—that "quasi-criminal institutions (i.e. those for offender patients) . . . have been a terrible failure, not only in the sense that they often failed to offer meaningful treatment, but also because they typically created an environment worse than prisons or mental institutions" (Stone, 1984, p. 49). Berman and Segel (1982) write admirably of the hazards and dilemmas of psychotherapy with the "captive client", but from a more encouraging viewpoint. However, the difficulty of achieving areas of relative freedom of thought for detained patients should not be underestimated. How free are patients to talk openly of thoughts, wishes, and fantasies, as they need to do if any psychodynamic therapy is to stand a chance without the content being "taken down", as it were, and used against them? Such second thoughts based upon a real fear was encapsulated by a patient of my own in a ward round: "You know that fantasy I told you about last week", he said, "well it wasn't true!" It is our task to be fully aware of the extraordinary dilemmas and sometimes perverse incentives that our institutional structures impose upon patients. The culture has to be better for the patient than that of "keep your head down and keep mum", which is often the quickest way to proceed through the hoops of the detention system. It is for this reason that "institutional" shared experiences and a culture of "openness" as, for example, in that of the therapeutic community—and in its *much* diluted form, so-called "milieu therapy"—are so suited to the therapeutic task with the offender patient.

Cox (1983) makes the case for the presence of the psychotherapist as a constituent member of the eclectic, multi-disciplinary team, basing his model on work in a Special Hospital, to which however it is not confined. He describes the mutual contributions which the forensic psychiatrist and the dynamic psychotherapist can offer one another. He comments, however, that most psychotherapists have a "relative lack of experience of that watershed in which intrapsychic forces burst their bounds and interpersonal disaster ensues" (p. 91). It is in this area that the forensic psychotherapist has a particular role to play in balancing the possibilities for psychotherapeutic work with the risk of the patient's dangerous enactment either against himself, the therapist, or others.

Much psychotherapeutic work with offenders involves the provision of psychological "support", although *how* that is done is the source of much debate: evaluation of this is even more difficult than the evaluation of "change". Psychodynamically the work of Winnicott (1960) and the "holding" environment, and Bion (1970) and the "container and contained", are central concepts. The concept of "projective identification"—well described in a demystified way by Jureidini (1990)—and of splitting are also crucial. Etchegoyen (1992) remarks that (psychologically speaking) "support is the most common instrument of psychotherapy, the one most available to the general practitioner (or simply to anyone who has to do with inter-personal relations)" (p. 311).

Group, Family and Individual

Coming to a group and individual level of forensic psychotherapy practice, the therapist focuses predominantly upon the individual either within the group or family, or singularly, and upon his or her psychopathology, although context and the social "ecology" are, of course, still fundamentally important. Welldon (1998) provides an account of group therapy with offenders, and specifically with victims and perpetrators of incest. A first attempt at work with families where the therapeutic work is between offenders and their (family) victims in a Regional Secure Unit is described by Cordess (1991).

Assessment

Neither the seriousness of offending, nor the gravity of some forms of psychiatric illness, for example, chronic psychoses or depression, nor indeed evidence of low intellectual performance (Sinason, 1992), should preclude assessment and consideration for *some* form of psychotherapeutic help, alongside the involvement of other professionals providing a range of different treatments. The question is: What sort of psychotherapy and when? Cox and Theilgaard (1987) have written of the importance of the therapist's attentiveness and accurate empathy, to be attendant upon the moments when an offender patient may be receptive to offers of "talking" therapy and support, or to the prospect of change which psychological treatments can offer: moments like these may be brought about, for example, by acute feelings of depression, or appropriate shame or of guilt.

Such attentiveness should be the aim of all staff who are in contact with offender patients.

However, we need to be clear in our own minds about the primary and secondary aims of "psychotherapy". In a given case, is it the changing of the offensive behaviour (which becomes a largely criminological task); or the relief of an underlying condition (for example depression); or is it a more holistic, existential goal, responding to the subject's experience in order to improve the patient's general sense of well-being, and thereby his adaptation to the environment (i.e. his social relationships and social functioning)? Aims are multiple and vary according to circumstances, but we cannot and should not aim *only* to reduce the rate or gravity or re-offending, even though that is a hoped-for consequence. Robertson (1989) specifically argues against the use of re-offending rates in the evaluation of any treatment of the offender, and states that the criteria used to judge therapeutic effectiveness for offenders should not differ from those used in all other forms of care.

The relationship between the offending behaviour and psychological state is invariably complex. Part of the specifically forensic psychotherapeutic task consists of the elucidation of this relationship by understanding the individual and the context in which the offending occurs. Common to most clinical analyses of offending behaviour is an analysis of:

1. the offender himself—his behaviour, cognitions and personal psychodynamics, and the relation of these to personal and family history and present circumstances;
2. the criminal act; and
3. the situation and environmental conditions in which it occurs.

For example, in a given act of violence, the assessor will want to know what the perpetrator feels he did it for: was it self-protection (reactive) or was it in the pursuit of gratification (i.e. sadistic)? He will want to know the minute details of the antecedents to the act, the act itself, and what happened afterwards: also, is this a recurrent behaviour and are there specific, repeated characteristics, for example of the type of victim(s) or of the circumstances?

For assessment, and possibly later treatment to occur, the first step is necessarily one of management and of containment within the least restrictive environment that provides safety for the patient as well as for society. This may be achieved emotionally within a "holding" relationship or may require physical containment, e.g. admission to a locked ward. Although community and outpatient treatment of the offender is the aim—where it is practicable—it is frequently the case that treatment will begin as an in-patient, or in residential care, as part of a plan of working towards later care for the particular individual in the community. In Winnicott's phrase "there is first a need for environmental care and then for psychotherapy" (Winnicott, 1956, p. 309). Only then, when these preconditions are satisfied, can assessment and therapeutic work begin. He adds that therapists need to be realistic about what can be achieved because of the amount of secondary gain that accrues to offending behaviour.

However, the fact that many offender patients are contained for long periods of time within intensively staffed settings provides, at least, the external conditions for their engagement in an extended treatment alliance. By contrast, some of the apparently more motivated offenders who present to out-patient settings often break off treatment peremptorily for what they think are compelling reasons. Whilst, rarely, this may be a reasonable reaction to external demands, sabotage of offers of help by leaving therapy is invariably a possibility with the offender, since he or she frequently deals with emotions and psychological stress by action rather than words. The dangers of inexperienced or unsupervised psychotherapists taking into therapy difficult, perverse, and damaged offender patients was emphasized at the beginning of this chapter. Precisely because offender patients frequently make intense and intensively dependent relationships, frequently with powerful projective and introjective identificatory confusions, suitability for group and individual psychotherapies are dependent upon the level of training as well as supervision of staff. There is no getting round this and no short cuts. Adventures of curiosity for the untrained may have rewards of excitement for the novice (or may be disastrous). For the patient they may repeat an interaction—for example, of hope and then rejection—which sadly repeats what, at core, is his or her life experience and major difficulty. To this extent such unprepared therapeutic "forays" may do more harm than good. For example, see Symington (1980). Thus, part of the assessment for psychotherapy is in terms of who is the therapist going to be; what level of training has he/she had; is he/she being supervised; how long and how frequently can he/she see the patient; is he/she committed to the task, etc.?

Functionally psychotic patients being treated with medication present different challenges to those of the borderline and anti-social, personality disordered, patient. Particularly in the case, for example, of psychotic patients, psychotherapy will be but one amongst several therapeutic ingredients, including the use of major tranquillizers. Too frequently the use of medication has been seen as oppositional to psychodynamic psychotherapy rather than complementary: in severely ill populations there is a need to study the benefits of the *combined* effects of pharmacotherapy and psychotherapy (Karasu, 1982a).

Research and Audit

Maxwell (1984) describes a number of criteria by which a *general* psychotherapy service may be judged. They are:

1. relevance or appropriateness;
2. equity (for example, the relative failure to provide psychotherapy services to members of ethnic minorities);
3. accessibility;

4. acceptability;
5. effectiveness; and
6. efficiency.

However, although easy to state, such title headings hide a mass of complexities which are too frequently ignored. Parry (1992) has provided a useful account of the application of findings from research and audit in order to improve provision of psychotherapy services.

Karasu (1982b) has summarized many of the main issues of evaluation of psychotherapy, and they, too, are equally of relevance to the evaluation of psychotherapy with the offender patient. In particular, he emphasizes

> the fact that traditional diagnostic categories may be of limited reliability and validity . . . (and that) diagnostic labels are too narrow. Psychodynamic variables such as conflicts, defences, and patient therapist relationships also need to be evaluated in order to meaningfully discriminate patients who have been given the same diagnosis (p. 789).

He continues, "it is unclear at the present time whether the conflict between the research demands of reproducibility and standardisation will ever be reconciled with the clinician's need for flexibility, creativity and sensitivity to the uniqueness of their individual patients" (p. 789). At the extreme ends of forensic practice—for example, when engaged with homicide within the family—this argument has an especially compelling edge.

Peay and Shapland (1992, p. 126) state that "the historical lessons in clinical criminology of the attempts to evaluate treatment have shown that proper individual therapy is almost always impossible to continue with rigorous evaluation where all is held constant but the treatment".

There are, thus, major difficulties (both methodological and ethical) and, therefore, major disputes about the amenability of forensic psychotherapy to meaningful and useful research.

In much general psychotherapy outcome research the methods of natural science and aspirations towards the rigour of the randomized control trial are in the ascendant. The demands of "evidence-based" medicine, of Cochrane standards, and growing demands of cost–benefit studies within Health Service research increasingly influence the flow of resources and service development.

Although relatively lacking (yet) in forensic psychotherapy research, there are, increasingly, examples of a creative interplay of psychotherapy research and practice: see, for example, Horowitz (1997) on stress response syndromes, a subject-matter intimately related and adaptable to forensic psychotherapy research. Also there is room, and much need, for evaluations of the economic impact of psychotherapy in forensic practice, along the lines of Gabbard et al. (1997); they found psychotherapy to reduce "a range of costs when used to treat patients with the most severe psychiatric disorders" (p. 147). This has been started by Dolan and Norton (1991).

Taking consideration of these difficulties, I will structure part of this account in an adversarial form.

The Case Against

Robertson (1997, p. 501), a distinguished forensic clinical researcher, expresses a Luddite view, which I quote at length:

> Since, in forensic psychiatry, we are unlikely ever to discover or uncover anything of practical use, the taint of money is not an issue in our research. Extraneous factors none the less influence the formation of the questions asked and the agendas of funding bodies may not lend themselves to answerable, relevant, or meaningful questions. Only our oldest universities can contemplate research activity generated because a question is "interesting". More than ever before it would seem that simple and short-term behavioural principles govern research activity. It is with mixed feelings that the rest of us watch eminent professors behaving like children in an infants class, motivated and rewarded by the collection of gold stars.

He continues:

> The need for young doctors to "do" some research in order to advance their careers also encourages short-term planning. Funders, and the recipients of funds, tend to think and act in terms of two- or three-year blocks of financial support. This time-span can accommodate research enquiries into the administrative aspects of forensic psychiatry, but it mitigates against the development of the long-term, in-depth study of the human subjects being administered. The problem is largely attributable to the way in which so-called success is measured. If short-term planning characterizes research activity, short-sightedness marks the evaluation of that activity— "Never mind the quality, count the number".

However, he mitigates these views:

> Lastly, although truths may be few and far between in forensic psychiatric research, as they are in any subject, there are plenty of facts still to be uncovered. The bias towards administrative research is understandable given the nature of the speciality and its relative youthfulness. But things are changing, and it is to be hoped that as the subject matures, there will be more emphasis on research into the psychiatric aspects of the discipline. What other area of psychiatric (*and psychotherapeutic*) practice now allows (*potentially*) for the study of *long-term* course and progress of psychotic illnesses in a contained environment? (p. 502).

Dell (1997) succinctly, too, puts her considerable finger on another aspect of current dangers in the pursuit of research in the forensic field:

> In forensic psychiatry (*and, therefore, forensic psychotherapy*), research access and funding usually depend on those running the services or institutions. Inevitably, they would rather not have publicity for unwelcome findings. It might be expected that academic institutions would take a robust stand in such circumstances. But academics depend on the grants, and prefer to avoid conflicts with their fundings. The situation is not a healthy one (p. 691, my italics).

She gives a particularly worrying example of bowdlerization of some of her own research findings.

Furthermore, Gunn (1996), referring to the formidable (or overwhelming) problems that research in forensic psychotherapy presents, expresses a (forlorn?) wish that: "perhaps forensic psychotherapy can not only show that it is possible to treat the untreatable, but also that it is possible to research the unresearchable" (p. xviii).

If there are many pitfalls in the area of *meaningful* and relevant research within forensic psychiatry, then, since forensic psychotherapy essentially deals in meaning, it has a formidable core problem of its own.

The Case For

Evans, Carlyle, and Dolan (1996) in an overview of forensic psychotherapy research write,

> in an ideal world we would review a large number of publications that would form a coherent body [of evidence]. However we believe that we do not live in that ideal world . . . the way forward is for forensic psychotherapists to consider the parentage of their discipline and to look anew at the variety of research methods open to it (p. 509).

They go on to discuss the particularity of the clientele who may be offered formal psychotherapy by the forensic psychotherapist—paradigmatically they take the "sex offender" and the (legally defined) "psychopathically disordered" patient, with the addition of other personality disorders such as narcissistic, borderline, and antisocial types.

They emphasize the difficulties in terms of severity of clinical problems; the fact that "forensic" patients are frequently defined by criminological or behavioural categories; and the invariable presence of a "third party" between client/patient and therapist/practitioner, namely that of the representative of the Criminal Justice System, whether in the form of a requirement to attend for treatment, or in the form of the locked doors and walls of a secure institution.

These authors further raise the question of whether forensic psychotherapy should ally its "research" methods with those of:

1. the humanities, for example within *hermeneutics* (see Mooij, 1996); or
2. the almost religiously venerated *natural sciences*; or
3. their hybrid progeny, the *human or social sciences*.

There is, for example, wide agreement that the Randomized Control Trial (RCT) is not appropriate for dynamic psychotherapy in general (Higgitt & Fonagy, 1992) and for forensic psychotherapy in particular. These authors, like others, emphasize the importance of the single case study and of qualitative research which, although currently unfashionable, does not abandon the individual "internal world" and motivations of the offender patient.

Hopefully, new paradigms and methodologies will become available.

Since the possible range of this subject is so vast—and the actual products relatively few—I shall focus this discussion on two particularly promising areas of development.

1. The area of "attachment" research and criminology offers the prospect of a real breakthrough in the challenge of moving from *qualitative* research and subjective mental state and "internal world" representation, to a *quantification* of those internal world phenomena. Building on the work of Bowlby (1988) and the "strange situation" test for infants developed by Ainsworth, Blehar, Waters, and Wall (1978), Main and Hesse (1992) have developed the Adult Attachment Interview (AAI)—a semi-structured interview, which allows for categorization and quantification of degrees of psychological attachment of an individual to his or her developmentally "primary" (significant) figures. By extension, offenders' psychological attachment status to current partners or other significant people, and the establishment of data of attachment for individual offenders and different offender groups, becomes a reality. A pathway of possible causation from early parenting failures, disruptive behaviour problems, and the continuity into criminal careers can thereby be critically examined. The possibility of studying the multiple and significant variables in the course towards delinquency and criminality offers an incisive and truly powerful methodology, leading to possible ameliorative intervention. Levinson and Fonagy (1999) have, for example, studied a cohort of prisoners with psychiatric diagnoses using the AAI, and matched them with two control groups—one of severe personality disorders, and the other neither criminal nor "psychiatric", i.e. "normal". In summary, they found greater "secure" attachments in the normal control group, and greater proportions of "dismissive" or failed attachments amongst the prison cohort. Overall they concluded that "criminality arises in the context of weak bonding with individuals and social institutions and the relatively ready dismissal of attachment objects" (Fonagy et al., 1997, p. 255). An overview of this whole subject, entitled "Morality, disruptive behaviour, borderline personality disorder, crime and their relationships to security of attachment" gives a flavour of this pioneering work (Fonagy et al., 1997).

2. A range of psychodynamic perspectives on psychopathic and anti-social personality disorders are contained in a volume edited by van Marle (1997). This includes a brief account by Pfäfflin of empirical paradigms of process research in psychotherapy, and specifically of the need for its application to "forensic" populations, as exemplified by the Ulm Text Book (UTB) based at the Department of Psychotherapy of Ulm University, Germany (Mergenthaler & Kächele, 1991). This contains "the largest collection of reports, test protocols, tapes and transcripts" (Pfäfflin, 1997, p. 27). So far this paradigm of empirical, therapy transcript evaluations remains relatively undeveloped, but it does provide a potential new route to replace that

merely of cherished—but largely untested—beliefs and assertions which constitute too much of forensic psychotherapeutic practice at the present time.

CONCLUSION

Since psychodynamic psychotherapy focuses upon the meaning of the ways of being and acting of an individual, group, or institution, its concepts and modes of understanding clearly have massive import and relevance to the perpetrators and victims of anti-social acts, and our societal and institutional responses to them; the remit, that is, of forensic psychotherapy. This chapter has attempted to provide an outline of that relevance, whilst acknowledging the considerable difficulties inherent in a demonstration of efficacy of psychotherapeutic intervention, and of outcome evaluation—and especially the use of *quantitative* measures—which this sort of endeavour presents.

In an era when evidence-based medicine in some areas of physical treatment is salient, the subtleties of the *necessarily* subjective, and interpersonal—relationship-based—psychological aspects of offending behaviour, and our responses to it and its perpetrators, are in danger of marginalization and neglect.

Whilst there has been a huge growth of complex research methodologies aimed at addressing the essentially human, mental, and "internal world" phenomena of the "offender"—without which any account must be considered at best intellectually impoverished, and at worst irrelevant—the fact remains that the dynamic therapies, and forensic psychotherapy in particular, have a monumental—if not impossible—task if they are to demonstrate their relevance within the restricted bounds of much current evaluative thinking. The funding of both clinical—therapeutic—initiatives, and research, needs to take this heuristic dilemma on board if—in this writer's view—there is not to be a lamentable throwing out of the forensically dangerous subject (the "baby") with the narrowly evidentially based bath water.

Individual case studies *still* have enormous relevance (for example, see Smith, 1993), largely *because* they preserve the essential individuality of (in our case) the human subject and his or her reasons for offensive behaviour. As Walker (1990) writes:

> Forensic Psychiatry (and thereby forensic psychotherapy) obliges practitioners as well as courts to study the individual ... [But] social scientists have moved away from case studies in the hunt for larger samples, with a corresponding increase in the superficiality ... of the data: The information tends to take the form of "hard" measurable data: age, sex, marital status, occupational group, educational level, employment record, performance in tests (p. v).

This frequently loses the essence of the significant variables. Walker continues:

> measurability can be a will-o'-the-wisp: the easier something is to measure, the less likely it is to be what one really wants to know. And it ends in the formulation of

weak generalisations masquerading as natural laws of human behaviour, with a plethora of unspecifiable exceptions.

This is not to deny the place for psychological measures in our subject; some of this chapter has made reference to new and more sensitive methods of measurement. It does warn us against a too facile and simplistic approach to multi-determined and over-determined problems.

The task then becomes one of

1. assessing the subjective mental states of an individual in all their complexity;
2. finding effective ways of addressing the pathological aspects of these states interpersonally; and
3. attempting to evaluate changes in mental representations and ways of being, feeling and thinking—as well as behaving.

A challenge, indeed, for all forensic psychotherapists, but also all clinical forensic practitioners and researchers.

REFERENCES

Ainsworth, M., Blehar, M., Waters, E., & Wall, S. (1978). *Patterns of attachment: A psychological study of the strange situation*. Hillsdale, NJ: Erlbaum.

Alexander, F. (1935). *Roots of crime*. New York: Knopf.

Berman, E., & Segel, R. (1982). The captive client: Dilemmas of psychotherapy in the psychiatric hospital. *Psychotherapy, Research and Practice, 19*, 31–42.

Bion, W. R. (1970). Container and contained. In W. Bion, *Attention and interpretation*. London: Maresfield Reprints.

Bolton, D., & Hill, J. (1996). *Mind, meaning and mental disorder*. Oxford, UK: Oxford University Press.

Bowlby, J. (1946). *Forty-four juvenile thieves: Their character and homelife*. London: Ballière, Tyndall & Cox.

Bowlby, J. (1988). *A secure base: Clinical application of attachment theory*. London: Routledge.

Cleckley, H. (1941). *The mask of sanity*. St Louis, MO: Mosby.

Cleckley, H. (1976). *The mask of sanity* (6th ed). St Louis, MO: Mosby.

Cordess, C. (1991). Family therapy with psychotic offenders and family victims in a forensic psychiatric secure unit. *Law and Mental Health—Proceedings of the 17th International Academy of Law and Mental Health*, Leuven, Belgium, 366–380.

Cordess, C. (1992). Pioneers in forensic psychiatry. Edward Glover (1888–1972): Psychoanalysis and crime—A fragile legacy? *Journal of Forensic Psychiatry, 3*, 509–530.

Cordess, C. (1993). Understanding: Exoneration and condemnatio (Editorial). *Journal of Forensic Psychiatry, 4*, 423–426.

Cordess, C., & Cox, M. (1996). *Forensic psychotherapy. Crime, psychodynamics and the offender patient*. London: Jessica Kingsley.

Cox, M. (1983). The contribution of dynamic psycho-therapy to forensic psychiatry and vice versa. *International Journal of Law and Psychiatry, 6*, 89–99.

Cox, M. (1996). Psychodynamics and the Special Hospital: Road blocks and thought blocks. In C. Cordess & M. Cox, *Forensic psychotherapy: Crime, psychodynamics and the offender patient*. London: Jessica Kingsley.

Cox, M., & Theilgaard, A. (1987). *Mutative metaphors in psychotherapy. The Aeolian mode.* London: Tavistock.

Cullen, E. (1994). Grendon: The therapeutic prison that works. *Therapeutic Communities, 15*(4), 301–311.

Dell, S. (1997). Research on the supervision of restricted patients in the community. (Letter). *The Journal of Forensic Psychiatry, 8*(3), 691.

Dolan, B., & Coid, J. (1993). *Psychopathic and antisocial personality disorders, treatment and research issues.* London: Royal College of Psychiatrists/Gaskell.

Dolan, B. M., & Norton, K. (1991). The predicted impact of the NHS white paper upon the use and funding of a specialist psychiatric service for personality disordered patients. *Psychiatric Bulletin, 15*, 402–404.

Ellenberger, H. (1970). *The discovery of the unconscious.* New York: Basic Books.

Etchegoyen, R. H. (1992). *The fundamentals of psychoanalytic technique.* London, New York: Karnac Books.

Evans, C., Carlyle, J., & Dolan, B. (1996). Research: An overview. In C. Cordess & M. Cox (Eds.), *Forensic psychotherapy: Crime, psychodynamics and the offender patient* (pp. 509–542). London: Jessica Kingsley.

Fonagy, P., Target, M., Steele, H., Steele, M., Leigh, T., Levinson, A., & Kennedy, R. (1997). Morality, disruptive behaviour, borderline personality disorder, crime and their relationship to security of attachment. In L. Atkinson & K. Zucker (Eds.), *Attachment and psychopathology.* New York, London: The Guildford Press.

Freud, S. (1905). *Three essays on the theory of sexuality* (Stan. Ed., Vol. 7, pp. 125–243). London: The Hogarth Press.

Freud, S. (1911). *Psycho-analytic notes on an autobiographical account of a case of paranoia* (Stan. Ed., Vol. 12, pp. 3–82). London: The Hogarth Press.

Freud, S. (1916a). *Some character types met with in psychoanalytic work. I. The exceptions.* (Stan. Ed., Vol. 14, pp. 311–315). London: The Hogarth Press.

Freud, S. (1916b). *Some character types met with in psychoanalytic work. III. Criminals from a sense of guilt* (Stan. Ed., Vol. 14, pp. 332–333). London: The Hogarth Press.

Freud, S. (1921). *Group psychology and the analysis of the ego* (Stan. Ed., Vol. 18, pp. 67–143). London: The Hogarth Press.

Frith, U. (1989). *Autism: Explaining the enigma* (pp. 1–97). Oxford, UK: Blackwell.

Gabbard, G. (1989). Splitting in hospital treatment. *American Journal of Psychiatry, 146*, 444–451.

Gabbard, G. O., Lazar, S. G., & Hornberger, J. et al. (1997). The economic impact of psychotherapy: A review. *American Journal of Psychiatry, 154*, 147–155.

Gallwey, P. (1996). Psychotic and borderline processes. In C. Cordess & M. Cox (Eds.), *Forensic psychotherapy: Crime, psychodynamics and the offender patient* (pp. 153–174). London: Jessica Kingsley.

Genders, E., & Player, E. (1995). *Grendon: A study of a therapeutic prison.* Oxford, UK: Oxford University Press.

Gilligan, J. (1996). *Violence.* New York: G.P. Putnam.

Glover, E. (1960). *The roots of crime.* London: Imago.

Gunn, J. (1996). Foreword. In C. Cordess & M. Cox (Eds.), *Forensic psychotherapy: Crime, psychodynamics and the offender patient.* London: Jessica Kingsley.

Gunn, J., & Robertson, G. (1982). Therapeutic communities for offenders. An evaluation of Grendon prison. In J. Gunn & D. P. Farrington (Eds.), *Abnormal offenders, delinquency and the criminal justice system.* Chichester, UK: Wiley.

Gunn, J., &, Taylor, P. (1993). *Forensic psychiatry. Clinical, legal and ethical issues.* London: Butterworth–Heinemann.

Hazlitt, W. (1991). On the pleasure of hating. In J. Gross (Ed.), *The Oxford book of essays.* Oxford, UK: Oxford University Press. (Original work published 1828.)

Herman, J., Perry, J., & van der Kolk, B. A. (1989). Childhood trauma in borderline personality disorder. *American Journal of Psychiatry, 146*, 490–495.

Higgitt, A., & Fonagy, P. (1992). Psychotherapy in borderline and narcissistic personality disorder (Review article). *British Journal of Psychiatry*, *161*, 23–43.

Hinshelwood, R. D. (1993). Locked in role: A psychotherapist within the social defence system of a prison. *Journal of Forensic Psychiatry*, *4*, 427–440.

Holmes, J. (1998). Psychodynamics, narrative and "intentional causality" (Editorial). *British Journal of Psychiatry*, *173*, 279–280.

Horowitz, M. J. (1997). *Stress response syndromes, PTSD, grief and adjustment disorders*. Northvale NJ: Jason Aronson.

Huesmann, L., Eron, L., Lekkowitz, M., & Walder, L. (1984). Stability of aggression over time and generations. *Developmental Psychology*, *20*, 1120–1134.

Jaspers, K. (1963). *General psychopathology* (J. Hoenig & Max Hamilton, Trans.) Manchester, UK: Manchester University Press. (Original work published 1923.)

Jones, M. (1952). *Social psychiatry*. London: Tavistock Books.

Jureidini, J. (1990). Projective identification in gneral pychiatry. *British Journal of Psychiatry*, *157*, 656–660.

Karasu, T. B. (1982a) Psychotherapy and pharmacotherapy: Toward an integrative model. *American Journal of Psychiatry*, *139*, 1102–1111.

Karasu, T. B. (1982b). Proving the efficacy of psychotherapy to government: A bureaucratic solution? *American Journal of Psychiatry*, *139*, 789–790.

Klein, M. (1934). On criminality. In *M. Klein: The writings of Melanie Klein* (Vol. 1). London: The Hogarth Press.

Klein, M. (1975). Criminal tendencies in normal children. In *Love, guilt and reparation* (pp. 170–185). London: The Hogarth Press. (Original work published 1927.)

Leslie, A. M. (1987). Pretence and representation: The origins of "theory of mind". *Psychological Review*, *94*, 412–426.

Levi, P. (1988). *The drowned and the saved* (p. 53). New York: Summit Books.

Levinson, A., & Fonagy, P. (1999). Criminality and attachment: The relationship between interpersonal awareness and offending in a prison population. Manuscript submitted for publication.

Main, M., & Hesse, E. (1992). Disorganised/disorientated behaviour in the strange situation, lapses in the monitoring of reasoning and discourse during the parent's adult attachment interview, and dissociative states. In M. Ammanati & D. Stern (Eds.), *Attachment and psychoanalysis*. Rome: Guis, Laterza & Figli.

Maxwell, R. J. (1984). Quality assessment in health. *British Medical Journal*, *288*, 1470–1472.

Meloy, J. R. (1992). *The psychopathic mind: Origins, dynamics and treatment*. Northvale, NJ, London: Jason Aronson.

Menzies Lyth, I. (1988). *Containing anxiety in institutions. Selected essays* (Vol. I). London: Free Association Books.

Mergenthaler, E., & Kächele, H. (1991). University of Ulm: The Ulm text bank research program. In L. E. Beutler (Ed.), *Psychotherapy research, an international review of programmatic studies*. Washington, DC: American Psychological Association.

Mooij, A. (1996). Hermeneutics. In C. Cordess & M. Cox (Eds.), *Forensic psychotherapy: Crime, psychodynamics and the offender patient* (pp. 67–73). London: Jessica Kingsley.

Mullen, P. (1990). The long-term influence of sexual assault on the mental health of victims. *Journal of Forensic Psychiatry*, *1*, 13–24.

Mullen, P., Martin, J., Anderson, J., Romans, S., & Herbison, G. (1993). Childhood sexual abuse and mental health in adult life. *British Journal of Psychiatry*, *163*, 721–732.

Norton, K. (1996). The personality-disordered forensic patient and the therapeutic community. In C. Cordess & M. Cox (Eds.), *Forensic psychotherapy: Crime, psychodynamics and the offender patient* (pp. 401–421). London: Jessica Kingsley.

Parry, G. (1992). Improving psychotherapy services: Applications of research, audit and evaluation. *British Journal of Clinical Psychotherapy*, *31*, 3–19.

Peay, J., & Shapland, J. (1992). Introduction: Special issue: Clinical criminology, *International Journal of Law and Psychiatry*, *15*, 125–128.

Pfäfflin, F. (1997). Forensic psychotherapy and the empirical paradigm. In H. van Marle (Ed.), *Challenges in forensic pychotherapy*. London: Jessica Kingsley.

Robertson, G. (1989). Treatment for offender patients: How should success be measured? *Medicine, Science and the Law*, *29*(4), 363.

Robertson, G. (1997). Research in forensic psychiatry (Editorial). *The Journal of Forensic Psychiatry*, *8*(3), 501–503.

Schetsky, D. H. (1990). A review of the literature on the long term effects of childhood sexual abuse. In R. P. Khuft (Ed.), *Incest related syndromes of adult psychopathology* (pp. 35–54). Washington, DC: American Psychiatric Press.

Simon, R. (1996). *Bad men do what good men dream*. Washington, DC: American Psychiatric Press.

Sinason, V. (1992). *Mental handicap another human condition. New approaches from the Tavistock*. London: Free Association Books.

Smith, J. (1993). The case study. In R. Byrne & P. Nicolson (Eds.), *Counselling and psychology for health professionals*. London: Chapman & Hall.

Stanton, R., & Schwarz, M. S. (1954). *The mental hospital*. London: Tavistock.

Stevenson, R. L. (1979). *The strange case of Dr Jekyll and Mr Hyde*. London: Penguin Books.

Stone, A. (1984). *Law, psychiatry and morality*. Washington, DC: American Psychiatric Press.

Symington, N. (1980). The response aroused by the psychopath. *International Review of Psychoanalysis*, *7*, 291–298.

Travers, J. A. (1994). On not fearing the Devil. In J. Travers (Ed.), *Psychotherapy and the dangerous patient*, pp. 141–150. New York, London: The Howarth Press.

van Marle, H. (Ed.) (1997). *Challenges in forensic psychotherapy*. London: Jessica Kingsley.

Walker, N. (1990). Foreword. In R. Bluglass & P. Bowden (Eds.), *Principles and practice of forensic psychiatry*. London, New York: Churchill Livingstone.

Welldon, E. (1998). Group therapy for victims and perpetrators of incest. *Advances in Psychiatric Treatment*, *4*, 82–88.

Welldon, E., & Van Velsen, C. (1997). *A practical guide to forensic psychotherapy*. London: Jessica Kingsley.

Williams, H. (1982). Adolescence, violence and crime. *Journal of Adolescence*, *5*, 125–134.

Winnicott, D. (1960). The theory of the parent–infant relationship. In D. W. Winnicott (Ed.), *The maturational process and the facilitating environment*. London: The Hogarth Press.

Winnicott, D. W. (1991). The antisocial tendency. In D. W. Winnicott (Ed.), *Collected papers: Through paediatrics to psychoanalysis*. London: Karnac Books. (Original work published 1958.)

Zulueta, F. de (1993). *From pain to violence: The traumatic roots of destructiveness*. London: Whurr.

Part IV

Assessment and Treatment of Offenders

Chapter 22

Adult Sexual Offenders Against Women

William L. Marshall
Queen's University, Kingston, Ontario, Canada

INTRODUCTION

It is essential first to clarify what the topic of this chapter involves. There are various legal descriptions of sexual assaults against adult females, and across jurisdictions the same terms can mean quite different offenses. Primarily the offenses discussed in this chapter will match what is usually meant by rape and that term will be used interchangeably with sexual assault, as generic descriptors. However, rape is in practice a problematic term because it has traditionally meant forced, non-consenting vaginal penetration by the male assailant's penis. Such a restricted definition caused so many problems (e.g. having to prove that penile–vaginal penetration took place) that Canada wisely amended its laws in 1983 to eliminate the word rape by replacing all the relevant laws with one that specified the meaning of different levels of sexual assault. Concern about whether or not vaginal penetration occurred was replaced by specifications of the degree of forcefulness, coercion, or the imbalance of power. In this sense, a sexual assault is any unwanted direct sexual contact. This allows us to consider frotteurism within the same category as rape, a position that some researchers (Langevin, 1983) have suggested is more appropriate than viewing them as different behaviours.

The sexual assault of females by males has a very long history. Indeed, socio-biological accounts claim that rape was a common practice in the very earliest part of our history as a species (Quinsey & Lalumière, 1995; Thornhill & Thornhill, 1992). It is also evident that rape occurs in all societies, whether they are industrial, or pre-industrial, or even pre-agricultural societies (Sanday, 1981; Schiff, 1971).

Handbook of Offender Assessment and Treatment. Edited by C. R. Hollin.
© 2000 John Wiley & Sons Ltd.

Incidence and prevalence studies reveal that the sexual assault of adult females occurs with frightening frequency in Western countries. For example, Koss, Gidycz, and Wisniewski (1987) report that more than half their national sample of women in the United States said they had been sexually victimized sometime after age 14 years. Similarly, 44% of the Californian women Russell (1984) interviewed told her they had been sexually assaulted as adults. Interestingly, only 8% of these women reported the assault to the police. Deriving their data from official police records, and then correcting for the police estimates of unreported rapes, Marshall and Barrett (1990) concluded that every seven minutes an adult Canadian woman is either raped or is the victim of an attempted rape. Prevalence data from various European countries, including the United Kingdom, reveal very similar rates of sexual assault (van Dijk & Mayhew, 1992). The effects on victims and their families, and the cost to society of these assaults, is both devastating and extensive (Koss & Harvey, 1991). This is obviously a very serious social problem that calls for a comprehensive response, one part of which is to deal effectively with identified offenders.

THE NATURE OF THE OFFENDER

Although researchers have made persistent efforts over many years to discern distinctive features of rapists, and while group differences have been found on several variables, it is clear that these offenders are a good deal more like other men than most people would like to think. Research has typically examined one of two populations of men who have engaged in sexually coercive behaviours:

1. men convicted of sexually assaulting adult females (usually incarcerated offenders); or
2. men not identified by the legal system but who either admit to having forced a woman to have sex or who say they would be likely to do so if they knew they could get away with it.

Malamuth and his colleagues (Malamuth, 1986; Malamuth, Heavey, & Linz, 1993) have been the foremost researchers adopting the latter strategy. While Malamuth's research is methodologically exemplary, the underlying assumption that examining males who indicate some likelihood of raping will tell us about the characteristics of men who actually assault women, seems to be problematic. First, these subjects may not all mean the same thing when they rate their likelihood of raping. One man may assume that the context of the possible rape is within his normal living circumstances, whereas another may assume unusual circumstances, such as being stranded on a desert island with a lone woman. Such studies, therefore, have dubious relevance for understanding actual offenders.

However, examining only incarcerated offenders also has its problems. The investigatory and judicial systems are selective, although they presumably do not intend to be so. The rigorous pursuit of an investigation of sexual assault, the decision to prosecute, the likelihood of conviction, and the sentence handed down upon conviction, all appear to be influenced by factors such as race, socioeconomic status, intelligence, style of presentation, admission of guilt, and the expression of remorse, in addition to the facts of the offense.

Unfortunately there is little research available on the characteristics of men who rape outside of those studied in prisons. In addition to the selective processes of the investigative and prosecutorial systems, many women who are raped do not report the offense and this is probably more true when the offender is a boyfriend or a husband. Indeed, in many jurisdictions a husband is still exempt from prosecution for raping his wife. The majority of the data available on rapists, then, represents a distorted picture but it is, unfortunately, the only picture we have. The rest of this chapter will perforce be restricted to a discussion of those rapists who have been identified by the judicial system.

CHARACTERISTICS AND ASSESSMENT OF THE OFFENDER

Few rapists seem to be characterized by the sort of evident psychopathology that the public expects in these offenders. No more than 5%–8% of rapists suffer from either psychosis, serious brain dysfunction, or mental retardation (Abel, Rouleau, & Cunningham-Rathner, 1986; Seghorn, Prentky, & Boucher, 1987).

It is not possible to discuss all of the features of rapists that have been examined in the literature. The following will focus on those features that most clinicians appear to consider relevant to assessment and treatment. Table 22.1 lists some of the more appropriate measures used to assess these various features.

Social Skills

Although it has been expected that rapists would display deficient social skills, in fact the evidence is at best equivocal and some subtypes of rapists appear to be satisfactorily socially competent (Knight, Rosenberg, & Schneider, 1985). While Segal and Marshall (1985) found that all their incarcerated offenders (rapists, child molesters, and non-sexual offenders) were equally skilled and all were less socially skilled than community males, Overholser and Beck (1986) found that rapists tended to be more appropriately assertive than child molesters. Finally, Stermac and Quinsey (1985) found that incarcerated offenders were more deficient than a community group, but the rapists did not display unique social deficits.

Table 22.1 Assessment methods

Problems	Measures
Assertiveness	Rathus Assertiveness Scale (Rathus, 1973).
Intimacy/loneliness	Social Intimacy Scale (Miller & Lefcourt, 1982). Fear of Intimacy Scale (Descutner & Thelen, 1991). UCLA Loneliness Scale (Russell, Peplau, & Cutrona, 1980).
Empathy	Rapist Empathy Measure (Fernandez & Marshall, 1998). Empathy for Women (Hanson & Scott, 1995).
Self-esteem	Social Self-esteem Inventory (Lawson, Marshall, & McGrath, 1979).
Cognitive distortions	Rape Scale (Bumby, 1996). Rape Myth Acceptance Scale (Burt, 1980). Hostility Toward Women Scale (Check, 1984).
Sexual preferences	Phallometric tests (Murphy & Barbaree, 1994). Multiphasic Sex Inventory (Nichols & Molinder, 1984).
Personality	Psychopathy Checklist–Revised (Hare, 1991).
Substance abuse	Michigan Alcoholism Screening Test (Selzer, 1971). Drug Abuse Screening Test (Skinner, 1982).
Anger	State–Trait Anger Expression Inventory (Speilberger, 1988).

Two studies have suggested that rapists may have problems with specific aspects of general social skills. Lipton, McDonel, and McFall (1987) demonstrated that rapists typically either failed to recognize a rebuff by a woman or took the woman's response to reflect a positive interest in them. Marshall, Barbaree, and Fernandez (1995) found that the rapists judged aggressive behaviours to be more socially appropriate than either normal assertiveness or underassertiveness. Perhaps these offenders misread cues from women and consider aggression to be the proper response in dealing with others.

Three other aspects of the social behaviour of rapists have revealed reasonably consistent findings over the past few years.

Intimacy Problems

Marshall (1989) outlined the potential extent of intimacy difficulties and their relationship to the etiology and maintenance of sexual abuse. He suggested that rapists failed to acquire the capacity for intimacy as a result of their poor childhood relationships with their parents and, as a consequence, did not develop the skills and confidence necessary to form satisfactory relationships as adults. Subsequent research has demonstrated that rapists are deficient in intimacy and suffer from emotional loneliness (Garlick, Marshall, & Thornton, 1996; Smallbone & Dadds, in press).

Empathy Deficits

There now exists a reasonably extensive body of literature on empathy deficits in sexual offenders (see the reviews by Hanson, 1997; Marshall, Hudson, Jones, & Fernandez, 1995). Presumably emotional recognition is an essential first step to empathy, and Hudson et al. (1993) showed that rapists had problems recognizing emotions in others. The particular emotions these men confused were anger, disgust, and fear; that is, just the sort of emotions we might expect victims to display. Having subjects respond to vignettes describing adult heterosexual interactions which varied from acceptable behaviours to explicit rape, Hanson and Scott (1995) found that rapists were deficient in perspective taking. Interestingly, those rapists who were intoxicated at the time of their offense, and those who used the least amount of force, were the most accurate in perceiving the distress of the women in the vignettes.

Fernandez and Marshall (1998) developed a measure to assess the capacity of rapists to recognize harm suffered by a woman, and to feel distress over her suffering. Rapists were as empathic as non-offenders toward a woman who had been disfigured in an accident and they were somewhat more compassionate toward the woman who had been raped by someone else. However, they were markedly deficient in empathy toward their own victim. Fernandez and Marshall took their results to indicate that the primary problem for rapists was not so much a generalized deficiency in empathy, but rather an inability to acknowledge the harm they had done. Thus, the apparent empathy deficits among rapists were seen as just another aspect of their ubiquitous, and self-serving, cognitive distortions.

Self-esteem

Marshall, Anderson, and Champagne (1996) suggested that sexual offenders have low self-esteem and that this is both causally related to their offending and problematic for engaging their cooperation in treatment. Self-esteem, and particularly that aspect having to do with confidence in social relationships, has its source in the person's childhood experiences, most notably with their parents. Learning to have confidence in oneself and confidence that others will be trustworthy and positive is largely dependent on the quality of the person's relationship with their parents. Rapists, so Marshall et al. claim, have childhood experiences that make them either cynical of others or self-denigrating.

Recently, Fernandez, Anderson, and Marshall (1997) evaluated the self-esteem of rapists across a number of domains (e.g. in social situations, sexual contexts, occupational functioning, and in personal appearance and athletic performance). They report idiosyncratic patterns of self-confidence across these domains among individual rapists, although all were lacking in self-esteem generally.

Cognitive Distortions

For many years theorists and clinicians have declared that sexual offenders display manifold cognitive distortions. However, a problem with these ideas, and much of the subsequent research, is that it is not always clear what is meant by cognitive distortions. For example, are deliberate misrepresentations (denial and minimization) properly thought of as cognitive distortions, or simply lying? Barbaree (1991), for example, found that 54% of rapists denied having committed an offense and Schlank and Shaw (1997) report that minimization is common. Both denial and minimization must be addressed in treatment whether or not they are construed as distortions.

Abel et al. (1989) developed a scale to measure distortions in child molesters and, although they presented convincing data, other researchers have had trouble replicating these findings (Hanson, Gizzarelli, & Scott, 1994). Hanson et al. suggested that these failures to replicate are due to the transparent nature of the questions which allow the respondents to readily identify the "correct" answer.

Bumby (1996) has devised a scale similar to Abel's to assess distortions in men who sexually assault adult females. His items reflect misinterpretations of the woman's behavior, distorted views of women's sexuality and of the victim's responsibility, as well as denial of harm. Bumby demonstrated that scores on his scale were reliable, were uncontaminated by a socially desirable response set, and distinguished rapists from non-sexual offenders.

Rapists have also been found to harbor attitudes toward women, violence, and rape that are offense-supportive (Burt, 1980). However, other studies have failed to detect differences between the attitudes of rapists and other men (Overholser & Beck, 1986; Segal & Stermac, 1984).

Sexual Preferences

Early studies of the phallometric assessment of rapists found differences between small groups of offenders and non-offenders (Abel, Barlow, Blanchard, & Guild, 1977; Barbaree, Marshall, & Lanthier, 1979; Quinsey, Chaplin, & Varney, 1981). Subsequently, however, large-scale studies have failed to replicate these early findings, with rapists in these recent studies appearing to match non-rapists (Baxter, Barbaree, & Marshall, 1986; Hall, 1989; Wormith, Bradford, Pawlak, Borzecki, & Zohar, 1988). It may be that in the earlier studies there were an unusual number of very vicious or sadistic offenders who we may expect to be highly aroused by the sexual violence depicted in the stimuli (Barbaree, 1990).

Personality Problems

While some authors (e.g. Kalichman, 1991) claim that rapists have distinctive personalities, Marshall and Hall (1995), in their review of MMPI studies, concluded that "there appears to be little support for the claim that any version of MMPI profiles, or any of its derived scales, distinguishes rapists from other subjects" (pp. 211–212). Research on psychopathy, on the other hand, has consistently shown that a proportion of rapists meet the criteria for psychopathy. For example, Quinsey, Rice, and Harris (1990) report that over 30% of sexual offenders scored above the cutoff on Hare's (1991) Psychopathy Checklist—Revised Scale. However, the offenders in these studies were housed in institutions created specifically to accommodate the most dangerous and chronic sexual offenders. When Serin, Malcolm, Khanna, and Barbaree (1994) examined sexual offenders in Ontario prisons, they found only 12.2% of rapists scored above the cutoff on Hare's measure.

Other Problems

Substance use and abuse problems (usually alcohol) appear to be common in rapists (Seto & Barbaree, 1995). We should not infer from these observations, however, that rapists are typically alcoholics or drug addicts. In a re-examination of some early data collected in Canadian prisons, Marshall (1996a) found that 70% of the rapists were intoxicated at the time of their offense, but only 60% of these intoxicated offenders (i.e. 42% of the total) had persistent problems with substance use and even less met the criteria for alcoholism or drug dependence.

Some theories of rape identify anger as a fixed disposition of the offender (e.g. Groth, Burgess, & Holmstrom, 1977), and researchers have found anger to be an immediate precursor to an offense (Pithers, Beal, Armstrong, & Petty, 1989). Marshall and Hambley (1996) found rapists to be hostile toward women, and Hudson and Ward (1997) reported that rapists displayed high levels of trait anger.

Finally, there is evidence that a limited number of rapists have elevated levels of one or another of the sex steroids (Bradford, 1990). Hormonal assays, in those cases where either deviant fantasies are persistent and powerful or behavioral controls are tenuous, appear to be valuable and an appropriate referral should be made.

TREATMENT

Cognitive–behavioural programs appear to be the most popular approach to the treatment of rapists. These programs arose out of strictly behavioral interventions for various other sexual deviations that were developed in the 1960s. When applied to sexual offenders, these programs were progressively modified throughout the 1970s. By the early 1980s they had assumed most of their current form after relapse prevention procedures were co-opted from the field of addictions.

In the first description of a behavioral intervention specifically designed for rapists, Marshall (1973) aimed at modifying deviant sexual preferences. This goal was consistent with the behavioral thesis of the time that acquired sexual preferences drove overt sexual behavior (McGuire, Carlisle, & Young, 1965). While this was a reasonable proposition, it was gradually deemed to be incomplete and theories about sexual offending became progressively more complex, invoking a vast array of factors. As a consequence, assessment and treatment have become far more elaborate. These comprehensive programs are now in widespread use in many countries (Marshall, Fernandez, Hudson, & Ward, 1998).

Marshall and Eccles (1995) have distinguished what they call "offense-specific" treatment targets from "offense-related" targets. The former refer to those features that are thought to be critical to the treatment of all sexual offenders while the latter are seen as relevant to some but not all offenders. This section will describe only the offense-specific components of treatment; other sources describe offense-related components (Schwartz & Cellini, 1997).

Treatment for sexual offenders is typically carried out in groups of 8–10 offenders with one or two therapists. Generally, individual counselling is avoided as it is thought to be uneconomical, unproductive, and lends itself to inadvertent collusion with the offender.

Self-esteem and Treatment Processes

The enhancement of self-esteem is best achieved in three ways:

1. by providing an environment which is conducive to the development of positive self-worth;
2. by adopting a therapist style that encourages trust and respects the client's dignity; and
3. by the use of specific clinical procedures.

While it is certainly difficult to create appropriate circumstances outside the group room, it is part of the treatment providers' responsibility to make every effort to achieve these conditions.

At present there is little information on what constitutes an effective therapist style with sexual offenders. Marshall (1996b), and Kear-Colwell and Pollack (1997) have made a case against using a confrontational approach. Both sets of authors, basing their claims on the work of earlier therapists (e.g. Carl Rogers, Jerome Frank) advocate a more supportive but firmly challenging style that directs attention to the offender's behavior rather than to his character.

In terms of procedures to enhance self-esteem, encouraging clients to increase the frequency and range of their social and pleasurable activities has been shown to increase self-confidence (Khanna & Marshall, 1978) as has having them rehearse positive self-statements (Marshall & Christie, 1982).

Finally, a combination of these treatment approaches significantly improved the self-worth of sexual offenders (Marshall, Champagne, Sturgeon, & Bryce, 1997). While increasing offenders' self-esteem seems valuable in itself, it is essential if we are effectively to engage sexual offenders in treatment. Research with addictions indicates that increasing self-esteem markedly improves compliance with treatment and significantly reduces post-treatment relapse rates (Miller & Rollnick, 1991).

Cognitive Distortions

Many treatment programs do not include deniers or those who markedly minimize what they did or their responsibility for the offense. Unfortunately this seems likely to exclude those offenders most at risk for reoffending or most at risk to reoffend in a particularly damaging way. However difficult these offenders may be to treat, society will be best served by attempting to treat them. Specific programs that deal with denial and minimization have been shown to be effective (Schlank & Shaw, 1997). All other aspects of cognitive distortions (e.g. distorted views of their victim's behavior, seeing others as responsible rather than themselves, various rape-supportive attitudes) are dealt with in treatment by having the offender discuss in detail his offense and challenging any distortions, rationalizations, and justifications as they arise.

Social Skills

Most programs attempt to enhance the offender's general social skills such as assertiveness and conversational skills. Most aspects of general social skills are best shaped throughout the whole program, making a specific component unnecessary. However, empathy and intimacy skills are usually targeted separately.

Empathy

The primary goal here is to sensitize the offender to the harm his sexual assaults cause. However, on this issue therapists must be careful to avoid increasing the satisfaction of the sadistic rapists in the group. For this component, and possibly for the whole program, it may be better to treat the sadists independently.

The focus in this component is on having the offender develop an understanding of the problems victims face as a result of being sexually assaulted, and on generating remorse in the offender. Since rapists appear to be deficient at recognizing emotions, it may be necessary to initially train them in emotional recognition. The full details of empathy training have been described elsewhere (Marshall, O'Sullivan, & Fernandez, 1996) and this report indicates that empathy was effectively enhanced by these procedures.

Intimacy

Marshall, Bryce, Hudson, Ward, and Moth (1996) have described in detail their approach to enhancing intimacy skills and they have demonstrated its effectiveness. Skills involved in romantic relationships are identified, discussed, and prac-tised. Issues around jealousy, loneliness, effective communication, sexuality, and myths about sex are topics for discussion. These various issues are integrated for each offender and he is encouraged to extend his range of friendships, approach relationships with caution, and deepen his capacity for intimacy.

Deviant Sexuality

It may not always be necessary directly to target deviant sexual preferences in rapists. As we have seen, few of them show deviant preferences at phallometric evaluations, so it would seem inappropriate to have all rapists participate in arousal modification procedures. However, even with those rapists who reveal deviant preferences at assessment, Marshall (1997) has shown that deviant pref-erences can be normalized without specifically targeting these preferences. Of course, many therapists are unlikely to adopt this approach and will prefer to employ specific interventions.

Behavioral methods aimed at changing sexual preferences include aversion therapy, masturbatory reconditioning, and covert sensitization. Aversion therapy, however, seems to have lost its early popularity (Quinsey & Earls, 1990). Mas-turbatory reconditioning combines directed masturbation up to orgasm while fantasizing appropriate sexual acts, with immediate post-orgasm repetition of deviant fantasies. The evidence in support of these procedures is encouraging but not strong (Laws & Marshall, 1991). Covert sensitization associates thoughts of deviant sex with thoughts of unpleasant consequences. Unfortunately, no study has clearly demonstrated any positive effects for covert sensitization with sexual offenders.

Pharmacological interventions seem to be at least as effective as behavioral methods in giving sexual offenders greater control over their urges. Bradford and Pawlak (1993) demonstrated that cyproterone acetate (an antiandrogen) specifi-cally reduced arousal to deviant fantasies while enhancing arousal to appropri-ate stimuli. Federoff (1993) has reviewed the evidence on the value of serotonin reuptake inhibitors, and concluded that they can be effective in bringing deviant sexual urges under control.

Relapse Prevention

Relapse prevention provides both an integrative framework and specific proce-dures for developing post-treatment maintenance strategies. Some programs, most notably those in California (Marques, Day, Nelson, & Miner, 1989) and Vermont (Pithers, Martin, & Cumming, 1989) have very extensive relapse pre-vention components, both within treatment and during post-release supervision. Offenders are rigorously taught the language and meaning of the relapse pre-vention approach. They are required to provide detailed accounts of their offense chain, identify all the factors that may put them at risk, and generate an extensive set of plans to avoid or deal with risks. Upon release offenders in these programs are required to enter community treatment and are very thoroughly supervised by trained staff. While this approach has obvious appeal, it does not necessarily follow that it will actually reduce risk. In fact, such comprehensive training and post-release supervision may serve to convince the offender that he cannot function effectively on his own. Once their sentence expires, supervisory control also expires and such a sudden change may precipitate an offense. A less intense approach involving a graduated shift to self-management would seem more sensible.

A review (Marshall & Anderson, 1996) of relapse prevention programs has shown that relapse rates are lower when post-release supervision is less extensive than that employed in the Californian or Vermont programs. In addition, these apparently more effective programs did not employ very extensive within-treatment training in relapse prevention. It may, in fact, be unnecessary to ensure that offenders learn the meaning of relapse prevention terminology. The whole relapse prevention package has largely been adopted without question just because it seems to make such apparent sense, and there have been few attempts to criticize or evaluate the specific procedures of relapse prevention with the exception of the work of Ward and his colleagues (e.g. Ward, Hudson, & Siegert, 1995).

Treatment Benefits

Reviews of treatment outcome with sexual offenders (e.g. Furby, Weinrott, & Blackshaw, 1989; Marshall, Jones, Ward, Johnston, & Barbaree, 1991) have differed in their conclusions about its effectiveness and debate continues. Whatever the eventual outcome of this debate, even the optimists agree that treatment is somewhat less effective with rapists than with child molesters (Marshall & Pithers, 1994). It has been suggested that we need to modify some aspects of treatment with these offenders (Marshall, 1993; Pithers, 1993). However, those who claim treatment does not work (e.g. Quinsey, Harris, Rice, & Lalumière, 1993) reject these suggestions. They advocate withdrawing funding from treatment and diverting it into long-term intensive supervision. Unfortunately, there is no evidence that such supervision reduces recidivism, and the evidence regarding relapse prevention approaches suggests that this might not be a wise decision.

What is important to realize is that continuing to do treatment is the only way we will develop better techniques, and it does not have to be very effective to realize benefits. Employing a cost–benefit analysis, Marshall (1992) demonstrated that eliminating the risk to reoffend in just one or two sexual offenders out of every 100 treated is enough to cover the costs of treatment. While this analysis is impressive, it does not illustrate the true value of saving future innocent women from suffering at the hands of an effectively treated rapist.

REFERENCES

Abel, G. G., Barlow, D. H., Blanchard, E. B., & Guild, D. (1977). The components of rapists' sexual arousal. *Archives of General Psychiatry, 34*, 894–903.

Abel, G. G., Gore, D. K., Holland, C. L., Camp, N., Becker, J. V., & Rathner, J. (1989). The measurement of the cognitive distortions of child molesters. *Annals of Sex Research, 2*, 135–152.

Abel, G. G., Rouleau, J. L., & Cunningham-Rathner, J. (1986). Sexually aggressive behavior. In W. Curran, A. L. McGarry, & S. A. Shah (Eds.), *Forensic psychiatry and psychology: Perspectives and standards for interdisciplinary practice* (pp. 289–313). Philadelphia: Davis.

Barbaree, H. E. (1990). Stimulus control of sexual arousal: Its role in sexual assault. In W. L. Marshall, D. R. Laws, & H. E. Barbaree (Eds.), *Handbook of sexual assault: Issues, theories, and treatment of the offender* (pp. 115–142). New York: Plenum.

Barbaree, H. E. (1991). Denial and minimization among sex offenders: Assessment and treatment outcome. *Forum on Corrections Research, 3*, 30–33.

Barbaree, H. E., Marshall, W. L., & Lanthier, R. D. (1979). Deviant sexual arousal in rapists. *Behaviour Research and Therapy, 14*, 215–222.

Baxter, D. J., Barbaree, H. E., & Marshall, W. L. (1986). Sexual responses to consenting and forced sex in a large sample of rapists and nonrapists. *Behaviour Research and Therapy, 24*, 513–520.

Bradford, J. M. W. (1990). The antiandrogen and hormonal treatment of sex offenders. In W. L. Marshall, D. R. Laws, & H. E. Barbaree (Eds.), *Handbook of sexual assault: Issues, theories, and treatment of the offender* (pp. 297–310). New York: Plenum.

Bradford, J. M. W., & Pawlak, A. (1993). Double-blind placebo crossover study of cyproterone acetate in the treatment of paraphilias. *Archives of Sexual Behavior, 22*, 383–402.

Bumby, K. M. (1996). Assessing the cognitive distortions of child molesters and rapists: Development and validation of the molest and rape scales. *Sexual Abuse: A Journal of Research and Treatment, 8*, 37–54.

Burt, M. (1980). Cultural myths and supports for rape. *Journal of Personality and Social Psychology, 38*, 217–230.

Check, J. V. (1984). *The hostility towards women scale.* Unpublished doctoral dissertation, University of Manitoba, Winnipeg.

Descutner, C., & Thelen, M. H. (1991). Development and validation of the fear of intimacy scale. *Psychological Assessment: A Journal of Consulting and Clinical Psychology, 3*, 218–225.

Federoff, J. P. (1993). Serotonic drug treatment of deviant sexual interests. *Annals of Sex Research, 6*, 105–121.

Fernandez, Y. M., Anderson, D., & Marshall, W. L. (1997, October). *The relationship between empathy, cognitive distortions and domain specific self-esteem in sexual offenders.* Paper presented at the 16th Annual Research and Treatment Conference of the Association for the Treatment of Sexual Abusers, Arlington, VA.

Fernandez, Y. M., & Marshall, W. L. (1998). *The rapist empathy scale.* Manuscript submitted for publication.

Furby, L., Weinrott, M. R., & Blackshaw, L. (1989). Sex offender recidivism: A review. *Psychological Bulletin, 105*, 3–30.

Garlick, Y., Marshall, W. L., & Thornton, D. (1996). Intimacy deficits and attribution of blame among sexual offenders. *Legal and Criminological Psychology, 1*, 251–258.

Groth, A. N., Burgess, A. W., & Holmstrom, L. L. (1977). Rape: Power, anger, and sexuality. *American Journal of Psychiatry, 134*, 1239–1243.

Hall, G. C. N. (1989). Sexual arousal and arousability in a sexual offender population. *Journal of Abnormal Psychology, 98*, 145–149.

Hanson, R. K. (1997). Invoking sympathy—Assessment and treatment of empathy deficients among sexual offenders. In B. K. Schwartz & H. R. Cellini (Eds.), *The sex offender: New insights, treatment innovations and legal developments* (Vol. II, pp. 6.1–6.7). Kingston, NJ: Civic Research Institute.

Hanson, K., Gizzarelli, R., & Scott, H. (1994). The attitudes of incest offenders: Sexual entitlement and acceptance of sex with children. *Criminal Justice and Behavior, 21,* 187–202.

Hanson, K., & Scott, H. (1995). Assessing perspective taking among sexual offenders, nonsexual criminals and nonoffenders. *Sexual Abuse: A Journal of Research and Treatment, 7,* 259–277.

Hare, R. D. (1991). *Manual for the revised psychopathy checklist.* Toronto, Canada: Multi-Health Systems.

Hudson, S. M., Marshall, W. L., Wales, D., McDonald, E., Bakker, L. W., & McLean, A. (1993). Emotional recognition skills of sex offenders. *Annals of Sex Research, 6,* 199–211.

Hudson, S. M., & Ward, T. (1997). Rape: Psychopathology and theory. In D. R. Laws & W. O'Donohue (Eds.), *Sexual deviance: Theory, assessment, and treatment* (pp. 332–355). New York: Guilford.

Kalichman, S. C. (1991). Psychopathology and personality characteristics of criminal sexual offenders as a function of victim age. *Archives of Sexual Behavior, 20,* 187–197.

Kear-Colwell, J., & Pollack, P. (1997). Motivation or confrontation: Which approach to the child sex offender? *Criminal Justice and Behavior, 24,* 20–33.

Khanna, A., & Marshall, W. L. (1978, November). *A comparison of cognitive and behavioral approaches for the treatment of low self-esteem.* Paper presented the 12th Annual Convention, Association for Advancement of Behavior Therapy, Chicago.

Knight, R. A., Rosenberg, R., & Schneider, B. (1985). Classification of sexual offenders: Perspectives, methods and validation. In A. W. Burgess (Ed.), *Rape and sexual assault: A research handbook* (pp. 222–293). New York: Garland Press.

Koss, M. P., Gidycz, C. A., & Wisniewski, N. (1987). The scope of rape: Incidence and prevalence of sexual aggression and victimization in a national sample of higher education students. *Journal of Consulting and Clinical Psychology, 55,* 162–170.

Koss, M. P., & Harvey, M. R. (1991). *The rape victim: Clinical and community interventions* (2nd ed.). Newbury Park, CA: Sage.

Langevin, R. (1983). *Sexual strands: Understanding and treating sexual anomalies in men.* Hillsdale, NJ: Lawrence Erlbaum.

Laws, D. R., & Marshall, W. L. (1991). Masturbatory reconditioning: An evaluative review. *Advances in Behaviour Research and Therapy, 13,* 13–25.

Lawson, J. S., Marshall, W. L., & McGrath, P. (1979). The social self-esteem inventory. *Educational and Psychological Measurement, 39,* 803–811.

Lipton, D. N., McDonel, E. C., & McFall, R. M. (1987). Heterosocial perception in rapists. *Journal of Consulting and Clinical Psychology, 55,* 17–21.

Malamuth, N. M. (1986). Predictors of naturalistic sexual aggression. *Journal of Personality and Social Psychology, 50,* 953–962.

Malamuth, N. M., Heavey, C. L., & Linz, D. (1993). Predicting men's antisocial behavior against women: The interaction model of sexual aggression. In G. C. N. Hall, R. Hirschman, J. R. Graham, & M. S. Zaragoza (Eds.), *Sexual aggression: Issues in etiology, assessment and treatment* (pp. 63–97). Washington, DC: Taylor & Francis.

Marques, J. K., Day, D. M., Nelson, C., & Miner, M. H. (1989). The sex offender treatment and evaluation project: California's relapse prevention program. In D. R. Laws (Ed.), *Relapse prevention with sex offenders* (pp. 96–104). New York: Guilford.

Marshall, W. L. (1973). The modification of sexual fantasies: A combined treatment approach to the reduction of deviant sexual behavior. *Behaviour Research and Therapy, 11,* 557–564.

Marshall, W. L. (1989). Intimacy, loneliness and sexual offenders. *Behaviour Research and Therapy, 27,* 491–503.

Marshall, W. L. (1992). The social value of treatment for sexual offenders. *Canadian Journal of Human Sexuality, 1*, 109–114.

Marshall, W. L. (1993). A revised approach to the treatment of men who sexually assault adult females. In G. C. N. Hall, R. Hirschman, J. R. Graham, & M. S. Zaragoza (Eds.), *Sexual aggression: Issues in etiology, assessment and treatment* (pp. 143–165). Bristol, PA: Taylor & Francis.

Marshall, W. L. (1996a). Assessment, treatment, and theorizing about sex offenders: Development over the past 20 years and future directions. *Criminal Justice and Behavior, 23*, 162–199.

Marshall, W. L. (1996b). The sexual offender: Monster, victim, or everyman. *Sexual Abuse: A Journal of Research and Treatment, 8*, 317–335.

Marshall, W. L. (1997). The relationship between self-esteem and deviant sexual arousal in nonfamilial child molesters. *Behavior Modification, 21*, 86–96.

Marshall, W. L., & Anderson, D. (1996). An evaluation of the benefits of relapse prevention programs with sexual offenders. *Sexual Abuse: A Journal of Research and Treatment, 8*, 209–221.

Marshall, W. L., Anderson, D., & Champagne, F. (1996). The importance of self-esteem in sexual offenders. *Psychology, Crime, and Law, 3*, 81–106.

Marshall, W. L., Barbaree, H. E., & Fernandez, Y. M. (1995). Some aspects of social competence in sexual offenders. *Sexual Abuse: A Journal of Research and Treatment, 7*, 113–127.

Marshall, W. L., & Barrett, S. (1990). *Criminal neglect: Why sex offenders go free.* Toronto: Doubleday.

Marshall, W. L., Bryce, P., Hudson, S. M., Ward, T., & Moth, B. (1996). The enhancement of intimacy and the reduction of loneliness among child molesters. *Journal of Family Violence, 11*, 219–235.

Marshall, W. L., Champagne, F., Sturgeon, C., & Bryce, P. (1997). Increasing the self-esteem of child molesters. *Sexual Abuse: A Journal of Research and Treatment, 9*, 321–333.

Marshall, W. L., & Christie, M. M. (1982). The enhancement of social self-esteem. *Canadian Counsellor, 16*, 82–89.

Marshall, W. L., & Eccles, A. (1995). Cognitive-behavioral treatment of sex offenders. In V. M. B. Hasselt & M. Hersen (Eds.), *Sourcebook of psychological treatment manuals for adult disorders* (pp. 295–332). New York: Plenum.

Marshall, W. L., Fernandez, Y. M., Hudson, S. M., & Ward, T. (Eds.) (1998). *Sourcebook of treatment programs for sexual offenders.* New York: Plenum.

Marshall, W. L., & Hall, G. C. N. (1995). The value of the MMPI in deciding forensic issues in accused sexual offenders. *Sexual Abuse: A Journal of Research and Treatment, 7*, 203–217.

Marshall, W. L., & Hambley, L. S. (1996). Intimacy and loneliness, and their relationship to rape myth acceptance and hostility toward women among rapists. *Journal of Interpersonal Violence, 11*, 586–592.

Marshall, W. L., Hudson, S. M., Jones, R. L., & Fernandez, Y. M. (1995). Empathy in sex offenders. *Clinical Psychology Review, 15*, 99–113.

Marshall, W. L., Jones, R. L., Ward, T., Johnston, P., & Barbaree, H. E. (1991). Treatment outcome with sex offenders. *Clinical Psychology Review, 11*, 465–485.

Marshall, W. L., O'Sullivan, C., & Fernandez, Y. M. (1996). The enhancement of victim empathy among incarcerated child molesters. *Legal and Criminological Psychology, 1*, 95–102.

Marshall, W. L., & Pithers, W. D. (1994). A reconsideration of treatment outcome with sex offenders. *Criminal Justice and Behavior, 21*, 10–27.

McGuire, R. J., Carlisle, J. M., & Young, B. G. (1965). Sexual deviations as conditioned behavior: A hypothesis. *Behaviour Research and Therapy, 2*, 185–190.

Miller, R. S., & Lefcourt, H. M. (1982). The assessment of social intimacy. *Journal of Personality Assessment, 46*, 514–518.

Miller, W. R., & Rollnick, S. (1991). *Motivational interviewing: Preparing people to change addictive behavior.* New York: Guilford.

Murphy, W. D., & Barbaree, H. E. (1994). *Assessments of sex offenders by measures of erectile response: Psychometric properties and decision-making.* Brandon, VT: Safer Society Press.

Nichols, H. R., & Molinder, I. (1984). *Multiphasic sex inventory manual.* Tacoma, WA: Author.

Overholser, J. C., & Beck, S. (1986). Multimethod assessment of rapists, child molesters, and three control groups on behavioral and psychological measures. *Journal of Consulting and Clinical Psychology, 54*, 682–687.

Pithers, W. D. (1993). Treatment of rapists: Reinterpretation of early outcome data and explanatory constructs to enhance therapeutic efficacy. In G. C. N. Hall, R. Hirschman, J. R. Graham, & M. S. Zaragoza (Eds.), *Sexual aggression: Issues in etiology, assessment, and treatment* (pp. 167–196). Washington, DC: Taylor & Francis.

Pithers, W. D., Beal, L. S., Armstrong, J., & Petty, J. (1989). Identification of risk factors through clinical interviews and analysis of records. In D. R. Laws (Ed.), *Relapse prevention with sex offenders* (pp. 77–87). New York: Guilford.

Pithers, W. D., Martin, G. R., & Cumming, G. F. (1989). Vermont treatment program for sexual aggressors. In D. R. Laws (Ed.), *Relapse prevention with sex offenders* (pp. 292–310). New York: Guilford.

Quinsey, V. L., Chaplin, T. C., & Varney, G. (1981). A comparison of rapists' and non-sex offenders' sexual preferences for mutually consenting sex, rape, and physical abuse of women. *Behavioral Assessment, 3*, 127–135.

Quinsey, V. L., & Earls, C. M. (1990). The modification of sexual preferences. In W. L. Marshall, D. R. Laws, & H. E. Barbaree (Eds.), *Handbook of sexual assault: Issues, theories, and treatment of the offender* (pp. 279–295). New York: Plenum.

Quinsey, V. L., Harris, G. T., Rice, M. E., & Lalumière, M. L. (1993). Assessing treatment efficacy in outcome studies of sex offenders. *Journal of Interpersonal Violence, 8*, 512–523.

Quinsey, V. L., & Lalumière, M. L. (1995). Evolutionary perspectives on sexual offending. *Sexual Abuse: A Journal of Research and Treatment, 1*, 301–315.

Quinsey, V. L., Rice, M. E., & Harris, G. T. (1990). Psychopathy, sexual deviance, and recidivism among sex offenders released from a maximum security institution. *Penetanguishene Research Report 7*(1).

Rathus, S. A. (1973). A 30-item schedule for assessing assertive behavior. *Behavior Therapy, 4*, 398–406.

Russell, D. E. H. (1984). *Sexual exploitation: Rape, child sexual abuse, and workplace harassment.* Newbury Park, CA: Sage.

Russell, D., Peplau, L. A., & Cutrona, C. A. (1980). The revised UCLA loneliness scale. *Journal of Personality and Social Psychology, 39*, 472–480.

Sanday, P. R. (1981). The socio-cultural context of rape: A cross-cultural study. *The Journal of Social Issues, 37*, 5–27.

Schiff, A. F. (1971). Rape in other countries. *Medicine, Science and the Law, 11*, 139–143.

Schlank, A. M., & Shaw, T. (1997). Treating sexual offenders who deny—A review. In B. K. Schwartz & H. R. Cellini (Eds.), *The sex offender: New insights, treatment innovations and legal developments* (Vol. II, pp. 6.1–6.7). Kingston, NJ: Civic Research Institute.

Schwartz, B. K., & Cellini, H. R. (Eds.) (1997). *The sex offender: New insights, treatment innovations and legal developments.* Kingston, NJ: Civic Research Institute.

Segal, Z. V., & Marshall, W. L. (1985). Heterosexual social skills in a population of rapists and child molesters. *Journal of Consulting and Clinical Psychology, 53*, 55–63.

Segal, Z. V., & Stermac, L. E. (1984). A measure of rapists' attitudes towards women. *International Journal of Law and Psychiatry, 7*, 437–440.

Seghorn, T. K., Prentky, R. A., & Boucher, R. J. (1987). Childhood sexual abuse in the lives of sexually aggressive offenders. *Journal of the American Academy of Child and Adolescent Psychiatry, 26,* 262–267.

Selzer, M. L. (1971). The Michigan alcoholism screening test (MAST): The quest for a new diagnostic instrument. *American Journal of Psychiatry, 127,* 1653–1658.

Serin, R. C., Malcolm, P. B., Khanna, A., & Barbaree, H. E. (1994). Psychopathy and deviant sexual arousal in incarcerated sexual offenders. *Journal of Interpersonal Violence, 9,* 3–11.

Seto, M. C., & Barbaree, H. E. (1995). The role of alcohol in sexual aggression. *Clinical Psychology Review, 15,* 545–556.

Skinner, H. A. (1982). The drug abuse screening test. *Addictive Behaviors, 7,* 363–371.

Smallbone, S. W., & Dadds, M. R. (in press). Childhood attachment and adult attachment in incarcerated adult male sex offenders. *Journal of Interpersonal Violence.*

Speilberger, C. D. (1988). *State–trait anger expression inventory: Professional manual research edition.* Odessa, FL: Psychological Assessment Resources.

Stermac, L. E., & Quinsey, V. L. (1985). Social competence among rapists. *Behavioral Assessment, 8,* 171–185.

Thornhill, R., & Thornhill, N. W. (1992). The evolutionary psychology of men's coercive sexuality. *Behavioral and Brain Sciences, 15,* 363–375.

van Dijk, J. J. M., & Mayhew, P. (1992). *Criminal victimization in the industrial world.* The Hague, Netherlands: Directorate for Crime Prevention.

Ward, T., Hudson, S. M., & Siegert, R. J. (1995). A critical comment on Pithers' relapse prevention model. *Sexual Abuse: A Journal of Research and Treatment, 7,* 167–175.

Wormith, J. S., Bradford, J. M. W., Pawlak, A., Borzecki, M., & Zohar, A. (1988). The assessment of deviant sexual arousal as a function of intelligence, instructional set and alcohol ingestion. *Canadian Journal of Psychiatry, 33,* 800–808.

Chapter 23

The Assessment and Treatment of Sexual Offenders Against Children

Tony Ward
University of Melbourne, Melbourne, Australia
Stephen M. Hudson
and
Thomas R. Keenan
University of Canterbury, Christchurch, New Zealand

INTRODUCTION

Sexual offending against children remains a socially significant and complex problem. It is becoming increasingly evident that the psychological and emotional costs to victims and their families are profound, with many victims experiencing major difficulties in adjusting to the demands of adult life (Cole & Putnam, 1992). In addition, the high reoffending rate and financial costs of incarceration underlines the need to both understand, and to treat effectively, men who sexually abuse children. In the past two decades a number of innovations have led to improved treatment of these difficult men (Hudson & Ward, 1997). Factors such as low self-esteem, intimacy deficits, problems empathizing with victims, distorted beliefs, and deviant sexual preferences have all been suggested as causal strands in the genesis of sexual abuse (Marshall, 1996). From a cognitive–behavioural perspective, the problems child molesters present with can be addressed by teaching them more adaptive ways of thinking about children, establishing core social competencies, and increasing their repertoire of coping skills. We suggest that effective treatment needs to

Handbook of Offender Assessment and Treatment. Edited by C. R. Hollin.
© 2000 John Wiley & Sons Ltd.

be based on an understanding of the variables associated with sexual abuse of children.

The evaluation of treatment outcomes has recently has received considerable attention, particularly since the Furby, Weinrott, and Blackshaw (1989) review of recidivism, which argued that because of profound methodological inadequacies in existing data it was not possible to establish whether treatment reduced recidivism (e.g. Quinsey, Harris, Rice, & Lalumière, 1993). However, the most optimistic evaluators have concluded that despite numerous methodological problems inherent in the best of the existing research, there is evidence that comprehensive cognitive–behavioural programmes, and those that combine antiandrogens with psychological treatment, are associated with ecologically significant reductions in recidivism for treated sex offenders (Hall, 1995; Hudson & Ward, 1997; Marshall, Jones, Ward, Johnston, & Barbaree, 1991; Marshall & Pithers, 1994).

In this chapter we present a model of assessment and treatment for individuals who sexually offend against children. We describe the key components of assessment and treatment and finish with some general comments on future directions. In the description of treatment components we draw upon our experience with the Kia Marama treatment programme for child molesters (Hudson, Marshall, Ward, Johnston, & Jones, 1995).

ASSESSMENT

Effective treatment of child molesters requires a dedicated and systematic assessment period targeting a number of domains, and utilizing a number of methods to collect clinical information. These methods include a clinical interview, the administration of psychological scales, and phallometric testing. It is important to use multiple methods to gather clinically relevant data; relying on just one source of data, for example self-report, is risky (Ward & Haig, 1997). While self-report is a valuable source of information, limitations in cognitive processing and the distorting effects of psychological defences and memory, make it likely that exclusive reliance on this type of data might result in a formulation that bears little resemblance to an individual's real problems. The assessment process should culminate in a clinical formulation (Ward & Haig, 1997) which serves to guide the customization of the programme content to the individual. A comprehensive clinical formulation of sexually aggressive behaviour needs to consider an individual's background, psychological vulnerabilities, current stresses, and the problem behaviour itself.

Comprehensive coverage of the important content areas (as identified in the empirical literature and with clinical experience) will enable the clinical decisions that arise from assessment to be based on the most accurate and scientific information available. These areas include developmental history, social competency, self-regulation, sexual functioning and preferences, beliefs and attitudes towards children and women, capacity for empathy and perception of victim harm, and offence-related information (Barbaree & Seto, 1997; Hudson & Ward, 1997;

Marshall, 1996). The latter category includes degree of denial and cognitive distortions related to the sexual offence, offence antecedents, degree and type of planning, amount of force used to subdue the victim, and emotional states evident throughout the offence process.

The clinical interview is the most common assessment device available to the clinician. However, as noted above, data collected in this fashion, especially from men accused of sexual assault, may be unreliable. This means that collateral information is essential for corroborating or challenging the material obtained during the interview. For example, any records held by the police, including details provided by victims or mental health professionals' reports at the time or during previous arrests, are extremely useful. It is also invaluable in helping formulate interview strategies, as well as predict relevant issues and the excuses given by an offender (Ward, Hudson, Johnston, & Marshall, 1997). The process issues can be divided into those that set the stage for the interview and those designed to manage the interview process itself. Ethical standards require informed consent, which means that the offender, or accused, understands the purpose of the interview and the inevitable limits to confidentiality. Offender disclosure is likely to be enhanced by an honest discussion of the benefits and risks of co-operation.

Denial and the various ways in which offenders minimize their offending are the major problems facing the interviewer (Marshall, 1996); accuracy and completeness is important. An acceptable level of completeness means that while the offender may not fully accept the amount of damage he has done to the victim, he has at least taken physical responsibility for the acts committed. Aggressive confrontation is unlikely to be successful for at least two reasons; namely, these men are skilled at maintaining their privacy, and aggression is likely to increase defensiveness. Overcoming denial depends heavily on the interviewer's ability to demonstrate a genuine awareness and understanding of the offender's situation. Viewing him as a whole person rather than as *the sex offender* is likely to help the process. Reframing disclosure as a fresh beginning can also be helpful. Maximizing retrospective caring about the victim, as in "you may not have thought much about her at the time but it would be great if you were to consider how you could help her now" can also assist the process.

We recommend that all clients undergo phallometric testing to identify the presence or absence of deviant attraction to either children and/or aggressive themes (Earls & Marshall, 1983; Laws & Osborne, 1983). We are aware of the controversy surrounding phallometric assessment (for a discussion of these issues see Hudson & Ward, 1997) and are seeking to develop alternative measures of sexual interest. In essence, the early promise of phallometry to discriminate between offenders and non-offenders has generally not been sustained. For example, exhibitionists are not distinguishable from controls and it has been difficult to distinguish rapists from matched non-offenders, with approximately one-third of both groups demonstrating arousal to rape cues (Hudson & Ward, 1997). However, on the whole child molesters, at least those of the non-familial type, fare a little better, but even here discriminent validity is modest (Barbaree & Marshall, 1989). An additional issue concerns the poor reliability of phallometric assessment, with a seminal study finding that data from 75% of their sample of rapists and non-offenders were unreliable (Barbaree, Baxter, & Marshall, 1989). However, until alternative measures are fully available we believe there to be sufficient utility in this process, at least for child molesters, to justify continuing. We see phallometric testing as an essential component of the assessment process and it should be explicitly covered in the consent form. In our experience, most men accept the therapist's explanation that it is needed to set appropriate treatment goals and to help reduce their risk of reoffending. The link between deviant sexual arousal and offending is also drawn explicitly in the "Understanding Offending" module (see below).

Concerning the selection of psychological scales and tests, we recommend that clinicians select measures that cover the following domains:

1. Sexual attitudes, beliefs, and behaviours, including views of sexual activity between an adult and a child, attitudes and fantasies about various sexual activities, hostile attitudes and acceptance of violence towards women.
2. Emotional functioning, particularly anger, anxiety and depression.
3. Interpersonal competence, particularly issues of self esteem, attachment, intimacy, and loneliness.
4. Personality, using primarily the Millon Clinical Multiaxial Inventory, 2nd Edition (Millon, 1987).

Both the scales and the phallometric assessment are repeated at the completion of treatment. It may also be useful for therapists to complete the Hare Psychopathy Checklist—Revised (Hare, 1991) at the end of treatment, as this instrument can help to formulate an assessment of future risk.

TREATMENT

Overall Structure

The majority of cognitive–behavioural treatment programmes are entirely group-based with individual therapy kept to a minimum, that is, sufficient only to enable a resident to participate in a group. Group treatment is more effective both in terms of use of time in that more men can be dealt with at once, and, we believe, in terms of efficacy in that processes such as credible challenges by other offenders and vicarious learning are not available in individual treatment. In our treatment programme (Hudson et al., 1995) groups are selected on the basis of release dates and currently consist of eight men with one therapist. We suggest that seven core components or modules underlie effective cognitive–behavioural treatment for child molesters. The Kia Marama programme described below incorporates these modules, and runs for 31 weeks with groups meeting for three, two-and-a-half hour sessions per week. Non-therapy time is spent engaged in homework assignments, therapy-related activities, prison work (e.g. kitchen or garden), or at leisure.

Module 1: Norm Building

The primary aim for this module is to establish the rules of conduct that are essential if the group is to function effectively, and to provide an overview of the treatment philosophy, that is the "the big picture". At the first session, the underlying social learning model of human behaviour change is described. The men are told that we do not intend to cure them of their problems, but rather to teach them to control their behaviour by helping them break dysfunctional habits and learn prosocial ways of satisfying their needs. Although each group generates its own set of rules which are in a sense unique to the group, most groups would typically include rules covering confidentiality (prohibiting the discussion of issues raised in group concerning other group members, with people outside the group) and communication procedures (using "I" statements, one person speaking at a time, speaking to each other not about each other, and demonstrating active listening skills). Additional rules may emphasize the importance of accepting responsibility for one's own issues (by facing up to challenges, and by asking questions when something is not understood) and challenging other members constructively and assertively rather than aggressively or colluding.

Module 2: Understanding Offending (Cognitive Restructuring)

Sexually aggressive behaviour is often facilitated and justified by distorted thinking (Ward et al., 1997). In this module the distorted views these offenders so frequently have of their offences are challenged and more accurate and constructive alternative ways of thinking about these issues developed. This process is partially facilitated by encouraging the man to develop a thorough understanding of his offence cycle. We base this process on the descriptive model we have developed regarding the typical offending pathways (Ward, Louden, Hudson, & Marshall, 1995; Ward & Hudson, in press).

In our model child molesters show at least nine discriminable steps in the offence chain. In brief, these are as follows (see Ward et al., 1995). Stage 1 are proximal background factors, such as the offender's perception of his general circumstances and his prevailing mood. Stage 2, distal planning, involves three possibilities: covert planning and chance contact, together with a third route, explicit planning, which may be associated with positive affect. Contributing factors here include the influence of circumstances such as structured contact with the victim, alcohol, victim vulnerability, cognitive distortions, and finally sexual arousal.

Stage 3 involves non-sexual contact with the victim for the purpose of offending. Stage 4 involves the offender re-evaluating his present circumstances and often changing his perception of his relationship with the victim in order to allow offending to occur. There are two major outcome states from this process, i.e. negative and positive affect, both of which involve increasing levels of sexual arousal and a belief that the cause is uncontrollable.

Stage 5, proximal planning, concerns the immediate precursors to the sexual offence and involve behaviours such as getting into bed with the child. Three subcategories were distinguishable: a self-focus, where the offender's needs were paramount; victim focus, where he justifies his offending in terms of caring for the child; and finally a mutual focus or caring relationship with a willing partner. Each of these were associated with different offence styles, with a self-focus being associated with short duration but high intrusiveness, and a mutual focus showing typically longer duration, more perceived reciprocity, and typically less intrusiveness.

Stage 6 is the sexual offence. Stage 7 is the evaluative process occurring in reaction to having committed the offence. Cognitive distortions were evident in the manner in which men appraised their behaviour. A negative evaluation involved feeling guilt or shame and was associated with self-blaming (an abstinence violation effect). While some men who negatively evaluated their behaviour acknowledged that their perceptions of victim willingness were mistaken, they also tended to minimize. Men starting with positive affect typically remained positive. Stage 8, resolutions regarding future behaviour, were largely determined by the affective tone of their post-offence appraisals.

Using a collaborative approach, with help from group members, the man is expected to develop an understanding of how background factors, such as low mood, lifestyle imbalances, sexual difficulties, intimacy difficulties (Hudson & Ward, 1997b; Ward, Hudson, & Marshall, 1996) set the scene for offending. The next two sections of the chain, distal planning and entering the high-risk situation, in which both proximal planning and the offence behaviours occur, are distinguished by the presence of a potential victim (Hudson & Ward, 1996) or being in a situation where the presence of a potential victim is highly probable, for example being in a park at around 3 pm on a school day. The individual's appraisal and emotional response to the initial lapse is carefully described and noted. The final part of the chain involves a description of the types of reactions the man has to having offended, and how these reactions inevitably add to his difficulties and therefore increase the likelihood of the chain continuing. Each man completes this chain during one group session. After receiving feedback from the therapist and other group members he then has a further opportunity to refine his understanding during a further session. The flexibility and scope of our model allows therapists to acknowledge the existence of different offence patterns, and also to look out for changes in mood and cognitions throughout the offence process.

Module 3: Arousal Reconditioning

Inappropriate or deviant sexual arousal to children is hypothesized to be an important factor causing and maintaining sexual offending (Marshall & Barbaree, 1990), and indeed is described as an important part of the problem behaviour process (Ward et al., 1995). Even where there is no phallometric evidence of sexual arousal to children, and this is not uncommon (see Marshall & Eccles, 1991 for a review), our belief is that any extensive pairing of orgasm and children means that it is likely that under circumstances of risk (for example, a negative mood state and the presence of a potential victim) the man will experience deviant sexual arousal.

In terms of the procedures used in this module, there is a limited amount of evidence suggesting that reconditioning strategies can reduce inappropriate sexual arousal in some categories of child molesters (Johnston, Hudson, & Marshall, 1992; Laws & Marshall, 1991). There are three components to this intervention. Covert sensitization comprises the first of these. Each man identifies the process or sequence involved in his most recent or most typical sexual assault and operationalizes this by preparing a personalized fantasy divided into four parts:

1. a neutral scene involving boredom;
2. a scene involving gradual build-up to hands-on contact with a victim, but which ends before sexual contact is actually made;
3. a scene involving detection, arrest, going to jail, humiliation, etc., i.e. negative consequences; and
4. an escape scene involving "coming to his senses" and getting out of the situation, feeling relieved and "very pleased with himself".

Scenes 1 and 2 are repeatedly paired with both scenes 3 and 4. The men are encouraged to activate the escape scene at progressively earlier points in the previous scenes. These are then written on pocket-sized cards and the offender is required to regularly review these behaviour sequences.

The remaining components in this module are designed to decrease deviant sexual arousal, on the one hand, and to strengthen sexual arousal to appropriate images and thoughts on the other. Directed masturbation, where the man is encouraged to become aroused by what ever means is necessary, but once aroused to masturbate to consensual images involving an adult, is designed to pair arousal with thoughts of appropriate sexual activity in order to strengthen these associations. Once the man has ejaculated, and becomes at least relatively refractory to sexual stimulation (Masters & Johnston, 1966), he is asked to carry out the satiation procedures suggested by Marshall (1979). These involve him repeatedly verbalizing components of his deviant sexual fantasies, for at least 20 minutes, whilst in this state of minimal sexual arousal. This pairing of deviant sexual material with both low arousal and arousability is likely to reduce its positive valence.

Module 4: Victim Impact and Empathy

A lack of empathy for their victims, and an inability or refusal to seriously consider the traumatic effects of sexual abuse appear to be common features of sex offenders (Marshall, Hudson, Jones, & Fernandez, 1995). We attempt to enhance each man's understanding of the impact of offending on victims by having the group "brainstorm" immediate effects, post-abuse effects, and long-term consequences (Briere & Runtz, 1993; Cole & Putnam, 1992; Downs, 1993). Any gaps in understanding are filled by the therapist.

Typically, a general deficiency in the capacity to be empathic is seen as facilitating offending, where things that are manifestly harmful are done to others. We doubt this is the case (Marshall et al., 1995) and indeed have evidence (Marshall, 1996) that the deficit is quite selective to the man's own victim, and as such most likely reflects dysfunctional cognitions specifically related to his own offending (Ward et al., 1997). The victim impact material may serve to reinstate offenders' capacity to empathize with potential victims, and reduce the future risk of reoffending.

To enhance this process we have the men engage in several other tasks. They read aloud accounts of sexual abuse and view videotapes of victims describing their experiences. We also have an abuse survivor come in to the group, as a guest speaker; she facilitates a discussion about the impact of abuse, both in general and specifically to her. They then write an "autobiography" from their own victim's perspective. This covers the distress they suffered and the ongoing consequences to having been abused by him. Finally, we have the man role-play both roles between himself and his victim. The group assists in these processes, challenging and suggesting additional material, and provides, along with the therapist, final approval. Marshall (1996) suggests that these procedures produce significant improvements in reported empathic responding specifically focused upon the men's own victims. This work constitutes an excellent beginning but needs to be replicated across other groups.

Module 5: Mood Management

Negative mood states are a frequent precipitating stimulus for the offence chain, usually depression or feelings of rejection, or more rarely anger (Pithers, 1990). Therefore deficiencies in affect regulation are a critical part of the management of risk. However, it is important to keep in mind that positive mood states can also be associated with sexual offending for some individuals (Ward, Hudson, & Keenan, 1998). The men are presented with a cognitive–behavioural model of mood as an overarching framework. They are taught to identify and distinguish between a range of affects including anger, fear, and sadness. They are then asked to identify particular moods that are, for them, especially associated with their offending process and are then taught the physiological, cognitive, and behavioural skills to manage these moods. Cognitive strategies include techniques aimed at challenging or interrupting negative thoughts and include stress inoculation. Behavioural techniques include teaching, and role-playing, effective communication styles for expressing emotions, including assertiveness training, anger management, and conflict resolution techniques. Lastly, problem-solving and time-management strategies are briefly introduced.

Module 6: Relationship Skills

In our clinical and research work we have been struck by the apparent difficulty child molesters have in the area of social competence (Ward et al., 1996). Not only do these difficulties in relating to others result in unmet needs, they also relate to difficulties in regulating affect (Ward et al., 1996). It is therefore of considerable importance to enhance interpersonal functioning. In this module we focus particularly on intimate relationships, first establishing their benefits and then examining ways in which they can be enhanced. The four main areas we focus upon here involve:

- conflict and its resolution;
- the constructive use of shared leisure activities;
- the need to be communicative, supportive and rewarding of each other; and
- finally, intimacy, which is the key issue around which all the others revolve.

We have argued that sex offenders are particularly deficient in their capacity for intimacy and we have provided evidence to support this (Seidman, Marshall, Hudson, & Robertson, 1994) as well as the existence of the related negative emotional states such as loneliness and anger (Hudson & Ward, 1997b).

We pay attention to the relationship style described or exhibited by each man, and identify aspects which may serve to block the development of an intimate relationship. We then examine approaches to relationships which might more effectively serve to develop intimacy. This is completed through the use of brain-storming, role-playing, discussion of prepared handouts, and homework assignments. We also traverse issues relevant to sexuality and sexual dysfunction as part of this module, providing educational material, through handouts and videos, as required to correct misinformation or challenge unhelpful attitudes. We discuss sexuality as an aspect of intimacy, and consider attitudes and behaviours that make for a mutually fulfilling encounter. Two recent studies have provided evidence for the efficacy of self-esteem enhancement (Marshall, Champagne, Sturgeon, & Bryce, 1997) and intimacy skills training with child-molesters (Marshall, Bryce, Hudson, Ward, & Moth, 1996).

Module 7: Relapse Prevention

The overarching framework of the programme is that of a relapse prevention (RP) view of offending, and we introduce RP constructs early in treatment. In this sense the final intervention module of the programme comes as no surprise to the men, and forms a natural extension of the earlier components. The distinction between internal and external management (Pithers, 1990) has utility and we make use of it in structuring this module.

The internal management component involves the man presenting a more refined understanding of his offense chain, and describing the skills he has acquired to manage his risk factors. This approach is based on the assumption that the goal of treatment is to enhance self-monitoring and control over sexually abusive behaviour, rather than to cure the offender. The acquisition of behavioural and cognitive skills and attitudes is designed to enable individuals to meet their needs in more prosocial ways. The emphasis upon understanding the various links in the offense process also encourages attempts to "break the chain" as early as possible. Thus, this module helps the offender to identify the external and internal factors that put him at risk for further sexually abusive behaviour, and to ameliorate these by utilizing appropriate coping responses.

The external management aspect involves the man identifying friends and/or family who are prepared to support him in his goal of avoiding reoffending, and the preparation, and presentation, of his personal statement. This critical component is the bridge between the whole intervention effort and the community in which the offender plans to live. The personal statement articulates the factors or steps in his offending cycle and outlines a plan for both the avoidance of high-risk situations and ways to escape from one if it develops. It also describes the external cues or signs signifying to others that he is at risk for further offending, for example irritable behaviour. This process serves to facilitate good communication between the sex offender and those responsible for his management upon release (community corrections officer), as well as those people who have agreed to assist his self-management process.

Risk Assessment

The assessment of the level of risk for reoffending has become an integral task for treatment providers, particularly where legislators enact "sexual predator" laws (see Anderson, 1992). Hanson and Bussière's (1996) meta-analysis found positive predictive relationships for history of prior sex offences (especially if they exhibited variety), deviant sexual preferences (at least for child molesters), victim profile (interactions between gender and relationship to perpetrator, with offenders with related female children as victims being less likely to reoffend than those with unrelated males as victims), age (younger), and some aspects of developmental adversity (see Chapter 24). This list is quite similar to those variables found by Quinsey, Rice, and Harris (1995) to be related to sexual reoffending in men released from the Oak Ridge facility. It also parallels our own strategies, based on Barbaree's (1991) recommendations, which includes offence variables (length of history, versatility, presence of violence, and victim profile), and personality variables, most notably the Psychopathy Checklist—Revised (Hare, 1991).

CONCLUSIONS

The assessment and treatment of men who sexually offend against children presents many difficulties for clinicians. Only a small proportion of men who behave in sexually abusive ways get to be treated (Hudson & Ward, 1997a). Thus one of the major issues facing treatment providers is what type of client to select for inclusion in their programme. Some authors have argued that entry criteria ought to be set according to who is most likely to benefit from treatment (e.g. Marques, Day, Nelson, & Miner, 1989; Pithers, 1990). Certainly, where the major consequence of a treatment failure is the possibility of the programme being closed down, this strategy confers short-term advantage. An alternative perspective suggests that we ought to treat as wide a range of sex offenders as possible, with as customized an intervention as possible, and assess the results (Hudson & Ward, 1997a). To do otherwise means we are faced with substantial limitations on our ability to generalize from treatment studies. Marshall's more recent suggestions of a tiered approach, where intensive long-term interventions are reserved for those at higher risk of reoffending (Marshall, 1996), provides needed structure to the customization process.

The other area requiring urgent attention is treatment outcome research (Hanson, 1997). The cold facts are that the majority of treatment programmes have not been formally evaluated, and there has been even less attention given to dismantling comprehensive programmes (Barbaree & Seto, 1997). While it appears that effective treatment needs to contain multiple ingredients, it is not clear whether all of the seven components described earlier are essential for good treatment outcome. The second area of concern is the lack of sound evaluation studies. The problem of low base rates of recidivism, and the accompanying issue of statistical power, mean that multi-site studies are essential if we want to establish the efficacy of sex offender treatment. The evidence at this stage is suggestive, but it is still preliminary. We owe it to sexually abused children to do everything we can to improve our ability to treat these difficult men, and to continue to advance the field.

REFERENCES

Anderson, N. W. (Ed.) (1992). Predators and politics: A symposium on Washington's Sexual Violent Predators Statute. *University of Puget Sound Law Review, 15*, 507–987.

Barbaree, H. E. (1991, October). *Assessment of risk in sex offenders.* A workshop presented at the Annual Research and Treatment Meeting of the Association for the Treatment of Sexual Abusers, Fort Worth, TX.

Barbaree, H. E., Baxter, D. J., & Marshall, W. L. (1989). The reliability of the rape index in a sample of rapists and nonrapists. *Violence and Victims, 4*, 299–306.

Barbaree, H. E., & Marshall, W. L. (1989). Erectile response amongst heterosexual child molesters, father–daughter incest offenders, and matched nonoffenders: Five distinct age preference profiles. *Canadian Journal of Behavioral Science, 21*, 70–82.

Barbaree, H. E., & Seto, M. C. (1997). Pedophilia: Assessment and treatment. In D. R. Laws & W. O'Donohue (Eds.), *Sexual deviance: Theory, assessment, and treatment* (pp. 175–193). New York: Guilford.

Briere, J., & Runtz, M. (1993). Childhood sexual abuse: Long-term sequelae and implications for psychological assessment. *Journal of Interpersonal Violence, 8*, 312–330.

Cole, P. M., & Putnam, F. W. (1992). Effects of incest on self and social functioning: A developmental psychopathology perspective. *Journal of Consulting and Clinical Psychology, 60*, 174–184.

Downs, W. R. (1993). Developmental considerations for the effects of childhood sexual abuse. *Journal of Interpersonal Violence, 8*, 331–345.

Earls, C. M., & Marshall, W. L. (1983). The current state of technology in laboratory assessment of sexual arousal patterns. In J. G. Greer & I. R. Stuart (Eds.), *The sexual aggressor: Current perspectives on treatment* (pp. 336–362). New York: Van Nostrand Reinhold.

Furby, L., Weinrott, M. R., & Blackshaw, L. (1989). Sex offender recidivism: A review. *Psychological Bulletin, 105*, 3–30.

Hall, G. C. N. (1995). Sexual offender recidivism revisited: A meta-analysis of treatment studies. *Journal of Consulting and Clinical Psychology, 63*, 802–809.

Hanson, R. K. (1997). How to know what works with sexual offenders. *Sexual Abuse: A Journal of Research and Treatment, 9*, 129–145.

Hanson, R. K., & Bussière, M. T. (1996). *Predictors of sexual offender recidivism: A meta-analysis*. Ottawa, Canada: Solicitor General Canada.

Hare, R. D. (1991). *Manual for the Revised Psychopathy Checklist*. Toronto, Canada: Multi-Heath Systems.

Hudson, S. M., Marshall, W. L., Ward, T., Johnston, P. W., & Jones, R. L. (1995). Kia Marama: A cognitive–behavioural program for incarcerated child molesters. *Behaviour Change, 12*, 69–80.

Hudson, S. M., & Ward, T. (1996). Relapse prevention: Future directions. *Sexual Abuse: A Journal of Research and Treatment, 8*, 249–256.

Hudson, S. M., & Ward, T. (1997a). Future directions. In D. R. Laws & W. O'Donohue (Eds.), *Sexual deviance: Theory, assessment, and treatment* (pp. 481–500). New York: Guilford.

Hudson, S. M., & Ward, T. (1997b). Intimacy, loneliness, and attachment style in sex offenders. *Journal of Interpersonal Violence, 12*, 323–339.

Johnston, P. W., Hudson, S. M., & Marshall, W. L. (1992). The effects of masturbatory reconditioning with nonfamilial child molesters. *Behaviour Research and Therapy, 30*, 559–561.

Laws, D. R., & Marshall, W. L. (1991). Masturbatory reconditioning: An evaluative review. *Advances in Behaviour Therapy, 13*, 13–25.

Laws, D. R., & Osborne, C. A. (1983). How to build and operate a behavioural laboratory to evaluate and treat sexual deviance. In J. G. Greer & I. R. Stuart (Eds.), *The sexual aggressor: Current perspectives on treatment* (pp. 293–335). New York: Van Nostrand Reinhold.

Marques, J. K., Day, D. M., Nelson, C., & Miner, M. H. (1989). The Sex Offender Treatment and Evaluation Project: California's relapse prevention program. In D. R. Laws (Ed.), *Relapse prevention with sex offenders*. New York: Guilford.

Marshall, W. L. (1979). Satiation therapy: Changing sexual choice through controlling masturbatory fantasies. *Journal of Behaviour Therapy and Experimental Psychiatry, 1*, 263–271.

Marshall, W. L. (1996). Assessment, treatment, and theorizing about sex offenders. *Criminal Justice and Behavior, 23*, 162–199.

Marshall, W. L., & Barbaree, H. E. (1990). An integrated theory of the etiology of sexual offending. In W. L. Marshall, D. R. Laws, & H. E. Barbaree (Eds.), *Handbook of sexual assault: Issues, theories, and treatment of the offender* (pp. 257–275). New York: Plenum.

Marshall, W. L., Bryce, P., Hudson, S. M., Ward, T., & Moth, B. (1996). The enhancement of intimacy and the reduction of loneliness among child molesters. *Journal of Family Violence, 11*, 219–235.

Marshall, W. L., Champagne, F., Sturgeon, C., & Bryce, P. (1997). Increasing the self-esteem of child molesters. *Sexual Abuse: A Journal of Research and Treatment, 9*, 321–333.

Marshall, W. L., & Eccles, A. (1991). Issues in clinical practice with sex offenders. *Journal of Interpersonal Violence, 6*, 90–96.

Marshall, W. L., Hudson, S. M., Jones, R. J., & Fernandez, Y. M. (1995). Empathy in sex offenders. *Clinical Psychology Review, 15*, 99–113.

Marshall, W. L., Jones, R. L., Ward, T., Johnston, P., & Barbaree, H. E. (1991). Treatment outcome with sex offenders. *Clinical Psychology Review, 11*, 465–485.

Marshall, W. L., & Pithers, W. D. (1994). A reconsideration of treatment outcome with sex offenders. *Criminal Justice and Behavior, 21*, 10–27.

Masters, W. H., & Johnson, V. E. (1966). *Human sexual response*. Boston, MA: Little, Brown.

Millon, T. (1987). *Manual for the Millon Multiaxial Clinical Inventory* (2nd Ed.). Minneapolis, MN: National Computer Systems.

Pithers, W. D. (1990). Relapse prevention with sexual aggressors: A method for maintaining therapeutic gain and enhancing external supervision. In W. L. Marshall, D. R. Laws, & H. E. Barbaree (Eds.), *Handbook of sexual assault: Issues, theories, and treatment of the offender* (pp. 343–361). New York: Plenum.

Quinsey, V. L., Harris, G. T., Rice, M. E., & Lalumière, M. L. (1993). Assessing treatment efficacy in outcome studies of sex offenders. *Journal of Interpersonal Violence, 8*, 512–523.

Quinsey, V. L., Rice, M., & Harris, G. T. (1995). Actuarial prediction of sexual recidivism. *Journal of Interpersonal Violence, 10*, 85–105.

Seidman, B., Marshall, W. L., Hudson, S. M., & Robertson, P. J. (1994). An examination of intimacy and loneliness in sex offenders. *Journal of Interpersonal Violence, 9*, 518–534.

Ward T., & Haig, B. (1997). Abductive reasoning and clinical assessment. *Australian Psychologist, 32*, 93–100.

Ward, T., & Hudson, S. M. (in press). Relapse prevention: Conceptual innovations. In D. R. Laws, S. M. Hudson, & T. Ward (Eds.), *Relapse prevention with sex offenders: Reconceptualizations, revisions, innovations* (2nd Ed.). New York: Guilford.

Ward, T., Hudson, S. M., Johnston, L., & Marshall, W. L. (1997). Cognitive distortions in sex offenders: An integrative review. *Clinical Psychology Review, 17*, 479–507.

Ward, T., Hudson, S. M., & Keenan, T. R. (1998). A self-regulation model of the sexual offense process. *Sexual Abuse: A Journal of Research and Treatment, 10*, 141–157.

Ward, T., Hudson, S. M., & Marshall, W. L. (1996). Attachment style in sex offenders: A preliminary study. *Journal of Sex Research, 33*, 17–26.

Ward, T., Louden, K., Hudson, S. M., & Marshall, W. L. (1995). A descriptive model of the offence process. *Journal of Interpersonal Violence, 10*, 453–473.

Chapter 24

Adolescent Sexual Offenders: Assessment and Treatment

Stephen M. Hudson
University of Canterbury, Christchurch, New Zealand
and
Tony Ward
University of Melbourne, Melbourne, Australia

INTRODUCTION

There are few areas of social concern as distressing as sexual assault; this is even more the case when it is young males that are perpetrating these attacks on others. Not surprisingly this area involves considerable controversy with the understandable concern generated by sexual assaults by adolescents leading to polarized positions being taken by both individuals and various systems. The minimization of such assaults reflects the considerable anxiety these issues generate, but the "it is just experimentation" and "they will grow out of it" is not a competent response. It ignores both the need to respond appropriately to the victim and the fact that at least some young men continue on from these initial abusive episodes to essentially careers of sexually assaulting others. The alternate extreme, while reflecting good sentiments involving the prevention of abuse, has led to abused boys being responded to as if they are automatically, and inevitably, on an increasingly deviant trajectory (Cavanagh-Johnson, 1998). This fails both to respond appropriately to their need for support and assistance, as well as risking a self-fulfilling prophecy. The recent position statement on juvenile sexual offenders promulgated by the board of the major professional body in this area (Association for the Treatment of Sexual Abusers, 1997) supports the more moderate ground. They note that there is little evidence that the majority of juvenile sexual offenders are destined to show an offending trajectory into adulthood,

Handbook of Offender Assessment and Treatment. Edited by C. R. Hollin.
© 2000 John Wiley & Sons Ltd.

going as far as to suggest that there is recent evidence to the contrary. Finally, the additional issue, raised again and again in this literature, is that there are important distinctions between juvenile and adult sexual offenders, particularly with respect to the reasons they abuse, and that juvenile offenders are heterogeneous. A response to these themes and thus how to respond appropriately to this distressing social problem constitute the core dilemmas in this area.

DEFINITIONS

Sexually abusive behavior has never been as straightforward to define as we would imagine or hope. In essence it is a range of sexually relevant behaviors carried out against someone's will, without their consent or carried out in an aggressive or exploitative style. And it is not only the behaviors involved, if at all, in the sense that many sexual behaviors are generally considered acceptable, if unusual, provided mutual consent exists. Some of these behaviors may even be illegal in some places, for example anal intercourse. In the case of rape the issues are often not about the sexual behaviors specifically, but rather that the processes involve force and a lack of consent.

The situation of two juveniles behaving sexually makes the issues even more difficult to define, especially if the behaviors involved are at the low end of the intrusiveness and aggression dimensions. The conventional use of a five-year age differential to define abuse may frequently not work. Ryan (1997) usefully suggests that attention to three factors is needed to define an abuse incident adequately. First, equality, which involves developmental age as well as physical age, and the integrally related issue of power differential. Second, consent, which is essentially that the person is seen as understanding what is happening and able to evaluate aspects like risk and alternatives. It also means that the person is able to comprehend the meanings associated with various behaviors that are being proposed and can voluntarily make the decision to participate. Ryan (1997) notes that compliance is not equivalent to cooperation and that therefore this is not equal to consent. Finally, coercion, which can range from the covert use of power, authority, and size, or the presence of secondary gains and losses to ensure the sexual behaviors are carried out, through to the use of overt threats and violence. Attention to these factors as part of a full clinical formulation is needed in order to ensure adequate treatment planning.

PREVALENCE/INCIDENCE

Estimates of the incidence of sexual assaults perpetrated by adolescents range from 20% to 30% of rapes and from 30% to 60% of instances of child molestation (Association for the Treatment of Sexual Abusers, 1997; Becker, Kaplan, Cunningham-Rathner, & Kavoussi, 1986; Brown, Flanagan, & McLeod, 1984; Davis & Leitenberg, 1987; Deisher, Wenet, Paperny, Clark, & Fehrenback, 1982;

Fehrenback, Smith, Monastersky, & Deisher, 1986). These figures are unlikely to be an accurate reflection of the true rates. There is every possibility, given the enduring tendency to minimize such assaults, that the detection rate is even lower than for adult perpetrators which themselves require inflating by a factor of between 3 and 10 depending on the type of assault (Hudson & Ward, 1997b). The community sampling work, for example Koss, Gidycz, and Wisniewski (1987), Gavey (1991), and Finklehor, Hotalling, Lewis, and Smith (1989) lend substance to these figures by suggesting that very approximately one in four women and one in ten men have experienced some form of serious sexual assault. This means that, one way or another, adolescents, typically male (Worling, 1998), are offending in very significant ways.

Furthermore, isolated instances of sexual aggression are rare in that most adolescent sexual offenders referred for initial assessments have a history of undetected offenses (Gray & Pithers, 1993; Worling, 1998). What remains unclear, but drives a significant amount of interest in the area, is what proportion of adolescents continue to offend as adults. Rubinstein, Yeager, Goodstein, and Lewis (1993) report that 37% of an untreated violent adolescent sexual offender sample had re-offended sexually as adults. While data from the reverse perspective does not really help us answer this question, there are certainly strong beliefs, and some evidence, that as many as 50% of adult sexual offenders begin offending during their teenage years (Abel, Mittleman, & Becker, 1985; Becker & Abel, 1985; Longo & Groth, 1982; Prenkty & Knight, 1993).

Regardless of how inadequate these data are, the core issue that they inform is: "Is the problem of sufficient proportions to justify intervention?" Our belief is that despite the problems noted above, these data are convincing in this regard. Not only are there a large number of assaults being carried out, but a significant proportion of these young men continue on to offend as adults. Furthermore, it is likely that the implicit theories about others (Ward, in press) held by these young men that support offending are more unstable at this age, and thus intervention has a greater chance of being successful. Put another way, the distal causes for many adult offenders may well still be proximal with adolescents, and therefore be more amenable to real treatment rather than long-term management.

ASSESSMENT

Assessment ought to reflect etiology, at least in the sense of the proximal causes for offending behavior. So what are the causes of sexual aggression in juveniles? That we do not have a definitive answer ought to surprise no one. Moreover, we have argued that the absence of an integrated approach to theory building in the general area of sexual offending is a major problem (see Ward & Hudson, 1998a, for an extended discussion of these points). In brief, the lack of a meta-theory has resulted in the *ad hoc* proliferation of theories that often overlap, confuse levels of theory, and frequently neglect each other's existence. We have suggested that there is considerable utility in using a two-dimensional organizational system; according to level, on the one hand, and temporally, in terms of distal to proximal, on the other.

Level I, or multifactorial theories, use a loosely grouped set of constructs that serve as a framework. Marshall and Barbaree's (1990) integrated model is an example of theory at this level and since it addresses some of the issues relevant to adolescents we present a brief overview here. They suggest that biology provides the major developmental challenge for a young male around puberty in that he needs to acquire the socially required control over both sexuality and aggression. Those males with a history of developmentally adverse events, such as harsh parenting, physical and sexual abuse, are unlikely to reach puberty with an adequate level of skill to cope with the challenges involved. Poor social skills, inappropriate attitudes towards the rights of others, together with loneliness and anger result in it being even less likely that the vulnerable young male will be able to meet his social needs in prosocial ways. These vulnerability factors interact with transient situation factors to produce the offense.

Level II (i.e. single-factor theories) typically take one variable of interest, often suggested by a level I theory, and describe the relevant structures and processes, and their interrelationships. Examples of theories at this level are empathy deficits (Marshall, Hudson, Jones, & Fernandez, 1995), intimacy deficits and attachment styles (Marshall, 1989; Marshall, Hudson, & Hodkinson, 1993; Ward, Hudson, Marshall, & Siegert, 1995), the role of developmental adversity (Bentovim & Williams, 1998), and the development of fantasy and deviant sexual preferences in offending (Marshall & Eccles, 1993). Little work has been done in these areas with adolescents but their direct relevance to assessment is at least supported. For example, we have suggested that attachment style may assist our understanding of how difficulties in forming and managing relationships might happen in sexually aggressive men. We have suggested that the three insecure attachment styles are likely to be involved in different types of sexual offending (e.g. child molesting versus raping adults), and to be associated with different psychological characteristics (loneliness and anger in particular).

Level III, or micro theories, involve building descriptive models of the offense process (e.g. Gray & Pithers, 1993; Ward, Louden, Hudson, & Marshall, 1995). The relapse prevention model as applied to adolescent sexual offenders (Gray & Pithers, 1993) predominantly focuses on factors proximal to offending, describing the process as typically beginning with negative affect (e.g. loneliness, confusion, or anger). Negative affect leads to fantasies of performing sexually abusive acts that are seen as learned ways of reducing negative feelings. These fantasies are often associated with a stream of dysfunctional cognitions that serve to rationalize deviant sexuality. The offender then begins to plan and carry out an assault. Ryan and Lane have developed a similar model, the sexual assault cycle, with their specific experience with adolescents (Lane, 1997; Ryan, Lane, Davis, & Isaac, 1987). This model describes a process where some event, interpersonal interaction, or problem triggers negative perceptions of self and a sense of hopelessness in an offender. This event is responded to in light of previous life experiences, which are hypothesized to be sufficiently negative to cause expectations that the future will be similarly negative. This in turn generates more hopelessness that results in more avoiding dealing with the problems. The lack of success of these coping maneuvers leads to more energy being expended in the form of responding to feeling resentful by attempting to exert control over others in non-sexual ways such as aggression. The typical brevity of such "positive" feelings leads in turn to further thoughts of other "power based" behaviors and things such as sex that would make him feel good. Thus the exertion of control is expressed sexually. The aftermath of the sexual assault is seen as involving concern about being caught and the consequent need to use distorted thinking to minimize post-offending distress.

While the relapse prevention model has been hugely beneficial, it has substantial limitations (Ward & Hudson, 1996). Our most recent model of the relapse process (Ward & Hudson, 1998b) has the potential to overcome these problems. Specifically it suggests that there are likely to be at least four discriminable pathways involved in offending. These are defined in essence by the nature of the self-regulatory deficits, if any, and second by the nature of the goals relevant to deviant sexual activity (inhibitory versus appetitive). Thus it is likely that one pathway will reflect both a commitment to avoid offending and under-regulation, a second pathway reflects the same goal but with mis-regulation (active but flawed strategies). The first of the approach goal pathways involves an under-regulatory style, and finally those people with no self-regulatory deficits (intact style) who choose to engage in sexually deviant or aggressive ways supported by relevant global belief systems or implicit theories (Ward, in press). This modeling of the offense process is still "work in progress" and needs to be validated with adult offenders, as well as extended to adolescents. It is likely that a greater variety or heterogeneity will be reflected in the process with adolescents. However, it is important to note that these descriptions, driven largely as they are by what offenders tell us they actually do when they offend, provide the touchstone for the other levels of theorizing; it is these processes that need to be explained. They also define the types of issues and areas that must be assessed in order for a comprehensive "theory" which explains, at least tentatively, the offending process for an individual adolescent offender.

In summary, we do not yet know enough about how vulnerability to offending develops, nor what offender-specific processes turn that vulnerability into an initial offense. These processes often occur in adolescence, the most critical and the most poorly studied period of sexual development. The form of these triggers, despite their significance to explaining sexual aggression, remain critically under-explored. Finally, while some appropriate work is beginning to be carried out, for example our work in empathy deficits, generally insufficient attention has been paid to both the temporal instability and the situational specificity of many of the factors suggested to be important in bringing about deviant sexuality.

Given the absence of an adequate and integrated set of models concerning the development and maintenance of sexual offending it is essential to ensure that an assessment is comprehensive. Moreover, assessment needs to at least provide a plausible, if tentative model of how the individual has ended up doing what he has done in a manner that ultimately informs his treatment. The clinician should examine a wide range of pertinent content areas. These ought to be determined by the empirical literature and clinical experience, and need to consider an individual's background (cultural, biological, and familial), psychological vulnerability, his strengths and weaknesses (Dougher, 1995) as well as the problem behavior process itself and its situational context.

Another issue to complicate this process is that the aim of assessment, i.e. the goals and associated strategies, can vary substantially according to where in the process it is taking place. For example, an assessment designed to assist the judicial processes involved in establishing guilt, and level of risk in order to rationally plan disposition, is likely to be different from one aiming to assess motivation and amenability for treatment (Marshall & Barbaree, 1989, McGrath, 1991). Finally, any evaluation at the conclusion of treatment ought to rely on an accurate assessment (Hanson, Cox, & Woszczyna, 1991), particularly as risk assessments have important implications for both the safety of the community and the future lifestyle of the offender.

The clinical interview is frequently the primary assessment device, but gathering collateral information from as many sources as possible is essential. It is also likely that the issues of readiness and motivation for assessment, let alone treatment, are even more problematic with adolescent perpetrators than with adults, if for no other reason than confrontation and coercion are especially available when working with this population (Jenkins, 1998). This has the potential to create a situation where therapists have more motivation than their clients. Jenkins (1990, 1998) has articulated an approach that is intensely collaborative and which aims to separate what the individual has done from who he is. There is an acute need to avoid these core adolescent identity issues in a way that leaves the young person room to explore what he has done. Jenkins approach, termed "invitations to responsibility", is essentially a systemic approach (White, 1995). It serves to contextualize the more main steam intervention styles such as psychoeducational approaches and relapse prevention. It is entirely congruent with the respectful position that many people have been suggesting for some time, and provides a means of achieving an intervention appropriate climate (Beech & Fordham, 1997).

The other significant process issue specific to this area is the implications of carrying out an assessment where the perpetrator is still in the family situation where he offended (Worling, 1998). There is potential for him re-offending while the assessment is proceeding. One of the consequences of this is that the treatment agency may well find itself doing child protection services work, where these services do not act for some reason. This confusion of roles can be damaging, for example the perception that the treatment agency will act to remove children from the home can adversely affect future referrals (Worling, 1998). However, as Graham, Richardson, and Bhate (1998) note, while adolescents perpetrate about one-third of sexual assaults, the majority will escape prosecution because either disclosure is delayed or evidence is inadequate. So restricting involvement only to where the young person has been adjudicated is probably unduly restrictive.

In overview, assessment targets have been usefully conceptualized as specific and generic (Graham et al., 1998). Specific factors involve getting a detailed understanding about the offense, and the context within which it has been enacted. We believe that the use of adequate models of this process assist assessment in so far as they help by structuring the typical steps involved, such as self-regulatory style, types of goals, and planning (e.g., Ward & Hudson, 1998b; Ward, Louden, Hudson, & Marshall, 1995). The processes associated with this core behavior chain, such as deviant sexuality and masturbatory fantasies, past abuse experiences that may be linked to sexual knowledge and attitudes, and issues around victim harm (awareness of the impact of abuse on victims and other cognitive distortions) are all critical assessment targets. The characteristics of the victim, issues such as age, gender, and physical characteristics, particularly vulnerabilities, inform clinical judgments regarding preferences as well as motivational issues. For example, an offender who indecently assaults a younger sibling is likely to be following a different offense process than someone intent on dominating, hurting, or humiliating an age peer in the context of a general antisocial behavioral style (France & Hudson, 1993). These distinctions reflect an offense style that in turn is related to type of victim, degree of violence used, and the nature of the underlying models of relationships being used. Finally, motivation for treatment needs to be both assessed and enhanced.

The generic factors contextualize this core by examining the young person's social competency (personal and relationship skills and academic functioning) and his family context. This is where the developmental context becomes critical. The Reed Committee (Reed, 1992) recommendations were clear that adolescents were not appropriately treated as adults and that the developmental task of transition to adulthood needed to be both respected and encouraged in positive ways (Graham et al., 1998). As Marshall and his colleagues have noted, puberty marks the beginning of significant changes in biological, personal, and social domains and is a critical period for the male with respect to controlling his sexual behavior (Marshall & Barbaree, 1990; Marshall & Eccles, 1993). It is clear that young men with problematic histories replete with adversity are not well equipped (under-socialized) to cope with these dramatic changes, and not too surprisingly constitute a significant proportion of those young men who end up being sexually abusive (Bentovim & Williams, 1998). Low social competency is increasingly being viewed as critical to the development of sexually deviant behavior (Hudson & Ward, in press; Ward, Hudson, & Marshall, 1996). As noted above we have suggested that attachment theory can provide a useful theoretical framework for studying the interpersonal deficits in sexual offenders, both adult and adolescent (Hudson & Ward, 1997a; Marshall, 1989; Marshall, Hudson, & Hodkinson, 1993; Ward, Hudson, Marshall, & Siegert 1995).

Most of these assessment targets are not controversial or particularly noteworthy in either the adult or adolescent context. However, special mention is required with respect to the use of phallometry in assessing deviant sexual interests. Such assessment is contentious, even in the adult literature (Hudson & Ward, 1997b). The debate focuses on adolescence as a time of emerging development, with exposure to phallometric stimuli having the potential to distort these processes (see also Laws & Marshall, 1990). There are no systematic data concerning negative effects of phallometric assessment with adolescents but Worling (1998) reports anecdotal material suggesting that humiliation is a common experience. Also the reliability and validity of these procedures is contentious, especially with adolescents. For example, arousal data are thought to be related to both an offender's age (Kaemingk, Koselka, Becker, & Kaplan, 1995), denial, and an abuse history (Becker, Kaplan, & Tenke, 1992). Moreover, phallometric responding is reported to be not reliably associated with offense history variables as is the case, at least to some extent, with adults (Hunter, Goodwin, & Becker, 1994). At the very least ATSA has recently recommended that only auditory stimuli be used and that the young person must be at least 14 years of age.

These assessment processes ought to lead to both a clinical formulation, to inform treatment, and to a dispositional recommendation, i.e. security and treatment need driven triage. The heart of the latter is in the assessment of risk. Graham et al. (1998) suggest useful criteria for making these clinical judgments and the associated dispositional decisions with respect to programs (see Table 24.1). Adolescents assessed as showing low risk need an intervention that is likely to involve a mix of structured group work supported by individual and family work delivered via an outpatient clinic. Those youg men deemed to present a medium risk (see Table 24.1) are likely to need interventions that involve them being seen in an outreach capacity to the children's residential facilities; that is structured programs developed by specialist staff are delivered by residential social workers. Those presenting high risk are likely to be in residential secure

Table 24.1 Risk assessent criteria

Level of risk	Frequency of offending	Intrusiveness	Victim type	Family support	Social integration	Deviant sexual preoccupal
Low	Low	Low	Intra and extra familial	Yes	At least some	Usually absent
Medium	Higher	Limited violence	Intra and extra familial	Limited	Low	Some
High	Variable	Very high—violent	Typically extra familia	Low	Low	High

Adapted from Graham et al. (1998).

facilities if they are under 15 years of age, or prison if they are older. Alternatively, especially if they have co-morbid psychiatric conditions (psychosis or psychopathic disorder), they will be in a secure hospital unit. Programs for these offenders are likely to be similar to thoe developed for medium risk offenders, in that they involve structured group work, but with more emphasis on the violent and sexually deviant aspects of their offending.

As a final comment, almost all writers in this area note the problem posed by a typical lack of integration of services. Cellini (1995) argues persuasively that the sheer number of agencies involved with an adolescent offender (health, probation, criminal justice, and social services), together with a continuing and significant level of denial by some professionals and lay people alike, means that problems abound. He argues for an explicit inter-agency policy of cooperation and information transfer. While the involvement of several agencies is often a problem even with adult offenders, this is a particular problem with adolescents (Worling, 1998) especially as many do not come before the courts (Graham et al., 1998). Worling suggests that a case conference for all involved parties, parents, offender, probation officer, custody facility, child protection worker, and the treatment provider, is critical. The purpose of this "business" meeting is to share information regarding assessment and treatment procedures, limits of confidentiality, and expectations concerning a coordinated approach to re-offense prevention. Second, it provides a forum for discussion of long-term goals and biases and mandates, and finally gives everyone access to the most recent information about the case.

TREATMENT

The explicit guiding principle for treatment delivery to adolescents is based upon the notion that models and techniques derived from work with adults ought not to be used. Indeed, it is possible to see treatment as assisting the young person to manage the developmental tasks of adolescence in order to make as functional a transition to adulthood as possible. However, the most popular, at least by program self-report, and widely recognized intervention style is cognitive–behavioral, including relapse prevention. Moreover, programs for adolescents tend to be simplifications of those developed for adults. The specific differences, where developmental level is thought to be problematic, concern the role of deviant sexual arousal, abusive fantasies, and cognitive distortions in the early development of abusive behavior. However, the usual targets of treatment look remarkably familiar: motivational enhancement, disclosure, psycho-educational interventions, for example, with drug misuse, sexuality and attitudes, cognitive distortions (denial, mimimization, and accountability), understanding abusive behavior, victim harm issues, social skills training, modification of arousal and fantasy, and relapse prevention. In terms of group process many suggestions reflect the need to reduce the cognitive complexity of the processes involved for the offender. For example, Becker and Kaplan (1993) suggest that concreteness, shorter time frames (one hour), repetition, and use of games are key issues. Similarly, Worling (1998) suggests that the offense process needs to be simplified to: situation—strong feelings—sexual thoughts—thinking errors—planning—high-risk situations—sexual assault—strong feelings. Other process issues, such as group rules, are familiar: respecting others and their contribution, no leaving the group except for emergencies, no lateness, one person speaking at a time, no shouting, stay seated, and no violence (Becker & Kaplan, 1993). In negotiating these rules it is useful to note that the individuals are being taught to be clients and to overcome the understandable initial anxiety and confusion that they bring to the first group (Ryan & Lane, 1997). Some treatment providers run their groups with the clients sitting at a table because this is seen as being less threatening (Becker & Kaplan, 1993).

In terms of treatment format the received wisdom is that group-based is the most efficient and efficacious. The rationale for this usually includes that it is good to see others take risks in disclosing as this encourages the observer to also take the same risks later. Group members are quicker and more accurate in spotting denial in the accounts of offending presented by other group members as they share a greater similarity of experience with each other than with therapists. Seeing the distortions and minimizations in other offenders aids the process of identifying them in oneself. This format also models and promotes relationships and provides a relatively benign, or at least moderately controlled, environment in which to attempt new ways of relating to others. In other words, there is the possibility of exposure to disconfirming attachment experiences, provided the therapeutic climate is rational and non-abusive. In this regard confrontation between the therapist and the group member needs to be managed carefully. It must be well timed (enough of it and when both the therapist and client are ready), occur in an appropriate relationship context (empathy and concern), and have measured impact (an appropriate level of discomfort with his thoughts and behavior sufficient to motivate desired change) (Ryan & Lane, 1997).

In overview, treatment, as we have described in treating adults, begins with understanding the offense process. This ought to provide a touchstone for interventions; if it is a significant aspect of the process, then it ought to be addressed in the intervention. Central elements, in addition to comprehension of the offending process, are likely to be cognitive restructuring for offense supportive beliefs and attitudes, deviant arousal, empathy for victims, and issues of victim harm. Finally, most programs seek to help the person develop a relapse safety plan.

Ryan and Lane (1997) use their offense cycle, first in generic form, and then expect the adolescent to personalize it. The initial work will very likely involve the young person learning to discriminate situations, thoughts, feelings, and behavior. This process includes defining what constitutes sexual abuse; the issues of consent, equality, and coercion need to be very clearly covered. These tasks are often a challenge for adult offenders. Lots of illustrations of cyclical phenomena (arguments with parents for example) are used to broaden and deepen the young person's understanding. Several things happen as a result of these processes, and they are not unique to this population. Insight into mental states (desires and beliefs) develops. Distorted thinking (see Ward, in press, for a discussion of the central and organizing role implicit theories play) and minimizations are challenged. These can be presented as an examination of the "things that you told yourself to make it OK to do what you did". Intervention often uses analogies and role-playing a wide range of abusive situations (Becker & Kaplan, 1993). The typical themes that arise here are lack of empathy, objectification of victims, views of sex in personal gratification terms, lack of remorse, over-commitment to autonomy such that that no one has the right to criticize or interfere with what he wants, and general acceptance of violence. Triggers, grooming behaviors (including stalking), along with other motivating forces such as deviant fantasies, are identified. Any progression in abusive patterns is also identified. The keeping of a journal as an aid to this intense process of self-examination is frequently recommended (Becker & Kaplan, 1993). All programs have components that aim to assist the young person control arousal. Covert sensitization is frequently used to interrupt the pleasurable associations and anticipations that the young person has previously experienced (Ryan & Lane, 1997). This goal is usually achieved by using visualizations of extremely negative and shaming outcomes (mentally aversive scenarios) part way through the sequence, then an escape-reward scene. Recommended dose is 4 hours broken down into 20 minute sessions. Satiation (an extinction paradigm) is less frequently recommended because of the difficulties in adherence. Becker and Kaplan (1993) use verbal satiation but they require these sessions (8 at 30 minutes duration) to be carried out at the clinic while attached to a phallometric device. They continue for usually no more than 16 sessions (2 blocks). They use this technique alone, instead of the broader package involving directed masturbation (Hudson, Wales, & Ward, 1998). This procedure reflects problems they report such as a lack of privacy and masturbatory prohibitions.

Modules designed to address the deficiencies in social competency are common. Usual targets include mood management (developing assertiveness and managing anger in particular), and general social skills such as conversational skills (especially developing sensitivity to non-verbal cues), and relationship issues (especially to do with intimacy). Similarly, sex education, despite having a greater current emphasis within the school system, is still frequently required. Topics typically covered include sexual development (structure and function), disposing of various myths (cannot get pregnant if you withdraw prior to ejaculation), issues of pregnancy and sexually transmitted diseases, the various emotional and physical needs that are met though sexual contact, and sexual values, emphasizing issues of consent. Finally, a relapse prevention module is covered where the need to develop a customized plan that includes safety measures to avoid relapse is addressed.

Outside of what are often modified mainstream adult interventions the significant difference for this population lies in the role of the family. The central point is that adolescents are separating from their family of origin but have not, by definition, completed this task; this makes them different from adult offenders. The complications that flow from this are to do with the role of the family in treatment (family difficulties may have contributed to offending, for example with instability and abuse issues), and they may well be involved in external supervision. This is likely to be both confusing and demanding. Additionally, some issues especially around concerns about abuse issues, sibling violence and the abuse of pets are frequently overlooked in assessment (Ryan & Lane, 1997).

CONCLUSIONS

We still do not have accurate data on how many adolescent offenders will continue with their assaultive behavior, and it may well be the case that we never will. However, as we commented at the outset of this chapter, it is our belief that enough young men do pose the risk of continuing to offend to make the task of intervening in these processes critical. Given this we ought to be striving to do as good a job as possible. The obvious areas that are desperately in need of research are what specifically generates a vulnerability to the development of deviant sexual behaviors and what processes are involved in the transition between being vulnerable to having begun to abuse. We know all to little about offense processes in adults and arguably we know even less in adolescents. Similarly, the central explanatory constructs of empathy deficits, intimacy and attachment, deviant sexual arousal and fantasies, and dysfunctional cognitive processes have yet to be fully investigated in adult offenders, particularly concerns about temporal instability and situational specificity (Hudson & Ward, 1997c). The optimism about the amount of change that is possible for adolescents (founded or otherwise) as well as the significant potential to reduce victim numbers, makes this an intriguing and important group of offenders to address well.

REFERENCES

Abel, G. G., Mittleman, M. S., & Becker, J. V. (1985). Sex offenders: Results of assessment and recommendations for treatment. In M. H. Ben-Aron, S. J. Hucker, & C. D. Webster (Eds.), *Clinical criminology: The assessment and treatment of criminal behavior* (pp. 207–220). Toronto, Canada: M & M Graphics.

Association for the Treatment of Sexual Abusers (1997). *Position on the legal management of juvenile offenders.* Beaverton, OR: Author.

Becker, J. V., & Abel, G. G. (1985). Methodogical and ethical issues in evaluating and treating adolescent sexual offenders. In E. M. Otey & G. D. Ryan (Eds.), *Adolescent sex offenders: Issues in research and treatment* (pp. 109–129). Rockville, MD: Department of Health and Human Services.

Becker, J. V., & Kaplan, M. S. (1993). Cognitive behavioral treatment of the juvenile sex offender. In H. E. Barbaree, W. L. Marshall, & S. M. Hudson (Eds.), *The juvenile sex offender* (pp. 264–277). New York: Guilford.

Becker, J. V., Kaplan, M. S., Cunningham-Rathner, J., & Kavoussi, R. J. (1986). Characteristics of adolescent incest sexual perpetrators: Preliminary findings. *Journal of Family Violence, 1*, 85–97.

Becker, J. V., Kaplan, M. S., & Tenke, C. E. (1992). The relationship of abuse history, denial, and erectile response: Profiles of adolescent perpetrators. *Behavior Therapy*, *23*, 87–97.

Beech, A., & Fordham, A. S. (1997). Therapeutic climate of sexual offender treatment programs. *Sexual Abuse: A Journal of Research and Treatment*, *9*, 219–237.

Bentovim, A., & Williams, B. (1998). Children and adolescents: Victims who become perpetrators. *Advances in Psychiatric Treatment*, *4*, 101–107.

Brown, E. J., Flanagan, T. J., & McLeod, M. (1984). *Sourcebook of criminal justice statistics—1983*. Washington, DC: Bureau of Justice Statistics.

Cavanagh-Johnson, T. (1998). Children who molest. In W. L. Marshall, Y. M. Fernandez, S. M. Hudson, & T. Ward (Eds.), *Sourcebook of treatment programs for sexual offenders* (pp. 337–351). New York: Plenum.

Cellini, H. R. (1995). Assessment and treatment of the adolescent offender. In B. K. Schwartz & H. R. Cellini (Eds.), *The sex offender: Corrections, treatment and legal practice* (pp. 6.1–6.12). Kingston, NJ: Civic Research Institute.

Davis, G., & Leitenberg, H. (1987). Adolescent sex offenders. *Psychological Bulletin*, *101*, 417–427.

Deisher, R. W., Wenet, G. A., Paperny, D. M., Clark, T. F., & Fehrenback, P. A. (1982). Adolescent sexual offense behavior: The role of the physician. *Journal of Adolescent Health Care*, *2*, 279–286.

Dougher, M. J. (1995). Clinical assessment of sex offenders. In B. K. Schwartz & H. R. Cellini (Eds.), *The sex offender: Corrections, treatment, and legal practice* (pp. 11.1–11.13). Kingston, NJ: Civic Research Institute.

Fehrenback, P. A., Smith, W., Monastersky, C., & Deisher, R. (1986). Adolescent sexual offenders: Offender and offense characteristics. *American Journal of Orthopsychiatry*, *56*, 225–233.

Finklehor, D., Hotalling, G., Lewis, I., & Smith, C. (1989). Sexual abuse and its relationship to later sexual satisfaction, marital status, religion and attitudes. *Journal of Interpersonal Violence*, *4*, 379–399.

France, K. G., & Hudson, S. M. (1993). The conduct disorders and the juvenile sex offender. In H. E. Barbaree, W. L. Marshall, & S. M. Hudson (Eds.), *The juvenile sex offender* (pp. 225–234). New York: Guilford.

Gavey, N. (1991). Sexual victimizaton prevalence among New Zealand university students. *Journal of Consulting and Clinical Psychology*, *59*, 464–466.

Graham, F., Richardson, G., & Bhate, S. R. (1998). Development of a service for sexually abusive adolescents in the northeast of England. In W. L. Marshall, Y. M. Fernandez, S. M. Hudson, & T. Ward (Eds.), *Source book of treatment programs for sexual offenders* (pp. 367–382). New York: Plenum.

Gray, A. S., & Pithers, W. D. (1993). Relapse prevention with sexually aggressive adolescents and children: Expanding treatment and supervision. In H. E. Barbaree, W. L. Marshall, & S. M. Hudson (Eds.), *The juvenile sex offender* (pp. 289–320). New York: Guilford.

Hanson, R. K., Cox, B., & Woszczyna, C. (1991). Assessing treatment outcome for sexual offenders. *Annals of Sex Research*, *4*, 177–208.

Hudson, S. M., Wales, D. S., & Ward, S. M. (1998). Kia marama: A treatment program for child molesters in New Zealand. In W. L. Marshall, Y. M. Fernandez, S. M. Hudson, & T. Ward (Eds.), *Source book of treatment programs for sexual offenders* (pp. 17–28). New York: Plenum.

Hudson, S. M., & Ward, T. (1997a). Intimacy, loneliness, and attachment style in sexual offenders. *Journal of Interpersonal Violence*, *12*, 323–339.

Hudson, S. M., & Ward, T. (1997b). Rape: Psychopathology and theory. In D. R. Laws & W. O'Donohue (Eds.), *Sexual deviance: Theory assessment and treatment* (pp. 332–335). New York: Guilford.

Hudson, S. M., & Ward, T. (1997c). Future directions. In D. R. Laws & W. O'Donohue (Eds.), *Sexual deviance: Theory assessment and treatment* (pp. 481–500). New York: Guilford.

Hudson, S. M., & Ward, T. (in press). Interpersonal competency in sexual offenders. *Behavior Modification*.

Hunter, J. A., Goodwin, D. W., & Becker, J. V. (1994). The relationship between phallometrically measured deviant sexual arousal and clinical characteristics in juvenile sexual offenders. *Behaviour Research and Therapy, 32*, 533–538.

Jenkins (1990). *Invitations to responsibility*. Adelaide, Australia: Dulwich Centre.

Jenkins, A. (1998). Invitations to responsibility: Engaging adolescents and young men who have abused. In W. L. Marshall, Y. M. Fernandez, S. M. Hudson, & T. Ward (Eds.), *Source book of treatment programs for sexual offenders* (pp. 163–189). New York: Plenum.

Kaemingk, K. L., Koselka, M., Becker, J. V., & Kaplan, M. S. (1995). Age and adolescent sexual offender arousal. *Sexual Abuse: A Journal of Research and Treatment, 7*, 249–257.

Koss, M. P., Gidycz, C. A., & Wisniewski, N. (1987). The scope of rape: Incidence and prevalence of sexual aggression and victimization in a national sample of higher education students. *Journal of Consulting and Clinical Psychology, 55*, 162–170.

Lane, S. (1997). The sexual abuse cycle. In G. Ryan & S. Lane (Eds.), *Juvenile sexual offending* (pp. 77–121). San Francisco, CA: Jossey-Bass.

Laws, D. R., & Marshall, W. L. (1990). A conditioning theory of the etiology and maintenance of deviant sexual preference and behavior. In W. L. Marshall, D. R. Laws, & H. E. Barbaree (Eds.), *Handbook of sexual assault: Issues, theories, and treatment of the offender* (pp. 209–229). New York: Plenum.

Longo, R. E., & Groth, A. N. (1982). Juvenile sexual offenses in the histories of adult rapists and child molesters. *International Journal of Offender Therapy and Comparative Criminology, 27*, 150–155.

Marshall, W. L. (1989). Invited essay: Intimacy, loneliness, and sexual offenders. *Behaviour Research and Therapy, 11*, 557–564.

Marshall, W. L., & Barabaree, H. E. (1989). Sexual violence. In K. Howells & C. R. Hollin (Eds.), *Clinical approaches to violence* (pp. 205–246). New York: Wiley.

Marshall, W. L., & Barabaree, H. E. (1990). An integrated theory of the etiology of sexual offending. In W. L. Marshall, D. R. Laws, & H. E. Barbaree (Eds.), *Handbook of sexual assault: Issues, theories, and treatment of the offender* (pp. 343–361). New York: Plenum.

Marshall, W. L., & Eccles, A. (1993). Pavlovian conditioning processes in adolescent offenders. In H. E. Barbaree, W. L. Marshall, & S. M. Hudson (Eds.), *The juvenile sex offender* (pp. 118–142). New York: Guilford.

Marshall, W. L., Hudson, S. M., & Hodkinson, S. (1993). The importance of attachment bonds in the development of juvenile offending. In H. E. Barbaree, W. L. Marshall, & S. M. Hudson (Eds.), *The juvenile sex offender* (pp. 164–181). New York: Guilford.

Marshall, W. L., Hudson, S. M., Jones, R. L., & Fernandez, Y. M. (1995). Empathy in sex offenders. *Clinical Psychology Review, 15*, 99–113.

McGrath, R. J. (1991). Sex offender risk assessment and disposition planning: A review of the empirical and clinical findings. *International Journal of Offender Therapy and Comparative Criminology, 35*, 328–350.

Prenkty, R. A., & Knight, R. A. (1993). Age of onset of sexual assault: Criminal and life history correlates. In G. C. N. Hall, R. Hirschman, J. R. Graham, & M. S. Zaragoza (Eds.), *Sexual aggression: Issues in etiology, assessment, and treatment* (pp. 43–62). Washington, DC: Taylor & Francis.

Reed, J. (1992). *Review of health and social services for mentally disordered offenders and others requiring similar services*. Report of the official working group on services for young people with special needs. London: Home Office, Department of Health.

Rubinstein, M., Yeager, C. A., Goodstein, C., & Lewis, D. O. (1993). Sexually assaultive male juvenile: A follow-up. *American Journal of Psychiatry, 150*, 262–265.

Ryan, G. (1997). Sexually abusive youth: Defining the population. In G. Ryan & S. Lane (Eds.), *Juvenile sexual offending: Causes, consequences, and correction* (pp. 3–9). San Francisco, CA: Jossey-Bass.

Ryan, G., & Lane, S. (1997). Integrating theory and method. In G. Ryan & S. Lane (Eds.),

Juvenile sexual offending: Causes, consequences, and correction (pp. 267–391). San Francisco, CA: Jossey-Bass.

Ryan, G., Lane, S., Davis, J., & Isaac, C. (1987). Juvenile sexual offenders: Development and correction. *Child Abuse & Neglect, 3,* 385–395.

Ward, T. (in press). Sexual offenders cognitive distortions as implicit theories.

Ward, T., & Hudson, S. M. (1996). Relapse prevention: A critical analysis. *Sexual Abuse: A Journal of Research and Treatment, 8,* 177–200.

Ward, T., & Hudson, S. M. (1998a). The construction and development of theory in the sexual offending area: A metatheoretical framework. *Sexual Abuse: A Journal of Research and Treatment, 10,* 47–63.

Ward, T., & Hudson, S. M. (1998b). A model of the relapse process in sexual offenders. *Journal of Interpersonal Violence, 13,* 700–725.

Ward, T., Hudson, S. M., & Marshall, W. L. (1996). Attachment style in sex offenders: A preliminary study. *Journal of Sex Research, 33,* 431–437.

Ward, T., Hudson, S. M., Marshall, W. L., & Siegert, R. J. (1995). Attachment style and intimacy deficits in sexual offenders: A theoretical framework. *Sexual Abuse: A Journal of Research and Treatment, 7,* 317–334.

Ward, T., Louden, K., Hudson, S. M., & Marshall, W. L. (1995). A descriptive model of the offense chain in child molesters. *Journal of Interpersonal Violence, 10,* 452–472.

White, M. (1995). *Re-authoring lives.* Adelaide, Australia: Dulwich Centre.

Worling, J. R. (1998). Adolescent sexual offender treatment at the SAFE-T program. In W. L. Marshall, Y. M. Fernandez, S. M. Hudson, & T. Ward (Eds.), *Source book of treatment programs for sexual offenders* (pp. 353–365). New York: Plenum.

Chapter 25

Criminal Justice Programmes for Men Who Assault Their Partners

Russell P. Dobash
and
R. Emerson Dobash
University of Manchester, Manchester, UK

THE EMERGENCE OF ABUSER PROGRAMMES

The problem of "wife abuse" or men's use of violence against an intimate partner was initially brought to wide-scale public attention by the women's movement in Britain and the United States in the early 1970s (Dobash & Dobash, 1979). It is now acknowledged to be a world-wide problem warranting explicit attention at the 1995 United Nations Conference in Beijing. Within a few years of the discovery of "battered wives" and the establishment of refuges in Britain, North America, several European countries, Australia, New Zealand and elsewhere, programmes for abusers began to appear in the United States (Dobash & Dobash, 1992). Today, there are hundreds of such programmes delivering direct forms of intervention to men who violently abuse intimate partners. Some are voluntary in nature while others are attached to the justice system usually through probation orders for offenders.

Abuser programmes developed in several different ways. Most emerged through the influence of the battered women's movement with its analysis of battering as related to issues of gender and power. Some of these programmes were staffed by women who had worked in women's shelters and had come to recognize that there was a need to respond to the men who perpetrated violence against their partners. One of the best known is the Duluth Domestic Abuse

Handbook of Offender Assessment and Treatment. Edited by C. R. Hollin.

Intervention Project (DAIP), located in Minnesota, USA, and founded in 1980 by Ellen Pence and Michael Paymar (Pence & Paymar, 1993). Others were created by men's organizations who were in philosophical agreement with the women's groups and began programmes to challenge these offenders. EMERGE, established in Boston in 1977, was the first of this kind, and ManAlive of Marin, California, is another well-known "men only" group (Adams, 1988; Sinclair, 1989). A few therapists have developed influential programmes that combine feminist insights with more traditional approaches to offenders (Ganley, 1981). These pioneering programmes have served as models for the development of scores of abuser programmes in many countries including Britain. Two Scottish programmes, CHANGE (established in 1989) and the Lothian Domestic Violence Probation Project (established in 1990), were strongly influenced by these models and were the first criminal justice based programmes for abusers to be established in Britain or in any European country (Dobash, Dobash, Cavanagh, & Lewis, 1995; Morran & Wilson, 1997). Other abuser programmes have developed within the context of more orthodox forms of psychotherapy, casework, and probation. Overall, the prevailing approach in most programmes combines a mixture of feminist knowledge with cognitive–behavioural methods and the vast majority of programmes are educational rather than psychodynamic in orientation.

PROGRAMMES FOR ABUSERS AND FORMS OF INTERVENTION

While in practice there is considerable overlap between many of the existing programmes in terms of general philosophy and techniques of intervention, it is possible to consider them separately in order to examine those aspects that characterize the different approaches. The terms "pro-feminist" and "cognitive–behavioural" are often used with respect to the same programmes. When combined, the terms usually reflect a common view about the nature of the problem as generated within a context of gender relations, socialization and learning, and an orientation to treatment that focuses on changing behaviour and ways of thinking. The general orientation is one in which men who use violence against a woman partner are deemed to be acting within a culturally constructed context of relationships between "husbands" and "wives" in which the man has greater power and authority over the woman and violence is used to control and punish. Violence is seen as intentional behaviour, usually occurring against a background of intimidation, coercion, and other forms of controlling behaviour. Violence is learned behaviour and is chosen as a resource in settling conflicts and disputes and as a means of maintaining authority (Adams, 1988; Pence & Paymar, 1993). The issues in dispute typically involve sexual jealousy, the man's sense of ownership of the woman (proprietariness), domestic labour including housework and child care, the distribution and use of household resources including money, mobility and time as well as contests over power, control and authority (Dobash

& Dobash, 1998). Offenders are deemed to be highly self-oriented, lack empathy, and frequently deny responsibility, minimize the harm done, and deflect blame onto others, particularly the woman.

The basic approach to intervention focuses on learning new attitudes and orientations toward women, particularly wives or intimate partners, and learning new forms of behaviour and ways of responding to conflicts of interest and disputes between partners (Ptacek, 1988; Pence & Paymar, 1993; Morran & Wilson, 1997). A primary focus is on the violence and associated behaviours. The violent event is often "dissected" in great detail as men begin to see stages in its development from the initial source of conflict through to the violent attack as decisions and choices are made at each stage that may escalate into violence. Group work is the preferred approach rather than individual therapy. Within the context of the group, men are challenged to accept responsibility for their violent behaviour, for the harm done to others, and for their need to change their own behaviour and attitudes. Accepting responsibility for their own behaviour and acknowledging the consequences of their violence are deemed to be essential starting points. Within this pro-feminist framework, it is argued that if men do not accept responsibility for their own acts, then they will see no need for change. If they do not see such acts as serious or consequential, then they will have no need to change. In short, if men are not motivated to change or cannot be brought to that point, then it is impossible for change to occur.

Techniques for changing behaviours and cognitions include focusing on issues of conflict, reconstructing violent events, thinking within the context of action, and identifying how one's behaviour is related to others. Abuser programmes are highly structured, didactic, or educational in approach and involve skills training and behavioural re-enactments. Men learn to monitor their own behaviour and orientations through the use of various techniques including daily homework completed between group sessions which is reported back to the group and forms a part of its work (Pence & Paymar, 1993; Morran & Wilson, 1997).

Some programmes adopt a cognitive–behavioural approach to learning new behaviours and cognitions but do so without using the feminist analysis of the phenomenon of violence with its focus on power and gender relations. For example, some anger management programmes emphasize the control of emotions and learning of specific techniques for dealing with anger once aroused but do so without considering the issues that give rise to the anger itself. With such an approach, the anger is de-contextualized and one of its principal sources, gender relations, need not be addressed (Gondolf, 1985).

Within an "insight" or psychodynamic approach, there is a diversity of models and treatment interventions. One of the main assumptions within such psychodynamic approaches is that violence is caused by childhood trauma such as the witnessing and/or experiencing of abuse, and anger about these traumas results in attachment disorders that are displaced onto adult relationships (Saunders, 1996). Uncontrolled anger resulting from unresolved conflicts with parents may, for example, result in "displacement of anger and aggression onto the most convenient targets in his life", e.g. wife or girlfriend (Schlesinger, Benson, & Zornitzer, 1982). These approaches attempt to create relatively unstructured, non-didactic group relationships (Jennings, 1987). Within a supportive environment, men are meant to re-experience childhood traumas and thereby grieve for them and overcome the trauma through such insight. The focus of treatment includes discussions of childhood loss and rejections, experience with violence, and emotional safety in the group. Focus on the distant past is prominent in this sort of intervention which is markedly different from the work conducted in cognitive–behavioural programmes (Saunders, 1996).

More recent efforts, particularly those associated with the work of clinical psychologists, have been aimed at assessing the supposed psychological disorders of violent offenders. Using traditional psychometric measures such as the Millon Clinical Multiaxial Inventory (MCMI), the Beck Depression Inventory (BDI), and the Novaco Anger Scale (NAS), therapists attempt to differentiate violent from non-violent men and to create typologies of offenders based on psychological disorders (Hamberger, Lohr, Bonge, & Tolin, 1996) which are, in turn, meant to be used in the context of intervention. However, the relationships among personality disorders, violent behaviour, and treatment modalities are not always direct or clear. Additionally, some psychometric and many psychodynamic approaches have been criticized for failing to deal directly with issues of the man's responsibility for his own violent behaviour and for not considering wider socio-cultural issues such as power and gender (Adams, 1988; Dobash & Dobash, 1992; Holtzworth-Munroe & Saunders, 1996; Saunders, 1996).

There are concerns and controversies with respect to each approach. Profeminists programmes explicitly focus on issues of women's safety and express concern that other approaches do not. They also focus on issues of power and gender as primary factors leading to violence and are concerned about approaches that ignore these wider dynamics in favour of a more narrow focus limited solely to issues such as anger and its control. There is also a concern about who delivers abuser programmes and about the possibility of collusion between male programme staff and men who use violence (Hart, 1988). Representatives of the justice system who would use abuser programmes as a sentencing option express concern that programmes should have an effect on the offending behaviour, that they should be clearly structured, men's behaviour should be monitored, and information about their progress should be provided to the court and probation. Those who operate programmes with a more psychodynamic approach express concern about other approaches that foreground the violence and challenge men's behaviour fearing that such an approach will not create a supportive environment in which childhood trauma can be explored. Still others are concerned about focusing exclusively on the offender and his behaviour rather than on the couple.

EVALUATIONS OF ABUSER PROGRAMMES

There have been a number of attempts to assess the effects of participation on an abuser programme and several reviews have summarized Canadian and

American research (Eisikovits & Edleson, 1989; Burns, Meredith, & Paquette, 1991; Gondolf, 1996). In general, the research shows that abuser programmes do have some impact on the reoccurrence of violent behaviour and that 50%–80% of programme participants remain violence-free for up to a year or more after the intervention (Bersani, Chen, & Denton, 1988; Chen, Bersani, Myers, & Denton, 1989; Dutton, 1986, 1995; Edleson & Grusznski, 1988; Edleson & Syers, 1990; Gondolf, 1988; 1996; Hamm & Kite, 1991; Harrell, 1991; Saunders, 1996; Saunders & Hanusa, 1986; Tolman & Bennett, 1990). The vast majority of existing evaluations have assessed men who have volunteered to participate on an abuser programme rather than men who have been court mandated. Here, we will discuss examples of some of the very few studies that have examined the effectiveness of abuser programmes operating within the justice system with men participating as a condition of probation (Chen et al., 1989; Hamm & Kite, 1991; Dutton, 1995; Dobash, Dobash, Cavanagh, & Lewis, 1995, 1999a).

Hamm and Kite (1991) conducted a quasi-experimental study of 166 men all of whom were on probation and participated in a mandatory batterers anonymous programme. The programme included 10 weekly sessions held in the local jail and used a cognitive–behavioural approach. Two comparison groups were established, comprised of men who were defined as a "good risk" (i.e. no prior record of a police call to the residence) and those who were defined as a "poor risk" (i.e. at least one prior police call to the residence). The only indicator of success or failure was that of re-arrest. It was found that 80% of the 166 men in the study had not been re-arrested after 54 months. Of those defined as a "poor risk", 34% were re-arrested during the follow-up period while only 8% of the "good risk" category had a subsequent arrest during the same period. Failure came fairly quickly during the follow-up period, usually within the first six months (Hamm & Kite, 1991).

Dutton (1995) assessed the impact of a four-month, court mandated, cognitive–behavioural programme with weekly group sessions. Using the arrest records and self-reports of men who had been convicted of "wife assault" and reports of women partners, he compared 50 men in the abuser programme with 50 "untreated" men. The follow-up period varied from six months to three years. Using police data, he found that the recidivism rate within six months was 16% for "untreated" men and 4% for "treated" men; the recidivism rate within two and one-half years was 40% and 4%, respectively. Using data from self-reports of a sub-sample of men and of women partners from the "treated" group, he found that levels of violence and verbal aggression dropped after the completion of the programme. Dutton's findings further suggest that the "surveillance" associated with a probation order is a "useful means of diminishing the rate of wife assault with men who have something to lose from another assault conviction" (1995, p. 275).

Dobash et al. (1995, 1999a, 1999b) undertook a non-equivalent control group study with a total sample of 256 men and women. This included 122 men who had been found guilty of an offence in which violence had been used against a woman partner and 134 women partners of abusive men processed through the courts. The sample contained 95 intact couples. All cases included in the study had been processed through the justice system and resulted in a conviction. For the purposes of the research, two groups were compared: those on the abuser programme and those receiving other forms of intervention from the justice system. Men receiving mandatory treatment on an abuser programme had weekly sessions for a six-month period which were highly structured and used a pro-feminist, cognitive–behavioural approach. The comparison group contained men who received all other forms of sentence (e.g. fine, probation, prison). Women partners were similarly categorized. Men and women partners were studied at three points during a one-year period: at intervention, three months after initial contact, and one year after initial contact. At Time One, men and women partners were interviewed in-depth. At Times Two and Three, they were sent postal questionnaires.

Standardized, validated measurements were used to obtain data about violence, controlling behaviours, injuries, and quality of life in order to study changes in these factors before and after intervention (Violence Assessment Index, VAI; Injury Assessment Index, IAI; Controlling Behaviour Index, CBI; Quality of Life Index, QLI) (Dobash et al., 1999b). Using the reports of women partners, the findings show that after one year 66% of those men who completed the abuser programme remained violence-free compared with only 25% of the men who received other sanctions from the justice system. In addition, programme men also reduced their use of other forms of intimidation and controlling behaviour. Women partners of men in the programme group were more likely than those in the other group to report an improvement in their quality of life and sense of well-being and personal safety.

Although the small body of research on court-mandated abuser programmes, like all research, is not without its limitations and methodological problems, the findings are encouraging for those who would intervene with men who perpetrate this form of violence.

ISSUES IN EVALUATION RESEARCH

Evaluations of abuser programmes have gone through several stages of development in recent years beginning with assessments by programme staff of the "effectiveness" of their own programmes and/or of staff satisfaction (Pirog-Good & Stets, 1986). It is essential that evaluation research in this area includes a consideration of the issue or "phenomenon" meant to be addressed by the intervention (e.g. violence and other coercive behaviour) and that this outcome is related to the form of intervention. "Outcome" measures limited to "course completion" by clients and/or "staff satisfaction", while relevant with respect to those particular issues, do not constitute an assessment of the impact of any form of intervention upon the subsequent use of violence. While staff satisfaction and programme completion are certainly important, they are more properly defined as monitoring and do not provide evidence for judging the effects of the intervention upon the phenomenon of concern. This requires a research design and measurement tools that can directly address questions about the effect of the intervention upon violent behaviour and orientations, about which aspects of the intervention are most successful in changing behaviour and orientations, and about the sustainability of any observed changes over a period of time. Thus, a valid evaluation needs to identify the nature and extent of any effects of the intervention, to delineate the processes whereby such outcomes are achieved, and to examine the sustainability of changes over a period of time.

More recently, some studies have employed quasi-experimental or randomized experimental designs to examine the effectiveness of programmes in changing subsequent violent behaviour (for reviews of this research, see Edleson & Grusznski, 1988; Edleson & Syers, 1990; Dobash et al., 1995; Dutton, 1995; Gondolf, 1996; Saunders, 1996). Despite the more rigorous nature of these approaches, limitations and problems in implementation still remain and include: small sample sizes, lack of comparison groups, absence of pre-testing of violent behaviour, reliance on official data such as arrest and/or self-reports of offenders as the sole indicator of the reoccurrence of violence, no period of follow-up or relatively short periods of follow-up, and others. With respect to evaluations of criminal-justice-based abuser programmes, some of the quasi-experimental designs have failed to examine the issue of potential selection bias that might be introduced because of the nature of processing offenders through the justice system (i.e. selective arrest, prosecution, and/or sentencing). In addition, all studies that aim to examine the re-reoccurrence of violence within a given relationship need to attend to the issue of "separation effects" (i.e. the woman who has left the relationship) in order properly to consider whether the woman remained at risk of further violence. This is not to say that divorced or separated women are not necessarily at risk of subsequent violence since some men may continue to follow or harass them after separation; however, it is necessary to consider whether there is a continued risk.

Although randomized designs are not common in this area of study (cf. Harrell, 1991), some researchers express support for this approach as a means of dealing with the problems of selection bias (Saunders, 1996). At the same time, other researchers have raised pragmatic and ethical concerns about the use of randomized designs. The use of randomized designs to evaluate the outcome of an intervention requires the random allocation of the type of intervention (e.g. men's programme, arrest only, fine, traditional probation, prison, etc.) on the basis of chance with some individuals allocated to a *treatment* group (e.g. men's programme) with others assigned to a *control* group (other criminal justice responses). For a classic statement of this approach, see Campbell and Stanley (1963). At the practical and ethical levels, there are several issues to be considered. Practical issues include the willingness of judges, magistrates, and probation officers to assign a sanction based on random procedures set by researchers rather than in accordance with their own judgement. Even if agreed in principle, it is difficult to maintain such designs in the field as practitioners and professionals often are unwilling or unable to adhere to such strict allocation procedures. Following this, it is often difficult for the researcher who may be somewhat distanced from these processes to know whether the strict rules of allocation necessary for the design have been implemented in the field. At the practical level of incorporating findings from research into intervention programmes, it is necessary to have specific and detailed information concerning the content of programmes and what may or may not have had an effect on the outcome. Randomized designs usually rely solely on outcome measures (i.e. a reduction or elimination of violence) and do not examine the processes whereby these outcomes have been achieved. The lack of specific information about the processes that lead to the outcome means that those who would use the findings of research to help build abuser programmes have little information that can be brought to that purpose (Pawson & Tilly, 1996).

One of the main ethical issues of random assignment involves that of informed consent. That is, it is the responsibility of researchers to inform the "participants" that they are involved in an experimental field trial and of the possible implications for them. It is also necessary to obtain their explicit consent. Additionally, in this area of study, it is essential to ask from whom consent is to be obtained? The abuser, the victim, or both? While the consent of women partners may not be sought and they may not be informed either of the experiment or of its possible implications for themselves and their children, they nonetheless have a stake in the process and its outcome. Here, the safety of women is an important issue for consideration. These concerns about ethics and procedures have not usually been addressed in research on abuser programmes although there are some examples of research designs that have considered these ethical issues (Dobash et al., 1999a, 1999b; Hamm & Kite, 1991). Dutton has raised another ethical and practical issue concerning the use of random assignment of offenders stating that ". . . withholding treatment for men who need it because they fall by chance into a 'control group' . . . may be featured by the man's defence lawyer should he re-offend" (1995, p. 279). Overall, the issues of the adequacy of research design and the validity and utility of findings will continue to be of importance and the subject of debate in this field of study as in all others where evidence-based policy and practice are important (for the debate about evaluations of programmes for sex offenders, see Marshall, Jones, Ward, & Johnston, 1991, and McPherson, Chein, Maren, & Swenson, 1994).

CONCLUSIONS

Prior to the 1970s, men who used violence against a wife or intimate partner were not usually considered to be offenders or treated as such. While they sometimes came to the attention of the police, they were rarely prosecuted or sanctioned. Instead, this form of violence was deemed to be a private matter and not one of concern to the state or the justice system, and those who perpetrated it were not usually the subject of official concern. Since then, the problem of "domestic violence" or wife abuse has been recognized throughout most of the world as a serious problem which affects a substantial proportion of the population and one that can no longer be left within the private domain. Initial concern was focused on abused women and their need for safety and accommodation, and this has continued and expanded, although there is still need for further resources and development. This has involved the strengthening of protection orders in order to enhance women's safety and the provision of refuges in order to provide temporary accommodation. In the early stages of recognition of the problem, little attention was paid to the perpetrators of this violence. This began to change, particularly in the United States, as various groups began to develop specialized programmes for abusers. The programme that set the scene for much of the subsequent development was the "Duluth" model with its pro-feminist, cognitive–behavioural, educational approach that focuses on the man, the violence, the man's responsibility for the violence, and the man's need to change. This model is based on the idea that violence is used within a context of power and control and involves men's beliefs about women and intimate relationships with them. These factors are explicitly addressed in the programmes for abusers. Increasingly, abuser programmes are being linked to the justice system, usually as a sanction attached to a probation order. In this way, the positive response to addressing the problem of continued violence usually involves some form of surveillance and control, necessary if men are to enter a programme and remain until it is completed, along with "treatment" focused on the violence and its elimination. While only a few valid evaluations of such interventions have now been completed, the results suggest that an intervention combining a criminal justice sanction with a cognitive–behavioural programme focused on the offence and the offending behaviour is more successful than other sanctions at eliminating subsequent violence, and that such changes are more likely to be sustained over a longer period of time.

REFERENCES

Adams, D. (1988). Treatment models for men who batter: A pro-feminist analysis. In K. Yllo & M. Bogard (Eds.), *Feminist perspectives on wife abuse* (pp. 176–199). Beverly Hills, CA: Sage.

Bersani, C., Chen, H. J., & Denton, R. (1988). Spouse abusers and court-mandated treatment, *Crime and Justice, 11*, 43–59.

Burns, N., Meredith, C., & Paquette, C. (1991). *Treatment programs for men who batter: A review of the evidence of their success*. Ontario, Canada: Abt Associates of Canada.

Campbell, D. T., & Stanley, J. C. (1963). *Experimental and quasi-experimental designs for research*. London: Houghton Mifflin.

Chen, H. T., Bersani, C., Myers, S. C., & Denton, R. (1989). Evaluating the effectiveness of a court-sponsored abuser treatment programme. *Journal of Family Violence, 4*, 309–322.

Dobash, R. E., & Dobash, R. P. (1979). *Violence against wives*. New York: The Free Press.

Dobash, R. E., & Dobash, R. P. (1992). *Women, violence and social change*. London: Routledge.

Dobash, R. E., & Dobash, R. P. (1998). Violent men and violent contexts. In R. E. Dobash & R. P. Dobash (Eds.), *Rethinking violence against women* (pp. 141–168). Newbury Park, CA: Sage.

Dobash, R. P., Dobash, R. E., Cavanagh, K., & Lewis, R. (1995). Evaluating programmes for violent men: Can violent men change? In R. E. Dobash, R. P. Dobash, & L. Noaks (Eds.), *Gender and crime* (pp. 358–389). Cardiff: University of Wales Press; Concord, MA: Paul.

Dobash, R. P., Dobash, R. E., Cavanagh, K., & Lewis, R. (1999a). A research evaluation of British programmes for violent men. *Journal of Social Policy*, *28*(2), 205–233.

Dobash, R. P., Dobash, R. E., Cavanagh, K., & Lewis, R. (1999b). *Changing violent men*, Thousand Oaks, CA: Sage.

Dutton, D. G. (1986). The outcome of court-mandated treatment for wife assault: A quasi-experimental evaluation. *Violence and Victims*, *1*, 163–175.

Dutton, D. G. (1995). *The domestic assault of women: Psychological and criminal justice perspectives*. Vancouver, Canada: UBC Press.

Edleson, J. L., & Grusznski, R. J. (1988). Treating men who batter: Four years of outcome data from a domestic abuse project. *Journal of Social Service Research*, *12*, 3–22.

Edleson, J. L., & Syers, M. (1990). Relative effectiveness of group treatments for men who batter. *Social Work Research & Abstracts*, *26*, 10–17.

Eisikovits, Z., & Edleson, J. (1989). Intervening with men who batter: A critical review of the literature. *Social Science Review*, *37*(3), 385–414.

Ganley, A. L. (1981). *Participant's manual: Court-mandated therapy for men who batter—A three day workshop for professionals*. Washington, DC: Center for Women Policy Studies.

Gondolf, E. W. (1985). Anger and oppression in men who batter: Empiricist and feminist perspectives and their implications for research. *Victimology*, *10*, 311–324.

Gondolf, E. W. (1988). The effects of batterer counselling on shelter outcome. *Journal of Interpersonal Violence*, *3*, 275–289.

Gondolf, E. W. (1996). Batterer programs. What we know and need to know. *Journal of Interpersonal Violence*, *12*(1), 83–98.

Hamberger, L. K., Lohr, J. M., Bonge, D., & Tolin, D. F. (1996). A large sample empirical typology of male spouse abusers and its relationship to dimensions of abuse. *Violence and Victims*, *11*(4), 277–292.

Hamm, M. S., & Kite, J. C. (1991). The role of offender rehabilitation in family violence policy: The batterers anonymous experiment. *Criminal Justice Review*, *16*(2), 227–248.

Harrell, A. (1991). *Evaluation of court-ordered treatment for domestic violence offenders* (Final Report). Washington, DC: Urban Institute.

Hart, B. (1988). *Safety for women: Monitoring the batterers' programs*. Harrisburg, PA: Pennsylvania Coalition Against Domestic Violence.

Holtzworth-Munroe, A., & Saunders, D. G. (1996). Men who batter: Recent history and research. *Violence and Victims*, *11*(4), 273–276.

Jennings, J. L. (1987). History and issues in the treatment of battering men. A case for unstructured group therapy. *Journal of Family Violence*, *2*, 193–214.

Marshall, W. L., Jones, R., Ward, T., & Johnston, P. (1991). Treatment outcomes with sex offenders. *Clinical Psychology Review*, *11*, 465–485.

McPherson, M., Chein, D., Maren, V., & Swenson, D. (1994). *Sex offender treatment programs*. St. Paul, MN: State of Minnesota, Office of the Legislative Auditor, Program Evaluation Division.

Morran, D., & Wilson, M. (1997). *Men who are violent to women: A groupwork practice manual*. Lyme Regis, UK: Russell House.

Pawson, R., & Tilly, J. (1996). *Realistic evaluations*. London: Sage.

Pence, E., & Paymar, M. (1993). *Education groups for men who batter*. New York: Springer.

Pirog-Good, M. A., & Stets, J. (1986). Male batterers and battering prevention programs: A national survey. *RESPONSE (to Violence in the Family and Sexual Assault)*, *8*, 8–12.

Ptacek, J. (1988). Why do men batter their wives? In K. Yllo & M. Bogard (Eds.), *Feminist perspectives on wife abuse* (pp. 133–157). Beverly Hills, CA: Sage.

Saunders, D. G. (1996). Feminist–cognitive–behavioral and process–psychodynamic treat-ments for men who batter: Interaction of abuser traits and treatment models. *Violence and Victims, 11*(4), 393–413.

Saunders, D. G., & Hanusa, D. (1986). Cognitive–behavioral treatment for men who batter: The short-term effects of group therapy. *Journal of Family Violence, 1,* 357–372.

Schlesinger, L. B., Benson, M., & Zornitzer, M. (1982). Classification of violent behavior for the purposes of treatment planning: A three-pronged approach. In M. Roy (Ed.), *The abusive partner: An analysis of domestic battering* (pp. 148–169). New York: Van Nostrand Reinhold.

Sinclair, H. (1989). *Manalive: An accountable advocacy batterer intervention program.* Marin County, CA: Marin Abused Women's Services.

Tolman, R. M., & Bennett, L. W. (1990). A review of quantitative research on men who batter. *Journal of Interpersonal Violence, 5,* 87–118.

Chapter 26

Firesetters

David J. Kolko
University of Pittsburgh, School of Medicine; Western Psychiatric Institute and Clinic, Pittsburgh, USA

SIGNIFICANCE OF THE PROBLEM

Children and youth account for a significant proportion of the fires set in the United States. On the basis of figures reported by the National Fire Protection Association (NFPA), children playing with fire committed 98 410 fires that were reported to US fire departments, causing an estimated 408 civilian deaths, 3130 civilian injuries, and millions of dollars in property damages (see Hall, 1995; National Fire Protection Association, 1995). Fireplay was the leading cause of death among preschoolers. Child victims who survive may suffer burn trauma and its serious medical (e.g. hospitalization) and psychological (e.g. post-traumatic stress, depression) sequelae (see Cella, Perry, Kulchycky, & Goodwin, 1988; Stoddard, Norman, Murphy, & Beardslee, 1989). Other significant consequences of firesetting include an arrest for arson. In fact, juvenile firesetters accounted for a majority of the arrests for arson in this country in 1994, making arson the only crime to have had a higher proportion of juvenile than adult involvement (US Federal Bureau of Investigations, 1995).

PREVALENCE AND RECIDIVISM

Prevalence rates have been reported in a small number of samples from medium to large-sized cities. In a large community survey conducted in Rochester, New York, 38% of the 770 children (ages 6–14 years) surveyed reported ever having played with fire and 14% reported fireplay since the school year began (Grolnick, Cole, Laurenitis, & Schwartzman, 1990; Kafry, 1980). Older children reported the highest percentage of recent fireplay within the past six months (23).

Handbook of Offender Assessment and Treatment. Edited by C. R. Hollin.
© 2000 John Wiley & Sons Ltd.

In addition to child age, access to fire-related materials, expectations of no parental response, and fire responsibility predicted the children's involvement in fireplay. A study of 736 children in Lund, Sweden, found that 255 (35%) reported playing with fire "fairly often" and 50 children (7%) played "often or quite often" (Terjestam & Ryden, 1996). Here, too, the number of children who played with fire increased five-fold from grades 1–3 to 7–9. Developmental competence deserves further consideration as a construct that may help to determine the level of a child's involvement with fire, which may be related to variables that reflect both antecedents and consequences of firesetting involvement (e.g. exposure, limited consequences).

Among psychiatric samples, high prevalence rates have been found for firesetting (i.e. an incident of burning with property damages) and matchplay (play with matches or lighters with no damages) in outpatients (19.4%, 24.4%) and inpatients (34.6%, 52.0%), respectively, and for multiple firesetting incidents among inpatients in the metropolitan Pittsburgh area (Kolko & Kazdin, 1988b). Moderate rates of recurrent firesetting have been found among children seen in the fire department (65%; Parrish et al., 1985) or psychiatric centers (23%–58%; Kolko & Kazdin, 1988b; Stewart & Culver, 1982).

A two-year follow-up study of 268 patient and non-patient children (ages 6–13 yrs) used fire history reports to classify cases into one of three mutually exclusive categories in order to determine how many children engaged in firesetting or matchplay only (Kolko & Kazdin, 1995). On the basis of aggregated reports of children and their parents, both patients and non-patients reported high levels of follow-up firesetting (49%, 64%) and matchplay (57%, 76%), though the frequency of each behavior was generally higher for patients than non-patients for both firesetting (M's = 4.2, 1.0) and matchplay (M's = 3.1, 0.9). At initial assessment, there were 50 firesetters (31.3%), 15 matchplayers (9.4%), and 95 non-firesetters (59.4%) in a non-patient sample; similar percentages of firesetters (24.4% or 39), matchplayers only (20.0% or 32), and non-firesetters (55.6% or 89) were found for the follow-up period. In a patient sample, there were 44 firesetters (51.2%), 10 matchplayers only (11.6%), and 32 non-firesetters (37.2%); similar percentages of firesetters (43.3% or 37), matchplayers only (12.8% or 11), and non-firesetters (44.2% or 38) were found for the follow-up period. In each sample, 25 of 50 non-patients (50%) and 26 of 44 patients (59%) were recidivists, whereas 14 of 110 non-patients (13%) and 11 of 42 patients (26%) became late-starters. Such findings highlight the prevalence of firesetting in disturbed and non-disturbed youth, and the continuity of firesetting over time.

Recidivism rates or predictors or subsequent firesetting behavior have been infrequently reported. One prospective study that followed a sample of 138 children for one year showed that 14 of 78 non-firesetters (18%) later had set their first fire, and that 21 of 60 firesetters (35%) had set an additional fire by follow-up (Kolko & Kazdin, 1992). "Late-starting" was associated with limited family sociability, whereas recidivism was associated with child knowledge about combustibles and involvement in fire-related activities, community complaints about fire contact, child hostility, lax discipline, family conflict, and limited parental acceptance, family affiliation, and family organization. A few of these predictors have been identified as correlates of adult arson in other samples (Rice & Harris, 1991). A study of young arsonists receiving forensic evaluations found a recidivism rate of approximately 33% over an average of a seven-year follow-up period (Repo & Virkkunen, 1997).

A more recent study examined fire-specific and general psychosocial measures as predictors of follow-up firesetting and matchplay, separately for patients and non-patients (Kolko & Kazdin, 1995). Early firesetting and matchplay were significant predictors of follow-up fire involvement in both samples. The psychosocial predictors of firesetting that added incremental variance beyond this fire history varied by sample. In the non-patients, two predictors were found (i.e. exposure to fire models, parental psychological control). In the patients, several variables served as predictors (e.g. fire competence, complaints about the child, parental distress, harsh punishment, social service contact). Different predictors in the two samples also were found for matchplay. These findings highlight some of the potential risk factors for later involvement with fire which included, not surprisingly, prior firesetting and matchplay.

DESCRIPTIVE AND CLINICAL CHARACTERISTICS

No specific "profile" of the juvenile firesetter has been identified. In fact, the background and clinical characteristics of firesetting children and youth are quite diverse. Descriptive details of the firesetting incidents and children's motives point to some of the factors that may influence the severity of this problem. Empirical studies have examined group differences between firesetting and non-firesetting samples obtained in different settings, such as community, outpatient, or residential settings.

Studies have examined demographic, diagnostic, and clinical characteristics of firesetting youth. Based on controlled studies, firesetting has been found to be associated with various forms of child dysfunction, such as heightened aggression and social skills deficits (Kolko, Kazdin, & Meyer, 1985). On parent reports, firesetters have been found to exhibit greater covert behavior such as lying, stealing, or running away, than both matchplayers and non-firesetters (Kolko & Kazdin, 1991b). Both firesetters and matchplayers have been found to differ from non-firesetters on other measures of dysfunction (e.g. aggression, externalizing behaviors, impulsivity, emotionality, hostility), but did not differ from one another. It is noteworthy that far fewer differences between firesetters and matchplayers were observed on child than parent self-report measures (e.g. aggression, unassertion, low self-esteem). Heightened aggression and other antisocial behaviors in firesetters have been reported elsewhere (Cole et al., 1986, 1993; Gaynor & Hatcher, 1987; Jacobson, 1985a, 1985b; Kolko et al., 1985; Showers & Pickrell, 1987; Stewart & Culver, 1982). Some studies also have reported a relationship between firesetting and the diagnosis of conduct disorder (see American Psychiatric Association, 1987; see Heath, Hardesty, Goldfine, & Walker, 1985; Kelso &

Stewart, 1986), though others have not (Kolko et al., 1985; Kolko & Kazdin, 1989a, 1989b).

Studies using projective assessments with youth in residential treatment have identified an array of psychological characteristics that were more common among firesetters than non-firesetters (Sakheim, Vigdor, Gordon, & Helprin, 1985; Sakheim & Osborn, 1986). These characteristics include greater problems with sexual excitement, anger at mother and father, rage and fantasies of revenge, sexual conflicts or dysfunction, poor social judgment, difficulty verbalizing anger, and a diagnosis of conduct disorder. The youth's firesetting was viewed as providing the means to exercise power over adults (Sakheim & Osborn, 1994). Similar variables have been found more common in "high-risk" (i.e., deliberate or persistent fires) than "low-risk" (i.e., accidental or occasional fires) residential youth, such as anger and rage, poor judgment, impulsivity, little guilt, animal cruelty, and aggressive conduct disorder (Sakheim, Osborn, & Abrams, 1991). In an inpatient sample, other types of psychopathology that distinguished firesetters from non-firesetters included a greater history of sexual abuse and higher scores on the schizophrenia and mania scales of the MMPI (Moore, Thompson-Pope, & Whited, 1994).

Parental factors have also emerged as correlates of firesetting behavior. For example, parents of firesetters have reported higher levels of personal or relationship problems (e.g. psychiatric distress, marital discord, less child acceptance) and greater difficulties with parenting practices (e.g. less monitoring, discipline, and involvement in prosocial activities) than parents of non-firesetters (Kazdin & Kolko, 1986; Kolko & Kazdin, 1991a). Firesetters have described their parents' child-rearing practices as reflecting greater anxiety induction, lax discipline, and non-enforcement of rules or consequences, with scores for matchplayers generally falling between firesetters and controls. At the family level, firesetters have been found to experience more stressful life events than non-firesetters (Kolko & Kazdin, 1991a). These findings may implicate both deviant parental practices and parental dysfunction in the etiology of firesetting.

The prevalence of psychiatric disorders and criminal recidivism was examined among 45 male arsonists (ages 15–21 years) from Finland who were referred for a forensic evaluation (Repo & Virkkunen, 1997). At intake, almost 65% of the sample had a history of conduct disorder with aggressive features. Alcohol dependence was common, despite the young age of the sample. A six-year follow-up revealed that 73% had repeated general crimes. History of conduct disorder was not significantly related to recidivist firesetting. A related comparison study found that juvenile arsonists had more use of public health services for treatment of psychiatric symptoms, heightened suicidality, and were relieved of their responsibilities for the crime than juvenile crimes of violence (Rasanen, Hirvenoja, Hakko, & Vaisanen, 1995). However, the only difference between delinquents adjudicated for arson or another crime was a greater history of past firesetting in the arson group (Hanson, Mackay-Soroka, Staley, & Poulton, 1994).

These descriptive characteristics provide a general overview of the characteristics of firesetting children and, more recently, adolescents and their family backgrounds. Of course, the precipitants for a child's recent incident of firesetting may or may not be related to any of these documented variables, nor reflect the potential influence of other features, such as the child's interest in or attraction to fire, exposure to fire materials, idiosyncratic motives, and limited fire competence (see Cole et al., 1983, 1986; Kafry, 1980; Kolko & Kazdin, 1989a, 1989b). Also, there is considerable variability in the clinical pictures of firesetting youth, given that the behavior has multiple motives, antecedent conditions, and consequences. Thus, it is important to understand that firesetters may vary significantly in level of personal dysfunction, parental effectiveness, family integrity, and exposure to fire-related factors. We know even less about differences between children who present with varying forms of involvement with fire, such as those who set fires, play with matches, mix chemicals and create bombs, or just smoke. While some research findings have suggested similarities between firesetters and match-players on certain variables, findings indicate group differences on others (see Kolko & Kazdin, 1991a, 1991b).

ASSESSMENT AND EVALUATION

Many of the types of clinical problems shown by firesetting youth or their families have been described in the aforementioned section. Certainly, several individual, family, and environmental factors may contribute to a child's firesetting behavior and may warrant assessment and attention during intervention (see Kolko & Kazdin, 1986). In this section, specific measures for evaluating specific incidents and fire-related risk factors will be examined.

Children's Firesetting Incidents

There are several methods to obtain information regarding children's incidents that have expanded upon the initial screening instruments developed by the FEMA (1979, 1983, 1987). Other important aspects of children's firesetting incidents include the child's intention and social context, personal and environmental reactions, and the consequences or impact of the fire (see Cole et al., 1993). The Fire Incident Analysis for Parents (FIA-P; Kolko & Kazdin, 1991c) is a structured parent interview designed to document parameters of a child's firesetting incident that was based on items from other measures (FEMA, 1979) and the general literature (see Kolko, 1989; Wooden & Berkey, 1984). The FIA-P includes coded responses for several questions. Factor analysis of several items yielded three general motive factors (curiosity, anger, attention/help-seeking) and two other items (accident, peer pressure or destructiveness) designed to understand the presumed reason for the fire.

The FIA-P also evaluated details/characteristics of firesetting incident (e.g. how materials were obtained, site of fire, type of property damage), levels of behavioral and emotional correlates just prior to the fire (e.g. aggression/defiance, depression/withdrawal, rule violations), and consequences following the fire, such as family/disciplinary (e.g. family discipline, child was talked to or counseled by someone outside of the family), financial (e.g. value of damages), medical (i.e. injury, death), legal (e.g. criminal record, removal from home), and social/peer (e.g. peer acceptance, peer rejection/avoidance). This study reported several descriptive details of the children's fires. Other findings comparing children with different firesetting motives showed that heightened curiosity was associated with greater fire involvement out of the house and less costly fire damages, whereas heightened anger was associated with greater aggression/defiance just prior to the fire and peer rejection following the fire.

A parallel study of 95 firesetters described responses to the Fire Incident Analysis for Children which included some of the same items in the FIA-P (FIA-C; Kolko & Kazdin, 1994). The FIA-C consists of 21 questions that identified details/characteristics (e.g. how materials were obtained, site, severity of damages, forethought, planning), primary motives (curiosity/experimentation, anger/revenge/manipulation), consequences from family members and friends (e.g. discipline, attention) and reactions to the incident, and the impact of the incident on future firesetting (e.g. desire to set fire again). Among the study's findings, access to incendiaries, lack of child remorse and parental consequences, and motives of curiosity and fun were reported frequently. Four descriptive characteristics of the fire predicted the overall severity of the child's involvement in fire at follow-up (i.e. fire out of home, acknowledgement of being likely to set another fire, a neutral/positive reaction to the fire, no parental response to the fire). Although the FIA-C and FIA-P provide a quantitative evaluation of the parameters of a firesetting incident, more research is needed to determine how well these measures perform across settings and populations.

Similar descriptive details have been reported in the large Swedish study mentioned earlier (Terjestam & Ryden, 1996). In that study, 9% of the children played with fireworks frequently and 13% played with candles frequently, though the majority of children had set fire to an object (54%); another 43% lit paper, leaves, or grass. Seven percent of the children reported that they had lost control over a fire they had lit. Interestingly, most children reported a motive of wanting to see the fire burn, followed next by being bored and wanting to destroy something, though a high percentage of cases reported that they did not know the reason. Perhaps, then, it is not surprising that 36% of the sample experienced fire as exciting, 60% as nice and cozy, and only 26% as frightful. Finally, the older children in the study did not seem to have a much better understanding of the flammability of different materials than younger children. These data further emphasize the potential role of self-stimulation in firesetting and the need to pay more attention to the types and impact of children's knowledge about fire.

Fire-Related Risk Factors

Turning to other measures, fire-specific and psychosocial factors may increase a child's risk for setting an initial or even a subsequent fire. Drawing upon items in the FEMA (1979, 1983) interviews, we have operationalized certain risk factors in separate interview measures for parents (the Firesetting Risk Inventory or FRI; Kolko & Kazdin, 1989a) and children (Children's Firesetting Inventory or CFI; Kolko & Kazdin, 1989b). The FRI examines several factors specific to fire (e.g. curiosity about fire, involvement in fire-related activities, early experiences with fire, exposure to peer/family models, knowledge of fire safety, fire skill/competence), and more general factors (e.g. positive and negative behavior, frequency and efficacy of harsh punishment). Compared with non-firesetters, parents of firesetters acknowledged significantly higher scores on measures of firesetting contact (e.g. curiosity about fire, involvement in fire-related acts, exposure to peers/family fire models), general child/parent behavior (e.g. negative behavior), and family environment (e.g. use of harsh punishment, less effective mild punishment).

The CFI items were developed to evaluate the children's primary motives, skills, or experiences as potential targets for intervention. Specifically, the following six factors are examined:

- curiosity about fire (e.g. how much do you want to play with fire; how special or magical is fire to you?),
- involvement in fire-related activities (e.g. how many times did you pull a fire alarm?),
- knowledge about things that burn (e.g. will clothes, like a shirt or pair of pants, burn?),
- fire competence (e.g. what steps would you follow to light a fire in a fireplace?),
- exposure to models/materials (e.g. how many of your friends have you seen playing with matches or lighting fire?), and
- supervision/discipline (e.g. how often are you disciplined at home?).

Based on group comparisons, firesetters have shown more curiosity about involvement in fire-related acts, exposure to friends or family who smoke, and, somewhat surprisingly, knowledge of things that burn, although they only tended to show less fire competence (safety skills) on role-plays than non-firesetters.

In sum, several characteristics merit evaluation in cases where children have been implicated in a fire. In the context of understanding the child's behavioral and emotional problems, it is important to evaluate other considerations, some of which are shown in Tables 26.1 and 26.2. These include the presence of psychiatric diagnoses (e.g. attention deficit/hyperactivity disorder, conduct disorder), developmental limitations that reflect poor judgment or contact with reality, medication use, interpersonal or emotional expressiveness difficulties, and involvement with delinquent or deviant peers. Areas of parental or family dysfunction that merit evaluation include parental monitoring and supervision, parental effectiveness, parental drug or alcohol use/abuse, abuse or neglect history, child stimulation, family activities and structure, and the safety of the home environment (see Kolko, 1994).

Table 26.1   Representative clinical characteristics and domains for evaluation

Fire incident and cause/origin report
Fire history
Fire motive and precipitants
Fire consequences and related discipline
Services/community responses
Developmental level/IQ
Psychiatric disorders and history
Child cognitive–behavioral repertoire; affect regulation and expressiveness
Parental functioning and practices
Family environment, functions, and structure
Social supports and activities

Table 26.2   Sample questions for assessment

What happened?
What's the history?
Why fire now?
Does child understand the dangers of fire?
Does child have a learning or psychiatric disorder?
What outside influences make fire exposure and involvement possible?
How does the parent or family contribute to the child's fire problem?
Is there sufficient structure, use of rules, and consequences?
What interactions in the child's environment are stressful?
What threats to the child's safety exist in the environment?

INTERVENTION AND TREATMENT

Overview

Intervention methods may vary in the degree to which they target the child's fire-specific experiences or interest, the child's behavior, or the psychosocial or ecological context in which the fire occurred (Gaynor & Hatcher, 1987; Kolko, 1989, Wooden & Berkey, 1984). This may reflect the fact that fire education is conducted primarily by the fire service, whereas psychological treatment is conducted primarily by mental health practitioners. Programs in the fire department have generally emphasized instruction in fire safety skills, but have expanded to include access to psychosocial interventions, evaluations of child and family characteristics associated with firesetting, and follow-up assessments of outcome (Kolko, 1988). Many of these components have been integrated in novel comprehensive programs.

Fire Safety Skills/Prevention Education

The most common approach to working with the firesetter involves fire safety or prevention education consisting of instruction in various fire safety skills/practices. Information or practice is typically provided in such concepts as recognizing fire, understanding the dangers of fire, making emergency calls or requesting assistance, putting fires out or getting it off of one's clothes (e.g. stop/drop/roll), or other emergency plans or drills. In some cases, training is provided in the appropriate and safe use of fire. Technical manuals that describe interviews for evaluating a child's "risk status" and intervention procedures have been well disseminated (Interviewing and Counseling Juvenile Firesetter Program [ICJF]; Federal Emergency Management Agency [FEMA], 1979, 1983; National Fire Protection Association [NFPA], 1979), although there are few evaluations of their impact on firesetting behavior. Some information has documented improved fire-safety knowledge in trained, relative to control, classroom students (NFPA, 1978). Low recidivism rates have been reported following participation in fire department programs, such as the 6.2% (4/65) figure that was reported using mailings or phone calls over an unspecified time period (Porth, 1996).

Evaluations of various fire evacuation and assistance skills have been conducted with young children (see Jones, Kazdin, & Haney, 1981; Jones, Ollendick, & Shinske, 1989), which have incorporated fear-reduction techniques. For example, Williams and Jones (1989) found improvements in fire emergency responding and less fear of fire following a fire safety skills training group and a combined fire safety/fear reduction group, relative to two control groups. The combined group performed at a higher level at five-month follow-up than the other groups. Elaborative rehearsal strategies have been found to enhance the effects of behavioral rehearsal on acquisition of fire emergency skills and the reduction of fear of fire (Jones, Ollendick, McLaughlin, & Williams, 1989). Children with post-traumatic stress disorder may benefit from the use of these procedures.

A group fire safety/prevention skills training (FSST) program with hospitalized firesetters based on the aforementioned work has been found beneficial relative to individual fire awareness/discussion (FAD; Kolko, Watson, & Faust, 1991). FSST included four sessions devoted to the following content:

1. characteristics and functions of fire (e.g. damages),
2. discriminating objects that are okay or not okay for children to use (e.g. matches are tools),
3. function and use of matches (e.g. return matches if you find them), and
4. personal fire/burn safety (e.g. get help, stop-drop-roll).

Relative to FAD, FSST was associated with significantly less contact with fire-related toys and matches in an analog play room, and an increase in fire safety knowledge, relative to FAD children. Parent-report measures at six-month follow-up showed that FSST children had engaged less often in firesetting or matchplay than FAD children (16.7% vs. 58.3%). Such findings are encouraging and highlight the need to expand both the skills and scope of this type of intervention.

A similar application of fire safety and prevention education in an inpatient and residential treatment setting made use of the "Smokey the Bear" theme (DeSalvatore & Hornstein, 1991) to train children to understand the fire triangle, hazards, camp fires, and match safety, and to report fires. The program was novel in its efforts to train parents to serve as educators for their children and to encourage family participation in completing fire safety assignments. Only one of 35 children who were followed for one year was found to have set another fire. Although the absence of a control or comparison group makes it difficult to determine the overall effectiveness of the program, the report nonetheless shows that conducting fire safety skills training in controlled settings is viable.

Other recent work has extended the application of fire awareness and prevention training sessions with parents and other adults. Pinsonneault (1996) describes a fire awareness curriculum for foster parents or child protective services workers that includes helpful strategies for identifying the motives of child firesetting and different subgroups of juvenile firesetters. The manual includes brief recommendations for creating a safe environment to minimize a family's risk for another fire, and promote positive relationships, home safety, and discussions of current events involving fire. Numerous practical exercises make this program easily applicable to most circumstances where caregiver participation is a necessary element of intervention.

Another important advance is the integration of multiple approaches or procedures, such as the integration of fire safety materials and psychological procedures. Johnston (1996) has developed an eight-session, group treatment and fire safety education program for younger children with innovative lesson plans that target feelings and behaviors, peer pressure, and identification of appropriate choices in response to challenging interpersonal situations. The inclusion of worksheets and group activities to convey certain fire safety concepts (e.g. understand fire's destructive capability, conduct home fire safety checks, describe fire interventions for the home) is a nice feature of this manual. As is true of many of the program developments in this area, there is still a need to conduct field testing and psychometric evaluations of these manuals and their impact on both firesetting and fire safety.

Psychosocial Intervention and Treatment

Several treatment procedures have been used to enhance the firesetter's prosocial repertoire, parental practices, or family functions. Among the many clinical approaches that are applied in practice, case reports and empirical studies have reported the use of structural and behavioral family therapies (Eisler, 1974; Madanes, 1981; Minuchin, 1974). One of the earliest behavioral procedures reported to be effective was negative practice (repeatedly lighting matches), a technique designed to satiate the child's interest in fire (Holland, 1969; Kolko, 1983; McGrath, Marshall, & Prior, 1979). Perhaps due to the potential controversy about encouraging fireplay in this population, the procedure has been less often reported in recent years. Other behavioral methods, such as the use of contingency management, have been applied both to discourage contact with fire and reinforce positive behaviors or the use of more appropriate materials (Adler, Nunn, Laverick, & Ross, 1988), including the use of stories designed to weaken the child's interest in fire (Stawar, 1976).

The graphing technique has been used at the outset of treatment to represent the personal and environmental context of a fire (Bumpass, Fagelman, & Brix, 1983). This procedure solicits information from the child about the antecedents and consequences of the fire, such as the emotional or cognitive precipitants of the fire (e.g. anger, perception of being unfairly treated). Graphs have been applied during individual and/or family psychotherapy (Bumpass, Brix, & Preston, 1985). The procedure may help to enhance rapport, document the child's responsibility for the fire, and identify potential clinical targets for intervention.

Youth who set fires in response to affective distress have been taught various prosocial, cognitive–behavioral skills to facilitate appropriate expression of anger and emotional arousal (Kolko & Ammerman, 1988; McGrath et al., 1979) and assertive problem-solving behavior (DeSalvatore & Hornstein, 1991). These clinical reports describe multicomponent treatments that target the child's interpersonal repertoire, the functional context of firesetting, and parental use of punishment and reinforcement. Other clinical techniques have been recommended to alter child and family factors related to firesetting, such as the use of communication training and family problem-solving (see Cole et al., 1993; Gaynor & Hatcher, 1987; Kolko, 1989, 1996). For the more serious cases, it seems reasonable to consider applying several procedures during treatment, such as skills training in appropriate behaviors, discussions of the child's motives, the introduction of immediate consequences for both positive and negative behavior, and parental or family monitoring of suspicious behavior that may be associated with firesetting.

Some recent applications have implemented different combinations of cognitive–behavioral and contingency management procedures with psychiatrically referred children and youth, such as home-based reinforcement and response-cost contingencies (Kolko, 1983), graphing of prior incidents and psychological skills training (Kolko & Ammerman, 1988), and fire safety assessment/skills training and parent management training (Cox-Jones, Lubetsky, Fultz, & Kolko, 1990). These interventions were associated with reduced firesetting behavior and improved behavioral adjustment at follow-up. Similarly, diverse psychological services that included cognitive–behavioral assessment information (e.g. functional analysis) and treatment (e.g. social skills, coping and relaxation, assertion training, covert sensitization), in addition to facial surgery, have been found helpful with a young adult (Clare, Murphy, Cox, & Chaplin, 1992). At four-month follow-up, no further firesetting or related behavior had been reported. These clinical reports suggest that there is some benefit to targeting the child's behavioral repertoire and/or environmental contingencies in the home. Moreover, the use of covert sensitization by Clare et al. (1992) highlights the potential for modifying the firesetter's inappropriate attraction to fire which has been targeted in prior reports (see Stawar, 1976). However, all these studies are based on single-case reports or designs. Thus, these psychological procedures have not been evaluated in the context of large-scale, controlled outcome studies.

Among the developments for treating firesetting youth is the articulation of novel assessment methods and conceptualizations of the clinical factors that bear implications for subsequent firesetting and treatment planning. In conjunction with the Oregon Office of State Fire Marshall, a treatment strategies task force has developed a "needs assessment" protocol to assess mental health needs, take an accurate firesetter history, determine precipitating stressors and a firesetter typology, and make appropriate treatment and supervision recommendations (Humphreys & Kopet, 1996). This assessment is designed to suggest potential areas and systems that should be targeted by treatment. For example, the protocol includes suggested interview questions in various domains (e.g. family, social, trauma, mental health, fire) that yield typology scores (e.g. curiosity, delinquent) which allow the evaluator to develop a formulation about case diagnosis, prognosis, and treatment. Practical, clinically oriented questions and assessment guidelines are provided to facilitate application of the protocol.

A related model outlining some of the psychological and environmental factors proposed to influence the likelihood of recidivism has been developed by this task force to promote a more systematic approach to the selection of relevant mental health treatments (Oregon Treatment Strategies Task Force). This model recognizes the importance of understanding the various subtypes of firesetters noted above. Four overlapping cycles or rings are proposed in the model, each representing a domain that may influence a child's and family's behavior:

1. emotional/cognitive (e.g. thinking errors, believes life is unfair, boredom or anger),
2. behavioral (e.g. limit testing, power struggles, covert behaviors),
3. family (e.g. initial response to fire, stressors, ineffective discipline), and
4. community/social (e.g. special services, institutional conflicts, community resources).

The specific reactions proposed in each domain cycle are examined to determine the likelihood of recidivism and to identify necessary steps to intervention designed to minimize the child's use of fire. For example, specific interventions may target the child (e.g. eliminate negative peer influences, restitution, anger management), family (e.g. communication training, logical discipline, fire safety education), or fire department (e.g. fire education, contract). The model emphasizes how various systems that serve firesetting youth can both help and exacerbate the problem, and demonstrates how solutions to the firesetting problem require a coordinated network of agencies (e.g. school, law enforcement, mental health). The model is exploratory at this point due to the absence of needed information regarding its feasibility in applied settings and psychometric adequacy. For example, it would be useful to determine which of the components of the cycle in each domain are most commonly identified in clinical practice and how easy it is to make changes in these components. Other practical recommendations have been described by members of the Oregon Treatment Task Force to help parents and families address the behavioral and clinical needs of the youthful firesetter. A noteworthy feature of these recommendations is their incorporation of an array of intervention procedures, such as installing smoke alarms, teaching fire safety information and skills, monitoring children's possessions for fire-related materials, encouraging the expression of affective states, establishing structure and consequences in the home, and addressing systemic problems in family therapy (Humphreys, Kopet, & Lajoy, 1994). Humphreys et al. offer several tips to help parents monitor, teach, and manage a child's firesetting, regardless of the level of child or family dysfunction (e.g. remove matches, monitor television habits, discuss consequences in advance, forbid fireplay).

Delinquent firesetters have also been targeted by a group program developed by Campbell and Elliott (1996). The program includes lessons that cover many of the concepts commonly found in cognitive–behavioral treatments, such as communication, assertion, and anger-control, conscience, thinking errors, and relapse prevention plans, as well as how to work with parents. The program is strengthened by the inclusion of discussion questions, homework exercises, and a post-test evaluation. An extension of this work for application to adolescents has incorporated both restitution and fire education components through which the youth completes a community impact report and participates in community service (Clackamas County Juvenile Firesetting Intervention Network, 1996).

Treatment Research and Outcome Studies

As noted earlier, studies that evaluate intervention procedures are rare. One of the few controlled evaluations of alternative approaches to working with children (5–16 years) who were classified as either curiosity and pathological firesetters was conducted in Australia (Adler, Nunn, Northam, Lebnan, & Ross, 1994). Curious and non-dysfunctional firesetters were randomly assigned to either education (fire safety information to child and parents, discussion of fire awareness) or a combined condition (education, satiation, response cost for fires, graphing of fire) with both interventions being conducted by a fire fighter at home, whereas pathological cases were offered psychiatric referral and treatment by a specialist in a children's hospital clinic and then randomized either to the same education alone or combined condition.

The findings revealed a significant reduction in the frequency of firesetting following the intervention but no difference between the home/specialist and education/combined conditions. The overall mean rates of firesetting were 7.1 and 1.5 at each of these two respective time periods. There was also a reduction in the severity of firesetting. Of 80 children considered improved, 59 (42.8%) set no fires during the 12-month post-treatment period and an additional 21 (15.2%) no longer met the referral criterion as they set less than three fires during that period. Home-based (vs. specialist) cases tended to have a higher proportion of improvement (73% vs. 52%) and a lower percentage of dropout (20% vs. 35%). The combined (vs. education only) group also tended to have a higher dropout rate (35% vs. 21%). Although the 28% attrition rate and absence of treatment integrity or child behavior date are limitations, this study is the first controlled outcome study based on these common procedures and it demonstrates that even minimal intervention may be effective in reducing firesetting over a long period of time.

A study in the United States is examining the relative efficacy of fire service and mental health interventions conducted in a "clinic" setting (Kolko, 1996). Firesetting boys, aged 5–13, were randomly assigned to either Fire Safety Education (FSE) conducted by trained firefighters or therapist-delivered cognitive-behavioral treatment (CBT) and compared with cases that were assigned to a brief condition consisting of a Home Visit from a Firefighter (FHV) that was designed to reflect a routine fire service practice. Intervention was designed to be short-term, directed to children and their parents, executed by specialists, and evaluated using multiple measures. FSE involved training in fire safety education principles and tasks (e.g. stop-drop-roll, emergency phone calls, exiting a burning house, declining an invitation to engage in matchplay), whereas CBT involved teaching self-control and problem-solving skills, establishing environmental conditions to encourage prosocial behavior, and altering the motive to use fire. FHV included a brief discussion of fire dangers and firefighting, executing a "no-fire contract", and distributing safety materials (e.g. coloring books). Thus, two intensive programs are being compared with one another and then with a third, minimal contact condition.

Preliminary analyses of outcome data suggest that all three interventions resulted in reductions in child- and parent-reported incidents of firesetting and matchplay. However, both CBT and FSE were associated with even greater improvements than FHV for child-reported firesetting incidents. Only FSE led to improvements in children's fire safety skill. There were few group differences in improvements in child and parent dysfunction. These acute effects will be supplemented with one-year follow-up data. The study will also identify predictors of firesetting recidivism.

Summary of Intervention Procedures

The aforementioned anecdotal, clinical, and limited empirical evidence suggests that there may be some advantage to targeting both fire-specific experiences and skills (e.g. children's involvement with, exposure to, and interest in fire) and the child's behavior and environmental context (e.g. aggression, parental practices). However, the clinical impact of these interventions has been demonstrated with a few, limited empirical studies. Program evaluation and controlled studies of both fire safety education and psychosocial treatment would certainly advance our understanding of interventions for childhood firesetters. An evaluation of the separate and combined effects of these two complementary interventions is warranted because firesetters who set multiple fires may also exhibit significant psychosocial maladjustment, and are often referred for multiple services. The procedures used in these two areas also seem to be quite compatible and may enhance one another's effectiveness.

PROGRAM DEVELOPMENT, ORGANIZATION, AND DISSEMINATION

Collaborative Programs

The National Juvenile Firesetter/Arson Control and Prevention Program (NJF/ACP) of 1987 was sponsored by the Office of Juvenile Justice and Delinquency Prevention (OJJDP) and US Fire Administration (USFA) to "conceptualize, design, develop, and evaluate a variety of community-based approaches to prevent and control juvenile firesetting" (FEMA, 1994, p. 1). The initiative was conducted in different stages (assessment of problem, development of comprehensive approach and training and technical materials, testing and dissemination of materials) and led to the identification of seven components common to effective juvenile firesetter programs (i.e. program management, screening and evaluation, intervention services, referral mechanisms, publicity and outreach, monitoring systems, and developing relationships with juvenile justice), which have been articulated in several guidebooks published by FEMA (1994, FA-145-149). These resources identify various steps to developing a collaborative program.

A large-scale evaluation was conducted of the initial application of the NJF/ACP model for developing fire-department-based programs. As reported by Bourque, Cronin, and Han (1993), this evaluation examined the implementation of a program model in three jurisdictions (Parker, Colorado; Oklahoma City, Oklahoma; West Valley, Utah), tested the effectiveness of the model in controlling firesetting, and suggested modifications to the model and related program materials. Interestingly, about two-thirds of the cases referred to two of the sites were rated as needing a mental health evaluation. In general, the evaluation found that regional evaluations were helpful and that the program guides were useful in developing new programs. Thus, these programs highlight the potential utility of the program guidebooks upon which they were based. However, certain assessed cases were not referred to services. Furthermore, it is not clear whether these programs actually altered the incidence of firesetting following their implementation. Nevertheless, the JFACCP material offers one of the first systematic approaches to the application of field-tested concepts and methods in the organization of multiple services for juvenile firesetters.

Several comprehensive networks of services in different cities were in operation prior to the NJF/ACP initiative but are clearly consistent with its content, such as the combined mental health and fire department program reported in Dallas, Texas (Bumpass et al., 1985). This program is noteworthy for its novel use of the graphing technique, fire safety films, and activities to promote community involvement. Helpful program evaluation data showed before–after improvements for recidivist cases (32% vs. 2%), number of reported juvenile fires reported (204 vs. 141), and fire costs ($1 031 606 vs. $536 102), though these changes were not statistically evaluated. Integrated community-based services also have extended the use of fire department and mental health screening evaluations to select appropriate interventions, incorporated engagement, liaison, and outreach strategies, and provided a range of services that cover school-based curricula, fire education and mental health services, and intensive treatment (Webb, Sakheim, Towns-Miranda, & Wagner, 1990).

Service or Program Networks

Multidisciplinary collaboration in the administration of services for firesetting youth has become an important advance in this area and, in recent years, represents more the rule than the exception. This is due, in part, to the accumulation of evidence suggesting the relevance of fire safety and mental health considerations in understanding the problem of juvenile firesetting, and to the recognition of the roles being played by professionals in the juvenile justice, burn care and other medical, educational, and social service systems. At the same time, there is a strong need to expand the scope and comprehensiveness of intervention programs in this area and level of regional support and resources received by various programs to ensure their long-term viability.

In the last few years several states have developed organized networks of affiliated programs that share common policies and procedures, as reflected in one network's ongoing newsletter (see *The Strike Zone*, Fall, 1997). For example, the Massachusetts Coalition for Juvenile Firesetter Programs represents 12 program sites through the state (e.g. Lowell, Barnstable, West Springfield, River Valley). Staff at each site have received specialty training in various areas (e.g. screening, interviewing, assessment, education, treatment) to serve the various aspects of the firesetting problem. These programs benefit from the participation of experts from multiple disciplines (e.g. fire service, mental health, social services, law enforcement) and include an array of innovative services and resources, such as a weekend "fire school", the use of teachers and firefighter/emergency services technicians as educators, and specialized manuals and audio-visual aids. An interesting development in the State of Massachusetts is the passage of legislation that requires a worker from the Department of Social Services to refer children with a history of either firesetting or sexual offending for a specialized risk-management assessment to identify appropriate treatments and placement options. Coalition members will be participating in the assessment and disposition process with these cases, which, to date, reflects one of the largest collaborative networks established between social services and firesetter programs.

State-wide programs in Oregon have been coordinated by the Office of State Fire Marshall which has developed innovative collaborations and specialized materials (see Juvenile Firesetter Intervention Program's *Hot Issues*, 1998). A newsletter published by the coordinator of these programs disseminates various stories, program descriptions, practical suggestions, and information related to training opportunities and conferences at both the regional and national level. More recently, *The Idea Bank* has developed a web site that provides access to news, announcements, articles, technical resources, and program descriptions throughout the country (Idea Bank, 1997). All these materials are likely to facilitate a discussion of program developments in the field and enhance the quality of care and professional competence in this area.

Of course, there are still many obstacles to developing and maintaining an effective collaborative program in most communities. A task force on juvenile firesetting convened by the NFPA in 1993 reported on several impediments and some potential solutions (NFPA, 1993). To promote greater public and professional awareness of the problem of firesetting, suggestions were made to train juvenile firesetter professionals in community coalition building strategies, educate media professionals, develop fire science information and parent education materials, enlist fire service leaders in juvenile programs, and train mental health professionals in intervention techniques. The need to access existing resources through the establishment of a national clearinghouse that could disseminate information on program descriptions and outcomes also was discussed. Finally, the need to use data effectively was considered important in terms of describing, planning, and revising program components. A follow-up task force meeting identified other needs for the field, including the identification of a "niche" or organization that embraces the juvenile firesetting problem, the need for greater technical assistance to existing programs, and maintenance of communication at a regional and national level (NFPA, 1995).

One of the practical problems in the field reflects the uncertainty about the role of assessment information. A recent study of firesetting youth found that parent ratings on a child behavior checklist were not examined prior to the fire department's referral of the case for services (Pierce & Hardesty, 1997). Significant levels of psychopathology were not found to contribute to the child's future referral for mental health services. Such findings highlight the importance of working collaboratively with mental health practitioners in identifying the most appropriate services for juvenile firesetters.

FUTURE DIRECTIONS

The delivery of services for juvenile firesetters is enriched but also complicated by the inclusion of multiple disciplines and, thus, requires considerable thought to ensure long-term program viability. One practical solution to the development of an efficient and cost-effective approach to the fire problem is to develop "clinical pathways" that specify the order in which specific intervention components are to be implemented based on screening and evaluation information. For example, the most simple procedure (e.g. providing a short brochure on the dangers of fire) may prove useful with a large number of cases referred for services. Some type of informational pack, such as this, may provide tips or suggestions to address a child's interest or initial involvement with fire. Of course, other more intensive and direct procedures may be needed, such as child training in fire safety/prevention skills or parent training in effective child or contingency management techniques. Next, there may be a need to encourage clinical involvement in treatment that focuses on cognitive–behavioral skills, parental counseling, and/or family treatment. Involvement with restitution may be a useful intervention, especially for older firesetters, with or without concurrent juvenile justice involvement. Finally, some children may require hospitalization or residential treatment to address serious forms of psychopathology and family dysfunction. The relative advantage of developing a hierarchy of interventions and their most judicious use merits further conceptual elaboration and empirical evaluation.

As shown in Table 26.3, there are several areas worth examining in research studies. There is a need to understand better the nature of firesetting in children and youth, such as whether there is a continuum of fire behavior that reflects a progression to more serious involvement with fire. For example, fire interest or curiosity may be precursors to matchplay or fireplay, which may stimulate involvement in firesetting. Precipitants of serious firesetting and arson are also important to evaluate. Psychometric evaluation of new fire materials and models, such as the Oregon Cycle of Firesetting Model, is needed to determine their practical utility. We also need to know the relationship between childhood firesetting and adult arson to understand the continuity of this behavior over time. Follow-up studies would help us document the natural history of children's involvement with fire and predictors of recidivism.

In terms of interventions, there is an urgent need to examine the feasibility and efficacy of different interventions, and the overall impact of services at two levels:

1. the individual firesetter, and
2. the community at large.

Whether psychosocial interventions impact upon both firesetting behavior and other behavior problems is also unknown. Likewise, studies should examine the

Table 26.3 Topics for research

Assessment of fire-specific risk factors, including child's attraction to fire
Evaluation of a typology of child motives for firesetting
Outcomes of alternative or comparative interventions
Predictors of program response and follow-up recidivism
Documentation of the effects of preventive programs
Examination of specialized audio-visual materials and curricula

relative utility of fire safety skills training with different groups of children who vary in psychological disturbances in order to determine its generality. The efficacy of both interventions with children who show a heightened attraction to and interest in fire is certainly important to document as few methods have been evaluated in this context. A similar argument could made regarding the need to treat children whose firesetting results in significant avoidance of fire-related stimuli and heightened anxiety. Exposure-based treatments have been effective in such cases (see Jones, Ollendick, McLaughlin et al., 1989). Data collected in community settings could examine both short-term impact and long-term outcome. Finally, it would be of interest to examine the relative benefits of multicomponent interventions that integrate diverse approaches with more simplified interventions that lend themselves to efficient administration, such as films or groups.

Even with advances in intervention, there may be an even greater benefit to the application of primary prevention programs in this area. Prevention programs can be efficiently implemented in multiple naturalistic settings and by a range of community participants (e.g. schools, community centers). In all likelihood, the scope of impact following a media campaign (e.g. public service announcements) designed to reduce exposure to incendiary materials, child matchplay, and other fire-related risk factors may be much greater than those generated by interventions with known firesetters. Effective suppression and prevention of juvenile firesetting will no doubt require advances in scientific knowledge about its etiology and management, the integration of diverse educational and clinical services, and the dedicated efforts of a cadre of community practitioners.

ACKNOWLEDGMENTS

Preparation of this chapter was supported, in part, by a renewal of grant MH-39976 to the author from the National Institute of Mental Health. The author acknowledges the contribution of the staff associated with Project SAFETY (Services Aimed at Fire Education and Training for Youth). Many of the initial background studies reviewed herein were conducted in collaboration with Alan E. Kazdin, Ph.D. Reprint requests can be obtained from David J. Kolko, Director, WPIC/Special Services Unit, Western Psychiatric Institute and Clinic, 3811 O'Hara St., Pittsburgh, PA 15213, USA. E-mail: kolkodj@msx.upmc.edu.

REFERENCES

Adler, R. G., Nunn, R. J., Laverick, J., & Ross, R. (1988, October). *Royal Children's Hospital/Metropolitan Fire Brigade juvenile fire awareness and intervention program: Research and intervention protocol*. Unpublished paper.

Adler, R. G., Nunn, R., Northam, E., Lebnan, V., & Ross, R. (1994). Secondary prevention of childhood firesetting. *Journal of the American Academy of Child and Adolescent Psychiatry*, *33*, 1194–1202.

American Psychiatric Association (1987). *Diagnostic and statistical manual of mental disorders-revised* (3rd ed., Rev.). Washington, DC: Author.

Bourque, B. B., Cronin, R. C., & Han, M. (1993, November). *Controlling juvenile fireset-ting: An evaluation of three regional pilot programs.* Final report, submitted to the Office of Juvenile Justice and Delinquency Prevention, Office of Justice Programs, US Depart-ment of Justice. Washington, DC: American Institutes for Research.

Bumpass, E. R., Brix, R. J., & Preston, D. (1985). A community-based program for juve-nile firesetters. *Hospital and Community Psychiatry, 36,* 529–533.

Bumpass, E. R., Fagelman, F. D., & Brix, R. J. (1983). Intervention with children who set fires. *American Journal of Psychotherapy, 37,* 328–345.

Campbell, C., & Elliott, E. J. (1996). Skills building curriculum for juvenile firesetters. Salem, OR: Oregon Office of State Fire Marshal.

Cella, D. F., Perry, S. W., Kulchycky, S., & Goodwin, C. (1988). Stress and coping in rela-tives of burn patients: A longitudinal study. *Hospital and Community Psychiatry, 39,* 159–166.

Clackamas County Juvenile Firesetting Intervention Network (1996). Adolescent fireset-ters: An intervention—A restitution model with fire education emphasis. Salem, OR: Office of State Fire Marshall.

Clare, I. C. H., Murphy, G. H., Cox, D., & Chaplin, E. H. (1992). Assessment and treatment of firesetting: A single-case investigation using a cognitive-behavioral model. *Criminal Behaviour and Mental Health, 2,* 253–268.

Cole, R. E., Grolnick, W. S., McCandrews, M. M., et al. (1986). *Rochester fire-related youth project, progress report, Vol. 2.* Rochester, NY: New York State Office of Fire Preven-tion and Control.

Cole, R. E., Grolnick, W., & Schwartzman, P. (1993). Fire Setting. In R. T. Ammerman, C. Last, & M. Hersen (Eds.), *Handbook of prescriptive treatments for children and adolescents.* Boston, MA: Allyn & Bacon.

Cole, R. E., Laurenitis, L. R., McCandrews, M. M., et al. (1983). *Final report of the 1983 fire-related youth program development project.* Rochester, NY: New York State Office of Fire Prevention and Control.

Cox-Jones, C., Lubetsky, M., Fultz, S. A., & Kolko, D. J. (1990). Inpatient treatment of a young recidivist firesetter. *Journal of the American Academy of Child Psychiatry, 29,* 936–941.

DeSalvatore, G., & Hornstein, R. (1991). Juvenile firesetting: Assessment and treatment in psychiatric hospitalization and residential placement. *Child and Youth Care Forum, 20,* 103–114.

Eisler, R. M. (1974). Crisis intervention in the family of a firesetter. *Psychotherapy: Theory, Research and Practice, 9,* 76–79.

Federal Emergency Management Agency (1979). *Interviewing and counseling juvenile firesetters.* Washington, DC: US Government Printing Office.

Federal Emergency Management Agency (1983). *Juvenile firesetter handbook: Dealing with children ages 7 to 13.* Washington, DC: US Government Printing Office.

Federal Emergency Management Agency (1987). *Juvenile firesetter handbook: Dealing with adolescents ages 14 to 18.* Washington, DC: US Government Printing Office.

Federal Emergency Management Agency (1994). *The national juvenile firesetter/Arson control and prevention program* (Executive summary). Washington, DC: US Fire Administration.

Gaynor, J., & Hatcher, C. (1987). *The psychology of child firesetting: Detection and inter-vention.* New York: Brunner/Mazel.

Grolnick, W. S., Cole, R. E., Laurenitis, L., & Schwartzman, P. I. (1990). Playing with fire: A developmental assessment of children's fire understanding and experience. *Journal of Clinical Child Psychology, 19,* 128–135.

Hall, J. R. (1995, August). *Children playing with fire: U.S. experience, 1980–1993.* Quincy, MA: National Fire Protection Association.

Hanson, M., Mackay-Soroka, S., Staley, S., & Poulton, L. (1994). Delinquent firesetters:

A comparative study of delinquency and firesetting histories. *Canadian Journal of Psychiatry*, *39*, 230–232.

Heath, G. A., Hardesty, V. A., Goldfine, P. E., & Walker, A. M. (1985). Diagnosis and child-hood firesetting. *Journal of Clinical Psychology*, *41*, 571–575.

Holland, C. J. (1969). Elimination by the parents of firesetting behavior in a 7-year old boy. *Behaviour Research & Therapy*, *7*, 135–137.

Humphreys, J., Kopet, T., & Lajoy, R. (1994). Clinical considerations in the treatment of juvenile firesetters. *The Behavior Therapist*, *17*, 13–15.

Humphreys, J., & Kopet, T. (1996, March). *Manual for juvenile firesetter needs assessment protocol*. Salem, OR: Office of State Fire Marshal.

The Idea Bank (1997). Juvenile firesetter resources. Santa Barbara, CA: The Idea Bank, 1139 Alameda Padre Serra (Info@the ideabank.com).

Jacobson, R. R. (1985a). Child firesetters: A clinical investigation. *Journal of Child Psychology and Psychiatry*, *26*, 759–768.

Jacobson, R. R. (1985b). The subclassification of child firesetters. *Journal of Child Psychology and Psychiatry*, *26*, 769–775.

Johnston, K. (1996). *A step by step approach to group treatment and fire safety education: An eight session intervention program for child firesetters*. Salem, OR: Office of State Fire Marshal.

Jones, R. T., Kazdin, A. E., & Haney, J. I. (1981). Social validation and training of emergency fire safety skills for potential injury prevention and life saving. *Journal of Applied Behavior Analysis*, *14*, 249–260.

Jones, R. T., Ollendick, T. H., McLaughlin, K. J., & Williams, C. E. (1989). Elaborative and behavioral rehearsal in the acquisition of fire emergency skills and the reduction of fear of fire. *Behavior Therapy*, *20*, 93–101.

Jones, R. T., Ollendick, T. H., & Shinske, F. K. (1989). The role of behavioral versus cognitive variables in skill acquisition. *Behavior Therapy*, *20*, 293–302.

Juvenile Firesetter Intervention Program (1998). *Hot Issues*, *8*. Salem, OR: Office of State Fire Marshall.

Kafry, D. (1980). Playing with matches: Children and fire. In D. Canter (Ed.), *Fires and human behavior* (pp. 41–60). Chichester, UK: Wiley.

Kazdin, A. E., & Kolko, D. J. (1986). Parent psychopathology and family functioning among childhood firesetters. *Journal of Abnormal Child Psychology*, *14*, 315–329.

Kelso, J., & Stewart, M. A. (1986). Factors which predict the persistence of aggressive conduct disorder. *Journal of Child Psychology and Psychiatry*, *27*, 77–86.

Kolko, D. J. (1983). Multicomponent parental treatment of firesetting in a developmentally-disabled boy. *Journal of Behavior Therapy and Experimental Psychiatry*, *14*, 349–353.

Kolko, D. J. (1988). Community interventions for childhood firesetters: A comparison of two national programs. *Hospital and Community Psychiatry*, *39*, 973–979.

Kolko, D. J. (1989). Fire setting and pyromania. In C. Last & M. Hersen (Eds.), *Handbook of Child Psychiatric Diagnosis* (pp. 443–459). New York: Wiley.

Kolko, D. J. (1994). Conduct Disorder. In M. Hersen, R. T. Ammerman, & L. Sisson (Eds.), *Handbook of aggressive and destructive behavior in psychiatric patients* (pp. 363–394). New York: Plenum.

Kolko, D. J. (1996). Education and counseling for child firesetters: A comparison of skills training programs with standard practice. In E. D. Hibbs & P. S. Jensen (Eds.), *Psychosocial treatments for child and adolescent disorders: Empirically based strategies for clinical practice* (pp. 409–433). Washington, DC: American Psychological Association.

Kolko, D. J., & Ammerman, R. T. (1988). Firesetting. In M. Hersen & C. Last (Eds.), *Child behavior therapy casebook* (pp. 243–262). New York: Plenum.

Kolko, D. J., & Kazdin, A. E. (1986). A conceptualization of firesetting in children and adolescents. *Journal of Abnormal Child Psychology*, *14*, 49–62.

Kolko, D. J., & Kazdin, A. E. (1988a). Parent–child correspondence in identification of fire-setting among child psychiatric patients. *Journal of Child Psychology and Psychiatry*, *29*, 175–184.

Kolko, D. J., & Kazdin, A. E. (1988b). Prevalence of firesetting and related behaviors in child psychiatric inpatients. *Journal of Consulting and Clinical Psychology*, *56*, 628–630.

Kolko, D. J., & Kazdin, A. E. (1989a). Assessment of dimensions of childhood firesetting among child psychiatric patients and nonpatients. *Journal of Abnormal Child Psychology*, *17*, 157–176.

Kolko, D. J., & Kazdin, A. E. (1989b). The Children's Firesetting Interview with psychiatrically referred and nonreferred children. *Journal of Abnormal Child Psychology*, *17*, 609–624.

Kolko, D. J., & Kazdin, A. E. (1991a). Matchplay and firesetting in children: Relationship to parent, marital, and family dysfunction. *Journal of Clinical Child Psychology*, *19*, 229–238.

Kolko, D. J., & Kazdin, A. E. (1991b). Aggression and psychopathology in matchplaying and firesetting children: A replication and extension. *Journal of Clinical Child Psychology*, *20*, 191–201.

Kolko, D. J., & Kazdin, A. E. (1991c). Motives of childhood firesetters: Firesetting characteristics and psychological correlates. *Journal of Child Psychology and Psychiatry*, *32*, 535–550.

Kolko, D. J., & Kazdin, A. E. (1992). The emergence and recurrence of child firesetting: A one-year prospective study. *Journal of Abnormal Child Psychology*, *20*, 17–37.

Kolko, D. J., & Kazdin, A. E. (1994). Children's descriptions of their firesetting incidents: Characteristics and relationship to recidivism. *Journal of the American Academy of Child Psychiatry*, *33*, 114–122.

Kolko, D. J., & Kazdin, A. E. (1995). *Two-year follow-up of child firesetters: Late-starting and recidivism*. Poster presented at the Annual Meeting of the Association for the Advancement of Behavior Therapy, Washington, DC.

Kolko, D. J., Kazdin, A. E., & Meyer, E. C. (1985). Aggression and psychopathology in childhood firesetters: Parent and child reports. *Journal of Consulting and Clinical Psychology*, *53*, 377–385.

Kolko, D. J., Watson, S., & Faust, J. (1991). Fire safety/prevention skills training to reduce involvement with fire in young psychiatric inpatients: Preliminary findings. *Behavior Therapy*, *22*, 269–284.

Madanes, C. (1981). *Strategic family therapy*. San Francisco, CA: Jossey-Bass.

McGrath, P., Marshall, P. T., & Prior, K. (1979). A comprehensive treatment program for a firesetting child. *Journal of Behavior Therapy and Experimental Psychiatry*, *10*, 69–72.

Minuchin, S. (1974). *Families and family therapy*. San Francisco, CA: Jossey-Bass.

Moore, J. M., Thompson-Pope, S. K., & Whited, R. M. (1994). MMPI-A profiles of adolescent boys with a history of firesetting. *Journal of Personality Assessment*, *67*, 116–126.

Moos, R. H., Insel, P. M., & Humphrey, B. (1974). *Family work and group environment scales*. Palo Alto, CA: Consulting Psychologists Press.

National Fire Protection Association (1978). *Executive summary report of the Learn Not to Burn Curriculum*. Quincy, MA: Author.

National Fire Protection Association (1979). *Learn Not to Burn Curriculum*. Quincy, MA: Author.

National Fire Protection Association (1993, October). *Report of the NFPA task force on juvenile firesetting* (Inaugural meeting). Norwood, MA: Author.

National Fire Protection Associatio (1995, September). *Report of the NFPA firesetter practitioners' forum*. Braintree, MA: Author.

Oregon Treatment Strategies Task Force (1996). *The cycles of firesetting: An Oregon model*. Salem, OR: Office of State Fire Marshall.

Parrish, J. M., Capriotti, R. M., Warzak, W. J., Handen, B. L., Wells, T. J., Phillipson, S. J., & Porter, C. A. (1985). *Multivariate analysis of juvenile firesetting*. Paper presented at the

Annual Meeting of the Association for the Advancement of Behavior Therapy, Houston, TX.

Pierce, J. L., & Hardesty, V. A. (1997). Non-referral of psychopathological child firesetters to mental health services. *Journal of Clinical Psychology*, *53*, 349–350.

Pinsonneault, I. (1996). *Fire awareness: Training for foster parents*. Fall River, MA: F.I.R.E. Solutions.

Porth, D. (1996). A report on the juvenile firesetting problem. *The Portland Report '95*. Portland, OR: Portland Fire Bureau.

Rasanen, P., Hirvenoja, R., Hakko, H., & Vaisanen, E. (1995). A portrait of the juvenile arsonist. *Forensic Science International*, *73*, 41–47.

Repo, E., & Virkkunen, M. (1997). Young arsonists: History of conduct disorder, psychiatric diagnoses and criminal recidivism. *Journal of Forensic Psychiatry*, *8*, 311–320.

Rice, M. E., & Harris, G. T. (1991). Firesetters admitted to a maximum security psychiatric institution: Offenders and offenses. *Journal of Interpersonal Violence*, *6*, 461–475.

Sakheim, G. A., & Osborn, E. (1986). A psychological profile of juvenile firesetters in residential treatment: A replication study. *Child Welfare*, *45*, 495–503.

Sakheim, G. A., & Osborn, E. (1994). *Firesetting children: Risk assessment and treatment*. Washington, DC: Child Welfare League of America.

Sakheim, G. A., Osborn, E., & Abrams, D. (1991). Toward a clearer differentiation of high-risk from low-risk fire-setters. *Child Welfare*, *45*, 489–503.

Sakheim, G. A., Vigdor, M. G., Gordon, M., & Helprin, L. M. (1985). A psychological profile of juvenile firesetters in residential treatment. *Child Welfare*, *44*, 453–476.

Showers, J., & Pickrell, E. P. (1987). Child firesetters: A study of three populations. *Hospital and Community Psychiatry*, *38*, 495–501.

Stawar, T. L. (1976). Fable mod: Operantly structured fantasies as an adjunct in the modification of firesetting behavior. *Journal of Behavior Therapy and Experimental Psychiatry*, *7*, 285–287.

Stewart, M. A., & Culver, K. W. (1982). Children who set fires: The clinical picture and a follow-up. *British Journal of Psychiatry*, *140*, 357–363.

Stoddard, F. J., Norman, D. K., Murphy, J. M., & Beardslee, W. R. (1989). Psychiatric outcome of burned children and adolescents. *Journal of the American Academy of Child and Adolescent Psychiatry*, *28*, 589–595.

The Strike Zone (1997, Fall). *Massachusetts coalition for juvenile firesetter programs*, 1–8.

Terjestam, P. Y., & Ryden, O. (1996). Fire-settings as normal behavior: Frequencies and patterns of change in the behavior of 7–16 year old children. *Research report* (pp. 21–147/96). Karlstad, Sweden: Swedish Rescue Services Agency.

US Federal Bureau of Investigation (1995). *Uniform crime reports*. Washington, DC: Author.

Webb, N. B., Sakheim, G. A., Towns-Miranda, L., & Wagner, C. R. (1990). Collaborative treatment of juvenile firesetters: Assessment and outreach. *American Journal of Orthopsychiatry*, *60*, 305–310.

Williams, C. E., & Jones, R. (1989). Impact of self-instructions on response maintenance and children's fear of fire. *Journal of Clinical Psychology*, *18*, 84–89.

Wooden, W., & Berkey, M. L. (1984). *Children and arson: America's middle class nightmare*. New York: Plenum.

Chapter 27

Assessment and Treatment: Violent Offenders

Devon L. L. Polaschek
Victoria University of Wellington, Wellington, New Zealand
and
Nikki Reynolds
Department of Corrections Psychological Service,
Lambton Quay, Wellington, New Zealand

INTRODUCTION

Violent offending is considered by many to be on the increase. Regardless of whether this is true, violent offenders are an increasing proportion of correctional populations in many parts of the Western world. Non-sexual violence constitutes an extensive and disparate category of human behaviours which, despite its seriousness, has not received the level of attention accorded to sexual offending by clinicians and correctional practitioners. However, interest is growing, especially in the area of treatment provision, although many fundamental research questions remain. The focus of this chapter is generally on violent juvenile and adult male offenders; for convenience the male pronoun will be used throughout. Because of space constraints, readers are referred to more detailed reviews and sources wherever possible.

ASSESSMENT

The aims of treatment-oriented assessment are to develop a sophisticated conceptual model of the offender, his offence characteristics and personal vulnerabilities; to determine which of these are criminogenic, and then to match

Handbook of Offender Assessment and Treatment. Edited by C. R. Hollin.
© 2000 John Wiley & Sons Ltd.

the offender with a programme that addresses these. Working with violent offenders whether at the assessment or treatment stage poses challenges. Violent offenders often are resistant to fully admitting their offending, to taking responsibility for it, and to committing themselves to behavioural change. Additionally they often bring to assessment an aggressive, hostile, or intimidating interpersonal style. This forms an obstacle to gaining accurate information, challenges rapport building, and can be aversive and stressful for the assessor. Lastly, because few violent offenders are specialists (Reiss & Roth, 1993; Simon, 1997) many have extensive and diverse histories of criminal behaviour. Alongside similar childhood, adolescent, and adult features, these histories render them essentially indistinguishable from frequent offenders (Capaldi & Patterson, 1996; Farrington, 1994), and suggest an underlying criminal propensity that includes the potential for violent behaviour (Farrington, 1994; Reiss & Roth, 1993).

Comprehensive assessment currently relies as much on clinical experience and tradition as it does on the empirical literature, and there is a dearth of standardised assessment measures (Correctional Service of Canada, 1995). Foci are diverse, ranging from early developmental issues to the details of the current offence. The framework used here for organising these foci is the *offence chain* or *problem behaviour process* (Ward, Louden, Hudson, & Marshall, 1995), where assessment topics are structured around the goal of understanding the role of developmental, cognitive, affective, social/contextual, and behavioural factors and interactions as they impinge on the offending concerned, and as each offence sequence unfolds over time (Ward, McCormack, Hudson, & Polaschek, 1997). However, a number of other useful assessment structures exist (see Goldstein & Keller, 1987; Megargee, 1995).

The overall goal of assessment is to develop an individual case formulation for the assessed offender that, regardless of whether treatment is to be provided individually, via a group "package", or a combination of the two, will give a basis for reviewing that individual's progress in treatment and their status at its completion relative to their assessed treatment needs. Empirically derived criminogenic needs assessments for violent offenders are yet to be conducted; assessment is driven largely by clinical practice, theory, and speculation about the relevance to violent offenders of needs assessment with other offender groups (Howells, Watt, Hall, & Baldwin, 1997).

Assessment Methods

Ideally assessment should take place over a number of sessions and include a combination of interview, self-report (e.g. *in vivo* thought sampling), psychometric instruments, interviews with significant others (family, friends, prison and probation staff, psychiatric nurses), response evaluation (Goldstein & Keller, 1987), and behavioural observation. Existing documentation such as previous psychological or psychiatric reports, probation reports, court summaries and sentencing notes, institutional files, and official conviction histories will assist in developing a longitudinal perspective of the individual.

In addition to developing a case formulation, the assessor may simultaneously be involved in "selling" the programme to the participant, where programme participation is not mandatory. Interviewing strategies typically helpful in gaining rapport with offenders, developing a collaborative relationship, and motivating behavioural change, assist with this goal and in improving the quality of self-disclosure by the offender (e.g. McGrath, 1990; Miller & Rollnick, 1991). Issues of cultural and gender appropriateness, and reading level of the client population being assessed need to be considered in making choices about assessors, assessment instruments, and methods that will be used.

Assessment Areas

Essentially areas for assessment include a range of factors found to be common to frequent offenders and a number of issues that are thought to be particularly relevant to violence. Because of the heterogeneity of the violent offender group the list of assessment topics needs to be wide ranging. Clearly in some areas, topics will be directly related to treatment targets, whereas others (e.g. developmental history) may give an indication of the degree of risk or the pervasiveness or entrenchment of a propensity for violent behaviour. The existing literature suggests that the following areas are of potential relevance, but the list is not inclusive. In particular, areas that commonly are included in a general mental health screen (e.g. major psychiatric disorders) may be highly relevant to particular populations but are omitted because of space considerations. Where appropriate psychometric measures exist for a particular area, they are noted. In many areas measurement is in its infancy. Goldstein and Keller (1987) and the Correctional Service of Canada (1995) provide lists of additional suggested measures.

Offender Characteristics

Cognitive Processes and Products

A variety of cognitive or information-processing biases have been implicated in both anger- and violence-proneness. Copello and Tata (1990) found that adult male violent offenders were more likely than non-violent offenders and non-offenders to interpret ambiguous sentences as threatening, similar to the hostile attributional biases found in aggressive children by Dodge and colleagues (e.g. Lochman & Dodge, 1994). Such biases are conceptualised as arising from the influence of established schema (Serin & Kuriychuk, 1994), or behavioural scripts (Huesmann, 1988). Although there is little research, Novaco and Welsh's (1989) suggestions about information-processing mechanisms in the cognitive mediation of anger and aggression may provide a working assessment model. They propose five types of information-processing biases: attentional cueing, perceptual matching, attribution error, false consensus, and anchoring effects, and make suggestions about assessment methodology.

Few psychometric measures of cognitive products such as aggressive beliefs exist. The use of vignettes with coding of responses to probes appears promising (Serin & Kuriychuk, 1994; see also Slaby & Guerra, 1988).

Impulsivity and Self-Regulation Deficits

Impulsivity can be conceptualised as a cognitive processing deficit (Serin & Kuriychuk, 1994). Self-regulation refers to both self-initiated, well-organised, goal-directed activity and to self-control, particularly restraint, and the ability to delay gratification and tolerate tension when there are significant benefits to doing so (Ward, Hudson, & Keenan, 1998). Most often self-regulatory failure in violent offenders has been viewed simply as a failure to inhibit responding to immediate cues (Serin & Kuriychuk, 1994). Typically such offenders appear to respond violently to the many cues they interpret as provoking (e.g. perceived slights to self-image), without consideration of the costs.

Barratt's (1994) research on impulsiveness suggests that the concept has motoric and cognitive components. Impulsiveness is viewed as being responsible for aggression associated with a "hair-trigger" temper, that results in thoughtless violence, often followed afterwards by guilt and remorse and a resolution not to aggress again, which is not adhered to. However, he notes that two or more types of violence (e.g. impulsive and planned) often occur in the same individual, thus causing confusion for researchers and therapists. A variety of forms of self-regulatory failure not associated with impulsivity may also occur. For example, over a much longer period of time, an individual may brood over a grievance, disrupting internal self-control mechanisms by developing offence-supportive cognitive distortions and escalating anger. Several distinct types of self-regulatory problems have been proposed for sex offending (Ward et al., 1998), and may apply as well to violent offending. Measures of impulsivity currently in use include Barratt's BIS-11 (Barratt, 1994) and Eysenck's 1.7 scale (Eysenck & Eysenck, 1977).

Anger and Hostility

Anger is a subjective emotion which while neither necessary nor sufficient for violence to occur, has a causal relationship to violence in that it operates as a mediator of the relationship between subjectively aversive events and behaviour intended to harm (Novaco, 1994). Novaco proposes a conceptual framework for anger with cognitive, behavioural, and physiological domains. The subjective affect of anger results from the highly automatic cognitive labelling of arousal. Violent offenders often appear to overlabel arousal so that their predominant emotional experience is anger.

Anger is often perceived as unpleasant and individuals may undertake a variety of actions to alleviate or avoid it. However, the individual's perceptions of the experience of being angry should be assessed. Some violent offenders find anger very satisfying, and may deliberately expose themselves to situations and cues that will arouse them. Such individuals may have pathways to violence in which by getting angry they are then justified in acting violently. In this sense, exposure to reliably provoking cues can be seen as a form of covert planning on the offender's part.

A variety of aspects of anger can be assessed. Existing scales provide measures of situations that are anger provoking, the extensiveness of anger responding or anger as a trait, how anger is expressed, and the degree to which it is controllable. Novaco's most recent scale (Novaco Anger Scale; 1994) assesses anger across cognitive (attentional focus, suspicion, rumination, and hostile attitude), arousal (intensity, duration, somatic tension, and irritability), and behavioural (impulsive reaction, verbal aggression, physical confrontation, and indirect expression) domains, and also provides an index of anger intensity in various provoking situations.

Other scales with reasonable psychometric properties include the Buss–Durkee Hostility Inventory (Buss & Durkee, 1957), and the State–Trait Anger Expression Inventory (Spielberger, 1988). A new scale recommended by Gendreau, Goggin, and Paparozzi (1996) is the Aggression Questionnaire (Buss & Perry, 1992). Measures of hostility, anger, and aggression may be highly correlated, and there is little evidence that offenders differ from non-offenders on these constructs (Serin & Kuriychuk, 1994). However, the measures are potentially useful in identifying those who do.

Empathy

Empathy deficits can be pervasive and enduring (e.g. in psychopathy) or situation- or affect-specific. Assessment needs to establish which is the case for a particular offender since this will determine the type and extent of intervention required. The four-stage information-processing model suggested by Marshall, Hudson, Jones, and Fernandez (1995) also has assessment implications in that it enables fine-grained analysis of the sources of empathy deficits. The four steps are:

1. recognising the other's emotion;
2. taking their perspective;
3. experiencing a matching or appropriate emotional response from that perspective; and
4. generating a well-formulated behavioural response.

Marshall et al. argue that a precursor deficit to step 1 may be an inability to identify one's own emotional state. This appears common in violent offenders.

There are a number of scales for measuring empathy, including the Interpersonal Reactivity Index (Davis, 1983) and the Hogan empathy scale (Hogan, 1969). Measures of specific victim empathy may also be needed.

Social Competence

Traditional conceptualisations of social skills deficits are being replaced by multi-staged models of social competence. McFall's (1990) information-processing model provides one useful assessment framework. McFall proposes that social competence is a function of the adequacy of social task performance in a particular circumstance, as evident to the individual performer or observers. Social skills are the underlying component processes involved in competent task performance. Three sequential processes are involved:

1. Decoding skills such as correctly perceiving and interpreting incoming information such as social cues.
2. Decision skills as seen in generating possible responses, matching them to the requirements of the situation, choosing the most suitable, checking whether it is behaviourally available, and evaluating its likely outcome relative to other options.
3. Enactment skills such as carrying out the chosen behavioural routine, including smooth performance, monitoring and adjusting to achieve the intended impact (McFall, 1990).

The advantages of using this model are clear; social competence across a wide range of settings will require an extensive behavioural repertoire. Some offenders will have an impoverished range of social behaviours from which to select, while others will have a good range of choices but will fail to utilise an appropriate option because of misperception of others' behavioural intentions or misjudgement about which behaviours will best achieve their goals.

Social Support for Violence

Violent offenders may be socially isolated individuals or have extensive involvement with a supportive peer group. A supportive social context provides plentiful opportunities for (1) developing relationships with potential co-offenders; (2) developing a wider repertoire of violent behaviours with supervised training, rehearsal and practice; and (3) social reinforcement for violence, through gaining peer approval, a sense of belonging, and enhanced status. Even if support in the wider society is limited, significant subcultural pockets exist in many Western countries that support warrior values (McCarthy, 1994), including a code of honour (Nisbett, 1993), physically risky and courageous behaviour, or machismo (Zaitchik & Mosher, 1993). Perhaps the most explicit example is gang membership. Assessment of social support for proviolent and prosocial behaviour needs to consider both how willing the individual is to relinquish subcultural values supporting diverse forms of violence, and the likely accessibility of an attractive non-violent, actively prosocial support network.

Assessment of alcohol and drug use patterns, co-existing psychiatric and personality disorders may also have relevance to the choice of treatment options. General and violent recidivism risk (see Gendreau et al., 1996; Serin, 1995) and readiness to undertake treatment (Serin & Kennedy, 1997) should also be considered in a thorough assessment.

Offence Characteristics

A detailed picture of how the typical or current offence unfolded over time should be constructed with the offender. Interviewing, police and court records, and other file information are essential to this phase. It is important to assess whether there are a variety of offence patterns for an individual offender since diversity seems more typical than does a single repeated pattern. As part of understanding the offence chains of an offender, a full assessment of the range of violent acts committed, the range of victims, the duration of offending, the motives and goals involved should be undertaken. This will identify physical and emotional high-risk situations (Serin & Brown, 1996).

A number of specific foci of enquiry may assist in establishing a clear offence picture. For example, did alcohol or drugs facilitate the offending, or was there a sudden absence of drugs used routinely to manage violence precursors such as anger and boredom? Similarly, did anger feature prominently, and if so at what stages? What relationship did it have to the level of violence used, and to victim resistance? Were there pre-existing violent fantasies? There has been a dearth of research on the role of fantasies or cognitive rehearsal in violent offending, although it is often seen in assessment. Elaborative rumination is thought likely to make overlearned aggressive scripts both more accessible in memory and more generalised (Huesmann, 1988). In adults, general fantasy elaboration may become an established strategy for enhancing emotional well-being, while fantasising in a ruminative way about a particular individual seems clinically to be most often associated with individuals who "hold grudges" and plan revenge, sometimes over very extended periods of time.

As with sexual offending, a number of different types of planning may be discerned in the early portions of the offence chain. Planning may be explicit and elaborate or an offence may at first be presented as impulsive. Closer examination and greater familiarity with the individual's offence style may suggest covert or implicit planning in the early "apparently irrelevant decisions" that help create a situation in which violence is imminent. Lastly, some offenders demonstrate planned opportunism (Pithers, 1993), where they engage in a variety of offending-related high-risk situations on a routine, recreational basis, and can readily respond violently if a suitable situation presents itself. Such violence will appear impulsive on superficial analysis (e.g. getting into fights in bars).

Historically, the motives underlying violent behaviour have been classified into two categories: expressive and instrumental. More recently, multidimensional scaling research suggested four categories of motive: hostile, instrumental, normative, or status-related (Campbell, Muncer, & Bibel, 1985). In reality more than one goal (e.g. hostile and status-related) may be operating simultaneously, and goals and motives may change as the interaction unfolds. In the traditional clinical literature, status-related violence has been given less attention than some argue it deserves (e.g. Indermaur, 1995). Predominant motives may change as the offender's career matures. Indermaur's research on offenders committing acts of violence in the course of property crimes suggests that mixed expressive and instrumental goals are common. Instrumental violence not associated with significant affective arousal (e.g. anger, excitement, fear) may be confined to psychopathic individuals (Cornell et al., 1996; Dempster et al., 1996).

Co-offending is especially common for robbery and street fights (Farrington, 1994) and gang-related crime, but is rarely discussed in the treatment literature. Assessment would include examining the relationship between co-offenders prior to the offence, the relative contribution of each to planning and execution, and how relationship dynamics contributed to the progression of events during the offence. Also of interest is whether the offender persistently recruits younger offenders with whom to commit violent crimes (Farrington, 1994), and whether he has organised or "set up" other offenders to commit violent crimes on his behalf, such as robberies or beatings. In particular, assessment of status-related offending requires analysis of the role of onlookers and co-offenders.

Although there is little evidence of specialisation within types of violent offending, assessment should examine whether offenders target particular victim groups, such as women, men or strangers, the degree of victim injury, the pattern of interaction between victim and offender, and how weapons are used.

Post-offence reactions can range from satisfaction to despair and shock, and enquiry can reveal more information about offence goals and their relationship to actual behaviour as well as whether or not the behaviour is consistent with the offender's personal behavioural standards. Emotional reactions such as remorse and self-disgust, and the resolution to make changes to avoid further violence suggest the existence of some internal constraints against violent behaviour, whereas satisfaction and other positive mood states may suggest that violence is congruent with the offender's self image.

TREATMENT

Recent meta-analyses of offender rehabilitation programmes have done much to refute the contention that "nothing works" and have offered guidance about general principles associated with effective correctional programming. Cullen and Gendreau (1989) confirm in an important review of the literature on correctional rehabilitation, that the most effective theoretical bases for programmes are: social learning theory, cognitive models, skills training, differential association, and behavioural systems including family therapy. Effective intervention components include: anti-criminal modelling, problem-solving, use of community resources, high-quality interpersonal relationships, firm but fair discipline, and relapse prevention/self-efficacy. Non-directive approaches, punishment paradigms, deterrence, and medical model approaches were most often associated with ineffective styles of intervention.

Unlike sexual offending against children, violent offending has not traditionally attracted the funding necessary systematically to develop and evaluate interventions (Blackburn, 1988). Although violent offender programmes currently are proliferating in several countries, especially within North America (J. Bush, personal communication, 18 November 1996; Serin & Brown, 1997), there are few outcome studies to guide the development of these programmes, and methodological problems are frequently found. However, a small group of studies from both the juvenile and adult arenas provides some guidance for treatment programme development. Priority here has been given to studies with higher methodological standards, programmes that appear to be targeting higher-risk rather than low-risk offenders, and those that contain more than one treatment component. Often these programmes are provided in a group or mixed group-and-individual format. For a purely individual case-formulation-based approach to violent offender treatment, see Browne and Howells (1996). Van Voorhis, Cullen, and Applegate (1995) provide guidelines on programme evaluation.

Juvenile Treatment Programmes

A number of secondary and tertiary prevention programmes appear promising with violent or potentially violent youth (see Guerra, Tolan, & Hammond, 1994; Tate, Reppucci, & Mulvey, 1995, for reviews). Goldstein and his colleagues (e.g. Goldstein, 1988) have developed an elaborate behavioural skills curriculum that includes components of anger control, prosocial skills, and prosocial values. Goldstein and Glick (1994) report several evaluations suggesting that Aggression Replacement Training (ART) has the potential to effect positive changes in participants on a number of relevant outcome indices, for a variety of populations and settings, including incarcerated violent youths and adolescent gangs.

A newer approach, the EQUIP programme (Gibbs, Potter, & Goldstein, 1995), integrates a peer-helping group format with cognitive–developmental and social information processing skills adapted from Goldstein's ART and Prepare (Goldstein, 1988) curricula, and Yochelson and Samenow's (1977) work. Seven to nine youths meet daily for 1 to 1.5 hours. The first treatment goal is to develop a prosocial group culture to motivate change. Once this is achieved, the teaching of the EQUIP curriculum commences (Gibbs, Potter, Barriga, & Liau, 1996). An outcome study in which incarcerated juveniles were randomly assigned either to EQUIP or to one of two control groups found significant reductions in self-reported misconduct and staff-reported misconduct in the treated group. General recidivism for the treatment group was 15% at both 6 and 12 months following release; significantly lower than the control groups' 29.7% recidivism at 6 months and 40.5% at 12 months (Leeman, Gibbs, & Fuller, 1993). No data on specific changes in violent behaviour were reported (see Gibbs et al., 1996).

Unlike the adult programme literature, where the offenders themselves tend to be the only direct programme recipients, programmes for youth have better incorporated significant others in treatment delivery. Tate et al. (1995) report preliminary evidence of effectiveness with violent youth for programmes such as Multisystemic Therapy (MST), that include a social–cognitive component and are directed at solving multiple problems across the various contexts in which the youth is embedded; family, peers, school, and neighbourhood.

Henggeler and colleagues have obtained extensive empirical support for MST with serious juvenile offenders. MST is based on social ecology and family systems models and delivers high-quality, individually tailored interventions to youth and their families, at times and places of their choosing (Henggeler, Melton, Brondino, Scherer, & Hanley, 1997; see Henggeler, 1997, for a review). MST has been implemented in four randomised clinical trials with over 300 offenders and their families. Improvements were found in rates of arrest (25–70% reduction) and out of home placement (50–64% reduction). MST has proved equally effective with African–American as with European–American youths.

Programmes for Adult Violent Offenders

The provision of psychological treatment to adult violent offenders predominantly has been limited to clinically unique approaches for individual offenders (Browne & Howells, 1996), or has focused on links between violence and anger (Hollin & Howells, 1989). Particularly vexing has been the absence of an adequate conceptual model to guide theoretically coherent programme development (Howells et al., 1997; Serin & Brown, 1996).

In New Zealand, low intensity anger management (AM) programmes have been offered for over a decade and remain the most common interventions for imprisoned violent offenders, despite few outcome data. A similar trend has been observed in other correctional populations (e.g. Australia: Howells et al., 1997; Canada: Serin & Brown, 1997). These programmes typically are based on Novaco's (1975, 1977) stress inoculation-coping skills approach, perhaps because Novaco provides an elaborate conceptual framework for anger and aggression (Novaco & Welsh, 1989).

In a recent review of outcome evaluations of AM, Novaco (1997) notes that few involve seriously violent participants, few report on the impact of their programmes on violent behaviour, and reconviction has not been examined. Inadequate descriptions of treatment content and process are common, but many may omit significant treatment targets (e.g. aggression-supportive beliefs; see Guerra & Slaby, 1990) and the level of service, often less than 25 hours, is unlikely to have an impact on all but the lowest risk offenders (Andrews, Bonta, & Hoge, 1990). Additional criticisms include the absence of evidence that violent offenders experience anger at pathological levels of frequency or intensity, rather than simply having developed dysfunctional methods of anger expression, and that an exclusive anger control focus ignores other common motivational bases for violence (Guerra et al., 1994) such as its normative and status-restorative functions. The observation of a number of writers that this narrow focus on the role of anger in violent offending can be seen to parallel the role ascribed to deviant sexual arousal in sexual offending models a decade ago, is encouraging given the current status of treatment models for sex offenders.

Several approaches show promise with violent offenders. The Cognitive Skills Training (CST) programme comprises 36 two-hour sessions delivered by staff coaches to groups of up to 10 offenders, combining didactic teaching of cognitive skills with group and individual skill practice. Based on the work of Ross and Fabiano (1985), CST deals with a variety of cognitive deficits identified as common to offender populations, including poor interpersonal, decision-making, goal-setting, and general thinking skills. Developed in Canada in the late 1980s, it has been completed by more than 5500 federal offenders in institutional and community settings (Robinson, 1995) and is being implemented internationally.

Robinson (1995) presents outcome data on a sample of 2125 offenders who have been receiving community supervision for at least 12 months following release. Of these, 67.9% were programme completers, 14.2% were drop-outs, and 17.8% were untreated waiting list controls. Within the 12 months, 44.5% of programme completers and 50.1% from the waiting list were readmitted. There were no differences between treated and untreated participants on technical parole violations but there was a 20% reduction in official reconvictions for programme completers. Violent offenders had approximately a 35% reduction in reconviction, except for robbers, whose recidivism rates were unchanged. The programme was most effective with low-risk offenders and Robinson concludes that this is because only relatively high-risk offenders are referred to the programme, so that the lowest risk offenders in the sample are high-risk offenders relative to the remainder of the correctional population. However, an alternative interpretation is that this is a relatively low to medium intensity programme (i.e. apparently 72 hours of programme in total), and thus is not suited to the highest risk offenders (cf. Bush, 1995b).

Another cognition-based programme, for male and female violent offenders, is the Cognitive Self Change (CSC) programme of the Vermont Department of Corrections. First implemented in 1988 (Bush, 1995a), it was developed from the work of Yochelson and Samenow (1977). It targets attitudes, beliefs, and thinking patterns that support violent behaviour. Groups are run by specifically trained prison staff and parole workers and the programme is delivered in three phases; the first two in prison and the third in the community. During Phase I, groups meet twice a week for 8 to 10 weeks, and undertake general programme orientation. In Phase II offenders identify their own high-risk thinking patterns (i.e. thinking associated with past criminal or violent behaviour), learn techniques for controlling and disrupting such thinking, and use what they have learned to develop relapse prevention plans for managing high-risk thinking in the community. Lastly, in Phase III offenders meet twice weekly for a year in maintenance groups after release into the community, and report high-risk situations they have experienced and their strategies for controlling their thinking in these situations (see Bush, 1995b, for details). Recent outcome data suggest significant reductions in parole violation and any rearrest for those who attended the programme for more than six months (Bush, 1995b). Of these, 45.5% had recidivated at three years compared with 76.7% of the untreated group. In an independent evaluation, Henning and Frueh (1996) found that of 55 treated offenders, 50% obtained a new criminal charge in the two years following release, compared with 70.8% of the 141 offenders in the control group. Like CST, this programme's central components are relevant to both violent and non-violent offending, focusing on the cognitive–emotional process leading to rule violation. Data are presented for violent rearrest, but the methodology prohibits drawing firm conclusions because a dichotomous (rearrest/none) measure was used. Since violent offenders are generalists, their first reoffence is likely to be a non-violent one. This will result in underestimation of post-programme violent recidivism.

In 1987 a residential community-based group programme for violent offenders, the Montgomery House Violence Prevention Project (VPP), was implemented in Hamilton, New Zealand. The VPP consisted of a series of three-month programmes for five to eight offenders on either parole or community supervision for violent convictions. The programme was cognitive–behavioural in content and method, but was embedded in a therapeutic community milieu in which group processes were used to develop mutual trust and skills practice (Dixon & Wikaira, 1988). Because 78% of programme participants were New Zealand Maaori, traditional Maaori customs and protocol were incorporated in the programme process. Participants attended up to 40 hours of structured modular group programming per week, including anger management and altering attitudes to violence, communication, relationship and parenting skills, social problem-solving, alcohol and drug intervention, and tikanga and te reo Maaori (Maaori culture and language) instruction. Forty-six offenders commenced and 33 completed the programme in the first two years. Reconvictions over an average 2.3 years of follow-up were compared with conviction rates for completers in the two years prior to programme admission. Both parolees and community-sentenced participants showed reductions in frequency and seriousness of violent offending (Polaschek & Dixon, 1997). Because of insufficient statistical power, effect size statistics were used to examine recidivism in a long-term (five-year) follow-up with a matched control group. The results found a medium reduction in general reconvictions and a large reduction in violent reconvictions for treated offenders, with insubstantial reductions on both indices for the control group (Dixon & Behrnes, 1996).

Guidelines for Treatment Provision

Treatment of violent offenders should conform to the risk, need, and responsivity principles identified in the rehabilitation literature (Andrews et al., 1990). With low-risk offenders, it may be possible to provide an adequate level of treatment on an individual basis, tailored to violence-related needs identified in assessment. However, provision of low intensity programmes that focus only on anger regulation is unlikely to reduce violence risk in those with an extensive and varied history of violence. For these individuals, it is likely that a more intensive, group treatment programme that contains a variety of treatment methods, and targets affect regulation and violence-related cognitive processes and products, that teaches a range of cognitive and social skills and strategies, and tackles other common correlates such as alcohol and drug abuse will be necessary.

The question of whether offenders in intensive violent offender programmes should be at high risk generally or at high risk of violence remains to be investigated, and depends conceptually on whether a programme is targeting factors relating to all types of offending, or factors hypothesized to be especially relevant to violent offending. Some programmes clearly do both (e.g. CSC, VPP) while others are specifically designed to address violent offending (e.g. Correctional Service of Canada, 1995). Future investigation needs to establish whether these concerns are relevant to reconviction outcomes. Needs assessment research on violent offenders (Howells et al., 1997) would assist in clarifying these issues and in developing more sophisticated conceptual models.

Existing programmes suggest a variety of development options for violent offending-based treatment. Most are cognitive–behavioural and provide a combination of approaches designed to challenge biases in information processing and distorted cognitions, and teach a range of other cognitive and interpersonal skills to manage violence risk. Preliminary interventions to enhance motivation and treatment responsivity and a maintenance or external relapse prevention phase may be added.

There is much work to be done to develop interventions with violent offenders to the level of sophistication of current sex offender programmes. Areas requiring development for this heterogeneous population include: assessment batteries (self-report questionnaires, vignette, and role-play measures) that are both sufficiently robust to assess treatment changes and empirically related to recidivism; comprehensive needs assessments for violent offender populations; risk measures that differentiate between general recidivism and violent recidivism; and lastly, methodologically sophisticated evaluation of programme innovations. Violent offender treatment is entering an exciting era that holds promise in providing a constructive alternative or adjunct to lengthy imprisonment sentences, and in reducing the enormous associated social costs.

REFERENCES

Andrews, D. A., Bonta, J., & Hoge, R. D. (1990). Classification for effective rehabilitation: Rediscovering psychology. *Criminal Justice and Behavior, 17*, 19–52.

Barratt, E. S. (1994). Impulsiveness and aggression. In J. Monahan & H. J. Steadman (Eds.), *Violence and mental disorder: Developments in risk assessment* (pp. 21–79). Chicago, IL: University of Chicago.

Blackburn, R. (1988). Cognitive behavioural approaches to understanding and treating aggression. In K. Howells & C. R. Hollin (Eds.), *Clinical approaches to aggression and violence* (pp. 6–23). Leicester, UK: The British Psychological Society.

Browne, K., & Howells, K. (1996). Violent offenders. In C. R. Hollin (Ed.), *Working with offenders: Psychological practice in offender rehabilitation* (pp. 188–210). Chichester, UK: Wiley.

Bush, J. (1995a). *Cognitive self change: A program manual.* Burlington, VA: Vermont Department of Corrections.

Bush, J. (1995b). Teaching self-risk management to violent offenders. In J. McGuire (Ed.), *What works: Reducing reoffending—Guidelines from research and practice* (pp. 139–154). Chichester, UK: Wiley.

Buss, A., & Durkee, A. (1957). An inventory for assessing different kinds of hostility. *Journal of Consulting and Clinical Psychology, 21,* 342–349.

Buss, A. H., & Perry, M. (1992). The aggression questionnaire. *Journal of Personality and Social Psychology, 63,* 452–459.

Campbell, A., Muncer, S., & Bibel, D. (1985). Taxonomies of aggressive behavior: A preliminary report. *Aggressive Behavior, 11,* 217–222.

Capaldi, D. M., & Patterson, G. R. (1996). Can violent offenders be distinguished from frequent offenders: Prediction from childhood to adolescence. *Journal of Research in Crime and Delinquency, 33,* 206–231.

Copello, A. G., & Tata, P. R. (1990). Violent behaviour and interpretative bias: An experimental study of the resolution of ambiguity in violent offenders. *British Journal of Clinical Psychology, 29,* 417–428.

Cornell, D. G., Warren, J., Hawk, G., Stafford, E., Oram, G., & Pine, D. (1996). Psychopathy in instrumental and reactive violent offenders. *Journal of Consulting and Clinical Psychology, 64,* 783–790.

Correctional Service of Canada (1995). *Persistently violent (nonsexual) offenders: A program proposal* (Report No. R-42). Ottawa, Canada: Author.

Cullen, F. T., & Gendreau, P. (1989). The effectiveness of correctional rehabilitation—reconsidering the "nothing works" debate. In L. Goodstein & D. L. McKenzie (Eds.), *The American prison: Issues in research policy* (pp. 23–44). New York: Plenum.

Davis, M. H. (1983). Measuring individual differences in empathy: Evidence for a multidimensional approach. *Journal of Personality and Social Psychology, 44,* 113–126.

Dempster, R. J., Lyon, D. R., Sullivan, L. E., Hart, S. D., Smiley, W. C., & Mulloy, R. (1996, August). *Psychopathy and instrumental aggression in violent offenders.* Poster session presented at the annual meeting of the American Psychological Association, Ontario, Canada.

Dixon, B. G., & Behrnes, S. (1996). *Violence prevention project reconviction study: Overview of study and findings.* Unpublished report, New Zealand Department of Corrections Psychological Service.

Dixon, B. G., & Wikaira, R. G. (1988, September). *The violence prevention project: Development of residential training programmes for violent offenders.* Poster paper presented at the XXIV International Congress of Psychology, Sydney, Australia.

Eysenck, S., & Eysenck, H. (1977). The place of impulsiveness in a dimensional system of personality description. *British Journal of Social and Clinical Psychology, 16,* 57–68.

Farrington, D. P. (1994). Human development and criminal careers. In M. Maguire, R. Morgan & R. Reiner (Eds.), J. Pepler & K. H. Rubin (Eds.), *The Oxford handbook of criminology* (pp. 511–584). Oxford: Clarendon Press.

Gendreau, P., Goggin, C., & Paparozzi, M. (1996). Principles of effective assessment for community corrections. *Federal Probation, 60*(3), 64–70.

Gibbs, J. C., Potter, G. B., Barriga, A. Q., & Liau, A. K. (1996). Developing the helping skills and prosocial motivation of aggressive adolescents in peer group programs. *Aggression and Violent Behavior, 1,* 283–305.

Gibbs, J. C., Potter, G., & Goldstein, A. P. (1995). *The EQUIP program: Teaching youth to think and act responsibly through a peer-helping approach.* Champaign, IL: Research Press.

Goldstein, A. P. (1988). *The prepare curriculum: Teaching prosocial competencies.* Champaign, IL: Research Press.

Goldstein, A. P., & Glick, B. (1994). *The prosocial gang: Implementing aggression replacement training*. Thousand Oaks, CA: Sage.

Goldstein, A. P., & Keller, H. (1987). *Aggressive behavior: Assessment and intervention*. New York: Pergamon.

Guerra, N. G., & Slaby, R. G. (1990). Cognitive mediators of aggression in adolescent offenders: 2. Intervention. *Developmental Psychology, 26*, 269–277.

Guerra, N. G., Tolan, P. H., & Hammond, W. R. (1994). Prevention and treatment of adolescent violence. In L. D. Eron, J. H. Gentry, & P. Schlegel (Eds.), *Reason to hope: A psychosocial perspective on violence and youth* (pp. 383–403). Washington, DC: American Psychological Association.

Henggeler, S. W. (1997). *Multisystemic therapy with serious juvenile offenders and their families: Program design, implementation and outcomes*. Unpublished manuscript.

Henggeler, S. W., Melton, G. B., Brondino, M. J., Scherer, D. G., & Hanley, J. H. (1997). Multisystemic therapy with violent and chronic juvenile offenders and their families: The role of treatment fidelity in successful dissemination. *Journal of Consulting and Clinical Psychology, 65*, 821–833.

Henning, K. R., & Frueh, B. C. (1996). Cognitive–behavioral treatment of incarcerated offenders: An evaluation of the Vermont Department of Corrections' cognitive self-change program. *Criminal Justice and Behavior, 23*, 523–541.

Hogan, R. (1969). Development of an empathy scale. *Journal of Consulting and Clinical Psychology, 33*, 307–316.

Hollin, C. R., & Howells, K. (1989). An introduction to concepts, models and techniques. In K. Howells & C. R. Hollin (Eds.), *Clinical approaches to violence* (pp. 3–24). Chichester, UK: Wiley.

Howells, K., Watt, B., Hall, G., & Baldwin, S. (1997). Developing programmes for violent offenders. *Legal and Criminological Psychology, 2*, 117–128.

Huesmann, L. R. (1988). An information processing model for the development of aggression. *Aggressive Behavior, 14*, 13–24.

Indermaur, D. (1995). *Violent property crime*. Sydney, Australia: Federation Press.

Leeman, L. W., Gibbs, J. C., & Fuller, D. (1993). Evaluation of a multicomponent group treatment program for juvenile delinquents. *Aggressive Behavior, 19*, 281–292.

Lochman, J. E., & Dodge, K. A. (1994). Social–cognitive processes of severely violent, moderately aggressive, and nonaggressive boys. *Journal of Consulting and Clinical Psychology, 62*, 366–374.

Marshall, W. L., Hudson, S. M., Jones, R., & Fernandez, Y. M. (1995). Empathy in sex offenders. *Clinical Psychology Review, 15*, 99–113.

McCarthy, B. (1994). Warrior values: A socio-historical survey. In J. Archer (Ed.), *Male violence* (pp. 105–120). London: Routledge.

McFall, R. M. (1990). The enhancement of social skills: An information-processing analysis. In W. L. Marshall, D. R. Laws, & H. E. Barbaree (Eds.), *Handbook of sexual assault: Issues, theories, and treatment of the offender* (pp. 311–330). New York: Plenum.

McGrath, R. J. (1990). Assessment of sexual aggressors: Practical clinical interviewing strategies. *Journal of Interpersonal Violence, 5*, 507–519.

Megargee, E. I. (1995). Assessing and understanding aggressive and violent patients. In J. N. Butcher (Ed.), *Clinical personality assessment: Practical approaches* (pp. 395–409). New York: Oxford University Press.

Miller, W. R., & Rollnick, S. (1991). *Motivational interviewing: Preparing people to change addictive behavior*. New York: Guilford.

Nisbett, R. E. (1993). Violence and U.S. regional culture. *American Psychologist, 48*, 441–449.

Novaco, R. W. (1975). *Anger control: The development and evaluation of an experimental treatment*. Lexington, MA: D. C. Heath.

Novaco, R. W. (1977). Stress inoculation: A cognitive therapy for anger and its application to a case of depression. *Journal of Consulting and Clinical Psychology, 45*, 600–608.

Novaco, R. W. (1994). Anger as a risk factor for violence. In J. Monahan & H. J. Steadman (Eds.), *Violence and mental disorder: Developments in risk assessment* (pp. 21–59). Chicago, IL: University of Chicago Press.

Novaco, R. W. (1997). Remediating anger and aggression with violent offenders. *Legal and Criminological Psychology, 2,* 77–88.

Novaco, R. W., & Welsh, W. N. (1989). Anger disturbances: Cognitive mediation and clinical prescriptions. In K. Howells & C. R. Hollin (Eds.), *Clinical approaches to violence* (pp. 39–60). Chichester, UK: Wiley.

Pithers, W. D. (1993). Treatment of rapists: Reinterpretation of early outcome data and exploratory constructs to enhance therapeutic efficacy. In G. C. N. Hall, R. Hirschman, J. R. Graham, & M. S. Zaragoza (Eds.), *Sexual aggression: Issues in etiology, assessment, and treatment* (pp. 167–196). Washington, DC: Taylor & Francis.

Polaschek, D. L. L., & Dixon, B. G. (1997). *The violence prevention project: The development and evaluation of a program for violent offenders.* Manuscript under review.

Reiss, A. J., & Roth, J. A. (Eds.) (1993). *Understanding and preventing violence.* Washington: National Academy.

Robinson, D. (1995). *The impact of cognitive skills training on post-release recidivism among Canadian federal offenders* (Report No. R-41). Ottawa, Canada: Correctional Service of Canada, Correctional Research and Development.

Ross, R. R., & Fabiano, E. A. (1985). *Time to think: A cognitive model of delinquency prevention and offender rehabilitation.* Johnson City, TN: Institute of Social Sciences and Arts.

Serin, R. (1995). Assessment and prediction of violent behaviour in offender populations. In T. A. Leis, L. L. Motiuk, & J. R. P. Ogloff (Eds.), *Forensic psychology: Policy and practice in Corrections* (pp. 69–90). Ontario, Canada: Correctional Service of Canada.

Serin, R., & Brown, S. (1996). Strategies for enhancing the treatment of violent offenders. *Forum on Corrections Research, 8*(3), 45–48.

Serin, R., & Brown, S. (1997). Treatment programs for offenders with violent histories: A national survey. *Forum on Corrections Research, 9*(2) (Available at http://198.103.98.138/crd/forum/e092/e092h.htm).

Serin, R., & Kennedy, S. (1997). *Treatment readiness and responsivity: Contributing to effective correctional programming.* (Report No. R54). Ottawa, Canada: Correctional Service of Canada, Correctional Research and Development. (Available at http://www.csc-scc.gc.ca/crd/reports/r54e.htm).

Serin, R. C., & Kuriychuk, M. (1994). Social and cognitive processing deficits in violent offenders: Implications for treatment. *International Journal of Law and Psychiatry, 17,* 431–441.

Simon, L. M. J. (1997). Do criminal offenders specialize in crime types? *Applied and Preventative Psychology, 6,* 35–53.

Slaby, R. G., & Guerra, N. G. (1988). Cognitive mediators of aggression in adolescent offenders: 1. Assessment. *Developmental Psychology, 24,* 580–588.

Spielberger, C. D. (1988). *State-trait anger expression inventory: Research edition professional manual.* Odessa, FL: Psychological Assessment Resources.

Tate, D. C., Reppucci, N. D., & Mulvey, E. P. (1995). Violent juvenile delinquents: Treatment effectiveness and implications for future action. *American Psychologist, 50,* 777–781.

Van Voorhis, P., Cullen, F. T., & Applegate, B. (1995). Evaluating interventions with violent offenders: A guide for practitioners and policymakers. *Federal Probation, 59*(2), 17–28.

Ward, T., Hudson, S. M, & Keenan, T. (1998). A self-regulation model of the sexual offense process. *Sexual Abuse: A Journal of Research and Treatment, 10,* 141–157.

Ward, T., Louden, K., Hudson, S. M., & Marshall, W. L. (1995). A descriptive model of the offence chain in child molesters. *Journal of Interpersonal Violence, 10,* 452–472.

Ward, T., McCormack, J., Hudson, S. M., & Polaschek, D. (1997). Rape: Assessment and treatment. In D. R. Laws & W. O'Donohue (Eds.), *Sexual deviance: Theory, assessment and treatment* (pp. 356–393). New York: Guilford.

Yochelson, S., & Samenow, S. (1977). *The criminal personality, Vol 2: The change process.* New York: Jason Aronsen.

Zaitchik, M. C., & Mosher, D. L. (1993). Criminal justice implications of the macho personality constellation. *Criminal Justice and Behavior*, 20, 227–239.

Chapter 28

Offenders with Major Mental Disorders

Sheilagh Hodgins
Université de Montréal, Montréal, Québec, Canada
and
Karolinska Institute, Stockholm, Sweden

THE MAJOR MENTAL DISORDERS

The major mental disorders[1] include schizophrenia, major depression, bipolar disorder, delusional disorder, and atypical psychoses. While much is known about the first three of these disorders, knowledge of the latter two continues to elude us. There is relatively good consensus among researchers and clinicians about the diagnoses of schizophrenia and bipolar disorder. The present criteria identify populations of individuals that share a core of symptoms, biological and behavioural characteristics, and similar outcomes. The current diagnosis of major depression, however, is unsatisfactory; it identifies a population that is heterogeneous as to symptomatology, biological characteristics, and outcome (Hodgins, 1996).

Schizophrenia affects just less than 1% of adult men and women and bipolar disorder approximately 1.6%. While the prevalence of schizophrenia is thought to have remained stable at least since the beginning of the century, there is evidence to suggest that the prevalence of bipolar disorder is increasing among the relatives of those affected. Major depression, according to the most recent and methodologically sound investigations, affects 12.7% of men and 21.3% of women (Kessler et al., 1994), and the prevalence is increasing while the age of

---

[1]Throughout this chapter the terms major mental disorder and mental illness will be used interchangeably to refer to these five disorders.

Handbook of Offender Assessment and Treatment. Edited by C. R. Hollin.

onset decreases. Among adolescents, rates as high as 21% have been reported (Klerman & Weissman, 1992; Lewinsohn, Rohde, Seeley, & Fischer, 1993). In most cases, the major mental disorders onset in late adolescence or early adulthood and are chronic. These disorders inflict unmeasurable suffering on those who are affected and on their family and close friends. They limit all aspects of an individual's functioning. Acute episodes characterized by severe symptoms of psychosis, mania, and/or depression are interspersed with periods in which fewer symptoms are present, but psychosocial functioning remains impaired.[2] These disorders are associated with increased risks for premature death, both from disease and suicide, for certain personality disorders, and for alcohol and drug use disorders (Hodgins, 1996).

PREVALENCE OF CRIMINALITY AMONG PERSONS WITH MAJOR MENTAL DISORDERS

Persons who develop major mental disorders are more likely than persons with no mental disorders to be convicted of criminal offences. Three types of investigations support this conclusion. First, there are studies of birth cohorts followed from pregnancy through adulthood which compare the criminal records of persons who develop major mental disorders and are hospitalized with those of persons with no admission for a major mental disorder. (In these studies, persons with other types of mental disorders and with mental retardation are examined separately.) Five studies of this type using cohorts born between 1944 and 1966 have been conducted and all have obtained similar results (Hodgins, 1998a). More of the persons who developed a major mental disorder as compared with those with no disorder were convicted of a crime. The differences between the disordered and non-disordered groups were greater for violent than for non-violent crime, and the associations between mental disorder and criminality and violent criminality were stronger for women than for men.

A second type of investigation which demonstrates that persons who develop major mental disorders are at increased risk for criminal conviction are follow-up studies which compare the criminal activities of persons discharged from inpatient psychiatric wards with those of non-disordered persons living in the same community. Since the middle to late 1960s, studies of persons with major mental disorders living in the community have consistently reported that more of them than their non-disordered neighbours are convicted of crimes. As in the birth cohort studies, the results of most of these investigations indicate that

---

[2] Contrary to popular clinical lore, recent empirical evidence demonstrates that the major affective disorders are recurrent in almost all cases. In addition, psychosocial functioning between the acute episodes is impaired (Coryell et al., 1993; Klerman & Weissman, 1992; Harrow, Goldberg, Grossman, & Meltzer, 1990; Stoll et al., 1993; Tohen, Waternaux, & Tsuang, 1990).

the association between the major mental disorders and violence is stronger than that between the major mental disorders and non-violent crime (Hodgins, 1993).

Third, studies conducted in North America find higher prevalence rates for the major mental disorders among convicted offenders than among age and gender matched samples from the general population (Hodgins & Côté, 1990). This is not the case in the United Kingdom (Gunn, Maden, & Swinton, 1991). In addition, among unbiased samples of homicide offenders prevalence rates for the major mental disorders far exceed general population rates (Hodgins, 1994a).

FACTORS THAT INFLUENCE THE PREVALENCE OF CRIMINALITY AMONG PERSONS WHO DEVELOP MAJOR MENTAL DISORDERS

Individual Factors

A number of individual and contextual factors have been identified that influence criminality among persons who suffer from major mental disorders. Consider first the individual factors. Evidence suggests that among persons who develop major mental disorders, there is a sub-group who are characterized by antisocial behaviour from a young age throughout their lives (Hodgins, Côté, & Toupin, 1998; Hodgins, 1998a). We have hypothesized that this sub-group may be proportionately larger among the mentally ill born since the mid-1940s than among those born previously (Hodgins, 1999). These data have led us to hypothesize that there are two types of persons who develop major mental disorders and who commit crimes. The early-starters are characterized by stable antisocial behaviour across the lifespan. They begin their criminal careers in adolescence, often before the onset of the major mental disorder. The criminality of the early-starters is, we propose, linked to this antisocial personality and lifestyle. By contrast, the late-starters show no evidence of antisocial or aggressive behaviour before the onset of the symptoms of the major mental disorder. Their illegal behaviours are more likely to be the consequence, or at least associated with, the symptoms of the major mental disorder.

A second, individual factor associated with the increased prevalence of criminality among persons who develop major mental disorders is their increased likelihood of aggressive behaviour. A number of studies have found that persons with major mental disorders are more likely than non-disordered persons to behave aggressively towards others (Link, Andrews, & Cullen, 1992; Steadman & Felson, 1984; Swanson, Holzer, Ganju, & Jono, 1990). For example, in samples of persons being discharged from psychiatric wards in three US cities, 35% of the women and 39% of the men reported aggressive behaviour in a two-month period (Steadman et al., 1993). This rate increased by 26% when the reports of collaterals were combined with the subjects' reports (Steadman et al., 1994).

A third individual factor that affects the rate of criminality among those with major mental disorders is the tendency for the late-starters to stay at the scene of the crime and/or to confess to a crime that they have committed (Lapalme, Jöckel, Hodgins, & Müller-Isberner, submitted; Robertson, 1988). Consequently, this sub-group of offenders with major mental disorders would be more likely to be arrested and successfully prosecuted than other offenders.

Another factor that influences the rate of criminality among those who develop major mental disorders is alcohol and drug use. Both disorders (abuse, dependence) and intoxication are associated with an increased risk of illegal behaviour. While the presence or history of an alcohol and/or drug use disorder increases the likelihood of illegal and particularly violent behaviour (Eronen, Tiihonen, & Hakola, 1996), such disorders do not characterize all mentally ill offenders (Lindqvist, 1986), nor are all mentally disordered offenders intoxicated when they commit an offence. Studies have systematically shown that alcohol and drugs are associated with the offending of some, but not all, mentally disordered persons. The ways in which alcohol and drug use increase the likelihood of illegal behaviours, and especially aggressive behaviour, are multiple and complex. This is true both for persons with and without major mental disorders, but those who develop major mental disorders may have a specific vulnerability for abuse/ dependence. Persons with major mental disorders are more likely than non-disordered persons living in the same community to develop alcohol and drug use disorders (Helzer & Przybeck, 1988; Hodgins, 1994b), and more likely to engage in substance abuse as children or young adolescents (Hodgins & Janson, in press). We have hypothesized that the association between alcohol and drugs and criminality is different for the early and late-start offenders with major mental disorders. Among the early-starters it begins in adolescence and is an integral part of their antisocial life-style. Among the late-starters, abuse and dependence may be less important than intoxication (Hodgins et al., 1998).

Another individual factor that increases the risk of violent behaviour among persons with major mental disorders is the presence of certain types of psychotic symptoms labelled threat-control/override (Link & Stueve, 1994; Swanson, Borum, Swartz, & Monahan, 1996). Like alcohol or drug use, these symptoms constitute a risk factor since they increase the likelihood of violent behaviour, but characterize only some proportion of offenders with major mental disorders at the time of their offence (Lapalme et al., submitted). Some studies have suggested that in fact such symptoms are present during the offending of only a small group of offenders with major mental disorders (Hodgins, 1998b).

Contextual Factors

Initially when data began to accumulate showing higher prevalence rates of criminality among persons who develop major mental disorders than those with no disorders, it was often proposed that this was due to discrimination against the mentally ill by police and the judicial system. While one US investigation did find that police were more likely to arrest a mentally ill than a non-mentally ill suspect (Teplin, 1984), all other data suggest that in most countries a great effort is made to divert mentally ill persons from the criminal justice system. Some studies have even found that mentally ill persons are subject to positive discrimination in that their aggressive behaviours lead to prosecution less often than similar behaviours by non-disordered persons (Link et al., 1992; Steadman & Felson, 1984).

While discrimination does not explain the higher rates of criminality among persons who develop major mental disorders, there are societal factors that clearly do influence these rates. Some of these factors are associated with crime among both the disordered and the non-disordered (Hodgins, 1998a), while others specifically influence criminality among persons who develop major mental disorders. Existing data suggest that the prevalence of criminality among persons who develop major mental disorders has increased dramatically since the middle to late 1960s (Hodgins & Lalonde, 1999; Hodgins, 1999). During this period in most Western industrialized countries mental health policies and practices were drastically changed. Mental health care for the major disorders no longer involved life-time hospitalization in large asylums, but rather short stays in hospital and appointments in outpatient clinics, in many cases limited to evaluations of medications. During this same period, in most countries the criteria for involuntary hospitalization were strengthened and patients were accorded rights to refuse treatment. In retrospect, it seems clear that the implementation of the policy of deinstitutionalizing mental health care and the amendments to laws that were adopted at approximately the same time to limit the legal powers of mental health professionals to impose treatment against the will of a client, have been associated with an increase in the prevalence of criminality among persons who develop major mental disorders. This conclusion suggests that criminality in this population is affected by the quality, type, and intensity of treatment and services that they receive. As will be seen in the latter part of this chapter, this conclusion is further supported by the results of evaluation studies of specialized community treatment programmes for offenders with major mental disorders.

GOALS OF TREATMENT

The primary goal of treatment for persons with major mental disorders is to end, or at least reduce, their suffering. More specifically, the goal is to address and resolve the multiple behavioural, cognitive, and emotional problems that these individuals present in the most humane and least restrictive ways possible. One of the problems that persons with major disorders often present is suicide. Consequently, it is now taken for granted that mental health professionals have a particular responsibility, and in most countries specific legal powers, to prevent suicide. As noted above, another problem that many persons with major mental disorders present is repetitive aggressive behaviour towards others and non-violent criminal activity. In fact, the results of many investigations document rates of aggressive behaviour and criminality that are as high or higher than the rates of suicide. It can be argued, then, that mental health professionals, in addition to their role in treating the symptoms of the major mental disorder, also have a responsibility to evaluate the risks for aggressive behaviour towards others and criminality, and if they are present to intervene to prevent them. Blackburn has put it well:

> ... The rehabilitation "ideal" is aimed at increasing personal effectiveness, of which avoiding further offending is only one component ... this implies that the targets of intervention are those cognitive, emotional and interpersonal disabilities which impede social reintegration. Reduced recidivism is therefore a necessary but not sufficient criterion of the effectiveness of intervention (1996, p. 133).

In order to succeed in meeting these goals, treatment programmes for offenders with major mental disorders must have the following characteristics. First, they must be long-term because major mental disorders are chronic and in most cases involve cognitive, behavioural, and emotional deficits which can be reduced but not eliminated. Second, they must include multiple components because offenders with major disorders present multiple disorders involving both the lack of appropriate skills necessary for autonomous living and the presence of inappropriate behaviours and cognitions. Third, they must be co-ordinated with social services because many of these persons lack the skills to be financially independent and some even lack the skills necessary to eat nutritionally and clothe themselves appropriately for the weather. Fourth, they must include the possibility of legally imposing either inpatient or outpatient care in order to ensure compliance with the various aspects of treatment which are deemed necessary to prevent violence or non-violent criminality.

ORGANIZATION AND CO-ORDINATION OF SERVICES

As noted in the previous sections of this chapter, a great deal of evidence has accumulated since the mid-1960s, indicating that many persons who will or who have already developed a major mental disorder are involved in criminal activities. Consequently, the so-called forensic psychiatric populations and traditional psychiatric populations are no longer distinct. For example, in many countries, large proportions of patients with major mental disorders treated in the emergency, inpatient, and outpatient services of general and psychiatric hospitals have a criminal record. In some countries, many such persons are homeless substance abusers whose only contact with services is the use of medical emergency rooms for the treatment of drug overdoses or to detoxify themselves so that a smaller quantity of drug will have a more powerful psychological effect (Côté & Hodgins, 1996).

Regardless of where and when they are first identified, persons with major mental disorders, especially those who have a history of criminal behaviour, present multiple problems requiring treatment and services over many years. In order to successfully limit their suffering, prevent them from committing crimes, and allow them to live under the least restrictive conditions while keeping the costs of hospitalization and incarceration to a minimum, a long-term stable multi-component programme is required which co-ordinates mental health and social services and respects conditions laid out by criminal and civil law. The goals described above can be achieved if a long-term perspective is taken and the mental health professionals responsible for treatment can access different types of services to address the individual client's needs, which will vary over time. While most of the treatment can be effectively and safely provided in the community, in many cases both long-term inpatient care on psychiatric wards with varying degrees of security and short-term rapid hospitalization are necessary.

There are no empirical studies that indicate which types of patients benefit from which type of inpatient care. This is partially due to the fact that in many instances inpatient care is ordered by a criminal court following the commission of a crime. Some jurisdictions provide inpatient care in general hospitals, while others have specialized forensic hospitals with various levels of security (see, for example, the special issue of the *International Journal of Law and Psychiatry*, *16* (1/2) 1993). In some cases, such hospitals exist within a correctional facility. Empirical research has not as yet provided data on the effective use of various types of inpatient settings—general psychiatric wards, high, medium, and low security hospitals (see, for example, Taylor, Maden, & Jones, 1996).

Setting up long-term co-operation between different authorities—health, social, justice—proves difficult in many jurisdictions (see, for example, Petch, 1996; Wormith & McKeague, 1996). Yet, there is a consensus that the continuity of treatment is essential (Heilbrun & Griffin, 1993; McGreevy, Steadman, Dvoskin, & Dollard, 1991; Steadman, McCarty & Morrissey, 1989; Wiederanders, Bromley, & Choate, 1997; Wiederanders & Choate, 1994). A model programme set up in Vancouver which illustrates such co-ordination has been described (Corrado, Doherty, & Glackmen, 1989) and evaluated (Wilson, Tien, & Eaves, 1995). In many countries, offenders with major mental disorders are convicted and sentenced to incarceration in correctional facilities where treatment needs to be begun or continued. Models for treatment inside such facilities have been described (Cohen & Dvoskin, 1992; Metzner, 1993). The importance of continuity in the provision of long-term treatment to persons with major mental disorders is demonstrated in the evaluation studies of case management (Brekke, Long, Nesbitt, & Sobel, 1997; Ryan, Sherman, & Bogart, 1997; Wolff et al., 1997).

These investigations have not yet succeeded in identifying programmes that are effective for all sub-groups of persons with major mental disorders, nor in identifying criteria for matching clients to programmes. As in all forms of mental health treatment, some of these programmes have produced positive results, some no results, and others negative results (Ryan et al., 1997).

ASSESSMENT[3]

Identification

Offenders with major mental disorders come into contact with mental health professionals in different ways and at different times in the development of their disorder, depending largely on the laws, policies, and practices of the country or state where they live. Despite these national differences, two situations are common. An individual in an acute episode of psychosis, mania, or depression is brought to the emergency room of a hospital. The immediate concern is to reduce the acute symptoms and protect the individual from harming him/herself. If the individual has committed a violent crime in the previous hours or days, the risk of suicide may be particularly elevated (Hillbrand, Krystal, Sharpe, & Foster, 1994). The other commonly occurring situation that brings offenders with major mental disorders into contact with mental health professionals is arrest and incarceration. In this situation the difficulties are twofold: first, identifying the mentally ill person; second, obtaining adequate and appropriate treatment for him/her. In most countries, mental health professionals do not assess all persons who are arrested. Consequently, it is necessary to develop a cost-effective screening procedure in order to identify those in need of treatment. Such a procedure would be constructed so that initially all new admissions would be assessed by non-clinicians or by questionnaires and only those who were judged to present certain symptoms would undergo a diagnostic interview. The challenge in developing such a screening procedure is to ensure that no one with a serious disorder is missed at the initial stage, and as few as possible of those without such disorders are identified for further assessment. The major mental disorders are especially difficult to identify by non-clinicians. Even the best of the diagnostic instruments designed to be used by lay interviewers in epidemiological investigations fails to identify significant numbers of cases of major mental disorders (Hodgins, 1995). Not surprisingly, then, attempts to develop such screening procedures for use in jails have had varying success (Hart, Roesch, Corrado, & Cox, 1993; Teplin & Swartz, 1989). Even when arrestees with major mental disorders are identified, obtaining appropriate and adequate treatment requires co-operation between criminal justice and mental health authorities and services. Models for such co-operation have been described (Ogloff, Tien, Roesch, & Eaves, 1991; Rowlands, Inch, Rodger, & Soliman, 1996; Solomon & Draine, 1995; Walsh & Bricourt, 1996).

---

[3] Assessment here refers to a mental health assessment and not an assessment requested by a criminal court, for example to determine responsibility for an offence, to identify mitigating circumstances to be considered in sentencing an offender, or to predicting the future risk of criminality.

Three Stages of Assessment

The Primary Disorder

Assessments of individuals suffering from major mental disorders include several steps. Depending on the mental state of the individual and the context in which the assessment is being conducted, these steps may be completed within a few days, weeks, or months. The first step obviously involves accurately diagnosing the major disorder. In most cases this poses no problem for experienced clinicians if they have adequate time to interview and observe the individual in question. However, among persons who suffer from these disorders and who offend there are obstacles to making accurate diagnoses of the primary disorder. The first obstacle to accurately diagnosing the primary disorder is the presence of other disorders. Research has shown that most persons with major mental disorders who commit crimes present several co-morbid disorders (Côté & Hodgins, 1990; Lapalme et al., submitted).

A second obstacle to accurately diagnosing the presence of a major mental disorder, particularly among offenders, is their reluctance to acknowledge the presence of symptoms. Males with a well-established antisocial life-style, who have often been part of a criminal sub-culture since adolescence, have an abhorrence of being labelled "crazy" or mentally ill. And in fact, in their world, either a correctional facility or the community, there probably are very real negative consequences associated with such a label, such as physical abuse and being put in isolation cells (Hodgins & Côté, 1991). This refusal to acknowledge the presence of symptoms was well illustrated by findings from a study that a colleague and I conducted in Canada. We promised a representative sample of penitentiary inmates complete confidentiality (except if they represented an immediate threat to themselves or someone else) if they participated in a diagnostic interview. To our astonishment we found that less than half of those who received a diagnosis of a major mental disorder had ever spoken to anyone about their symptoms, despite the fact that the disorder had been present for several years (Hodgins & Côté, 1990).

Paranoid symptoms are another obstacle to accurate diagnosis of persons with major mental disorders who are at risk for crime and for violence. While it has long been thought that paranoid symptoms are associated with violence, very little is known about this association nor about delusional disorder, simply because persons with these symptoms are reticent to talk to either clinicians or researchers. Also, in certain sub-cultures and contexts, for example jails and prisons, it is often difficult for a mental health professional to discern if stories of predators, threats, car chases, listening devices, etc. are true or delusional (Côté, Lesage, Chawky, & Loyer, 1997; Hodgins et al., 1998).

Another obstacle to accurately diagnosing major mental disorders among offenders or persons with a history of antisocial behaviour is that they are often intoxicated when they first come into contact with a mental health professional.

As noted above, alcohol and drug use disorders are more prevalent among those who offend than among those with the same disorders who do not.

Assessment of the immediate risk of harm to self and others must be included at this initial step. However, as this initial assessment usually takes place when the individual is in an acute psychotic, manic, or depressive state, the evaluation is limited to assessing the likelihood of acting out behaviour before medication can reduce the acute symptomatology. It is important to note that the factors associated with aggressive behaviour on an inpatient ward are different from those that influence these behaviours in the community (Davis, 1991; Quinsey & Maguire, 1986).

Co-morbid Disorders and Accompanying Problems

The second step in an assessment involves diagnosing co-morbid disorders and it must wait until the symptoms characterizing the acute episode have been reduced or eliminated. Given current mental health policy and practice in many countries, it is often difficult to hospitalize a person with a major mental disorder long enough to do this. However, it is necessary to accurately identify co-morbid disorders among persons suffering from major mental disorders. Research has shown that accurate diagnoses of alcohol and drug problems (Bryant, Rounsaville, Spitzer, & Williams, 1992), and no doubt personality disorders, can only be made when acute symptoms have been reduced and when detoxification is complete.

This step in the assessment also includes obtaining a detailed history of aggressive and all other illegal behaviours. In taking such a history, it is critical to:

1. distinguish aggressive or violent behaviour from non-violent criminality;
2. document the age when these behaviours first occurred and relate this to the onset of the symptoms of the major disorder;
3. document the situations in which these illegal behaviours occur—for example, when the acute symptoms of the disorder are present, when intoxicated, when disagreeing with another person, when perceiving ridicule or humiliation;
4. document the motives for the behaviour; and
5. document the level of impulsivity associated with these behaviours (Bjørkly, 1997).

It is essential to collect information not only from the individual being assessed but from as many other sources as possible. Family members and friends can be an invaluable source of information on all of the points described above. Note that in the study reported above, the frequency of aggressive behaviour by patients living in the community increased by 25% when information from a collateral was added to the subject's self-report (Steadman et al., 1994). However, in numerous cases family and friends are reticent to describe the individual's aggressive behaviours, often seeing it as betrayal of a loved one who is ill. Mental health professionals have to take time to meet with these persons and to reassure them that accurate descriptions of their family member's or friend's behaviour is of critical importance for his/her treatment and ultimate welfare. Records of previous mental health assessments, inpatient and outpatient treatment, assessments done for the court, criminal activities, records of both behaviour and academic performance at school, and records of employment can add information which is critical to clarifying the client's reports and planning treatment.

The accuracy and breadth of information collected at this stage in the assessment will determine to a large extent the effectiveness of the treatment programme to be designed for the client and thereby, in some cases, the safety of others. This point is well illustrated by a tragic example which is reminiscent of so many other cases both with respect to the characteristics and history of the patient and the response to him by the mental health and criminal justice systems. Mr Christopher Clunis had suffered from schizophrenia for a number of years. After he stabbed to death another man on a subway platform in London, the North East Thames and South East Thames Regional Health Authorities conducted an inquiry into the treatment and care he had received prior to the murder. In piecing together this man's history, the commission of inquiry found that information concerning incidents of aggressive behaviour, even of incidents that had occurred in the presence of mental health professionals, was not passed on from one treating clinician to the next. While in retrospect a clear pattern emerged of aggressive behaviour increasing in frequency and severity over time, this information was unknown to those responsible for Mr Clunis's care before the murder. Collecting such information is time consuming and sometimes frustrating and difficult. However, it is critical to effectively treating this population and to preventing violent and criminal behaviours among them (Hodgins, 1994a).

Optimal Treatment Conditions

The final step in the assessment involves measuring treatability and identifying what are the optimal conditions for effective treatment for this particular person. For example, most persons who suffer from major mental disorders require medication on a long-term basis. Not only is it necessary to identify the most effective medications for the person, but also to assess the amount and type of supervision that will be required to ensure that the individual continues to take the medication as prescribed, and as well to assess what training the individual requires in order to be able to monitor symptoms and side-effects, to recognize signs indicating the necessity of medical intervention, and if necessary, knowing how to quickly contact the appropriate physician. Medications are only one part of the treatment required by offenders with major mental disorders. It may not be helpful at this stage in the assessment to use a medical model to think about the co-morbid disorders. This would lead, for example, in the case of antisocial personality disorder which will characterize large numbers of such persons, to unwarranted scepticism about even embarking on treatment. A behavioural or behavioural–cognitive approach may be of more use. Such an approach would involve a systematic description of the problems presented by the individual that hinder autonomous living in the community. In addition to these concrete descriptions of the multiple problems that characterize mentally disordered offenders, an evaluation of the individual's capacity to change and to tolerate the different treatments is needed. Many of the possible treatments will involve skills training that requires concentration, memory, a certain level of intelligence, and an ability to tolerate the presence of others. Some of the programmes, for example those designed to end substance abuse, may well require the ability to cope with stressful and frustrating situations and to think abstractly. Most of these programmes will be offered in a group context and require tolerance by each client of the other. Thus, assessments of the problems that need to be addressed by various components of the treatment programme and the personal resources that the individual brings to treatment are essential to ensure that treatment goals are realistic. Furthermore, such information allows the treatment staff to create some success experiences relatively quickly once treatment begins, thereby increasing compliance.

This final step in the assessment involves evaluating the need for supervision in order to ensure that the client follows the treatment programme and does not commit crimes before these interventions have beneficial effects. For the same client, the levels of supervision required for different problems or to ensure compliance with different components of treatment will vary, and will, if treatment is effective, be reduced over time. For example, an individual suffering from schizophrenia who regularly steals money for beer and food when his or her own runs out at the end of the month requires supervision until he/she learns how to manage a monthly income. An individual suffering from bipolar disorder requires supervision to monitor the onset of manic episodes which usually involve paranoid symptoms and are accompanied by aggressive behaviour towards his wife and children. A client with a history of major depression and alcohol abuse requires supervision to prevent binge drinking which in the past has been associated with fighting.

TREATMENT

Offenders with major mental disorders require all of the treatments and services needed by non-offenders who suffer from these disorders, plus additional treatment components which teach them skills for autonomous living and the skills necessary to prevent further aggressive behaviour and/or non-violent criminality. Given the paucity of evaluation studies of such multi-component treatment programmes for this population, the diversity of the clientele, and the broad array of problems that they present, only a brief outline of such programmes and the necessary components will be discussed.

Specialized Inpatient Care

Evaluation studies of inhospital care for offenders with major mental disorders are non-existent. As noted above, no studies have provided information on the types of offenders with major mental disorders who require inhospital treatment with varying levels of security, on the optimal length of inpatient care, and on the components of inpatient care. A major contribution in this direction was made by a group of Canadian researchers (Rice, Harris, Quinsey, & Cyr, 1990). They surveyed the problems presented by the patients in two secure psychiatric hospitals. They then reviewed the empirical literature and identified treatments that directly addressed each type of problem. They concluded that:

> ... Interventions have been developed that are relevant to all of the problem types most commonly exhibited by patients in secure facilities ... the degree to which these treatments have received rigorous evaluations varies but there is at least some encouraging evidence for the efficacy of all of the interventions we recommend (p. 215).

This pioneering study provides a framework and methodology for progress in this area. While the general treatment philosophy presented by Rice and her colleagues has been adopted elsewhere (see, for example, Müller-Isberner, 1993, 1998), evaluation studies are virtually non-existent.

Specialized Community Care

Despite the multiple and complex problems presented by offenders with major mental disorders and the necessity of co-ordinating interventions by mental health, social service, and criminal justice authorities over long periods of time, there is empirical evidence of successful community programmes that prevent recidivism among even high risk cases.[4] In 1993, Heilbrun and Griffin authored a review of studies which had evaluated community-based treatments for insanity acquittees in the United States. While the lengths of the follow-up periods, the combinations of treatment components, social services, and legal contexts varied considerably across studies, the outcomes were generally positive. Similarly, Wiederanders has evaluated services and supervision for insanity acquittees in California (Wiederanders, 1992; Wiederanders & Choate, 1994) and compared them with programmes offered in Oregon and New York State (Wiederanders,

---

[4] A discussion of the appropriate outcome measures for such treatment programmes is beyond the scope of this chapter. However, measures of effectiveness would include assessments of symptoms, levels of psychosocial functioning, quality of life, client's subjective assessment of suffering and of success, and counts of the frequency of suicide attempts, criminal offending, aggressive behaviour towards others, alcohol use, and drug use.

Bromley, & Choate, 1997). Again, the results were positive and demonstrated a crime prevention effect. The programme in Vancouver, referred to above, recruited clients in a correctional facility and compared those admitted to the programme with a group of clients with similar problems and histories who refused admission, for whom there was no place available, or who moved away from the city (Wilson et al., 1995). Another programme in Germany (Müller-Isberner, 1996) and one in Québec (Hodgins, Lapalme, & Toupin, in press) compared offenders with mental disorders who were treated in a specialized forensic after-care programme and general psychiatry outpatient clinics. Again, the specialized programmes designed for offenders with major mental disorders all demonstrated positive crime prevention effects. Not only are these programmes effective in preventing recidivism, they are highly cost-effective. The community programme in Oregon that has been identified as a model of effectiveness for offenders with major mental disorders (Buckley, 1994) has been estimated to cost 14% that of hospital care (Bigelow, Bloom, & Williams, 1990). The specialized forensic community programme in Germany described above, plus housing provided by the social authorities, is estimated to cost 37% that of inpatient care (Müller-Isberner, personal communication).

As Wiederanders and his colleagues noted (1997), problems of comparability abound in this small but burgeoning outcome literature on treatment of offenders with major mental disorders. Despite this fact, these programmes, which have had positive results, share a number of features in common. One, the goals of the programmes are to treat the major mental disorder, the co-morbid disorders that hinder autonomous functioning in the community, and to prevent crime and aggressive behaviour. Two, the programmes are structured, intense, and diversified and include specific components designed to address the multiple problems presented by offenders with major mental disorders. Three, the programmes involve outreach, or what has been referred to as assertive case management. Four, in most cases compliance with the community-based treatment was compulsory. Five, the mental health professionals running the programme had the right to re-hospitalize clients, for short periods, relatively rapidly and easily. As Heilbrun and Griffin (1993) noted, the importance of research in identifying the active and essential components of such programmes cannot be overemphasized. This echoes the conclusion of Rice and her colleagues (1990) with respect to inhospital treatment (Hodgins & Müller-Isberner, 2000).

CONCLUSION

The empirical data available today suggest that much of the criminality and violence perpetrated by persons suffering from major mental disorders could be prevented if policy decisions and the allocation of funds were based on empirical evidence, and programme evaluation was used to continually increase the effectiveness of treatment programmes. Such programmes are long-term and usually involve care both in and out of hospital. Each programme is developed on an individual basis, after extensive assessment of the client, which involves not only interviewing and observing him/her, but also collecting information from family members and friends, other mental health and social service professionals who have treated the client, and if possible records of performance at school, in the military, and at work. Criminal records, both juvenile and adult, are essential. The results of outcome studies available suggest that effective treatment programmes include:

1. components that have been shown to be effective in the treatment of the major mental disorders;
2. components that specifically address the co-morbid disorders or problems in autonomous living presented by most offenders with major mental disorders;
3. varying levels of supervision for different problems;
4. legal obligation for community treatment if compliance is a problem;
5. possibility of involuntary rehospitalization for short periods of time; and
6. adequate social services (income, housing).

The outcome literature on the major mental disorders indicates that such programmes will have a greater likelihood of success if the key staff person organizing the various aspects of the treatment programme and who is in continual contact with the client over the long-term remains stable.

As noted, progress in implementing effective treatment programmes for offenders with major mental disorders will be made only if such programmes are based on empirical data on the effectiveness of the various components of treatment and on knowledge of the major mental disorders and of offenders who suffer from these disorders. All of the interventions described in Chapters 11–22 that have proven to be effective with non-disordered offenders are worth adapting and evaluating with offenders with major mental disorders (Harris & Rice, 1997; Müller-Isberner, 1998). Research is urgently needed in order to identify the social services necessary for the various sub-groups of offenders with major mental disorders and ways to provide these services that are acceptable to the clients. For example, men suffering from schizophrenia who have a history of antisocial behaviour from early adolescence are more likely to be homeless than offenders with schizophrenia but no childhood history of antisocial behaviour (Lapalme et al., submitted). They are also more likely to present substance abuse (Mueser, Drake, Alterman, Miles, & Noordsy, 1997). Getting them settled in stable accommodations with an income sufficient for food and clothing may well be a first step to ensuring compliance with the other components of the treatment programme. Civil and criminal laws that support and promote effective treatment under the least restrictive conditions need to be identified. Particularly urgent is the need in several countries for laws providing for compulsory treatment in the community. Finally, the effect of factors known to increase criminality among non-disordered persons needs to be investigated with reference to persons with major mental disorders, and particularly the consequences of living in high crime areas where alcohol, drugs, and firearms are readily available.

Several sub-topics within this area have not yet even been addressed. Notable is the absence of descriptions and evaluations of treatment programmes for female offenders with major mental disorders. Another glaring lack of knowledge concerns the parenting skills of offenders with major mental disorders who have children and the effect that both their offending and their mental disorder is having on their children. Finally, while knowledge is available which could be used to implement programmes designed to prevent offending and related problems such as substance abuse among children and adolescents at high risk for the development of major mental disorders, to our knowledge this is not being done.

REFERENCES

Bigelow, D. A., Bloom, J. D., & Williams, M. H. (1990). Costs of managing insanity acquittees under a psychiatric security review board system. *Hospital and Community Psychiatry*, *41*, 613–614.

Bjørkly, S. (1997). Clinical assessment of dangerousness in psychotic patients: Some risk indicators and pitfalls. *Aggression and Violent Behavior*, *2*, 167–178.

Blackburn, R. (1996). Mentally disordered offenders. In C. R. Hollin (Ed.), *Working with offenders: Psychological practice in offender rehabilitation* (pp. 119–149). Chichester, UK: Wiley.

Brekke, J. S., Long, J. D., Nesbitt, N., & Sobel, E. (1997). The impact of service characteristics on functional outcomes from community support programs for persons with schizophrenia: A growth curve analysis. *Journal of Consulting and Clinical Psychology*, *65*, 464–475.

Bryant, K. J., Rounsaville, B., Spitzer, R. L., & Williams, J. B. W. (1992). Reliability of dual diagnosis. Substance dependence and psychiatric disorders. *The Journal of Nervous and Mental Disease*, *180*, 251–257.

Buckley, M. C. (1994). A model for management and treatment of insanity acquittees. *Hospital and Community Psychiatry*, *45*, 1127–1131.

Cohen, F., & Dvoskin, J. (1992). Inmates with mental disorders: A guide to law and practice. *Mental and Physical Disability Law Reporter*, *16*, 462–470.

Corrado, R. R., Doherty, D., & Glackman, W. (1989). A demonstration program for chronic recidivists of criminal justice, health, and social service agencies. *International Journal of Law and Psychiatry*, *12*, 211–229.

Coryell, W., Scheftner, W., Keller, M., Endicott, J., Maser, J., & Klerman, G. L. (1993). The enduring psychosocial consequences of mania and depression. *American Journal of Psychiatry*, *150*, 720–727.

Côté, G., & Hodgins, S. (1990). Co-occurring mental disorders among criminal offenders. *Bulletin of American Academy of Psychiatry and the Law*, *18*, 271–281.

Côté, G., & Hodgins, S. (1996). *Problèmes d'alcool, problèmes de drogue et conduite antisociale chez les sujets en demande d'aide psychologique dans une salle d'urgence*. Research report, Conseil Québécois de la Recherche Sociale.

Côté, G., Lesage, A., Chawky, N., & Loyer, M. (1997). Clinical specificity of prison inmates with severe mental disorders: A case control study. *British Journal of Psychiatry*, *170*, 571–577.

Davis, S. (1991). Violence by psychiatric inpatients: A review. *Hospital and Community Psychiatry*, *42*, 585–590.

Eronen, M., Tiihonen, J., & Hakola, P. (1996). Schizophrenia and homicidal behavior. *Schizophrenia Bulletin*, *22*, 83–89.

Gunn, J., Maden, A., & Swinton, M. (1991). Treatment needs of prisoners with psychiatric disorders. *British Medical Journal, 303*, 338–340.

Harris, G. T., & Rice, M. E. (1997). Mentally disordered offenders: What research says about effective service. In C. D. Webster & M. A. Jackson (Eds.), *Impulsivity* (pp. 361–393). New York: Guilford.

Harrow, M., Goldberg, J. F., Grossman, L., & Meltzer, H. (1990). Outcome in manic disorders. *Archives of General Psychiatry, 47*, 665–671.

Hart, S. D., Roesch, R., Corrado, R. R., & Cox, D. N. (1993). The referral decision scale. *Law and Human Behavior, 17*, 611–623.

Heilbrun, K., & Griffin, P. A. (1993). Community-based forensic treatment of insanity acquittees. *International Journal of Law and Psychiatry, 16*, 133–150.

Helzer, J. E., & Przybeck, T. R. (1988). The co-occurrence of alcoholism with other psychiatric disorders in the general population and its impact on treatment. *Journal of Studies on Alcohol, 49*, 219–224.

Hillbrand, M., Krystal, J. H., Sharpe, K. S., & Foster, H. G. (1994) Clinical predictors of self-mutilation in hospitalized forensic patients. *The Journal of Nervous and Mental Disease, 182*, pp. 9–13.

Hodgins, S. (1993). The criminality of mentally disordered persons. In S. Hodgins (Ed.), *Mental disorder and crime* (pp. 1–21). Newbury Park, CA: Sage.

Hodgins, S. (1994a). Schizophrenia and violence: Are new mental health policies needed? *Journal of Forensic Psychiatry, 5*, 473–477.

Hodgins, S. (1994b). Letter to the Editor. *Archives of General Psychiatry, 51*, 71–72.

Hodgins, S. (1995). Assessing mental disorder in the criminal justice system: Feasibility versus clinical accuracy. *International Journal of Law and Psychiatry, 18*, 15–28.

Hodgins, S. (1996). The major mental disorders: New evidence requires new policy and practice. *Canadian Psychology, 37*, 95–111.

Hodgins, S. (1998a). Epidemiological investigations of the association between major mental disorders and crime: Methodological limitations and validity of the conclusions. *Social Psychiatry and Epidemiology.*

Hodgins, S. (1998b). Research in forensic hospitals: Possibilities and limitations. *Criminal Behaviour and Mental Health, 8*, 7–12.

Hodgins, S. (1999). Studying the etiology of crime and violence among persons with major mental disorders: Challenges in the definition and measurement of interactions. In L. Bergman & B. Cairns (Eds.), *Developmental Science and the holistic approach.* (pp. 317–337). Los Angeles, CA: Lawrence Erlbaum Associates.

Hodgins, S., & Côté, G. (1990). The prevalence of mental disorders among penitentiary inmates. *Canada's Mental Health, 38*, 1–5.

Hodgins, S., & Côté, G. (1991). The mental health of penitentiary inmates in isolation. *Canadian Journal of Criminology, 33*, 175–182.

Hodgins, S., Côté, G., & Toupin, J. (1998). Major mental disorders and crime: An etiological hypothesis. In D. Cooke, A. Forth, & R. D. Hare (Eds.), *Psychopathy: Theory, research and implications for society* (pp. 231–256). Dordrecht, The Netherlands: Kluwer.

Hodgins, S., & Janson, C.-G. (in press). *Criminality and violence among the mentally disordered: The Stockholm metropolitan project.* Cambridge, UK: Cambridge University Press.

Hodgins, S., & Lalonde, N. (1999). Major mental disorders and crime: Changes over time? In P. Cohen, L. Robins, & C. Slomkowski (Eds.), *Where and when: Geographical and historical aspects of psychopathology* (pp. 57–83). Mahwah, NJ: Erlbaum.

Hodgins, S., & Müller-Isberner, R. (2000). *Violence, crime and mentally disordered offenders: Concepts and methods for effective treatment and prevention.* Chichester, UK: Wiley.

Hodgins, S., Lapalme, M., & Toupin, J. (in press). Criminal activities and substance use of patients with major affective disorders and schizophrenia: A two-year follow-up. *Journal of Affective Disorders*

Kessler, R. C., McGonagle, K. A., Zhao, S., Nelson, C. B., Hughes, M., Eshleman, S., Wittchen, H. -U., & Kendler, K. S. (1994). Lifetime and 12-month prevalence of DSM-III-R psychiatric disorders in the United States, *Archives General of Psychiatry, 51*, 8–19.

Klerman, G. L., & Weissman, M. M. (1992). The course, morbidity, and costs of depression. *Archives of General Psychiatry, 49*, 831–834.

Lapalme, M., Jöckel, D., Hodgins, S., & Müller-Isberner (submitted). The management and treatment of offenders with major mental disorders: The role of antisocial personality disorder.

Lewinsohn, P. M., Rohde, P., Seeley, J. R., & Fischer, S. A. (1993). Age-cohort changes in the lifetime occurrence of depression and other mental disorders. *Journal of Abnormal Psychology, 102*(1), 110–120.

Lindqvist, P. (1986). Criminal homicide in Northern Sweden 1970–1981: Alcohol intoxication, alcohol abuse and mental disease. *International Journal of Law and Psychiatry, 8*, 19–37.

Link, B. G., Andrews, H., & Cullen, F. T. (1992). The violent and illegal behaviour of mental patients reconsidererd. *American Sociological Review, 57*, 275–292.

Link, B. G., & Stueve, A. (1994). Psychotic symptoms and the violent/illegal behavior of mental patients compared to community control. In J. Monahan & H. Steadman (Eds.), *Violence and mental disorder. Developments in risk assessment* (pp. 137–159). Chicago, IL: University of Chicago Press.

McGreevy, M. A., Steadman, H. J., Dvoskin, J. A., & Dollard, N. (1991). New York State's system of managing insanity acquittees in the community. *Hospital and Community Psychiatry, 42*, 512–517.

Metzner, J. L. (1993). Guidelines for psychiatric services in prisons. *Criminal Behavior and Mental Health, 3*, 252–267.

Mueser, K. T., Drake, R. E., Alterman, A. I., Miles, K. M., & Noordsy, D. L. (1997). Antisocial personality disorder, conduct disorder, and substance abuse in schizophrenia. *Journal of Abnormal Psychology, 106*, 473–477.

Müller-Isberner, R. (1993). Managing insane offenders: The practice of hospital order treatment in the forensic psychiatric hospital. *International Bulletin of Law and Mental Health, 4*, (1 and 2), 28–30.

Müller-Isberner, J. R. (1996). Forensic psychiatric aftercare following hospital order treatment. *International Journal of Law and Psychiatry, 19*, 81–86.

Müller-Isberner, R. (1998). Ein differenziertes Behandlungskonzept für den psychiatrischen Maßregelvollzug: Organisationsfragen und methodische Aspekte. In E. Wagner & W. Werdenich (Eds.), *Forensische Psychotherapie: Psychotherapie im Zwangskontext von Justiz, Medizin und sozialer Kontrolle* (pp. 197–209). Vienna: Facultas Universitötsverlag.

Ogloff, J. R. P., Tien, G., Roesch, R., & Eaves, D. (1991). A model for the provision of jail mental health services: An integrative, community-based approach. *The Journal of Mental Health Administration, 18*, 209–222.

Petch, E. (1996). Mentally disordered offenders: Inter-agency working. *The Journal of Forensic Psychiatry, 7*, 376–382.

Quinsey, V. L., & Maguire, A. (1986). Maximum security psychiatric patients: Actuarial and clinical prediction of dangerousness. *Journal of Interpersonal Aggression, 1*, 143–171.

Rice, M. E., Harris, G. T., Quinsey, V. L., & Cyr, M. (1990). Planning treatment programs in secure psychiatric facilities. In D. N. Weisstub (Ed.), *Law and mental health: International perspectives, Vol. 5* (pp. 162–230). New York: Pergamon Press.

Robertson, G. (1988). Arrest patterns among mentally disordered offenders. *British Journal of Psychiatry, 153*, 313–316.

Rowlands, R., Inch, H., Rodger, W., & Soliman, A. (1996). Diverted to where? What happens to the diverted mentally disordered offender. *Journal of Forensic Psychiatry, 7*, 284–296.

Ryan, C. S., Sherman, P. S., & Bogart, L. M. (1997). Patterns of services and consumer outcome in an intensive case management program. *Journal of Consulting and Clinical Psychology*, *65*, 485–493.

Solomon, P., & Draine, J. (1995). Issues in serving the forensic client. *Social Work*, *40*, 25–33.

Steadman, H. J., & Felson, R. B. (1984). Self-reports of violence—Ex-mental patients, ex-offenders, and the general population. *Criminology*, *22*, 321–342.

Steadman, H, J., McCarty, D. W., & Morrissey, J. P. (1989). *The mentally ill in jail: Planning for essential services.* New York: Guilford.

Steadman, H. J., Monahan, J., Appelbaum, P. S., Grisso, T., Mulvey, E. P., Roth, L. H., Robbins, P. C., & Classen, D. (1994). Designing a new generation of risk assessment research. In J. Monahan & H. J. Steadman (Eds.), *Violence and mental disorder: Developments in risk assessment* (pp. 297–318). Chicago, IL: The University of Chicago Press.

Steadman, H. J., Monahan, J., Robbins, P. A., Applebaum, P., Grisso, T., Klassen, D., Mulvey, E., & Roth, L. (1993). From dangerousness to risk assessment: Implications for appropriate research strategies. In S. Hodgins (Ed.), *Mental disorder and crime* (pp. 39–62). Newbury Park, CA: Sage.

Stoll, A. L., Tohen, M., Baldessarini, R. J., Goodwin, D. C., Stein, S., Katz, S., Geenens, D., Swinson, R., Goethe, J. W., & Glashan, T. (1993). Shifts in diagnostic frequencies of schizophrenia and major affective disorders at six North American psychiatric hospitals. *American Journal Psychiatry*, *150*, 1668–1673.

Swanson, J. W., Borum, R., Swartz, M., & Monahan, J. (1996). Psychotic symptoms and disorders and the risk of violent behavior in the community. *Criminal Behaviour and Mental Health*, *6*, 309–329.

Swanson, J. W., Holzer, C. E., Ganju, V. K., & Jono, R. T. (1990). Violence and psychiatric disorder in the community: Evidence from the epidemiologic catchment area surveys. *Hospital and Community Psychiatry*, *41*, 761–770.

Taylor, P. J., Maden, A., & Jones, D. (1996). Long-term medium-security hospital units: A service gap of the 1990s? *Criminal Behaviour and Mental Health*, *6*, 213–229.

Teplin, L. (1984). Criminalizing mental disorder: The comparative arrest rate of the mentally ill. *American Psychologist*, *39*, 794–803.

Teplin, L., & Swartz, M. (1989). Screening for severe mental disorder in jails: The development of the referral decision scale. *Law and Human Behavior*, *13*, 1–18.

Tohen, M., Waternaux, C. M., & Tsuang, M. T. (1990). Outcome in mania: A 4-year prospective follow-up of 75 patients utilizing survival analysis. *Archives General of Psychiatry*, *47*, 1106–1111.

Walsh, J., & Bricourt, J. (1996). Improving jail lindages of detainees with mental health agencies: The role of family contact. *Psychiatric Rehabilitation Journal*, *20*, 73–76.

Wiederanders, M. R. (1992). Recidivism of disordered offenders who were conditionally vs. unconditionally released. *Behavioral Sciences and the Law*, *10*, 141–148.

Wiederanders, M. R., Bromley, D. L., & Choate, P. A. (1997). Forensic conditional release programs and outcomes in three states. *International Journal of Law and Psychiatry*, *20*, 249–257.

Wiederanders, M. R., & Choate, P. A. (1994). Beyond recidivism: Measuring community adjustments of conditionally released insanity acquittees. *Psychological Assessment*, *6*, 61–66.

Wilson, D., Tien, G., & Eaves, D. (1995). Increasing the community tenure of mentally disordered offenders: An assertive case management program. *International Journal of Law and Psychiatry*, *18*, 61–69.

Wolff, N., Helminiak, T. W., Morse, G. A., Calsyn, R. J., Klinkenberg, W. D., & Trusty, M. L. (1997). Cost-effectiveness evaluation of three approaches to case management for homeless mentally ill clients. *American Journal of Psychiatry*, *154*, 341–348.

Wormith, J. S., & McKeague, F. (1996). A mental health survey of community correctional clients in Canada. *Criminal Behaviour and Mental Health*, *6*, 49–72.

Chapter 29

Offenders with Mental Retardation

Kenneth Day
University of Newcastle, Newcastle upon Tyne, UK

INTRODUCTION

Mentally retarded offenders differ significantly from other mentally disordered offenders. Much of their offending is developmental in origin, mental illness is rarely a direct or associated factor, sex offences and arson are over-represented, and the prognosis is generally more favourable. The typical mentally retarded offender is a young man functioning in the mild to borderline intellectual range with poor social, interpersonal, and communication skills, who is underachieving educationally, often has a minor physical disability, and who usually but not invariably comes from a dysfunctional family. Female offenders are uncommon. More details about individual offender types are given below. The reader is referred to other texts for a fuller account of clinical features and psychopathology (Day, 1990, 1993, 1997).

IDENTIFICATION

In most countries specific mechanisms are triggered under mental health and criminal legislation once an offender is identified as mentally retarded. Major problems regarding admissibility of statements and disposal arise when this does not occur (Murphy & Mason, 1999). Mentally retarded people may have an impaired understanding of a caution and their legal rights, may too readily agree with suggestions made to them out of a desire to please and are prone to make false confessions to gain attention. Gudjonssen has been a pioneer in this field

Handbook of Offender Assessment and Treatment. Edited by C. R. Hollin.
© 2000 John Wiley & Sons Ltd.

developing a Suggestibility Scale, to aid the retrospective validation of statements made to the police, and a simple Checklist to assist the police and others in the identification of underlying mental retardation (Gudjonsson, Clare, Rutter, & Pearse, 1993).

ASSESSMENT

Comprehensive, multidisciplinary, ongoing assessment provides the basis for the formulation of the treatment plan, the assessment of progress, and decisions about eventual discharge from all or part of the treatment programme. It also forms the basis for reports to the courts. The key components of assessment are listed in Table 29.1. The aim is to build up a global picture of the individual with particular reference to his/her offence history and the factors pertinent to current and previous offending.

Table 29.1 Examination of the mentally retarded offender (adapted from Day, 1990)

History	
Current offence	Nature, circumstances, solitary/joint, impulsive/ planned, motive, contextual factors, e.g. life events, conflicts, pressures, temptations, level of support and supervision, alcohol
Previous offence history	Include incidents not prosecuted Dates, nature, outcome
Neuropsychiatric and medical history	Full details of other conduct/behaviour disorders, mental illness, epilepsy, medical problems, hospitalization
Personality	Features, friends, interests, relationships, gangs Pathological type
Family and background factors	FH mental illness, mental retardation, delinquency, criminality or other psychopathology. Dysfunctional family
Examination	
Mental state	Intellectual level and functioning mental illness Fitness to plead, concept of right and wrong, knowledge of the law and social codes, attitude to offence and its consequences, attitude to treatment
Physical examination	Note particularly any minor defects
Investigations	
Psychometry	IQ, educational attainments, adaptive behaviour, structured analysis of offence behaviour
Electroencephalography and brain scan	If organic brain disease suspected
Chromosome studies	If behavioural phenotype suspected

Particular attention should be paid to the following.

Fitness to Plead

Fitness to plead requires an understanding of the difference between right and wrong and of the nature and possible consequences of the charge and the ability to instruct counsel, follow evidence in court, and challenge a juror. Most mentally retarded offenders are fit to plead but each case must be judged individually with the greatest weight being given to understanding the charge and the difference between a plea of guilty and not guilty. Care should be taken to avoid coaching.

Index Offence

The nature and circumstances of the index offence together with previous offending history should be thoroughly explored with particular attention to contributory and precipitating factors, attitude to the offence, victim empathy, concepts of right and wrong, and the offence pattern and cycle. Wherever possible a structured analysis of offence behaviour should be made utilizing available scales and schedules. Aspects of the personal history relevant to the offence, e.g. sexual history, should be explored in depth. The account given by the patient should always be supplemented by collateral information from as many other sources as possible, including victim and witness statements, photographic material, and previous medical, psychiatric, social and criminal records.

Risk Assessment

Risk assessment is crucial in shaping the treatment plan, in the decision to admit for treatment, and in the evaluation of progress, discharge, and the discontinuation of treatment. Special factors to be considered in the mentally retarded are concepts of right and wrong, knowledge and understanding of the law and social codes, level of comprehension of the nature of the offence and its consequences, predisposing factors, such as impulsivity and other behaviour problems, precipitating factors, including life events and situational factors, and offender typology.

LEGAL PROCESSES

Court Diversion Schemes

Court diversion schemes aim to divert mentally disordered offenders accused of a less serious offence directly into the treatment services obviating the need for a court appearance. Success has been reported with mentally ill offenders but such iniatives are likely to be of limited value in the management of mentally retarded offenders where learning about the social consequences of behaviour is a key therapeutic gaol (Brier, 1994). For this reason victims and the police should always be encouraged to press charges, which they are often reluctant to do on learning that an offender is mentally retarded (Day, 1994; Lyall, Holland, Collins, & Styles, 1995). A further potential complication is an offender's incapacity or unwillingness to co-operate with treatment and the possible need for and the associated difficulties in applying a civil section under the mental health legislation.

Sentencing Options

When faced with a mentally retarded offender the court will look for expert professional guidance on disposal. There are a number of options, each with its advantages and disadvantages, depending upon the needs of the individual, the perceived risk to the public, and the availability of services (Day, 1990). The majority of mentally retarded offenders can be managed in the community with support from the social, probation, and the specialist mental retardation services. Most are able to remain with their family or in their regular residential placement, but a special residential placement may be necessary if additional support is needed or there is bad feeling in the neighbourhood about the offence. Sometimes a conventional sentence, such as a small fine or conditional discharge, may be indicated if care and treatment needs are already satisfactorily in place but there is a therapeutic need to mark the event.

Hospital treatment is indicated if: the offence is serious and would normally have attracted a custodial sentence; the offender is judged to pose a significant danger to the public (not necessarily only on the basis of the current offence); an in-depth assessment is required or there is a general need for care, training, supervision, and control which cannot be properly carried out or provided in the community; and for persistent multiple offenders who have proved unresponsive to treatment in the community (Day, 1993).

Co-operation with treatment is frequently a problem and some form of legal restraint under mental health and/or criminal legislation is usually advisable for both community and hospital care. Pharmacological and behavioural therapies require specific consent. Valid consent requires an understanding of the nature of the treatment and why it is proposed, its principal benefits and risks, the consequences of not receiving the treatment, and the available options. Most mentally retarded offenders are able to consent to treatment provided the explanation and advice is pitched at the correct level.

TREATMENT PROGRAMME

Offending in the mentally retarded is usually rooted in undersocialization, impaired internal controls, and faulty social learning compounded by educational

Table 29.2 Treatment programme for mentally retarded offenders—key components

General
  Life skills training
  Treatment of psychiatric and/or medical problems
  Counselling and general support
  Self-regulation and offence behaviour management
  Socialization programmes
  Family and carer support

Offence-specific interventions

Sex offenders	Sex education, socio-sexual skills training
	Antilibidinal medication
	Behavioural programmes for deviant sexuality
Firesetters	Assertiveness training
Aggressive offenders	Anger management training, relaxation therapy
	Mood stabilizing medication
Delinquency/property offenders	Constructional approaches
	Socialization programmes

Rehabilitation, aftercare, and relapse prevention
  General and specific support
  Continuation of specific treatment modalities

underachievement, poor social, interpersonal and occupational skills, and low self-esteem. The aims of treatment, therefore, are to assist maturation, improve self-control, instil a sense of personal worth and responsibility, establish acceptable social mores, improve social, occupational and educational skills, and address any offence-specific factors. The principal components of the treatment programme are listed in Table 29.2. Mentally retarded offenders are not an homogeneous group and programmes should be specifically tailored to meet individual needs.

General Measures

Deficiencies in life skills are often potent contributory factors and in some cases the key factor in offending behaviour. Training should be linked to individual needs, practically orientated, and focused on the knowledge and skills that will be of use in everyday life, e.g. obtaining information and assistance; survival cooking; managing finances; and use of public facilities. Recreational training should capitalize on any personal interests. Occupational training should focus on the work ethic and general work skills rather than training for a specific job. Advantage should be taken of the special courses increasingly offered by Further Education facilities. Role-play is an invaluable technique in the crucially important, but far more difficult, area of improving interpersonal skills.

Treatment of Psychiatric and Medical Problems

Approximately one-third of mentally retarded offenders have a history of psychiatric illness (Day, 1993). The possibility of an associated mental illness should therefore always be explored and, if present, treated accordingly. This may be all that is necessary in those few cases where active mental illness is a direct cause of the offending behaviour (Day, 1988, 1994).

Minor but often highly visible physical disabilities are surprisingly common and a potent source of low self-esteem and self-confidence (Day, 1988). If present they should be carefully reviewed with a view to further treatment or correction or counselling to assist adjustment. Unrecognized or inadequately treated epilepsy is not uncommon and better seizure control can substantially improve the longer-term outcome (Milne & O'Brien, 1997).

Families and Carers

This is a neglected area. Families need reassurance and help to understand and come to terms with their offspring's offending, and sometimes advice and support in handling community hostility if the offence has involved a close neighbour or is particularly serious. Families and carers should be acquainted with the treatment plan and its rationale at an early stage. Wherever possible common goals, attitudes, and rules should be established across all settings, including the home. A family therapy approach may be indicated, particularly if there is a high level of expressed emotion, but the family's capacity to co-operate and benefit must be carefully assessed before therapy begins. In most cases contact between the offender and his family can be used productively to bring about positive therapeutic benefits and is to be encouraged. Some families, however, are so dysfunctional that such contact can be extremely damaging and should be positively discouraged or kept to a minimum. In these situations treatment should be directed at helping the offender come to terms with the family's shortcomings and insulating him/her against their bad influences.

Socialization Programmes

Socialization programmes aim to link behaviour with its consequences—a major deficit in many mentally retarded offenders—utilizing token economy procedures. Many programmes have been described and all share common features, the principal differences being in the detail of the reward system and its application. In some schemes points or tokens are issued immediately following a behavioural event and in others on a daily or weekly basis; some apply to all aspects of behaviour whilst others specifically target antisocial behaviour. For a fuller account and references, see Day (1990, 1993).

Token economy schemes require a controlled environment and experienced staff for successful implementation and can only satisfactorily be operated in a specialized residential unit. They provide an invaluable framework for the general running of such units and are able to operate with a high degree of fairness. Token economy schemes have been criticized on the grounds that such a blanket approach cannot meet individual needs and that it is difficult to transfer skills acquired to the everyday environment. Good results have, however, been reported and individualized packages of skills training and offence-specific interventions are essential features of most schemes (Day, 1990).

Self-Regulation and Offence Behaviour Management

Deficiencies in self-management, understanding the offence cycle and coping skills are common features in mentally retarded offenders. A range of psychological interventions have been developed for their management, some adapted from procedures used with non retarded offenders. Although described separately below they are almost always used in combination in practice.

Anger Management

This technique has been developed for use with the mildly mentally retarded by Benson (1994). Offenders are taught to recognize angry feelings and the contextual and precipitating events which activate them and then to self-regulate utilizing verbal statements such as "stay cool" and "take it easy". Training is carried out in a group setting utilizing role-play and examples from everyday life such as criticism, teasing, and common frustrations, and is frequently combined with training in problem solving and relaxation therapy.

Offence Behaviour Management Programmes

Offence behaviour management aims to get the offender to recognize and accept responsibility for his/her offending behaviour; change attitudes to this behaviour; understand the "offence cycle"; recognize high-risk situations; and develop avoidance and coping strategies. Victim empathy, dealing with denial and minimization, and rectifying cognitive distortions are key components. Such programmes have been used successfully in the management of mentally retarded sex offenders (see Day, 1997).

Most practitioners employ group techniques and utilize a range of cognitive, behavioural, or psychotherapeutic techniques including peer pressure and confrontation. A three-stage approach is adopted. Stage 1 is concerned with setting up the group, establishing the goals and guidelines, developing trust and confidence, and assisting effective communication. Stage 2 involves an in-depth exploration of offence behaviour and its consequences linked to personal responsibility in both general and individual terms. In Stage 3 offenders are taught (through detailed analysis and "walking through" their offence) to recognize and understand the cognitive, emotional, and situational factors that underlie and maintain *their* offence cycle and how to recognize, avoid, and cope with high-risk situations using verbal self-regulation and other strategies.

Programmes usually run for one to three years and require a high degree of patient motivation and co-operation. Participants must be carefully selected on the basis of their ability to co-operate and it is advisable to require them to sign a "treatment contract". Small groups, of no more than seven or eight, short and frequent sessions (30–90 minutes once or twice weekly), and a categorical learning approach are recommended.

Psychopharmacotherapy

Overprescription in the past has made the use of psychotropic drugs in the absence of symptoms of mental illness unpopular. However judiciously used they can be a valuable adjunct to management. The neuroleptics, lithium, and certain antiepileptics are all effective mood stabilizers, particularly where organic brain damage is present (Clarke, 1997). They may be useful as an interim measure during assessment, for crisis management, and in facilitating co-operation with behavioural and social training programmes where impulsivity, unpredictability, and aggressivity are problems.

The antilibidinal drugs, such as cyproterone acetate and medroxyprogesterone acetate, are highly effective in reducing sex drive and sex response in the mentally retarded (Clarke, 1989). They are indicated as an initial short-term measure during assessment and the formulation of the treatment programme, as an adjunct to sex behaviour management programmes, to provide symptomatic relief and additional control during periods of stress, and as the principal therapeutic intervention where all other approaches have failed (Day, 1997).

Drug choice depends upon individual need and response. Regimes should be carefully planned and regularly monitored and dosage levels titrated according to the desired effect: it is not necessary, for example, to completely eliminate sex drive, only to reduce it to a level which the patient can control. Mood stabilizers should be given in adequate dosage for a sufficient duration before they are regarded as ineffective. Drug therapy should never be abruptly withdrawn or reduced or discontinued during potentially vulnerable periods such as discharge from hospital, transfer between services, or a significant life event.

Psychotherapy

Counselling and supportive psychotherapy is a common component of most treatment programmes for mentally retarded offenders (Day, 1990, 1993) but psychoanalytical psychotherapy has only recently begun to be used in the field of mental retardation (Hollins, Sinason, & Thompson, 1994; Gaedt, 1995).

Psychotherapeutic techniques are employed in some sex behaviour management programmes with this group of offenders (Cox-Lindenbaum & Lindenbaum, 1994) and mixed groups of mentally retarded offenders (Hollins & Sinason, personal communication).

MANAGEMENT OF SPECIFIC OFFENDER TYPES

Sex Offenders

Mentally retarded sex offenders can be classified into three groups each with specific treatment needs (Day, 1994, 1997).

A *developmental group*, the largest numerically, who tend to be shy, immature individuals, deficient in sexual knowledge and experience, who show little evidence of other psychosocial pathology and usually come from warm and caring, if somewhat overprotective, families. Their sex offending is essentially the consequence of crude attempts to fulfil normal sexual impulses in the absence of normal outlets compounded by poor adaptive behaviour, sexual naivety, poor impulse control, and social ineptness. Treatment for this group should focus on increasing overall social skills and self-confidence, sex education, including the law and social codes, improving interpersonal and courtship skills, and providing opportunities for mixing with an appropriate peer group of the opposite sex (see Day, 1997). Antilibidinal drugs may sometimes be indicated as an initial measure and occasionally, where there are particular difficulties with self-control and understanding, a sex behaviour management programme.

A smaller *antisocial group* are markedly damaged individuals whose sex offending is part of a generalized antisocial behaviour disorder. They show a high prevalence of psychosocial pathology, other maladaptive behaviours, and personality disorder; they are more likely to become persistent sex offenders and to commit serious offences. This group require intensive treatment, including sex behaviour management programmes and anger management, and often antilibidinal drugs, in the structured and controlled environment of a specialist treatment unit.

A small group of *sexually deviant* mentally retarded offenders, who engage exclusively in homosexual or paedophilic behaviour, exhibitionism, cross-dressing or other fetishisms and have similar characteristics and treatment needs as non-retarded offenders in these categories (Day, 1994, 1997). Success has been reported with a range of behavioural techniques aimed at reducing deviant sexual orientation and establishing normal sexual orientation (see Day, 1997, for references). However, the results are difficult to assess with accuracy owing to the previous tendency to assign all such behaviour in the mentally retarded to deviant sexual orientation. Sex behaviour management programmes and/or antilibidinal drugs may offer more realistic and successful options in most cases (Day, 1997).

Firesetters

Firesetting in the mentally retarded is usually the consequence of displaced aggression and functions as a communication vehicle in passive individuals with poor verbal communication skills and difficulty in expressing appropriate anger to others (McKerracher & Dacre, 1966; O'Sullivan & Kelleher, 1987). Incidents of firesetting frequently occur in situations of conflict and stress (Yesevage, Benezech, Ceccaldi, Bourgeois, & Addad, 1983; Clare, Murphy, Cox, & Chaplin, 1992) which the offender feels powerless to change, or where there is no "person target" (Jackson, Glass, & Hope, 1987). A low incidence of aggression to others and a high incidence of self-injury, attempted suicide, and aggression to property are common features.

Treatment approaches have therefore focused on assertiveness training, understanding the offence cycle, improving interactive communication skills and training in coping strategies such as relaxation, self-talk and escape and avoidance techniques (Jackson et al., 1987; Clare et al., 1992; Stewart, 1993). This approach needs to be coupled with sensible practical precautions to minimize the risk of further episodes such as a complete ban on personal matches and lighters, close supervision when the patient is smoking, and staff/carer awareness of risk situations. Treatment in a closed residential setting is usually indicated, at least in the initial stages of treatment.

Aggressive Offenders

Although the incidence of violent offences is low, a significant number of mentally retarded offenders display irritability and a low frustration tolerance which impairs social interaction and their ability to co-operate with treatment. Anger management training is a key component of treatment and mood stabilizing medication may also be indicated on a short-term basis, or sometimes as a longer term measure, particularly where there is evidence of underlying organic brain damage.

Delinquency

Property and technical offences are the commonest offences committed by the mentally retarded and, as in the general population, are usually adaptive in origin and rooted in faulty upbringing, poor parental models, and neighbourhood crime. Solitary delinquent acts are uncommon and peer group pressure, poor self-control, and gullibillity are common factors (Day, 1990).

Most offenders in this category can be managed in the community and often require no more than general measures to improve their social functioning and self-esteem, day care, and support. Specific treatment initiatives should focus on improving awareness and self-control, self-monitoring, self-evaluation and coping strategies, and insulation against adverse environmental factors (Cole, Gardner, & Karan, 1985). Constructional approaches which attempt to offer attractive, acceptable alternatives to offending behaviour have also been advocated (Donnellan, LaVigna, Negri-Shoultz, & Fassbender, 1988; Cullen, 1993) but await evaluation. Serious and persistent offenders may require a period of residential treatment where socialization programmes form the mainstay of the management programme (Day, 1988, 1990).

Female Offenders

Female mentally retarded offenders are uncommon and their treatment and management has received little attention. They are invariably severely damaged and disturbed individuals with appalling histories of social deprivation and physical and sexual abuse who present intractable problems. Aggression towards others and property, arson, self-wounding and mutilation, attempted suicide, and other behaviour disorders including sexual misdemeanours are the common presenting problems (McKerracher, Street, & Segal, 1966; Robertson, 1981) and occasionally the rare and unusual crime of baby stealing (d'Orban, 1990).

They pose enormous management problems, are extremely difficult to help, and invariably require medium to long-term care and treatment in a specialist unit with highly skilled and experienced staff. Treatment should be directed at increasing self-esteem, femininity, and self-worth through personal skills and relationship training coupled with socialization programmes, self-control procedures, and specific interventions for offences such as arson or baby stealing. The possibility of previous physical or sexual abuse should be carefully explored (Beail & Warden, 1995) and, where appropriate, treatment offered utilizing approaches developed for the non-retarded (Jehu, 1991).

REHABILITATION AND AFTERCARE

Rehabilitation after a period of hospital treatment should be a carefully phased process with gradually extended periods of supervised community leave. High-quality, comprehensive aftercare is crucial in improving the prognosis and reducing reconviction rates (see Day, 1990, 1993) and is particularly important during the first year following discharge when the risk of breakdown is greatest (Day, 1988). A comprehensive rehabilitation and aftercare plan with clear goals, covering all aspects of care, is essential. A key worker should be appointed to implement and monitor the plan and families and community staff adequately prepared. Statutory supervision for a period is advisable for serious offenders where compliance is judged to be a likely problem.

OUTCOME AND PROGNOSIS

Studies show that 40%–60% of hospitalized mentally retarded offenders are reconvicted after discharge and nearly one-third are rehospitalized or imprisoned, but that very few commit serious offences. Many reoffend during the first year but long-term studies reveal a low but persistent tendency towards recidivism, particularly in sex offenders and arsonists. Reconviction rates alone, however, paint an unduly pessimistic picture and global assessments using a range of measures indicate a rather better outcome in terms of social adjustment.

Adequate duration of treatment and good-quality aftercare are associated with a better outcome, and a history of previous convictions and a poor response to inpatient treatment with a poor outcome. Offenders against the person have a better prognosis than property offenders—problems in the former being rooted essentially in problems of poor self-control and immaturity with the potential to respond to treatment, whilst in the latter they are more a function of overall lifestyle and subcultural influences to which the offender so frequently returns. For a full account and references, see Day (1990, 1993).

SERVICE PROVISION

Mentally retarded offenders are disadvantaged and vulnerable in generic forensic psychiatry services where they are in the minority, staff lack the necessary expertise, and it is difficult if not impossible to establish specialist training programmes. Specialist services developed within mental retardation psychiatric services are required (Day, 1993, 1995). A model specialist forensic service has been described by Day (1993): the elements are shown in Table 29.3. The minimal requirements are an assessment and treatment unit, long-stay care, and rehabilitation facilities. It is argued by some that control in treatment units is best effected by high staffing levels, but others consider that secure settings offer a more relaxed and therapeutic environment for both patients and staff.

Because of the small numbers of patients and their specialized treatment needs, specialist forensic services can only viably be provided on a subre-

Table 29.3 Key elements of a comprehensive specialist forensic psychiatric service for mentally retarded offenders

Appropriately trained and experienced staff
Specialist treatment programmes
Specialist community-based services, including support personnel and a range of
    residential and day facilities, for assessment, treatment, aftercare and continuing care
Open units for assessment and treatment of less serious offenders and for rehabilitation
Units with varying levels of security for more dangerous offenders
Secure facilities for longer term care
Rehabilitation programmes and hostels

gional/regional basis. A single provider for the total service facilitates flexibility and continuity of care for the patient and is to be preferred. Successful community management requires good multiagency co-operation, and the availability of an adequate range of services and experienced personnel. Regular community services for the mentally retarded are not geared to meeting the needs of mentally retarded offenders and specialist facilities are required.

REFERENCES

Beail, N., & Warden, S. (1995). Sexual abuse of adults with learning disabilities. *Journal of Intellectual Disability Research, 39*, 382–387.

Benson, B. (1994). Anger management training: A self controlled programme for persons with mild mental retardation. In N. Bouras (Ed.), *Mental health in mental retardation* (pp. 224–232). Cambridge, UK: Cambridge University Press.

Brier, N. (1994). Targetted treatment for adjudicated youths with learning disabilities: Effects on recidivism. *Journal of Learning Disability Research, 27*(4), 215–222.

Clare, I. C. H., Murphy, G. H., Cox. D., & Chaplin, E. H. (1992). Assessment and treatment fire setting: A single case study. *Criminal Behaviour and Mental Health, 2*, 253–268.

Clarke, D. J. (1989). Antilibidinal drugs and mental retardation: A review. *Medicine, Science and the Law, 29*, 136–148.

Clarke, D. (1997). Physical treatment. In S. G. Read (Ed.), *Psychiatry in Learning Disability* (pp. 350–379). London: W. J. Saunders.

Cole, C. L., Gardner, W. I., & Karan, O. C. (1985). Self management training of mentally adults presenting severe conduct difficulties. *Applied Research in Mental Retardation, 6*, 337–347.

Cox-Lindenbaum, D., & Lindenbaum, L. (1994). A modality for treatment of aggressive behaviour and sexual disorders in people with mental retardation. In N. Bouras (Ed.), *Mental health in mental retardation* (pp. 244–254). Cambridge, UK: Cambridge University Press.

Cullen, C. (1993). The treatment of people with learning disabilities who offend. In K. Howells & C. R. Hollin (Eds.), *Clinical approaches to the mentally disordered offender* (pp. 145–163). Chichester, UK: Wiley.

Day, K. (1988). A hospital based treatment programme for male mentally handicapped offenders. *British Journal of Psychiatry, 153*, 635–644.

Day, K. (1990). Mental retardation: Clinical aspects and management. In R. Bluglass & P. Bowden (Eds.), *Principles and Practice of Forensic Psychiatry* (pp. 399–418). Edinburgh, UK: Churchill Livingstone.

Day, K. (1993). Crime and mental retardation: A review. In K. Howells & C. R. Hollin (Eds.), *Clinical approaches to the mentally disordered offender* (pp. 111–144). Chichester, UK: Wiley.

Day, K. (1994). Male mentally handicapped sex offenders. *British Journal of Psychiatry, 165*, 630–639.

Day, K. (1995). Specialist psychiatric services for mentally retarded offenders. In R. Fletcher, D. McNelis, & L. Fusaro (Eds.), *Proceedings of International Congress II on the dually diagnosed* (pp. 102–106). New York: NADD.

Day, K. (1997). Sex offenders with learning disabilities. In S. G. Read (Ed.), *Psychiatry in learning disabilities* (pp. 278–306). London: Saunders.

Donnellan, A. M., LaVigna, G. W., Negri-Shoultz, N., & Fassbender, L. L. (1988). *Progress without punishment: Effective approaches for learners with behaviour problems*. New York: Teachers College Press.

d'Orban, P. T. (1990). Kidnapping, abduction and child stealing. In R. Bluglass & P. Bowden (Eds.), *Principles and practice of forensic psychiatry* (pp. 797–804). Edinburgh, UK: Churchill Livingstone.

Gaedt, C. (1995). Psychotherapeutic approaches in the treatment of mental illness and behavioural disorders in mentally retarded people: The significance of a psycho-analytic perspective. *Journal of Intellectual Disability Research, 39*, 233–239.

Gudjonssen, G., Clare, I., Rutter, S., & Pearse, J. (1993). *Persons at risk during interviews in police custody: The identification of vulnerabilities.* London: HMSO.

Hollins, S., Sinason, V., & Thompson, S. (1994). Individual, group and family psychother-apy. In N. Bouras (Ed.), *Mental health in mental retardation* (pp. 233–243). Cambridge, UK: Cambridge University Press.

Jackson, H. F., Glass, C., & Hope, S. (1987). A functional analysis of recidivistic arson. *British Journal of Clinical Psychology, 26*, 175–185.

Jehu, D. (1991). Clinical work with adults who were sexually abused in childhood. In C. R. Hollin & K. Howells (Eds.), *Clinical approaches to sex offenders and their victims* (pp. 229–260). Chichester, UK: Wiley.

Lyall, I., Holland, T., Collins, S., & Styles, P. (1995). Incidence of persons with a learning disability detained in police custody: A needs assessment for service development. *Science, Medicine and the Law, 35*(1), 61–71.

McKerracher, D. W., & Dacre, A. J. I. (1966). A study of arsonists in a special security hospital. *British Journal of Psychiatry, 112*, 1151–1154.

McKerracher, D., Street, D. R. K., & Segal, L. J. (1966). A comparison of the behaviour problems presented by male and female subnormal offenders. *British Journal of Psychiatry, 122*, 891–897.

Milne, E., & O'Brien, G. (1997). Epilepsy in learning disabled offenders: Prevalence, diag-nosis and impact on treatment. *Epilepsia, 38*(Suppl. 3), 111.

Murphy, G., & Mason, J. (1999). People with learning disabilities who offend. In N. Bouras (Ed.), *Psychiatric and behavioural disorders in developmental disabilities and mental retardation* (pp. 226–245). Cambridge, UK: Cambridge University Press.

O'Sullivan, G. H., & Kelleher, M. J. (1987). A study of fire setters in the south west of Ireland. *British Journal of Psychiatry, 151*, 818–823.

Robertson, G. (1981). The extent and pattern of crime amongst mentally handicapped offenders. *Journal of the British Institute of Mental Handicap, 90*, 1–8.

Stewart, L. A. (1993). Profile of female fire setters: Implications for treatment. *British Journal of Psychiatry, 163*, 248–256.

Yesavage, J. A., Benezech, M., Ceccaldi, S., Bourgeois, M., & Addad, M. (1983). Arson in mentally ill and criminal populations. *Journal of Clinical Psychiatry, 44*, 128–130.

Chapter 30

Offenders with Personality Disorders

Mary McMurran
Centre for Applied Psychology, University of Leicester, Leicester, UK

INTRODUCTION

The aim of this chapter is to examine psychiatric approaches to personality disorder. Psychiatric diagnoses have medico-legal significance in that they are the basis on which an offender may be diverted to health services. In England and Wales, for example, an offender may be legally classified as suffering from "psychopathic disorder" under the terms of the Mental Health Act (1983) if he or she is deemed by psychiatrists to meet the definition of suffering from a persistent disorder or disability of mind which results in abnormally aggressive or seriously irresponsible conduct. Offenders legally classified as suffering from "psychopathic disorder" will be referred to as legal psychopaths throughout this chapter. A "persistent disorder or disability of mind" in this context may be taken to mean a personality disorder. As we shall see, there is no personality disorder called psychopathy in the major diagnostic systems, although the issue of psychopathy is clinically important and will be addressed. Provided the personality disorder is deemed treatable, and depending upon the perceived level of risk of harm to self or others, the person legally classified as suffering from "psychopathic disorder" may be detained involuntarily in hospital for treatment or treated in the community by virtue of a compulsory treatment order. Since psychiatric diagnoses of personality disorder can contribute to legal decisions that have significant implications for the disposal and treatment of an offender, the issue of personality disorder warrants examination.

Handbook of Offender Assessment and Treatment. Edited by C. R. Hollin.
© 2000 John Wiley & Sons Ltd.

PERSONALITY DISORDERS

Psychiatric diagnostic criteria for personality disorders are defined in the *Diagnostic and Statistical Manual of Mental Disorders—IV* (DSM-IV; American Psychiatric Association, 1994) and the *International Classification of Diseases—10* (ICD-10; World Health Organization, 1992). The personality disorders are listed in Table 30.1, along with a brief description of each identifying the most salient features of that disorder. Stone (1993) observes that the personality disorders defined in DSM and ICD are a narrow group compared with the maladaptive

Table 30.1   DSM-IV and ICD-10 personality disorders (adapted from Tyrer, 1992)

DSM-IV	ICD-10
Cluster A	
Paranoid	Paranoid
Distrust and suspiciousness	Sensitivity and suspiciousness
Schizoid	Schizoid
Socially and emotionally detached	Emotionally cold and detached
Schizotypal	No equivalent
Social and interpersonal deficits; cognitive or perceptual distortions	
Cluster B	
Antisocial	Dyssocial
Violation of the rights of others	Callous disregard of others, irresponsibility, and irritability
Borderline	Emotionally unstable
Instability of relationships, self-image and mood	(a) Borderline
	Unclear self-image, and intense, unstable relationships
	(b) Impulsive
	Inability to control anger, quarrelsome, and unpredictable
Histrionic	Histrionic
Excessive emotionality and attention-seeking	Dramatic, egocentric, and manipulative
Narcissistic	No equivalent
Grandiose, lack of empathy, need for admiration	
Cluster C	
Avoidant	Anxious
Socially inhibited, feelings of inadequacy, hypersensitivity	Tense, self-conscious, and hypersensitive
Dependent	Dependent
Clinging and submissive	Subordinates personal needs, and needs constant reassurance
Obsessive–compulsive	Anankastic
Perfectionist and inflexible	Indecisive, pedantic, and rigid

personalities generally recognizable in people at large, and describe conditions that are of interest to clinicians; they do not purport to describe personality in general. Psychological approaches to the study of normal personality traits and maladaptive extremes of these may do better justice to the diversity of human personality and dimensional approaches might be the key to the future (e.g. Costa and Widiger, 1994). At present, however, categorical approaches have more practical relevance and so are the focus of this chapter.

Personality disorder classifications suffer problems with both validity and reliability. Descriptions of personality disorders consist of a mixture of both psychological traits (e.g. impulsivity, anxiety, sensitivity) and behaviour (e.g. self-mutilation, miserliness, law-breaking), leading to doubt as to whether these diagnoses identify "true" personality disorders (i.e. traits) or social deviance (i.e. behaviour). In general, the reliability of clinical diagnosis of personality disorders is only poor to fair, except for those disorders that are primarily described in terms of overt behaviours, antisocial personality disorder diagnosis being particularly reliable (Stone, 1993). Reliance on observable behaviour as a means of identifying a personality disorder may improve the reliability of diagnosis, but introducing operational criteria before the disorder is thoroughly understood may diminish validity.

There are also problems with co-morbidity in that multiple personality disorders are frequently observed in the same person, and personality disorders frequently co-exist with Axis 1 disorders (e.g. psychosis, mood disorders, and substance use disorders). It is quite possible that a person may suffer two conditions at the same time, and co-morbidity may be taken as a measure of the severity of disorder (Tyrer & Johnson, 1996). Co-morbidity of personality disorders may indicate that the descriptive features of several personality disorders overlap and so diagnosticians cannot easily distinguish one from the other. Widiger and Trull (1994), for example, point out that violent behaviour is a defining feature of two of DSM-IV personality disorders (borderline and antisocial), which may explain the high degree of co-morbidity of these two disorders. Co-morbidity of particular groupings of personality disorders is evident, and in DSM-IV they are presented as three clusters—Cluster A: odd or eccentric (paranoid, schizoid, and schizotypal); Cluster B: dramatic or flamboyant (comprising antisocial, borderline, histrionic, and narcissistic); and Cluster C: anxious or fearful (avoidant, dependent, and obsessive–compulsive).

PERSONALITY DISORDERED OFFENDERS

Legal psychopaths are of particular interest to clinicians in that they, in comparison with mentally ill offenders, are more likely to reoffend after discharge from hospital (Bailey & MacCulloch, 1992; Steels et al., 1998). The range of personality disorders that may feature in a group of legal psychopaths is illustrated in a study by Reiss, Grubin, and Meux (1996), where 30 patients in a maximum security psychiatric hospital (a "special" hospital) included those diagnosed as borderline, antisocial, schizoid, narcissistic, schizotypal, and paranoid, many with multiple diagnoses. Similarly, Coid (1992) in a study of male and female patients, all legal psychopaths in special hospitals, and male prisoners held in special units for dangerous or disruptive prisoners found a wide range of DSM-III (American Psychiatric Association, 1980) personality disorders in these groups, with significantly more female patients receiving a diagnosis of borderline personality disorder, and significantly more male prisoners receiving diagnoses of antisocial, narcissistic, paranoid, passive-aggressive, and histrionic disorders (see Table 30.2). A study of female prisoners referred to prison psychiatrists similarly reveal high levels and a broad range of DSM-III-R (American Psychiatric Association, 1987) disorders (Dolan & Mitchell, 1994; see Table 30.2).

Personality disordered offenders may be defined according to the medico-legal definition and disposal but, as the studies by Coid (1992) and Dolan and Mitchell (1994) show, many personality disordered offenders are located within prisons. These personality disordered prisoners may not be involved in treatment by health service personnel because they are deemed untreatable, do not wish to receive treatment, or simply have never been referred to a psychiatrist.

The relationship between personality disorder and offending is complex. Care must be taken to avoid using diagnoses tautologically. For example, persistent aggressive behaviour may lead the clinician to diagnose antisocial personality disorder, and then the diagnosed disorder is simply used to explain aggression, which it plainly does not—the diagnosis merely describes the behaviour. Theoretically driven aetiological studies are important in understanding how a disorder develops, progresses, and remits, and, in the case of offenders, how the disorder relates to particular types of offending (violence, sexual offending, firesetting, and so on).

Table 30.2 Percentage of male and female special hospital patients and male prisoners receiving DSM-III/DSM-III-R personality disorder diagnoses (adapted from Coid, 1992, and Dolan & Mitchell, 1994)

Diagnosis	Female special hospital patients ($n = 93$)	Male special hospital patients ($n = 86$)	Male prisoners ($n = 64$)	Female prisoners ($n = 50$)
Borderline	91	56	55	60
Antisocial	44	38	86	44
Narcissistic	37	45	61	34
Paranoid	46	28	67	52
Passive-aggressive	28	16	50	26
Schizotypal	25	19	30	38
Histrionic	19	13	42	40
Avoidant	36	8	19	32
Dependent	25	20	14	34
Schizoid	11	13	11	28
Compulsive	11	14	5	20
Masochistic	9	4	6	—

Information from such studies is important in determining relevant treatment goals. Some critics would say that a personality disorder diagnosis is of very limited value in identifying treatment goals and that an analysis of the individual's behaviour in historical and current contexts, including cognitive, behavioural, and psychosocial elements, is more productive (Rice & Harris, 1997). This may be true, but research into the aetiology of personality disorders provides information that helps direct the clinician's assessment, as well as revealing implications for prevention and treatment. Biopsychosocial approaches, which look at biologically-based personal characteristics as they interact with the social environment, may hold most promise. Research into antisocial personality disorder, for example, identifies an early history of hyperactivity, impulsivity, and attention problems (Maughan, 1993; Widiger & Trull, 1994). There is evidence that these characteristics may have a biological basis, for example neurochemical or brain dysfunction (Carey & Goldman, 1997; Raine, 1997), but that the resultant antisocial behaviour can best be explained by looking at how biological predispositions interact with the social environment over time.

In summary, the information presented above suggests that all personality types figure in criminal populations, both patients and prisoners, and if professionals intend to offer treatment for personality disordered offenders, then attention should be paid to all diagnoses. An individual approach to problem analysis is the best way to identify treatment needs for any one person, but biopsychosocial research into the aetiology of personality disorders can inform clinical assessment and treatment, as well as provide directions for prevention.

DIAGNOSIS

Psychiatrists may diagnose by clinical interview with reference to the relevant criteria, but there are a number of semi-structured interview schedules to guide the clinician (Van Elzen & Emmelkamp, 1996). These interview schedules present questions matching the diagnostic criteria contained in DSM or ICD and provide scoring systems that identify a diagnosis or otherwise. These schedules are the Structured Clinical Interview for DSM-IV Axis II Personality Disorders (First, Gibbon, Spitzer, Williams, & Benjamin, 1997); the Personality Disorder Examination (Loranger, Susman, Oldham, & Russakoff, 1987); the International Personality Disorder Examination (Loranger et al., 1994); and the Structured Interview for DSM Personality Disorders (Stangl Pfohl, Zimmerman, Bowers, & Corenthal, 1985; Pfohl, Blum, & Zimmerman, 1995). Interview schedules show improved test–retest reliability and inter-rater reliability over clinical diagnosis, yet this is still only moderately good (Zimmerman, 1994). Whilst there is good agreement between interview schedules on continuous scores, diagnostic concordance is moderate, and the match with clinical diagnosis is only fairly good, and so none should be taken as superior (Pilkonis et al., 1995; Van Elzen & Emmelkamp, 1996).

PSYCHOPATHY

Cleckley (1941) defined psychopathy as cluster of personality traits, including lack of guilt, lack of anxiety, inability to learn from punishment, impoverished emotions, inability to form lasting emotional ties, egocentricity, and superficial charm. He argued that these characteristics may be associated with antisocial behaviour, but that this is not necessarily the case. These personality characteristics are captured in the ICD-10 definition of dyssocial personality disorder. Critics of the personality-based approach to diagnosis have argued that it is based too much upon inference and value judgement, and that psychopathy should be operationalized in terms of readily agreed antisocial behaviours (Lilienfeld, 1994). DSM-IV's criteria for antisocial personality disorder are largely behavioural, based upon law-breaking, recklessness, and irresponsibility. Because of the emphasis on antisocial behaviour, a large proportion of criminals meet the criteria for antisocial personality disorder, although they would not meet the criteria for psychopathy as a personality-based disorder.

Hare has incorporated both personality and behaviour in the Psychopathy Checklist—Revised (PCL–R; Hare, 1991). The PCL–R consists of 20 items which are scored from interview, official records, and corroborative checks with significant others. Each item may score absent (0), somewhat applicable (1), or definitely applicable (2), with the resultant range of scores being 0–40. The higher the score, the more psychopathic the individual. Hare recommends a cut-off point of 30 for determining psychopathy, although researchers may use continuous scores or different cut-off points (e.g. Cooke, 1995). The PCL–R is a reliable measure, and two factors may be defined—Factor 1, which measures interpersonal and affective characteristics such as selfishness and callousness, and Factor 2, which measures an antisocial, unstable, and deviant lifestyle (Hare et al., 1990).

A meta-analysis of studies using the PCL–R showed that psychopaths were three times more likely than non-psychopaths to commit further offences and about four times more likely to commit further violent offences (Hemphill, Hare, & Wong, 1998). Correlations between Factor 2 and general recidivism were stronger than for Factor 1, and both factors correlated equally with violent recidivism. Personality disorder diagnoses were not as accurate as PCL–R scores at predicting recidivism. A meta-analysis of treatment outcome indicates that high PCL–R scorers benefit least from psychological therapies (Garrido, Esteban, & Molero, 1996).

TREATMENT OF PERSONALITY DISORDERED OFFENDERS

Offenders with a personality disorder can be legally compelled to participate in treatment only if they are deemed treatable. Decisions about treatability are based upon a number of factors, including the availability of an effective treatment for the identified disorder, the resources currently available to provide an offender with the effective treatment, perceptions of the offender's motivation to change based upon previous engagement in and response to therapy, and the offender's current willingness to engage in the treatment on offer. The first of these issues is the one of primary interest here. Are there effective treatments for personality disorders, and if so what are they?

Where treatment of personality disorder is concerned, there is a fundamental issue of what is to be treated. Should practitioners address the socially deviant behaviour *per se* or the underlying maladaptive personality traits or a combination of the two? Regarding personality disordered offenders in health services, Blackburn (1993) suggests the following position:

> Since it is mental disorder rather than offending which justifies the diversion of mentally disordered offenders to the mental health system, alleviation of the disorder is a necessary outcome criterion, but reduced recidivism will be one indication of successful outcome in the case of personality disorder. Reduced recidivism is therefore a necessary but not sufficient outcome criterion. The primary need is to identify and target the *mediators* of antisocial behaviour, and to establish which treatments influence those mediators (p. 184).

With respect to personality disordered offenders located in the criminal justice system (i.e. prisons or on probation), one may paraphrase Blackburn's statement and argue that since it is crime rather than personality disorder that is the reason that offenders are in the criminal justice system, reduced recidivism will be the indicator of successful outcome, but that this is likely to be achieved by identifying and targeting the mediators of antisocial behaviour. If one accepts both of the above premises (and they are not mutually exclusive), the likely net result would be that treatment programmes for personality disordered offenders in the health services and in the criminal justice system would be indistinguishable, although the ultimate service evaluation criterion might differ between the two settings.

Harris and Rice (1997) suggest that appropriate target outcomes might be a reduction of recidivism, decreases in symptom severity and health service usage, and improvements in community adjustment, quality of life, and general happiness. Direct offence-focused work and the treatment of disorders strongly related to offending (e.g. alcohol and drug use) are clearly relevant but, since other chapters in this book address these specific treatments, they will not be addressed here.

The role of pharmacological treatments for personality disorders is arguably more limited than that of psychosocial interventions, but is nonetheless important to consider. Pharmacological treatments should target specific personality disorder symptoms which are believed to be mediated by neurotransmitter pathologies. Reviews of pharmacological treatments permit the conclusion that symptoms of anger and impulsivity, leading to aggression and violence, can be successfully treated in a number of ways: antidepressants for those who are depressed and irritable, agitated, and impulsive; lithium or anticonvulsants for those with mood lability and impulsivity; low dose antipsychotics for anger and impulsivity related to cognitive–perceptual symptoms; and selective serotonin reuptake inhibitors for the highly anxious and impulsive (Karper & Krystal, 1997; Soloff, 1998). Pharmacological treatments show modest clinical effects, should be used for limited periods, and should not be seen as a cure for personality disorder. They can, however, optimize functioning and minimize disability (Soloff, 1998), and may enhance a person's ability to benefit from psychosocial interventions.

Meta-analyses of what works with offenders in general have revealed that structured, cognitive–behavioural approaches that address criminogenic needs hold most promise in reducing recidivism (Andrews et al., 1990; Lipsey, 1992). Harris and Rice (1997) point out that the same risk factors predict recidivism in mentally disordered and non-mentally disordered offenders alike, therefore the same treatments may be used to address offending behaviour. Most psychosocial treatment approaches for personality disorders are broad-based, addressing interpersonal styles, cognitions, attitudes, beliefs, and emotion control.

Therapeutic communities (TCs) aim to address maladaptive interpersonal styles in a democracy where residents confront each other with the impact of their behaviours. In a study of personality disordered patients referred to a hospital, Copas, O'Brien, Roberts, and Whiteley (1984) found that, at three- and five-year follow-ups, fewer TC participants had further convictions or hospitalizations compared with those assessed but not admitted, and those who stayed in the TC for nine months or longer fared best. In a study of TC participants at the same hospital, Dolan (1997) measured change in symptomatology using the Symptom Checklist 90—Revised (Derogatis, 1975), showing a highly significant reduction in psychological distress. McMurran, Egan, and Ahmadi (1998) examined the criminal recidivism of predominantly personality disordered offenders who had either participated in a hospital-based TC for an average of 17 months or had been rejected after an assessment period averaging two months. At a mean follow-up time of almost five years, there was a significant reduction in crime for the whole sample when comparing pre-admission and post-discharge offences, but there were no significant differences between the two groups in terms of reconvictions, suggesting that the TC intervention had no effect on offending and that personality disordered offenders improved regardless. If an intervention has no effect, then it may be seen at best as a waste of resources and at worst as unethical practice when other more effective interventions could have been used. There is evidence, however, that TCs have done more harm than good with some mentally disordered offenders. Rice, Harris, and Cormier (1992) carried out a retrospective evaluation of a TC in a maximum security institution for mentally disordered offenders, matching the TC participants with comparable assessment-only group. Follow-up at a mean of 10.5 years after discharge showed a modest overall degree of success for the TC (success being no reconviction, revocation of parole, or reincarceration), but those TC participants scoring 25 or more on the PCL–R showed higher rates of recidivism, particularly violent recidivism, than a comparable non-treated group. That is, treatment in a TC made "psychopaths" worse than if they had had no treatment at all. TCs probably have some value in treating personality disordered offenders, but careful attention needs to be paid to who is selected, what is addressed, and how the TC operates (McMurran et al., 1998).

Hughes, Hogue, Hollin, and Champion (1997) describe a structured cognitive–behaviour therapy (CBT) programme for male legal psychopaths who were detained in a maximum security hospital. The programme included a range of groups targeting cognitive, emotional and skills functioning, for example assertiveness, self-esteem, cognitive skills, problem-solving, and emotional awareness, in which patients participated as necessary. Preliminary results on nine patients who have completed the programme show a net overall global positive change on a range of measures relevant to the problems addressed. In this sample there was a significant negative correlation between PCL–R scores and clinical improvement, this relationship being with PCL–R Factor 1 and not Factor 2. These results provide tentative support for CBT with personality disordered offenders who have lower PCL–R Factor 1 scores, in that they lead to clinical improvement, although the effect this has on recidivism remains to be seen.

A unit at Broadmoor Hospital for young male patients, most of whom were legal psychopaths, was based upon a combination of CBT and psychodynamic psychotherapy, run both individually and in groups (Grounds et al., 1987; Reiss et al., 1996). A comparison was made between patients who had undertaken this treatment programme and a matched group from other wards in the hospital. Amongst those discharged into the community, similar numbers in each group committed a further serious offence, but a higher proportion of those treated in the unit showed a good social outcome, and this was predictive of not reoffending.

Dialectical behaviour therapy (DBT) is a broad-based, cognitive–behavioural programme developed specifically to teach those with borderline personality disorders how to regulate their emotions (Linehan, 1993a, 1993b). This treatment is based on the premise that borderline personality disorder is typified by a failure to regulate emotions, which has developed as a result of a biologically-based emotional vulnerability in combination with an invalidating environment, that is where the child's private experiences are denied, contradicted, or punished by significant others (Linehan, 1993a, 1993b). A group skills training programme addressing problem-solving, interpersonal skills, and maladaptive cognitions is conducted in conjunction with individual therapy. Outcome studies with non-offender populations show reduced parasuicidal behaviour, inpatient psychiatric treatment, and anger, and improved social adjustment (Linehan, 1993a). Preliminary results of DBT with female mentally disordered offenders in a secure psychiatric hospital show reduced self-harm, suicidal ideation, depression, and dissociative experiences, along with improved survival and coping beliefs (Low, 1998).

Beck and Freeman (1990) base their cognitive therapy on the notion that cognitive schemas, or controlling beliefs, are the filter through which all incoming information is processed and thus determine affect and behaviour. They see these schemas as the fundamental units of personality. The purpose of therapy is to effect change in these schemas and so influence emotions and behaviour. Evidence for the effectiveness of this approach is limited, but single case studies of patients with borderline ($n = 7$) or antisocial ($n = 5$) personality disorders revealed improvements on targets relevant to each individual, for example anger, irritability, and self-control (Davidson & Tyrer, 1996). Walters (1995a, 1995b, 1996) has identified criminal thinking styles which may be useful to address in cognitive therapy.

CONCLUSION

The treatment of personality disordered offenders, particularly within health services, is a contentious matter. There are ethical objections to "treating" people for violation of social norms (Blackburn, 1992), yet it is clear that this group of offenders, and particularly those with high psychopathy scores, may be responsible for greater amounts of crime, especially violent crime, than mentally ill offenders or non-personality disordered offenders. Ethical admission of personality disordered offenders into health services for treatment requires that mental health professionals can identify the person's disorder, what the goals of treatment are, what treatments are effective, what type of person might benefit from the treatments on offer, and how long the treatment might take. Only when these issues are clarified is it possible for all involved to decide what is the fairest course of action. The vexed question of whether psychopaths, as defined by high PCL–R scores, should be admitted for treatment at all arises from the evidence of poor outcomes in this particular sub-group. Without clear information about what treatments are offered, their goals, and likely effectiveness, the patient is merely detained for the equivalent of respite care and, whilst this may be defensible, the situation should at least be plain to all those involved. Researchers and clinicians working in the field of personality disordered offenders, as in many other clinical areas, are searching for answers to the fundamental question, "What works best with whom under which conditions?" There will never be a simple, one-line answer to this important and socially relevant question.

ACKNOWLEDGMENT

I wish to thank Professor Conor Duggan and Dr Vincent Egan for their help and advice.

REFERENCES

American Psychiatric Association (1980). *Diagnostic and statistical manual of mental disorders* (3rd ed.). Washington, DC: Author.

American Psychiatric Association (1987). *Diagnostic and statistical manual of mental disorders* (3rd ed., Rev.). Washington, DC: Author.

American Psychiatric Association (1994). *Diagnostic and statistical manual of mental disorders* (4th ed.). Washington, DC: Author.

Andrews, D. A., Zinger, I., Hoge, R. D., Bonta, J., Gendreau, P., & Cullen, F. T. (1990). Does correctional treatment work? A clinically relevant and psychologically informed meta-analysis. *Criminology, 28,* 369–404.

Bailey, J., & MacCulloch, M. (1992). Characteristics of 112 cases discharged directly to the community from a new special hospital and some comparisons of performance. *Journal of Forensic Psychiatry, 3,* 91–112.

Beck, A. T., & Freeman, A. (1990). *Cognitive therapy of personality disorders.* New York: Guilford.

Blackburn, R. (1992). Criminal behaviour, personality disorder, and mental illness: The origins of confusion. *Criminal Behaviour and Mental Health, 2,* 66–77.

Blackburn, R. (1993). Clinical programmes with psychopaths. In K. Howells & C. R. Hollin (Eds.), *Clinical approaches to the mentally disordered offender.* Chichester, UK: Wiley.

Carey, G., & Goldman, D. (1997). The genetics of antisocial behavior. In D. M. Stoff, J. Brieling, & J. D. Maser (Eds.), *Handbook of antisocial behavior.* New York: Wiley.

Cleckley, H. (1941). *The mask of sanity.* St Louis, MO: Mosby.

Coid, J. (1992). DSM-III diagnosis in criminal psychopaths: A way forward. *Criminal Behaviour and Mental Health, 2,* 78–79.

Cooke, D. J. (1995). Psychopathic disturbance in the Scottish prison population: The cross-cultural generalisability of the Hare Psychopathy Checklist. *Psychology, Crime, and Law, 2,* 101–108.

Copas, J., O'Brien, M., Roberts, J., & Whiteley, S. (1984). Treatment outcome in personality disorder. *Personality and Individual Differences, 5,* 565–573.

Costa, P. T., & Widiger, T. A. (Eds.) (1994). *Personality disorders and the five factor model of personality.* Washington, DC: American Psychological Association.

Davidson, K. M., & Tyrer, P. (1996). Cognitive therapy for antisocial and borderline personality disorders: Single case study series. *British Journal of Clinical Psychology, 35,* 413–429.

Derogatis, L. R. (1975). *Symptom Checklist 90—Revised.* Minneapolis, MN: National Computer Systems.

Dolan, B. (1997). A community based TC: The Henderson Hospital. In E. Cullen, L. Jones, & R. Woodward (Eds.), *Therapeutic communities for offenders.* Chichester, UK: Wiley.

Dolan, B., & Mitchell, E. (1994). Personality disorder and psychological disturbance of female prisoners: A comparison with women referred for NHS treatment of personality disorder. *Criminal Behaviour and Mental Health, 4,* 130–143.

First, M. B., Gibbon, M., Spitzer, R. L., Williams, J. B. W., & Benjamin, L. S. (1997). *Structured clinical interview for DSM-IV Axis II personality disorders.* Washington, DC.: American Psychiatric Press.

Garrido, V., Esteban, C., & Molero, C. (1996). The effectiveness in the treatment of psychopathy: A meta-analysis. In D. J. Cooke, A. E. Forth, J. Newman, & R. D. Hare (Eds.), *International perspectives on psychopathy. Issues in criminological psychology, No. 24.* Leicester, UK: The British Psychological Society.

Grounds, A. T., Quayle, M. T., France, J., Brett, T., Cox, M., & Hamilton, J. R. (1987). A unit for "psychopathic disorder" patients in Broadmoor Hospital. *Medicine, Science and Law, 27,* 21–31.

Hare, R. D. (1991). *The Hare Psychopathy Checklist—Revised.* Toronto, Canada: Multi-Health Systems.

Hare, R. D., Harpur, T. J., Hakstian, A. R., Forth A. E., Hart, S. D., & Newman, J. P. (1990). The Revised Psychopathy Checklist: Reliability and factor structure. *Psychological Assessment, 2,* 338–341.

Harris, G. T., & Rice, M. E. (1997). Mentally disordered offenders: What research says about effective service. In C. D. Webster & M. A. Jackson (Eds.), *Impulsivity: Theory, assessment and treatment*. New York: Guilford.

Hemphill, J. F., Hare, R. D., & Wong, S. (1998). Psychopathy and recidivism: A review. *Legal and Criminological Psychology*, *3*, 139–170.

Hughes, G., Hogue, T., Hollin, C., & Champion, H. (1997). First-stage evaluation of a treatment programme for personality disordered offenders. *Journal of Forensic Psychiatry*, *8*, 515–527.

Karper, L. P., & Krystal, J. H. (1997). Pharmacotherapy of violent behaviour. In D. M. Stoff, J. Brieling, & J. D. Maser (Eds.), *Handbook of antisocial behavior*. New York: Wiley.

Lilienfeld, S. O. (1994). Conceptual problems in the assessment of psychopathy. *Clinical Psychology Review*, *14*, 17–38.

Linehan, M. M. (1993a). *Cognitive–behavioral treatment of borderline personality disorder*. New York: Guilford.

Linehan, M. M. (1993b). *Skills training manual for treating borderline personality disorder*. New York: Guilford.

Lipsey, M. W. (1992). Juvenile delinquency treatment: A meta-analytic enquiry into the variability of effects. In R. S. Cook, H. Cooper, D. S. Cordray, H. Hartmann, L. V. Hedges, R. J. Light, T. A. Louis, & F. Mosteller (Eds.). *Meta-analysis for explanation* (pp. 83–125). New York: Springer-Verlag.

Loranger, A. W., Sartorius, N., Andreoli, A., Berger, P., Buchheim, P., Channabasavanna, S. M., Coid, B., Dahl, A., Diekstra, R. F. W., Ferguson, B., Jacobsberg, L. B., Mombour, W., Pull, C., Ono, Y., & Regier, D. A. (1994). The international personality disorder examination. *Archives of General Psychiatry*, *51*, 215–224.

Loranger, A. W., Susman, V. L., Oldham, J. M., & Russakoff, M. (1987). The personality disorder examination: A preliminary report. *Journal of Personality Disorders*, 11–13.

Low, G. (1998). Treatment of mentally disordered women who self-harm. Paper presented at the III European Congress on Personality Disorders, University of Sheffield, Sheffield, UK.

Maughan, B. (1993). Childhood precursors of aggressive offending in personality disordered adults. In S. Hodgin (Ed.), *Mental disorder and crime*. Newbury Park, CA: Sage.

McMurran, M., Egan, V., & Ahmadi, S. (1998). A retrospective evaluation of a therapeutic community for mentally disordered offenders. *Journal of Forensic Psychiatry*, *9*, 103–113.

Pfohl, B., Blum, N., & Zimmerman, M. (1995). *Structured interview for DSM-IV personality disorders (SIDP-IV)*. University of Iowa, Department of Psychiatry.

Pilkonis, P. A., Heape, C. L., Proietti, J. M., Clark, S. W., McDavid, J. D., & Pitts, T. E. (1995). The reliability and validity of two structured diagnostic interviews for personality disorders. *Archives of General Psychiatry*, *52*, 1025–1033.

Raine, A. (1997). Antisocial behavior and psychophysiology: A biosocial perspective and a prefrontal dysfunction hypothesis. In D. M. Stoff, J. Brieling, & J. D. Maser (Eds.), *Handbook of antisocial behavior*. New York: Wiley.

Reiss, D., Grubin, D., & Meux, C. (1996). Young "psychopaths" in special hospital: Treatment and outcome. *British Journal of Psychiatry*, *168*, 99–104.

Rice, M. E., & Harris, G. T. (1997). The treatment of mentally disordered offenders. *Psychology, Public Policy, and Law*, *3*, 126–183.

Rice, M. E., Harris, G. T., & Cormier, C. A. (1992). An evaluation of a maximum security therapeutic community for psychopaths and other mentally disordered offenders. *Law and Human Behavior*, *16*, 399–412.

Soloff, P. H. (1998). Symptom-oriented psychopharmacology for personality disorders. *Journal of Practical Psychiatry and Behavioral Health*, *4*, 3–11.

Stangl, D., Pfohl, B., Zimmerman, M., Bowers, W., & Corenthal, C. (1985). A structured interview for the DSM-III personality disorders. *Archives of General Psychiatry*, *42*, 591–596.

Steels, M., Roney, G., Larkin, E., Jones, P., Croudace, T., & Duggan, C. (1998). Discharged from special hospital under restrictions: A comparison of the fates of psychopaths and the mentally ill. *Criminal Behaviour and Mental Health, 8,* 39–55.

Stone, M. H. (1993). *Abnormal personalities: Within and beyond the realm of treatment.* New York: W.W. Norton.

Tyrer, P. (1992). Flamboyant, erratic, dramatic, borderline, antisocial, sadistic, narcissistic, histrionic and impulsive personality disorders: Who cares which? *Criminal Behaviour and Mental Health, 2,* 95–104.

Tyrer, P., & Johnson, T. (1996). Establishing the severity of personality disorder. *American Journal of Psychiatry, 153,* 1593–1597.

Van Elzen, C. J. M., & Emmelkamp, P. M. G. (1996). The assessment of personality disorders: Implications for cognitive and behavior therapy. *Behavior Research and Therapy, 34,* 655–668.

Walters, G. D. (1995a). The psychological inventory of criminal thinking styles, Part I: Reliability and validity. *Criminal Justice and Behavior, 22,* 307–325.

Walters, G. D. (1995b). The psychological inventory of criminal thinking styles, Part II: Identifying simulated response sets. *Criminal Justice and Behavior, 22,* 437–445.

Walters, G. D. (1996). The psychological inventory of criminal thinking styles, Part III: Predictive validity. *International Journal of Offender Therapy and Comparative Criminology, 40,* 105–112.

Widiger, T. A., & Trull, T. J. (1994). Personality disorders and violence. In J. Monahan & H. J. Steadman (Eds.), *Violence and mental disorder: Developments in risk assessment.* Chicago, IL: University of Chicago Press.

World Health Organisation (1992). *10th revision of the international classification of diseases (ICD-10).* Geneva: WHO.

Zimmerman, M. (1994). Diagnosing personality disorders: A review of issues and research methods. *Archives of General Psychiatry, 51,* 225–245.

Chapter 31

Offenders with Drink and Drug Problems

Mary McMurran
Centre for Applied Psychology, University of Leicester,
Leicester, UK

INTRODUCTION

Offenders, as others, may drink or take drugs to the detriment of their physical, psychological, and interpersonal well-being, and they will benefit from help with their substance use to alleviate such problems. Whilst clinical goals are relevant to substance-using offenders, criminological goals also need to be addressed, in that a major aim is to reduce the likelihood of further crime. The means to clinical and criminological goals are often the same, for example reducing drug consumption will improve overall functioning, as well as moderate the likelihood of crime. Yet additional issues need to be taken into account in designing adequate interventions, such as targeting the connection between substance use and crime, and altering criminal lifestyles. The purpose of this chapter is to draw on what is known about offenders, their substance use, and related crime to derive substance use interventions with "added value" for this group of clients.

Meta-analyses of interventions with offenders show that cognitive–behavioural and multi-modal programmes hold most promise in reducing crime (see review by Lösel, 1995). Whilst awaiting the results of a meta-analysis of the outcomes of interventions with substance-using offenders (Lipton, 1995), the same overall conclusion has been drawn from reviewing the literature (Husband & Platt, 1993; McMurran, 1995). Peters and May (1992) report on a six-week cognitive–behavioural programme and relapse prevention with imprisoned adult drug users, which resulted in an improvement in participants' coping strategies and a lower re-offending rate at one year post-discharge, as compared with programme drop-outs. Platt, Perry, and Metzger (1980) describe a programme of

Handbook of Offender Assessment and Treatment. Edited by C. R. Hollin.
© 2000 John Wiley & Sons Ltd.

behavioural group work, problem-solving skills training, and community reintegration for imprisoned young male heroin users, and showed that those who completed this programme had lower reconviction rates and better adjustment
at follow-up compared with a matched control group. Shewan, Macpherson,
Reid, and Davies (1996) have evaluated a residential prison drug reduction
programme, including education, group work, counselling, and a reduction-
prescribing programme, and found that participants used fewer drugs, less often,
and in lower amounts during their stay in prison, in comparison with those who
did not complete the programme. Baldwin et al. (1991) compared a skills-based
alcohol education group with a talk-based education group for young offenders
referred by the courts. Those in the skills group drank significantly less after intervention, although both groups showed a reduction in re-offending. Participants
in prison therapeutic communities for substance users, in which reintegration into
the community is an important goal, show lower rearrest and reincarceration
rates compared with no-treatment controls (Wexler, 1997).

Multi-modal programmes, such as those described above, accord with the literature on "what works", yet they do not provide information on what works
with whom. Components of an intervention should be selected according to individual needs, and assessment is the key to appropriate programme design.

ASSESSMENT

There are two purposes of assessment. The first is to understand the nature and
extent of substance use and crime so that goals for change may be set and progress
monitored. The second purpose is to understand the reasons why substance use
and crime developed and how they are maintained in the present. This provides
information about the issues that need to be targeted to achieve the goals set.

Nature and Extent of Substance Use and Crime

Factual information is required in the course of assessment, answering basic
questions such as: What substances do people use, how much, how often, and with
whom? What kind of offences do people commit, how serious, how often, and
with whom? In collecting this information, it is important to look at drinking and
the use of a range of illicit drugs. Miller and Welte (1986), in a study of prisoners, found that those who used alcohol *and* illicit drugs were most likely to have
committed crimes of violence, followed by those who used only alcohol. Drug
only users were most likely to have committed property offences. Loza (1993)
surveyed prisoners in relation to their substance use, treatment needs, and
psychopathy, as measured by Hare's (1991) Psychopathy Checklist—Revised. He
found that polysubstance users were the most numerous, over drug only users or
alcohol only users, and that they have most treatment needs and greatest psychopathic deviance. He says that programmes should be designed with the nature
of substance use in mind, with attention paid to polysubstance use.

Information about the nature and extent of substance use and crime is typically gathered through a combination of interviews, diaries, and corroborative checks with official records or significant others (e.g. McMurran & Hollin, 1993). Therapists are frequently dubious about the accuracy of information obtained from the client, yet there is usually no alternative source of complete information. Ensuring that the client is motivated to provide the most accurate information is possible by adopting a motivational style throughout. Indeed, a comprehensive assessment with feedback given in a motivational style can effect behaviour change without further intervention (Miller & Sovereign, 1989).

The Relationship between Substance Use and Crime

Having established the nature and extent of both substance use and crime, one may address the more complex issue of what this person brings to specific situations such that substance use and crime occur. This will be revealed by examining the development of both substance use and crime over the individual's lifespan (see also McMurran, 1996). It is evident that risk factors throughout the lifespan are highly similar for both delinquency and substance use (Hawkins, Catalano, & Miller, 1992), and a developmental sequence describing the major risk factors will be offered here. There is evidence that this pathway describes those offenders who display a continuity of disruptive and problematic behaviours from early childhood, through adolescence and beyond (Farrington & Hawkins, 1991; Loeber, 1990). There is no inevitability about this pathway, however, and it is worth emphasizing that, whilst most antisocial adults have a history of childhood conduct problems, conduct problems in childhood are not strong predictors of adult antisocial behaviour (Lynam, 1996). That is, most children grow out of troublesome behaviour, and protective factors may operate to prevent progression into substance use and crime. Others may experience some, but not all, of the risk factors, and grow into and out of substance use and crime at various stages of development.

The earliest manifestation of problems is a constellation of hyperactivity/inattention/impulsivity behaviours. This characteristic may be called different things across the lifespan—difficult temperament in babies, hyperactivity in childhood, sensation-seeking in adolescence, and personality disorder in adults. Longitudinal research indicates that this characteristic is a risk factor independently for both substance use and crime (Klinteberg, Andersson, Magnusson, & Stattin, 1993; White et al., 1994). In the study by Klinteberg et al. (1993), 540 boys were rated by teachers for hyperactivity (motor restlessness and concentration difficulties) at age 13 years, and were followed up until they were 26 years old, with information being collected about alcohol use and violent offending. The hyperactive boys were three times more likely to develop alcohol problems, and eight times more likely to become violent offenders. Of the violent offenders, the presence of an alcohol problem increased the risk of violence 10-fold. The overall conclusion of the study was that "childhood hyperactive behaviour is closely linked to later alcohol problems and violent offending *in the same people*"

(Klinteberg et al., 1993, p. 385). Adult patients in treatment for substance abuse also show high levels of impulsivity, with higher levels for multiple substance users compared with single substance users (O'Boyle & Barratt, 1993).

A difficult child may stress parents, who consequently fall into family management styles that are associated with the child's later delinquency and substance use, namely unclear expectations for behaviour, lax monitoring of behaviour, harsh discipline, and few rewards for positive behaviours (Farrington & Hawkins, 1991; Hawkins et al., 1992). Under such circumstances the child is unlikely to learn to control his or her behaviour, and experiences harshness as a means of behavioural control. Furthermore, some parents may turn to drink or drugs (licit or illicit) to help them cope with stress, which may exacerbate poor family management practices and also provide the child with a model of substance use.

The child who cannot control his or her behaviour is less likely to do well at school, leading to poor academic achievement, which may set the scene for later problems with employment (Le Blanc, 1994). The child is a handful for the teacher and is probably unpopular with prosocial peers. Being frequently scolded and being unpopular allows for the development of a belief that the world is hostile, a belief possibly started at home with harsh parenting. Hostile belief systems are predictive of violence (Dodge, Price, Bachorowski, & Newman, 1990; Serin & Kuriychuk, 1994). Through being scolded and punished, as well as failing in class, the child comes to dislike school, which may lead to truancy.

Peer influence is understood to influence both delinquency and substance use. Young people both select peer groups who are similar to themselves and are socialized into the norms of their peer group (Kandel, 1985), thus truants gravitate towards other truants and delinquency and substance use are the normative pastimes. Longitudinal studies have shown that bonding with delinquent peers predicts later delinquency and drug use in that order, that is, delinquency comes first (Elliott, Huizinga, & Ageton, 1985). Thus, in the early stages at least, drinking and drug use do not cause crime. Early on, it is easiest for youngsters to become involved in petty crimes, such as vandalism and theft, and, perhaps through having money from theft, the next easiest thing is to buy alcohol, the widely available licit drug. From there, some will go on to illicit drug use.

Substance use affects behaviour, with the nature of the effect dependent upon the type of drug, dosage, and characteristics of the consumer. Most laboratory research has focused on the relationship between alcohol and violence. Alcohol consumption has been shown to increase aggression in direct relationship to the quantity consumed, especially in people with an aggressive disposition (Taylor & Chermack, 1993). Alcohol adversely affects higher-order cognitive activities, reducing the recognition of cues which might otherwise inhibit aggression, and limiting the recognition of the potential outcomes of behaving aggressively. There is some evidence that other depressant drugs (e.g. diazepam) have similar effects (Taylor & Chermack, 1993). The individual's hostile beliefs exacerbate the likelihood of violence.

The frequent co-occurrence of substance use and crime leads to the develop-

Table 31.1 Summary of risk factors

* Hyperactivity/inattention/impulsivity
* Poor family management
* Family models of substance use
* Hostile beliefs
* Poor school performance
* Truancy
* Association with delinquent peers
* Intoxicants disrupting information processing
* Criminogenic outcome expectancies in relation to substance use
* Criminal lifestyle
* Antisocial attitudes

ment of criminogenic outcome expectancies. There is evidence, for example, that rapists who have offended under the influence of alcohol expect that they are more likely to do something sexually risky after drinking (McMurran & Bellfield, 1993). Such expectancies are both a representation of past experience and a predictor of future behaviour.

All along the line, involvement in conventional society, i.e. commitment to the family, school, work, and non-offending peers, protects against the development of delinquency (Farrington & Hawkins, 1991). For many, however, opportunities for involvement in conventional society decrease as time goes by and a lifestyle of substance use and crime develops (Walters, 1994). Lifestyles of crime and substance use lead people into social contexts which breed further crime and substance use through adherence to cultural norms. Lifestyles of crime and substance use make relationships difficult to sustain, job prospects diminish, and alternative lifestyles seem impossible. The person is trapped in an antisocial lifestyle. Offenders rationalize their behaviour, developing and strengthening beliefs that crime is a reasonable way to live, e.g. "I only steal from people who are insured" and "Violence is the only language some people understand".

The risk factors in this developmental sequence are set out in Table 31.1. Some of these risk factors cannot be corrected in retrospect and they indicate the need for prevention efforts, which include providing support to parents and helping them manage their children effectively, as well as interventions aimed at improving the child's affiliation to school, including changes to school organization, classroom management, and teaching practices (Mulvey, Arthur, & Repucci, 1993). Later in life, other risk factors can be addressed in individual or group work with adolescents and adults.

INTERVENTIONS

The psychosocial developmental model described above, and the risk factors thereby identified, enable the specification of a comprehensive list of the relevant components of intervention, which should be selected according to the indi-

Table 31.2 Components of intervention

	Stage of change
Motivating offenders to change	PC/C
Changing antisocial attitudes and hostile beliefs	C
Criminological harm reduction	PA/A
Changing alcohol and drug outcome expectancies	PA/A
Reducing drinking and drug use	A
Emotion control	A
Impulse control	A
Interpersonal skills enhancement	A
Relapse prevention	M
Lifestyle modification	M

Note: PC = precontemplation; C = contemplation; PA = preparation; A = action; M = maintenance.

vidual's particular needs (see Table 31.2). A considerable amount of research has been directed at identifying stages of change in substance users, and determining which interventions are appropriate at each stage (Prochaska, DiClemente, & Norcross, 1992). The stages are precontemplation, contemplation, preparation, action, and maintenance, and the relevance of the components of intervention at each stage is identified in the table. Components of intervention will be described briefly, the main aim here being to provide an outline of effective interventions with directions for further reading. The criteria of success of intervention will be reductions in offending and substance use, but progress in each component should also be monitored, and advice is given about measurement.

Motivating Offenders to Change

Motivational interviewing is a style of interacting with the client to encourage behaviour change and is described in a text edited by Miller and Rollnick (1991). The essence of motivational interviewing is to avoid confrontation and instead to facilitate the expression and resolution of ambivalence by the client. One motivational strategy that seems particularly useful is to ask people to list the good and bad outcomes of substance use for them, and then to balance the outcomes for abstinence, light, moderate, and heavy use, thus illustrating at least that over-indulgence is costly (e.g. McMurran & Thomas, 1991). Motivation to change in therapy may be measured by the "stages of change" questionnaire (McConnaughy, Prochaska, & Velicer, 1983; McConnaughy, DiClemente, Prochaska, & Velicer, 1989).

Antisocial Attitudes and Hostile Beliefs

Antisocial attitudes and hostile beliefs are addressed throughout the entire process of therapy. Rather than challenge attitudes and beliefs through confrontation, argue for a change in behaviour, so that what clients do gets them largely what they want, but without being antisocial in the process. Beck and Freeman (1990) describe this approach as moving people from a position of basic, unqualified self-interest to qualified self-interest, whereby they take into account the feelings of others in specific situations when there is something to gain by doing so. People who expect hostility from others usually elicit the very behaviour they expect as a result of their style of interaction, thus confirming their beliefs. The therapist should provide disconfirming experiences and model equable behaviour. A useful measure of attitudes and beliefs is the Psychological Inventory of Criminal Thinking Styles (Walters 1995a, 1995b, 1996).

Criminological Harm Reduction

Criminological harm reduction focuses on risk factors that are relatively straightforward to alter and leads to a list of rules regarding the circumstances of drinking or drug use, with the principal aim of staying out of trouble. Rules for reducing the risk of crime should be personal and specific, and may include changing substance-using companions and venues. Examples of such rules for a drinker who gets into trouble fighting are as follows: "I will not drink with Bob on Saturday nights" (where Bob is someone who is often present when fights break out, and Saturday seems to be the night most fights occur), and "Before I go out, I will separate out the money for a taxi fare, I will leave the club ten minutes before closing time, and I will take a taxi straight home" (to avoid trouble on the streets). A measure of the number of offences monitors progress towards this goal.

Change Outcome Expectancies

Learning what to expect from substance use is a process that starts from an early age through messages conveyed by the media, instruction from parents and peers, observation of others, and personal experience. Some of these expectancies may predispose a person to use substances under certain conditions; for example, the belief that alcohol has a relaxing effect may lead to drinking to alleviate tension. Goldman (1994) reviews the general expectancy concept, prevention, and treatment.

One method of expectancy challenge reported by Darkes and Goldman (1993) was to provide moderate to heavy drinking male college students with drinks, some containing alcohol and others not, without them knowing who has actually consumed alcohol. After a group task, a word game or debate, participants were asked to identify who had drunk alcohol, with everyone making some errors. This was followed by a discussion about expectancies. Students in this treatment subsequently reduced their drinking more than comparable students in alcohol education or assessment only.

Particularly relevant here are outcome expectancies that may be criminogenic, that is, they dispose a person to commit crime under the influence. Expectancy challenge attempts to address these criminogenic self-fulfilling prophecies.

1. Identify the client's personal outcome expectancies by asking "What effect does [substance] (e.g. alcohol, speed, crack, etc.) have on you?
2. Identify the potential trouble these expectancies might cause, e.g. arguments, fights, sexual indiscretion, trouble with the police.
3. Examine and test these expectancies, through questioning. How does [substance] have this effect? What evidence do you have for this? Are all [substance] users affected this way? Are you always affected this way after using [substance]? Is there evidence that you can use [substance] without being affected this way? (see Beck, Wright, Newman, & Liese, 1993).

There are no instruments specifically designed to measure criminogenic expectancies, however, there exist a number of alcohol and drug expectancy questionnaires (e.g. Goldman, Brown, & Christiansen, 1987; Jaffe & Kilbey, 1994).

Reduce Drinking and Drug Use

Behavioural self-control training (BSCT) is the process of teaching people to monitor their substance use, set goals for change, identify and alter antecedents and consequences, make changes to drinking styles, is incentives for maintaining change. The effectiveness of BSCT for drinking is well established (see Miller, 1992). Procedures are best described in the self-help book *Let's Drink to Your Health!* (Heather & Robertson, 1996), and there is evidence for its effectiveness (e.g. Heather, Robertson, MacPherson, Allsop, & Fulton, 1987). The measure of progress in this component is quantity and frequency of substance use.

Techniques based on classical conditioning, such as cue exposure with response prevention (Rohsenow, Niaura, Childress, Abrams, & Monti, 1991), and covert sensitization (Miller & Dougher, 1989), have a role to play in enhancing resistance to temptation.

Emotion Control

Aggression and violence attract particular concern in substance-using offenders. Novaco's (1975) model of anger and aggression holds that an adverse external event (e.g. insult, inequity, or assault) is appraised by the individual in a hostile fashion, who labels the consequent physiological arousal as anger, and then behaves aggressively or violently. The individual's behaviour impacts on the external event and at least short-term positive outcomes maintain aggressive and violent responses. Novaco's model can be augmented to explain substance-related anger and aggression, in that contexts of substance use may increase the likelihood of encountering an adverse event; intoxication interferes with how the brain processes information, and so cognitive appraisal of events is affected; and the regulation of physiological arousal may be impaired when intoxicated. This emphasizes the need to alter lifestyle and reduce substance use as a means of controlling anger, aggression, and violence; nonetheless specific emotion control interventions are also important.

Novaco's approach includes identification of anger triggers, construction of a provocation hierarchy, modifying appraisals, reducing arousal through relaxation techniques, learning negotiation and assertiveness skills, and practising coping skills under increasingly difficult conditions. Evidence of success with offenders is summarized in a review by Novaco (1996). Measures of progress towards anger control are behaviour ratings, self-reported anger, and the State-Trait Anger Expression Inventory (Spielberger, 1996).

Other emotional problems, such as depression and anxiety, should not be ignored (see Beck et al., 1993).

Impulse Control

A combination of impulsivity and the persistent choice of antisocial solutions to problems, repeating ingrained patterns with little flexibility of response, can be addressed in problem-solving skills training. D'Zurilla and Goldfried (1971) specify the skills to be taught in five separate stages:

1. *Orientation*: Learning to recognize a problem when one occurs by attending to "bad feelings". Instead of ignoring or enduring these bad feelings, they should be seen as a cue to stop and think about what the problem is.
2. *Problem definition and goal setting*: The problem is clarified and defined, then realistic goals are set.
3. *Generation of alternatives*: A variety of options for attaining these goals is generated. In this stage, impractical and even antisocial solutions should not be excluded, to encourage creativity.
4. *Decision-making and action*: The options produced are analysed in terms of their viability, the best ones selected, and an action plan specified. In this stage, antisocial solutions can be challenged in terms of their costs versus benefits.
5. *Evaluation*: After the action plan has been implemented, success or failure is assessed. If success has not been achieved, then reasons for this can be examined and issues such as skills deficits, problematic beliefs and attitudes, or substance use may be identified as targets to be addressed. Social problem solving skills may be measured using the Social Problem Solving Inventory—Revised (D'Zurilla, Nezu, & Maydeu-Olivares, in press).

Interpersonal Skills Enhancement

Enhancing interpersonal skills, such as assertiveness, negotiation, and communication, in close relationships is typically conducted by role-play, using modelling, rehearsal, and feedback (e.g. Monti, Abrams, Kadden, & Cooney, 1989). Interpersonal skills training has sufficient empirical support to allow this component a place in treatment for substance use (Chaney, 1989; Hawkins, Catalano, & Wells, 1986). Methods of measurement include self-report, role-play assessment, and observation (Becker & Heimberg, 1988).

Relapse Prevention

Relapse prevention (RP) prepares the client to maintain change by identifying situations which may present a risk for relapse (e.g. interpersonal conflict, emotional distress, cravings), teaching skills to cope with these situations, and enabling the client to limit lapses should they occur. Procedures are explained fully by Marlatt and Gordon (1985) and Wanigaratne, Wallace, Pullin, Keaney, and Farmer (1990), and one outcome measure is the Situational Confidence Questionnaire (Annis, 1982). In a recent review of clinical trials, Carroll (1996) suggests that RP is more effective than no-treatment controls, particularly for smoking, but less convincingly superior to other active interventions. There is evidence of a delayed effect, where RP reduces the severity of lapses when they do occur, and that RP is more effective with severely impaired substance users.

Lifestyle Modification

Lifestyle modification is a holistic approach facilitating the development of a reinforcing non-drug, non-criminal lifestyle by arresting the old lifestyle. Walters (1998) suggests the following process:

1. Identify what is being met by the antisocial lifestyle, i.e. what will the client miss if s/he stops drinking, drug use, and crime?
2. Select substitute activities which will satisfy these needs, through work, relationships, and leisure activities.
3. Encourage commitment to a new lifestyle by reviewing the decision to change, enhancing social support, and abandoning the "addict" or "criminal" identity.

The community reinforcement approach, which includes job finding, marital therapy, and enhancing social reinforcement, has been shown to improve sobriety and social adjustment (Meyers & Smith, 1995). Broad measures of social integration, for example employment, leisure pursuits, and friendships, measure progress in changing lifestyle.

CONCLUSION

Substance use is an important area of offender treatment. Whilst there is a comprehensive general substance abuse treatment literature on which to rely for guidance, treatment outcome studies with offenders are scarce. Interventions for offenders need to be further tested and developed, and hopefully this chapter will prove a starting point for some therapists.

REFERENCES

Annis, H. M. (1982). *Situational confidence questionnaire*. Toronto, Canada: Addictions Research Foundation.

Baldwin, S., Heather, N., Lawson, A., Robertson, I., Mooney, J., & Braggins, F. (1991). Comparison of effectiveness: Behavioural and talk-based courses for court-referred young offenders. *Behavioural Psychotherapy, 19*, 157–192.

Beck, A. T., & Freeman, A. (1990). *Cognitive therapy of personality disorders*. New York: Guilford.

Beck, A. T., Wright, F. D., Newman, C. F., & Liese, B. S. (1993). *Cognitive therapy of substance use*. New York: Guilford.

Becker, R. E., & Heimberg, R. G. (1988). Assessment of social skills. In A. S. Bellack & M. Hersen (Eds.), *Behavioral assessment*. New York: Pergamon.

Carroll, K. M. (1996). Relapse prevention as a psychosocial treatment: A review of controlled clinical trials. *Experimental and Clinical Psychology, 4*, 46–54.

Chaney, E. F. (1989). Social skills training. In R. K. Hester & W. R. Miller (Eds.), *Handbook of alcoholism treatment approaches*. New York: Pergamon.

Darkes, J., & Goldman, M. S. (1993). Expectancy challenge and drinking reduction. *Journal of Consulting and Clinical Psychology, 61*, 344–353.

Dodge, K. A., Price, J. M., Bachorowski, J., & Newman, J. P. (1990). Hostile attributional bias in severely aggressive adolescents. *Journal of Abnormal Psychology, 99*, 385–392.

D'Zurilla, T. J., & Goldfried, M. R. (1971). Problem solving and behavior modification. *Journal of Abnormal Psychology, 78*, 107–126.

D'Zurilla, T. J., Nezu, A. M., & Maydeu-Olivares, A. (in press). *Manual for the social problem solving inventory—Revised*. North Tonawanda, NY: Multi-Health Systems Inc.

Elliott, D. S., Huizinga, D., & Ageton, S. S. (1985). *Explaining delinquency and drug use*. Newbury Park, CA: Sage.

Farrington, D. P., & Hawkins, J. D. (1991). Predicting participation, early onset, and later persistence in officially recorded offending. *Criminal Behaviour and Mental Health, 1*, 1–33.

Goldman, M. S. (1994). The alcohol expectancy concept: Applications to assessment, prevention, and treatment of alcohol abuse. *Applied and Preventive Psychology, 3*, 131–144.

Goldman, M. S., Brown, S. A., & Christiansen, B. A. (1987). *Alcohol expectancy questionnaire*. Odessa, FL: Psychological Assessment Resources.

Hare, R. D. (1991). *Hare Psychopathy Checklist—Revised*. Odessa, FL: Psychological Assessment Resources.

Hawkins, J. D., Catalano, R. F., & Miller, J. Y. (1992). Risk and protective factors for alcohol and other drug problems in adolescence and early adulthood: Implications for substance abuse prevention. *Psychological Bulletin, 112*, 64–105.

Hawkins, J. D., Catalano, R. F., & Wells, E. A. (1986). Measuring effects of a skills intervention for drug abusers. *Journal of Consulting and Clinical Psychology, 54*, 661–664.

Heather, N., & Robertson, I. (1996). *Let's Drink to Your Health!* (2nd ed.). Leicester, UK: The British Psychological Society.

Heather, N., Robertson, I., MacPherson, B., Allsop, S., & Fulton, A. (1987). Effectiveness of a controlled drinking self-help manual: One year follow-up results. *British Journal of Clinical Psychology, 26*, 279–287.

Husband, S. D., & Platt, J. J. (1993). The cognitive-component in substance abuse treatment in correctional settings: A brief review. *Journal of Drug Issues, 23*, 31–42.

Jaffe, A. J., & Kilbey, M. M. (1994). The cocaine expectancy questionnaire (CEQ). *Psychological Assessment, 6*, 18–26.

Kandel, D. B. (1985). On processes of peer influence in adolescent drug use: A developmental perspective. *Advances in Alcohol and Substance Use, 4*, 139–163.

Klinteberg, B. A., Andersson, T., Magnusson, D., & Stattin, H. (1993). Hyperactive behavior in childhood as related to subsequent alcohol problems and violent offending: A longitudinal study of male subjects. *Personality and Individual Differences, 15*, 381–388.

Le Blanc, M. (1994). Family, school, delinquency, and criminality: The predictive power of an elaborated social control theory for males. *Criminal Behaviour and Mental Health, 4*, 101–117.

Lipton, D. S. (1995). CDATE: Updating the effectiveness of correctional treatment 25 years later. *Journal of Offender Rehabilitation, 22*, 1–20.

Loeber, R. (1990). Development and risk factors of juvenile antisocial behavior and delinquency. *Clinical Psychology Review, 10*, 1–41.

Lösel, F. (1995). The efficacy of correctional treatment: A review and synthesis of meta-evaluations. In J. McGuire (Ed.), *What works: Reducing reoffending—Guidelines from research and practice* (pp. 79–111). Chichester, UK: Wiley.

Loza, W. (1993). Different substance abusing offenders require a unique program. *International Journal of Offender Therapy and Comparative Criminology, 37*, 351–358.

Lynam, D. R. (1996). Early identification of chronic offenders: Who is the fledgling psychopath? *Psychological Bulletin, 120*, 209–234.

Marlatt, G. A., & Gordon, J. R. (Eds.) (1985). *Relapse prevention*. New York: Guilford.

McConnaughy, E. A., DiClemente, C. C., Prochaska, J. O., & Velicer, W. F. (1989). Stages of change in psychotherapy: A follow-up report. *Psychotherapy, 26*, 494–503.

McConnaughy, E. A., Prochaska, J. O., & Velicer, W. F. (1983). Stages of change in psychotherapy: Measurement and sample profiles. *Psychotherapy: Theory, Research and Practice, 20*, 368–375.

McMurran, M. (1995). Alcohol interventions in prisons: Towards guiding principles for effective intervention. *Psychology, Crime and Law, 1*, 215–226.

McMurran, M. (1996). Substance use and delinquency. In C. R. Hollin & K. Howells (Eds.), *Clinical approaches to working with young offenders* (pp. 209–235). Chichester, UK: Wiley.

McMurran, M., & Bellfield, H. (1993). Sex-related alcohol expectancies in rapists. *Criminal Behaviour and Mental Health, 3*, 76–84.

McMurran, M., & Hollin, C. R. (1993). *Young offenders and alcohol-related crime: A practitioner's guidebook*. Chichester, UK: Wiley.

McMurran, M., & Thomas, G. (1991). An intervention for alcohol-related offending. *Senior Nurse, 11*, 33–36.

Meyers, R. J., & Smith, J. E. (1995). *Clinical guide to alcohol treatment: The community reinforcement approach*. New York: Guilford.

Miller, B. A., & Welte, J. W. (1986). Comparisons of incarcerated offenders according to use of alcohol and/or drugs prior to offence. *Criminal Justice and Behavior, 13*, 366–392.

Miller, W. R. (1992). The effectiveness of treatment for substance abuse. *Journal of Substance Abuse Treatment, 9*, 93–102.

Miller, W. R., & Dougher, M. J. (1989). Covert sensitisation: Alternative treatment procedures for alcoholism. *Behavioural Psychotherapy, 17*, 203–220.

Miller, W. R., & Rollnick, S. (Eds.) (1991). *Motivational interviewing: Preparing people to change addictive behaviour*. New York: Guilford.

Miller, W. R., & Sovereign, R. G. (1989). The check-up: A model for early intervention in addictive behaviors. In T. Loberg, W. R. Miller, P. E. Nathan, & G. A. Marlatt (Eds.), *Addictive behaviors: Prevention and early intervention* (pp. 219–231). Amsterdam, The Netherlands: Swets & Zeitlinger.

Monti, P. M., Abrams, D. B., Kadden, R. M., & Cooney, N. L. (1989). *Treating alcohol dependence*. London: Cassell.

Mulvey, E. P., Arthur, M. W., & Repucci, N. D. (1993). The prevention and treatment of juvenile delinquency: A review of the research. *Clinical Psychology Review, 13*, 133–167.

Novaco, R. W. (1975). *Anger control: The development and evaluation of an experimental treatment*. Lexington, MA: D.C. Heath.

Novaco, R. W. (1996). Remediating anger and aggression with violent offenders. *Legal and Criminological Psychology, 2*, 77–88.

O'Boyle, M., & Barratt, E. S. (1993). Impulsivity and DSM-III-R personality disorders. *Personality and Individual Differences, 14*, 609–611.

Peters, R. H., & May, R. (1992). Drug treatment services in jails. In C. J. Leukefeld & F. M. Tims (Eds.), *Drug abuse treatments in prisons and jails* (NIDA Research Monograph 118, pp. 38–50). Rockville, MD: US Department of Health and Human Services.

Platt, J. J., Perry, G. M., & Metzger, D. S. (1980). The evaluation of a heroin addiction treatment program within a correctional environment. In R. R. Ross & P. Gendreau (Eds.), *Effective correctional treatment* (pp. 421–437). Toronto, Canada: Butterworths.

Prochaska, J. O., DiClemente, C. C., & Norcross, J. C. (1992). In search of how people change: Applications to addictive behaviors. *American Psychologist, 47*, 1102–1104.

Rohsenow, D. J., Niaura, R. S., Childress, A. R., Abrams, D. B., & Monti, P. M. (1991). Cue reactivity in addictive behaviours: Theoretical and treatment implications. *International Journal of the Addictions, 25*, 957–993.

Serin, R. C., & Kuriychuk, M. (1994). Social and cognitive processing deficits in offenders. *International Journal of Law and Society, 17*, 431–441.

Shewan, D., Macpherson, A., Reid, M. M., & Davies, J. B. (1996). The impact of the Edinburgh Prison (Scotland) drug reduction programme. *Legal and Criminological Psychology, 1*, 83–94.

Spielberger, C. D. (1996). *State–trait anger expression inventory*. Odessa, FL: Psychological Assessment Resources.

Taylor, S. P., & Chermack, S. T. (1993). Alcohol, drugs and human physical aggression. *Journal of Studies on Alcohol* (Suppl. 11), 78–88.

Walters, G. D. (1994). *Drugs and crime in lifestyle perspective*. Thousand Oaks, CA: Sage.

Walters, G. D. (1995a). The psychological inventory of criminal thinking styles: Part I: Reliability and preliminary validity. *Criminal Justice and Behavior, 22*, 307–325.

Walters, G. D. (1995b). The psychological inventory of criminal thinking styles: Part II: Identifying simulated response sets. *Criminal Justice and Behavior, 22*, 437–445.

Walters, G. D. (1996). The psychological inventory of criminal thinking styles: Part III: Predictive validity. *International Journal of Offender Therapy and Comparative Criminology, 40*, 105–112.

Walters, G. D. (1998). *Changing lives of crime and drugs*. Chichester, UK: Wiley.

Wanigaratne, S., Wallace, W., Pullin, J., Keaney, F., & Farmer, R. (1990). *Relapse prevention for addictive behaviours: A manual for therapists*. Oxford: Blackwell.

Wexler, H. (1997). Therapeutic communities in American prisons. In E. Cullen, L. Jones, & R. Woodward (Eds.), *Therapeutic communities for offenders* (pp. 161–179). Chichester, UK: Wiley.

White, J. L., Moffitt, T. E., Caspi, A., Bartusch, D. J., Needles, D. J., & Stouthamer-Loeber, M. (1994). Measuring impulsivity and examining its relationship to delinquency. *Journal of Abnormal Psychology, 103*, 192–205.

Chapter 32

Property Offences

James McGuire
University of Liverpool, Liverpool, UK

INTRODUCTION

Property offences constitute the majority of known illegal acts. In England and Wales, for example, theft and burglary together account for more than three-quarters of recorded crimes (Maguire, 1994; Walker, 1995). When criminal damage and fraud are added the proportion rises to over 90%. This pattern is typical of most countries in which criminal statistics are published. The pattern for recorded crime is also reflected in that for total crime as estimated from victim surveys (Walker, 1995).

What do we understand by "property crime"? This is a collective and somewhat loosely defined category. It is generally distinguished from offences *against the person* and presumed to contain acquisitive crimes such as theft, burglary, fraud, and other acts in which the objective of the perpetrator is to secure by unlawful means goods or money which are another person's property. It is also frequently taken to encompass vandalism in which the aim is to cause damage to property. Yet there remain untidy overlaps with other types of offences. For example, arson is very destructive of property but is understandably regarded as a manifestation of considerable aggression. Robbery, though acquisitive, is a combination of theft and instrumental aggression. Drug trafficking, while primarily an economically-motivated crime, has been studied mainly as an adjunct to investigation of drug abuse itself. For the purpose of the present chapter, attention will be restricted to those criminal offences which involve action by one person to appropriate another individual's possessions by illegal means. Excluded from the chapter will be any discussion of criminal damage (for an excellent overview, see Goldstein, 1996); offences of deception; and embezzlement or other "white-collar" monetary crimes.

Handbook of Offender Assessment and Treatment. Edited by C. R. Hollin.
© 2000 John Wiley & Sons Ltd.

MODELS AND MOTIVATIONS

Most theorizing and planned intervention in relation to property crime has been founded predominantly on sociological, rather than psychologically-based, models of criminal action. To date, however, no clear answers can be given to the question of whether there are any factors which specifically contribute to property as opposed to other types of offences. In traditional criminological research in which patterns of illegal activity were studied in larger social groupings, it was initially hypothesized that property crime emerged in identifiable social-developmental pathways. Thus in Merton's Strain Theory, for example, acquisitive crimes are classed as a form of *innovation* in attempting to resolve the conflict between cultural aims of material success set against restricted opportunities to achieve this through legitimate means. In Cloward and Ohlin's study of sub-cultural delinquency, a relationship was hypothesized between the existence of patterns of property crime in the surrounding adult environment and the absorption of aspiring delinquents into that culture. Where opportunities for lucrative property crime were available, such activity would flourish. Where this was not the case, alternative patterns of *aggressive* (gang-fighting) or *retreatist* (drug-taking) delinquency would appear instead (Maguire, 1994).

Property crimes by their essence are assumed to be economically motivated. Evidence in support of this proposition comes from several directions. First, Field (1990) analysed trends in crime in England and Wales since 1900 and their relationship to economic indicators. A similar pattern of inter-relationships was found in France, the United States, and Japan. While all forms of crime increased in the long term, the rate of change for property crime was inversely correlated with the overall prosperity of society. Thus during periods when personal consumption declined, the rate of property crime increased; whilst for personal crimes, the reverse was the case. Second, interviews with offenders have tended, by and large, to confirm the role of economic motives in property crimes. But rates of such crimes also vary in accordance with the numbers and movements of goods in society; and for goods to be stolen they must share certain features, including accessibility, transportability, and demand for them through re-sale outlets (Cohen & Felson, 1979; Felson, 1994). Thus, it has been suggested that the overall level of property crime in society fluctuates in as yet uncharted ways in response to the scale of the market for stolen goods (Sutton, 1993).

Nevertheless, sheer acquisitiveness is not the sole reason for the occurrence of property offences, and in any case that motive itself requires full understanding. The model embodied within economic theory takes material acquisitiveness as a self-evident "given" amongst human motives: there is no pressure to analyse it further. But for a proportion of property offenders, there are established links between law-breaking and substance abuse (Jarvis & Parker, 1989; Walters, 1998). The concept of carefully considered action is unlikely to be applicable here in its pure form. In this connection, other research has indicated that the capacities of those who persistently offend may, in relation to some elements of rational thought and action, be limited or deficient (Ross & Fabiano, 1985). Still other studies have confirmed the view that some offending, especially theft of motor vehicles, is motivated by a quest for excitement or status-seeking amongst peers (e.g. Light, Nee, & Ingham, 1993). Finally, for a small proportion of offenders, criminal acts may fulfil other personal or emotional needs. In relation to several types of crime, then, motives may be very complex; and the balance between them may vary for different age-groups, or even for the same individual at different times.

CRIME PREVENTION

The principal intervention utilized in tackling much property crime, and one that has received considerable official promotion and resourcing, is *crime prevention* (Gilling, 1997; Pease, 1994). This involves a wide range of initiatives variously described as situational or "target-hardening" (the use of steering column locks on cars; installation of burglar alarms and ensuring their visibility; property coding; employment of store detectives; video surveillance); "designing out crime" by maximizing inter-visibility of dwellings or improved lighting; and community crime prevention, for example through the introduction of neighbourhood watch schemes, or publicity campaigns ("together we'll crack it"). The cumulative aim of these activities is to reduce the frequency of criminal acts at the point of potential occurrence.

The systematic application of these measures in recent years has been underpinned by the convergence of two theoretical frameworks. The first is *Routine Activity Theory*, within which the essential ingredients of a "predatory contact offence" (mainly property crimes) are the availability of a suitable target and the absence of capable guardians (Felson, 1994). The intersection of these is the principal focus of study. Discussion of psychological variables is explicitly avoided in order not to distract attention from analysis of the criminal act. The model thus takes for granted the presumption of a "likely offender" but leaves the nature of this unspecified. Cohen and Felson (1979) adduced a great deal of evidence concerning relationships, for example between increasing rates of house burglary and changes in the extent to which houses were left unoccupied by day, as a result of evolving patterns of work and leisure.

The second is the *Rational Choice* perspective. Here the offender is cast in the mould of the calculating and self-interested consumer or decision-maker envisioned within macro-economic theory (Clarke & Felson, 1993). A criminal act is a result of a careful weighing up of relative gains and potential risks. In relation to breaking-and-entering, evidence supporting the view that would-be burglars analyse these components was obtained from several studies. For example, Maguire (1982) showed that houses varied in their degree of victimization as a function of potential for burglary, influenced by aspects of their location (ease of access and escape, visibility from other dwellings, and so on). Interviews with burglars by Bennett and Wright (1984) and by Walsh (1986) furnished further support for this view. Other studies have embraced the concept of "bounded rationality" or reasoned action within a confined frame of reference (e.g. Carroll & Weaver, 1986).

The implementation of situational crime prevention involves an initial stage of *Crime Analysis* (Ekblom, 1988). This analysis is designed to establish features and patterns of crime affecting particular targets, following which a course of action is planned and implemented (Cooper, 1989). In the United Kingdom, the largest-scale departure in this respect has been the *Safer Cities Programme* (Ekblom, Law, & Sutton, 1996). Where crime prevention measures comprised "target-hardening" alone, their impact was fairly marginal; where they were more elaborate and combined with "community mobilization" the outcome was considerably better (Tilley & Webb, 1994). A particularly successful scheme within this field was the *Kirkholt Burglary Project* which combined "situational" and "community" crime prevention methods. Rates of domestic burglary in the targeted area fell by 75% over the duration of that project (Forrester, Frenz, O'Connell, & Pease, 1990). It has been argued that interventions of this kind run the risk of merely "displacing" crime from one area, or one type of offence, to another. Research has shown that the interactions of the types of crime prevention measure taken and a variety of outcome variables are considerably more complex (Tilley, 1995).

The models of crime on which situational prevention is based have made an indispensable contribution to our understanding of criminal events. They do not, however, explicate the nature of many of the factors which might be at play in contributing to decisions to commit crimes in the first place (the "likely" or "motivated" offender). The question of the relationship between routine-activity, rational-choice, and "dispositional" perspectives on offending has not been resolved. Trasler (1993) has rightly drawn attention to the need for an integrative account within which these perspectives can be fruitfully combined. Probably the most concerted attempt towards integrative theorizing was undertaken by Cohen and Machalek (1988), who applied ideas from evolutionary theory and behavioural ecology to an understanding of 'expropriative' crime, simultaneously incorporating aspects of differential association, social learning, and control theory perspectives.

PSYCHOLOGICAL APPROACHES

Psychological research and theorizing in this field is currently cast in terms of a series of *risk–need* factors which have been empirically demonstrated to be associated with the emergence and potential persistence of patterns of criminality. Recent comprehensive reviews of this research, for example by Andrews (1995), Blackburn (1993), or Farrington (1996), have resulted in general accounts which integrate individual and social variables. Their conclusions rest first on evidence which has been obtained with a high degree of consistency from a series of longitudinal studies conducted in many countries. Here, a very wide range of variables has been isolated as being linked with the appearance of juvenile offending and its persistence, where this occurs, into adulthood. Such "risk factors" operate cumulatively, such that the greater the number which are applicable in any given case, the greater the likelihood of offending. Second, meta-analytic reviews of cross-sectional studies examining relationships between individual variables and offence behaviour have identified a set of similar factors. These "criminogenic" factors include: anti-social or pro-criminal attitudes and values; pro-criminal associates; temperamental and personality factors such as impulsivity and egocentrism; limited social, self-control, and problem-solving skills; familial factors including poor parental supervision and discipline practices; and low levels of attainment in educational, vocational, and financial domains (Andrews, 1995).

Assessment

On this basis, it is important to conduct individualized assessment of offenders. This is much more likely to happen when the offence committed is one of a violent or sexual nature. Recent research on the outcomes of work with offenders has emphasized the need for proper assessment and allocation to appropriate services, whatever the type of offence. As a first stage in this, evidence from the meta-analytic reviews virtually dictates that use be made of a validated *risk–needs* assessment instrument. Regrettably, despite the obvious potential value of such measures, the choice remains limited and extensive validation research is required. Several approaches to risk–needs assessment have been reviewed by Bonta (1996). The available inventories generally take into account "static" demographic and historical variables such as an individual's past pattern of offending, together with "dynamic" factors including aspects of present circumstances, current perceived problems, attitudes, and skills.

In a second stage of assessment, selected measures can be introduced to evaluate the extent to which problems in the areas of social skill, self-control, anti-social attitudes, or problem-solving capacities such as alternative or means–end thinking may have influenced the individual's risk of re-offending. This inquiry might be widened to include aspects of an individual's life-style which may be conducive to or supportive of crime, and Walters (1998) has described a number of assessment methods which can be utilized in this area.

Thirdly, to supplement the use of population-based measures, an idiographic approach can be adopted, for example following some of the guidelines provided by McGuire and Priestley (1985). This level of assessment can be carried out within the context of a semi-structured interview and might entail a form of functional analysis with an individual, focused initially on a selected offence (probably the most recent). The circumstances and motivational state of the individual can be explored using, for example, a simple scheme such as the *5WH*; inviting the offender to describe when and where the offence occurred; who was involved and affected by it; what precisely happened; and why in his or her view the events took place. The same procedure is then applied to a series of the individual's offences, with any common patterns being noted: such as criminal associates, links to features of lifestyle, specific life events, or states of mind. Thus for one

15-year-old boy, who had committed a series of car thefts and been involved in a number of high-speed car chases, a relatively focused and concrete beginning (by analysing offence incidents) led to a clarification and understanding of the motives and triggers which maintained his risk of re-offending. Further exploration of attitudes and readiness to change can be undertaken using for example *force field analysis* (compiling parallel lists of reasons for offending versus "going straight"); an *A-B-C* diary of events surrounding the criminal act; and a dysfunctional thoughts record or "thinking report" of cognitions at key decision-points in the offence sequence.

Finally, for more in-depth forensic or psycho-legal assessment where required, an extensive range of standardized psychometric methods can be drawn upon, as outlined by Melton, Petrila, Poythress, and Slobogin (1997). The importance of dynamic variables in risk prediction has recently been illustrated in a study by Zamble and Quinsey (1997) of a sample of 311 high-risk recidivists, approximately one-third of whom had committed a new offence of burglary or theft. The factors identified as preceding their re-offences included ongoing personal problems, dysphoric mood states, life crises, and low levels of coping and self-management skills.

Methods of Intervention

Research findings indicate that the majorities of both juvenile and adult offenders placed on intensive supervision programmes in the community have committed property offences (Bottoms, 1995; Mair, Lloyd, Nee, & Sibbitt, 1995). The differential impact of sentences on rates of recidivism for property crime as opposed to other types of offences is impossible to evaluate as the relevant evidence is simply not available. Evaluation of the outcomes of different sentences *per se* shows negligible differential impact of sentence type (Lloyd, Mair, & Hough, 1994). Probation Centre programmes produce effects which are enormously variable (Mair & Nee, 1992). The principal forms of sentencing "disposal" reserved for serious property offenders do not, in a nutshell, "work" in yielding any discernible effect in reduced recidivism.

Is there any evidence which might indicate the prospect of effective "tertiary prevention" with adjudicated property offenders? Research on criminal careers shows that most offenders are "versatile" or "generalists" who commit a variety of different types of offence (Farrington, 1996). Even in the case of those found guilty of assaults, the majority have only one conviction of this type, the remainder of their records consisting of various other offences (Levi, 1994). There is now a large research literature on effective methods for treatment of offenders and reduction of recidivism (Harland, 1996; McGuire, 1995; Ross, Antonowicz, & Dhaliwal, 1995; Sherman et al., 1997). In the vast majority of the studies subsumed within the published meta-analyses, those participating had committed a variety of offence types. Nevertheless, in one recent meta-analytic review (Redondo, Sànchez-Meca, & Garrido, 1999) it was found that the outcome "effect size" for reductions in rates of property offences was lower than that for personal crimes. The number of studies reviewed was, however, fairly small. Overall, there-fore, no firm conclusions regarding offence-specific treatments or outcomes are yet permissible. Until further studies appear which focus on offence type as a variable, it can be tentatively suggested that the conclusions drawn from the meta-analytic reviews, and which clarify the respective components of more and less successful interventions, are in principle applicable to property offenders. The best advice which might be given therefore for the design and delivery of sys-tematic intervention with these groups, must be to follow the same guidelines as have been generally extracted from the "what works" treatment–outcome lit-erature. Beyond this, several reports are available of work conducted specifically addressed towards reduction of property offences. In the remainder of this chapter, this work will be briefly outlined.

Theft

Stealing can be a conduct problem amongst children prior to the onset of "official" delinquency, and several studies have addressed this issue. Reid and Patterson (1976) reported a series of seven cases of children with high rates of stealing and aggression. These problems were significantly reduced utilizing a parent-directed behaviour modification programme. Stumphauzer (1976) described elimination of stealing in a 12-year-old girl using a combination of self-reinforcement of alternative behaviour and a family-based contingency contract. Henderson (1981) outlined 10 cases of children treated with individually adapted combinations of self-control training, coupled with the involvement of a signifi-cant adult. A follow-up of between two and five years revealed that only two of the children had resumed stealing. Finally Hollin (1990) reported on the use of a behaviourally based approach with two brothers, aged 11 and 12, involved in stealing from shops. Assessment included a detailed analysis of the patterns of offending, and self-monitoring of behaviour by the boys. The intervention involved drawing up a set of rules jointly between the boys and their parents, and which were linked to a contingency contract. A one-year follow-up through the parents indicated that the boys' stealing had stopped, though this could not be corroborated from other sources.

However, most existing research on stealing is focused on shoplifting by adults. Studies show that there are several distinct motives for engaging in shoplifting. They are preeminently economic; but may include an admixture of other factors such as excitement, peer influence, and emotional dysphoria, the balance of which is likely to change over the life span (McGuire, 1997). Here, too, some interven-tions have entailed the use of behaviourally-based methods. The procedures employed include systematic desensitization (Marzagao, 1972); contingency man-agement (Guidry, 1975); covert sensitization (Gauthier & Pellegrin, 1982; Glover, 1985); self-management training (Aust, 1987); and activity scheduling for an indi-vidual with concomitant depressive symptoms (Gudjonsson, 1987). All of these studies entailed single-case designs, and in every instance successful outcomes were reported.

In a contrasting vein, other studies have been carried out using cognitive therapies and allied approaches, or semi-structured counselling. Kolman and Wasserman (1991) planned a delivered group counselling session aimed exclusively at women offenders. Solomon and Ray (1984) described a group therapy programme employing methods drawn from Rational Emotive Therapy. A more broadly-based, eclectic approach was adopted by Edwards and Roundtree (1982) integrating methods derived from reality therapy, transactional analysis, assertiveness training, and behaviour modification. MacDevitt and Kedzierzawski (1990) developed a six-session group programme of struc- tured psycho-educational methods. Two studies have been undertaken of diver- sion programmes for first-offence shoplifters (Casey & Shulman, 1979; Royse & Buck, 1991). The second of these incorporated community service and a series of group sessions utilizing rational behaviour therapy. The outcomes of all of these studies are encouragingly positive, but few employed controlled designs.

Finally, however, Glasscock, Rapoff, and Christophersen (1988) carried out a comparative review of the treatment of convicted shoplifters, and preventive measures in retail outlets, and concluded that the latter would be likely to have a more substantial impact on rates of theft from shops.

Car Crime

The volume of research available on car crime is not large, and falls into two prin- cipal categories. The first consists of studies of young offenders involved in car crime, often with an explicit aim of collecting information which might assist crime prevention initiatives. Individuals have been interviewed and asked about their preferences for different models of cars, or which types of security measures are most likely to deter them, combining this interview material with police data on reported crimes (Gow & Peggrem, 1991; McGillivray, 1993; Webb & Laycock, 1992). Other research has emphasized the symbolic importance of cars as objects of general cultural significance (McCaghy, Giordano, & Henson, 1977).

Two studies have delineated the evolution of a "car crime career" (Light et al., 1993; Spencer, 1992). This commences with vehicle-taking as a form of excitement in which at the outset (in the early-to-mid teenage years) entire groups participate. The motivations include the "buzz" or exhilaration of the theft and of fast driving, peer-group expectations, and the possibility of making money, set against an arid background of boredom and a wish to escape from it. In later teenage years, a proportion of those involved in car theft may graduate to vehicle- taking for financial gain, sometimes stealing designated vehicles to order. This change in the balance of motives and proportions of an age-cohort participating has parallels with that suggested for shop theft, and of course reflects the general evidence on age as related to crime.

Second, a variety of initiatives has been taken in attempts to reduce car crime, particularly by focusing upon the needs of those at risk of becoming involved. One such strategy is described by Spencer (1992) who monitored patterns of car theft on an urban housing estate before and after the injection of a new set of local provisions. These included the introduction of community youth workers, and allocation of police officers to school-based crime education work. Following the commencement of these services, there was a decline in recorded vehicle theft on the estate of 27%.

A more commonly favoured option, however, has been the development of specialized interventions for those with convictions for car crime, collectively referred to as "motor projects", generally run by either youth justice services or by the probation service. In the typical case, projects of this type combine a legitimate activity such as go-kart or "banger" racing with a more formal element such as attendance at group sessions. However, formats vary a great deal as do the settings and total amounts of time demanded of the offender (Martin & Webster, 1994). The overall objective is generally one of inculcating positive attitudes towards responsible road use. The formal components of a programme may include: instruction on the laws related to driving; sessions on vehicle maintenance and on road safety; visits to hospitals to meet road-accident victims; discussions with police officers; and offence-focused work on motivations for offending and alternatives to it.

Concerning those projects established for juveniles, very little evaluation work has been carried out. Figures supplied by the National Association of Motor Projects, an informal body with the aim of maintaining contact between staff involved in this work, are quoted by McGillivray (1993). These show that whilst 80% of those sent to prison for car theft re-offended within two years, the corresponding figure for participants in motor projects who continued to attend for a three-month period was 30%.

Regrettably, none of the projects surveyed by Martin and Webster (1994) had been subjected to a properly controlled evaluation. More recent evidence, however, indicates that projects of these kinds may have a positive effect. The strongest and most direct evidence comes from evaluation of the *Ilderton Motor Project*, based in London, where a follow-up evaluation has demonstrated significant reductions in re-offending (Wilkinson & Morgan, 1995). Over a three-year follow-up period, the re-offence rate amongst programme participants was 62%, whilst that amongst a comparison sample was 100%. There was also a significant difference in the proportions receiving custodial sentences (15% as against 46%), though the sample sizes were relatively small. Complementing this, an alternative form of evaluation was employed for the *Turas* project in Belfast (Chapman, 1995; Marks & Cross, 1992). This innovative project involved a programme of activities and the running of sessions for potential and actual joyriders between 10.00 p.m. and 3.00 a.m., the highest-risk times of day. A sizeable proportion of known joyriders who joined in the programme activities subsequently left having desisted from stealing cars. During the first year of the project's operation, while the rate of car crime increased by 57% in adjoining police divisions, that in the target area rose by only 4%.

Car crime projects for adults mounted by the West Midlands Probation Service were evaluated by Davies (1993). Those offenders completing projects were compared with non-completers, yielding re-conviction rates of 54% and 100%, respectively. While only 27% of the completers were convicted of another motoring offence within two years, the corresponding figure for non-completers was 61%. This study did not unfortunately contain a genuine control group, therefore there may have been other differences between completers and non-completers which account for the obtained effect.

Evaluative studies of motor projects have recently been reviewed by the Leicestershire Community Projects Trust (1997). The sample sizes in most studies have been relatively small and only one study to date (Ilderton) employed a comparison sample. However, using "benchmark" data such as anticipated rates of re-offending based on prediction studies, it was concluded that there are grounds for optimism concerning the impact of these programmes, both on re-offending itself and on the attitudes towards safe driving of those taking part.

Burglary

The number of evaluated "tertiary prevention" or treatment programmes which have been directly or exclusively addressed towards burglary offenders is extremely small. Manning (1994) surveyed a number of projects run by probation services which consisted of group programmes with an offence-specific focus on burglary, or involved victim–offender conciliation. However, evaluative follow-up data was available for only one of these initiatives. There was tentative evidence for a group programme based in Lincolnshire, that the burglary recidivism rate over a monitoring period of 21 months was 5%, set alongside a rate of 33% for a comparison custody sample. Wilkinson (1996) conducted a long-term study to compare two probation-based projects in London, one dealing with burglary, the other with car crime. The former, but not the latter, utilized "offence-focused" work within the programme, and was associated with a reduction in recidivism after one year. By a two-year follow-up, however, this effect had disappeared.

Multi-Modal Programmes

Almost all the interventions just described have consisted of a single ingredient; in some instances a behavioural procedure such as contingency contracting, in other cases a community-based initiative involving a programme of legitimate activities. There appear to be no multi-modal programmes specifically designed for property offenders as there are for other selected groups such as those who have committed violent or sexual assaults.

The exception is the *Reasoning and Rehabilitation* programme (Ross & Ross, 1995) which has been employed with a variety of offender groups, in both custodial and community settings, and in several countries. Regrettably, however, results concerning the impact of the programme upon recidivistic property offenders are somewhat inconsistent. Delivery of the programme to a large sample ($n = 4072$) of federal offenders in Canadian prisons produced a significant reduction in offences involving sex, violence, and drugs at 22-month follow-up, but no impact on re-convictions for property offenders (Robinson, 1995). By contrast in a probation setting in the United Kingdom there was a measurable impact on serious offending, including burglary rates, at one-year follow-up (Knott, 1995). While the overall impact on re-convictions had disappeared by a two-year follow-up, there remained evidence of a reduction in burglary recidivism (Raynor & Vanstone, 1997). Both these findings and that reported by Wilkinson (1996) indicate the possible need for "booster" sessions for programme participants to help maintain any gains made during an intervention.

CONCLUSION

There is evidently a marked need for much more research on the psycho-social factors which contribute to the emergence of the "likely offender" depicted by routine activity theory. Contemporary research on cognitive skills programmes indicates one potentially valuable direction for such efforts. Alongside this, comparatively little is known concerning the most appropriate components of interventions designed for "tertiary prevention" of property offences, and here too much more research is required.

REFERENCES

Andrews, D. A. (1995). The psychology of criminal conduct and effective treatment. In J. McGuire (Ed.), *What works: Reducing reoffending—Guidelines from research and practice*. (pp. 35–62). Chichester, UK: Wiley.

Aust, A. (1987, December). Gaining control of compulsive shop theft. *National Association of Probation Officers' Journal*, 145–146.

Bennett, T., & Wright, R. (1984). *Burglars on burglary: Prevention and the offender*. Aldershot: Gower.

Blackburn, R. (1993). *The psychology of criminal conduct*. Chichester, UK: Wiley.

Bonta, J. (1996). Risk–needs assessment and treatment. In A. T. Harland (Ed.), *Choosing correctional options that work: Defining the demand and evaluating the supply* (pp. 18–32). Thousand Oaks, CA: Sage.

Bottoms, A. E. (1995). *Intensive community supervision for young offenders: Outcomes, process and cost*. Cambridge, UK: Institute of Criminology Publications.

Carroll, J., & Weaver, F. (1986). Shoplifters' perceptions of crime opportunities: A process-tracing study. In D. B. Cornish & R. V. Clarke (Eds.), *The reasoning criminal: Rational choice perspectives on offending* (pp. 19–38). New York: Springer-Verlag.

Casey, L. R., & Shulman, J. L. (1979). Police–Probation shoplifting reduction programme in San José, California: A synergetic approach. *Crime Prevention Review, 6*, 1–9.

Chapman, T. (1995). Creating a culture of change: A case study of a car crime project in Belfast. In J. McGuire (Ed.), *What works: Reducing reoffending—Guidelines from research and practice* (pp. 127–138). Chichester, UK: Wiley.

Clarke, R. V., & Felson, M. (1993). Introduction: Criminology, routine activity and rational choice. In R. V. Clarke & M. Felson, (Eds.), *Routine activity and rational choice. Advances in criminological theory, Vol. 5* (pp. 1–14). New Brunswick; London: Transaction.

Cohen, L. E., & Felson, M. (1979). Social change and crime rate trends: A routine activity approach. *American Sociological Review*, *44*, 588–608.

Cohen, L. E., & Machalek, R. (1988). A general theory of expropriative crime: An evolutionary ecological approach. *American Journal of Sociology*, *94*, 465–501.

Cooper, B. (1989). *The management and prevention of juvenile crime problems* (Crime Prevention Unit Paper 20). London: Home Office.

Davies, H. (1993). *Evaluation of motor offender projects*. Birmingham, UK: West Midlands Probation Service.

Edwards, D., & Roundtree, G. (1982). Assessment of short-term treatment groups with adjudicated first offender shoplifters. *Journal of Offender Counselling, Services and Rehabilitation*, *6*, 8–102.

Ekblom, P. (1988). *Getting the best out of crime analysis* (Crime Prevention Unit Paper 10). London: Home Office.

Ekblom, P., Law, H., & Sutton, M. (1996). *Domestic burglary schemes in the safer cities programme* (Research Findings No. 42). London: Home Office Research and Statistics Directorate.

Farrington, D. P. (1996). The explanation and prevention of youthful offending. In J. D. Hawkins (Ed.), *Delinquency and crime: Current theories*. Cambridge, UK: Cambridge University Press.

Felson, M. (1994). *Crime and everyday life: Insight and implications for society*. Thousand Oaks, CA: Pine Forge Press.

Field, S. (1990). *Trends in crime and their interpretation: A study of recorded crime in postwar England and Wales* (Home Office Research Study 119). London: HMSO.

Forrester, D., Frenz, S., O'Connell, M., & Pease, K. (1990). *The Kirkholt burlary prevention project: Phase II* (Crime Prevention Unit Paper 23). London: Home Office.

Gauthier, J., & Pellegrin, D. (1982). Management of compulsive shoplifting through covert sensitization. *Journal of Behavior Therapy and Experimental Psychiatry*, *13*, 73–75.

Gilling, D. (1997). *Crime prevention: Theory, policy and politics*. London: UCL Press.

Glasscock, S., Rapoff, M., & Christophersen, E. (1988). Behavioral methods to reduce shoplifting. *Journal of Business and Psychology*, *2*, 272–278.

Glover, J. H. (1985). A case of kleptomania treated by covert sensitization. *British Journal of Clinical Psychology*, *24*, 213–214.

Goldstein, A. P. (1996). *The psychology of vandalism*. New York: Plenum.

Gow, J., & Peggrem, A. (1991). *Car crime culture? A study of motor vehicle theft by juveniles*. Cardiff, UK: Barnardos.

Gudjonsson, G. H. (1987). The significance of depression in the mechanism of "compulsive" shoplifting. *Medicine, Science and the Law*, *27*, 171–176.

Guidry, L. S. (1975). Use of a covert punishment contingency in compulsive stealing. *Journal of Behavior Therapy and Experimental Psychiatry*, *6*, 169.

Harland, A. T. (Ed.) (1996). *Choosing correctional options that work: Defining the demand and evaluating the supply*. Thousand Oaks, CA: Sage.

Henderson, J. Q. (1981). A behavioral approach to stealing: A proposal for treatment based on ten cases. *Journal of Behavior Therapy and Experimental Psychiatry*, *12*, 231–236.

Hollin, C. R. (1990). *Cognitive–behavioral interventions with young offenders*. New York: Pergamon.

Jarvis, G., & Parker, H. (1989). Young heroin users and crime: How do the "new users" finance their habits? *British Journal of Criminology*, *29*, 175–185.

Knott, C. (1995). The STOP programme: Reasoning and rehabilitation in a British setting. In J. McGuire (Ed.), *What works: Reducing reoffending—Guidelines from research and practice* (pp. 115–126). Chichester, UK: Wiley.

Kolman, A. S., & Wasserman, C. (1991). Theft groups for women: A cry for help. *Federal Probation*, *55*, 48–54.

Leicestershire Community Projects Trust (1997). *Motorvate: An evaluation of its impact on re-offending, self-esteem and attitudes to safety*. Leicester, UK: Author.

Levi, M. (1994). Violent crime. In M. Maguire, R. Morgan, & R. Reiner (Eds.), *The Oxford handbook of criminology* (pp. 295–353). Oxford, UK: Clarendon Press.

Light, R., Nee, C., & Ingham, H. (1993). *Car theft: The offender's perspective* (Home Office Research Study 130). London: HMSO.

Lloyd, C., Mair, G., & Hough, M. (1994). *Explaining reconviction rates: A critical analysis* (Home Office Research Study 136). London: HMSO.

MacDevitt, J. W., & Kedzierzawski, G. D. (1990). A structured group format for first offence shoplifters. *International Journal of Offender Therapy and Comparative Criminology, 34*, 155–164.

Maguire, M. (1982). *Burglary in a dwelling: The offence, the offender and the victim.* London: Heinemann.

Maguire, M. (1994). Crime statistics, patterns and trends: Changing perceptions and their implications. In M. Maguire, R. Morgan, & R. Reiner (Eds.), *The Oxford handbook of criminology* (pp. 233–291). Oxford, UK: Clarendon Press.

Mair, G., Lloyd, C., Nee, C., & Sibbitt, R. (1995). *Intensive probation in England and Wales: An evaluation* (Home Office Research Study 133). London: HMSO.

Mair, G., & Nee, C. (1992). Day centre reconviction rates. *British Journal of Criminology, 32*, 329–339.

Manning, J. (1994). *A study of burglary victim/offender programmes in the United Kingdom.* Manchester, UK: The Rhodes Foundation.

Marks, J., & Cross, G. (1992). *An evaluation of the Turas project.* Belfast: Centre for Independent Research and Analysis of Crime (CIRAC).

Martin, J. P., & Webster, D. (1994). *Probation motor projects in England and Wales.* Manchester, UK: Home Office.

Marzagao, L. R. (1972). Systematic desensitization treatment of kleptomania. *Journal of Behavior Therapy and Experimental Psychiatry, 3*, 327–328.

McCaghy, G., Giordano, P., & Henson, T. (1977). Auto theft: Offender and offense characteristics. *Criminology, 15*, 367–385.

McGillivray, M. (1993). *Putting the brakes on car crime.* London; The Children's Society; Cardiff: Mid Glamorgan County Council.

McGuire, J. (Ed.) (1995). *What works: Reducing reoffending—Guidelines from research and practice.* Chichester, UK: Wiley.

McGuire, J. (1997). Irrational shoplifting and models of addiction. In J. Hodge, M. McMurran, & C. R. Hollin (Eds.), *Addicted to crime?* (pp. 207–231). Chichester, UK: Wiley.

McGuire, J., & Priestley, P. (1985). *Offending behaviour: Skills and stratagems for going straight.* London: Batsford.

Melton, G. B., Petrila, J., Poythress, N. G., & Slobogin, C. (Eds.) (1997). *Psychological evaluations for the courts: A handbook for mental health professionals and lawyers.* New York: Guilford.

Pease, K. (1994). Crime prevention. In M. Maguire, R. Morgan, & R. Reiner (Eds.), *The Oxford handbook of criminology* (pp. 659–703). Oxford, UK: Clarendon Press.

Raynor, P., & Vanstone, M. (1997). *Straight thinking on probation (STOP): The Mid Glamorgan experiment* (Probation Studies Unit Report No. 4). University of Oxford, Centre for Criminological Research.

Redondo, S., Sànchez-Meca, J., & Garrido, V. (1999). The influence of treatment programmes on the recidivism of juvenile and adult offenders: A European meta-analytic review. *Psychology, Crime & Law, 5*, 251–278.

Reid, J. B., & Patterson, G. R. (1976). The modification of aggression and stealing behavior of boys in the home setting. In E. Ribes-Inesta & A. Bandura (Eds.), *Analysis of delinquency and aggression* (pp. 123–145). Hillsdale, NJ: Erlbaum.

Robinson, D. (1995). *The impact of cognitive skills training on post-release recidivism among Canadian federal offenders.* Ottawa, Canada: Correctional Services of Canada.

Ross, R. R., Antonowicz, D. H., & Dhaliwal, G. K. (Eds.) (1995). *Going straight: Effective delinquency prevention and offender rehabilitation.* Ottawa, Canada: Air Training and Publications.

Ross, R. R., & Fabiano, E. A. (1985). *Time to think: A cognitive model of delinquency prevention and offender rehabilitation.* Johnson City, TN: Institute of Social Sciences and Arts.

Ross, R. R., & Ross, R. D. (Eds.) (1995). *Thinking straight: The reasoning and rehabilitation programme for delinquency prevention and offender rehabilitation.* Ottawa, Canada: Air Training and Publications.

Royse, D., & Buck, S. A. (1991). Evaluating a diversion program for first offense shoplifters. *Journal of Offender Rehabilitation, 17,* 147–158.

Sherman, L. W., Gottfredson, D., MacKenzie, D., Eck, J., Reuter, P., & Bushway, S. (1997). *Preventing crime: What works, what doesn't, what's promising.* Washington, DC: US Department of Justice, Office of Justice Programs.

Solomon, G. S., & Ray, J. B. (1984). Irrational beliefs of shoplifters. *Journal of Clinical Psychology, 40,* 1075–1077.

Spencer, E. (1992). *Car crime and young people on a Sunderland housing estate* (Crime Prevention Unit Series Paper 40). London: Home Office Police Department.

Stumphauzer, J. S. (1976). Elimination of stealing by self-reinforcement of alternative behaviour and family contracting. *Journal of Behavior Therapy and Experimental Psychiatry, 7,* 265–268.

Sutton, M. (1993). From receiving to thieving: The market for stolen goods and the incidence of theft. *Research Bulletin, Home Office Research and Statistics Department, 34,* 3–8.

Tilley, N. (1995). *Thinking about crime prevention performance indicators* (Crime Detection and Prevention Series Paper 57). London: Home Office Police Department.

Tilley, N., & Webb, J. (1994). *Burglary reduction: Findings from safer cities schemes* (Crime Prevention Unit Series Paper 56). London: Home Office Police Department.

Trasler, G. (1993). Conscience, opportunity, rational choice, and crime. In R. V. Clarke & M. Felson, (Eds.), *Routine activity and rational choice. Advances in criminological theory, Vol. 5* (pp. 305–322). London: Transaction.

Walsh, D. (1986). Victim selection procedures among economic criminals: The rational choice perspective. In D. B. Cornish & R. V. Clarke (Eds.), *The reasoning criminal: Rational choice perspectives on offending* (pp. 40–52). New York: Springer-Verlag.

Walker, M. A. (1995). Statistics of offences. In M. A. Walker (Ed.), *Interpreting crime statistics* (pp. 4–23). Oxford, UK: Clarendon Press.

Walters, G. D. (1998). *Changing lives of crime and drugs: Intervening with substance-abusing offenders.* Chichester, UK: Wiley.

Webb, B., & Laycock, G. (1992). *Tackling car crime: The nature and extent of the problem* (Crime Prevention Unit Series Paper 32). London: Home Office Police Department.

Wilkinson, J. (1996). Does offence-focused work reduce offending in the long term? A follow-up of the first ILPS Demonstration Unit 1981–85. In B. Rowson & J. McGuire (Eds.), *What works: Making it happen* (pp. 53–61). Manchester, UK: What Works Group.

Wilkinson, J., & Morgan, D. (1995). *The impact of Ilderon motor project on motor vehicle crime and offending.* London: Inner London Probation Service.

Zamble, E., & Quinsey, V. L. (1997). *The criminal recidivism process.* Cambridge, UK: Cambridge University Press.

Chapter 33

Serial Offenders

David M. Gresswell
Lincolnshire District Healthcare NHS Trust, Lincoln, UK

INTRODUCTION

Consideration of the psychological literature on offending indicates that most offenders are "serial" in the sense of repeating their crimes many times. This pattern would seem to be true for most types of offenders and multiple offending is more common than single offending. The exceptions would appear to be very rare crimes such as murder where generally there is also a very low risk of recidivism (Blackburn, 1993).

Consideration of other offenders ranging from "joy-riders" (McMurran & Whitman, 1997) to sex offenders (Doren, 1998; Hanson, 1996; Soothill & Gibbens, 1978) and violent criminals (Hare & Hart, 1993; Hodge, 1997) indicates that multiple offending is common. Most assessment packages and treatment approaches make this assumption implicitly: Why offer treatment to offenders if recidivism is not assumed? Nevertheless when using the term "serial offender" most lay people, and indeed many professionals working in the field of criminology, first think of serious offences such as rape and murder rather than other less serious but more common forms of crime.

In this chapter this trend will largely be followed and the focus will be on serial serious offending, in particular murder.

There are a number of reasons for this bias toward applying the term "serial" primarily to serious offenders, however, the root of the problem may lay lie to a large extent within the nature of the offending itself. Serial murder is a very rare crime and most professionals working with offenders will never come into contact with a perpetrator. However, a clinician working in a busy out-patient forensic setting may well come across one or two offenders a year who have been referred because they are thought to have some of the features of a potential serial offender (extensive use of violent fantasy, social isolation, etc.) or who even

Handbook of Offender Assessment and Treatment. Edited by C. R. Hollin.
© 2000 John Wiley & Sons Ltd.

express the wish to be a serial killer. Such potential offenders cause alarm not least because in most cases the individual will not have a clear mental disorder, thus the clinician may have no statutory powers to intervene but may experience pressure to predict whether the client will be violent and "to do something".

Any anxiety experienced by the clinician is unlikely to be reduced by reference to the research on serial murder as there is comparatively little scientific literature, particularly in comparison with journalistic interest (Blackburn, 1993; Gresswell & Hollin, 1994). Furthermore, crimes with an obvious extrinsic gain (increased material wealth, comfort, the accolades of a deviant peer group) are perhaps easier to make sense of than serious serial offences where the motivation is often less obvious and would appear more intrinsic. Given all of the above the serial murderer is often perceived as a very different type of offender to other types of offender.

In this chapter the prevalence, aetiology, and behaviour patterns of serial murderers will be examined and assumptions such as those above will be challenged. It will be argued that serious serial offenders have features in common with other offenders and their offending can be assessed and understood in conventional psychological terms. It may be felt that since most detected serial murderers will never be released into the community, treatment in terms of attempts to address criminological issues is largely irrelevant. However, the study of such serious serial offenders may help to facilitate the identification and treatment of potential offenders who emerge from time to time in both clinical and forensic populations and who have many of the psychological features and interests of multiple murderers but who have not as yet committed serial offences.

DEFINITIONS

An immediate difficulty faced by the clinician attempting to understand serial murder is the lack of a universally agreed definition or typology. Clearly a central feature is repetition but there is even disagreement over the number of victims before the killer can be said to be a multiple murderer. There have been suggestions that two victims (Egger, 1984) are sufficient for the definition, while other authors have indicated three victims (Dietz, 1986) and four victims (Jenkins, 1988). The disagreement also extends to whether other factors such as the perpetrator's motivation (intrinsic versus extrinsic) and methods of killing ("hands-on" as opposed to impersonal using weapons) should be used in the definition (Dietz, 1986; Egger, 1984; Holmes & DeBurger, 1988; Levin & Fox, 1985; Lunde & Sigal, 1990). Generally, however, and for the purposes of this chapter, multiple murder will be defined as the killing of three or more people by one or more perpetrators.

It is possible to classify serial murder according to a number of relevant variables. The most widely used classification of multiple murder encompasses three sub-types: mass, spree, and serial, and is derived primarily from the number of victims, the pattern of the murders, the frame of mind of the killer, and the time period of the murders.

Mass murder is typically defined as three or more killings in the same general location, committed by a lone assassin who takes no steps to avoid detection. The killer's victims may have some symbolic or familial significance. Mass murders have been further divided into sub-types by a number of authors (Dietz, 1986; Rappaport, 1988; Rowlands, 1991) to include "pseudo-commandos" who tend to be younger men obsessed with firearms; "set and run killers" who, for example, poison food or set bombs but plan the lethal episode sufficiently well to escape; and "family annihilators" who are most typically senior males in a family who, suffering from depression or other mental illness, kill other members of their families "altruistically" before taking their own lives.

Spree murder is again typically defined involving three or more murders, but unlike mass murders the killings may take place over a longer time period: several hours up to several days. The murderer may kill his or her victims in different locations and is impulsive, making little effort to evade detection. Like a mass murderer the spree killer's victims may also have familial or symbolic significance to him, but unlike mass-murderers there is no "cooling off period" between the killings. It is this absence of the cooling off period between killings which differentiates spree and mass murder from the third form of multiple murder—serial murder.

Serial murder has best been defined by Egger (1984) as having six features: (1) There are two or more murders in which there is (2) generally no relationship between perpetrator and victim. (3) The murders are committed at different times and have no direct connection to previous or subsequent murders other than in the killer's mind and often (4) take place at different locations. (5) The murders are not committed for material gain but either are compulsive acts or satisfy needs developed through fantasy. (6) Subsequent victims may have characteristics in common with earlier or later victims.

In order to distinguish serial killers from spree killers Gresswell (1995) has suggested that a seventh characteristic must be added to Egger's list. This seventh feature is a "cooling off period", defined as "a return to normal patterns of daily living evident before the first murder for at least two days between each killing". This variable has good discriminative power and its inclusion in the definition reduces the number of perpetrators who could be labelled as serial killers.

Rowlands (1991) has suggested a number of subtypes of serial killer: *criminal spree killers*, who kill in the pursuit of other criminal activities; *functionaries of organized crime*, such as hired assassins; *custodial poisoners and asphixiators*, who kill their clients/patients; and *sexually sadistic psychopaths*. Holmes & De Burger (1988) and Ressler, Burgess, and Douglas (1988) have also suggested subtypes of serial killer depending on the killer's planning and organization (as determined from the crime scenes) and geographical stability (i.e. whether or not the killer kills in one or more places). The typical organized offender is often the first born son in the family with a better than average IQ, albeit that his employment record does not show this: the organized offender will generally have a skilled job but below his potential. The organized offender is usually socially adept and living with a partner at the time of the offence and is more likely to use a car and follow reporting of his crimes in the media. Although the organized offender's crime scene shows signs of planning, the victim may be chosen at random having wandered into a location that the offender has "staked out.' By contrast the disorganized offender is likely to be of below average intelligence to be of low birth status in the family, and to have an unstable work record similar to his father's. The disorganized offender tends to be socially inadequate, has never married, lives alone or with a parent, acts impulsively under stress, and will tend to be sexually incompetent. The crime scene left by the disorganized offender tends to show disarray and gives the impression that the crime was committed following no particular plan (Ressler et al., 1988).

Holmes and DeBurger (1988) have also offered four further sub-types of serial murder based on the apparent motivation of the killer. *Visionary killers* are those whose delusional beliefs lead them to kill particular victims; these killers are unusual in being psychotic. *Missionary killers* are individuals who have decided that they have the right to rid society of a certain group of people. *Hedonistic killers* are "lust-murderers" who kill for sexual enjoyment and for thrills: the sheer excitement of a novel and highly arousing experience. With this type of killer the killing is likely to be sadistic, with mutilation, dismemberment, and sexual activity with the victim before and after death. In the same hedonistic group, "comfort-oriented" killers kill for financial or psychological security. Finally, *"power and control"* killers wish to have complete life and death control over another person.

PREVALENCE

The prevalence of multiple killers is very hard to estimate. Serial killers in particular may conceal their murders and victims may not be discovered nor necessarily correctly attributed to the same killer. As noted above, the process of estimating the prevalence of multiple killers is further hampered by the lack of an agreed definition.

However, in using the definition of three or more killings attributed to the same killer or group of killers, then the prevalence of "official" multiple murder in England and Wales can be determined using Home Office data collected for the 10-year period 1982–1991. Home Office records show that there were 52 incidents of multiple murder (all types) in which a perpetrator could be identified during this period. Involved in these incidents were 58 perpetrators (five incidents had multiple perpetrators) claiming a total of 196 victims. However, there were a further eight incidents without a known perpetrator in which a further 42 victims were killed. This total figure of 238 victims represents about 3% of the total number of homicide victims for the same period.

These figures are likely to represent a conservative figure, however, as only victims who could be identified are included. For example, one killer in this sample claims to have killed 13 victims but because the parts of only six bodies could be identified only six victims are attributed to him. Similarly, the figures represent an underestimate of the number of perpetrators involved as it is now known that some killers were active during the period in question but were undiscovered.

In considering only serial killers using Jenkins' (1988) definition (also a rather conservative one) of four or more killings, then the prevalence serial killers in the United Kingdom is low with between one and five killers being detected each decade from 1940 to 1990. Over this period there is a total of 17 killers and 141 victims (figures reanalysed by Gresswell & Hollin, 1994). Figures for the United States are also comparatively small: Lunde and Sigal (1990) suggest 30 serial killers in the United States between 1970 and 1985. Other authors, however, quote much greater figures: Holmes and DeBurger (1988), for example, have estimated the number of serial killers who go unrecognized. They allowed for a number of "missing persons" to be attributed as victims of serial killers and suggested that there could be more than 300 such killers in the United States. These figures have been described as "preposterous" by Fox (1990) who questioned the assumptions on which the figures were based. Notwithstanding the figures given above, the difficulties in researching this field mean that it is likely that the real prevalence of serial killing will never be truly known.

Offender Characteristics

Although there have been these attempts to create classification systems for multiple killers, research samples to date are too small for detailed statistical analysis (Gresswell, 1995; Lunde & Sigal, 1990; Ressler et al., 1988). However, as Lunde and Sigal have noted "There do not appear to be consistent psychological differences between mass murderers and serial killers. Rather the important distinction is primarily between single and multiple-victim killers" (p. 625).

The bulk of the literature on multiple murder considers only male perpetrators (Holmes & DeBurger, 1988; Levin & Fox, 1985; Ressler et al., 1988) while Lunde and Sigal (1990) have one woman in their sample of 10 killers. It would appear that this gender bias only partially reflects the incidence of female perpetrators, Reccoppa, Burton, and McElroy as Myers (1993) comment on "isolated cases of female serial killers" (p. 439) and Gresswell and Hollin (1994) have noted that in England and Wales between 1982 and 1991 nearly 10% of multiple murderers were female. The multiple killer tends to be older than the single murderer but usually less than 35 years. They are predominantly white and tend to kill alone (Gresswell, 1995; Gresswell & Hollin, 1994; Lunde & Sigal, 1990; Myers et al., 1993).

When the issue of previous criminality is addressed, about 60% of multiple murderers emerge as having some form of a criminal record, predominantly for acquisitive or violent offences (Gresswell, 1995; Myers et al., 1993), although 44% of sexually motivated serial killers have a conviction for some kind of sexual offence (Hickey, 1991). Ressler et al. (1988) also noted histories of other antisocial behaviours including stealing (81%), chronic lying (68%), and "assaultative behaviour towards adults" (84%).

The prevalence of psychiatric disturbance amongst multiple killers is varied, with figures for the incidence of a psychiatric history ranging from 20% to 45% for all multiple murderers to 70% for perpetrators of sexual homicide (Myers et al., 1993; Gresswell, 1995). Although the patterns of behaviour described by Ressler et al. are consistent with a diagnosis of anti-social personality disorder, Ansevics and Doweiko (1991) have suggested that serial murder is a sub-type of borderline personality disorder. However, in common with much of the research in this field, this conclusion is based on a small sample of only 11 serial killers. Despite these figures, Jenkins (1988) reports that a defence of "not guilty on grounds of diminished responsibility" (an insanity defence) had only been used once successfully by a British serial killer between 1940 and 1985.

Based on an FBI study, Rowlands has offered a profile of a sexually sadistic serial murderer that suggests that they are most likely to be young, white, intelligent, sociable males who, in contrast to the figures given above, are unlikely to have a criminal record. The family background of this type of offender is reported to be characterized by a history of physical and emotional abuse in childhood along with a family history of alcohol, drug, and sexual abuse. The offender's parents are likely to have separated and to have moved around more than average. The personality of the offender is described by Rowlands as "aimless, rootless and with gender identity problems a history of substance and gambling abuse, of psychopathic relationships" and a history of "retreat into fantasy life". This type of offender"s crimes are characterized by using "intimate killing methods" to kill a victim who is "meaningful to the offender". There is a high risk of suicide after the crime.

ASSESSING AND TREATING SERIAL OFFENDERS

As with any assessment of an offender, the aim/starting point of the assessment of a multiple killer or potential killer is a detailed functional analysis. The analysis should be influenced by the psychological model of offending used (in this case a behavioural model), an understanding of the aetiology of the offending in question, and reference to the existing literature on the type of offender. Of particular significance with the serial offender is an understanding of not only the factors that maintain the offending (the offender's overt offending behaviour and covert processes such as physiological arousal, thoughts, feelings, attitudes) but also those environmental circumstances which have elicited the offending behaviour and/or may elicit it in the future.

Understanding the Origins of Multiple Murder

MacCulloch and Bailey (1993) have argued that one of the most important tasks facing a forensic clinician is making sense of the causes of violent behaviour and their meanings for the offender. Such an understanding can, in principle, lead to the design of effective treatment packages and more accurate predictions of the risk of offending.

Consideration of the literature on multiple murderers indicates that histories of sexual and physical abuse and abandonment are both common and thought to have causal status (Ansevics & Doweiko, 1991; Burgess, Hartman, Ressler, & Douglas, 1986; Levin & Fox, 1985; Liebert, 1985; MacCulloch, Bailey, & Robinson, 1995). Burgess et al., describe the failure of "empathic bonding" and developing attachment disorders in the child, with the child becoming increasingly cold and aloof.

In Burgess et al.'s (1986) model of the progression towards sexual murder, the failure of the child's carers to help the child to deal with the trauma of being abused is emphasized. These authors suggest that the child incorporates the trauma into violent/sadistic day-dreams and fantasies as a way of coping and finding relief from the pervasive feelings of fear and disempowerment. The child feels helpless but develops a private world where highly arousing fantasies give him a sense of power and control.

As time progresses and the child is not helped, Burgess et al. suggest that he becomes increasingly dependent on fantasy to meet his emotional needs. With continuing lack of effective intervention from his carers, the child's reliance on fantasy reduces his opportunities to acquire pro-social skills. Ultimately the child develops the increasingly anti-social belief that he is entitled to express himself in any way that he wishes. For Burgess et al. the key features in this psychological model of an individual who is progressing towards multiple murder are feelings of alienation, with the individual becoming increasingly socially isolated and devaluing/filtering out any feedback that could inhibit aggression.

As the offender matures so he becomes more reliant on fantasy to meet his emotional needs. These fantasies are often supported by pornography and violent films. For many of the serial offenders considered by Burgess et al., the offences are likely to be driven by the expectation of meeting needs that will typically have been developed and maintained by fantasies and "try-outs". Try-outs are essentially "trial runs" that attempt to enhance the power of the fantasies and make real experience match them.

MacCulloch, Sowden, Wood, and Mills (1983) studied 18 sadistic offenders detained in an English special hospital and found that 13 made habitual use of both sadistic masturbatory fantasy and recollections of previous offences. Several of the offenders in this group had acted out elements of their fantasy prior to committing their index offence. Ressler et al. (1988) note that some offenders collect trophies or souvenirs from offences/victims in order to later enhance their fantasies. Prentky et al. (1989) found that 86% of multiple killers disclosed using violent fantasy in comparison with 23% of single murderers. These authors also observed that sadistic offenders often aim to make reality match an idealized fantasy murder, however, the outcome of any violent interaction is difficult to predict and the match between fantasy and reality is likely to be imperfect: the reality is never quite as satisfying as the fantasy promises. The reinforcing effects of engagement in both violent fantasy and offending are therefore likely to be intense but short-lived and, in behavioural terms, give rise to schedules of rein-forcement that make the behaviour very likely to recur and be very persistent (Skinner, 1974).

With such a pattern of reliance on covert behavioural (private fantasy) processes to meet such a range of emotional and sexual needs, it would be pre-dicted that two primary patterns would emerge: Burgess et al. (1988) predict that in some cases the offender will progress through minor criminal acts to rape and murder; in other cases the change to overt violent offending may be more sudden. Gresswell and Hollin (1997) have suggested that for some potential offenders with some inhibitions against overt aggression there will nevertheless come a point when the individual becomes habituated to the effects of the fantasizing. Further incorporation of fantasy material no longer achieves the desired changes in affect and sexual arousal.

Applying behavioural theory to the process described above it would be pre-dicted that when the fantasies were no longer able to meet the needs of the poten-tial offender, then there would be the risk of an escalation in the behaviour of the offender as he struggled to meet his needs. Such a process would weaken any surviving inhibitions against overt aggression and reduce the strength of the trig-gers necessary to overcome existing inhibitions.

In the case of a person with murdererous escapist fantasies but with strong inhibitions against overt aggression (presumably the majority of clients who present for treatment but who have not progressed to overt aggression) the indi-vidual would have to adopt other strategies, for example seeking therapy for the experience of loss of power or depression. However, in the case of a person with weakened inhibitions against aggressing, the risk of acting out part or all of the fantasy and progression to murder would be high (Gresswell & Hollin, 1997).

In such a case, however, it could be argued that the potential offender has already desensitized himself to his victim's distress by fantasizing about it while masturbating. Furthermore, if this model is accepted, then the offenders will have only a limited capacity to empathize with others, will have learned to deperson-alize victims, and will have come to believe that violence against other is legiti-mate. There is the potential to commit a series of major offences when such conditions occur.

ANTECEDENTS AND TRIGGERS

Analyses such as those described above tentatively describe a potential to offend; in addition, there is a small literature considering situational factors and triggers that have consistently been found to be important in initiating a homicidal episode. Indeed, Prentky et al. (1989) found no differences in the degree of plan-ning used by a group of multiple murderers' prior to their first murder and mur-derers who only kill once. Ressler et al. also found that in 84% of cases a serial killer had not planned the first murder in a murder sequence but was in an "emo-tional state" that made him "open for opportunities". In 16% of cases the offender said that the first offence was spontaneous and unplanned. Triggers for murder in the Ressler et al. (1988) study included financial, legal, employment, marital, and other conflicts. Emotional states such as frustration, anger, hostile moods, and feeling agitated and excited were reported at a lower frequency.

Levin (1987) has offered a four-factor model of sudden indiscriminate mass killing. First, the potential offender has led a "life of frustration"; second, he has access to and the ability to use firearms; third, there is a significant destabilizing experience of a loss of "social controls" such as moving to a new area or the loss of an important relationship; fourth, there must be a precipitating event such as unemployment or divorce. Gresswell and Hollin (1994) have suggested that a more useful way of conceptualizing the "firearms" component could be to consider that a fascination with weapons is indicative of a style of coping with stress, frustration, and feelings of low self-esteem that includes the use of violent fantasy involving weapons. In such cases the nature of such fantasies may be the best predictor of a homicidal response to a stressful event.

TREATMENT

Given the above, the identification of offenders who become serial offenders is theoretically possible. If a potential offender is assessed and treated early in the offending sequence, then processes such as those described above could be interrupted before the client has escalated to murder.

Ansevics and Doweiko (1991) have suggested that the serial murderer "Reflects a variation of the borderline personality" (p. 115) and should be treated as such. However, the authors do not cite any outcome studies for this approach. In the sections above, a number of variables have been listed such as the experience of being sexually abused, feelings of hostility and entitlement, and continual reliance on fantasy; all these components have been researched individually and treatment approaches are available (Abel & Blanchard, 1974; Novaco, 1978; Salter, 1988). Gresswell and Hollin (1997) have suggested that clinical techniques drawn from the addictions field could also be relevant and quote from an interview with convicted serial killer Dennis Nilsen. Some clinicians may be anxious about exposing the offender's fantasies and talking about them for fear of making them worse, however, Nilsen, in talking about his fantasies, appears to be indicating that the opposite could be true:

> Having written them down they cease to be another world. It's like being in a house in the pitch black, the imagination runs wild, every sound takes on significance. Flick the switch—the lights come on: four walls. In writing down what happened to me what I was doing was switching the light on. Everything was suddenly then exposed and ceased (Gresswell & Hollin, 1997, p. 156).

While not every offender may experience the sudden relief that Nilsen claims, his account does leave room for optimism that significant changes are possible. Nevertheless, with any offender, but especially an offender with an extensive pattern of offending as well as fantasising careful assessment would be required before a clinician could place much confidence that risk had been significantly reduced.

PROFILES

Perhaps one of the most controversial areas of clinical and research work with multiple offenders is that of "offender profiling". Profiling is based on the assumption that serial offenders are motivated to behave in consistent ways, leaving some kind of "behavioural signature" in, for example, their choice of similar victims or in the methods and locations of their attacks. A further assumption is then made that analysis of the crime scene reveals significant features of the offender which are unique to that individual. Work of this type with serial offenders has attracted much media attention, for example with the film *Silence of the Lambs* and the British TV series *Cracker*, but whether offender profiling is possible in any meaningful way, and whether it can help police officers to either link crimes or identify perpetrators, remains to be seen. Certainly, much of the profiling research to date is based on very small populations and reveals a rather heterogeneous population of offenders, and potential offenders, who may only have in common the experience of small number of psychological processes that are hard to identify without detailed interviewing, and of course, the fact that they have killed more than once.

CONCLUSION

Multiple murderers make up a very small part of the criminal population and it is likely that most clinicians working in the forensic field will have no experience of working with them. It seems equally likely, however, that many clinicians will come across individuals who have many of the features of multiple killers and who may even warn professionals that they feel at risk of offending.

Hopefully this chapter will help the concerned professional recognize risk and be able to consider appropriate treatment strategies. It is also evident that this population has been under-researched to date despite considerable media interest and public concern. There are many questions about the progression to murder and the behaviour of multiple murderers that have yet to be answered, however, it would appear possible that further research with this rather extreme population would be worthwhile and could be helpful in understanding other serial offenders as well as correctly identifying future perpetrators.

REFERENCES

Abel, G. G., & Blanchard J. V. (1974). The role of fantasy in the treatment of sexual deviation. *Archives of General Psychiatry*, *30*, 467–475.

Ansevics, N. L., & Doweiko, H. E. (1991). Serial murderers: Early proposed developmental model and typology. *Psychotherapy in Private Practice*, *9*, 107–122.

Blackburn, R. (1993). *The psychology of criminal conduct: Theory, research and practice.* Chichester, UK: Wiley.

Burgess, A. W., Hartman, C. R., Ressler, R. K., & Douglas, J. E. (1986). Sexual homicide: A motivational model. *Journal of Interpersonal Violence*, *1*(3), 251–272.

Dietz, P. E. (1986). Mass, serial and sensational homicides. *Bulletin of the New York Acadamy of Medicine*, *62*, 447–490.

Doren, D. M. (1998). Recidivism base rates, predictions of sex offender recidivism, and the "sexual predator" commitment laws. *Behavioral Sciences and the Law*, *16*, 97–114.

Egger, S. A. (1984). A working definition of serial murder and the reduction of linkage blindness. *Journal of Police Science and Administration*, *12*, 348–357.

Fox, J. A. (1990). Murder they wrote. *Contemporary Psychology*, *35*, 890–891.

Gresswell, D. M. (1995). Multiple murder in England and Wales 1982–1991: An analysis. Unpublished PhD thesis, University of Birmingham, Birmingham, UK.

Gresswell, D. M., & Hollin, C. R. (1994). Multiple murder: A review. *The British Journal of Criminology*, *34*, 1–14.

Gresswell, D. M., & Hollin, C. R. (1997). Addictions and multiple murder: A behavioural perspective. In J. E. Hodge, M. McMurran, & C. R. Hollin (Eds.), *Addicted to crime?* (pp. 139–164). Chichester, UK: Wiley.

Hanson, R. K. (1996). Child molester recidivism. *Research Summary: Correction Research and Development*, *1*, 1–2.

Hare, R. D., & Hart, S. D. (1993). Psychopathy, mental disorder and crime. In S. Hodgins (Ed.), *Mental disorder and crime.* Newbury Park, CA: Sage.

Hickey, E. W. (1991). *Serial murderers and their victims.* Pacific Grove, CA: Brooks/Cole.

Hodge, J. E. (1997). Addiction to violence. In J. E. Hodge, M. McMurran, & C. R. Hollin, (Eds.), *Addicted to crime?* (pp. 87–104). Chichester, UK: Wiley.

Holmes, R. M., & DeBurger, J. (1988). *Serial murder.* Newbury Park, CA: Sage.

Jenkins, P. (1988). Serial murder in England 1940–1985. *Journal of Criminal Justice*, *16*, 1–15.

Levin, J. (1987, August 23). Why his last shot blew the truth away. *The Sunday Times*, p. 23.

Levin, J., & Fox, J. A. (1985). *Mass murder: America's growing menace.* New York: Plenum.

Liebert, J. A. (1985). Contributions of psychiatric consultation in the investigation of serial murder. *International Journal of Offender Therapy and Comparative Criminology*, *29*, 187–200.

Lunde, D., & Sigal, H. (1990). Multiple victim killers. In R. Bluglass & P. Bowden (Eds.), *Principles and practice of forensic psychiatry* (pp. 625–630) Edinburgh, UK: Churchill Livingstone.

MacCulloch, M. J., & Bailey, J. (1993). Issues in the management and rehabilitation of patients in maximum secure special hospitals. *Journal of Forensic Psychiatry*, *4*, 25–44.

MacCulloch, M. J., Bailey, J., & Robinson, C. (1995). Mentally disordered attackers and killers: Towards a taxonomy. *Journal of Forensic Psychiatry*, *6*, 41–61.

MacCulloch, M. J., Sowden, P. R., Wood, J. W., & Mills, H. E. (1983). Sadistic fantasy, sadistic behaviour and offending. *British Journal of Psychiatry*, *143*, 20–29.

McMurran, M., & Whitman, J. (1997). The development of a brief intervention for car theft. In J. E. Hodge, M. McMurran, & C. R. Hollin (Eds.), *Addicted to crime?* (pp. 191–206). Chichester, UK: Wiley.

Myers, W. C., Reccoppa, L., Burton, K., & McElroy, R. (1993). Malignant sex and aggression: An overview of serial sexual homicide. *Bulletin of the American Academy of Psychiatry and Law*, *21*, 435–451.

Novaco, R. W. (1978). Anger and coping with stress. In J. P. Foreyt & D. P. Rathjan (Eds.), *Cognitive behaviour therapy*. New York: Lexington Books.

Prentky, R. A., Burgess, A. W., Rokus, F., Lee, A., Hartman, C., Ressler, R., & Douglas, J. (1989). The presumptive role of fantasy in serial sexual homicide. *American Journal of Psychiatry*, *146*, 887–891.

Rappaport, R. C. (1988). The serial and mass murderer: Patterns, differentiation, pathology. *American Journal of Forensic Psychiatry*, *9*, 38–48.

Ressler, R. K., Burgess, A. W., & Douglas, J. E. (1988). *Sexual homicide: Patterns and motives.* Lexington, MA: Lexington Books.

Rowlands, M. (1991). Sex murder and the potential sex murderer. *Diseases of the Nervous System*, *26*, 640–646.

Salter, A. (1988). *Treating child sex offenders and victims.* Thousand Oaks, CA: Sage.

Skinner, B. F. (1974). *About behaviourism.* London: Jonathan Cape.

Soothill, K. L., & Gibbens, T. C. N. (1978). Recidivism of sexual offenders: A re-appraisal. *British Journal of Criminology*, *18*, 267–276.

Part V

Treatment in Context

Chapter 34

Treatment in High Security Hospitals

Ronald Blackburn
University of Liverpool, Liverpool, UK

INTRODUCTION

Maximum security hospitals originated as the "criminal lunatic asylums" of the mid-nineteenth century, and were set up to provide secure containment for offenders excused legal punishment by the courts on the grounds of insanity. Their location at the shifting interface of criminal justice and mental health policies and frequent scandals about standards of care have ensured regular attention to their roles and shortcomings in official reports and the media. Despite this scrutiny, empirical data on the efficacy of the clinical services they provide remains scant.

These institutions have a manifest function to treat mentally disordered offenders but this is frequently subordinated to the latent political function of preventive detention. Clinical resources beyond medication and nursing care have therefore often received a low priority. Nevertheless, psychological treatment for patients in high security has been reported from several institutions during the last two decades. This chapter summarizes these developments and their implications for clinical practice.

HIGH SECURITY HOSPITALS AND THEIR PATIENTS

Characteristics of High Security Hospitals

In Britain, high security hospital services are provided for some 1800 patients at Broadmoor, Rampton, and Ashworth hospitals and the State Hospital in Scot-

Handbook of Offender Assessment and Treatment. Edited by C. R. Hollin.
© 2000 John Wiley & Sons Ltd.

land. Under the Mental Health Act, these are designated *special hospitals* for patients who "require treatment under conditions of special security on account of their dangerous, violent or criminal propensities". Offenders can be subject to compulsory, and effectively indeterminate detention under a hospital order when they constitute "a grave and immediate danger to the public".

Until the 1970s, special hospitals were the base for forensic psychiatric services, but Regional Secure Units (RSUs) were subsequently developed to provide "medium" secure facilities. Differences between "high" or "maximum" and "medium" security are to some extent arbitrary. Although maximum security implies an escape-proof perimeter, some special hospitals and most RSUs rely more on internal security through strictly controlled access and staffing levels. Institutions designated as maximum security hospitals generally contain the more serious offenders and impose longer term detention.

Most jurisdictions have developed similar services. There are administrative variations, for example in the degree of control by the criminal justice system, but maximum security hospitals share several common features that affect clinical services (Rice, Harris, Quinsey, & Cyr, 1990; Webster, Hucker, & Grossman, 1993). First, their typical location in isolated areas not only limits contact of patients with relatives but may also isolate staff from developments in the wider professional community. Second, treatment staff usually have only limited control over admission and release, and may have to care for patients they believe should no longer be there. For example, more than one-third of patients in special hospitals are known to require long-term medium secure care rather than detention in maximum security (Maden, Curle, Meux, Burrow, & Gunn, 1993). Third, the balance between security and treatment is frequently tipped in favour of the former. Hospitalization then emphasizes containment rather than rehabilitation.

Characteristics of Patients in High Security

In some jurisdictions, most patients in secure facilities have been found not guilty by reason of insanity or unfit to plead. In Britain, however, a hospital order more usually follows a finding of guilt. The English Mental Health Act recognizes four categories of mental disorder:

1. *mental illness* includes the more serious mental disorders, such as schizophrenia;
2. *psychopathic disorder* covers personality disorders; and
3. *mental impairment* and
4. *severe mental impairment* covers learning disabilities.

These are legal categories, not clinical diagnoses, and psychopathic disorder should not be confused with the clinical concept of psychopathy (Blackburn, 1993a). About two-thirds of patients in special hospitals fall in the mental illness category, and this predominance of patients with psychotic disorder characterizes maximum security hospitals elsewhere.

Detained mentally disordered offenders are therefore clinically heterogeneous. They are also heterogeneous in criminal histories. About 70% have committed serious crimes such as murder, arson, or sexual assault, and many have
extensive criminal careers. However, high security hospitals also admit prisoners
who become mentally disordered, and psychiatric patients who are assaultive in
other hospitals. Detention is usually long term, the average length of stay in
Britain being eight years. Length of stay is often influenced more by offence than
disorder, particularly in the case of psychopathic disorder (Dell & Robertson,
1988).

Treatment Goals and Clinical Needs

Problems of patients in maximum security include not only the cognitive, emotional, and social dysfunctions suggested by the range of psychiatric diagnoses,
but also their dangerous behaviour. Service priorities and the objectives of treatment in maximum security are, however, frequently unclear. Forensic psychiatrists commonly view mentally disordered offenders as simply the mentally
disordered who happen to offend. Treatment of disorder is therefore the primary
goal, and offending behaviour is of secondary consideration.

Some psychologists, in contrast, argue that treatment should address those personal and social characteristics of which the dangerous behaviour is a function.
This neglects psychological dysfunctions not directly related to offending.
Although the relationship of many patient problems to subsequent dangerousness beyond the institution is unknown, attention to most of them can be justified in terms of the commitment of clinicians to alleviate distress and improve
patients' conditions (Rice et al., 1990). However, the clinical goals of "psychological improvement" and criminal targets may need to be addressed
separately, and it needs to be made explicit when the priority is the problems of
the patient and when it is the problems the patient causes for others (Blackburn,
1993b).

Clarification of the goals of individual treatment is critical to the evaluation
of *treatability*, which has become a major consideration in decisions to admit
patients to high security. Agreement between clinicians on treatability is low
(Quinsey, 1988), and this reflects both ambiguities in the concept and in the
decision-making task (Heilbrun et al., 1988). The prediction of an *outcome*, i.e.
response to treatment, has to be distinguished from the assessment of *amenability to treatment* as a constellation of personal and situational characteristics. The
latter includes not only motivation and history of prior response to treatment,
but also the availability of treatment resources (Heilbrun et al., 1988). As yet,
however, an appropriate methodology for assessing treatability is lacking.

There are few reports of systematic needs assessments in maximum security
hospitals. Neither legal category nor psychiatric diagnosis provides a clear guide
to patient need, particularly because of co-morbid or co-occurring diagnoses. For
example, more than a half of psychotic patients also exhibit personality disorders

(Blackburn, Crellin, Morgan, & Tulloch, 1990; Hodgins, 1995). Blackburn et al. (1990) concluded that problems of submissiveness, fear of competitiveness, poor self-esteem, affective insensitivity, and inappropriately expressed anger were as common among mentally ill patients as among those in the psychopathic disorder category, and that the treatment needs of the two groups overlapped.

Homogeneous groups among maximum security patients have been identified by means of multivariate statistics applied to personality test data and ratings of social and emotional problems (Blackburn, 1992; Quinsey, Cyr, & Lavallee, 1988; Rice et al., 1990). Quinsey et al. (1988) found that at two secure hospitals in Canada, the most frequent problems were anxiety, impulsivity, lack of consideration for others, poor use of leisure, anger, and crazy talk. Cluster analysis indicated seven patient groups: good citizens, social isolates, institutionalized psychotics, personality disorders, psychotics, institutional management problems, and a developmentally handicapped group. These groups formed the basis for reorganizing hospital wards and for identifying the kind of assessment and treatment methods required (Rice et al., 1990).

TREATMENT INTERVENTIONS IN HIGH SECURITY HOSPITALS

Most treatment methods developed in mental health services have been employed in maximum security hospitals. Pharmacological treatment is standard, but psychological interventions are applied with only a minority of patients, and individualized treatment is the exception rather than the rule. In a survey of 127 American forensic psychiatric units, Kerr and Roth (1986) found that pharmacological treatment was used in 98% of all units, and received by 61% of all residents, but only one-third received weekly individual psychotherapy.

Rice et al. (1990) provide a detailed review of the psychological treatment literature which demonstrates that interventions have been developed that are relevant to all the problems most frequently demonstrated by patients in secure facilities. These include, for example, social skills training to deal with problems of social withdrawal, psychodynamic and cognitive therapy for depression, and training in problem-solving, moral reasoning, and empathy to deal with criminal attitudes and thinking. The following discussion focuses on the areas that have received most attention.

Treatment of Psychotic Patients

The ubiquitous reliance on medication is as might be expected with predominantly long-stay, psychotic populations, and despite frequent concerns that mentally disordered offenders are overmedicated, surveys suggest that prescribing practices in special hospitals are similar to those elsewhere. However, although the efficacy of neuroleptic drugs in ameliorating positive symptoms of schizophrenia is well established, a significant number of psychotic patients in maximum security remain "treatment-resistant".

When lack of response to medication is a significant obstacle to discharge or transfer, this is usually because of associated behaviour problems of social interaction and aggression. These may often be more amenable to psychological interventions than to medication. Rice et al. (1990) point to evidence that behavioural treatments, such as social skills training for conversational skills, emotional recognition, and coping strategies, enhance the effectiveness of neuroleptic medication. Skills training methods can also be of some value in overcoming negative symptoms of psychosis, which are less likely to be responsive to medication. There is also a growing interest in the application of cognitive–behavioural methods to positive symptoms of schizophrenia (e.g. Fowler, Garety, & Kuipers, 1995), although there is as yet only limited indication of their application to mentally disordered offenders.

Violence and Institutional Management Problems

Patients in high security have been identified as dangerous in some situations, and a general aim of treatment is to alleviate those problems that mediate violence. This requires not only amelioration of symptoms of disorder but also the provision of generalizable skills for coping with provocative situations in the community. However, a high priority is accorded to behaviour problems which affect the management of patients within the institution. Most prominent are assaultive behaviours, impulsive, angry outbursts, property destruction, and self-harm.

Violent incidents have traditionally been dealt with by seclusion, mechanical restraints, the use of a "chemical straitjacket", or physical restraint techniques. These strategies may temporarily remove the problem, but do not produce new learning. Seclusion, the social isolation of a patient in a locked room, is often justified as therapeutic, but is now recognized as a coercive form of control. Behavioural interventions have been shown to provide a viable alternative.

Behavioural strategies for reducing aggression and disruptive behaviour in maximum security hospitals involve the consequation of aggressive behaviours complemented by the teaching of alternative prosocial skills (Howells, 1976; Rice et al., 1990). Behavioural techniques have included differential reinforcement of incompatible behaviours, time-out, overcorrection–restitution, and contingent shock, together with group skills training involving role-play and the rehearsal of responses to provocation. The synthesis of behaviour modification methods with other psychological approaches in the treatment of four chronically violent, psychotic patients was described by Becker, Love, and Hunter (1997). This approach successfully eliminated violence within six months and permitted the transfer of all four patients to less secure facilities.

Although behavioural methods have been employed most often with aggressive individuals, much of the variance in institutional aggression is accounted for by environmental factors such as crowding, lack of social structure, and coercive ward atmosphere (Harris & Rice, 1992). Victim characteristics such as age, stature, or authoritarian behaviour by staff also contribute to aggressive incidents. Some attempts have been made to deal with these factors. For example, the token economy and the therapeutic community can provide more structure to the institutional environment. Rice et al. (1990) also developed training workshops to improve staff skills for dealing with aggression.

Reductions in the frequency of aggressive acts in the ward setting can be achieved quite rapidly by contingency management methods, but generalization requires additional training in new situations. However, Harris and Rice (1992) identify several problems that weaken the integrity of institutional behavioural programmes. In particular, implementation is often dependent on staff co-operation, but staff may not reward skilled assertive behaviour by patients and may resist attempts to change environmental factors.

Recurrent acts of aggression are often mediated by proneness to excessive anger, and the cognitively oriented stress inoculation approach to *anger management* developed by Novaco (see Chapter 19) has been used on both an individual and group basis in several high security hospitals. Anger management is contraindicated for patients who use aggression instrumentally or who deny anger problems, but its potential value for violent patients for whom emotional dysregulation is a central problem has received only limited attention (Howells, 1989). Renwick, Black, Ramm, and Novaco (1997) describe a pilot study of anger management with four psychotic patients with a history of problems of anger and aggression. As well as using an extended, individually based version of Novaco's procedure, they also introduced a five-session preparatory phase to deal with issues of patient motivation and basic skills. No controlled evaluation was undertaken, but ratings from interviews with clinical staff at treatment termination indicated positive changes in manifestations of anger and aggression.

Anger management methods may also be appropriate to patients who engage in *self-harming behaviour* such as cutting or self-strangulation. Self-harm is a common problem in high security hospitals and is particularly prevalent among females. Staff responses are most frequently the use of medication, seclusion, or restraint (Burrow, 1992). However, self-harm is a means of coping with tension, distress, or perceived lack of control, and is a function of social factors in the ward environment as much as individual psychopathology (Liebling, Chipchase, & Velangi, 1997). Attempts to deal with self-harm should therefore include not only interventions aimed at individual emotional distress, but also changes in the therapeutic climate of wards and staff reactions. However, the efficacy of interventions to reduce self-harm has not been reported.

Sex Offenders in Maximum Security Hospitals

Sexual offenders are generally admitted to maximum security hospitals only when they are considered to have a psychiatric disorder, usually a personality disorder, but form a substantial minority of the populations of these hospitals. Many are "model citizens" within the institution, having been removed from the situations in which they pose a risk to others. They are, however, often unwilling to acknowledge sexual problems or to engage in treatment, and closed, male-dominated environments are not optimal settings in which to develop appropriate heterosocial skills or non-sexist attitudes.

It is also now accepted that interventions with sex offenders require continuing treatment and supervision within the community to prevent relapse. Nevertheless, many of the dysfunctions that mediate sexual offences have been treatment targets within high security settings. These include deviant sexual preferences, deficits in social competence, deficient sexual knowledge, and inappropriate beliefs about victims, as well as more general characteristics that may contribute to sex offences, such as poor self-esteem, anger control, or lack of empathy.

Antiandrogen medication has occasionally been used in attempts to reduce sexual "drive", but most interventions with this group are psychological. Cox (1980) describes the use of small group psychotherapy at Broadmoor. Treatment aims were to reduce defences against trusting relationships arising from early traumatic experiences and to promote self-esteem, but no necessary effects on recidivism were expected.

Early behavioural approaches assumed a heterosocial deficit as a major factor in sex offending. Crawford and Allen (1979) applied social skills training with a small group of sex offenders at Broadmoor, and demonstrated improved skills and reduced social anxiety following training, and at a two-year follow-up within the hospital. Others have focused on behavioural techniques for reducing deviant sexual arousal and increasing non-deviant arousal. Methods developed with sex offenders at Atascadero in California (e.g. Laws & Osborn, 1983) have included satiation, olfactory aversion, and orgasmic reconditioning. Studies of small groups or individual cases have generally demonstrated effectiveness of these methods in reducing deviant sexual interests. There is, however, little evidence of their longer term maintenance or their effectiveness in reducing recidivism.

Other approaches used in maximum security have attempted to deal with problems of self-control of sexual impulses or anxieties about sex, for example through sex education. However, sex offenders in maximum security are heterogeneous not only in their choice of victims and deviant interests, but also in the variety of social and sexual problems they exhibit (Crawford, 1979; Rice et al., 1990). Treatment programmes therefore need to be individualized and comprehensive. An example of a successful multimodal treatment for an aggressive exhibitionist is described by Blackburn (1993a).

Treatment of Personality Disorders and Psychopathy

The socially deviant behaviour of high security patients is commonly mediated by dispositions such as anger-proneness, social avoidance, or impulsivity. These traits are encompassed by current concepts of personality disorder, which also subsume the more specific concept of psychopathic personality. This classical concept of psychopathy is currently defined most clearly by Hare's Psychopathy Checklist (PCL–R: Hare, 1996). As was noted earlier, this concept is not equivalent to the legal category of psychopathic disorder.

Concerns about the treatability and risk of high security patients centre particularly on "psychopaths". Not only are psychopaths believed to be inherently antisocial, there is also a long-standing debate about whether it is appropriate to deal with them in a health care context. Many clinicians believe that psychopaths are untreatable. The treatment literature, however, provides no clear support for this view. Most reports of treatment are methodologically deficient and typically fail to define "psychopaths", treatment goals, or treatment programmes (Blackburn, 1993a; see also Chapter 31). Generalizations about the treatability of "psychopaths" are not therefore currently warranted.

Despite the prominence of personality disorders, relatively few programmes for these disorders have been described in maximum security hospitals. Nevertheless, psychological interventions in high security are frequently concerned with the dysfunctional traits that identify personality disorders, even though they may not be defined in these terms. However, personality disorder in these settings is typically associated not only with behaviour problems of violence or sex offending, but also with other clinical problems (Coid, 1992), and treatment therefore needs to address multiple problems.

Some psychotherapists argue that group psychotherapy within a therapeutic community is most likely to benefit personality disordered offenders. However, therapeutic communities have rarely been established in maximum security hospitals, and their utility for psychopaths is questioned by a recent long-term follow up study in Canada (see below). Components of the therapeutic community milieu have, however, been included in some recent programmes in combination with other forms of intervention. Reiss, Grubin, and Meux (1996) evaluated an eclectic programme for legally defined psychopaths at Broadmoor which combined group and individual dynamic psychotherapy in a structured milieu with social skills training, anger management, sex education, and cognitive therapy for depression and sexual problems. Positive outcomes in terms of clinical gains and later offending were observed. A psychological treatment ward for legal psychopaths at Rampton also combined a supportive ward milieu with cognitive–behavioural group treatments covering assertiveness, macho attitudes, cognitive skills, self-esteem, problem-solving, and emotional awareness (Hughes, Hogue, Hollin, & Champion, 1997). Preliminary evaluation for the first nine patients indicated a net positive effect on global estimates of change. Positive change was also negatively related to scores on the PCL—R.

These recent studies suggest that structured interventions within high security can benefit personality disordered offenders, at least in the short term. In the absence of controls, however, it cannot be asserted that these interventions were responsible for changes observed, nor is it clear which components of these multifaceted treatments are the most helpful.

LONG-TERM FOLLOW-UPS OF MAXIMUM SECURITY PATIENTS

Long-term follow-ups focus mainly on reoffending. Murray (1989) reviewed research on reoffending by released mentally disordered offenders, including six follow-up studies of the English special hospitals. Variable rates of reoffending reported reflect different periods of follow-up and differing criteria of recidivism. However, the most systematic study (Black & Spinks, 1985) reported a five-year follow-up during which 10% of the sample committed further serious assaults, 39% appeared in court for some offence, 29% were readmitted to a psychiatric hospital, and 51% survived in the community. Similar rates were found by Bailey and MacCulloch (1992) in a follow-up of up to 14 years of patients discharged from a new special hospital. Overall, 37% were reconvicted of any offence, and 17% of a serious offence.

These reoffending rates are somewhat lower than those found for released prisoners, but direct comparisons are hazardous. Several studies find higher rates for personality disordered offenders compared with mentally ill offenders. Bailey and MacCulloch (1992), for example, found that 55% of legal psychopaths re-offended compared with 21% of the mentally ill, while for serious reconvictions, the rates were 26% and 10%, respectively. These figures suggest that the majority of released patients do not commit further serious offences, and in these terms, maximum security hospitals cannot be considered unsuccessful (Webster et al., 1993). However, official recidivism figures are known to be underestimates of criminal activities. There are also continuing debates over the appropriateness of reoffending as an indicator of the performance of a maximum security hospital. Robertson (1989) questions whether it is the business of hospitals to "cure" criminality, and suggests that reduced recidivism is not an appropriate outcome criterion. MacCulloch and Bailey (1991), on the other hand, argue that reduced recidivism is the primary goal of interventions with mentally disordered offenders.

These follow-up studies address primarily the decision to release, and do not permit conclusions about the quality or effects of specific treatment programmes. Given the variety of treatment agents and environmental influences to which patients in maximum security are exposed, rigorous controlled studies of the efficacy of specific treatments may not be feasible. However, some evaluations of specific programmes have been reported from the Oak Ridge Division of the Penetanguishene Mental Health Centre in Ontario. A five-year follow-up of a token economy revealed that half the patients subsequently reoffended, but that outcome was unrelated to performance in the programme (Rice, Quinsey, & Houghton, 1990). Rice, Quinsey, and Harris (1991) also found no differences in reconviction for a sexual offence between child molesters who participated in aversion therapy and general institution programmes and child molesters who participated in institutional programmes alone. Although short-term effects of these behavioural programmes within the hospital were demonstrated, these findings suggest that treatment gains are not maintained or that the programmes are not directly relevant to offending in the community.

A 10-year evaluation of a therapeutic community at Oak Ridge also revealed little difference in violent recidivism between patients in the programme and a matched group of untreated prisoners (Rice, 1997; Harris, Rice, & Cormier, 1994). However, there was a significant interaction of treatment with psychopathy as defined by the PCL—R. Treated psychopaths had a worse outcome than untreated psychopaths, while treated non-psychopaths did better than untreated non-psychopaths. A therapeutic community may not therefore be a suitable modality for psychopaths, but non-psychopathic offenders may benefit. Some commentators, however, have argued that this programme was more coercive than other hospital-based therapeutic communities.

CONCLUSIONS

Despite the justifiable criticisms of high security hospitals as living environments, the available evidence suggests that they may not be wholly unsuccessful in rehabilitating their patients. However, the treatment findings to date provide little unequivocal guidance on which treatment methods work best and with which patients. Short-term behavioural changes have been demonstrated for a variety of psychological interventions, but controlled studies of specific treatments have been rare, and longer-term effects on community integration and recidivism remain to be established.

The unique features of treatment in maximum security arise from the institutional environment as much as from patient characteristics. Patients typically have multiple deficits but are frequently reluctant to engage in therapy, and organizational pressures on them to conform and demonstrate change are as likely to produce defensiveness as positive motivation. Security and organizational routines also commonly have priority over treatment activities, and the dominance of the "medical model" or a custodial culture poses significant obstacles to the implementation of innovative psychosocial treatments. Programme integrity is particularly dependent on institutional conditions, such as therapeutic ward atmosphere, rewards of ward staff by managers for implementing positive clinical programmes, rather than simply maintaining institutional routines, and specifically developed information systems (Rice, Harris et al., 1990).

Observations by clinicians who have attempted to develop treatment programmes in high security suggest several strategies that may improve treatment effectiveness. Particularly important are:

1. clarification of priorities through population needs assessments and specification of treatment goals at both an institutional and an individual level;
2. detailed multidisciplinary assessments of patient problems and deficits in the context of theory-based formulations;

3. individualised treatment that may include but does not rely on group methods or packages;
4. involvement of other staff as well as patients in treatment planning;
5. recognition of the need to work at the formation of a therapeutic alliance;
6. recognition of counter-transference issues and the stresses of working with violent patients through mutual support and supervision;
7. regular multimodal assessments that reliably document the extent of change.

Characteristics of innovative treatment programmes successfully established in other contexts are also likely to apply to the introduction of new programmes in maximum security hospitals (Backer, Liberman, & Kuehnel, 1986; Harris & Rice, 1992). Most prominent characteristics are interpersonal contact between potential adopters and those knowledgeable about innovations, outside consultation on the adoption process, organizational support for innovation, persistent championship by agency staff, adaptability of the innovation, and credible evidence of succcess.

REFERENCES

Backer, T. E., Liberman, R. P., & Kuehnel, T. G. (1986). Dissemination and adoption of innovative psychosocial interventions. *Journal of Consulting and Clinical Psychology*, *54*, 111–118.
Bailey, J., & MacCulloch, M. (1992). Characteristics of 112 cases discharged directly to the community from a new special hospital and some comparisons of performance. *Journal of Forensic Psychiatry*, *3*, 91–112.
Becker, M., Love, C. E., & Hunter, M. E. (1997). Intractability is relative: Behaviour therapy in the elimination of violence in psychotic patients. *Legal and Criminological Psychology*, *2*, 89–101.
Black, D. A., & Spinks, P. (1985). Predicting outcomes of mentally disordered and dangerous offenders. In D. P. Farrington & R. Tarling (Eds.), *Prediction in criminology* (pp. 35–49). Albany, NY: State University of New York Press.
Blackburn, R. (1992). Criminal behaviour, personality disorder, and mental illness: The origins of confusion. *Criminal Behaviour and Mental Health*, *2*, 66–77.
Blackburn, R. (1993a). Clinical programmes with psychopaths. In C. R. Hollin & K. Howells (Eds.), *Clinical approaches to the mentally disordered offender* (pp. 179–208). Chichester, UK: Wiley.
Blackburn, R. (1993b). *The psychology of criminal conduct: Theory, research and practice*. Chichester, UK: Wiley.
Blackburn, R., Crellin, M. C., Morgan, E. M., & Tulloch, R. M. B. (1990). Prevalence of personality disorders in a special hospital population. *Journal of Forensic Psychiatry*, *1*, 43–52.
Burrow, S. (1992). The deliberate self-harming behaviour of patients within a British special hospital. *Journal of Advanced Nursing*, *17*, 138–148.
Coid, J. W. (1992). DSM-III diagnosis in criminal psychopaths: A way forward. *Criminal Behaviour and Mental Health*, *2*, 78–94.
Cox, M. (1980). Personal reflections upon 3000 hours in therapeutic groups with sex offenders. In D. J. West (Ed.), *Sex offenders in the criminal justice system: Cropwood conference series No. 12* (pp. 56–68). Cambridge, UK: Institute of Criminology.

Crawford, D. A. (1979). Modification of deviant sexual behaviour: The need for a comprehensive approach. *British Journal of Medical Psychology*, *52*, 151–156.

Crawford, D. A., & Allen, J. V. (1979). A social skills training programme with sex offenders. In M. Cook & G. Wilson (Eds.), *Love and attraction* (pp. 527–536). Oxford, UK: Pergamon.

Dell, S., & Robertson, G. (1988). *Sentenced to hospital: Offenders in Broadmoor* (Maudsley Monographs, No. 32). Oxford, UK: Oxford University Press.

Fowler, D., Garety, P., & Kuipers, E. (1995). *Cognitive behaviour therapy for psychoses: Theory and practice.* Chichester, UK: Wiley.

Hare, R. D. (1996). Psychopathy: A clinical concept whose time has come. *Criminal Justice and Behavior*, *23*, 25–54.

Harris, G. T., & Rice, M. E. (1992). Reducing violence in institutions: Maintaining behavior change. In R. D. Peters, R. J. McMahon, & V. L. Quinsey (Eds.), *Aggression and violence throughout the lifespan* (pp. 263–284). Newbury Park, CA: Sage.

Harris, G. T., Rice, M. E., & Cormier, C. A. (1994). Psychopaths: Is a therapeutic community therapeutic? *Therapeutic Communities*, *15*, 283–289.

Heilbrun, K., Bennett, W. S., Evans, J. H., Offutt, R. A., Reiff, H. J., & White, A. J. (1988). Assessing treatability in mentally disordered offenders: A conceptual and methodological note. *Behavioral Sciences and the Law*, *6*, 479–486.

Hodgins, S. (1995). Major mental disorders and crime: An overview. *Psychology, Crime, and Law*, *2*, 5–17.

Howells, K. (1976). Interpersonal aggression. *International Journal of Criminology and Penology*, *4*, 319–330.

Howells, K. (1989). Anger management methods in relation to the prevention of violent behaviour. In J. Archer & K. Browne (Eds.), *Human aggression: Naturalistic approaches* (pp. 153–181). London: Routledge.

Hughes, G. V., Hogue, T. E., Hollin, C. R., & Champion, H. (1997). First-stage evaluation of a treatment programme for personality disordered offenders. *Journal of Forensic Psychiatry*, *8*, 515–527.

Kerr, C. A., & Roth, J. A. (1986). Populations, practices, and problems in forensic psychiatric facilities. *Annals of the American Academy of Political and Social Science*, *484*, 127–143.

Laws, D. R., & Osborn, C. A. (1983). Setting up shop: How to build and operate a laboratory to evaluate and treat sexual deviance. In J. G. Greer & I. R. Stuart (Eds.), *The sexual aggressor: Current perspectives on treatment* (pp. 293–335). New York: Van Nostrand Reinhold.

Liebling, H., Chipchase, H., & Velangi, R. (1997). Why do women self-harm at Ashworth special hospital? *Issues in Criminological and Legal Psychology, No. 27* (pp. 10–22). Leicester, UK: The British Psychological Society.

MacCulloch, M., & Bailey, J. (1991). Issues in the provision and evaluation of forensic services. *Journal of Forensic Psychiatry*, *2*, 247–265.

Maden, A., Curle, C., Meux, C., Burrow, S., & Gunn, J. (1993). The treatment and security needs of patients in special hospitals. *Criminal Behaviour and Mental Health*, *3*, 290–306.

Murray, D. J. (1989). *Review of research on reoffending of mentally disorderd offenders* (Research and Planning Unit Paper 55). London: Home Office.

Quinsey, V. L. (1988). Assessment of the treatability of forensic patients. *Behavioral Sciences and the Law*, *6*, 443–452.

Quinsey, V. L., Cyr, M., & Lavallee, Y. (1988). Treatment opportunities in a maximum security hospital: A problem survey. *International Journal of Law and Psychiatry*, *11*, 179–194.

Reiss, D., Grubin, D., & Meux, C. (1996). Young "psychopaths" in special hospital: Treatment and outcome. *British Journal of Psychiatry*, *168*, 99–104.

Renwick, S. J., Black, L., Ramm, M., & Novaco, R. W. (1997). Anger treatment with forensic hospital patients. *Legal and Criminological Psychology, 2*, 103–116.

Rice, M. E. (1997). Violent offender research and implications for the criminal justice
system. *American Psychologist, 52*, 414–423.

Rice, M. E., Harris, G. T., Quinsey, V. L., & Cyr, M. (1990). Planning treatment programmes
in secure psychiatric facilities. In D. N. Weisstub (Ed.), *Law and mental health: International perspectives, Vol. 5* (pp. 162–230). New York: Pergamon.

Rice, M. E., Quinsey, V. L., & Harris, G. T. (1991). Sexual recidivism among child molesters
released from a maximum security psychiatric institution. *Journal of Consulting and
Clinical Psychology, 59*, 381–386.

Rice, M. E., Quinsey, V. L., & Houghton, R. (1990). Predicting treatment outcome and
recidivism among patients in a maximum security token economy. *Behavioral Sciences
and the Law, 8*, 313–326.

Robertson, G. (1989). Treatment for offender patients: How should success be measured?
Medicine, Science and the Law, 29, 303–307.

Webster, C. D., Hucker, S. J., & Grossman, M. G. (1993). Clinical programmes for mentally
ill offenders. In K. Howells & C. R. Hollin (Eds.), *Clinical approaches to the mentally
disordered offender* (pp. 87–109). Chichester, UK: Wiley.

Chapter 35

Juvenile Offending: Treatment in Residential Settings

Roger Bullock
Dartington Social Research Unit, Dartington, Devon, UK

A HISTORY OF WELFARE POLICY

Historians naturally balk at generalizations but there does seem to be value in viewing treatment approaches to young offenders in their social as well as their clinical context.

Residential interventions have a long and varied tradition which makes such a view fruitful. Triseliotis (1992) cites a prototype residential service for youth at risk when monks in Byzantium took in homeless boys to ensure their religious upbringing. This monastic tradition has been important ever since and influenced provision in England long after its disappearance in the sixteenth century, an inheritance shown by the continuing use of titles such as sister and locations such as dormitory and cell. By the eighteenth century, however, many of the great medieval foundations had declined, become corrupt, or changed their function and it fell to the late Georgians and early Victorians to create a system based on sound moral principles and firm beliefs.

It need hardly be said that the nineteenth century was an era of great social and economic change and the growth in the numbers of unruly vagrant children was a constant concern. Throughout the century it was felt that something had to be done, one remedy being an expansion of residential facilities. Although private and voluntary reformatory schools had been established in various parts of the country from the end of the eighteenth century, the period of most rapid expansion began in the 1850s. This was marked by a Reformatory Schools Act, 1854, followed by an Industrial Schools Act in 1857 (Parker, 1990), statutes that remained the principal legislation for destitute and delinquent children until the

Handbook of Offender Assessment and Treatment. Edited by C. R. Hollin.

Children Act, 1908. Reformatory and industrial schools survived until 1933 when they were combined to form a single category of "approved" schools.

Changes in services for young offenders since the Second World War have sought to dismantle this institutional inheritance, mainly because of cost, poor outcomes for those sheltered, and better community services for the young. Approved schools have been closed and replaced by smaller units or community facilities and boarding schools for children with special needs have become much more open and homely. Only young offender institutions for older adolescents remain virtually intact.

In pursuing this policy of "deinstitutionalization", it is easy to forget the pioneering qualities of our predecessors. Faced with large numbers of unruly adolescents and few social and educational services, we too would probably opt for large-scale residential solutions, undoubtedly trying to make them as comfortable as possible. But, the difference between then and now is that the perceived benefits of institutional care accorded with the culture of the time, particularly in England. Public philanthropy was *de rigeur* among the wealthy and royal patronage was not unknown. Disputes between religious sects also fanned competition between providers (Bamford, 1967). Lambert, Millham, and Bullock (1975) argued that the growth of institutions was an attempt by the Victorians to apply the factory system to social problems, a policy aided by the growth of railways. Certainly, as one travels by train from London, distant campaniles, domes, and chimney stacks mark numerous institutions sheltering behind the trees and crumbling mansions pressed into unlikely service.

It must also be remembered that institutional solutions were used to solve all sorts of social problems, not just those of delinquency. Workhouses sheltered those who had fallen on hard times and much armed services, mercantile, and religious training as well as general education took place in residential settings. It seemed administratively tidy to create the right institution for the right problem.

The residential scene, however, was never tranquil. Scandals in places as varied as public schools, asylums, and training ships were constantly debated in parliament throughout the nineteenth century. Every year some commission reported and new laws were enacted in response to unease over residential care but the size of the problem and the difficulty of creating adequate and supervised alternatives meant that residential institutions flourished.

There is also a danger of underestimating the treatment efforts made. Much of what happened in asylums and reformatories may appear abusive today but there was often a conscious effort to link regime to problems. The reports of the Poor Law guardians and the managers of the industrial and reform schools, for instance, provide some of the first child care outcome studies. Worries about poor after care and the dilution of training effects once children had left residence were common concerns that are echoed today. But as objective clinical evidence was limited, compromises had to be made with other fashionable ideas. An example of this compromise is the design of the old St Thomas's Hospital in London which reflected such a therapeutic dispute between Florence Nightingale, who believed in the value of fresh air, and Sir John Simon (responsible for public health), who wanted a facility near to the poor. The product was a series of blocks with protruding wings, easily ventilated by exposure to prevailing winds and convenient for local people but hopelessly inefficient for sophisticated medical practice.

The First World War had an important but varied effect on all this. Many institutions were taken over by the military, often for hospitals or billets, and some never regained their former glory. On the other hand, the plethora of spinsters and war widows left after the Armistice provided cheap labour for whom the offer of on-site accommodation was particularly attractive. While the number of boys in the industrial and the reform schools declined, and by 1930 had fallen to 6000 compared with 25 000 at the turn of the century, new facilities were opened for groups with special needs, such as those with mental and physical disabilities. Moreover, the treatment philosophy was boosted by developments in psychology between the two world wars and by the perceived benefits of having a captive audience isolated from harmful influences, an opportunity grasped by many pioneers in special education (Bridgeland, 1971). Residential treatment was thus revived and given a new confidence; an ethos that led to a much larger expansion of facilities after 1945. Standards of care in much residential care, however, remained poor and there has been a steady stream of scandals right up the present day.

As a result of these concerns, the pendulum has swung back from the heady beliefs in therapy prevalent in pre- and immediate post-war decades. The history of residential treatment over the last 30 years has mostly been one of curtailment and declining belief, a more jaundiced view of its possibilities than envisaged in *Care and Treatment in a Planned Environment*, the blue print for provision for young offenders published by the Advisory Council on Child Care in 1970. Other factors, such as a growing awareness of the intractability of some problems, respect for consumers' rights, diminished public funding, and disappointing research results have all fuelled this scepticism. Between 1971 and 1991 the number of young people under the age of 18 years living in residential settings offering welfare and control (as opposed to private education) fell from 78 700 to 32 900, a drop of 58%, a pattern mirrored in most Western countries (Department of Health, 1998; Gooch, 1996).

As well as reductions in provision, the experiences of residents have also changed. Among the trends over the past two decades have been: the replacement of single-sex establishments by homes that are co-educational but which, in practice, are dominated by boys; the increasing age of residents on entry; more young people with health problems, behaviour disorders and disabilities; greater racial and ethnic mix; larger catchment areas, raising problems for educational continuity and contact with home; more provision by private agencies; less specialization by sector with a resulting wider mix of needs in each establishment; assessment by need criteria rather than social role categories, such as disabled or special educational needs; more generalist services; shorter stays; rising costs; more concerns about rights and protections; and further reductions in the size of units and in the numbers accommodated by the system (Gooch, 1996).

The influence of these factors will vary for each type of establishment so that the reasons for decline in private boarding schools will be different from those affecting provision for offenders. The important point, however, is that in virtually all sectors, viable alternatives have been created on a large enough scale to make a difference. In services primarily concerned with delinquent and disruptive adolescents, the emergence of a coherent system of community services, initially termed "intermediate treatment", has been significant, although there is still some dependency on residential services and imprisonment as a last resort.

These tensions between residential treatment and its alternatives became increasingly manifest during the 1960s. The term "treatment" was favoured by those who adopted a psychological position and viewed problem behaviours as deviant or abnormal, springing from adverse childhood experience, faulty learning, or trauma. This view encouraged a search for causes and informed effective treatments. The literature of the time abounds with studies searching for the special background characteristics of delinquents, the holy grail of the significant variable (Field, Hammond, & Tizard, 1973). Other researchers, attracted to a more sociological perspective, were sceptical, stressing that people with problems were usually orthodox in most other respects and that any deviance was usually contextual (Taylor, Walton, & Young, 1973). These beliefs stressed sub-cultures, blocked aspirations, identity, and career. Sociologists stressed that the labelling and separation associated with psychological approaches exacerbated young people's difficult situation. Residential care was strongly criticized for isolating inmates from the rest of society and exposing them to institutional cultures that reinforced deviant identities and aggravated their difficulties.

The fear of institutionalization had been highlighted by the powerful evidence (Goffman, 1961; Barton, 1959) that long residential stays in restrictive environments had detrimental effects on residents. Children in residential care were described as displaying shallow, attention-seeking over-friendliness and affectionless psychopathy (Wolkind & Rushton, 1994). The rituals and values of the institutions had little relevance to the outside world, interactions all took place in public, shows of emotion were discouraged, and social relationships were distorted by the absence of the very young, the elderly and, in some cases, the opposite sex. It was not surprising that as they emerged to the outside world, some leavers found it difficult to cope, a situation exacerbated by weakening links with home during the time spent away.

As a result of these and other pressures, such as rising costs and administrative changes during the 1970s, the reform (approved) schools closed and similar closures occurred in large mental hospitals and children's homes. For the first time, viable alternatives to residential care seemed possible for the majority of children. This change was aided by the creation of local authority social services departments in 1971 which brought together aspects of juvenile justice, mental health, and social services under a single administration, so facilitating flexibility and planning.

Nevertheless, it was becoming increasingly clear that for a small number of difficult young people, sophisticated treatment was not only necessary but could also only be delivered residentially. As a result, specialist residential "treatment" approaches were extended for a minority of those in need. There was a growth in secure accommodation (none of the approved schools had been secure and some training prisons (borstals) had been open) and new therapeutic communities were founded at places such as Peper Harrow and the Cotswold Community, both former approved schools. Initiatives based on behaviourist theories were developed at Aycliffe and Chelfham Mill and "treatment" initiatives were introduced at some borstals and prisons, such as Feltham and Grendon Underwood. The most ambitious development in England was the setting up of two Youth Treatment Centres at St Charles and Glenthorne. Here, the aim was to fashion a variety of treatment approaches that combined the best elements of education, health, and social work and so met the needs of troubled adolescents and young offenders for whom provision, particularly long-term and therapeutic, was lacking.

While this institutional diversity was welcomed by professionals seeking placement options, it did little to mollify critics of the "treatment" approach. Welfare economists questioned the evidence to justify the considerable expenditure these new developments required. Therapists argued about what precisely constituted treatment; for example, did simply keeping an adolescent safe qualify? Social workers expressed concern about those secondary effects of residence which could aggravate young people's situations, such as isolation from home and withering social links, while lawyers agonized over whether treatment could be enforced on grounds of welfare. The new interest in organizational management drew attention to the tendency for residential institutions to be readily filled and questioned whether the amount of available provision was driving the need for specialist services rather than the reverse. Treatment was thus criticized by the "left" and the "right" of the political spectrum. Much of the policy since the mid 1970s, of diversion, opening up residential units, and making life in them as normal as possible, reflects attempts to reconcile these differences in professional and political opinion.

This résumé of welfare policy is undoubtedly superficial but its purpose has not been so much to establish historical truth as to explain why, at the present time, the word "treatment" is somewhat out of fashion. Its use tends to be restricted to specific therapies for particular behaviour problems. While professionals speak confidently about "treatment" when dealing with depression or enuresis, the terms "intervention", "care plan" or "care strategy" are usually preferred when discussing the combination of difficult behaviours that many young offenders present. This change of language reflects the current practice of fashioning a package of services to meet a number of inter-related problems. It also reflects recent ethical developments in health and social care, such as greater user involvement and professional accountability.

THE NEW APPROACH

This new approach may seem to threaten residential treatment as it undermines its philosophy and limits the professional power on which it relies. On the other hand, a perspective starting with the needs of the individual and services required to meet them does give residential care a potential role in the continuum of services available to young people, even if it is to be used sparingly. The contemporary problem is thus more likely to be uncertainty about what works best rather than constraints on what can be offered. This caution is often manifest in psychiatric and psychological assessments of young offenders which seem more concerned with screening for formal mental illness and giving general indications, such as "a long stay in a therapeutic setting", than with making specific therapeutic prescriptions.

This complex role means that most long-stay treatment establishments are expected to fulfil a number of functions. There is usually a need for control—this may be expressed as security or a need for clear boundaries; for consistency and stability—to keep the young person in one place where demands and expectations are predictable; for supportive relations—with staff who are trained, sensitive, and informed; for safety—from self-harm or danger to the public; for assessment—the presenting behaviour is often difficult to understand; for planning the young person's future, and so on. Added to these is the need to provide opportunities for healthy psycho-social development and to help resolve particular problems. In a general context of support, care, and oversight, help is given with such things as remedial education, anger control, and self-esteem, according to the needs of each individual.

There will inevitably be conflicts between these functions. A question that frequently arises is: Does the mix of residents arising from one function (e.g. remand) limit the performance of others (e.g. treatment)? Even if residents have features in common, such as meeting the conditions for entry to secure accommodation, they will almost certainly differ considerably in others. In a study of admissions to the Youth Treatment Centres in the late 1980s, five distinct "career" groups were found among the young people even though they had all met the requirements just described (Bullock, Millham, & Little, 1998). The groups were: one-off grave offenders, persistent offenders who also committed a grave crime, adolescents who had long been looked after by social services, young people who had been in special education until their difficult behaviour necessitated transfer to social services, and adolescents whose behaviour had deteriorated dramatically in adolescence. Each group had a different previous history, presented different sorts of clinical and management problems, and had different prognoses for change.

In an ideal situation, a specific treatment effective in meeting young people's needs is consistently applied. However, as a result of client diversity and the varied functions of residential units, treatment approaches will inevitably be eclectic. A specific treatment appropriate for all residents is unlikely to be feasible and, in practice, psychotherapists will apply rewards and sanctions while behaviourists will probe the unconscious. This does not mean that validated treatment philosophies are unimportant but that because of the mix of residents there are limits to their application. But, even if "pure" therapy is difficult, treatment philosophies still shape the focus of the work, highlight factors and processes to be explored, indicate how resources should be deployed, determine the criteria for assessing behaviour, and suggest what activities and styles of relationships should be encouraged. The optimum situation, therefore, is one where there is a validated overarching treatment philosophy that is effective in meeting the needs of residents even though in reality practice may be somewhat eclectic. In addition, specific therapies will be applied to meet the idiosyncratic needs of each individual.

The key questions about residential approaches are, therefore:

1. What is the special contribution of a residential setting to treatment?
2. What factors are indicated by research as likely to produce an environment in which treatment can take place, i.e. what is a "good" establishment?
3. What aspects of regimes aid specific treatments for particular problems, i.e. how can clinical practice and effects be maximized?

THE SPECIAL CONTRIBUTION OF RESIDENTIAL SETTINGS

The strengths and weaknesses of residential care have been laid out in numerous publications (Bullock, Millham, & Little, 1993). Most of these studies are relevant to young offenders. To summarize, residential care can give shelter, education and good basic care, it can offer an ambience for sophisticated treatments, it can widen children's cultural horizons, provide opportunities for a range of non-affective relationships with adults, and offer support to ease young people's transition to independence. It also allows non-residential methods to flourish by siphoning off the most difficult cases.

There are many weaknesses with residential care. Like most substitute care, it does not provide unconditional love. It also offers limited stability to residents as staff turnover is high and children's stays are usually short. Continuities of education, family links, and peer friendships are often broken and regular health checks can be missed. Finally, residential units seem to find it difficult to involve young people's families in the treatment process. This difficulty seems to arise for a variety of reasons, particularly the long-standing division of labour between residential and field social workers which limits the scope of staff working in treatment settings. As most leavers go home (Bullock, Gooch, & Little, 1998), this failure to tackle family problems may diminish the effectiveness of the treatments offered and even exacerbate the problems that young people face after leaving.

It is also worth noting that residential care long enjoyed considerable control over the destinations of leavers. It was often part of a closed career avenue and even as recently as the 1970s most young offenders leaving approved schools found employment. Today this is not the case and the serene and predictable voyages to safe havens are no longer available. While few would wish to re-create the employment linkages of previous decades, the decline in work opportunities for leavers may explain why the problems of institutions surface in such an unsavoury way and why they face a crisis of confidence.

FEATURES OF A GOOD ESTABLISHMENT

Various research studies have explored the conditions that facilitate the strengths of residential approaches. A recent study of nine children's homes (Brown, Bullock, Hobson, & Little, 1998) found that a "good" home is one where the various components of the structure are complementary. The greater the concordance between the expectations of society, the law and professional guidance, the way the home is structured and resourced, and what staff believe they can achieve, the better the establishment. A concordant structure also leads to positive cultures among staff and children, creating a situation whereby group responses to common situations reinforce shared aims.

In another study of 48 children's homes, Sinclair and Gibbs (1998) found that a good home is likely to be one that is small, where the head of home feels that its role is clear, mutually compatible and not disturbed by frequent reorganisation, and that he or she is given adequate autonomy to get on with the job. It also helps if staff are agreed about how the home should be run and are not at odds with each other. Such a home is likely to help children by having low sickness rates among staff, infrequent running away by children, and good care plans for each resident as well as being a nice place to live, in terms of such things as the absence of bullying, feeling cared for, and being in a friendly place.

Looking more generally at residential settings, Bullock (1992) concluded that the following conditions were necessary for success.

1. The young people feel enriched by their residential experience and perceive staff as caring.
2. The young people see themselves as acquiring clear instrumental skills during their stay.
3. The institution pursues a set of goals which are matched to the primary rather than the secondary needs of the children; that is, to the needs which necessitated absence from home rather than those brought about by living away. These aims should be reiterated in a wide variety of ways and permeate the whole control process.
4. The demonstration of some consensus among staff, children, and parents about what these goals should be and how they should be achieved. To maintain this consensus, leadership should be clear and consistent. Staff should be reminded of the strengths of residential as well as warned against its weaknesses.

5. Efforts should be made to prevent staff and child cultures from cohering in a destructive way. It may be necessary to fragment the informal world of children by a variety of structural features, such as by creating small group situations, by appointing senior children to positions of responsibility, or by encouraging sensitive and informed staff/child relationships.

It should be emphasized that these conditions can be achieved in a variety of ways. For example, consensus among staff may be achieved just as effectively by bureaucratic process as by charismatic leadership; the important point being that if these characteristics are in place then the residential unit is likely to be a "good one". This in itself is a contribution to treatment as it wins young people's commitment, reduces disruptive behaviour, and provides an auspicious ambience for clinical work with individuals.

This impact on young people's behaviour while resident is very significant in the context of the tariff system and the associated process of status deterioration that affect juvenile offenders. Running away and violent behaviour usually result in transfer to more controlling environments so if this shift and accompanying growth of criminal identity can be prevented, then it is a contribution to welfare. In comparative studies of residential institutions for young offenders, Millham, Bullock, and Cherrett (1975) and Sinclair (1971) found large differences in the rates for premature transfer even when young people's background characteristics were taken into account, differences that closely reflected the regimes of the institutions.

Unfortunately, good outcomes for individuals do not automatically follow from good homes for a variety of reasons. Some persistent offenders become recidivists (Bullock, Millham et al., 1998) and young people can find the contrast between the caring home and the uncaring community too much to handle. Nevertheless, while there was much less difference in young people's reoffending rates after release, the pattern of good and bad homes was maintained, suggesting that the significant influence on young people's potentially damaging behaviour while resident is mirrored by a smaller but still significant effect on criminal behaviour after release (Millham et al., 1975).

The value of a residential approach is what it can offer the treatment process. There are many possible areas of "added value" but two are especially important for young offenders. The first is predictability in that much of the young person's life is enacted in the same value framework. This enables the treatment, whether it be analytic, cognitive, or behaviourist, to permeate education, relationships, and social development. Secondly, the staff and resident groups can be used creatively, to develop good relations with a range of adults, and to foster peer support and positive reinforcement. Given that persistent offenders are likely to have poor self-esteem and a jaundiced view of the world, some benefits in these areas resulting from a good experience should be apparent. Residential settings are powerful environments and if they are to be used effectively the treatment must be appropriate to the needs of the child and be morally acceptable in the demands they make.

THE EFFECTS OF SPECIFIC TREATMENTS

With regard to the effects of more specific residential treatments for offending behaviour, it is difficult to be conclusive. In a comprehensive review of the evidence, Sheldrake (1994) concludes, "the relative merits of different approaches have yet to be determined". Controlled trials and comparison studies (Cornish & Clarke, 1975; Bottoms & McClintock, 1973; Coates, Miller, & Ohlin, 1978) have all failed to identify any clear effects of residence other than those described on young people's behaviour while there. Moreover, in discussions about ways of dealing with offenders generally, where meta-analyses have indicated more clearly the components of effective remedies, residential options receive scant attention and are rarely seen as an essential part of provision (Sheldrake, 1994). The approach tends to be pragmatic: What can be done for young people who end up in residential settings for other reasons?

There is a danger of interpreting the absence of clear findings on effects as indicating that "nothing works". Although research findings on recidivism are generally disappointing, particularly for those working with persistent offenders (Millham et al., 1975; Rutter et al., 1998), and that residential care has not come up with the "silver bullet" that many hoped for in the 1960s, recent studies indicate some ways forward.

The first is to look more closely at the link between specific interventions and specific groups of adolescents. To do this, the taxonomies of young offenders constructed by West (1982) and Little (1990) need to be further developed and linked to a careful scrutiny of treatment processes. When this is done, more encouraging results emerge. For example, although persistent delinquency is obdurate, the outcomes for offenders who commit one-off grave crimes are quite encouraging (Bullock, Millham et al., 1998). In addition, although the trauma associated with some known contributory factors, such as child sexual abuse, is detrimental, sophisticated family therapy has been found to have some beneficial effects, including reduced criminal behaviour, on young offenders with conduct disorders (Bullock, Millham et al., 1998). The effects were more marked for some of the career groups described earlier and for sub-groups within them, such as those of gender and the extent of young people's social integration. Replication is obviously needed before findings can be considered authoritative, but initial results are promising. Although this more elaborate analysis is revealing, one should not hope for too much from more targeted interventions. Treatments address chronic conditions and the side-effects of some interventions, such as custody, are especially debilitating in the long run. Professionals can at best hope for improvements around 15%–20% in reconviction rates, the benefits are again most likely to be apparent while the young person is in residence (Rutter et al., 1998).

But even when differences are found, there remains the problem of separating treatment from other effects. Follow-up studies suggest that for disordered adolescents interventions have to be long and multi-faceted if they are to have any benefit (Hollin, Epps, & Kendrick, 1995). Progress is also variable; while there may be a slow general improvement in the young person's functioning, there are high and low points within it (Little & Kelly, 1995). Since randomized control trials are unlikely to be feasible with serious offenders, other methods of teasing out treatment effects have to be devised. One solution is to use research knowledge to make blind predictions of outcome at the point of entry and to compare actual with predicted results later on. An exploration of the experiences of leavers from long-stay secure treatment units based on this technique concluded that 75% of leavers had done better than expected, and that for 76% of these the residential experience seemed to have helped (Bullock, Millham et al., 1998). Nearly half (45%) of the leavers showed significantly changed behaviour in the areas which the treatment had addressed. However, again, the effects were better for some career groups than others. For example, those young people whose disruptive behaviour had escalated in adolescence and one-off grave offenders did better than the long-term care cases. In another study (of a therapeutic community), the treatment effect was found to have more impact on children with behaviour problems than on those in need of long-term protection (Little & Kelly, 1995). Thus, careful identification of needs groups and career pathways plus the application of predictive techniques is one way of clarifying the effects of residential interventions.

A second development is to view treatment in the wider context of the young person's needs and the services that best meet them. Meta-analyses of studies from around the world indicate that young offenders benefit most from targeted interventions that address offending behaviour using cognitive–behavioural methods and that if residential options are employed, then they need to be closely tied to community approaches (Hollin et al., 1995). But young people in residential care will almost certainly be difficult cases and for them different approaches may be needed. Certainly, the wider package of services available for young people and their families needs to be incorporated into the treatment as this will ensure that continuities are maintained and return problems forestalled. Contingency plans should also be made. The needs of disordered young people and their families cannot be compartmentalized and an undue emphasis on offending can lead to other of the young person's needs being ignored. So while the adolescent may be helped with violent behaviour, he/she can remain depressed. The philosophy underpinning the Children Act, 1989 in England and Wales facilitates both the focused approach that seems to work best and the wider strategies for helping children and families that research suggests are needed.

Residential treatment for offending, therefore, is best viewed as neither inherently good nor bad, but as whether it is appropriate. Current practice suggests that it is increasingly seen as less so although for some young people there does not seem to be any alternative, for example when some form of custody or control is required. In such cases it is helpful to look beyond the "treatment", sophisticated as this might be.

The starting point in adopting a treatment perspective is the needs of the young person and what is deemed necessary to meet them. The first question to be asked, therefore, is: What does the young person and his or her family need?

Does he or she need residential treatment, and if so what for, of what type, for how long and with what else? For those selected, the next question is: What regime and treatment approaches are shown by research to be the most effective for meeting those needs? To answer this properly, we again need to develop a validated taxonomy of young offenders and to consider the evidence on intervention and outcome for each group. To do this, the methodological and moral criteria employed to assess the effects of treatment have to be clearly specified.

This sequence of questions should focus attention on the aims of residential treatment and highlight gaps between desired and actual outcomes. Treatment is thus related to an individual's needs and seeks an auspicious setting with the application of specific therapies.

If these ideas inform answers to the three key questions posed earlier, then the place of residential treatment in a comprehensive service for persistent young offenders becomes clearer. Approaches to juvenile offending need to be multi-faceted; prevention and diversion can make important contributions as can residential treatment. A needs perspective has the advantage that when a new treatment approach comes on stream, its relevance can be quickly gauged and the unhelpful "for" and "against" stances taken by professionals are avoided. Considerable effort may be needed to develop these suggestions but the benefits of a comprehensive service should be apparent in improved outcomes for children and enhanced job satisfaction among professionals.

REFERENCES

Advisory Council on Child Care (1970). *Care and treatment in a planned environment.* London: Author.

Bamford, T. (1967). *The rise of the public schools.* London: Nelson.

Barton, R. (1959). *Institutional neurosis.* London: Wright.

Bottoms, A., & McClintock, F. (1973). *Criminals coming of age.* London: Heinemann.

Bridgeland, M. (1971). *Pioneer work with maladjusted children: A study of the development of therapeutic education.* London: Staples Press.

Brown, E., Bullock, R., Hobson, C., & Little, M. (1998). *Making residential care work: Structure and culture in children's homes.* Aldershot, UK: Ashgate.

Bullock, R. (1992). *Residential care: What we know and don't know.* London: National Children's Home.

Bullock, R., Gooch, D., & Little, M. (1998). *Children going home: The reunification of families.* Aldershot, UK: Ashgate.

Bullock, R., Millham, S., & Little, M. (1993). *Residential care: A review of the research.* London: HMSO.

Bullock, R., Millham, S., & Little, M. (1998). *Secure treatment outcomes: The care careers of very difficult adolescents.* Aldershot, UK: Ashgate.

Coates, R., Miller, A., & Ohlin, L. (1978). *Diversity in a youth correctional system.* Cambridge, MA: Ballinger.

Cornish, D., & Clarke, R. (1975). *Residential care and its effects on delinquency.* London: HMSO.

Department of Health (1998). *Caring for children away from home.* London: HMSO.

Field, E., Hammond, W., & Tizard, J. (1973). *Thirteen-year-old approved school boys in 1962.* London: HMSO.

Goffman, E. (1961). *Asylums*. New York: Doubleday.

Gooch, D. (1996). Home and away: the residential care, education and control of children in historical and political context. *Child and Family Social Work, 1*, 19–32.

Hollin, C., Epps, K., & Kendrick, D. (1995). *Managing behavioural treatment: Policy and practice with delinquent adolescents*. London: Routledge.

Lambert, R., Millham, S., & Bullock, R. (1975). *The chance of a lifetime? A study of boarding education*. London: Weidenfeld & Nicolson.

Little, M. (1990). *Young men in prison*. Aldershot, UK: Dartmouth.

Little, M., & Kelly, S. (1995). *A life without problems? The achievements of a therapeutic community*. Aldershot, UK: Arena.

Millham, S., Bullock, R., & Cherrett, P. (1975). *After Grace—teeth: A comparative study of the residential experience of approved school boys*. London: Human Context Books.

Parker, R. (1990). *Away from home: A history of child care*. Ilford, UK: Barnardos.

Rutter, M., Giller, M., & Hagell, A. (1998). *Antisocial behaviour by young people*. Cambridge, UK: Cambridge University Press.

Sheldrake, C. (1994). Treatment of delinquents. In Rutter, M., Taylor, E., & Hersov, L. (1994). *Child and adolescent psychiatry: Modern approaches* (pp. 968–982). Oxford, UK: Blackwell.

Sinclair, I. (1971). *Hostels for probationers*. London: HMSO.

Sinclair, I., & Gibbs, I. (1998). *Children's homes: A study in diversity*. Chichester, UK: Wiley.

Taylor, I., Walton, P., & Young, J. (1973). *The new criminology: For a theory of social deviance*. London: Routledge & Kegan Paul.

Triseliotis, J. (1992, September). *Key note address to conference on residential child care*. University of Glasgow, UK.

West, D. (1982). *Delinquency: Its roots, careers and prospects*. London: Heinemann.

Wolkind, S., & Rushton, A. (1994). Residential and family foster care. In Rutter, M., Taylor, E., & Hersov, L. (1994). *Child and adolescent psychiatry: Modern approaches* (pp. 252–266). Oxford, UK: Blackwell.

Chapter 36

Treatment in the Community

Gill McIvor
University of Stirling, Stirling, UK

INTRODUCTION

This chapter explores the effectiveness of community-based interventions with offenders. It is organized in three main sections: the first section describes the differing contexts in which community-based services and interventions may be delivered; the second section considers the advantages and disadvantages of intervention in the community; and the third section addresses the issue of effectiveness in the community context. Although increasing interest is being paid to the effectiveness of preventive efforts in domains such as the family, school, and community (see, for example, Sherman et al., 1997) the present concern is with those interventions aimed at reducing the risk, frequency, or seriousness of delinquent or criminal behaviour among known offenders.

WORKING WITH OFFENDERS IN THE COMMUNITY

The blanket term "treatment in the community" can be misleading since it implies a homogeneity of context and practice which does not, in reality, exist. Offenders may be under supervision in Britain, for example, at a variety of points in the criminal justice process, and the forms of supervision to which they are subject may vary considerably both in philosophy and in substance. Furthermore, even within Britain, organizational and legislative frameworks vary from country to country as do the particular forms of supervision which exist. In broad terms, however, it is possible to identify three distinct points in the criminal justice process at which offenders might be made subject to forms of supervision which are aimed directly or indirectly at addressing their risk of future offending: prior to prosecution; following conviction; and following release from a sentence of imprisonment.

Handbook of Offender Assessment and Treatment. Edited by C. R. Hollin.
© 2000 John Wiley & Sons Ltd.

Pre-prosecution Diversion

Since the 1970s a variety of measures have been introduced in Britain and North America with the explicit aim of diverting minor offenders from prosecution. Influenced strongly by labelling theory (see, for instance, Lilly, Cullen, & Ball, 1989; Schur, 1973) which emphasizes the potentially damaging consequences of criminal justice processing, mechanisms for pre-prosecution diversion—such as police cautioning in England and Wales—have frequently been developed with particular reference to younger offenders and predicated upon a philosophy of no or minimal intervention. In Scotland, however, which has a long-established tradition of independent prosecution (via the procurator fiscal) more formalized systems of pre-prosecution diversion have been developed. Although these developments have frequently been localized, they have included diversion to psychiatric (Duff & Burman, 1994) and psychological (Cooke, 1991, 1995) services; reparation and mediation (Warner, 1992); and diversion to social work and related services (Stedward & Millar, 1989).

To date research into diversion in Scotland has been largely descriptive, documenting the characteristics of cases referred to and accepted by the various programmes, the types of services provided, and the views of key stakeholders towards diversion as an alternative to prosecution. An exception is Cooke's (1991) comparative analysis of reconviction among accused persons diverted to psychological treatment and those considered for diversion but dealt with in other ways, which suggested that fewer of the former group were reconvicted. However, the number of accused persons in this study was relatively small and the two groups of accused persons are likely to have differed in other important respects. Further research into the effectiveness of intervention with minor offenders in the context of diversion from prosecution is clearly required, especially in view of the rather mixed findings from meta-analyses of diversion programmes in the United States (e.g. Gensheimer, Mayer, Gottschalk, & Davidson, 1986; Whitehead and Lab, 1989).

Community Sentences

Most statutory intervention with offenders in the community takes place under the auspices of community sentences (England and Wales) or community-based social work disposals (Scotland), with the probation order constituting the most common vehicle for work of this type. In both jurisdictions the courts can impose probation orders of between six months and three years upon offenders aged 16 years or over convicted in the adult courts and can attach an array of additional requirements to these orders to secure the co-operation of the offender in addressing the problems associated with his or her offending behaviour. In England and Wales, probation orders and other community sentences are supervised by probation officers, while in Scotland—where there is no separate probation service—offenders on supervision are the responsibility of the local authority social work departments. For a young person aged 17 or under in England and Wales an equivalent order called a supervision order may be set for periods up to three years, with the order supervised either by a probation officer or by a local authority social worker (for a more detailed exposition of the different forms of community supervision that offenders may be under, see McGuire, 1996).

Probation officers in England and Wales and social workers in Scotland are required to operate according to centrally developed national objectives and standards. In both jurisdictions the emphasis in probation practice has, accordingly, changed from a prior concern with gate-keeping and welfare issues to a more explicit focus upon addressing offending behaviour (Paterson & Tombs, 1998; Underdown, 1998). To this end the use of cognitive–behavioural methods by probation officers has increased dramatically in recent years. Burnett (1996), for example, found that around one-third of probation officers favoured a cognitive–behavioural approach in their work with offenders. By 1996, 39 of the 54 probation areas in England and Wales were running 191 intervention programmes which employed cognitive skills or cognitive–behavioural techniques, with general programmes more popular than those focusing upon a particular form of offending (Hedderman & Sugg, 1997). Half of these had been running for less than five years and a further quarter had been operational for less than a year.

Programmes which focused upon self-control (e.g. anger management) and sex offender interventions made the greatest use of cognitive skills training, while this was usually only one component of substance abuse and driving behaviour programmes. The predominance of groupwork as the preferred method of engaging with offenders was evident: almost two-thirds of programmes used groupwork only, one-third combined groupwork with individual sessions, and only four programmes relied upon one-to-one methods alone.

Just as the use of cognitive–behavioural approaches in general has increased rapidly in recent years, so too has there been a substantial growth in the availability of offence-specific programmes of intervention, with this being most apparent in the sex offender field. Barker and Morgan (1993), for example, identified 63 sex offender intervention programmes being run by 42 probation services in 1991, with 13 services having no such provision. By 1996, 109 probation-run programmes of this were in existence and only seven probation services had no provision of this type (Proctor & Flaxington, 1996).

There has also been a marked increase in partnership arrangements between the probation services and other service providers in England and Wales, a process that was formalized by the Home Office expectation (Home Office, 1990, 1992) that probation services would devote 5% of their budgets to the development of partnership projects involving other agencies (e.g. Cross, 1997; Smith, Paylor, & Mitchell, 1993). Hedderman and Sugg's (1997) review of the use of cognitive skills programmes by probation services revealed that 45% of programmes involved the participation of other agencies (most commonly alcohol or drugs workers, community theatre or arts workers, psychologists, and the police) while

29 of the 39 services providing programmes of this type made use of partnerships in just under half of the programmes they ran. Sex offender, driving behaviour, and substance misuse programmes were more likely than other types of programme to be run in partnership with other agencies. In Scotland, by contrast, the involvement of external agencies and individuals in the provision of services to offenders under supervision is not yet widespread and where it occurs is most likely to focus upon employment, substance misuse, and physical or mental health (McIvor & Barry, 1998a, 1998b).

Partnerships form an important element of community service, the other common form of supervision in the community, in which offenders aged 16 years and over are required to undertake between 40 and 240 (300 in Scotland) hours of unpaid work for the benefit of the community. Community service is not an expressly rehabilitative sanction—being first and foremost a fine on the offender's time—but it has long been postulated that the experience of carrying out work for individuals less fortunate than themselves might have a positive impact upon offenders' attitudes and behaviour (e.g. Carnie, 1991). Offenders may complete their community service orders alongside other offenders in supervised teams, in workshops or individually, in voluntary or statutory agencies where they are supervised by an agency member of staff. Research has revealed that the type of setting is less important than other qualities of the work experience. Offenders find community service more rewarding if it brings them into contact with the beneficiaries, if it enables them to acquire practical or interpersonal skills, and if it engages them in work that they can recognize as being of value to the recipients. It also appears that offenders whose experiences of community service are more rewarding are less frequently reconvicted and less likely to be reconvicted of property offences than offenders whose community service experiences are construed as less worthwhile (McIvor, 1992).

In broad terms, there is some evidence that the community supervision of offenders is at least as effective as imprisonment with respect to recidivism. For instance, in a study of probationers in Kent, Oldfield (1996) found that 40% of probationers were reconvicted after two years and 48% after five years in comparison with 49% and 63% of prisoners. The reconviction rate of probationers after five years compared favourably with a predicted rate of 56%, though the absence of a predicted rate at five years for prisoners prevents firm conclusions from being reached with respect to the relative effectiveness of these different disposals. Comparing predicted reconviction rates with actual reconviction rates (adjusted to take account of "pseudo-reconvictions") Lloyd, Mair, and Hough (1994) found that probation and community service produced adjusted rates that were slightly lower than predicted, while prison was associated with a rate of reconviction slightly higher than predicted.

If community disposals are, at the very least, no less effective than prison sentences in reducing offender risk, then there is ample evidence that the former are associated with significantly lower economic costs. For example, the Home Office estimated that in 1991/92 the average weekly cost of a custodial sentence was £1915 compared with £100 for a probation order and £95 for community service

(Home Office, 1993). More recent estimates of sentence costs in Scotland have suggested that a six-month prison sentence costs £13372 compared with £1700 for an average probation order and £1320 for community service (Scottish Office, 1998).

Post-release Supervision

The third broad context for community-based intervention with offenders is following release from a custodial sentence. Until relatively recently this was most likely to take the form of parole supervision, which requires active consent of the offender. Legislative changes throughout the United Kingdom have, however, resulted in an increased use of post-release supervision of a non-consensual nature. In England and Wales, for example, the 1991 Criminal Justice Act introduced a system of automatic conditional release for prisoners serving between one and four years and for those serving more than four years who do not qualify for parole. The former are released after serving half their sentences, are subject to active supervision for one-quarter of the sentence, and though not actively supervised are liable for return to prison if reconvicted of an imprisonable offence in the final quarter of the sentence. Long-term prisoners, on the other hand, are, unless granted parole, released after serving two-thirds of their sentence to be supervised by a probation officer in the community for the remaining third.

The Prisoners and Criminal Proceedings (Scotland) Act 1993 introduced a range of new measures for the post-release supervision of prisoners in Scotland. As in England and Wales a distinction is made between short- and long-terms prisoners, with the former (that is, those serving less than four years) normally eligible for unconditional release at the half-sentence point unless they have been made subject to a period of mandatory post-release supervision (a supervised release order) by the sentencing court. The spirit behind the supervised release order—which has similarities to the new custody probation orders in Northern Ireland—is to enable the courts to combine a short prison sentence with a period of post-release supervision for those offenders considered to present a risk of public harm, principally those convicted of violent and sexual offences (Scottish Office, 1996a, 1996b). Similar release arrangements apply in respect of long-term prisoners as pertain in England and Wales, with all long-term prisoners subject to supervision in the context of either a parole or a non-parole licence.

Post-release supervision is an area which has remained relatively under-researched, though the new arrangements in England and Wales were studied by Maguire, Peroud, and Raynor (1996) who have suggested that automatic conditional release—and the concept of throughcare more generally—is more obviously concerned with monitoring and practical resettlement than it is with ensuring the co-operation of offenders with rehabilitative programmes in the community. This was reflected, for instance, in probation managers' views that protecting the public and ensuring compliance with licence conditions were the most important objectives of supervision, with rehabilitative aims assuming considerably less importance. A primary focus of supervision for most probation officers was, accordingly, persuading offenders to comply with reporting requirements and providing practical assistance. A limited emphasis upon counselling and upon offenders' participation in groupwork programmes was attributed to the short licence periods involved, the lack of preparatory work in prisons, and the fact that ex-prisoners on automatic conditional release licences had not actively volunteered for probation assistance. Even so, most offenders expressed generally favourable views about post-release supervision, especially if they had had contact with their supervising officer prior to release. There was also some evidence in Maguire et al.'s (1996) study of positive changes in offenders' attitudes towards offending and towards the victims of offences, and some evidence that re-offending rates were lower than expected, though the data were acknowledged to have limitations.

The potential for tensions to arise in the context of post-release supervision was highlighted in McIvor and Barry's (1998b) study of community-based throughcare in Scotland. Here some conflict of opinion emerged between offenders and their supervising social workers with respect to the relative importance of offence-focused work and practical resettlement in the post-release period. Parolees in particular believed that social workers often placed undue emphasis upon addressing offending behaviour, at the expense of providing assistance of a more practical kind. For this reason, ex-prisoners were less likely than were probationers to express positive attitudes towards supervision (see also Ford, Pritchard, & Cox, 1997, and, with respect to short licence periods, Beaumont & Mistry, 1996) and, in comparison with probationers, the former were less often thought by their social workers to be less at risk of re-offending by the end of their period of supervision (McIvor and Barry, 1998a, 1998b).

THE ADVANTAGES AND DISADVANTAGES OF TREATMENT IN THE COMMUNITY

A key finding of recent meta-analyses of the offender treatment literature is that community-based interventions appear, in general, to be more effective than those delivered in prisons (Lipsey, 1992, 1995). One can as yet only speculate as to the reasons for the apparent superiority of community-based interventions. A possible explanation is that behavioural changes which are adaptive in the prison setting may have limited relevance to an individual's ability to sustain a law-abiding lifestyle on release. Ross and McKay (1978), for instance, concluded from a review of prison-based and community-based programmes that the former were ineffective with respect to reducing re-offending but were in some instances successful in achieving other objectives related to prisoner management.

It may also be the case that regardless of changes having been achieved in the prison setting, the environment to which prisoners return may exert a more powerful influence upon their attitudes and behaviour following release. Gendreau and Andrews (1990, p. 182), for example, have suggested that prison-based pro-grammes should be "structurally linked with community-based interventions where the strongest treatment effects have been found", though the British studies by Maguire et al. (1996) and McIvor and Barry (1998b) demonstrate that co-ordinated throughcare provision which promotes continuity is difficult to achieve.

By contrast, the primary advantage of community-based intervention lies in the opportunity it affords offenders to put into practice and rehearse in a real-life setting and with immediate effect skills that they have acquired. As we shall see, cognitive–behavioural methods of intervention, which have been derived from social learning theory and which promote the acquisition, applica-tion and rehearsal of cognitive skills, have been more consistently associated with positive behavioural outcomes than have other approaches aimed at preventing or reducing recidivism. McGuire (1996) has argued that realistic opportunities for learning and rehearsing skills are considerably more limited within a custo-dial setting which allows offenders to avoid accepting responsibility for their actions.

Working with offenders in the community offers a further advantage insofar as offenders are better able to maintain family and other social ties which might assist them in their endeavours to lead law-abiding lives. They also spend more time in the community interacting with non-offenders than they would do in prison (McGuire, 1996). The importance of supportive social networks has been highlighted by Haines (1990) in his review of the after-care literature: pro-grammes aimed at developing and strengthening positive community ties were found to be associated with reduced levels of recidivism. The juvenile offender decarceration experiment in Massachusetts in the 1970s (Coates, Miller, & Ohlin, 1978) further emphasized the significance of community networks. Here it was found that alternative community-based resources which had a higher number and higher quality of links with the local community also had lower levels of recidivism.

Although they may have actively consented to being placed under supervi-sion, offenders will vary significantly in terms of their motivation to engage with interventions aimed at effecting attitudinal and behavioural change (Maitland & Chapman, 1996). Furthermore, the potential effectiveness of community-based programmes may be undermined by strategies aimed at maintaining viable numbers for groupwork provision. Burnett (1996), for example, suggested that the offence types and offenders included in programmes being run by the pro-bation service were too diverse for their needs to be adequately addressed in a group setting and argued that greater attention should be focused on the criminogenic needs of individual offenders. A similar conclusion was reached by Hedderman and Sugg (1997, p. 51) who observed that "mixing offenders on parole with other subject to additional requirements and those attending volun-tarily may keep programme numbers high, but is unlikely to achieve programmes which are well-matched to the levels of risk, and criminogenic needs, of the offenders who attend".

THE EFFECTIVENESS OF INTERVENTION IN THE COMMUNITY

In stark contrast to the penal pessimism of the 1970s and 1980s, there is now a significant body of evidence that some interventions can have a positive impact upon recidivism with some offenders under some circumstances. Other approaches—such as unstructured, non-directive forms of counselling and therapy—appear at best to be ineffective or—in the case of approaches predicated more broadly upon punishment or deterrence—may even make offenders worse (Lipsey, 1992, 1995; Palmer, 1992, 1994). In addition to being community-based (as opposed to being implemented in a prison setting) it appears that more effective interventions target high-risk offenders, address criminogenic needs, employ cognitive–behavioural methods, and exhibit high levels of programme integrity (Hollin, 1995).

Support for these conclusions has been derived largely from a series of meta-analyses. For instance, Izzo and Ross's (1990) analysis of 46 juvenile offender studies found that programmes which incorporated a cognitive component were more than twice as effective as those that did not, with effective programmes targeting, in addition to cognition, behaviour and vocational or interpersonal skills. In their meta-analytic comparison of appropriate and inappropriate services, Andrews, Bonta, and Hoge (1990) reported that the former programmes had recidivism rates on average 53% lower than the latter. Appropriate services were defined as programmes which delivered more intensive treatment to higher risk offenders, targeted criminogenic needs associated with offending, and used cognitive or behavioural approaches. Inappropriate services, on the other hand, delivered treatment to low-risk offenders, failed to match the teaching styles of staff to offenders' learning styles, or used group approaches with no specific aims.

Antonowicz and Ross (1994) concluded that successful programmes were characterized by a sound conceptual model, a focus upon criminogenic needs, a responsiveness to offenders' learning styles (using the techniques of role-play and modelling), and the use of cognitive skills training. Lösel (1993, 1995) concluded from his review of meta-analyses that programmes that were cognitive–behavioural, skills-oriented, and multi-modal yielded the most encouraging results, while a similar conclusion was reached by Palmer (1994) who also drew attention to the comparative effectiveness of behavioural approaches with juvenile offenders.

McGuire (1996, p. 76) has argued that unstructured, non-directive approaches which are rooted in dynamic psychotherapies "may simply be inappropriate for the learning styles of individuals who are not mentally disordered, do not have intrapsychic problems but are beset by numerous everyday stressors. Neither in-depth analysis nor loosely formed group discussion will be seen by such individuals as relevant to their needs". McGuire's argument is consistent with the "responsivity principle" of supervision which recommends that services are delivered in such a way that the mode of delivery is consistent with the learning style of the offender. Andrews (1989, 1995) has further delineated the dimensions of supervision which appear to be associated with increased effectiveness. These include the firm but fair use of authority in such a way as to ensure that expectations are clearly conveyed and sanctions for non-compliance consistently enforced; the use of prosocial modelling and reinforcement in which positive alternative attitudes and behaviour are demonstrated and reinforced; concrete problem-solving in which obstacles to change are removed and the offender is equipped with the skills necessary to deal in future with problems in a more constructive way; advocacy and brokerage in which offenders are linked into a range of relevant services in the community; and relationships between offenders and their supervisors which are characterized by the latter adopting an open, enthusiastic, and caring approach.

Recent "consumer" studies of offenders under supervision identify the quality of relationships between offenders and supervisors as a crucial factor in motivating offenders towards change (Beaumont & Mistry, 1996; Mair & May, 1997; McIvor & Barry, 1998a; Rex, 1997). These studies have also highlighted the value offenders attach to receiving practical help or advice with respect to social or personal problems, while Rex (1997) draws attention additionally to the importance of prosocial modelling (see also Andrews & Keissling, 1980; Trotter, 1990, 1993), legitimacy, and active participation of the offender in the supervision process. These latter factors accord with Ross and McKay's (1978) earlier conclusion that successful community-based programmes were not imposed in an authoritarian fashion but instead involved offenders actively in the planning process.

Examples of more structured approaches in the United Kingdom include Deering, Thurston, and Vanstone's (1996) study of one-to-one probation supervision and the STOP programme in mid-Glamorgan. The latter employed the Reasoning and Rehabilitaion programme (Ross, Fabiano, & Ross, 1989) which aims to improve participants' cognitive skills. Early results from a comparison of actual and predicted reconviction rates for STOP participants and other groups of offenders given community sentences or custody were encouraging, with offenders who completed the STOP programme having significantly lower than expected reconviction rates after 12 months (Raynor & Vanstone, 1994). However, there was no significant difference between predicted and actual rates of reconviction at 24 months. Raynor and Vanstone (1996) have speculated that the lack of sustained impact of the STOP programme may have been partly attributable to probation officers failing systematically to address the other social and personal problems experienced by offenders on the programme.

McGuire et al. (1995) found in their evaluation of seven programmes delivered by the Greater Manchester Probation Service—in which only the drink-driving programme produced significant pre- and post-test differences on a range of measures—that there was an association between specific features of programmes and the outcomes achieved. They concluded that programmes delivered to high-risk offenders should be structured and directive and have clearly defined aims, and that offenders should be selected for programmes on the basis of offence type: in other words, offence-focused programmes may be more effective than programmes which address offending at a more generic level.

Positive outcomes have been reported in studies of community-based interventions focused upon specific types of offence behaviour, including violence/aggression (e.g. Leeman, Gibbs, & Fuller, 1993), domestic violence (Dobash, Dobash, Cavanagh, & Lewis, 1996), and sexual offending (e.g. Beckett, Beech, Fisher, & Fordham, 1994; Hedderman & Sugg, 1996; Marques, 1994). McGuire, Bloomfield, Robinson, and Rowson (1995) advocate the development of brief and focused offence-specific interventions to which, they argue, offenders with disorganized lifestyles may be better able to respond. Further support for the pursuit of specificity and diversity in provision comes from Coates et al. (1978) who found that areas that had developed a greater diversity of community-based options for young offenders produced lower recidivism rates than did areas in which resources were concentrated on one or two different types of programme.

There is, on the other hand, growing support from meta-analyses for the efficacy of multi-modal approaches—such as the STAC programme in Northern Ireland (Chapman & Maitland, 1995)—which draw upon a variety of methods to address a wide range of problems and needs. Vennard, Sugg, and Hedderman (1997) have highlighted Borduin et al.'s (1995) study of multi-systemic therapy as one specific example of a successful multi-modal approach which addresses the personal and social factors that are believed to be associated with delinquent behaviour among young people. Vennard et al. (1997, p. 21) concluded from their review of the use of cognitive–behavioural approaches with offenders that "the consistently strong effect of multi-modal combinations reported in several meta-analyses does suggest that there may be advantage, having assessed an offender's criminogenic needs, in seeking to address them within a single, integrated programme".

CONCLUSIONS

The supervision of offenders in the community is now underpinned by a more substantive, empirically informed knowledge base (see, for example, McGuire, 1995; Underdown, 1998). This, combined with a renewed sense of optimism in their ability to intervene to positive effect with offenders in the community, has enabled professionals such as probation officers to keep pace with a changing political agenda which places increased emphasis upon the inter-related issues of public protection and offender risk. A renewed interest in effectiveness has not, however, been matched by a widespread commitment to the evaluation of work with offenders in the community. As the recent probation inspectorate report illustrates, even in probation areas that have developed a range of intervention programmes which are broadly consistent with effectiveness principles, little or no attempt has usually been made to evaluate in a rigorous and systematic fashion the impact of the work (Underdown, 1998). Similar observations have been made by Barker and Morgan (1993) and Hedderman and Sugg (1997) in their surveys of probation practice.

As Mair (1993) has indicated, the development of programmes and initiatives by probation services is often a "bottom-up" process, driven by the interests and enthusiasm of practitioners rather than being the result of a strategic and co-ordinated approach to service development. Hedderman and Sugg (1997), for example, found that 44% of cognitive skills programmes run by probation services in England and Wales had been "championed" by a member of staff. Programmes of this kind are vulnerable, for a variety of reasons, if no attempt has been made to document their operation and impact. Echoing the respective calls by McIvor (1995) and Raynor (1996) for the development of a "culture of evaluation" and "culture of curiosity" in probation services, McGuire (1996, p. 86) has argued that "were evidence gathering and evaluation to become part of the culture of offender services, a habit as normal as doing the job itself, much more evidence would be available concerning effective interventions".

More research activity also needs to be directed towards the evaluation of mainstream probation work. As Raynor (1995) has pointed out, the majority of evaluative research in probation has concentrated on innovative or specialist projects. Whilst research of this kind has made a significant contribution to our understanding of which approaches to working with offenders in the community might be more likely to yield positive results, the projects concerned do not typify the majority of probation practice. Findings derived from specialist programmes consequently shed little light on what might realistically be achieved through the mainstream supervision of offenders in the community and in the absence of the high levels of enthusiasm and commitment and the more generous staffing ratios which often characterize "special" projects.

Whilst agreeing that recent meta-analyses have been of value in directing attention towards more promising approaches, Vennard et al. (1997, p. 27) concluded that important questions remained unanswered by these studies such as "the relative importance of the different components of programmes which appear to be effective, the criteria for assessing need and the theories which should guide the process of matching offender to programme content and mode of delivery". The concept of responsivity is also worthy of further exploration since much of what we know about the effectiveness of interventions with offenders in the community—or in prison for that matter—has been based upon programmes delivered to young white males.

There is good reason to be more optimistic than we were a decade ago about the potential to intervene effectively with offenders in the community. This optimism needs, however, to be tempered by the recognition that our understanding of what works in reducing re-offending is still relatively embryonic. An ongoing, and indeed increased, commitment to research and evaluation is required to further strengthen and refine the knowledge base which informs the development of interventions that can improve community safety and promote the inclusion of offenders in society.

REFERENCES

Andrews, D. A. (1989). Recidivism is predictable and can be influenced: Using risk assessments to reduce recidivism. *Forum on Corrections Research Volume 1, 2.* Canada: Correctional Service.

Andrews, D. A. (1995). The psychology of criminal conduct and effective treatment. In J. McGuire (Ed.), *What works: Reducing reoffending—guidelines from research and practice* (pp. 35–62), Chichester, UK: Wiley.

Andrews, D. A., Bonta, J., & Hoge, R. D. (1990). Classification for effective rehabilitation: Rediscovering psychology. *Criminal Justice and Behavior, 17*(1), 19–52.

Andrews, D. A., & Keissling, J. J. (1980). Program structure and effective correctional practices: A summary of the CaVIC research. In R. R. Ross & P. Gendreau (Eds.), *Effective correctional treatment* (pp. 441–463). Toronto, Canada: Butterworths.

Antonowicz, D., & Ross, R. R. (1994). Essential components of successful rehabilitation programs for offenders. *International Journal of Offender Therapy and Comparative Criminology, 38,* 97–104.

Barker, M., & Morgan, R. (1993). *Sex offenders: A framework for the evaluation of community-based treatment.* London: Home Office.

Beaumont, B., & Mistry, T. (1996). Doing a good job under duress. *Probation Journal, 43*(4), 200–204.

Beckett, R., Beech, A., Fisher, D., & Fordham, A. S. (1994). *Community-based treatment for sex offenders: An evaluation of seven treatment programmes.* London: Home Office.

Borduin, C. M., Mann, B. J., Cone, L. T., Henggler, S. W., Fucci, B. R., Blaske, D. M., & Williams, R. A. (1995). Multisystemic treatment of serious juvenile offenders: Long-term prevention of criminality and violence. *Journal of Consulting and Clinical Psychology, 63*(4) 569–578.

Burnett, R. (1996). *Fitting offenders to supervision: Assessment and allocation decisions in the probation service* (Home Office Research Study 153). London: Home Office.

Carnie, J. (1991). *Sentencers' perceptions of community service by offenders.* Edinburgh, UK: Scottish Office Central Research Unit.

Chapman, T., & Maitland, A. (1995). *Stop, think and change: An integrated and progressive programme of change for high risk offenders.* Belfast, UK: Probation Board for Northern Ireland.

Coates, R. B., Miller, A. D., & Ohlin, L. E. (1978). *Diversity in a youth correctional system.* Cambridge, MA: Ballinger.

Cooke, D. J. (1991). *Treatment as an alternative to prosecution volume one: Diversion to the Douglas Inch Centre.* Edinburgh, UK: Scottish Office Central Research Unit.

Cooke, D. (1995). Diversion from prosecution: A Scottish experience. In J. McGuire (Ed.), *What works: Reducing reoffending—guidelines from research and practice* (pp. 173–192). Chichester, UK: Wiley.

Cross, B. (1997). Partnership in practice: The experience of two probation services. *The Howard Journal, 36,* 62–79.

Deering, J., Thurston, R., & Vanstone, M. (1996). Individual supervision and reconviction: An experimental programme in Pontypridd. *Probation Journal, 43*(2), 70–76.

Dobash, R., Dobash, R. E., Cavanagh, K., & Lewis, R. (1996). *Research evaluation of programmes for violent men.* Edinburgh, UK: Scottish Office Central Research Unit.

Duff, P., & Burman, M. (1994). *Diversion from prosecution to psychiatric care.* Edinburgh, UK: Scottish Office Central Research Unit.

Ford, P., Pritchard, C., & Cox, M. (1997). Consumer opinions of the probation service: Advice, assistance, befriending and the reduction of crime. *The Howard Journal, 36*(1), 42–61.

Gendreau, P., & Andrews, D. A. (1990). Tertiary prevention: What the meta-analyses of the offender treatment literature tell us about "what works". *Canadian Journal of Criminology, 32*(1), 173–184.

Gensheimer, L. K., Mayer, J. P., Gottschalk, R., & Davidson, W. S. (1986). Diverting youth from the juvenile justice system: A meta-analysis of intervention efficacy. In S. J. Apter & A. P. Goldstein (Eds.), *Youth violence: Program and prospects* (pp. 39–57). Oxford, UK: Pergamon Press.

Haines, K. (1990). *After-care services for released prisoners: A review of the literature.* Cambridge, UK: University of Cambridge Institute of Criminology.

Hedderman, C., & Sugg, D. (1996). *Does treating sex offenders reduce offending?* (Research Findings No. 45). London: Home Office Research and Statistics Directorate.

Hedderman, C., & Sugg, D. (1997). The influence of cognitive approaches: A survey of probation programmes. In J. Vennard, D. Sugg, & C. Hedderman (Eds.), *Changing offenders' attitudes and behaviour: What works?* (pp. 39–60) (Home Office Research Study 171). London: Home Office.

Hollin, C. R. (1995). The meaning and implications of "programme integrity". In J. McGuire (Ed.), *What works: Reducing reoffending—guidelines from research and practice* (pp. 195–208). Chichester, UK: Wiley.

Home Office (1990). *Partnership in dealing with offenders in the community.* London: HMSO.

Home Office (1992). *Partnership in dealing with offenders in the community.* London: HMSO.

Home Office (1993). *Information on the criminal justice system in England and Wales.* London: Home Office Research and Statistics Department.

Izzo, R. L., & Ross, R. R. (1990). Meta-analysis of rehabilitation programs for juvenile delinquents. *Criminal Justice and Behavior, 17*(1), 134–142.

Leeman, L. W., Gibbs, J. C., & Fuller, D. (1993). Evaluation of a multi-component group treatment programme for juvenile delinquents. *Aggressive Behavior, 19*, 281–292.

Lilly, J. R., Cullen, F. T., & Ball, R. A. (1989). *Criminological theory: Context and consequences.* Newbury Park, CA: Sage.

Lipsey, M. (1992). Juvenile delinquency treatment: A meta-analytic enquiry into variability of effects. In T. D. Cook, H. Cooper, D. S. Cordray, H. Hartmann, L. V. Hedges, R. L. Light, T. A. Louis, & F. Mosteller (Eds.), *Meta-analysis for explanation* (pp. 83–127). New York: Russell Sage Foundation.

Lipsey, M. (1995). What do we learn from 400 research studies on the effectiveness of treatment with juvenile delinquents? In J. McGuire (Ed.), *What works: Reducing reoffending—guidelines from research and practice* (pp. 63–78). Chichester, UK: Wiley.

Lloyd, C., Mair, G., & Hough, M. (1994). *Explaining reconviction rates: A critical analysis* (Home Office Research Study 136). London: HMSO.

Lösel, F. (1993). The effectiveness of treatment in institutional and community settings. *Criminal Behaviour and Mental Health, 3*, 416–437.

Lösel, F. (1995). The efficacy of correctional treatment: A review and synthesis of meta-evaluations. In J. McGuire (Ed.), *What works: Reducing reoffending—guidelines from research and practice* (pp. 79–111). Chichester, UK: Wiley.

Maguire, M., Peroud, B., & Raynor, P. (1996). *Automatic conditional release: The first two years* (Home Office Research Study 156). London: Home Office.

Mair, G. (1993). *Specialist activities in probation: Confusion worse confounded?* Paper presented at the British Criminology Conference, University of Wales, Cardiff, UK.

Mair, G., & May, C. (1997). *Offenders on probation* (Home Office Research Study 167). London: Home Office.

Maitland, A., & Chapman, T. (1996). Learning to change: A motivational model for adults learning cognitive skills. In B. Rowson & J. McGuire (Eds.), *What works: Making it happen* (pp. 40–45). Manchester, UK: What Works Group.

Marques, J. (1994). Effects of cognitive–behavioural treatment on sex offender recidivism: Preliminary results of a longitudinal study. *Criminal Justice and Behavior, 21*, 28–54.

McGuire, J. (Ed.) (1995). *What works: Reducing reoffending—guidelines from research and practice.* Chichester, UK: Wiley.

McGuire, J. (1996). Community-based interventions. In C. R. Hollin (Ed.), *Working with offenders: Psychological practice in offender rehabilitation* (pp. 63–93). Chichester, UK: Wiley.

McGuire, J., Bloomfield, D., Robinson, C., & Rowson, B. (1995). Short-term effects of probation programs: An evaluative study. *International Journal of Offender Therapy and Comparative Criminology, 39*(1), 23–42.

McIvor, G. (1992). *Sentenced to serve: The operation and impact of community service by offenders.* Aldershot, UK: Avebury.

McIvor, G. (1995). Practitioner evaluation in probation. In J. McGuire (Ed.), *What works: Reducing reoffending—guidelines from research and practice* (pp. 209–219). Chichester, UK: Wiley.

McIvor, G., & Barry, M. (1998a). *Social work and criminal justice Volume 6: Probation.* Edinburgh, UK: The Stationery Office.

McIvor, G., & Barry, M. (1998b). *Social work and criminal justice Volume 7: Community-based throughcare.* Edinburgh, UK: The Stationery Office.

Oldfield, M. (1996). *The Kent reconviction survey: A 5 year survey of reconvictions amongst offenders made subject to probation orders in Kent in 1991.* Maidstone, UK: Kent Probation Service.

Palmer, T. (1992). *The re-emergence of correctional intervention.* Newbury Park, CA: Sage.

Palmer, T. (1994). *A profile of correctional effectiveness and new directions for research.* Albany, NY: State University of New York.

Paterson, F., & Tombs, J. (1998). *Social work and criminal justice Volume 1: The impact of policy.* Edinburgh, UK: The Stationery Office.

Proctor, E., & Flaxington, F. (1996). *Community-based interventions with sex offenders organised by the probation service.* London: Association of Chief Officers of Probation.

Raynor, P. (1995). Effectiveness now: A personal and selective overview. In G. McIvor (Ed.), *Working with offenders: Research highlights in social work 26* (pp. 182–193). London: Jessica Kingsley.

Raynor, P. (1996). Evaluating probation: The rehabilitation of effectiveness. In T. May & A. A. Vass (Eds.), *Working with offenders: Issues, contexts and outcomes* (pp. 242–258). London: Sage.

Raynor, P., & Vanstone, M. (1994). *Straight thinking on probation: Third interim report.* Bridgend, UK: Mid Glamorgan Probation Service.

Raynor, P., & Vanstone, M. (1996). Reasoning and rehabilitation in Britain: The results of the straight thinking on probation (STOP) programme. *International Journal of Offender Therapy and Comparative Criminology, 40*(4), 272–284.

Rex, S. (1997). *Desistance from offending: Experiences of probation.* Paper presented at the British Criminology Conference, The Queen's University Belfast, UK.

Ross, R. R., Fabiano, E. A., & Ross, B. (1989). *Reasoning and rehabilitation: A handbook for teaching cognitive skills.* Ottawa, Canada: The Cognitive Centre.

Ross, R. R., & McKay, H. B. (1978). Behavioral approaches to treatment in corrections: Requiem for a panacea. *Canadian Journal of Criminology, 20*, 279–295.

Schur, E. (1973). *Radical non-intervention: Rethinking the delinquency problem.* Englewood Cliffs, NJ: Prentice-Hall.

Scottish Office (1996a). *Making the punishment fit the crime.* Edinburgh, UK: Scottish Office Home Department.

Scottish Office (1996b). *Crime and punishment* (Cm 3302). Edinburgh, UK: HMSO.

Scottish Office (1998). *Costs, sentencing profiles and the Scottish criminal justice system 1996.* Edinburgh, UK: The Scottish Office.

Sherman, L., Gottfredson, D., MacKenzie, D., Eck, J., Reuter, P., & Bushway, S. (1997). *Preventing crime: What works, what doesn't, what's promising* (Report to the US Congress). Washington DC: National Institute of Justice.

Smith, D., Paylor, I., & Mitchell, P. (1993). Partnerships between the probation service and the independent sector. *The Howard Journal, 32*, 25–39.

Stedward, G. and Millar, A. (1989). *Diversion from prosecution Volume One: Diversion to social work*. Edinburgh, UK: Scottish Office Central Research Unit.

Trotter, C. (1990). Probation can work: A research study using volunteers. *Australian Social Work, 43*, 13–18.

Trotter, C. (1993). *The supervision of offenders: What works*. Melbourne, Australia: Victoria Office of Corrections.

Underdown, A. (1998). *Strategies for effective offender supervision: Report of the HMIP what works project*. London: Home Office.

Vennard, J., Sugg, D., & Hedderman, C. (1997). The use of cognitive–behavioural approaches with offenders: Messages from the research. In J. Vennard, D. Sugg, & C. Hedderman (Eds.), *Changing offenders' attitudes and behaviour: What works?* (pp. 1–35) (Home Office Research Study 171). London: Home Office.

Warner, S. (1992). *Making amends: Justice for victims and offenders*. Aldershot, UK: Avebury.

Whitehead, J. T., & Lab, S. P. (1989). A meta-analysis of juvenile correctional treatment. *Journal of Research in Crime and Delinquency, 26*, 276–295.

Author Index

Abbott, R.   244
Abel, G.G.   103, 335, 338, 365, 517
Aber, J.L.   60
Abidin, R.   58
Abney, V.D.   216
Abrams, D.B.   394, 488, 490
Achille, P.A.   103
Adams, D.   380, 382
Adams, G.R.   273, 277
Adams, H.E.   103
Addad, M.   462
Adler, R.G.   401, 403
Agee, V.L.   260, 262
Ageton, S.S.   484
Ahlstrom, W.   242, 249, 254
Ahmadi, S.   474
Aichhorn, A.   7, 314
Ainsworth, M.   324
Akers, R.L.   6, 140, 141, 142
Akhtar, N.   270, 271
Alexander, F.   6, 314
Alexander, J.F.   206, 208, 209
Allen, J.P.   60
Allen, J.V.   529
Allport, G.W.   112
Allsop, S.   488
Alper, J.S.   8
Alterman, A.I.   447
Amdur, R.   225
American Psychiatric Association   79,
    118, 393, 468, 470
Ammerman, R.T.   284, 401
Amos, N.L.   102
Anastasi, A.   114, 117
Anderson, D.   302, 337, 343
Anderson, J.   5, 316

Anderson, N.W.   358
Andersson, T.   483
Andrews, D.A.   10, 18, 20, 21, 22, 23, 28,
    30, 88, 101, 131, 174, 184, 187, 196,
    201, 424, 426, 474, 498, 499, 557, 558,
    559
Andrews, D.W.   249
Andrews, H.   435
Angelique, H.L.   233
Anglin, M.D.   163
Anguera, T.   10
Annis, H.M.   490
Ansevics, N.L.   514, 515, 517
Antonowicz, D.H.   10, 18, 21, 23, 276, 277,
    500, 558
Apfel, H.   246
Applegate, B.K.   197–198, 202, 423
Arbiter, N.   159, 163
Arbuthnot, J.   209, 241, 248, 253
Archer, M.A.   261
Argyle, M.   269, 270
Armstrong, J.   90, 339
Arthur, M.W.   485
Association for the Treatment of Sexual
    Abusers   99, 363, 364
Atwood, R.O.   261
Aubut, J.   102
Augimeri, L.   81
Aust, A.   501
Austin, J.   38, 190, 221
Austin, S.   270
Averbeck, M.   28
Avery-Clark, C.A.   103
Ayllon, T.   140, 146, 147
Azar, S.T.   55, 56, 58, 64, 65
Azrin, N.   146

Babiker, G.   59, 60
Bachorowski, J.   484
Backer, T.E.   533
Bailey, J.   469, 514, 515, 531
Bailey, W.C.   17
Baird, C.   200
Baker, S.L.   150
Baldwin, S.   66, 416, 482
Ball, R.A.   552
Balleweg, B.J.   285
Bamford, T.   538
Bandura, A.   5, 6, 88, 282
Barbaree, H.E.   99, 100, 101, 102, 103,
    104, 105, 272, 275, 301, 336, 338, 339,
    343, 350, 351, 352, 354, 358, 359, 366,
    368, 369
Barker, M.   553, 561
Barker, W.   55
Barlow, D.H.   100, 103, 338
Barnes, H.V.   7, 252
Barnett, L.W.   298
Barratt, E.S.   132, 418, 484
Barrera, F.   143, 144
Barrett, S.   334
Barriga, A.Q.   262, 264, 423
Barry, M.   554, 556, 557, 559
Barton, K.   208, 209
Barton, R.   540
Bass, D.   216
Basta, J.M.   18
Bauer, R.   189
Baxter, D.J.   338, 352
Beail, N.   463
Beal, L.S.   90, 339
Beardslee, W.R.   391
Beaumont, B.   556, 559
Beck, A.T.   475, 487, 488, 489
Beck, S.   335, 338
Becker, J.V.   103, 364, 365, 370, 371, 372,
    373
Becker, M.   527
Becker, R.E.   490
Beckett, R.C.   129–130, 560
Beckner, B.M.   287
Bednar, R.L.   144
Beech, A.   368, 560
Behrnes, S.   426
Belfrage, H.   79
Bellfield, H.   485
Belsky, J.   64, 66, 67
Benezech, M.   462
Bengit, C.L.   58
Benjamin, L.S.   471
Bennett, L.W.   383

Bennett, T.   497
Benson, B.   459
Benson, M.   381
Bentovim, A.   55, 59, 65, 66, 366, 369
Berkey, M.L.   395, 398
Berkowitz, L.   283
Berman, E.   317
Bersani, C.   383
Bersoff, D.N.   202
Beutler, L.E.   216
Bhate, S.R.   368
Bibel, D.   421
Bickford, M.E.   77
Bigelow, D.A.   446
Bion, W.R.   314, 318
Bis, J.S.   147
Bishop, D.S.   66
Bixby, F.L.   260
Bjørkly, S.   442
Black, D.A.   531
Black, E.L.   101
Black, L.   285, 291, 528
Blackburn, R.   6, 18, 21, 119, 283, 423,
    438, 473, 476, 498, 510, 524, 525, 526,
    529, 530
Blackshaw, L.   86, 302, 343, 350
Blader, J.C.   99, 102
Blakely, C.H.   196, 197, 226
Blanc, M. Le see Le Blanc, M.
Blanchard, E.B.   103, 338
Blanchard, J.V.   517
Blanchard, R.   101
Bland, R.   132
Blaske, D.M.   213
Blehar, M.   324
Bloom, J.D.   446
Bloomfield, D.   560
Blum, N.   471
Boddis, S.   29, 286
Boer, D.P.   79, 91
Bogart, L.M.   439
Bolton, D.   310
Bonge, D.   382
Bonta, J.   10, 22, 23, 86, 87, 88, 92, 124,
    126, 131, 187, 196, 197, 201, 424, 499,
    558
Booth, C.   207
Borduin, C.M.   205, 206, 212, 213, 214,
    560
Boren, J.J.   150
Bornstein, P.H.   285
Borum, R.   79, 284, 436
Borzecki, M.   338
Bottomley, A.   124

Bottomley, K.   3
Bottoms, A.E.   500, 546
Boucher, R.J.   335
Boulerice, B.   237
Bourgeois, M.   462
Bourque, B.B.   405
Bowers, W.   471
Bowlby, J.   6, 315, 324
Bradford, J.M.W.   338, 339, 342
Bradley, E.J.   270, 271
Bradlyn, A.S.   98
Branch, L.G.   298
Brassard, M.R.   62
Breakwell, G.M.   129
Brekke, J.S.   439
Brendtro, L.K.   260, 261
Brennan, P.A.   99
Breton, S.J.   55, 64, 65
Bricourt, J.   440
Bridgeland, M.   539
Brier, N.   456
Briere, J.   355
Briggs, D.   156
Brix, R.J.   401
Bromley, D.L.   439, 445–446
Brondino, M.J.   213, 214, 424
Bronfenbrenner, U.   212
Bronner, A.F.   6
Brook, L. Raven- *see* Raven-Brook, L.
Brown, E.   544
Brown, E.J.   364
Brown, G.D.   143
Brown, S.   421, 423, 424
Brown, S.A.   488
Brown, S.L.   201
Browne, K.D.   55, 56, 57–58, 65, 423, 424
Brunk, M.   213
Bry, B.H.   242, 250, 253, 254
Bryant, K.J.   442
Bryce, M.E.   207
Bryce, P.   340, 341, 357
Buchanan, B.D.   266
Buchsbaum, K.   270
Buck, S.A.   502
Buckley, M.C.   446
Bullock, R.   538, 542, 543, 544, 545, 546,
    547
Bumby, K.M.   90, 336, 338
Bumpass, E.R.   401, 406
Burchard, J.D.   143, 144
Burgess, A.W.   339, 511, 515, 516
Burgess, R.L.   141
Burkhead, M.   201
Burman, M.   552

Burnett, R.   553, 557
Burns, N.   383
Burrow, S.   524, 528
Burt, C.   8
Burt, M.   336, 338
Burton, K.   513
Bush, J.   423, 425
Buss, A.   283, 419
Bussière, M.T.   85, 86, 87, 88, 90, 91, 92,
    104, 358
Butzin, C.F.   155
Byrne, J.M.   200

Cadsky, O.   87, 88
Cahn, T.S.   283
Camacho, L.M.   155
Campbell, A.   421
Campbell, C.   403
Campbell, D.T.   385
Campbell, F.A.   241, 245, 246, 252, 254
Campbell, H.   102
Capaldi, D.M.   416
Card, R.D.   100, 101
Carducci, D.J.   262, 266
Carducci, J.B.   266
Carey, G.   471
Carlisle, J.M.   340
Carlson, V.   60
Carlyle, J.   323
Carnie, J.   554
Carrigan, W.F.   88, 101
Carroll, J.   498
Carroll, K.M.   490
Cartor, R.   125
Casanova, G.M.   98
Casey, L.R.   502
Caspi, A.   54
Castonguay, L.G.   102
Catalano, R.F.   244, 483, 490
Cattell, R.R.   5
Cavanagh-Johnson, T.   363
Cavanagh, K.   380, 383, 560
Cavanaugh, J.L.   101
Ceccaldi, S.   462
Cella, D.F.   391
Cellini, H.R.   340, 371
Center for Substance Abuse Treatment
    38, 44
Champagne, F.   337, 340, 357
Champion, H.   475, 530
Chan, L.K.S.   270–271
Chaney, E.F.   490
Chaplin, E.H.   401, 462
Chaplin, F.C.   88

Chaplin, T.C.   100, 101, 102, 103, 338
Chapman, T.   503, 557, 560
Chatham, L.R.   155
Chawky, N.   441
Check, J.V.   336
Checkley, K.L.   101
Chein, D.   386
Chemtob, C.M.   286, 288
Chen, H.J.   383
Chermack, S.T.   484
Cherrett, P.   545
Chiesa, J.   36–37
Childress, A.R.   488
Chipchase, H.   528
Choate, P.A.   439, 445–446
Christiansen, B.A.   488
Christie, M.M.   340
Christophe, D.   101
Christophersen, E.   502
Cicchetti, D.   60, 62
Clackamas County Juvenile Firesetting
    Intervention Network   403
Clare, I.C.H.   120, 401, 454, 462
Clark, C.A. Avery- see Avery-Clark, C.A.
Clark, T.F.   364
Clarke, D.J.   460
Clarke, R.V.G.   7, 10, 497, 546
Clarke, S.H.   241, 245, 252, 254
Clausen, A.E.I.   62
Cleckley, H.   77, 79, 314, 316, 472
Cleland, C.M.   10, 175, 184
Clements, C.B.   145, 146
Coates, R.B.   546, 557, 560
Cocozza, J.J.   71, 72
Cohen, A.K.   9
Cohen, F.   439
Cohen, H.L.   147
Cohen, J.   18, 239
Cohen, L.E.   496, 497
Cohen, M.A.   37, 38, 39
Coid, J.W.   316, 470, 530
Coie, J.D.   252
Cole, C.L.   463
Cole, P.G.   270–271
Cole, P.M.   349, 355
Cole, R.E.   391, 393, 395, 401
Coleman, C.   3
Collins, S.   456
Colman, A.D.   150
Colwell, J. Kear- see Kear-Colwell, J.
Conduct Problems Prevention Research
    Group   252
Conte, J.R.   59
Convit, A.   73, 127

Cooke, D.J.   19, 27, 28, 472, 552
Cooney, N.L.   490
Cooper, B.   498
Cooper, H.M.   205
Copas, J.   474
Copello, A.G.   417
Cordess, C.   7, 314, 315, 316, 318
Corenthal, C.   471
Cormier, C.A.   23, 75, 77, 86, 128, 474,
    532
Cornell, D.G.   422
Cornish, D.B.   7, 10, 546
Corrado, R.R.   439, 440
Corre, N.   120
Correctional Service of Canada   416, 417,
    427
Corsini, R.J.   29
Cortoni, F.   91
Coryell, W.   434
Costa, P.T.   469
Côté, G.   435, 438, 441
Côtè, M.   102, 103
Coutts, J.   102
Cox, B.   368
Cox, D.   77, 79, 401, 462
Cox, D.N.   440
Cox, M.   7, 313, 315, 317–318, 529, 556
Cox-Jones, C.   401
Cox-Lindenbaum, D.   461
Crawford, D.A.   529
Crawford, M.   87
Crellin, M.C.   526
Crick, N.R.   6, 270, 271
Crittenden, P.M.   62
Cronin, R.C.   405
Cross, B.   553
Cross, G.   503
Crouch, J.L.   213
Cullen, C.   463
Cullen, E.   157, 158, 317
Cullen, F.T.   9, 197, 202, 422, 423, 435, 552
Culver, K.W.   392, 393
Cumming, G.F.   298, 342
Cunliffe, T.   269
Cunningham, P.B.   206
Cunningham-Rathner, J.   335, 364
Curle, C.   524
Cutler, C.A.   55
Cutrona, C.A.   336
Cyr, M.   285, 445, 524, 526

Dacre, A.J.I.   462
Dadds, M.R.   336
Dakof, G.A.   206, 212

Daley, D.C.   297
Daly, A.   287
Dangel, R.F.   286, 287
Daniel, J.H.   55
Darkes, J.   487
Davidson, K.M.   476
Davidson, P.R.   103
Davidson, W.S.   10, 18, 24, 28, 196, 197,
    221–222, 224, 225, 226, 228, 229, 230,
    231, 232, 233, 552
Davies, H.   503
Davies, J.B.   482
Davis, G.   364
Davis, J.   366
Davis, M.H.   419
Davis, S.   442
Dawson, K.   29, 286
Day, B.T.   392
Day, D.M.   101, 342, 358
Day, K.   453, 454, 456, 458, 459, 460, 461,
    462, 463, 464
De Leon, G.   155, 159, 160, 163, 165
de Zulueta, F. see Zulueta, F. de
Dean, J.   55
Dean, K.   90
DeBono, E.   182
DeBurger, J.   510, 511, 512, 513
Deering, J.   559
Deisher, R.W.   364, 365
Delaney, J.   161
Dell, S.   158, 322–323, 525
Deluty, R.H.   284
Demorest, A.P.   271
Dempster, R.J.   422
Denton, R.   383
Department of Health and Social Security
    54
der Kolk, B.A. van see van der Kolk, B.A.
DeRisi, W.M.   147
Derogatis, L.R.   474
DeSalvatore, G.   399, 401
Deschner, J.P.   286
Descutner, C.   336
Dhaliwal, G.K.   500
Diamond, G.   206
Dibble, A.   101
DiClemente, C.C.   486
Dietz, P.E.   510, 511
Dijk, J.J.M. van see van Dijk, J.J.M.
Dinitz, S.   242, 249
Dishion, T.J.   237, 238, 249
Dixon, B.G.   426
Dobash, R.E.   128, 379, 380–381, 382, 383,
    560

Dobash, R.P.   128, 379, 380–381, 382, 383,
    384, 385, 386, 560
Dodge, K.A.   6–7, 180, 205, 270, 271, 417,
    484
Doherty, D.   439
Dolan, B.M.   316, 321, 323, 470, 474
Dollard, N.   439
Domanic, J.   98
Donahoe, C.P.   270
Donenberg, G.R.   216
Donnellan, A.M.   463
d'Orban, P.T.   463
Doren, D.M.   509
Doueck, H.J.   239
Dougher, M.J.   368, 488
Douglas, J.E.   511, 515
Douglas, K.S.   78, 79, 131
Doweiko, H.E.   514, 515, 517
Downes, D.   9
Downs, W.R.   355
Draine, J.   440
Drake, R.E.   447
Dubey, D.R.   286
Duff, P.   552
Durkee, A.   283, 419
Durlak, J.A.   237
Dutton, D.G.   383, 385
Dvoskin, J.A.   439
D'Zurilla, T.J.   489

Earls, C.M.   100, 342, 351
Earls, F.   238
Eaves, D.   78, 79, 131, 439, 440
Eccles, A.   102, 340, 354, 366, 369
Ecton, R.B.   286
Edleson, J.L.   383, 385
Edwards, D.   502
Egan, V.   474
Egeland, B.   62
Egger, S.A.   510, 511
Eisikovits, Z.   383
Eisler, R.M.   400
Ekblom, P.   498
Elias, A.   260
Ellenberger, H.   314
Elliott, D.S.   205, 484
Elliott, E.J.   403
Ellsworth, P.D.   150
Elrod, H.P.   272, 273
Elzen, C.J.M. Van see Van Elzen, C.J.M.
Emmelkamp, P.M.G.   471
Emshoff, J.   197, 226
Ennis, B.J.   72
Entwistle, S.R.   216

Epperson, D.L.   92
Epps, K.   11, 546
Epstein, N.B.   66
Erikson, E.   62
Eron, L.D.   80, 238, 316
Eronen, M.   436
Erwin, B.J.   197
Esteban, C.   472
Etchegoyen, R.H.   318
Evans, C.   323
Evans, J.H.   140
Evans, J.M. Lee- *see* Lee-Evans, J.M.
Everingham, S.S.   37
Ewles, C.D.   179, 197
Eysenck, H.J.   5, 6, 119, 140, 142, 418
Eysenck, S.B.G.   119, 418

Fabiano, E.A.   6, 7, 21, 179, 180, 184, 185,
   186, 197, 271, 425, 497, 559
Fagelman, F.D.   401
Fairbank, J.A.   98
Fairweather, G.W.   224
Falkin, G.P.   155, 168, 169, 170
Farmer, E.   61
Farmer, R.   297, 490
Farrall, W.   99
Farrell, A.D.   239, 240, 245
Farrington, D.P.   7, 80, 237, 238, 416, 422,
   483, 484, 485, 498, 500
Farrow, F.   207
Fassbender, L.L.   463
Faust, J.   399
Federal Emergency Management Agency
   395, 396, 399, 405
Federoff, J.P.   342
Fehrenback, P.A.   364–365
Feindler, E.L.   284, 285, 286
Feldman, L.H.   208
Felson, M.   496, 497
Felson, R.B.   435, 437
Fernandez, Y.M.   336, 337, 340, 341, 355,
   366, 419
Ferrara, M.L.   260
Ferraro, M.H.   55, 64, 65
Field, E.   540
Field, G.   155, 162, 170
Field, S.   496
Filipczak, J.A.   147, 242, 250, 253
Finkelhor, D.   58, 365
Fiquera-McDonough, J.   238
First, M.B.   471
Fischer, S.A.   434
Fisher, B.S.   202
Fisher, D.   560

Fishman, H.C.   206, 210
Fiske, A.   88
Fitzharding, S.   287
Flanagan, B.   103
Flanagan, T.J.   364
Flaxington, F.   553
Flynn, J.R.   116
Fonagy, P.   310, 323, 324
Foote, E.   211
Ford, P.   556
Fordham, A.S.   368, 560
Forrester, D.   498
Forth, A.E.   77
Foster, H.G.   440
Fowler, D.   527
Fox, J.A.   510, 513, 515
Frame, C.L.   180
France, K.G.   369
Fraser, M.W.   207, 208
Freedman, B.J.   270
Freeman, A.   475, 487
Freeman-Longo, R.   299
French, M.T.   38, 44, 47
Frenz, S.   498
Frenzel, R.R.   101
Freud, S.   5, 314
Freund, K.   90, 91, 100, 101, 102
Friedman, A.S.   210
Frisbie, L.V.   90
Frith, U.   310
Frodi, A.M.   98
Frude, N.   56, 57
Frueh, B.C.   426
Fuller, D.   259, 423, 560
Fulton, A.   488
Fulton, B.A.   201
Fultz, S.A.   401
Furby, L.   86, 302, 343, 350

Gabbard, G.   317, 321
Gaedt, C.   460
Gaffney, L.R.   271
Gallwey, P.   314
Ganju, V.K.   127, 435
Ganley, A.L.   380
Garbarino, J.   60, 61, 64
Gardner, W.   78
Gardner, W.I.   463
Garety, P.   527
Garlick, Y.   336
Garrett, C.J.   10, 261
Garrett, J.C.   18, 19, 21
Garrido, V.   10, 189, 472, 500
Gauthier, C.M.   79

Gauthier, J. 91, 501
Gavey, N. 365
Gaynor, J. 393, 398, 401
Genders, E. 317
Gendreau, P. 9, 10, 18, 20, 21, 22, 23, 26, 27, 30, 87, 90, 133, 195, 196, 197, 198, 200, 201, 202, 419, 420, 422, 556–557
Gensheimer, L.K. 10, 18, 24, 28, 221, 552
Gentry, M.R. 284
George, F.E. 250
George, R. 158
George, W.H. 298
Gerard, R.E. 146
Gibat, C.C. 297
Gibbens, T.C.N. 509
Gibbon, M. 471
Gibbs, I. 544
Gibbs, J.C. 259, 262, 263, 264, 270, 272, 423, 560
Gidycz, C.A. 334, 365
Gilligan, J. 309
Gilling, D. 497
Giordano, P. 502
Gizzarelli, R. 90, 338
Glackman, W. 439
Glass, C. 462
Glass, G.V. 18
Glasscock, R. 502
Glick, B. 266, 272, 423
Glover, E. 314, 317
Glover, J.H. 501
Goddard, M. 196
Goffman, E. 60, 64, 224, 540
Goggin, C. 20, 21, 22, 23, 27, 87, 200, 201, 419
Goldberg, J.F. 434
Goldfine, P.E. 393
Goldfried, M.R. 489
Goldman, D. 471
Goldman, M.S. 487, 488
Goldstein, A.P. 182, 259, 263, 266, 272, 286, 416, 417, 423, 495
Gondolf, E.W. 284, 381, 383, 385
Gooch, D. 539, 540, 543
Good, M.A. Pirog- see Pirog-Good, M.A.
Goodstein, C. 365
Goodwin, C. 391
Goodwin, D.W. 370
Gordon, A. 283
Gordon, D.A. 209, 241, 248, 253
Gordon, J.R. 55, 297, 298, 490
Gordon, M. 394
Gordon, R. 239

Gottfredson, D.C. 241, 246, 247, 248, 254
Gottfredson, D.M. 125
Gottfredson, G.D. 241, 246, 247, 248, 254, 261
Gottfredson, M.R. 87
Gottfredson, S.D. 125
Gottman, J.M. 98
Gottschalk, R. 10, 18, 24, 28, 221–222, 552
Gow, J. 502
Graham, F. 368, 369, 370, 371
Graubard, P.S. 145
Graves, K. 209
Graves, R. 273, 277
Gray, A.S. 365, 366
Gray, J.O. 55
Greathouse, L. 144
Greenwood, A. 23
Greenwood, P.W. 36–37
Gresswell, D.M. 510, 511, 513, 514, 516, 517
Griffin, P.A. 439, 445, 446
Grisso, T. 117, 118
Griswold, D. 19
Grolnick, W.S. 391
Gross, B.H. 124
Gross, D.M. 286
Grossman, L. 434
Grossman, L.S. 101
Grossman, M.G. 185, 524
Groth, A.N. 339, 365
Grounds, A.T. 475
Grove, W.M. 92, 93
Gruber, E. 261
Grubin, D. 469, 530
Grusznski, R.J. 383, 385
Gudjonsson, G.H. 111, 112, 113, 114–115, 116, 117, 118, 119, 140, 141, 453–454, 501
Guerra, N.C. 205
Guerra, N.G. 270, 418, 423, 424
Guidry, L.S. 501
Guild, D. 103, 338
Gulayets, M.J. 101
Gunn, J. 158, 315–316, 317, 323, 435, 524
Gunn, K. 216
Gustafson, K. 209

Haapala, D. 207
Haig, B. 350
Haines, K. 557
Hakko, H. 394
Hakola, P. 436
Haley, J. 213

Hall, G.C.N.   88, 101, 102, 338–339, 350, 416
Hall, J.R.   391
Haller, R.M.   284
Hamada, R.S.   286
Hamberger, L.K.   382
Hambley, L.S.   339
Hamm, M.S.   26, 383, 386
Hammond, W.R.   423, 540
Han, M.   405
Han, S.S.   216
Haney, C.   139
Haney, J.I.   399
Hanley, J.H.   213, 424
Hanson, K.   336, 337, 338
Hanson, M.   394
Hanson, R.K.   85, 86, 87, 88, 90, 91, 92, 93, 104, 301, 358, 359, 368, 509
Hanusa, D.   383
Harden, P.W.   237
Hardesty, V.A.   393, 407
Harding, T.   127
Hare, R.D.   76, 77, 78, 79, 87, 111, 116, 117, 119, 126, 336, 339, 352, 358, 472, 482, 509, 530
Harland, A.T.   500
Harrell, A.   383, 385
Harris, A.J.R.   90, 91
Harris, G.T.   23, 25–26, 27, 28, 30, 75, 76, 77, 78, 86, 87, 88, 92, 100, 101, 102, 104, 125, 126, 128, 131, 132, 134, 284, 285, 339, 343, 350, 358, 393, 445, 447, 471, 473, 474, 524, 528, 531, 532, 533
Harrison, L.D.   155
Harrow, M.   434
Hart, B.   382
Hart, S.D.   74, 77, 78, 79, 91, 131, 440, 509
Hart, S.N.   62
Hartman, C.R.   515
Harvey, M.R.   334
Hatcher, C.   393, 398, 401
Hathaway, S.R.   115
Havighurst, R.J.   242, 249, 254
Haward, L.R.C.   112, 114, 117, 118
Hawkins, J.D.   237, 238, 239, 240, 244, 245, 253, 254, 483, 484, 485, 490
Hayes, R.   29, 286
Haywood, T.W.   101
Hazelrigg, M.D.   205
Hazlitt, W.   311
Healy, W.   6
Heath, G.A.   393
Heather, N.   488
Heavey, C.L.   334

Hedderman, C.   553, 557, 560, 561
Hedges, L.V.   239
Heil, P.   91
Heilbrun, K.   112, 114, 439, 445, 446, 525
Heimberg, R.G.   490
Helprin, L.M.   394
Helzer, J.E.   436
Hemphill, J.F.   116, 119, 472
Henderson, J.Q.   501
Henderson, M.   269, 277
Henggeler, S.W.   205, 206, 207, 212, 213, 214, 215, 216, 424
Henning, K.R.   426
Henson, T.   502
Heras, P.   216
Herbert, M.   54, 55, 56, 57, 58, 62, 63, 64, 65
Herbison, G.   316
Herman, J.   316
Hersen, M.   284
Hervis, O.E.   211
Hesse, E.   324
Hickey, E.W.   513
Higgins, A.   260
Higgins, O. O'Connell see O'Connell Higgins, O.
Higgitt, A.   323
Hill, C.D.   77
Hill, J.   310
Hill, K.G.   244
Hillbrand, M.   440
Hinshelwood, R.D.   313
Hirschi, T.   9, 87
Hirschman, R.   102
Hirvenoja, R.   394
Hobbs, T.R.   146–147
Hobson, C.   544
Hodge, J.E.   509
Hodgins, S.   77, 433, 434, 435, 436, 437, 438, 440, 441, 443, 446, 526
Hodkinson, S.   366, 369
Hoffman, P.   125
Hogan, R.   419
Hoge, R.D.   22, 23, 187, 424, 558
Hogue, T.   475, 530
Holland, C.J.   400
Holland, T.   456
Hollin, C.R.   7, 10, 11, 24, 25, 26, 27, 29, 30, 140, 146, 269, 270, 271, 277, 284, 424, 475, 483, 501, 510, 513, 516, 517, 530, 546, 547, 558
Hollins, S.   460, 461
Holmes, J.   311
Holmes, R.M.   510, 511, 512, 513

Holmstrom, L.L. 339
Holt, M.M. 146–147
Holtzworth-Munroe, A. 382
Holzer, C.E. 127, 435
Home Office 553, 554–555
Hooper, R.M. 155
Hope, S. 462
Hopkins, R.E. 273, 277
Horan, J.J. 25, 285, 286
Hornstein, R. 399, 401
Horowitz, M.J. 321
Hotalling, G. 365
Hough, M. 19, 500, 554
Houghton, R. 531
Howells, K. 269, 282, 285, 416, 423, 424, 427, 527, 528
Howitt, D. 55
Hucker, S.J. 524
Hudson, S.M. 89, 90, 302, 303, 304, 305, 337, 339, 340, 341, 343, 349, 350, 351, 352, 353, 354, 355, 356, 357, 358, 359, 365, 366, 367, 369, 370, 373, 374, 416, 418, 419
Hudzik, J.K. 221, 222
Huesmann, L.R. 238, 316, 417, 421
Huff, G. 269
Hughes, G.V. 287, 475, 530
Huizinga, D. 205, 484
Humphreys, J. 402, 403
Hunt, W.A. 298
Hunter, J.A. 370
Hunter, M.E. 527
Huot, S.J. 92
Hurley, D. 260
Husband, S.D. 481

Ialongo, N. 239
The Idea Bank 407
Inch, H. 440
Inciardi, J.A. 155, 163, 173
Indermaur, D. 422
Ingham, H. 497
Ingram, G.L. 146
Irwin, M.J. 266
Isaac, C. 366
Isberner, J.R. Müller- see Müller-Isberner, J.R.
Iwaniec, D. 61
Iwata, M. 285
Izzo, R.L. 10, 18, 21, 184, 558

Jackson, D.N. 283
Jackson, H.F. 462
Jackson, J. 80

Jackson, M. 79
Jackson, P. 299, 302
Jacobson, N.S. 98
Jacobson, R.R. 393
Jacoby, J.E. 72
Jaeger, J. 73, 127
Jaffe, A.J. 488
Janson, C.-G. 436
Jarvis, G. 496
Jaspers, K. 310
Jayaratne, S. 250
Jeffery, C.R. 6, 7
Jehu, D. 463
Jenkins, A. 368
Jenkins, P. 510, 513, 514
Jenkins, W.O. 145, 150
Jennings, J.L. 382
Jensen, B. 286
Jensen, F.A.S. 73
Jesness, C.F. 147, 148
Jöckel, D. 436
Johnson, C. 221, 222
Johnson, J. 270
Johnson, T. 469
Johnson, T. Cavanagh see Cavanagh-Johnson, T.
Johnson, V.S. 24
Johnston, K. 400
Johnston, L. 88, 351
Johnston, P.W. 343, 350, 355, 386
Johnston, R. 301
Johnston, V.E. 355
Jones, C. Cox- see Cox-Jones, C.
Jones, D. 439
Jones, E.J. 274, 277
Jones, L. 157
Jones, M. 156, 158, 160, 260, 316
Jones, P.R. 125
Jones, R.L. 301, 337, 343, 350, 355, 366, 386, 419
Jones, R.T. 399, 409
Jono, R.T. 126, 435
Jureidini, J. 318

Kächele, H. 324
Kadden, R.M. 490
Kaduce, L. Lanza- see Lanza-Kaduce, L.
Kaemingk, K.L. 370
Kafry, D. 391, 395
Kalichman, S.C. 338
Kandel, D.B. 484
Kaplan, M.S. 130, 364, 370, 371, 372, 373
Karacki, L. 146
Karan, O.C. 463

Karasu, T.B.   320, 321
Karper, L.P.   474
Kassenbaum, G.   20
Kaul, J.D.   92
Kavanagh, C.   61
Kavoussi, R.J.   364
Kazdin, A.E.   77, 206, 209, 216, 262, 263,
    266, 392, 393, 394, 395, 396, 397, 399
Keaney, F.   297, 490
Kear-Colwell, J.   340
Kedzierzawski, G.D.   502
Keenan, T.R.   356, 418
Keissling, J.J.   559
Kellam, S.G.   239
Kelleher, M.J.   462
Keller, H.   286, 416, 417
Kelly, J.A.   98
Kelly, L.M.   200
Kelly, S.   547
Kelso, J.   393
Kempe, C.H.   55
Kendon, A.   269
Kendrick, D.   11, 546
Kennard, D.   156
Kennedy, S.   201, 421
Kerr, C.A.   526
Kessler, R.C.   433
Khanna, A.   339, 340
Kiessling, J.J.   28, 196
Kilbey, M.M.   488
Kingsley, R.B.   286
Kinney, J.   207
Kite, J.C.   383, 386
Klein, M.   314
Klein, P.   112
Klerman, G.L.   434
Klinteberg, B.A.   483–484
Knight, K.   155, 173, 174
Knight, R.A.   92, 101, 102, 335, 365
Knitzer, J.   208
Knott, C.   505
Koegl, C.   81
Köferl, P.   10, 18, 19
Kohlberg, L.   260
Kolbeinsson, H.   114
Kolk, B.A. van der see van der Kolk, B.A.
Kolko, D.J.   392, 393, 394, 395, 396, 397,
    398, 399, 400, 401, 404
Kolman, A.S.   502
Kolvin, I.   246
Konecni, V.J.   282
Konopasky, R.J.   100
Kopet, T.   402, 403
Korbin, J.   58

Koselka, M.   370
Koss, M.P.   85, 90, 334, 365
Kosterman, R.   244
Kotelchuck, M.   55
Koustenis, G.   250
Kressel, D.   155
Krisberg, B.   221
Krohn, M.D.   6
Kroner, D.G.   283
Kropp, P.R.   79
Krystal, J.H.   440, 474
Kuban, M.   90, 102
Kuehnel, T.G.   533
Kuipers, E.   527
Kulchycky, S.   391
Kuriychuk, M.   287, 417, 418, 419, 484
Kurtines, W.M.   206, 210, 211
Kurtz, L.   251

Lab, S.P.   10, 18, 552
Lajoy, R.   403
Lakatos, I.   86
Lalonde, C.   87
Lalonde, N.   437
Lalumière, M.L.   86, 102, 104, 126, 333,
    343, 350
Lam, T.   239, 240, 244
Lamb, M.E.   98
Lamb, R.   124
Lambert, E.W.   125
Lambert, R.   538
Lane, S.   366, 372, 373, 374
Lane, T.W.   237
Lang, R.A.   101, 103
Langevin, R.   100, 103, 333
Lanthier, R.D.   338
Lanza-Kaduce, L.   6
Lapalme, M.   436, 441, 447
LaTessa, E.   201
Launay, G.   87
Laurenitis, L.R.   391
Lavallee, Y.   526
Laverick, J.   401
LaVigna, G.W.   463
Law, H.   498
Law, M.   86
Laws, D.R.   26, 86, 88, 99, 100, 101, 103,
    125, 297, 299, 301, 302, 342, 351, 355,
    370, 529
Lawson, J.S.   336
Laycock, G.   502
Le Blanc, M.   484
Leavitt, S.   207
Lebnan, V.   403

Lee, A.F.S.   92
Lee, R.E.   260
Lee-Evans, J.M.   283
Leeman, L.W.   259, 265, 423, 560
Lefcourt, H.M.   336
Lefkowitz, M.M.   238
Leiber, M.J.   272, 274
Leicestershire Community Projects Trust
    504
Leitenberg, H.   364
Lekkowitz, M.   316
Lenin, V.I.   3
Lennings, C.J.   272, 275
Leon, G. De see De Leon, G.
Lesage, A.   441
Leslie, A.M.   310
Letourneau, E.   99, 100, 104
Levene, K.   81
Levi, M.   500
Levi, P.   309
Levin, J.   510, 513, 515, 517
Levinson, A.   324
Levinson, R.B.   146
Lewinsohn, P.M.   434
Lewis, D.O.   365
Lewis, I.   365
Lewis, R.   380, 383, 560
Lewis, R.V.   222, 223
Liau, A.K.   262, 423
Liberman, R.P.   533
Liddle, H.A.   206, 211, 212
Lidz, C.W.   77
Liebert, J.A.   515
Liebling, H.   528
Liese B.S.   488
Light, R.   497, 502
Lilienfeld, S.O.   472
Lilly, J.R.   552
Limandri, B.J.   127, 128
Lin, S.P.   73, 127
Lindenbaum, D. Cox- see Cox-
    Lindenbaum, D.
Lindenbaum, L.   461
Lindqvist, P.   436
Linehan, M.M.   475
Link, B.G.   284, 435, 436, 437
Linz, D.   334
Lipsey, M.W.   10, 18, 19, 20, 21, 24, 29,
    184, 474, 556, 558
Lipton, D.   17
Lipton, D.N.   270, 336
Lipton, D.S.   10, 11, 155, 161, 163, 164,
    168, 169, 170, 175, 184, 481
Lishner, D.M.   239

Little, M.   542, 543, 544, 546, 547
Little, T.   22, 87, 196, 201
Litwack, S.E.   263
Litwack, T.R.   72
Lloyd, C.   19, 500, 554
Lloyd, J.C.   207
Lochman, J.E.   243, 251, 270, 417
Loeber, M. Stouthamer- see Stouthamer-
    Loeber, M.
Loeber, R.   205, 237, 238, 483
Lohr, J.M.   382
Long, C.K.   142
Long, J.D.   439
Longo, R. Freeman- see Freeman-Longo,
    R.
Longo, R.E.   365
Loranger, A.W.   471
Lösel, F.   10, 18, 19, 22, 23–24, 28, 29, 184,
    481, 558
Louden, K.   302, 353, 366, 369, 416
Love, C.E.   527
Low, G.   475
Loyer, M.   441
Loza, W.   482
Lubetsky, M.   401
Lunde, D.   510, 513
Luque, E.   10
Lurigio, A.J.   200
Lusignan, R.   91
Lyall, I.   456
Lynam, D.R.   237, 483
Lynch, M.   55
Lyth, I. Menzies see Menzies Lyth, I.
Lytton, L.   271

McAnulty, R.D.   103
McCaghy, G.   502
McCanne, T.R.   98
McCarthy, B.   420
McCartney, C. Pask- see Pask-McCartney,
    C.
McCarty, D.W.   439
McClintock, F.   546
McColl, M.A.   274, 277
McCombs, D.   250
McConnaughy, E.   486
McCord, J.   249
McCorkle, L.   260
McCorkle, R.C.   140
McCormack, J.   90, 416
McCown, W.   270
MacCulloch, M.J.   469, 514, 515, 531
MacDevitt, J.W.   502
McDonel, E.C.   270, 336

McDonough, J. Fiquera- *see* Fiquera-
    McDonough, J.
McDougall, C.   27, 28, 29, 286
McDowell, H.   59
McElroy, R.   513
McFall, R.M.   90, 270, 271, 336, 420
McGee, R.A.   61, 65
McGillivray, M.   502, 503
McGrath, P.   336, 400, 401
McGrath, R.J.   368, 417
McGraw, B.   18
McGreen, P.   209
McGreevy, M.A.   439
McGuire, J.   7, 10, 11, 269, 499, 500, 501,
    553, 557, 558, 559, 560, 561
McGuire, R.J.   340
McIvor, G.   554, 556, 557, 559, 561
McKay, H.B.   556, 559
McKay, H.D.   9
Mackay-Soroka, S.   394
McKeague, F.   439
McKee, J.M.   140, 145, 146, 147, 148, 149
MacKeith, J.A.C.   111, 120
McKerracher, D.W.   462, 463
McKibben, A.   91, 102
MacKillop, B.   187
McKinley, J.C.   115
McLaughlin, K.J.   399, 409
McLeod, M.   364
McMain, S.   74, 125
McMurran, M.   474, 475, 481, 483, 485,
    486, 509
MacPherson, A.   482
MacPherson, B.   488
McPherson, M.   386
McWilliams, B.   262
Madanes, C.   400
Maden, A.   436, 439, 524
Magnusson, D.   238, 483
Maguire, A.   442
Maguire, M.   495, 496, 497, 555, 556, 557
Main, M.   324
Main, T.   156
Mair, G.   19, 500, 554, 559, 561
Maitland, A.   557, 560
Maiuro, R.D.   283
Malamuth, N.M.   90, 334
Malcolm, P.B.   101, 103, 339
Mann, B.J.   206
Mann, R.   305
Manning, J.   504
Maren, V.   386
Marks, J.   503
Marks-Tarlow, T.   80

Marlatt, G.A.   297, 298, 299, 301, 490
Marle, H. van *see* van Marle, H.
Marques, J.K.   297, 299, 342, 358, 560
Marriott, A.   285
Marshall, P.   158
Marshall, P.T.   400
Marshall, W.L.   89, 91, 99, 101, 102, 103,
    130, 272, 275, 301, 302, 334, 335, 336,
    337, 338–339, 340, 341, 342, 343, 349,
    350, 351, 352, 353, 354, 355, 356, 357,
    359, 366, 368, 369, 370, 386, 416, 419
Martin, F.P.   261
Martin, G.R.   298, 342
Martin, J.   316
Martin, J.P.   503
Martin, S.S.   155
Martinson, R.   9, 17, 18, 197
Marzagao, L.R.   501
Mason, J.   453
Mâsse, L.C.   251
Masters, W.J.   355
Matarazzo, J.D.   115
Mathews, J.W.   29
Mathias, R.E.   29
Mathiesen, T.   81
Mathur, S.R.   272, 275
Maughan, B.   471
Mawhorr, T.L.   272, 274
Maxwell, R.J.   320
May, C.   559
May, R.   481
Maydeu-Olivares, A.   489
Mayer, J.P.   10, 18, 24, 28, 221–222, 552
Mayer, L.S.   239
Mayhew, P.   334
Mazurick, J.L.   216
Meca, J. Sànchez- *see* Sànchez-Meca, J.
Meehl, P.E.   73, 92, 93, 119
Megargee, E.I.   416
Meichenbaum, D.   285
Meisner, M.   73, 127
Meloy, J.R.   316
Melton, G.B.   213, 214, 424, 500
Meltzer, H.   434
Menzies Lyth, I.   313
Menzies, R.J.   73, 74, 76, 125
Meredith, C.   383
Mergenthaler, E.   324
Merton, R.K.   9
Metzger, D.S.   481
Metzner, J.L.   439
Meux, C.   469, 524, 530
Mewhort, D.J.K.   100
Meyer, A.L.   239, 240, 245

Meyer, E.C. 393
Meyers, R.J. 490
Michie, C. 19
Milan, M.A. 140, 142, 145, 147, 148, 149
Miles, K.M. 447
Miller, A.D. 546, 552, 557
Miller, B.A. 482
Miller, G.A. 29
Miller, J.Y. 483
Miller, L.C. 59
Miller, R.S. 336
Miller, T.R. 37, 38
Miller, W.R. 292, 341, 417, 482, 483, 486, 488
Millham, S. 538, 542, 543, 545, 546, 547
Millon, T. 352
Mills, C.M. 196
Mills, H.E. 515
Millson, W.A. 187
Milne, E. 458
Milner, J.S. 57, 98
Miltenberger, R. 151
Miner, M.H. 101, 342, 358
Minor, K.I. 272, 273
Minuchin, S. 206, 210, 213, 400
Miranda, L. Towns- see Towns-Miranda, L.
Mistry, T. 556, 559
Mitchell, C. 197, 208, 225, 226
Mitchell, E. 470
Mitchell, P. 553
Mittleman, M.S. 365
Model, K.E. 36–37
Moffitt, T.E. 54, 238
Molero, C. 472
Molinder, I. 336
Monaghan, T. 226
Monahan, J. 73, 78, 81, 127, 133, 284, 436
Monastersky, C. 365
Montandon, C. 127
Monti, P.M. 488, 490
Mooij, A. 323
Moore, J.M. 394
Morgan, D. 503
Morgan, E.M. 526
Morgan, M.Y. 128
Morgan, R. 553, 561
Morran, D. 380, 381
Morris, T.P. 9
Morrissey, J.P. 439
Mosher, D.L. 420
Mossman, D. 125
Moth, B. 341, 357
Motiuk, L.L. 201

Moynihan, J. 3
Mueser, K.T. 447
Mullen, P. 284, 316
Müller-Isberner, J.R. 436, 445, 446, 447
Mulvey, E.P. 78, 205, 423, 485
Muncer, S. 421
Munroe, A. Holtzworth- see Holtzworth-Munroe, A.
Murakami, J. 237
Murphy, B.C. 20
Murphy, G. 453
Murphy, G.H. 401, 462
Murphy, J.M. 391
Murphy, R. 189
Murphy, R.R. 270
Murphy, W.D. 98, 99, 101, 103, 104, 105, 336
Murray, D.J. 531
Myers, S.C. 383
Myers, W.C. 513, 514

National Fire Protection Association 391, 399, 407
National Institute on Drug Abuse 266
Nee, C. 497, 500
Negri-Shoultz, N. 463
Neisser, U. 5
Nelson, C. 299, 302, 342, 358
Nelson, G.M. 101
Nelson, K.E. 206, 207
Nesbitt, N. 439
Ness, A.E. 261
Newberger, E.H. 55
Newcomb, T.M. 261
Newman, C.F. 488
Newman, J.P. 484
Newton, M. 158
Nezu, A.M. 489
Niaura, R.S. 488
Nichols, H.R. 336
Nietzel, M.T. 7
Nisbett, R.E. 420
Noble, P. 284
Noordsy, D.L. 447
Norcross, J.C. 486
Norman, D.K. 391
Northam, E. 403
Norton, K. 316, 321
Norton, R.N. 128
Novaco, R.W. 6, 282, 283, 284, 285, 286, 287, 288, 290, 291, 417, 418, 419, 424, 488–489, 517, 528
Nuffield, J. 125
Nunn, R.J. 401, 403

Oates, K. 59
O'Boyle, M. 484
O'Brien, G. 458
O'Brien, M. 474
O'Connell Higgins, O. 65
O'Connell, M. 498
O'Donohue, W. 99, 100, 104
O'Farrell, T. 38
Ogloff, J.R.P. 23, 440
Ohlin, L.E. 546, 557
Oldfield, M. 554
Oldham, J.M. 471
Olds, D.L. 246
Olivares, A. Maydeu- see Maydeu-
  Olivares, A.
Olkin, I. 239
Ollendick, T.H. 399, 409
Olsen, S.E. 100
Olweus, D. 239
Openshaw, D.K. 273, 277
Orn, H. 132
Osborn, C.A. 99, 529
Osborn, E. 394
Osborne, C.A. 351
Osgood, D.W. 261
Ostapiuk, E.B. 284
O'Sullivan, C. 341
O'Sullivan, G.H. 462
Otis, D. 191
Overholser, J.C. 335, 338
Owen, M. 61

Palmer, E.J. 270
Palmer, T. 222, 223, 558
Paparozzi, M. 196, 198, 199, 200, 201, 419
Paperny, D.M. 364
Paquette, C. 383
Parker, H. 496
Parker, R. 537
Parrish, J.M. 392
Parry, G. 321
Parsons, B.V. 206, 208, 209
Pask-McCartney, C. 266
Patel, H. 214
Paterson, F. 553
Patterson, G.R. 54, 57, 58, 416, 501
Paulus, P.B. 140
Pavlov, I. 5
Pawlak, A. 338, 342
Pawson, R. 386
Paylor, I. 553
Paymar, M. 380, 381
Pearse, J. 120, 454
Pearson, F.S. 10, 175, 184, 199

Pease, K. 3, 497, 498
Peay, J. 321
Peggrem, A. 502
Pekarik, G. 88
Pellegrin, D. 501
Pence, E. 380, 381
Peplau, L.A. 336
Perez-Vidal, A. 211
Peroud, B. 555
Perry, G.M. 481
Perry, J. 316
Perry, M. 419
Perry, S.W. 391
Petch, E. 439
Peters, J. 155
Peters, J.M. 105
Peters, R.H. 481
Petersilia, J. 197, 198, 199, 222
Petrila, J. 500
Petty, J. 90, 339
Petursson, H. 114
Pfäfflin, F. 324
Pfohl, B. 471
Pickrel, S.G. 213, 214
Pickrell, E.P. 393
Pierce, J.L. 407
Pihl, R.O. 237, 251
Pilkonis, P.A. 471
Pinsonneault, I. 400
Pirog-Good, M.A. 384
Pithers, W.D. 90, 99, 297, 298, 299, 302,
  303, 304, 339, 342, 343, 350, 356, 357,
  358, 365, 366, 421
Platt, J.J. 270, 481
Player, E. 317
Polaschek, D.L.L. 416, 426
Pollack, P. 340
Polvi, N. 79, 80
Pope, S.K. Thompson- see Thompson-
  Pope, S.K.
Porporino, F.J. 180, 185, 186, 187
Porth, D. 399
Potter, G.B. 259, 262, 263, 264, 423
Poulton, L. 394
Poythress, N.G. 500
Preiser, P. 161
Prentky, R.A. 92, 101, 102, 335, 365, 515,
  516
Preston, D. 401
Preston, D.L. 102
Price, J.M. 484
Priestley, P. 10, 269, 499
Prior, K. 400
Pritchard, C. 556

Prochaska, J.O.   486
Proctor, E.   553
Proctor, W.C.   101
Proulx, J.   91, 102, 103
Przybeck, T.   132, 436
Ptacek, J.   381
Pullen, S.   189
Pullin, J.   297, 490
Putnam, F.W.   349, 355

Quay, H.C.   146
Quinsey, V.L.   75, 77, 86, 88, 100, 101, 102, 103, 104, 125, 126, 128, 284, 285, 333, 335, 338, 339, 342, 343, 350, 358, 442, 445, 500, 524, 525, 526, 531

Radosevich, M.   6
Raine, A.   97, 98, 99, 141, 471
Rajkumar, A.S.   38, 44, 47
Ramey, C.T.   246, 254
Ramey, S.L.   254
Ramm, M.   285, 528
Rapoff, M.   502
Rapp, C.   226
Rappaport, J.   196, 224, 229
Rappaport, R.C.   511
Rasanen, P.   394
Rasp, R.R.   286
Rathner, J. Cunningham see Cunningham-Rathner, J.
Rathus, S.A.   336
Raven-Brook, L.   286
Ray, J.B.   502
Raynor, P.   188, 505, 555, 559, 561
Rebok, G.W.   239
Reccoppa, L.   513
Reckless, W.C.   242, 249
Reddon, J.R.   283
Redner, R.   197, 225, 226, 228, 229, 232
Redondo, S.   10, 18, 20, 21, 500
Reed, J.   369
Reed, R.B.   55
Reid, J.B.   501
Reid, M.M.   482
Reiss, A.J.   416
Reiss, D.   469, 475, 530
Reissman, F.   261
Renwick, S.J.   284, 285, 286, 289–290, 291, 293, 528
Repo, E.   393, 394
Repucci, N.D.   205, 423, 485
Ressler, R.K.   511, 512, 513, 514, 515, 516
Rex, S.   559

Rice, M.E.   23, 25–26, 27, 28, 30, 75, 77, 86, 87, 88, 92, 100, 101, 102, 104, 125, 126, 128, 284, 285, 339, 343, 350, 358, 393, 445, 446, 447, 471, 473, 474, 524, 525, 526, 527, 528, 529, 531, 532, 533
Richardson, G.   368
Rienzo, D.   102
Rio, A.T.   211
Rivard, J.C.   207
Roberts, J.   55, 156, 474
Roberts, M.D.   140, 147
Robertson, G.   158, 317, 319, 322, 436, 463, 525, 531
Robertson, I.   488
Robertson, P.J.   89, 357
Robins, L.N.   132, 238
Robinson, C.   515, 560
Robinson, D.   180, 185, 186, 187, 425, 505
Robinson, J.   17
Robinson, M.J.   196
Rodger, W.   440
Roesch, R.   440
Rogers, R.   77, 131
Rohde, P.   434
Rohrbeck, C.A.   65
Rohsenow, D.J.   488
Rollnick, S.   292, 341, 417, 486
Romans, S.   316
Rosenbaum, L.K.   246
Rosenberg, R.   335
Rosenblum, A.   168
Rosenthal, L.   270
Rosenthal, R.   19
Roshier, B.   4
Ross, B.   559
Ross, R.D.   504
Ross, R.R.   6, 7, 10, 18, 21, 23, 179, 184, 195, 196, 197, 271, 401, 403, 425, 497, 500, 504, 556, 558, 559
Rossman, S.B.   37
Roth, J.A.   416, 526
Rotter, J.   5
Rouleau, J.L.   335
Roundtree, G.   502
Rounsaville, B.   442
Rowland, M.D.   206
Rowlands, M.   511, 514
Rowlands, R.   440
Rowson, B.   560
Royse, D.   502
Rubama, I.   266
Rubin, D.B.   19
Rubin, H.B.   100
Rubinstein, M.   365

Runtz, M.   355
Rushe, R.H.   98
Rushton, A.   540
Rusilko, S.   250
Russakoff, M.M.   471
Russell, B.   4
Russell, D.E.H.   334, 336
Rutherford, R.B.   272, 275
Rutter, M.   238, 253
Rutter, S.   120, 454
Ryan, C.S.   439
Ryan, G.   364, 366, 372, 373, 374
Rydell, C.P.   36–37
Ryden, O.   392, 396

Sakheim, G.A.   394, 406
Salekin, R.T.   131
Saley, S.   74
Salter, A.   517
Samenow, S.E.   261, 423, 425
Sànchez-Meca, J.   10, 500
Sanchis, J.R.   189
Sanday, P.R.   333
Santisteban, D.A.   211
Saqi, S.   55, 57
Saunders, D.G.   381, 382, 383, 385
Saylor, C.Á.   196
Scaglione, R.   74, 125
Scarpa, A.   97, 98
Scavo, R.   266
Schaffer, H.R.   62
Schalling, D.   119
Scherer, D.G.   213, 424
Schetky, D.H.   316
Schiff, A.F.   333
Schillo, B.   226
Schlank, A.M.   338, 341
Schlesinger, L.B.   381
Schlichter, K.J.   25, 285, 286
Schlundt, D.G.   270
Schmidt, F.L.   86
Schmidt, S.E.   212
Schneider, B.   335
Schoenwald, S.K.   206, 207, 213, 214
Schon, D.   124
Schouten, P.G.W.   99
Schrink, J.L.   26
Schroeder, C.   208
Schur, E.   552
Schwartz, B.K.   340
Schwartzman, P.I.   391
Schwarz, M.S.   316
Schweinhart, L.L.   7, 243, 252, 254, 255
Scott, H.   85, 90, 336, 337, 338

Scottish Office   555
Seeley, J.A.   60, 64
Seeley, J.R.   434
Segal, L.J.   463
Segal, Z.V.   130, 335, 338
Segel, R.   317
Seghorn, T.K.   335
Séguin, J.R.   237, 252
Seidman, B.T.   89, 90, 357
Seidman, E.   196, 229
Seitz, V.   246
Selby, M.J.   283
Selzer, M.L.   336
Sepejak, D.S.   73, 74
Serin, R.C.   102, 201, 287, 339, 417, 418,
     419, 420, 421, 423, 424, 484
Seto, M.C.   90, 102, 339, 350, 359
Sewell, K.W.   131
Shadish, W.R.   205
Shah, S.A.   72–73, 75
Shapland, J.   321
Sharpe, K.S.   440
Shaw, C.R.   9
Shaw, T.   338, 341
Sheldrake, C.   546
Sheridan, D.J.   127, 128
Sherman, L.W.   500, 551
Sherman, P.S.   439
Shewan, D.   482
Shinske, F.K.   399
Shondrick, D.D.   102
Shortt, J.W.   98
Shoultz, N. Negri- see Negri-Shoultz, N.
Showers, J.   393
Shulman, J.L.   502
Shure, M.B.   270
Sibbitt, R.   500
Siegal, L.J.   4
Siegert, R.J.   343, 366, 369
Sigal, H.   510, 513
Sigurdsson, E.   114
Silva, P.A.   238
Simon, L.M.J.   416
Simon, R.   311
Simon, T.   99
Simonian, S.   270
Simpson, D.D.   155, 174
Sinason, V.   318, 460, 461
Sinclair, H.   380
Sinclair, I.   544, 545
Sindberg, R.M.   29
Sisson, L.A.   284
Skinner, B.F.   5, 516
Skinner, H.A.   336

Skuse, D.   55, 65, 66
Slaby, R.G.   270, 418, 424
Slobogin, C.   500
Sluckin, A.   63, 64
Sluckin, W.   63, 64
Smallbone, S.W.   336
Smith, C.   365
Smith, D.   553
Smith, E.   222, 225, 228, 233
Smith, G.   17
Smith, J.   325
Smith, J.E.   490
Smith, J.N.   287
Smith, L.A.   213
Smith, L.L.   287
Smith, M.   59, 65
Smith, M.L.   18
Smith, W.   365
Snowden, P.   81
Sobel, E.   439
Sockloskie, R.   90
Soliman, A.   440
Soloff, P.H.   474
Solomon, G.S.   502
Solomon, P.   440
Soothill, K.L.   509
Southard, M.J.   124
Sovereign, R.G.   483
Sowden, P.R.   515
Spence, S.H.   269, 271
Spencer, E.   502
Spielberger, C.D.   114, 283, 336, 419, 489
Spinks, P.   531
Spitzer, R.L.   442, 471
Spivack, G.   270
Staley, S.   125, 394
Stangl, D.   471
Stanley, J.C.   385
Stansky, L.   222
Stanton, R.   316
Stattin, H.   238, 483
Staub, H.   6
Stawar, T.L.   401
Steadman, H.J.   71, 72, 78, 284, 435, 436, 437, 439, 442
Stedward, G.   552
Steels, M.   469
Steffy, R.A.   85
Stein, R.   213
Stermac, L.E.   285, 335, 338
Stets, J.   384
Stevenson, R.L.   309
Stewart, L.A.   462
Stewart, M.A.   392, 393–394

Stichman, A.   201
Stoddard, F.J.   391
Stoll, A.L.   434
Stone, A.   317
Stone, M.H.   468, 469
Stone, S.B.   201
Stouthamer-Loeber, M.   237
Stratton, C. Webster- see Webster-Stratton, C.
Street, D.R.K.   463
Stuart, R.B.   242, 250, 253
Stueve, A.   436
Stueve, C.   284
Stumphauzer, J.S.   501
Sturgeon, C.   340, 357
Styles, P.   456
Sugg, D.   553, 557, 560, 561
Susman, V.L.   471
Sutherland, E.H.   6, 9, 141
Sutton, M.   496, 498
Swanson, J.W.   127, 284, 435, 436
Swartz, M.   284, 436, 440
Swenson, D.   386
Swinton, M.   435
Syers, M.   383, 385
Symington, N.   320
Szapocznik, J.   206, 210–211, 216

Tanaka, J.   90
Tarlow, T. Marks- see Marks-Tarlow, T.
Tarnowski, K.J.   270
Tata, P.R.   417
Tate, D.C.   205, 423
Taylor, I.   9, 540
Taylor, P.J.   284, 315–316, 439
Taylor, S.   88
Taylor, S.P.   484
Templeton, J.K.   269
Tenke, C.E.   370
Teplin, L.   437, 440
Terjestam, P.Y.   392, 396
Theilgaard, A.   112, 318
Thelen, M.H.   336
Thomas, G.   155, 486
Thompson-Pope, S.K.   394
Thompson, S.   460
Thornberry, T.P.   72, 205
Thornhill, N.W.   333
Thornhill, R.   333
Thornton, D.   92, 93, 158, 302, 336
Throckmorton, W.R.   148, 149
Thurston, R.   559
Tien, G.   439, 440
Tierney, J.   8, 9

Tiihonen, J. 436
Tilley, N. 498
Tilly, J. 386
Tipp, J. 132
Tizard, J. 540
Toch, H. 140, 283
Tohen, M. 434
Tolan, P.H. 205, 216, 423
Tolin, D.F. 382
Tolliver, R.M. 98
Tolman, R.M. 383
Tombs, J. 553
Tomko, L.A. 210
Tomlin, A.M. 270
Tong, L. 59
Toupin, J. 435, 446
Tovar, P. 208
Towl, G. 287
Towns-Miranda, L. 406
Trasler, G. 498
Travers, J.A. 312
Travis, L. 201
Tremblay, R.E. 237, 238, 243, 251, 254
Trevethan, S. 187
Tripodi, T. 250
Triseliotis, J. 537
Trotter, C. 559
Trower, P. 269
Trull, T.J. 469, 471
Tsuang, M.T. 434
Tulloch, R.M.B. 526
Tuma, J.M. 215
Turner, B.A. 272, 275
Turner, C.W. 209
Turner, S. 198, 199
Tyler, V.O. 143
Tyrer, P. 468, 469, 476

Underdown, A. 553, 560
Upfold, D. 103
Urbina, S. 114, 117
US Federal Bureau of Investigation 391
Utada, A. 210

Vaisanen, E. 394
Valciukas, J.A. 118
Valle, L.A. 98
Valliant, P.M. 276, 277, 286, 287
van der Kolk, B.A. 316
van Dijk, J.J.M. 334
Van Elzen, C.J.M. 471
van Marle, H. 315, 324
Van Velsen, C. 315

Van Voorhis, P. 423
Vanstone, M. 188, 505, 559
Varney, G.W. 284, 338
Velangi, R. 528
Velicer, W.F. 486
Velsen, C. Van see Van Velsen, C.
Venables, P.H. 99
Veneziano, C. 270
Veneziano, L. 270
Vennard, J. 560, 561
Vidal, A. Perez- see Perez-Vidal, A.
Vigdor, M.G. 394
Virkkunen, M. 393, 394
Vitaliano, P.P. 283
Vitaro, F. 251
Vizard, E. 59
Volavka, J. 73, 127
Voorhis, P. Van see Van Voorhis, P.
Vorrath, H.H. 260, 261

Wagner, B.C. 283
Wagner, C.R. 406
Wakefield, P.J. 216
Walder, L.O. 238, 316
Waldo, G. 19
Waldron, H. 209
Wales, D.S. 373
Walker, A.M. 393
Walker, G.L. 125
Walker, M.A. 495
Walker, N. 74, 325–326
Wall, S. 324
Wallace, W. 297, 490
Walsh, D. 497
Walsh, J. 440
Walter, T.L. 196
Walters, G.D. 476, 485, 487, 490, 496, 499
Walton, P. 9, 540
Wanigaratne, S. 297, 298, 299, 490
Warburton, J. 209
Ward, C.I. 271
Ward, D. 20
Ward, D.M. 214
Ward, T. 88, 90, 301, 302, 303, 304, 305, 339, 340, 341, 343, 349, 350, 351, 353, 354, 356, 357, 358, 359, 365, 366, 367, 369, 370, 373, 374, 386, 416, 418
Warden, S. 463
Warner, S. 552
Wasmund, W.C. 260, 261
Wasserman, C. 502
Waternaux, C.M. 434
Waters, E. 324
Watson, R.J. 101, 102

Watson, S.   399
Watt, B.   416
Weaver, F.   498
Webb, B.   502
Webb, J.   498
Webb, N.B.   406
Webster, C.D.   73, 74, 75, 78, 79, 80, 81,
   125, 128, 131, 132, 133, 524, 531
Webster, D.   503
Webster-Stratton, C.   54, 56, 57
Weikart, D.P.   7, 243, 252, 254
Weinberg, S.   144
Weinberger, L.E.   124
Weiner, I.B.   115
Weinrott, M.R.   86, 302, 343, 350
Weiss, B.   216
Weisser, C.E.   285
Weissman, M.M.   434
Weisz, J.R.   216
Welldon, E.   315, 318
Wells, E.A.   490
Welsh, W.N.   283, 417, 424
Welte, J.W.   482
Wenet, G.A.   364
Wessely, S.   284
West, D.   546
West, M.A.   101
Wexler, H.K.   155, 163, 165, 166, 167, 168,
   169, 170, 482
Wheeler, D.   100
Whelan, J.P.   213
White, J.L.   238, 483
White, M.   368
Whited, R.M.   394
Whitehead, J.T.   10, 18, 552
Whiteley, S.   474
Whitman, J.   509
Widiger, T.A.   469, 471
Wiederanders, M.R.   439, 445–446
Wiersema, B.   37, 38
Wierzbicki, M.   88
Wikaira, R.G.   426
Wilkinson, J.   503, 504, 505
Wilks, J.   17
Williams, B.   366, 369
Williams, C.E.   399
Williams, H.   314
Williams, J.B.W.   442, 471
Williams, M.   99
Williams, M.H.   446
Williams, R.E.   216

Willmott, P.   9
Wilner, D.   20
Wilson, D.   439, 446
Wilson, D.B.   10
Wilson, M.   380, 381
Wilson, P.H.   297
Wilson, R.J.   79, 91
Wilson, S.K.   65
Winnicott, D.W.   315, 318, 319
Wintrup, A.   78
Wishnie, H.   79
Wisniewski, N.   334, 365
Wodarski, J.S.   242, 250, 253
Wolfe, D.A.   56, 57, 61, 65, 98
Wolff, N.   439
Wolkind, S.   540
Wong, S.   23, 116, 472
Wood, J.W.   515
Wood, K.M.   208
Wood, L.F.   148, 149
Wooden, W.   395, 398
Woodward, R.   27, 157
Wookey, J.   56, 65
Worling, J.R.   365, 368, 370, 371, 372
Wormith, J.S.   10, 338, 439
Woszczyna, C.   368
Wright, F.D.   488
Wright, J.   197–198
Wright, N.A.   272, 276
Wright, R.   497
Wuthnow, R.   260

Yeager, C.A.   365
Yee, D.   10, 175, 184
Yesavage, J.A.   462
Yochelson, S.   261, 423, 425
Yoshikawa, H.   237
Young, B.G.   340
Young, J.   9, 540
Yuen, S.A.   65

Zaitchik, M.C.   420
Zamble, E.   180, 283, 500
Zegree, J.B.   283
Zelhart, P.F.   144
Zillmann, D.   282
Zimbardo, P.   139
Zimmerman, M.   471
Zohar, A.   338
Zornitzer, M.   381
Zulueta, F. de   315

Subject Index

Abecedarian Project 241, 245–246, 254
abuse *see* child abuse
abusers, characteristics 55
academic achievement *see* educational
   achievement
actuarial values
   in prediction of sexual recidivism
      92–93
   in prediction of violence 73, 76, 128,
      131–132
   in risk assessment 124–126, 131–132
Adolescent Diversion Project 223–228
   evaluation 228–233
adolescents *see* firesetters; young
   offenders; young people; young
   sexual offenders
Adult Attachment Interview 324
advocacy model, in adolescent diversion
   226–227, 230–231, 233
aggression *see* violence
Aichhorn, August 7
alcohol abuse *see* substance abuse
Amity Prison (US), Therapeutic
   Community programme 165–168
anger (*see also* domestic violence;
      violence)
   assessment of 290–291
   in domestic violence 283–284
   in psychiatric in-patients 284–285
   psychometric instruments 283,
      290–291, 419
   and psychotic symptoms 284
   in sexual offenders 336, 339
   and violence 282, 418–419, 424–425,
      488–489
   in violent offenders 418–419

in young offenders 284
anger management
   cognitive-behavioural therapy for 251,
      285–287, 288, 381
   in correctional institutes 287
   levels of treatment 287–289
   for mentally retarded offenders 459,
      462
   protocols 290
   in psychiatric hospitals 285–286,
      289–293, 528
   psycho-education for 286, 287, 288
   in school delinquency prevention
      projects 251
   selection of clients 282, 291
   studies 285–287, 424–426
   for young offenders 286
antisocial attitudes *see* negative attitudes
antisocial behaviour
   control of 143–144
   and mental illness 435
arsonists *see* firesetters
attachment (*see also* insecure attachment;
      parent-child attachment)
   problems with, and sexual offending
      89–90, 366
   research in 324

Beccaria, Cesare 4
behaviour *see* children, criminal
      behaviour; criminal behaviour
behavioural model, in adolescent
      diversion 226
behavioural self-control training 488
behavioural techniques (*see also*
      cognitive-behavioural therapy;

dialectical behaviour therapy)   7,
    143–151, 458–459
  for firesetters   400–401
  school delinquency prevention projects
    249–251, 253
  for violence   527–528
Bentham, Jeremy   4–5
bipolar disorder, prevalence   433
bonding see attachment; insecure
    attachment; parent-child attachment
burglary (see also property offences)
  interventions   504, 505

Canada, Reasoning and Rehabilitation
    programme   185–188, 504–505
car crime (see also property offences)
  interventions   502–504
case materials
  in assessment of sexual offenders
    350–351
  in risk assessment   126–128, 130–132,
    133
causality (see also determinism)
  concepts of   55, 310–311
Cellblock Token Economy   148–150
Chicago School   9
child abuse (see also child physical abuse;
    child sexual abuse; cycle of abuse;
    emotional abuse; neglect)
  definition   54
  risk assessment   65–67
Child Abuse Potential Inventory   57
child development, ecological approach
    66, 212–213, 215–216
child physical abuse
  definition   54
  perpetrators
    characteristics   55
    physiological responses   98
  risk factors   54–58
child sexual abuse
  cognitive-behavioural chain   299–300,
    303
  definition   54
  investigation of   58–60
  perpetrators
    assessment of   350–352
    cognitive behavioural therapy for
      352–358
    profiles   101
    risk assessment   358
    sexual arousal in   103, 104
    violence in   103

children (see also family-based treatment;
    firesetters; young offenders; young
    people; young sexual offenders)
  criminal behaviour, prediction of   77,
    98–99, 237–238, 483–485
  emotional needs (see also attachment)
    63
  in need, definition   61
  socialization   141, 142, 181
  theft by   501
  violence by, prediction of   80–81,
    483–485
Children Act (1989)   61, 62, 547
Children's Firesetting Risk Inventory
    397
children's homes see residential care
classical theory, of crime   4–5, 8, 10, 12
classroom management   143–146
  for delinquency reduction   238, 239,
    244–245, 253
clinical judgement, and risk assessment
    124, 125
clinical variables, in prediction of violence
    132
coercive spiral   58
cognitive-behavioural chain   299–300,
    302–303, 353–354
cognitive-behavioural model, of relapse
    prevention   298–300, 301, 303–305,
    366–367
cognitive-behavioural therapy (see also
    Reasoning and Rehabilitation
    programme)   7
  for anger management   251, 285–287,
    288, 381
  appropriateness, principles   22–24
  for domestic violence   381, 383–384
  effectiveness   21–22, 175, 184, 557, 558,
    560
  for firesetters   401–403
  for personality disordered offenders
    474–476, 530
  in probation work   553
  for property offences   501–502
  responsivity principle   22–23, 558–559
  for sexual offenders   339–343, 352–358,
    553
  for substance abusers   481–482
  for violence   425–426
  for young offenders   21, 558
  for young sexual offenders   371–374
cognitive distortions (see also social
    cognition)   263, 264

in sexual offenders   336, 337, 338, 341, 354
in violent offenders   417–418
cognitive psychology, and crime   6–7
cognitive restructuring   353–354
Cognitive Self Change   425–426
Cognitive Skills Training (see also Reasoning and Rehabilitation programme)   425
community-based interventions (see also family-based treatment; post-release supervision; probation and parole)   166, 187–188, 551–556
evaluation   556–560
and recidivism   554
community care, for mental illness   445–446
community sentences   552–555
community service   554–555
conditioning (see also behavioural techniques; socialization)
and criminal behaviour   141–142
contingency management, in firesetting   401–402
contingency plans, for treatment integrity   30
Cornerstone Therapeutic Community programme   162, 170–171
correctional institutes (see also Amity Prison (US); Grendon Prison (UK); high security hospitals; prison officers)
anger management in   287
behaviour management in   143–151
cognitive skills teaching see Reasoning and Rehabilitation programme
costs   554
interventions, effectiveness   556–557
substance abuse treatment see Therapeutic Community treatment
Correctional Program Evaluation Inventory   30
cost-benefit analysis
of treatment   37–39
case study   39–48
cost-effectiveness, of treatment   19, 36–37
costs
of correctional institutes   554
of crime   37–38, 40–41
discounting   45–46
of probation and parole   554–555
court diversion schemes (see also Adolescent Diversion Project)   552

for mentally retarded offenders   455–456
for young offenders   221–223
courts, sentencing options, for mentally retarded offenders   456
covert sensitization   355, 373
crime
classical theory   4–5, 8, 10, 12
costs of   37–38, 40–41
and decision-making   7, 10
deterrence see deterrence
prevention
cost benefits   19
for property offences   497–398
psychological theories   5–7
punishment of see punishment
and social learning theory   5, 6, 181
and social organization   9
statistics   3
criminal behaviour (see also children, criminal behaviour)
causation (see also cycle of abuse)   324
functional analysis   130, 499–500
and hyperactivity   483–484
and mental illness   434–437
and peer pressure   484
and psychophysiological responses   98–99
and socialization   141, 142, 181
and substance abuse   483–485
theory of   140–142
criminal sanctions see deterrence; punishment; sentencing options
criminals see offenders
criminogenic needs, treatment for   22
criminology   8–9, 17
cultural sensitivity, in therapy   216
cycle of abuse   54–55, 315–316

Dangerous Behaviour Rating Scheme   74–75, 78
dangerousness see violence
decision-making, and crime   7, 10
delinquency see latent delinquency; schools, delinquency programmes; young offenders
delusional disorders   441
demographic factors see actuarial values
depression, prevalence   433–434
desirable behaviour, increasing   144–146
determinism (see also causality)
and crime   7–8

deterrence
    development of   10
    principles of   4–5
    and recidivism   20
deviance see sexual deviance
dialectical behaviour therapy   475
Differential Association Theory   6, 9
differential reinforcement of other
        behaviour   147
Differential Reinforcement Theory   6
differentiation, in offenders   7, 8
directed masturbation   355
discipline (see also punishment)
    inappropriate   60–61
    and physical abuse   56, 57
discounting, of costs   45–46
diversion programmes see Adolescent
        Diversion Project; court diversion
        schemes
domestic violence perpetrators
    anger in   283–284
    physiological responses   98
    programmes for   379–382
    evaluation   382–386
drug abuse see substance abuse
dynamic risk factors   126
    in sexual recidivism   86, 88–91

Early Assessment Risk List—Boys'
        Version   80–81
ecological approach, to child development
        66, 212–213, 215–216
educational achievement (see also
        preschool interventions; schools)
    and behaviour reinforcement   145–146,
        147, 149–150
    and delinquency   237–238
effect sizes, in meta-analyses   19
emotional abuse
    definition   54, 60–62
    risk assessment   61, 62–65
emotional control see anger management;
        mood management; negative
        attitudes
empathy problems
    in sexual offenders   336, 337, 341,
        355–356
    in violent offenders   419
EQUIP programme   263–265, 423
erection see penile tumescence
ethics
    of phallometric testing   99, 370
    of randomized controlled trials
        385–386

ethos see institutional commitment;
        schools, ethos
evaluation, and treatment integrity   30
Eysenck, H.J.   140–141

families, of mentally retarded offenders,
        work with   458
family-based treatment (see also family
        preservation programmes; functional
        family therapy; multidimensional
        family therapy; multisystemic
        therapy; structural family therapy)
    definition   206
    effectiveness   205–206
    recommendations   215–217
family functioning, models   66
family preservation programmes
        207–208, 213
Family and School Consultation Project
        250
family therapy see family-based treatment
family violence see child physical abuse;
        domestic violence
fantasy (see also sexual fantasies)
    in serial murderers   515–516, 517
Fast Track Project   252
fathers see parents
females see women
Fire Incident Analysis for Children   396
Fire Incident Analysis for Parents
        395–396
fire safety skills   398–400
firesetters
    assessment   395–396, 402, 407
    characteristics   393–395, 397
    mentally retarded   462
    parents, characteristics   394
    prevention education   398–400
    programmes for   405–407
    psychometric instruments   395–397
    recidivism in   392–393
    research needs   408–409
    risk factors   396–398
    statistics   391–393
    therapy for   400–403
        evaluation   403–405
        selection   407–408
Firesetting Risk Inventory   396–397
fitness to plead, in mentally retarded
        offenders   455
forensic psychotherapy   310–312
    aims   319
    assessment for   318–320
    methods   315–320

origins   313–315
    research in   321–325
free will, and crime   5, 7, 8
Freud, Sigmund   5, 314
functional analysis   130, 499–500
functional family therapy   208–210
funding, for treatment   27

Grendon Prison (UK), Therapeutic
    Community Treatment in   156–158,
    317

HCR-20 rating scheme   78–79, 131–134
heart rate *see* psychophysiological
    responses
helping-skills, in peer groups   262, 263
high security hospitals
    anger management in   285–286,
        289–293, 528
    characteristics   523–524
    patients
        anger in   284–285
        assessment   525–526
        characteristics   524–526
        personality disordered   529–530
        recidivism in   531–532
        sexual offenders   528–529
        treatment   445, 526–530, 532–533
        violence in   284–285, 527–528
High/Scope   243, 252
historical variables *see* actuarial values
histories *see* case materials
hostility *see* anger
hyperactivity, and risk of criminal
    behaviour   483–484
hypothetico-deductive model, of risk
    assessment   124

ideographic measurement   112
impulsivity
    and risk of violence   132, 418
    and substance abuse   489
Impulsivity Checklist   79
in-patients *see* high security hospitals,
    patients
injury *see* child physical abuse; domestic
    violence; violence
insecure attachment
    and emotional abuse   64
    in young sexual offenders   366
institutional commitment, and treatment
    integrity   26–27, 28, 29–30
intensive supervision programmes
    197–198

effectiveness   198–200
interagency work
    with mental illness   439
    in probation services   553–554
    with young sexual offenders   371
intermediate sanctions (*see also* intensive
    supervision programmes)
    effectiveness   198–200
intermediate treatment *see* Adolescent
    Diversion Project; court diversion
    schemes
interpersonal skills *see* empathy; intimacy;
    relationships; social skills training
interviews (*see also* motivational
    interviewing)
    for risk assessment   129–130, 132, 133
intimacy, problems with, in sexual
    offenders   89–90, 336, 341–342, 357

joyriding *see* car crime
justice, conflict with treatment   7–8
juvenile delinquents *see* young offenders
juvenile firesetters *see* firesetters

Key–Crest Therapeutic Community
    programme   171–173
Kia Marama programme   352–358

latent delinquency, theory of   7
leadership, of treatment programmes
    28–29
learning disabled offenders *see* mentally
    retarded offenders
learning theory, and crime   6
legal psychopaths *see* personality
    disordered offenders
life skills training, for mentally retarded
    offenders   457
lifestyle modification, for substance
    abusers   490
linear rationalist model, of risk assessment
    124
Louiseville Behavior Checklist   59

McMaster model of family functioning
    66
management structures, and treatment
    integrity   26–27
mass murder, definition   511
masturbation, directed   355
matchplayers *see* firesetters
maximum security hospitals *see* high
    security hospitals
May Report   9

medication *see* psychopharmacotherapy
mental illness
    and antisocial behaviour   435
    assessment   440–444
    and co-morbidity   442–443
    diagnosis   441–442
    in mentally retarded offenders   458,
        461
    and prevalence of criminality   434–437
    and the Reasoning and Rehabilitation
        programme   191
    screening for   440
    in serial murderers   514
    services for   438–439
    statistics   433–434
    and substance abuse   436
    treatment   444–447, 526–527
        goals   437–438
        selection of   443–444, 447
    and violence   435–436, 442–443
        prediction of   71–73, 77, 78, 127–128,
            131, 132
mentally retarded offenders
    anger management for   459, 462
    assessment   454–455
    characteristics   453
    court diversion schemes   455–456
    female   463
    firesetters   462
    fitness to plead   455
    mental illness in   458, 461
    psychopharmacotherapy for   460
    recidivism in   464
    rehabilitation   463
    self-regulation skills   459–460
    sentencing options   456
    service provision for   464–465
    sexual offenders   460, 461
    socialization of   458–459
    suggestibility of   453–454
    treatment   456–464
    violence in   462
Metropolitan Area Child Study   252–
    253
Minnesota Sexual Offender Screening
    Tool   92
monitoring *see* evaluation
Montréal Longitudinal-Experimental
    Study   251
mood management (*see also* negative
    attitudes)   356
moral reasoning education, for
    delinquency prevention   248,
    253–254

mothers *see* parents
Motivating Offender Rehabilitation
    Environment   147
motivational interviewing   486
motor projects   503
multi-component peer groups   262–265
multidimensional family therapy
    211–212
multiple murderers *see* serial murder
multisystemic therapy   212–215, 424,
    560
murder *see* serial murder

need principle, in cognitive-behavioural
    therapy   22, 23
negative attitudes (*see also* mood
    management)
    and peer groups   260–261
    and risk of violence   132
    and sexual recidivism   90–91
    therapy for   486–487
neglect, definition   54
New Vision Therapeutic Community
    programme   173–174
nomothetic measurement   112
non-compliance *see* programme non-
    compliance
norm building, in cognitive-behavioural
    therapy   353

offenders (*see also* child physical abuse,
    perpetrators; child sexual abuse,
    perpetrators; domestic violence
    perpetrators; mentally retarded
    offenders; sexual offenders; young
    offenders; young sexual offenders)
    pathology of   7, 8, 12
    as victims   54–55, 315–316
operant conditioning *see* conditioning
outcome criteria, for treatment research
    19–20
outcome expectancies, in substance abuse
    487–488

paedophiles *see* child sexual abuse,
    perpetrators
paranoia   441
parent–child attachment   60–61, 63–64
Parent Opinion Questionnaire   65
parental care, and emotional needs   63
parents (*see also* reasonable parents)
    of firesetters, characteristics   394
    training, school delinquency prevention
        projects   251, 254

parole *see* post-release supervision; probation and parole
PATHE 248
pathology, of offenders 7, 8, 12
patients *see* high security hospitals, patients
pedophiles *see* child sexual abuse, perpetrators
Peer Culture Development programme 246–247
peer group therapy 260
    evaluation 261–262
    multi-component 262–265
    for offenders 261–262
    for young offenders 260–261, 263–265
peer pressure (*see also* social support)
    in behaviour reinforcement 145
    in criminal behaviour 484
penile tumescence, measures 99–100, 338, 351–352, 369–370
penitentiaries *see* correctional institutes
personality
    psychometric instruments for 119
    theory of 140–141
personality disordered offenders
    characteristics 469–471
    diagnosis 471–472
    treatment 472–476, 529–530
personality disorders
    co-morbidity in 469
    definition 468–469
    and risk of violence 132
    in serial murderers 514
personality problems, in sexual offenders 338–339
personality theory, and crime 6
phallometric testing 99–100, 338, 351–352, 369–370
pharmacotherapy *see* psychopharmacotherapy
philosophies, of treatment 7–8
physical abuse *see* child physical abuse; domestic violence; violence
physiological responses *see* psychophysiological responses
Positive Action Through Holistic Education 248
Positive Peer Culture 260, 261, 262, 263
post-release supervision 555–556
pre-prosecution diversion *see* court diversion schemes
PREP 250
Preparation through Responsive Educational Program 250

preschool interventions (*see also* High/Scope)
    for delinquency prevention 246, 252, 254
prevention *see* crime, prevention; deterrence; firesetters, prevention; relapse prevention
prison officers, role in treatment 29–30, 183
prisons *see* correctional institutes
probation and parole
    costs 554–555
    effectiveness 196, 198–200, 201, 555–556, 560–561
    and intensive supervision programmes 197–200
    recommended practices 201–202
    Straight Thinking on Probation 188, 505, 559
    and treatment provision 196, 199–200, 552–554
problem-solving skills 180, 182
programme drift 24
programme leaders, characteristics 28–29
programme manual, and treatment integrity 26
programme non-compliance 25
programme reversal 24–25
programmes *see* treatment programmes
projective tests, definition 112
Projects REFORM/RECOVERY 163–164
property offences
    definition 495
    offenders
        assessment 499–500
        interventions 500–505
        motivations 496–497, 501, 502
        risk-need factors 498–499
    prevention 497–498
psychiatric hospitals *see* high security hospitals
psychiatric illness *see* mental illness
psycho-education (*see also* social skills training)
    for anger management 286, 287, 288
psychoanalytical psychotherapy, for mentally retarded offenders 460–461
psychodynamic therapy (*see also* forensic psychotherapy) 310
    for domestic violence 381–382
    effectiveness 20–21, 558
    evaluation 320–321

for young offenders   7
psychological symptoms, and sexual
    recidivism   88
psychological theories, of crime   5–7
psychological vulnerabilities, psychometric
    instruments for   119–120
psychology, and criminology   8–9
psychometric assessment, usage   111, 114
psychometric instruments (*see also*
    interviews)
    administration   116, 133
    for anger   283, 290–291, 419
    for attachment   324
    batteries of   118
    description   111–112, 113–114
    in domestic violence   382, 384
    for emotional abuse   64–65
    for firesetting   395–397
    guidelines for use   114–118
    for impulsivity   79
    norms for   116–117
    for personality   119
    for personality disorders   471
    for physical abuse potential   57–58
    for psychological vulnerabilities
        119–120
    for psychopathy   75, 76–77, 111, 119,
        126–127, 472
    purpose   113–114, 116
    reliability   114–115
    for risk assessment, efficacy   119
    selection of   114–116
    for sexual abuse   59–60, 336, 338, 352
    test scores   113–114, 117–118
    validity   117
    for violence potential   74–81, 128,
        131–134
psychopathy (*see also* personality
    disorders)
    diagnosis of   472
    and risk of violence   131
    in sexual offenders   336, 339
    and sexual recidivism   87
Psychopathy Checklist—Revised   75,
    76–77, 111, 119, 126–127, 472
psychopharmacotherapy   473–474
    for mentally retarded offenders   460
    for psychotic patients   526–527
psychophysiological methods, definition
    97
psychophysiological responses
    and criminal behaviour   98–99
    in sexual arousal   99–104, 338, 351–352,
        369–370

in violent offenders   98
psychotherapy *see* forensic psychotherapy;
    psychoanalytical psychotherapy;
    psychodynamic therapy
psychotic symptoms (*see also*
    schizophrenia)
    and anger   284
punishment (*see also* deterrence;
    discipline; sentencing options)
    principles of   4–5
    and recidivism   20

randomized controlled trials, ethics
    385–386
Rapid Risk Assessment for Sexual
    Offence Recidivism   93
rapists
    recidivism in   104
    sexual arousal measures   101–102, 103
rating scales *see* psychometric instruments
Rational Choice perspective, of property
    offences   497–498
rational decision-making, and crime   7, 10
reasonable parents, concept of   62
Reasoning and Rehabilitation programme
    179–182
    in Canada   185–188, 504–505
    in community settings   187–188, 559
    evaluation   184–191, 559
    for property offences   504–505
    staff   183
recidivism (*see also* relapse prevention;
    risk assessment)
    and community-based interventions
        554
    and punishment   20
    reduction, cost benefits   19
    and treatment completion   87, 132, 133
records *see* case materials
rehabilitation *see* Reasoning and
    Rehabilitation programme; treatment
    programmes
relapse prevention (*see also* recidivism)
    cognitive-behavioural model   298–300,
        301, 303–305, 366–367
    criticisms   302, 343
    for sexual offenders   301–305, 342–343,
        357–358
    in substance abuse   297–298, 490
relationships (*see also* empathy; intimacy;
    social skills training)
    problems with
        and risk of violence   131
        and sexual recidivism   89–90

reoffending *see* recidivism
research *see* effect sizes; evaluation;
    outcome criteria; randomized
    controlled trials; test–retest
    reliability
residential care
    characteristics for success 544–545
    disadvantages 543–544
    functions 542
    history 537–541
    and recidivism 545, 546
    residents, characteristics 542
    treatment in 542–543, 546–548
Residential Substance Abuse Treatment
    for State Prisoners Program 155,
    164–165
response chaining 149–150
response cost 143–144, 146
responsiveness, and parent–child
    attachment 63
responsivity principle, in cognitive-
    behavioural therapy 22–23, 558–
    559
Right Living, in Therapeutic Communities
    159
risk assessment
    actuarial values 124–126, 131–132
    and case material 126–128, 130–132,
    133
    and clinical judgement 124, 125
    development of 124–126
    indicators for 200–201
    interviews for 129–130, 132, 133
    models 124
    psychometric instruments for 119
risk-needs assessment (*see also* HCR-20)
    126, 498–499
risk principle, in cognitive-behavioural
    therapy 22, 23–24
Routine Activity Theory 497

satiation techniques 373
schizophrenia 77, 433, 447, 526–527
schools (*see also* classroom management;
    educational achievement; preschool
    interventions)
    delinquency programmes
        advantages 237–238
        behavioural 249–251, 253
        evaluation 240–243, 253–254
        guidelines 254–255
        indicated 241–243, 246–252
        selective 241, 245–246, 253
        through organizational change 248

        through parent training 251, 254
        through school/work programmes
        249
        universal 239–240, 244–245, 252–
        253
    ethos, and delinquency 238
Seattle Social Development Project 240,
    244–245
secure accommodation *see* high-security
    hospitals; residential care
self-esteem
    in sexual offenders 336, 337
    therapy for 340–341
    through peer group therapy 261
self-harm, therapy for 528
self-regulation
    and anger management 288–289
    problems with
        in mentally retarded offenders
        459–460
        and sexual recidivism 89
        in violent offenders 418
    in sexual abuse, models 303–305, 367
    therapy, for substance abusers 488
sensitivity analysis, in cost–benefit analysis
    45, 47
sensitization, covert 355, 373
sentencing options (*see also* community
    sentences; correctional institutes;
    high-security hospitals; intermediate
    sanctions; probation and parole)
    for mentally retarded offenders 456
serial murder
    definition 510–512
    offenders
        assessment 514–517
        characteristics 511–512, 513–514
        profiling 518
        treatment 517–518
    prevalence 512–513
    triggers 516–517
sexual abuse (*see also* child sexual abuse;
    rapists; sexual offenders)
    causation 366–367
    cognitive-behavioural chain 299–300,
    302–303, 353–354
    definition 54, 58, 364
    psychometric instruments for 59–60,
    92, 336, 338, 352
    self-regulation models 303–305, 367
    statistics 334, 364–365
sexual arousal
    measures of 99–104, 338, 351–352,
    369–370

inappropriate uses   105
and sexual recidivism   104
therapy for   354–355
sexual assault cycle   366–367
sexual deviance
    in mentally retarded offenders   461
    and recidivism   86, 87, 104
    therapy for   340, 342, 354–355
sexual fantasies, and recidivism   91
Sexual Offender Screening Tool   92
sexual offenders (*see also* child sexual
        abuse, perpetrators; young sexual
        offenders)   334–35
    attachment problems   89–90, 366
    characteristics   335–339
    cognitive-behavioural therapy for
        339–343, 352–358, 553
    cognitive distortions in   336, 337, 338,
        341, 354
    empathy problems   336, 337, 341,
        355–356
    follow-up studies   86–88, 92
    in high security hospitals   528–529
    intimacy problems   89–90, 336,
        341–342, 357
    mentally retarded   460, 461
    recidivism
        actuarial risk scales   92–93
        prediction of   100–103, 358
        prevention   301–305, 342–343,
            357–358
        risk factors   86–92
        and sexual arousal   104
        social skills training   273, 276, 277,
            341–342, 356–357
    social support for   90
shoplifting *see* theft
significant harm, concept of   65
skills training (*see also* Cognitive Skills
        Training; life skills training; problem-
        solving skills; social skills training)
    for young offenders   263–265, 266
skin conductance *see* psychophysiological
        responses
Skinner, B.F.   5, 6
social cognition (*see also* cognitive
        distortions; empathy)
    and crime   6–7
    and peer groups   263
    and sexual recidivism   88–90
    in young offenders   270–271
social ecology *see* ecological approach
social education, for delinquency
        prevention   247

social learning theory, and crime   5, 6,
        181
social organization, and crime   9
social skills
    of sexual offenders   335–336
    of violent offenders   420
    of young offenders   270–271
    of young sexual offenders   369
social skills training (*see also* psycho-
        education; relationships)
    for offenders   182, 272, 274, 275, 276,
        277
    school delinquency prevention projects
        251, 254
    for sexual offenders   273, 276, 277,
        341–342, 356–357
    studies   271–277
    for substance abusers   490
    for young offenders   272, 273, 274–275,
        276, 277
social support
    for sexual offenders   90
    for violent behaviour   133, 420–421
socialization
    and criminal behaviour   141, 142, 181
    of mentally retarded offenders
        458–459
sociological criminology   8–9, 17
soldiers, behaviour reinforcement in
        150–151
spree murder, definition   511
staff (*see also* advocacy model;
        therapists)
    role in treatment   27–30, 183
State Hospital Anger Treatment Project
        289–293
Stay'n Out Therapeutic Community
        programme   162, 168–170, 174
stealing *see* theft
stigma, of offending   232–233
Straight Thinking on Probation   188, 505,
        559
Strategic Structural Systems Engagement
        211
stress
    and risk of violence   133
    and sexual recidivism   90–91
stress inoculation, for anger management
        285, 286
structural family therapy   210–211
Student Training Through Urban
        Strategies   247
substance abuse
    assessment   482–485

characteristics of offenders 482
and criminal behaviour 483–485
and mental illness 436
relapse prevention 297–298, 490
and risk of violence 128, 131, 484
in sexual offenders 336, 339
treatment (*see also* Therapeutic
   Community treatment) 485–490
benefits 44, 47
cognitive-behavioural 481–482
cost–benefit analysis 38, 39–48
cost-effectiveness 37
Reasoning and Rehabilitation
   programme 190–191
Residential Substance Abuse
   Treatment for State Prisoners
   Program 155, 164–165
for young people 210, 211–212,
   214
suggestibility, of mentally retarded
   offenders 453–454
supervision (*see also* intensive supervision
   programmes; post-release supervision;
   probation and parole)
for programme staff 29
Synanon 159

teaching methods, for delinquency
   reduction 239, 244–245, 253
test–retest reliability 115
theft (*see also* property offences)
interventions 501–502
Therapeutic Community treatment
   155–156, 316–317
evaluation 165–174, 317, 530, 532
for personality disordered offenders
   474–475
principles 157–158, 159–160, 165–166,
   171–172
and recidivism 158, 166–168, 169–171,
   172–174
in UK prisons 156–158, 317
in US prisons 160–174
therapists
effects on 312–313, 317
selection of 320
thinking skills *see* problem-solving skills;
   Reasoning and Rehabilitation
   programme; social cognition
time out 143–144
token economies, in behavioural
   programmes 143–145, 146–151,
   458–459
training, for staff 29, 183

treatment integrity 24
challenges to 24–25, 26–7, 28, 29–
   30
and contingency plans 30
and evaluation 30
and institutional commitment 26–27,
   28, 29–30
and the programme manual 26
and the theoretical basis 25–26
treatment programmes (*see also*
   behavioural techniques; cognitive-
   behavioural therapy; family-based
   treatment; forensic psychotherapy;
   multisystemic therapy;
   psychoanalytical psychotherapy;
   psychodynamic therapy; Therapeutic
   Community treatment)
assessment of 201
benefits 43–45, 47
comparability of 45–46
completion of, and recidivism 87, 132,
   133
conflict with justice 7–8
cost–benefit analyses 37–39
   case study 39–48
cost-effectiveness 19, 36–37
costs 40, 42–43, 47
decline of 9–10, 17–18, 197
effectiveness 10–11, 19, 23–24
facilities for 27
funding for 27
ineffective types 20–1
integrated 11, 311–312, 316–318, 371,
   439
leadership 28–29
meta-analyses of 18–20, 21–22
responsivity to 201
selection of 23
staff for (*see also* therapists) 27–30,
   183
tumescence *see* penile tumescence

undesirable behaviour, decreasing
   143–144, 145
utilitarianism, and crime 4–5

violence (*see also* anger; child physical
   abuse; domestic violence)
and anger 282, 418–419, 424–425,
   488–489
classroom curriculum on 245
and impulsivity 132, 418
in in-patients 284–285, 527–528
over-prediction of 71–72

prediction
    and actuarial values   73, 76, 128,
        131–132
    and case material   127–128
    in children   80–81, 483–485
    and mental illness   71–73, 77, 78,
        127–128, 131, 132
    psychometric instruments   74–81,
        128, 131–134
    and substance abusers   128, 131, 484
    techniques   73–75
    in women   78
    in sexual abusers   103
    and sexual arousal measures   103–104
Violence Prevention Project   426
Violence Risk Appraisal Guide   75–76,
    77, 128
violent offenders
    assessment   415–422
    characteristics   417–421, 435–436
        of offences   421–422
    mentally ill   435–436, 442–443
    mentally retarded   462
    motives   421–422
    social support for   133, 420–421
    treatment   422–423, 426–427
        for adults   424–426
        behavioural   527–528
        for young people   423–424
vocational achievement, and behaviour
    management   145, 147
vulnerabilities see psychological
    vulnerabilities

wife assault see domestic violence
women
    mentally retarded offenders   463
    prediction of violence in   78
    Therapeutic Community programmes
        for   169–170

young offenders (see also family-based
    treatment; firesetters; young sexual
    offenders)

anger in   284
anger management for   286
behaviour reinforcement in   143–145,
    146, 147–148
and car crime   502–503
cognitive-behavioural therapy for   21,
    558
diversion programmes see Adolescent
    Diversion Project; court diversion
    schemes
educational achievement   237–238
labelling, effects   232–233
multisystemic therapy   212–215
peer groups for   260–261, 263–265
psychodynamic therapy for   7
Reasoning and Rehabilitation
    programme   189–190
residential care for see residential
    care
skills training   263–265, 266
social cognition   270–271
social skills training   272, 273, 274–275,
    276, 277
theft by   501
violence, therapy for   423–424
young people (see also children)
    depression in   433–434
    substance abuse, therapy for   210,
        211–212, 214
young sexual offenders
    assessment   365–371
    causation   366–367
    cognitive-behavioural therapy for
        371–374
    prevalence   364–365
    risk assessment   370–371
    sexual assault cycle   366–367
Youth Development Project   249
youth intervention programmes
    cost-benefits   39
    cost-effectiveness   36–37
Youth Service Bureaus   221, 222–223

Index compiled by Sylvia Potter

Related titles
of interest...

Cognitive Behavioural Treatment of Sexual Offenders
WILLIAM MARSHALL, DANA ANDERSON and
YOLANDA FERNANDEZ
0471 975664   220pp   September 1999   Paperback

Handbook of the Psychology of Interviewing
AMINA MEMON and RAY BULL
0471 974439   380pp   February 1999   Hardback

The Handbook of Forensic Psychology
2nd Edition
ALLEN K. HESS and IRVING B. WEINER
0471 177717   832pp   December 1998   Hardback

Changing Lives of Crime and Drugs
Intervening with Substance-Abusing Offenders
GLENN D. WALTERS
0471 97658X   162pp   February 1998   Hardback
0471 978418   162pp   February 1998   Paperback

The Psychology of Criminal Conduct
RONALD BLACKBURN
0471 961752   506pp   1995   Paperback